Visual C# 2005 Recipes

A Problem-Solution Approach

Allen Jones
Matthew MacDonald
Rakesh Rajan

Apress®

Visual C# 2005 Recipes: A Problem-Solution Approach

Copyright © 2006 by Allen Jones, Matthew MacDonald, and Rakesh Rajan

ISBN (pbk): 1-59059-589-0

Printed and bound in the United States of America 9 8 7 6 5 4 3 2 1

Trademarked names may appear in this book. Rather than use a trademark symbol with every occurrence of a trademarked name, we use the names only in an editorial fashion and to the benefit of the trademark owner, with no intention of infringement of the trademark.

Lead Editor: Ewan Buckingham
Technical Reviewer: Christophe Nasarre
Editorial Board: Steve Anglin, Dan Appleman, Ewan Buckingham, Gary Cornell, Tony Davis, Jason Gilmore, Jonathan Hassell, Chris Mills, Dominic Shakeshaft, Jim Sumser
Associate Publisher: Grace Wong
Project Manager: Beckie Brand
Copy Edit Manager: Nicole LeClerc
Copy Editors: Marilyn Smith and Kim Wimpsett
Assistant Production Director: Kari Brooks-Copony
Production Editor: Ellie Fountain
Compositor: Kinetic Publishing Services, LLC
Proofreader: April Eddy
Indexer: Michael Brinkman
Artist: Kinetic Publishing Services, LLC
Interior Designer: Van Winkle Design Group
Cover Designer: Kurt Krames
Manufacturing Director: Tom Debolski

Distributed to the book trade worldwide by Springer-Verlag New York, Inc., 233 Spring Street, 6th Floor, New York, NY 10013. Phone 1-800-SPRINGER, fax 201-348-4505, e-mail orders-ny@springer-sbm.com, or visit http://www.springeronline.com.

For information on translations, please contact Apress directly at 2560 Ninth Street, Suite 219, Berkeley, CA 94710. Phone 510-549-5930, fax 510-549-5939, e-mail info@apress.com, or visit http://www.apress.com.

The source code for this book is available to readers at http://www.apress.com in the Source Code section.

For my fabulous wife Elena and my two lovely daughters, Anya and Alexia. Without your love and support, this book would not have been possible.

Allen Jones

Contents at a Glance

Contents

■CHAPTER 3   Application Domains, Reflection, and Metadata 65

■CHAPTER 4   Threads, Processes, and Synchronization 95

■CHAPTER 12   **Unmanaged Code Interoperability**.

■CHAPTER 13   **Commonly Used Interfaces and Patterns**

About the Authors

■**ALLEN JONES** is a Director of Principal Objective Ltd., a UK-based consultancy that provides independent IT strategy and solutions architecture services. Allen has more than 15 years of commercial experience, covering almost every aspect of IT; however, his true passion has been and always will be software development. In his spare time, Allen works—writing books and training material—or studies in an effort to find some form of enlightenment that has so far eluded him.

■**MATTHEW MACDONALD** is an author, educator, and MCSD developer. He is a regular contributor to programming journals and the author of more than a dozen books about .NET programming, including *User Interfaces in C#: Windows Forms and Custom Controls* (Apress), *Pro ASP.NET 2.0* (Apress), and *Microsoft .NET Distributed Applications* (Microsoft Press). In a dimly remembered past life, he studied English literature and theoretical physics.

■**RAKESH RAJAN** is a software engineer from India working with US Technology (http://www.ustri.com) at Technopark, Trivandrum in Kerala. He is a Microsoft MVP in C# and an MCSD in .NET. He has been working in .NET for the past three years. You can find him posting at newsgroups, writing articles, working on his own projects, or speaking about .NET. Visit his site at http://www.rakeshrajan.com or drop him an e-mail at rakeshrajan@mvps.org.

About the Technical Reviewer

 **CHRISTOPHE NASARRE** is a Development Architect for Business Objects, a company that develops desktop and Web-based business intelligence solutions. During his spare time, Christophe writes articles for *MSDN Magazine*, MSDN/Longhorn, and ASPToday and has reviewed books on Win32, COM, MFC, and .NET since 1996.

Acknowledgments

I would like to thank everyone at Apress for working so hard to bring this book to print. In particular, I would like to thank Christophe, whose exceptional efforts as technical reviewer and many good suggestions made this book far better than it would have been without him. I would also like to thank Joss Whedon for giving us Firefly, a truly inspirational and entertaining science-fiction masterpiece.

Allen Jones

Preface

Mastering the development of Microsoft .NET Framework applications in C# is less about knowing the C# language and more about knowing how to use the functionality of the .NET Framework class library most effectively. *Visual C# 2005 Recipes* explores the breadth of the .NET Framework class library and provides specific solutions to common and interesting programming problems. Each solution (or recipe) is presented in a succinct problem/solution format and most are accompanied by working code samples.

Visual C# 2005 Recipes is not intended to teach you how to program, nor to teach you C#. However, if you have even the most rudimentary experience programming applications built on the .NET Framework using C#, you will find this book to be an invaluable resource.

Ideally, when you are facing a problem, this book will contain a recipe that provides the solution, or at least it will point you in the right direction. Even if you just want to broaden your knowledge of the .NET Framework class library, *Visual C# 2005 Recipes* is the perfect resource to assist you.

However, you cannot become proficient with C# and the classes in the .NET Framework class library merely by reading about them. Rather, you must use them and experiment with them by writing code, code, and more code. The structure and content of this book and the real-world applicability of the solutions it provides offer the perfect starting point from which to kick-start your own experimentation.

Note This book is based on content previously published in the *C# Programmer's Cookbook* (Microsoft Press, 2004). All such content has been revised and updated for inclusion in this book. Whereas the *C# Programmer's Cookbook* targeted version 1.1 of the .NET Framework, *Visual C# 2005 Recipes* focuses on .NET Framework 2.0 and C# 2005. In many cases, you will find the recipes in this book still work on .NET Framework 1.1, except for those recipes that use features new to .NET Framework 2.0. In such cases, the recipe highlights the new .NET Framework 2.0 features being used and presents possible alternatives for those using .NET Framework 1.1.

CHAPTER 1

■■■

Application Development

This chapter covers some of the fundamental activities you will need to perform when developing your C# solutions. The recipes in this chapter describe how to do the following:

- Use the C# command-line compiler to build console and Windows Forms applications (recipes 1-1 and 1-2)

- Create and use code modules and libraries (recipes 1-3 and 1-4)

- Access command-line arguments from within your applications (recipe 1-5)

- Use compiler directives and attributes to selectively include code at build time (recipe 1-6)

- Access program elements built in other languages whose names conflict with C# keywords (recipe 1-7)

- Give assemblies strong names and verify strong-named assemblies (recipes 1-8, 1-9, 1-10, and 1-11)

- Sign an assembly with a Microsoft Authenticode digital signature (recipes 1-12 and 1-13)

- Manage the shared assemblies that are stored in the global assembly cache (recipe 1-14)

- Prevent people from decompiling your assembly (recipe 1-15)

- Manipulate the appearance of the console (recipe 1-16)

Note All the tools discussed in this chapter ship with the Microsoft .NET Framework or the .NET Framework software development kit (SDK). The tools that are part of the .NET Framework are in the main directory for the version of the framework you are running. For example, they are in the directory C:\WINDOWS\Microsoft.NET\Framework\v2.0.50727 if you install version 2.0 of the .NET Framework to the default location. The .NET installation process automatically adds this directory to your environment path.

The tools provided with the SDK are in the Bin subdirectory of the directory in which you install the SDK, which is C:\Program Files\Microsoft Visual Studio 8\SDK\v2.0 if you chose the default path during the installation of Microsoft Visual Studio 2005. This directory is *not* added to your path automatically, so you must manually edit your path in order to have easy access to these tools or use the shortcut to the command prompt installed in the Windows Start ➤ Programs menu of Visual Studio that calls vcvarsall.bat to set the right environment variables.

Most of the tools support short and long forms of the command-line switches that control their functionality. This chapter always shows the long form, which is more informative but requires additional typing. For the shortened form of each switch, see the tool's documentation in the .NET Framework SDK.

1-1. Create a Console Application from the Command Line

Problem

You need to use the C# command-line compiler to build an application that does not require a Windows graphical user interface (GUI) but instead displays output to, and reads input from, the Windows command prompt (console).

Solution

In one of your classes, ensure you implement a static method named Main with one of the following signatures:

```
public static void Main();
public static void Main(string[] args);
public static int Main();
public static int Main(string[] args);
```

Build your application using the C# compiler (csc.exe) by running the following command (where HelloWorld.cs is the name of your source code file):

```
csc /target:exe HelloWorld.cs
```

■**Note** If you own Visual Studio, you will most often use the Console Application project template to create new console applications. However, for small applications, it is often just as easy to use the command-line compiler. It is also useful to know how to build console applications from the command line if you are ever working on a machine without Visual Studio and want to create a quick utility to automate some task.

How It Works

By default, the C# compiler will build a console application unless you specify otherwise. For this reason, it's not necessary to specify the /target:exe switch, but doing so makes your intention clearer, which is useful if you are creating build scripts that will be used by others or will be used repeatedly over a period of time.

To build a console application consisting of more than one source code file, you must specify all the source files as arguments to the compiler. For example, the following command builds an application named MyFirstApp.exe from two source files named HelloWorld.cs and ConsoleUtils.cs:

```
csc /target:exe /main:HelloWorld /out:MyFirstApp.exe HelloWorld.cs ConsoleUtils.cs
```

The /out switch allows you to specify the name of the compiled assembly. Otherwise, the assembly is named after the first source file listed—HelloWorld.cs in the example. If classes in both the HelloWorld and ConsoleUtils files contain Main methods, the compiler cannot automatically determine which method represents the correct entry point for the assembly. Therefore, you must use the compiler's /main switch to identify the name of the class that contains the correct entry point for your application. When using the /main switch, you must provide the fully qualified class name (including the namespace); otherwise, you will get a CS1555 compilation error: "Could not find 'HelloWorld' specified for Main method."

If you have a lot of C# code source files to compile, you should use a response file. This simple text file contains the command-line arguments for csc.exe. When you call csc.exe, you give the name of this response file as a single parameter prefixed by the @ character. For example:

```
csc @commands.rsp
```

To achieve the equivalent of the previous example, commands.rsp would contain this:

```
/target:exe /main:HelloWorld /out:MyFirstApp.exe HelloWorld.cs ConsoleUtils.cs
```

The Code

The following code lists a class named ConsoleUtils that is defined in a file named ConsoleUtils.cs:

```csharp
using System;

namespace Apress.VisualCSharpRecipes.Chapter01
{
    public class ConsoleUtils
    {
        // A method to display a prompt and read a response from the console.
        public static string ReadString(string msg)
        {
            Console.Write(msg);
            return Console.ReadLine();
        }

        // A method to display a message to the console.
        public static void WriteString(string msg)
        {
            Console.WriteLine(msg);
        }

        // Main method used for testing ConsoleUtility methods.
        public static void Main()
        {
            // Prompt the reader to enter a name.
            string name = ReadString("Please enter your name : ");

            // Welcome the reader to Visual C# 2005 Recipes.
            WriteString("Welcome to Visual C# 2005 Recipes, " + name);
        }
    }
}
```

The HelloWorld class listed next uses the ConsoleUtils class to display the message "Hello, world" to the console (HelloWorld is contained in the HelloWorld.cs file):

```csharp
using System;

namespace Apress.VisualCSharpRecipes.Chapter01
{
    class HelloWorld
    {
        public static void Main()
        {
            ConsoleUtils.WriteString("Hello, world");

            Console.WriteLine("\nMain method complete. Press Enter.");
            Console.ReadLine();
        }
    }
}
```

Usage

To build HelloWorld.exe from the two source files, use the following command:

```
csc /target:exe /main:Apress.VisualCSharpRecipes.Chapter01.HelloWorld ➥
/out:HelloWorld.exe ConsoleUtils.cs HelloWorld.cs
```

1-2. Create a Windows-Based Application from the Command Line

Problem

You need to use the C# command-line compiler to build an application that provides a Windows Forms–based GUI.

Solution

Create a class that extends the System.Windows.Forms.Form class. (This will be your application's main form.) In one of your classes, ensure you implement a static method named Main. In the Main method, create an instance of your main form class and pass it to the static method Run of the System.Windows.Forms.Application class. Build your application using the command-line C# compiler, and specify the /target:winexe compiler switch.

■Note If you own Visual Studio, you will most often use the Windows Application project template to create new Windows Forms–based applications. Building large GUI-based applications is a time-consuming undertaking that involves the correct instantiation, configuration, and wiring up of many forms and controls. Visual Studio automates much of the work associated with building graphical applications. Trying to build a large graphical application without the aid of tools such as Visual Studio will take you much longer, be extremely tedious, and result in a greater chance of bugs in your code. However, it is also useful to know the essentials required to create a Windows-based application using the command line in case you are ever working on a machine without Visual Studio and want to create a quick utility to automate some task or get input from a user.

How It Works

Building an application that provides a simple Windows GUI is a world away from developing a full-fledged Windows-based application. However, you must perform certain tasks regardless of whether you are writing the Windows equivalent of Hello World or the next version of Microsoft Word, including the following:

- For each form you need in your application, create a class that extends the System.Windows.Forms.Form class.

- In each of your form classes, declare members that represent the controls that will be on that form, such as buttons, labels, lists, and textboxes. These members should be declared private or at least protected so that other program elements cannot access them directly. If you need to expose the methods or properties of these controls, implement the necessary members in your form class, providing indirect and controlled access to the contained controls.

- Declare methods in your form class that will handle events raised by the controls contained by the form, such as button clicks or key presses when a textbox is the active control. These methods should be private or protected and follow the standard .NET *event pattern* (described in recipe 13-11). It's in these methods (or methods called by these methods) where you will define the bulk of your application's functionality.

- Declare a constructor for your form class that instantiates each of the form's controls and configures their initial state (size, color, position, content, and so on). The constructor should also wire up the appropriate event handler methods of your class to the events of each control.

- Declare a static method named Main—usually as a member of your application's main form class. This method is the entry point for your application, and it can have the same signatures as those mentioned in recipe 1-1. In the Main method, call Application.EnableVisualStyles to allow XP theme support, create an instance of your application's main form, and pass it as an argument to the static Application.Run method. The Run method makes your main form visible and starts a standard Windows message loop on the current thread, which passes the user input (key presses, mouse clicks, and so on) to your application form as events.

The Code

The Recipe01-02 class shown in the following code listing is a simple Windows Forms application that demonstrates the techniques just listed. When run, it prompts a user to enter a name and then displays a message box welcoming the user to *Visual C# 2005 Recipes*.

```
using System;
using System.Windows.Forms;

namespace Apress.VisualCSharpRecipes.Chapter01
{
    class Recipe01_02 : Form
    {
        // Private members to hold references to the form's controls.
        private Label label1;
        private TextBox textBox1;
        private Button button1;

        // Constructor used to create an instance of the form and configure
        // the form's controls.
        public Recipe01_02()
        {
            // Instantiate the controls used on the form.
            this.label1 = new Label();
            this.textBox1 = new TextBox();
            this.button1 = new Button();

            // Suspend the layout logic of the form while we configure and
            // position the controls.
            this.SuspendLayout();

            // Configure label1, which displays the user prompt.
            this.label1.Location = new System.Drawing.Point(16, 36);
            this.label1.Name = "label1";
            this.label1.Size = new System.Drawing.Size(128, 16);
            this.label1.TabIndex = 0;
            this.label1.Text = "Please enter your name:";
```

```
        // Configure textBox1, which accepts the user input.
        this.textBox1.Location = new System.Drawing.Point(152, 32);
        this.textBox1.Name = "textBox1";
        this.textBox1.TabIndex = 1;
        this.textBox1.Text = "";

        // Configure button1, which the user clicks to enter a name.
        this.button1.Location = new System.Drawing.Point(109, 80);
        this.button1.Name = "button1";
        this.button1.TabIndex = 2;
        this.button1.Text = "Enter";
        this.button1.Click += new System.EventHandler(this.button1_Click);

        // Configure WelcomeForm, and add controls.
        this.ClientSize = new System.Drawing.Size(292, 126);
        this.Controls.Add(this.button1);
        this.Controls.Add(this.textBox1);
        this.Controls.Add(this.label1);
        this.Name = "form1";
        this.Text = "Visual C# 2005 Recipes";

        // Resume the layout logic of the form now that all controls are
        // configured.
        this.ResumeLayout(false);
    }

    // Event handler called when the user clicks the Enter button on the
    // form.
    private void button1_Click(object sender, System.EventArgs e)
    {
        // Write debug message to the console.
        System.Console.WriteLine("User entered: " + textBox1.Text);

        // Display welcome as a message box.
        MessageBox.Show("Welcome to Visual C# 2005 Recipes, "
            + textBox1.Text, "Visual C# 2005 Recipes");
    }

    // Application entry point, creates an instance of the form, and begins
    // running a standard message loop on the current thread. The message
    // loop feeds the application with input from the user as events.
    [STAThread]
    public static void Main()
    {
        Application.EnableVisualStyles();
        Application.Run(new Recipe01_02());
    }
  }
}
```

Usage

To build the Recipe01-02 class into an application, use this command:

```
csc /target:winexe Recipe01-02.cs.
```

The /target:winexe switch tells the compiler that you are building a Windows-based application. As a result, the compiler builds the executable in such a way that no console is created when you run your application. If you use the /target:exe switch to build a Windows Forms application instead of /target:winexe, your application will still work correctly, but you will have a console window visible while the application is running. Although this is undesirable for production-quality software, the console window is useful if you want to write debug and logging information while you're developing and testing your Windows Forms application. You can write to this console using the Write and WriteLine methods of the System.Console class.

Figure 1-1 shows the WelcomeForm.exe application greeting a user named Rupert. This version of the application is built using the /target:exe compiler switch, resulting in the visible console window in which you can see the output from the Console.WriteLine statement in the button1_Click event handler.

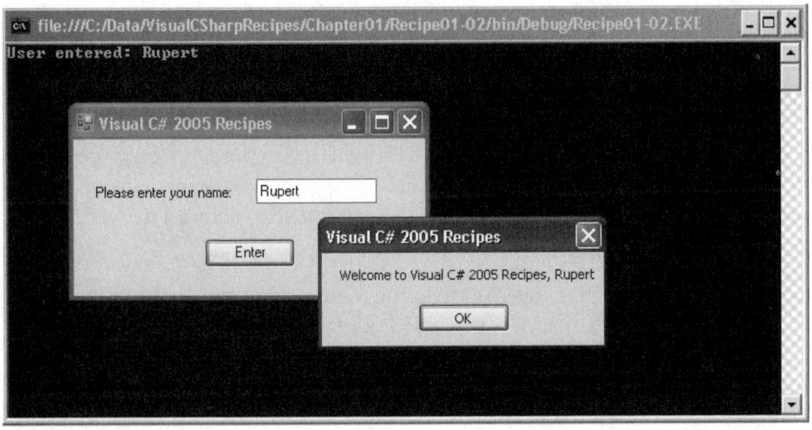

Figure 1-1. *A simple Windows Forms application*

1-3. Create and Use a Code Module

Problem

You need to do one or more of the following:

- Improve your application's performance and memory efficiency by ensuring the runtime loads rarely used types only when they are required
- Compile types written in C# to a form you can build into assemblies being developed in other .NET languages
- Use types developed in another language and build them into your C# assemblies

Solution

Build your C# source code into a module by using the command-line compiler and specifying the /target:module compiler switch. To incorporate existing modules into your assembly, use the /addmodule compiler switch.

How It Works

Modules are the building blocks of .NET assemblies. Modules consist of a single file that contains the following:

- Microsoft Intermediate Language (MSIL) code created from your source code during compilation
- Metadata describing the types contained in the module
- Resources, such as icons and string tables, used by the types in the module

Assemblies consist of one or more modules and an assembly manifest. When a single module exists, the module and assembly manifest are usually built into a single file for convenience. When more than one module exists, the assembly represents a logical grouping of more than one file that you must deploy as a complete unit. In these situations, the assembly manifest is either contained in a separate file or built into one of the modules.

By building an assembly from multiple modules, you complicate the management and deployment of the assembly, but under some circumstances, modules offer significant benefits:

- The runtime will load a module only when the types defined in the module are required. Therefore, where you have a set of types that your application uses rarely, you can partition them into a separate module that the runtime will load only if necessary. This offers the following benefits:

  - Improving performance, especially if your application is loaded across a network
  - Minimizing the use of memory

- The ability to use many different languages to write applications that run on the common language runtime (CLR) is a great strength of the .NET Framework. However, the C# compiler can't compile your Microsoft Visual Basic .NET or COBOL .NET code for inclusion in your assembly. To use code written in another language, you can compile it into a separate assembly and reference it. But if you want it to be an integral part of your assembly, then you must build it into a module. Similarly, if you want to allow others to include your code as an integral part of their assemblies, you must compile your code as modules. When you use modules, because the code becomes part of the same assembly, members marked as `internal` or `protected internal` are accessible, whereas they would not be if the code had been accessed from an external assembly.

Usage

To compile a source file named ConsoleUtils.cs (see recipe 1-1 for the contents) into a module, use the command `csc /target:module ConsoleUtils.cs`. The result is the creation of a file named ConsoleUtils.netmodule. The netmodule extension is the default extension for modules, and the filename is the same as the name of the C# source file.

You can also build modules from multiple source files, which results in a single file (module) containing the MSIL and metadata for all types contained in all the source files. The command `csc /target:module ConsoleUtils.cs WindowsUtils.cs` compiles two source files named ConsoleUtils.cs and WindowsUtils.cs to create the module named ConsoleUtils.netmodule. The module is named after the first source file listed unless you override the name with the /out compiler switch. For example, the command `csc /target:module /out:Utilities.netmodule ConsoleUtils.cs WindowsUtils.cs` creates a module named Utilities.netmodule.

To build an assembly consisting of multiple modules, you must use the /addmodule compiler switch. To build an executable named MyFirstApp.exe from two modules named WindowsUtils.netmodule and ConsoleUtils.netmodule and two source files named SourceOne.cs and SourceTwo.cs, use the command `csc /out:MyFirstApp.exe /target:exe /addmodule:WindowsUtils.netmodule,ConsoleUtils.netmodule SourceOne.cs SourceTwo.cs`. This command will result in an assembly consisting of the following files:

- MyFirstApp.exe, which contains the assembly manifest as well as the MSIL for the types declared in the SourceOne.cs and SourceTwo.cs source files

- ConsoleUtils.netmodule and WindowsUtils.netmodule, which are now integral components of the multifile assembly but are unchanged by this compilation process

---

■**Caution** If you attempt to run an assembly (such as MyFirstApp.exe) without any required netmodules present, a System.IO.FileNotFoundException is thrown the first time any code tries to use types defined in the missing code module. This is a significant concern because the missing modules will not be identified until runtime. You must be careful when deploying multifile assemblies.

1-4. Create and Use a Code Library from the Command Line

Problem

You need to build a set of functionality into a reusable code library so that multiple applications can reference and reuse it.

Solution

Build your library using the command-line C# compiler, and specify the /target:library compiler switch. To reference the library, use the /reference compiler switch when you build your application, and specify the names of the required libraries.

How It Works

Recipe 1-1 showed you how to build an application named MyFirstApp.exe from the two source files ConsoleUtils.cs and HelloWorld.cs. The ConsoleUtils.cs file contains the ConsoleUtils class, which provides methods to simplify interaction with the Windows console. If you were to extend the functionality of the ConsoleUtils class, you could add functionality useful to many applications. Instead of including the source code for ConsoleUtils in every application, you could build it into a library and deploy it independently, making the functionality accessible to many applications.

Usage

To build the ConsoleUtils.cs file into a library, use the command csc /target:library ConsoleUtils.cs. This will produce a library file named ConsoleUtils.dll. To build a library from multiple source files, list the name of each file at the end of the command. You can also specify the name of the library using the /out compiler switch; otherwise, the library is named after the first source file listed. For example, to build a library named MyFirstLibrary.dll from two source files named ConsoleUtils.cs and WindowsUtils.cs, use the command csc /out:MyFirstLibrary.dll /target:library ConsoleUtils. cs WindowsUtils.cs.

Before distributing your library, you might consider strong naming it so that nobody can modify your assembly and pass it off as being the original. Strong naming your library also allows people to install it into the global assembly cache (GAC), which makes reuse much easier. (Recipe 1-9 describes how to strong name your assembly, and recipe 1-14 describes how to install a strong-named assembly into the GAC.) You might also consider signing your library with an Authenticode signature, which allows users to confirm you are the publisher of the assembly—see recipe 1-12 for details on signing assemblies with Authenticode.

To compile an assembly that relies on types declared within external libraries, you must tell the compiler which libraries are referenced using the /reference compiler switch. For example, to compile the HelloWorld.cs source file (from recipe 1-1) if the ConsoleUtils class is contained in the ConsoleUtils.dll library, use the command csc /reference:ConsoleUtils.dll HelloWorld.cs. Remember these four points:

- If you reference more than one library, separate each library name with a comma or semicolon, but don't include any spaces. For example, use /reference:ConsoleUtils.dll,WindowsUtils.dll.

- If the libraries aren't in the same directory as the source code, use the /lib switch on the compiler to specify the additional directories where the compiler should look for libraries. For example, use /lib:c:\CommonLibraries,c:\Dev\ThirdPartyLibs.

- Note that additional directories can be relative to the source folder. Don't forget that at runtime, the generated assembly must be in the same folder as the application that needs it except if you deploy it into the GAC.

- If the library you need to reference is a multifile assembly, reference the file that contains the assembly manifest. (For information about multifile assemblies, see recipe 1-3.)

1-5. Access Command-Line Arguments

Problem

You need to access the arguments that were specified on the command line when your application was executed.

Solution

Use a signature for your Main method that exposes the command-line arguments as a string array. Alternatively, access the command-line arguments from anywhere in your code using the static members of the System.Environment class.

How It Works

Declaring your application's Main method with one of the following signatures provides access to the command-line arguments as a string array:

```
public static void Main(string[] args);
public static int Main(string[] args);
```

At runtime, the args argument will contain a string for each value entered on the command line after your application's name. Unlike C and C++, the application's name is not included in the array of arguments.

If you need access to the command-line arguments at places in your code other than the Main method, you can process the command-line arguments in your Main method and store them for later access. However, this is not necessary since you can use the System.Environment class, which provides two static members that return information about the command line: CommandLine and GetCommandLineArgs.

The CommandLine property returns a string containing the full command line that launched the current process. Depending on the operating system on which the application is running, path information might precede the application name. Microsoft Windows 2003, Windows NT 4.0, Windows 2000, and Windows XP don't include path information, whereas Windows 98 and Windows ME do. The GetCommandLineArgs method returns a string array containing the command-line arguments. This array can be processed in the same way as the string array passed to the Main method, as discussed at the start of this section. Unlike the array passed to the Main method, the first element in the array returned by the GetCommandLineArgs method is the filename of the application.

The Code

To demonstrate the access of command-line arguments, the Main method in the following example steps through each of the command-line arguments passed to it and displays them to the console. The example then accesses the command line directly through the Environment class.

```
using System;

namespace Apress.VisualCSharpRecipes.Chapter01
{
    class Recipe01_05
    {
        public static void Main(string[] args)
        {
            // Step through the command-line arguments.
            foreach (string s in args)
            {
                Console.WriteLine(s);
            }

            // Alternatively, access the command-line arguments directly.
            Console.WriteLine(Environment.CommandLine);

            foreach (string s in Environment.GetCommandLineArgs())
            {
                Console.WriteLine(s);
            }

            // Wait to continue.
            Console.WriteLine("\nMain method complete. Press Enter.");
            Console.ReadLine();
        }
    }
}
```

Usage

If you execute the Recipe01-05 example using the following command:

```
Recipe01-05 "one \"two\"    three" four 'five    six'
```

the application will generate the following output on the console:

```
one "two"    three
four
'five
six'
```

Notice that the use of double quotes (") results in more than one word being treated as a single argument, although single quotes (') do not. Also, you can include double quotes in an argument by escaping them with the backslash character (\). Finally, notice that all spaces are stripped from the command line unless they are enclosed in double quotes.

1-6. Include Code Selectively at Build Time

Problem

You need to selectively include and exclude sections of source code from your compiled assembly.

Solution

Use the #if, #elif, #else, and #endif preprocessor directives to identify blocks of code that should be conditionally included in your compiled assembly. Use the System.Diagnostics.ConditionalAttribute attribute to define methods that should be called conditionally only. Control the inclusion of the conditional code using the #define and #undef directives in your code, or use the /define switch when you run the C# compiler from the command line.

How It Works

If you need your application to function differently depending on factors such as the platform or environment on which it runs, you can build runtime checks into the logic of your code that trigger the variations in operation. However, such an approach can bloat your code and affect performance, especially if many variations need to be supported or many locations exist where evaluations need to be made.

An alternative approach is to build multiple versions of your application to support the different target platforms and environments. Although this approach overcomes the problems of code bloat and performance degradation, it would be an untenable solution if you had to maintain different source code for each version, so C# provides features that allow you to build customized versions of your application from a single code base.

The #if, #elif, #else, and #endif preprocessor directives allow you to identify blocks of code that the compiler should include in your assembly only if specified symbols are defined at compile time. Symbols function as on/off switches; they don't have values—either the symbol is defined or it is not. The #if..#endif construct evaluates #if and #elif clauses only until it finds one that evaluates to true, meaning that if you define multiple symbols (winXP and win2000, for example), the order of your clauses is important. The compiler includes only the code in the clause that evaluates to true. If no clause evaluates to true, the compiler includes the code in the #else clause.

You can also use logical operators to base conditional compilation on more than one symbol. Table 1-1 summarizes the supported operators.

Table 1-1. *Logical Operators Supported by the* #if..#endif *Directive*

Operator	Example	Description
==	#if winXP == true	Equality. Evaluates to true if the symbol winXP is defined. Equivalent to #if winXP.
!=	#if winXP != true	Inequality. Evaluates to true if the symbol winXP is *not* defined. Equivalent to #if !winXP.
&&	#if winXP && release	Logical AND. Evaluates to true only if the symbols winXP *and* release are defined.
||	#if winXP || release	Logical OR. Evaluates to true if either of the symbols winXP *or* release are defined.
()	#if (winXP || win2000) && release	Parentheses allow you to group expressions. Evaluates to true if the symbols winXP *or* win2000 are defined *and* the symbol release is defined.

■**Caution** You must be careful not to overuse conditional compilation directives and not to make your conditional expressions too complex; otherwise, your code can quickly become confusing and unmanageable—especially as your projects become larger.

To define a symbol, you can either include a #define directive in your code or use the /define compiler switch. Symbols defined using #define are active until the end of the file in which they are defined. Symbols defined using the /define compiler switch are active in all source files that are being compiled. To undefine a symbol defined using the /define compiler switch, C# provides the #undef directive, which is useful if you want to ensure a symbol is not defined in specific source files. All #define and #undef directives must appear at the top of your source file before any code, including any using directives. Symbols are case-sensitive.

A less flexible but more elegant alternative to the #if preprocessor directive is the attribute System.Diagnostics.ConditionalAttribute. If you apply ConditionalAttribute to a method, the compiler will ignore any calls to the method if the symbol specified by ConditionalAttribute is not defined at the calling point.

Using ConditionalAttribute centralizes your conditional compilation logic on the method declaration and means you can freely include calls to conditional methods without littering your code with #if directives. However, because the compiler literally removes calls to the conditional method from your code, your code can't have dependencies on return values from the conditional method. This means you can apply ConditionalAttribute only to methods that return void and do not use "out" modifiers on their arguments.

The Code

In this example, the code assigns a different value to the local variable platformName based on whether the winXP, win2000, winNT, or Win98 symbols are defined. The head of the code defines the symbols win2000 and release (not used in this example) and undefines the win98 symbol in case it was defined on the compiler command line. In ()addition, the ConditionalAttribute specifies that calls to the DumpState method should be included in an assembly only if the symbol DEBUG is defined during compilation.

```
#define win2000
#define release
#undef  win98
```

```
using System;
using System.Diagnostics;

namespace Apress.VisualCSharpRecipes.Chapter01
{
    class Recipe01_06
    {
        [Conditional("DEBUG")]
        public static void DumpState()
        {
            Console.WriteLine("Dump some state...");
        }

        public static void Main()
        {
            // Declare a string to contain the platform name
            string platformName;

            #if winXP        // Compiling for Windows XP
                platformName = "Microsoft Windows XP";
            #elif win2000    // Compiling for Windows 2000
                platformName = "Microsoft Windows 2000";
            #elif winNT      // Compiling for Windows NT
                platformName = "Microsoft Windows NT";
            #elif win98      // Compiling for Windows 98
                platformName = "Microsoft Windows 98";
            #else            // Unknown platform specified
                platformName = "Unknown";
            #endif

            Console.WriteLine(platformName);

            // Call the conditional DumpState method
            DumpState();

            // Wait to continue...
            Console.WriteLine("\nMain method complete. Press Enter.");
            Console.Read();
        }
    }
}
```

Usage

To build the example and define the symbols winXP and DEBUG (not used in this example), use the command csc /define:winXP;DEBUG ConditionalExample.cs.

Notes

You can apply multiple ConditionalAttribute instances to a method in order to produce logical OR behavior. Calls to the following version of the DumpState method will be compiled only if the DEBUG or TEST symbols are defined:

```
[System.Diagnostics.Conditional("DEBUG")]
[System.Diagnostics.Conditional("TEST")]
public static void DumpState() {//...}
```

Achieving logical AND behavior is not as clean and involves the use of an intermediate conditional method, quickly leading to overly complex code that is hard to understand and maintain. The following is a quick example that requires the definition of both the DEBUG *and* TEST symbols for the DumpState functionality (contained in DumpState2) to be called:

```
[System.Diagnostics.Conditional("DEBUG")]
public static void DumpState() {
    DumpState2();
}

[System.Diagnostics.Conditional("TEST")]
public static void DumpState2() {//...}
```

Note The Debug and Trace classes from the System.Diagnostics namespace use ConditionalAttribute on many of their methods. The methods of the Debug class are conditional on the definition of the symbol DEBUG, and the methods of the Trace class are conditional on the definition of the symbol TRACE.

1-7. Access a Program Element That Has the Same Name As a Keyword

Problem

You need to access a member of a type, but the type or member name is the same as a C# keyword.

Solution

Prefix all instances of the identifier name in your code with the at sign (@).

How It Works

The .NET Framework allows you to use software components developed in other .NET languages from within your C# applications. Each language has its own set of keywords (or reserved words) and imposes different restrictions on the names programmers can assign to program elements such as types, members, and variables. Therefore, it is possible that a programmer developing a component in another language will inadvertently use a C# keyword as the name of a program element. The at sign (@) enables you to use a C# keyword as an identifier and overcome these possible naming conflicts.

The Code

The following code fragment instantiates an object of type operator (perhaps a telephone operator) and sets its volatile property to true—both operator and volatile are C# keywords:

```
// Instantiate an operator object
@operator Operator1 = new @operator();

// Set the operator's volatile property
Operator1.@volatile = true;
```

1-8. Create and Manage Strong-Named Key Pairs

Problem

You need to create public and private keys (a key pair) so that you can assign strong names to your assemblies.

Solution

Use the Strong Name tool (sn.exe) to generate a key pair and store the keys in a file or cryptographic service provider (CSP) key container.

■**Note** A CSP is an element of the Win32 CryptoAPI that provides services such as encryption, decryption, and digital signature generation. CSPs also provide key container facilities, which use strong encryption and operating system security to protect any cryptographic keys stored in the container. A detailed discussion of CSPs and CryptoAPI is beyond the scope of this book. All you need to know for this recipe is that you can store your cryptographic keys in a CSP key container and be relatively confident that it is secure as long as nobody knows your Windows password. Refer to the CryptoAPI information in the platform SDK documentation for complete details.

How It Works

To generate a new key pair and store the keys in the file named MyKeys.snk, execute the command sn -k MyKeys.snk. (.snk is the usual extension given to files containing strong name keys.) The generated file contains both your public and private keys. You can extract the public key using the command sn -p MyKeys.snk MyPublicKey.snk, which will create MyPublicKey.snk containing only the public key. Once you have this file in hands, you can view the public key using the command sn -tp MyPublicKeys.snk, which will generate output similar to the (abbreviated) listing shown here:

```
Microsoft (R) .NET Framework Strong Name Utility  Version 2.0.50727.42
Copyright (C) Microsoft Corporation. All rights reserved.

Public key is
07020000002400005253413200040000010001002b4ef3c2bbd6478802b64d0dd3f2e7c65ee
6478802b63cb894a782f3a1adbb46d3ee5ec5577e7dccc818937e964cbe997c12076c19f2d7
ad179f15f7dccca6c6b72a

Public key token is 2a1d3326445fc02a
```

    The public key token shown at the end of the listing is the last 8 bytes of a cryptographic hash code computed from the public key. Because the public key is so long, .NET uses the public key token for display purposes and as a compact mechanism for other assemblies to reference your public key. (Recipes 11-14 and 11-15 discuss cryptographic hash codes.)

    As the name suggests, you don't need to keep the public key (or public key token) secret. When you strong name your assembly (discussed in recipe 1-9), the compiler uses your private key to generate a digital signature (an encrypted hash code) of the assembly's manifest. The compiler embeds the digital signature and your public key in the assembly so that any consumer of the assembly can verify the digital signature.

    Keeping your private key secret is imperative. People with access to your private key can alter your assembly and create a new strong name—leaving your customers unaware they are using modified code. No mechanism exists to repudiate compromised strong name keys. If your private key is compromised, you must generate new keys and distribute new versions of your assemblies that are strong named using the new keys. You must also notify your customers about the compromised keys and explain to them which versions of your public key to trust—in all, a very costly exercise in terms of both money and credibility. You can protect your private key in many ways; the approach you use will depend on several factors:

- The structure and size of your organization
- Your development and release process
- The software and hardware resources you have available
- The requirements of your customer base

■**Tip** Commonly, a small group of trusted individuals (the *signing authority*) has responsibility for the security of your company's strong name signing keys and is responsible for signing all assemblies just prior to their final release. The ability to delay sign an assembly (discussed in recipe 1-11) facilitates this model and avoids the need to distribute private keys to all development team members.

One feature provided by the Strong Name tool to simplify the security of strong name keys is the use of CSP key containers. Once you have generated a key pair to a file, you can install the keys into a key container and delete the file. For example, to store the key pair contained in the file MyKeys.snk to a CSP container named StrongNameKeys, use the command sn -i MyKeys.snk StrongNameKeys. (Recipe 1-9 explains how to use strong name keys stored in a CSP key container.)

An important aspect of CSP key containers is that they include user-based containers and machine-based containers. Windows security ensures each user can access only their own user-based key containers. However, any user of a machine can access a machine-based container.

By default, the Strong Name tool uses machine-based key containers, meaning that anybody who can log on to your machine and who knows the name of your key container can sign an assembly with your strong name keys. To change the Strong Name tool to use user-based containers, use the command sn -m n, and to switch to machine-based stores, use the command sn -m y. The command sn -m will display whether the Strong Name tool is currently configured to use machine-based or user-based containers.

To delete the strong name keys from the StrongNameKeys container (as well as delete the container), use the command sn -d StrongNameKeys.

1-9. Give an Assembly a Strong Name

Problem

You need to give an assembly a strong name for several reasons:

- So it has a unique identity, which allows people to assign specific permissions to the assembly when configuring code access security policy
- So it can't be modified and passed off as your original assembly
- So it supports versioning and version policy
- So it can be installed in the GAC and shared across multiple applications

Solution

When you build your assembly using the command-line C# compiler, use the /keyfile or /keycontainer compiler switches to specify the location of your strong name key pair. Use assembly-level attributes to specify optional information such as the version number and culture for your assembly. The compiler will strong name your assembly as part of the compilation process.

■**Note** If you are using Visual Studio, you can configure your assembly to be strong named by opening the project properties, selecting the Signing tab, and checking the Sign the Assembly box. You will need to specify the location of the file where your strong name keys are stored—Visual Studio does not allow you to specify the name of a key container.

How It Works

To strong name an assembly using the C# compiler, you need the following:

- A strong name key pair contained either in a file or in a CSP key container. (Recipe 1-8 discusses how to create strong name key pairs.)

- Compiler switches to specify the location where the compiler can obtain your strong name key pair:

    - If your key pair is in a file, use the /keyfile compiler switch, and provide the name of the file where the keys are stored. For example, use /keyfile:MyKeyFile.snk.

    - If your key pair is in a CSP container, use the /keycontainer compiler switch, and provide the name of the CSP key container where the keys are stored. For example, use /keycontainer:MyKeyContainer.

- Optionally, specify the culture that your assembly supports by applying the attribute System.Reflection.AssemblyCultureAttribute to the assembly. (You can't specify a culture for executable assemblies because executable assemblies support only the neutral culture.)

- Optionally, specify the version of your assembly by applying the attribute System.Reflection. AssemblyVersionAttribute to the assembly.

■**Note** If you are using the .NET Framework 1.0 or 1.1, the command-line C# compiler does not support the /keyfile and /keycontainer compiler switches. Instead, you must use the AssemblyKeyFileAttribute and AssemblyKeyNameAttribute assembly-level attributes within your code to specify the location of your strong name keys. Alternatively, use the Assembly Linker tool (al.exe), which allows you to specify the strong name information on the command line using the /keyfile and /keyname switches. Refer to the Assembly Linker information in the .NET Framework SDK documentation for more details.

The Code

The executable code that follows (from a file named Recipe01-09.cs) shows how to use the optional attributes (shown in bold text) to specify the culture and the version for the assembly:

```
using System;
using System.Reflection;

[assembly:AssemblyCulture("")]
[assembly:AssemblyVersion("1.1.0.5")]
```

```
namespace Recipe01_09
{
    class Recipe01_09
    {
        public static void Main()
        {
            Console.WriteLine("Welcome to Visual C# 2005 Recipes");

            // Wait to continue.
            Console.WriteLine("\nMain method complete. Press Enter.");
            Console.Read();
        }
    }
}
```

Usage

To create a strong-named assembly from the example code, create the strong name keys and store them in a file named MyKeyFile using the command sn -k MyKeyFile.snk. Then install the keys into the CSP container named MyKeys using the command sn -i MyKeyFile.snk MyKeys. You can now compile the file into a strong-named assembly using the command csc /keycontainer:MyKeys Recipe01-09.cs.

1-10. Verify That a Strong-Named Assembly Has Not Been Modified

Problem

You need to verify that a strong-named assembly has not been modified after it was built.

Solution

Use the Strong Name tool (sn.exe) to verify the assembly's strong name.

How It Works

Whenever the .NET runtime loads a strong-named assembly, the runtime extracts the encrypted hash code that's embedded in the assembly and decrypts it with the public key, which is also embedded in the assembly. The runtime then calculates the hash code of the assembly manifest and compares it to the decrypted hash code. This verification process will identify whether the assembly has changed after compilation.

If an executable assembly fails strong name verification, the runtime will display an error message or an error dialog box (depending on whether the application is a console or Windows application). If executing code tries to load an assembly that fails verification, the runtime will throw a System.IO.FileLoadException with the message "Strong name validation failed," which you should handle appropriately.

As well as generating and managing strong name keys (discussed in recipe 1-8), the Strong Name tool allows you to verify strong-named assemblies. To verify that the strong-named assembly Recipe01-09.exe is unchanged, use the command sn -vf Recipe01-09.exe. The -v switch requests the Strong Name tool to verify the strong name of the specified assembly, and the -f switch forces strong name verification even if it has been previously disabled for the specified assembly. (You can disable strong name verification for specific assemblies using the -Vr switch, as in sn -Vr Recipe01-09.exe; see recipe 1-11 for details about why you would disable strong name verification.)

If the assembly passes strong name verification, you will see the following output:

```
Microsoft (R) .NET Framework Strong Name Utility  Version 2.0.50727.42
Copyright (C) Microsoft Corporation. All rights reserved.

Assembly 'Recipe01-09.exe' is valid
```

However, if the assembly has been modified, you will see this message:

```
Microsoft (R) .NET Framework Strong Name Utility  Version 2.0.50727.42
Copyright (C) Microsoft Corporation. All rights reserved.

Failed to verify assembly --
Strong name validation failed for assembly 'Recipe01-09.exe'.
```

1-11. Delay Sign an Assembly

Problem

You need to create a strong-named assembly, but you don't want to give all members of your development team access to the private key component of your strong name key pair.

Solution

Extract and distribute the public key component of your strong name key pair. Follow the instructions in recipe 1-9 that describe how to give your assembly a strong name. In addition, specify the /delaysign switch when you compile your assembly. Disable strong name verification for the assembly using the -Vr switch of the Strong Name tool (sn.exe).

■**Note** If you are using Visual Studio, you can configure your strong-named assembly to be delay signed by opening the project properties, selecting the Signing tab, and checking the Delay Sign Only box.

How It Works

Assemblies that reference strong-named assemblies contain the public key token of the referenced assemblies. This means the referenced assembly must be strong named before it can be referenced. In a development environment in which assemblies are regularly rebuilt, this would require every developer and tester to have access to your strong name key pair—a major security risk.

Instead of distributing the private key component of your strong name key pair to all members of the development team, the .NET Framework provides a mechanism named *delay signing* with which you can partially strong name an assembly. The partially strong-named assembly contains the public key and the public key token (required by referencing assemblies) but contains only a placeholder for the signature that would normally be generated using the private key.

After development is complete, the signing authority (who has responsibility for the security and use of your strong name key pair) re-signs the delay-signed assembly to complete its strong name. The signature is calculated using the private key and embedded in the assembly, making the assembly ready for distribution.

To delay sign an assembly, you need access only to the public key component of your strong name key pair. No security risk is associated with distributing the public key, and the signing authority should make the public key freely available to all developers. To extract the public key component from a strong name key file named MyKeyFile.snk and write it to a file named MyPublicKey.snk, use the command `sn -p MyKeyFile.snk MyPublicKey.snk`. If you store your strong name key pair in a CSP key container named MyKeys, extract the public key to a file named MyPublicKey.snk using the command `sn -pc MyKeys MyPublicKey.snk`.

Once you have a key file containing, the public key, you build the delay-signed assembly using the command-line C# compiler by specifying the `/delaysign` compiler switch. For example, to build a delay-signed assembly from a source file named Recipe01-11, use this command:

```
csc /delaysign /keyfile:MyPublicKey.snk Recipe01-11.cs.
```

When the runtime tries to load a delay-signed assembly, the runtime will identify the assembly as strong named and will attempt to verify the assembly, as discussed in recipe 1-10. Because it doesn't have a digital signature, you must configure the runtime on the local machine to stop verifying the assembly's strong name using the command `sn -Vr Recipe01-11.exe`. Note that you need to do so on every machine on which you want to run your application.

■**Tip** When using delay-signed assemblies, it's often useful to be able to compare different builds of the same assembly to ensure they differ only by their signatures. This is possible only if a delay-signed assembly has been re-signed using the `-R` switch of the Strong Name tool. To compare the two assemblies, use the command `sn -D assembly1 assembly2`.

Once development is complete, you need to re-sign the assembly to complete the assembly's strong name. The Strong Name tool allows you to do this without changing your source code or recompiling the assembly; however, you must have access to the private key component of the strong name key pair. To re-sign an assembly named Recipe01-11.exe with a key pair contained in the file MyKeys.snk, use the command `sn -R Recipe01-11.exe MyKeys.snk`. If the keys are stored in a CSP key container named MyKeys, use the command `sn -Rc Recipe01-11.exe MyKeys`.

Once you have re-signed the assembly, you should turn strong name verification for that assembly back on using the `-Vu` switch of the Strong Name tool, as in `sn -Vu Recipe01-11.exe`. To enable verification for *all* assemblies for which you have disabled strong name verification, use the command `sn -Vx`. You can list the assemblies for which verification is disabled using the command `sn -Vl`.

■**Note** If you are using the .NET Framework 1.0 or 1.1, the command-line C# compiler does not support the `/delaysign` compiler switch. Instead, you must use the `System.Reflection.AssemblyDelaySignAttribute` assembly-level attributes within your code to specify that you want the assembly delay signed. Alternatively, use the Assembly Linker tool (al.exe), which does support the `/delaysign` switch. Refer to the Assembly Linker information in the .NET Framework SDK documentation for more details.

1-12. Sign an Assembly with an Authenticode Digital Signature

Problem

You need to sign an assembly with Authenticode so that users of the assembly can be certain you are its publisher and the assembly is unchanged after signing.

Solution

Use the Sign Tool (signtool.exe) to sign the assembly with your software publisher certificate (SPC).

■**Note** Versions 1.0 and 1.1 of the .NET Framework provided a utility called the File Signing tool (signcode.exe) that enabled you to sign assemblies. The File Signing tool is not provided with the .NET Framework 2.0 and has been superseded by the Sign Tool discussed in this recipe.

How It Works

Strong names provide a unique identity for an assembly as well as proof of the assembly's integrity, but they provide no proof as to the publisher of the assembly. The .NET Framework allows you to use Authenticode technology to sign your assemblies. This enables consumers of your assemblies to confirm that you are the publisher, as well as confirm the integrity of the assembly. Authenticode signatures also act as evidence for the signed assembly, which people can use when configuring code access security policy.

To sign your assembly with an Authenticode signature, you need an SPC issued by a recognized *certificate authority* (CA). A CA is a company entrusted to issue SPCs (along with many other types of certificates) for use by individuals or companies. Before issuing a certificate, the CA is responsible for confirming that the requesters are who they claim to be and also for making sure the requestors sign contracts to ensure they don't misuse the certificates that the CA issues them.

To obtain an SPC, you should view the Microsoft Root Certificate Program Members list at http:// msdn.microsoft.com/library/default.asp?url=/library/en-us/dnsecure/html/rootcertprog.asp. Here you will find a list of CAs, many of whom can issue you an SPC. For testing purposes, you can create a test SPC using the process described in recipe 1-13. However, you can't distribute your software signed with this test certificate. Because a test SPC isn't issued by a trusted CA, most responsible users won't trust assemblies signed with it.

Once you have an SPC, you use the Sign Tool to Authenticode sign your assembly. The Sign Tool creates a digital signature of the assembly using the private key component of your SPC and embeds the signature and the public part of your SPC in your assembly (including your public key). When verifying your assembly, the consumer decrypts the encrypted hash code using your public key, recalculates the hash of the assembly, and compares the two hash codes to ensure they are the same. As long as the two hash codes match, the consumer can be certain that you signed the assembly and that it has not changed since you signed it.

Usage

The Sign Tool provides a graphical wizard that walks you through the steps to Authenticode sign your assembly. To sign an assembly named MyAssembly.exe, run this command:

```
signtool signwizard MyAssembly.exe
```

Click Next on the introduction screen, and you will see the File Selection screen, where you must enter the name of the assembly to Authenticode sign (see Figure 1-2). Because you specified the assembly name on the command line, it is already filled in. If you are signing a multifile assembly, specify the name of the file that contains the assembly manifest. If you intend to both strong name and Authenticode sign your assembly, you must strong name the assembly first—see recipe 1-9 for details on strong naming assemblies.

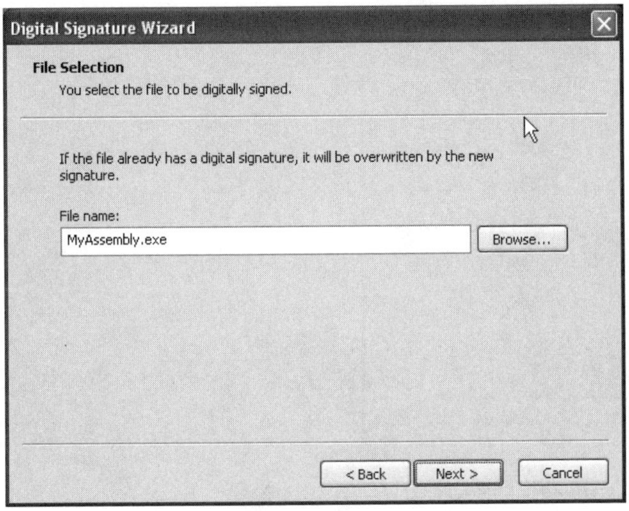

Figure 1-2. *The Sign Tool's File Selection screen*

Clicking Next takes you to the Signing Options screen (see Figure 1-3). If your SPC is in a certificate store, select the Typical radio button. If your SPC is in a file, select the Custom radio button. Then click Next.

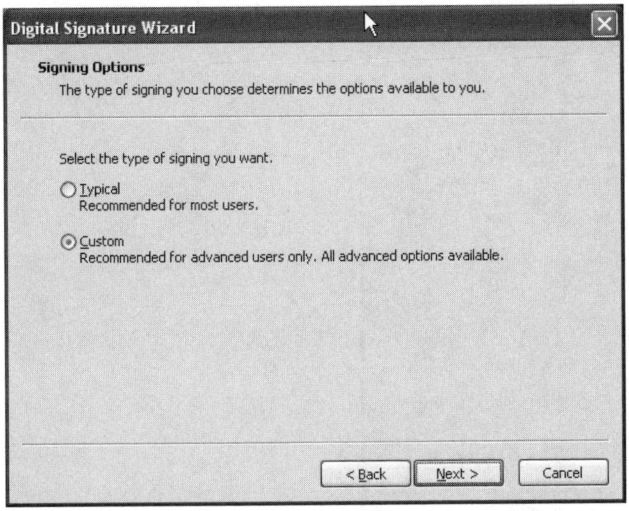

Figure 1-3. *The Sign Tool's Signing Options screen*

Assuming you want to use a file-based certificate (like the test certificate created in recipe 1-13), click the Select from File button on the Signature Certificate screen (see Figure 1-4), select the file containing your SPC certificate, and then click Next.

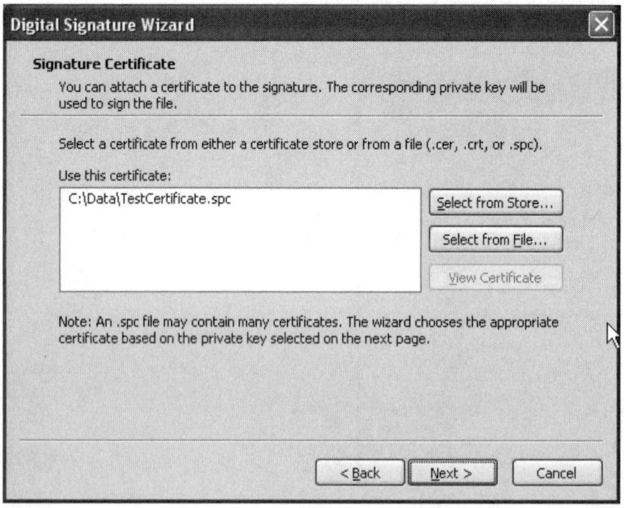

Figure 1-4. *The Sign Tool's Signature Certificate screen*

The Private Key screen allows you to identify the location of your private keys, which will either be in a file or in a CSP key container depending on where you created and stored them (see Figure 1-5). The example assumes they are in a file named PrivateKeys.pvk. When you click Next, if you selected to use a file, you will be prompted to enter a password to access the file (if required).

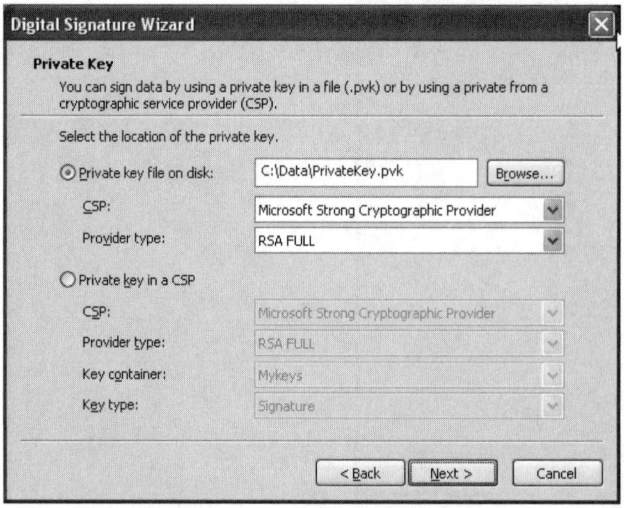

Figure 1-5. *The Sign Tool's Private Key screen*

You can then select whether to use the sha1 or md5 hash algorithm in the Hash Algorithm screen (see Figure 1-6). The default is sha1, which is suitable for most purposes. Pick an algorithm, and click Next.

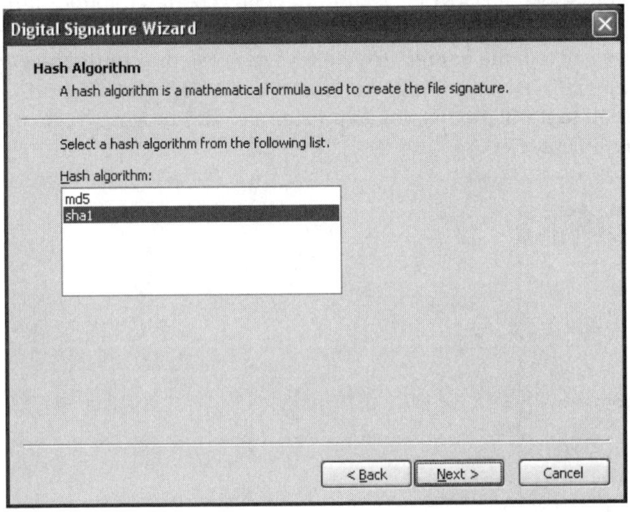

Figure 1-6. *The Sign Tool's Hash Algorithm screen*

Click Next to leave the default values for the Data Description screen and again for the Time-stamping screen. Finally, click Finish. If you are using a file-based private key that is password protected, you will once again be prompted to enter the password, after which the Sign Tool will Authenticode sign your assembly.

■Note The Sign Tool uses capicom.dll version 2.1.0.1. If an error occurs when you run signtool.exe that indicates capicom is not accessible or not registered, change to the directory where capicom.dll is located, and run the command `regsvr32 capicom.dll`.

1-13. Create and Trust a Test Software Publisher Certificate

Problem

You need to create an SPC to allow you to test the Authenticode signing of an assembly.

Solution

Use the Certificate Creation tool (makecert.exe) to create a test X.509 certificate and the Software Publisher Certificate Test tool (cert2spc.exe) to generate an SPC from this X.509 certificate. Trust the root test certificate using the Set Registry tool (setreg.exe).

How It Works

To create a test SPC for a software publisher named Allen Jones, create an X.509 certificate using the Certificate Creation tool. The command `makecert -n "CN=Allen Jones" -sk MyKeys TestCertificate.cer` creates a file named TestCertificate.cer containing an X.509 certificate and stores the associated private key in a CSP key container named MyKeys (which is automatically created if it does not exist). Alternatively, you can write the private key to a file by substituting the `-sk` switch with `-sv`. For example, to write the private key to a file named PrivateKeys.pvk, use the command `makecert -n " CN=Allen Jones" -sv PrivateKey.pvk TestCertificate.cer`. If you write your private key to a file, the Certificate Creation tool will prompt you to provide a password with which to protect the private key file (see Figure 1-7).

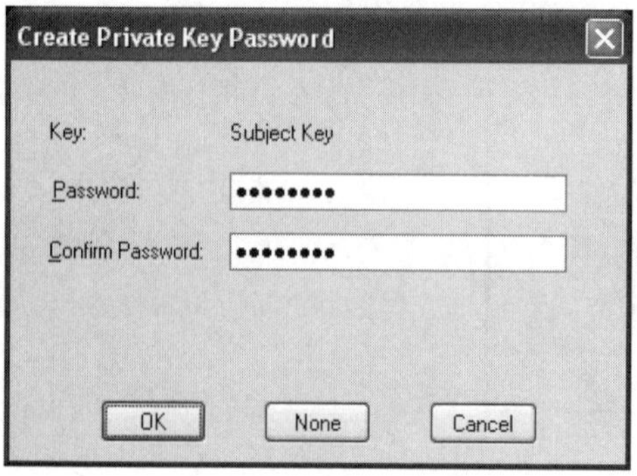

Figure 1-7. *The Certificate Creation tool requests a password when creating file-based private keys.*

The Certificate Creation tool supports many arguments, and Table 1-2 lists some of the more useful ones. You should consult the .NET Framework SDK documentation for full coverage of the Certificate Creation tool.

Table 1-2. *Commonly Used Switches of the Certificate Creation Tool*

Switch	Description
`-e`	Specifies the date when the certificate becomes invalid.
`-m`	Specifies the duration—in months—that the certificate remains valid.
`-n`	Specifies an X.500 name to associate with the certificate. This is the name of the software publisher that people will see when they view details of the SPC you create.
`-sk`	Specifies the name of the CSP key store in which to store the private key.
`-ss`	Specifies the name of the certificate store where the Certificate Creation tool should store the generated X.509 certificate.
`-sv`	Specifies the name of the file in which to store the private key.

Once you have created your X.509 certificate with the Certificate Creation tool, you need to convert it to an SPC with the Software Publisher Certificate Test tool (cert2spc.exe). To convert the certificate TestCertificate.cer to an SPC, use the command `cert2spc TestCertificate.cer TestCertificate.spc`. The Software Publisher Certificate Test tool doesn't offer any optional switches.

The final step before you can use your test SPC is to trust the root test CA, which is the default issuer of the test certificate. The Set Registry tool (setreg.exe) makes this a simple task with the command `setreg 1 true`. When you have finished using your test SPC, you must remove trust of the root test CA using the command `setreg 1 false`. You can now Authenticode sign assemblies with your test SPC using the process described in recipe 1-12.

1-14. Manage the Global Assembly Cache

Problem

You need to add or remove assemblies from the GAC.

Solution

Use the Global Assembly Cache tool (gacutil.exe) from the command line to view the contents of the GAC as well as to add and remove assemblies.

How It Works

Before you can install an assembly in the GAC, the assembly must have a strong name; see recipe 1-9 for details on how to strong name your assemblies. To install an assembly named SomeAssembly.dll into the GAC, use the command `gacutil /i SomeAssembly.dll`. You can install different versions of the same assembly in the GAC side-by-side to meet the versioning requirements of different applications.

To uninstall the SomeAssembly.dll assembly from the GAC, use the command `gacutil /u SomeAssembly`. Notice that you don't use the .dll extension to refer to the assembly once it's installed in the GAC. This will uninstall all assemblies with the specified name. To uninstall a particular version, specify the version along with the assembly name; for example, use `gacutil /u SomeAssembly,Version=1.0.0.5`.

To view the assemblies installed in the GAC, use the command `gacutil /l`. This will produce a long list of all the assemblies installed in the GAC, as well as a list of assemblies that have been precompiled to binary form and installed in the ngen cache. To avoid searching through this list to determine whether a particular assembly is installed in the GAC, use the command `gacutil /l SomeAssembly`.

■**Note** The .NET Framework uses the GAC only at runtime; the C# compiler won't look in the GAC to resolve any external references that your assembly references. During development, the C# compiler must be able to access a local copy of any referenced shared assemblies. You can either copy the shared assembly to the same directory as your source code or use the `/lib` switch of the C# compiler to specify the directory where the compiler can find the required assemblies.

1-15. Prevent People from Decompiling Your Code

Problem

You want to ensure people can't decompile your .NET assemblies.

Solution

Build server-based solutions where possible so that people don't have access to your assemblies. If you must distribute assemblies, you have no way to stop people from decompiling them. The best you can do is use obfuscation and components compiled to native code to make your assemblies more difficult to decompile.

How It Works

Because .NET assemblies consist of a standardized, platform-independent set of instruction codes and metadata that describes the types contained in the assembly, they are relatively easy to decompile. This allows decompilers to generate source code that is close to your original code with ease, which can be problematic if your code contains proprietary information or algorithms that you want to keep secret.

The only way to ensure people can't decompile your assemblies is to stop people from getting your assemblies in the first place. Where possible, implement server-based solutions such as Microsoft ASP.NET applications and Web services. With the security correctly configured on your server, nobody will be able to access your assemblies and therefore won't be able to decompile them.

When building a server solution is not appropriate, you have the following two options:

- Use an obfuscator to make it difficult to understand your code once it is decompiled. Some versions of Visual Studio include the Community Edition of an obfuscator named Dotfuscator. Obfuscators use a variety of techniques to make your assembly difficult to decompile; principal among these techniques are

  - Renaming of `private` methods and fields in such a way that it's difficult to read and understand the purpose of your code, and

  - Inserting control flow statements to make the logic of your application difficult to follow.

- Build the parts of your application that you want to keep secret in native DLLs or COM objects, and then call them from your managed application using P/Invoke or COM Interop. (See Chapter 12 for recipes that show you how to call unmanaged code.)

Neither approach will stop a skilled and determined person from reverse engineering your code, but both approaches will make the job significantly more difficult and deter most casual observers.

■**Note** The risks of application decompilation aren't specific to C# or .NET. A determined person can reverse engineer any software if they have the time and the skill.

1-16. Manipulate the Appearance of the Console

Problem

You want to control the visual appearance of the Windows console.

Solution

Use the `static` properties and methods of the `System.Console` class.

How It Works

Version 2.0 of the .NET Framework dramatically enhances the control you have over the appearance and operation of the Windows console. Table 1-3 describes the properties and methods of the Console class that you can use to control the console's appearance.

Table 1-3. *Properties and Methods to Control the Appearance of the Console*

Member	Description
Properties	
BackgroundColor	Gets and sets the background color of the console using one of the values from the System.ConsoleColor enumeration. Only new text written to the console will appear in this color. To make the entire console this color, call the method Clear after you have configured the BackgroundColor property.
BufferHeight	Gets and sets the buffer height in terms of rows.
BufferWidth	Gets and sets the buffer width in terms of columns.
CursorLeft	Gets and sets the column position of the cursor within the buffer.
CursorSize	Gets and sets the height of the cursor as a percentage of a character cell.
CursorTop	Gets and sets the row position of the cursor within the buffer.
CursorVisible	Gets and sets whether the cursor is visible.
ForegroundColor	Gets and sets the text color of the console using one of the values from the System.ConsoleColor enumeration. Only new text written to the console will appear in this color. To make the entire console this color, call the method Clear after you have configured the ForegroundColor property.
LargestWindowHeight	Returns the largest possible number of rows based on the current font and screen resolution.
LargestWindowWidth	Returns the largest possible number of columns based on the current font and screen resolution.
Title	Gets and sets text shown in the title bar.
WindowHeight	Gets and sets the width in terms of character rows.
WindowWidth	Gets and sets the width in terms of character columns.
Methods	
Clear	Clears the console.
ResetColor	Sets the foreground and background colors to their default values as configured within Windows.
SetWindowSize	Sets the width and height in terms of columns and rows.

The Code

The following example demonstrates how to use the properties and methods of the Console class to dynamically change the appearance of the Windows console:

```
using System;

namespace Apress.VisualCSharpRecipes.Chapter01
{
    public class Recipe01_16
    {
        static void Main(string[] args)
```

```csharp
{
    // Display the standard console.
    Console.Title = "Standard Console";
    Console.WriteLine("Press Enter to change the console's appearance.");
    Console.ReadLine();

    // Change the console appearance and redisplay.
    Console.Title = "Colored Text";
    Console.ForegroundColor = ConsoleColor.Red;
    Console.BackgroundColor = ConsoleColor.Green;
    Console.WriteLine("Press Enter to change the console's appearance.");
    Console.ReadLine();

    // Change the console appearance and redisplay.
    Console.Title = "Cleared / Colored Console";
    Console.ForegroundColor = ConsoleColor.Blue;
    Console.BackgroundColor = ConsoleColor.Yellow;
    Console.Clear();
    Console.WriteLine("Press Enter to change the console's appearance.");
    Console.ReadLine();

    // Change the console appearance and redisplay.
    Console.Title = "Resized Console";
    Console.ResetColor();
    Console.Clear();
    Console.SetWindowSize(100, 50);
    Console.BufferHeight = 500;
    Console.BufferWidth = 100;
    Console.CursorLeft = 20;
    Console.CursorSize = 50;
    Console.CursorTop = 20;
    Console.CursorVisible = false;
    Console.WriteLine("Main method complete. Press Enter.");
    Console.ReadLine();
    }
  }
}
```

CHAPTER 2

Data Manipulation

Most applications need to manipulate some form of data. The Microsoft .NET Framework provides many techniques that simplify or improve the efficiency of common data-manipulation tasks. The recipes in this chapter describe how to do the following:

- Manipulate the contents of strings efficiently to avoid the overhead of automatic string creation due to the immutability of strings (recipe 2-1)
- Represent basic data types using different encoding schemes or as byte arrays to allow you to share data with external systems (recipes 2-2, 2-3, and 2-4)
- Validate user input and manipulate string values using regular expressions (recipes 2-5 and 2-6)
- Create System.DateTime objects from string values, such as those that a user might enter, and display DateTime objects as formatted strings (recipe 2-7)
- Mathematically manipulate DateTime objects in order to compare dates or add/subtract periods of time from a date (recipe 2-8)
- Sort the contents of an array or an ArrayList collection (recipe 2-9)
- Copy the contents of a collection to an array (recipe 2-10)
- Use the standard generic collection classes to instantiate a strongly typed collection (recipe 2-11)
- Use generics to define your own general-purpose container or collection class that will be strongly typed when it is used (recipe 2-12)
- Serialize object state and persist it to a file (recipe 2-13)
- Read user input from the Windows console (recipe 2-14)

2-1. Manipulate the Contents of a String Efficiently

Problem

You need to manipulate the contents of a String object and want to avoid the overhead of automatic String creation caused by the immutability of String objects.

Solution

Use the System.Text.StringBuilder class to perform the manipulations and convert the result to a String object using the StringBuilder.ToString method.

How It Works

String objects in .NET are immutable, meaning that once created their content cannot be changed. For example, if you build a string by concatenating a number of characters or smaller strings, the common language runtime (CLR) will create a completely new String object whenever you add a new element to the end of the existing string. This can result in significant overhead if your application performs frequent string manipulation.

The StringBuilder class offers a solution by providing a character buffer and allowing you to manipulate its contents without the runtime creating a new object as a result of every change. You can create a new StringBuilder object that is empty or initialized with the content of an existing String object. You can manipulate the content of the StringBuilder object using overloaded methods that allow you to insert and append string representations of different data types. At any time, you can obtain a String representation of the current content of the StringBuilder object by calling StringBuilder.ToString.

Two important properties of StringBuilder control its behavior as you append new data: Capacity and Length. Capacity represents the size of the StringBuilder buffer, and Length represents the length of the buffer's current content. If you append new data that results in the number of characters in the StringBuilder object (Length) exceeding the capacity of the StringBuilder object (Capacity), the StringBuilder must allocate a new buffer to hold the data. The size of this new buffer is double the size of the previous Capacity value. Used carelessly, this buffer reallocation can negate much of the benefit of using StringBuilder. If you know the length of data you need to work with, or know an upper limit, you can avoid unnecessary buffer reallocation by specifying the capacity at creation time or setting the Capacity property manually. Note that 16 is the default Capacity property setting. When setting the Capacity and Length properties, be aware of the following behavior:

- If you set Capacity to a value less than the value of Length, the Capacity property throws the exception System.ArgumentOutOfRangeException. The same exception is also thrown if you try to raise the Capacity setting above the value of the MaxCapacity property. This should not be a problem except if you want to allocate more that 2 gigabytes (GB).

- If you set Length to a value less than the length of the current content, the content is truncated.

- If you set Length to a value greater than the length of the current content, the buffer is padded with spaces to the specified length. Setting Length to a value greater than Capacity automatically adjusts the Capacity value to be the same as the new Length value.

The Code

The ReverseString method shown in the following example demonstrates the use of the StringBuilder class to reverse a string. If you did not use the StringBuilder class to perform this operation, it would be significantly more expensive in terms of resource utilization, especially as the input string is made longer. The method creates a StringBuilder object of the correct capacity to ensure that no buffer reallocation is required during the reversal operation.

```
using System;
using System.Text;

namespace Apress.VisualCSharpRecipes.Chapter02
{
    class Recipe02_01
    {
        public static string ReverseString(string str)
        {
            // Make sure we have a reversible string.
            if (str == null || str.Length <= 1)
```

```
    {
        return str;
    }

    // Create a StringBuilder object with the required capacity.
    StringBuilder revStr = new StringBuilder(str.Length);

    // Loop backward through the source string one character at a time and
    // append each character to the StringBuilder.
    for (int count = str.Length - 1; count > -1; count--)
    {
        revStr.Append(str[count]);
    }

    // Return the reversed string.
    return revStr.ToString();
}

public static void Main()
{
    Console.WriteLine(ReverseString("Madam Im Adam"));

    Console.WriteLine(ReverseString(
      "The quick brown fox jumped over the lazy dog."));

    // Wait to continue.
    Console.WriteLine("\nMain method complete. Press Enter");
    Console.ReadLine();
}
    }
}
```

2-2. Encode a String Using Alternate Character Encoding

Problem

You need to exchange character data with systems that use character-encoding schemes other than UTF-16, which is the character-encoding scheme used internally by the CLR.

Solution

Use the System.Text.Encoding class and its subclasses to convert characters between different encoding schemes.

How It Works

Unicode is not the only character-encoding scheme, nor is UTF-16 the only way to represent Unicode characters. When your application needs to exchange character data with external systems (particularly legacy systems) through an array of bytes, you may need to convert character data between UTF-16 and the encoding scheme supported by the other system.

The abstract class Encoding and its concrete subclasses provide the functionality to convert characters to and from a variety of encoding schemes. Each subclass instance supports the conversion of characters between UTF-16 and one other encoding scheme. You obtain instances of the encoding-specific classes using the static factory method Encoding.GetEncoding, which accepts either the name or the code page number of the required encoding scheme.

Table 2-1 lists some commonly used character-encoding schemes and the code page number you must pass to the GetEncoding method to create an instance of the appropriate encoding class. The table also shows static properties of the Encoding class that provide shortcuts for obtaining the most commonly used types of encoding objects.

Table 2-1. *Character-Encoding Classes*

Encoding Scheme	Class	Create Using
ASCII	ASCIIEncoding	GetEncoding(20127) or the ASCII property
Default (current Microsoft Windows default)	Encoding	GetEncoding(0) or the Default property
UTF-7	UTF7Encoding	GetEncoding(65000) or the UTF7 property
UTF-8	UTF8Encoding	GetEncoding(65001) or the UTF8 property
UTF-16 (Big Endian)	UnicodeEncoding	GetEncoding(1201) or the BigEndianUnicode property
UTF-16 (Little Endian)	UnicodeEncoding	GetEncoding(1200) or the Unicode property
Windows OS	Encoding	GetEncoding(1252)

Once you have an Encoding object of the appropriate type, you convert a UTF-16 encoded Unicode string to a byte array of encoded characters using the GetBytes method. Conversely, you convert a byte array of encoded characters to a string using the GetString method.

The Code

The following example demonstrates the use of some encoding classes.

```
using System;
using System.IO;
using System.Text;

namespace Apress.VisualCSharpRecipes.Chapter02
{
    class Recipe02_02
    {
        public static void Main()
        {
            // Create a file to hold the output.
            using (StreamWriter output = new StreamWriter("output.txt"))
            {
                // Create and write a string containing the symbol for pi.
                string srcString = "Area = \u03A0r^2";
                output.WriteLine("Source Text : " + srcString);

                // Write the UTF-16 encoded bytes of the source string.
                byte[] utf16String = Encoding.Unicode.GetBytes(srcString);
                output.WriteLine("UTF-16 Bytes: {0}",
                    BitConverter.ToString(utf16String));
```

```
        // Convert the UTF-16 encoded source string to UTF-8 and ASCII.
        byte[] utf8String = Encoding.UTF8.GetBytes(srcString);
        byte[] asciiString = Encoding.ASCII.GetBytes(srcString);

        // Write the UTF-8 and ASCII encoded byte arrays.
        output.WriteLine("UTF-8  Bytes: {0}",
            BitConverter.ToString(utf8String));
        output.WriteLine("ASCII  Bytes: {0}",
            BitConverter.ToString(asciiString));

        // Convert UTF-8 and ASCII encoded bytes back to UTF-16 encoded
        // string and write.
        output.WriteLine("UTF-8  Text : {0}",
            Encoding.UTF8.GetString(utf8String));
        output.WriteLine("ASCII  Text : {0}",
            Encoding.ASCII.GetString(asciiString));
    }

    // Wait to continue.
    Console.WriteLine("\nMain method complete. Press Enter");
    Console.ReadLine();
    }
  }
}
```

Usage

Running the code will generate a file named output.txt. If you open this file in a text editor that supports Unicode, you will see the following content:

```
Source Text : Area = πr^2
UTF-16 Bytes: 41-00-72-00-65-00-61-00-20-00-3D-00-20-00-A0-03-72-00-5E-00-32-00
UTF-8  Bytes: 41-72-65-61-20-3D-20-CE-A0-72-5E-32
ASCII  Bytes: 41-72-65-61-20-3D-20-3F-72-5E-32
UTF-8  Text : Area = πr^2
ASCII  Text : Area = ?r^2
```

Notice that using UTF-16 encoding, each character occupies 2 bytes, but because most of the characters are standard characters, the high-order byte is 0. (The use of little-endian byte ordering means that the low-order byte appears first.) This means that most of the characters are encoded using the same numeric values across all three encoding schemes. However, the numeric value for the symbol pi (emphasized in bold in the preceding output) is different in each of the encodings. The value of pi requires more than 1 byte to represent. UTF-8 encoding uses 2 bytes, but ASCII has no direct equivalent and so replaces pi with the code 3F. As you can see in the ASCII text version of the string, 3F is the symbol for an English question mark (?).

■**Caution** If you convert Unicode characters to ASCII or a specific code page encoding scheme, you risk losing data. Any Unicode character with a character code that cannot be represented in the scheme will be ignored.

Notes

The Encoding class also provides the static method Convert to simplify the conversion of a byte array from one encoding scheme to another without the need to manually perform an interim conversion to UTF-16. For example, the following statement converts the ASCII-encoded bytes contained in the asciiString byte array directly from ASCII encoding to UTF-8 encoding:

```
byte[] utf8String = Encoding.Convert(Encoding.ASCII, Encoding.UTF8,asciiString);
```

2-3. Convert Basic Value Types to Byte Arrays

Problem

You need to convert basic value types to byte arrays.

Solution

The static methods of the System.BitConverter class provide a convenient mechanism for converting most basic value types to and from byte arrays. An exception is the decimal type. To convert a decimal type to or from a byte array, you need to use a System.IO.MemoryStream object.

How It Works

The static method GetBytes of the BitConverter class provides overloads that take most of the standard value types and return the value encoded as an array of bytes. Support is provided for the bool, char, double, short, int, long, float, ushort, uint, and ulong data types. BitConverter also provides a set of static methods that support the conversion of byte arrays to each of the standard value types. These are named ToBoolean, ToUInt32, ToDouble, and so on.

Unfortunately, the BitConverter class does not provide support for converting the decimal type. Instead, write the decimal type to a MemoryStream instance using a System.IO.BinaryWriter object, and then call the MemoryStream.ToArray method. To create a decimal type from a byte array, create a MemoryStream object from the byte array and read the decimal type from the MemoryStream object using a System.IO.BinaryReader instance.

The Code

The following example demonstrates the use of BitConverter to convert a bool type and an int type to and from a byte array. The second argument to each of the ToBoolean and ToInt32 methods is a zero-based offset into the byte array where the BitConverter should start taking the bytes to create the data value. The code also shows how to convert a decimal type to a byte array using a MemoryStream object and a BinaryWriter object, as well as how to convert a byte array to a decimal type using a BinaryReader object to read from the MemoryStream object.

```
using System;
using System.IO;

namespace Apress.VisualCSharpRecipes.Chapter02
{
    class Recipe02_03
    {
        // Create a byte array from a decimal.
        public static byte[] DecimalToByteArray (decimal src)
        {
            // Create a MemoryStream as a buffer to hold the binary data.
            using (MemoryStream stream = new MemoryStream())
```

```csharp
{
    // Create a BinaryWriter to write binary data to the stream.
    using (BinaryWriter writer = new BinaryWriter(stream))
    {
        // Write the decimal to the BinaryWriter/MemoryStream.
        writer.Write(src);

        // Return the byte representation of the decimal.
        return stream.ToArray();
    }
}
}

// Create a decimal from a byte array.
public static decimal ByteArrayToDecimal (byte[] src)
{
    // Create a MemoryStream containing the byte array.
    using (MemoryStream stream = new MemoryStream(src))
    {
        // Create a BinaryReader to read the decimal from the stream.
        using (BinaryReader reader = new BinaryReader(stream))
        {
            // Read and return the decimal from the
            // BinaryReader/MemoryStream.
            return reader.ReadDecimal();
        }
    }
}

public static void Main()
{
    byte[] b = null;

    // Convert a bool to a byte array and display.
    b = BitConverter.GetBytes(true);
    Console.WriteLine(BitConverter.ToString(b));

    // Convert a byte array to a bool and display.
    Console.WriteLine(BitConverter.ToBoolean(b,0));

    // Convert an int to a byte array and display.
    b = BitConverter.GetBytes(3678);
    Console.WriteLine(BitConverter.ToString(b));

    // Convert a byte array to an int and display.
    Console.WriteLine(BitConverter.ToInt32(b,0));

    // Convert a decimal to a byte array and display.
    b = DecimalToByteArray(285998345545.563846696m);
    Console.WriteLine(BitConverter.ToString(b));

    // Convert a byte array to a decimal and display.
    Console.WriteLine(ByteArrayToDecimal(b));

    // Wait to continue.
    Console.WriteLine("Main method complete. Press Enter");
    Console.ReadLine();
```

```
            }
        }
}
```

Tip The `BitConverter.ToString` method provides a convenient mechanism for obtaining a `String` representation of a byte array. Calling `ToString` and passing a byte array as an argument will return a `String` object
containing the hexadecimal value of each byte in the array separated by a hyphen, for example "34-A7-2C".
Unfortunately, there is no standard method for reversing this process to obtain a byte array from a string with this
format.

2-4. Base64 Encode Binary Data

Problem

You need to convert binary data into a form that can be stored as part of an ASCII text file (such as
an XML file) or sent as part of a text e-mail message.

Solution

Use the `static` methods `ToBase64CharArray` and `FromBase64CharArray` of the `System.Convert` class
to convert your binary data to and from a Base64-encoded `char` array. If you need to work with
the encoded data as a string value instead of a `char` array, you can use the `ToBase64String` and
`FromBase64String` methods of the `Convert` class instead.

How It Works

Base64 is an encoding scheme that enables you to represent binary data as a series of ASCII characters
so that it can be included in text files and e-mail messages in which raw binary data is unacceptable.
Base64 encoding works by spreading the contents of 3 bytes of input data across 4 bytes and ensuring
each byte uses only the 7 low-order bits to contain data. This means that each byte of Base64-encoded
data is equivalent to an ASCII character and can be stored or transmitted anywhere ASCII characters
are permitted.

The `ToBase64CharArray` and `FromBase64CharArray` methods of the `Convert` class make it straightforward to Base64 encode and decode data. However, before Base64 encoding, you must convert your
data to a byte array. Similarly, when decoding, you must convert the byte array back to the appropriate
data type. See recipe 2-2 for details on converting string data to and from byte arrays and recipe 2-3
for details on converting basic value types. The `ToBase64String` and `FromBase64String` methods of
the `Convert` class deal with string representations of Base64-encoded data.

The Code

The example shown here demonstrates how to Base64 encode and decode a byte array,
a Unicode string, an `int` type, and a `decimal` type using the `Convert` class. The `DecimalToBase64`
and `Base64ToDecimal` methods rely on the `ByteArrayToDecimal` and `DecimalToByteArray` methods
listed in recipe 2-3.

```
using System;
using System.IO;
using System.Text;
```

```csharp
namespace Apress.VisualCSharpRecipes.Chapter02
{
    class Recipe02_04
    {
        // Create a byte array from a decimal.
        public static byte[] DecimalToByteArray (decimal src)
        {
            // Create a MemoryStream as a buffer to hold the binary data.
            using (MemoryStream stream = new MemoryStream())
            {
                // Create a BinaryWriter to write binary data the stream.
                using (BinaryWriter writer = new BinaryWriter(stream))
                {
                    // Write the decimal to the BinaryWriter/MemoryStream.
                    writer.Write(src);

                    // Return the byte representation of the decimal.
                    return stream.ToArray();
                }
            }
        }

        // Create a decimal from a byte array.
        public static decimal ByteArrayToDecimal (byte[] src)
        {
            // Create a MemoryStream containing the byte array.
            using (MemoryStream stream = new MemoryStream(src))
            {
                // Create a BinaryReader to read the decimal from the stream.
                using (BinaryReader reader = new BinaryReader(stream))
                {
                    // Read and return the decimal from the
                    // BinaryReader/MemoryStream.
                    return reader.ReadDecimal();
                }
            }
        }

        // Base64 encode a Unicode string.
        public static string StringToBase64 (string src)
        {
            // Get a byte representation of the source string.
            byte[] b = Encoding.Unicode.GetBytes(src);

            // Return the Base64-encoded string.
            return Convert.ToBase64String(b);
        }

        // Decode a Base64-encoded Unicode string.
        public static string Base64ToString (string src)
        {
            // Decode the Base64-encoded string to a byte array.
            byte[] b = Convert.FromBase64String(src);

            // Return the decoded Unicode string.
            return Encoding.Unicode.GetString(b);
        }
```

```csharp
// Base64 encode a decimal.
public static string DecimalToBase64 (decimal src)
{
    // Get a byte representation of the decimal.
    byte[] b = DecimalToByteArray(src);

    // Return the Base64-encoded decimal.
    return Convert.ToBase64String(b);
}

// Decode a Base64-encoded decimal.
public static decimal Base64ToDecimal (string src)
{
    // Decode the Base64-encoded decimal to a byte array.
    byte[] b = Convert.FromBase64String(src);

    // Return the decoded decimal.
    return ByteArrayToDecimal(b);
}

// Base64 encode an int.
public static string IntToBase64 (int src)
{
    // Get a byte representation of the int.
    byte[] b = BitConverter.GetBytes(src);

    // Return the Base64-encoded int.
    return Convert.ToBase64String(b);
}

// Decode a Base64-encoded int.
public static int Base64ToInt (string src)
{
    // Decode the Base64-encoded int to a byte array.
    byte[] b = Convert.FromBase64String(src);

    // Return the decoded int.
    return BitConverter.ToInt32(b,0);
}

public static void Main()
{
    // Encode and decode a general byte array. Need to create a char[]
    // to hold the Base64 encoded data. The size of the char[] must
    // be at least 4/3 the size of the source byte[] and must be
    // divisible by 4.
    byte[] data = { 0x04, 0x43, 0x5F, 0xFF, 0x0, 0xF0, 0x2D, 0x62, 0x78,
        0x22, 0x15, 0x51, 0x5A, 0xD6, 0x0C, 0x59, 0x36, 0x63, 0xBD, 0xC2,
        0xD5, 0x0F, 0x8C, 0xF5, 0xCA, 0x0C};

    char[] base64data =
        new char[(int)(Math.Ceiling((double)data.Length / 3) * 4)];

    Console.WriteLine("\nByte array encoding/decoding");
    Convert.ToBase64CharArray(data, 0, data.Length, base64data, 0);
    Console.WriteLine(new String(base64data));
```

```
        Console.WriteLine(BitConverter.ToString(
            Convert.FromBase64CharArray(base64data, 0, base64data.Length)));

        // Encode and decode a string.
        Console.WriteLine(StringToBase64
            ("Welcome to Visual C# Recipes from Apress"));
        Console.WriteLine(Base64ToString("VwBlAGwAYwBvAG0AZQAgAHQAbwA" +
            "gAFYAaQBzAHUAYQBsACAAQwAjACAAUgBlAGMAaQBwAGUAcwAgAGYAcgB" +
            "vAG0AIABBBAHAAcgBlAHMAcwA="));

        // Encode and decode a decimal.
        Console.WriteLine(DecimalToBase64(285998345545.563846696m));
        Console.WriteLine(Base64ToDecimal("KDjBUPO7BoEPAAAAAAAAJAA=="));

        // Encode and decode an int.
        Console.WriteLine(IntToBase64(35789));
        Console.WriteLine(Base64ToInt("zYsAAA=="));

        // Wait to continue.
        Console.WriteLine("\nMain method complete. Press Enter");
        Console.ReadLine();
    }
  }
}
```

■**Caution** If you Base64 encode binary data for the purpose of including it as MIME data in an e-mail message, be aware that the maximum allowed line length in MIME for Base64-encoded data is 76 characters. Therefore, if your data is longer than 76 characters, you must insert a new line. For further information about the MIME standard, consult RFCs 2045 through 2049.

2-5. Validate Input Using Regular Expressions

Problem

You need to validate that user input or data read from a file has the expected structure and content. For example, you want to ensure that a user enters a valid IP address, telephone number, or e-mail address.

Solution

Use regular expressions to ensure that the input data follows the correct structure and contains only valid characters for the expected type of information.

How It Works

When a user inputs data to your application or your application reads data from a file, it's good practice to assume that the data is bad until you have verified its accuracy. One common validation requirement is to ensure that data entries such as e-mail addresses, telephone numbers, and credit card numbers follow the pattern and content constraints expected of such data. Obviously, you cannot be sure the actual data entered is valid until you use it, and you cannot compare it against values that are known to be correct. However, ensuring the data has the correct structure and content is a good first step to determining whether the input is accurate. Regular expressions provide an excellent mechanism for evaluating strings for the presence of patterns, and you can use this to your advantage when validating input data.

The first thing you must do is figure out the regular expression syntax that will correctly match the structure and content of data you are trying to validate. This is by far the most difficult aspect of using regular expressions. Many resources exist to help you with regular expressions, such as The Regulator (http://regex.osherove.com/) and RegExDesigner.NET by Chris Sells (http://www.sellsbrothers.com/tools/#regexd). The RegExLib.com web site (http://www.regxlib.com/) also provides hundreds of useful prebuilt expressions.

Regular expressions are constructed from two types of elements: *literals* and *metacharacters*. Literals represent specific characters that appear in the pattern you want to match. Metacharacters provide support for wildcard matching, ranges, grouping, repetition, conditionals, and other control mechanisms. Table 2-2 describes some of the more commonly used regular expression metacharacter elements. (Consult the .NET SDK documentation for a full description of regular expressions.)

Table 2-2. *Commonly Used Regular Expression Metacharacter Elements*

Element	Description
.	Specifies any character except a newline character (\n)
\d	Specifies any decimal digit
\D	Specifies any nondigit
\s	Specifies any white-space character
\S	Specifies any non-white-space character
\w	Specifies any word character
\W	Specifies any nonword character
^	Specifies the beginning of the string or line
\A	Specifies the beginning of the string
$	Specifies the end of the string or line
\z	Specifies the end of the string
|	Matches one of the expressions separated by the vertical bar; for example, AAA|ABA|ABB will match one of *AAA*, *ABA*, or *ABB* (the expression is evaluated left to right)
[abc]	Specifies a match with one of the specified characters; for example, [AbC] will match *A*, *b*, or *C*, but no other character
[^abc]	Specifies a match with any one character except those specified; for example, [^AbC] will not match *A*, *b*, or *C*, but will match *B*, *F*, and so on
[a-z]	Specifies a match with any one character in the specified range; for example, [A-C] will match *A*, *B*, or *C*
( )	Identifies a subexpression so that it's treated as a single element by the regular expression elements described in this table
?	Specifies one or zero occurrences of the previous character or subexpression; for example, A?B matches *B* and *AB*, but not *AAB*
*	Specifies zero or more occurrences of the previous character or subexpression; for example, A*B matches *B*, *AB*, *AAB*, *AAAB*, and so on
+	Specifies one or more occurrences of the previous character or subexpression; for example, A+B matches *AB*, *AAB*, *AAAB*, and so on, but not *B*
{n}	Specifies exactly *n* occurrences of the preceding character or subexpression; for example, A{2} matches only *AA*

Element	Description
{n,}	Specifies a minimum of *n* occurrences of the preceding character or subexpression; for example, A{2,} matches *AA, AAA, AAAA*, and so on, but not *A*
{n, m}	Specifies a minimum of *n* and a maximum of *m* occurrences of the preceding character; for example, A{2,4} matches *AA, AAA*, and *AAAA*, but not *A* or *AAAAA*

The more complex the data you are trying to match, the more complex the regular expression syntax becomes. For example, ensuring that input contains only numbers or is of a minimum length is trivial, but ensuring a string contains a valid URL is extremely complex. Table 2-3 shows some examples of regular expressions that match against commonly required data types.

Table 2-3. *Commonly Used Regular Expressions*

Input Type	Description	Regular Expression
Numeric input	The input consists of one or more decimal digits; for example, 5 or 5683874674.	`^\d+$`
Personal identification number (PIN)	The input consists of four decimal digits; for example, 1234.	`^\d{4}$`
Simple password	The input consists of six to eight characters; for example, *ghtd6f* or *b8c7hogh*.	`^\w{6,8}$`
Credit card number	The input consists of data that matches the pattern of most major credit card numbers; for example, 4921835221552042 or 4921-8352-2155-2042.	`^\d{4}-?\d{4}-?\d{4}-?\d{4}$`
E-mail address	The input consists of an Internet e-mail address. The [\w-]+ expression indicates that each address element must consist of one or more word characters or hyphens; for example, somebody@adatum.com.	`^[\w-]+@([\w-]+\.)+[\w-]+$`
HTTP or HTTPS URL	The input consists of an HTTP-based or HTTPS-based URL; for example, http://www.apress.com.	`^https?://([\w-]+\.)+ [\w-]+(/[\w-./?%=]*)?$`

Once you know the correct regular expression syntax, create a new System.Text. RegularExpressions.Regex object, passing a string containing the regular expression to the Regex constructor. Then call the IsMatch method of the Regex object and pass the string that you want to validate. IsMatch returns a bool value indicating whether the Regex object found a match in the string. The regular expression syntax determines whether the Regex object will match against only the full string or match against patterns contained within the string. (See the ^, \A, $, and \z entries in Table 2-2.)

The Code

The ValidateInput method shown in the following example tests any input string to see if it matches a specified regular expression.

```
using System;
using System.Text.RegularExpressions;
```

```
namespace Apress.VisualCSharpRecipes.Chapter02
{
    class Recipe02_05
    {
        public static bool ValidateInput(string regex, string input)
        {
            // Create a new Regex based on the specified regular expression.
            Regex r = new Regex(regex);

            // Test if the specified input matches the regular expression.
            return r.IsMatch(input);
        }

        public static void Main(string[] args)
        {
            // Test the input from the command line. The first argument is the
            // regular expression, and the second is the input.
            Console.WriteLine("Regular Expression: {0}", args[0]);
            Console.WriteLine("Input: {0}", args[1]);
            Console.WriteLine("Valid = {0}", ValidateInput(args[0], args[1]));

            // Wait to continue.
            Console.WriteLine("\nMain method complete. Press Enter");
            Console.ReadLine();
        }
    }
}
```

Usage

To execute the example, run Recipe02-05.exe and pass the regular expression and data to test as command-line arguments. For example, to test for a correctly formed e-mail address, type the following:

```
Recipe02-05 ^[\w-]+@([\w-]+\.)+[\w-]+$ myname@mydomain.com
```

The result would be as follows:

```
Regular Expression: ^[\w-]+@([\w-]+\.)+[\w-]+$
Input: myname@mydomain.com
Valid = True
```

Notes

You can use a Regex object repeatedly to test multiple strings, but you cannot change the regular expression tested for by a Regex object. You must create a new Regex object to test for a different pattern. Because the ValidateInput method creates a new Regex instance each time it's called, you do not get the ability to reuse the Regex object. As such, a more suitable alternative in this case would be to use a static overload of the IsMatch method, as shown in the following variant of the ValidateInput method.

```
// Alternative version of the ValidateInput method that does not create
// Regex instances.
public static bool ValidateInput(string regex, string input)
```

```
{
    // Test if the specified input matches the regular expression.
    return Regex.IsMatch(input, regex);
}
```

2-6. Use Compiled Regular Expressions

Problem

You need to minimize the impact on application performance that arises from using complex regular expressions frequently.

Solution

When you instantiate the `System.Text.RegularExpressions.Regex` object that represents your regular expression, specify the `Compiled` option of the `System.Text.RegularExpressions.RegexOptions` enumeration to compile the regular expression to Microsoft Intermediate Language (MSIL).

How It Works

By default, when you create a `Regex` object, the regular expression pattern you specify in the constructor is compiled to an intermediate form (not MSIL). Each time you use the `Regex` object, the runtime interprets the pattern's intermediate form and applies it to the target string. With complex regular expressions that are used frequently, this repeated interpretation process can have a detrimental effect on the performance of your application.

By specifying the `RegexOptions.Compiled` option when you create a `Regex` object, you force the .NET runtime to compile the regular expression to MSIL instead of the interpreted intermediary form. This MSIL is just-in-time (JIT) compiled by the runtime to native machine code on first execution, just like regular assembly code. You use a compiled regular expression in the same way as you use any `Regex` object; compilation simply results in faster execution.

However, a couple downsides offset the performance benefits provided by compiling regular expressions. First, the JIT compiler needs to do more work, which will introduce delays during JIT compilation. This is most noticeable if you create your compiled regular expressions as your application starts up. Second, the runtime cannot unload a compiled regular expression once you have finished with it. Unlike as with a normal regular expression, the runtime's garbage collector will not reclaim the memory used by the compiled regular expression. The compiled regular expression will remain in memory until your program terminates or you unload the application domain in which the compiled regular expression is loaded.

As well as compiling regular expressions in memory, the `static Regex.CompileToAssembly` method allows you to create a compiled regular expression and write it to an external assembly. This means that you can create assemblies containing standard sets of regular expressions, which you can use from multiple applications. To compile a regular expression and persist it to an assembly, take the following steps:

1. Create a `System.Text.RegularExpressions.RegexCompilationInfo` array large enough to hold one `RegexCompilationInfo` object for each of the compiled regular expressions you want to create.

2. Create a `RegexCompilationInfo` object for each of the compiled regular expressions. Specify values for its properties as arguments to the object constructor. The following are the most commonly used properties:

- IsPublic, a bool value that specifies whether the generated regular expression class has public visibility

- Name, a String value that specifies the class name

- Namespace, a String value that specifies the namespace of the class

- Pattern, a String value that specifies the pattern that the regular expression will match (see recipe 2-5 for more details)

- Options, a System.Text.RegularExpressions.RegexOptions value that specifies options for the regular expression

3. Create a System.Reflection.AssemblyName object. Configure it to represent the name of the assembly that the Regex.CompileToAssembly method will create.

4. Execute Regex.CompileToAssembly, passing the RegexCompilationInfo array and the AssemblyName object.

This process creates an assembly that contains one class declaration for each compiled regular expression—each class derives from Regex. To use the compiled regular expression contained in the assembly, instantiate the regular expression you want to use and call its method as if you had simply created it with the normal Regex constructor. (Remember to add a reference to the assembly when you compile the code that uses the compiled regular expression classes.)

The Code

This line of code shows how to create a Regex object that is compiled to MSIL instead of the usual intermediate form:

```
Regex reg = new Regex(@"[\w-]+@([\w-]+\.)+[\w-]+", RegexOptions.Compiled);
```

The following example shows how to create an assembly named MyRegEx.dll, which contains two regular expressions named PinRegex and CreditCardRegex.

```
using System;
using System.Reflection;
using System.Text.RegularExpressions;

namespace Apress.VisualCSharpRecipes.Chapter02
{
    class Recipe02_06
    {
        public static void Main()
        {
            // Create the array to hold the Regex info objects.
            RegexCompilationInfo[] regexInfo = new RegexCompilationInfo[2];

            // Create the RegexCompilationInfo for PinRegex.
            regexInfo[0] = new RegexCompilationInfo(@"^\d{4}$",
                RegexOptions.Compiled, "PinRegex", "", true);

            // Create the RegexCompilationInfo for CreditCardRegex.
            regexInfo[1] = new RegexCompilationInfo(
                @"^\d{4}-?\d{4}-?\d{4}-?\d{4}$",
                RegexOptions.Compiled, "CreditCardRegex", "", true);

            // Create the AssemblyName to define the target assembly.
            AssemblyName assembly = new AssemblyName();
```

```
        assembly.Name = "MyRegEx";

        // Create the compiled regular expression
        Regex.CompileToAssembly(regexInfo, assembly);
    }
  }
}
```

2-7. Create Dates and Times from Strings

Problem

You need to create a System.DateTime instance that represents the time and date specified in
a string.

Solution

Use the Parse or ParseExact method of the DateTime class.

■**Caution** Many subtle issues are associated with using the DateTime class to represent dates and times in
your applications. Although the Parse and ParseExact methods create DateTime objects from strings as described
in this recipe, you must be careful how you use the resulting DateTime objects within your program. See the article titled
"Coding Best Practices Using DateTime in the .NET Framework" (http://msdn.microsoft.com/netframework/
default.aspx?pull=/library/en-us/dndotnet/html/datetimecode.asp) for details about the problems
you may encounter.

How It Works

Dates and times can be represented as text in many different ways. For example, 1st June 2005,
1/6/2005, 6/1/2005, and 1-Jun-2005 are all possible representations of the same date, and 16:43 and
4:43 p.m. can both be used to represent the same time. The static DateTime.Parse method provides
a flexible mechanism for creating DateTime instances from a wide variety of string representations.

The Parse method goes to great lengths to generate a DateTime object from a given string. It will
even attempt to generate a DateTime object from a string containing partial or erroneous information
and will substitute defaults for any missing values. Missing date elements default to the current date,
and missing time elements default to 12:00:00 a.m. After all efforts, if Parse cannot create a DateTime
object, it throws a System.FormatException exception.

The Parse method is both flexible and forgiving. However, for many applications, this level of
flexibility is unnecessary. Often, you will want to ensure that DateTime parses only strings that match
a specific format. In these circumstances, use the ParseExact method instead of Parse. The simplest
overload of the ParseExact method takes three arguments: the time and date string to parse, a format
string that specifies the structure that the time and date string must have, and an IFormatProvider reference that provides culture-specific information to the ParseExact method. If the IFormatProvider
value is null, the current thread's culture information is used.

The time and date must meet the requirements specified in the format string, or ParseExact
will throw a System.FormatException exception. You use the same format specifiers for the format
string as you use to format a DateTime object for display as a string. This means that you can use
both standard and custom format specifiers.

The Code

The following example demonstrates the flexibility of the Parse method and the use of the ParseExact method. Refer to the documentation for the System.Globalization.DateTimeFormatInfo class in the .NET Framework SDK document for complete details on all available format specifiers.

```csharp
using System;

namespace Apress.VisualCSharpRecipes.Chapter02
{
    class Recipe02_07
    {
        public static void Main(string[] args)
        {
            // 1st September 2005 00:00:00
            DateTime dt1 = DateTime.Parse("Sep 2005");

            // 5th September 2005 14:15:33
            DateTime dt2 = DateTime.Parse("Monday 5 September 2005 14:15:33");

            // 5th September 2005 00:00:00
            DateTime dt3 = DateTime.Parse("5,9,05");

            // 5th September 2005 14:15:33
            DateTime dt4 = DateTime.Parse("5/9/2005 14:15:33");

            // Current Date 14:15:00
            DateTime dt5 = DateTime.Parse("2:15 PM");

            // Display the converted DateTime objects.
            Console.WriteLine(dt1);
            Console.WriteLine(dt2);
            Console.WriteLine(dt3);
            Console.WriteLine(dt4);
            Console.WriteLine(dt5);

            // Parse only strings containing LongTimePattern.
            DateTime dt6 = DateTime.ParseExact("2:13:30 PM", "h:mm:ss tt", null);

            // Parse only strings containing RFC1123Pattern.
            DateTime dt7 = DateTime.ParseExact(
                "Mon, 05 Sep 2005 14:13:30 GMT",
                  "ddd, dd MMM yyyy HH':'mm':'ss 'GMT'", null);

            // Parse only strings containing MonthDayPattern.
            DateTime dt8 = DateTime.ParseExact("September 05", "MMMM dd", null);

            // Display the converted DateTime objects.
            Console.WriteLine(dt6);
            Console.WriteLine(dt7);
            Console.WriteLine(dt8);

            // Wait to continue.
            Console.WriteLine("\nMain method complete. Press Enter");
            Console.ReadLine();
        }
    }
}
```

2-8. Add, Subtract, and Compare Dates and Times

Problem

You need to perform basic arithmetic operations or comparisons using dates and times.

Solution

Use the DateTime and TimeSpan structures, which support standard arithmetic and comparison operators.

How It Works

A DateTime instance represents a specific time (such as 4:15 a.m. on September 5, 1970), whereas a TimeSpan instance represents a period of time (such as 2 hours, 35 minutes). You may want to add, subtract, and compare TimeSpan and DateTime instances.

Internally, both DateTime and TimeSpan use *ticks* to represent time. A tick is equal to 100 nanoseconds. TimeSpan stores its time interval as the number of ticks equal to that interval, and DateTime stores time as the number of ticks since 12:00:00 midnight on January 1 in 0001 C.E. (C.E. stands for Common Era and is equivalent to A.D. in the Gregorian calendar.) This approach and the use of operator overloading makes it easy for DateTime and TimeSpan to support basic arithmetic and comparison operations. Table 2-4 summarizes the operator support provided by the DateTime and TimeSpan structures.

Table 2-4. *Operators Supported by* DateTime *and* TimeSpan

Operator	TimeSpan	DateTime
Assignment (=)	Because TimeSpan is a structure, assignment returns a copy and not a reference	Because DateTime is a structure, assignment returns a copy and not a reference
Addition (+)	Adds two TimeSpan instances	Adds a TimeSpan instance to a DateTime instance
Subtraction (-)	Subtracts one TimeSpan instance from another TimeSpan instance	Subtracts a TimeSpan instance or a DateTime instance from a DateTime instance
Equality (==)	Compares two TimeSpan instances and returns true if they are equal	Compares two DateTime instances and returns true if they are equal
Inequality (!=)	Compares two TimeSpan instances and returns true if they are not equal	Compares two DateTime instances and returns true if they are not equal
Greater than (>)	Determines if one TimeSpan instance is greater than another TimeSpan instance	Determines if one DateTime instance is greater than another DateTime instance
Greater than or equal to (>=)	Determines if one TimeSpan instance is greater than or equal to another TimeSpan instance	Determines if one DateTime instance is greater than or equal to another DateTime instance

(Continued)

Table 2-4. *Continued*

Operator	TimeSpan	DateTime
Less than (<)	Determines if one TimeSpan instance is less than another TimeSpan instance	Determines if one DateTime instance is less than another DateTime instance
Less than or equal to (<=)	Determines if one TimeSpan instance is less than or equal to another TimeSpan instance	Determines if one DateTime instance is less than or equal to another DateTime instance
Unary negation (-)	Returns a TimeSpan instance with a negated value of the specified TimeSpan instance	Not supported
Unary plus (+)	Returns the TimeSpan instance specified	Not supported

The DateTime structure also implements the AddTicks, AddMilliseconds, AddSeconds, AddMinutes, AddHours, AddDays, AddMonths, and AddYears methods. Each of these methods allows you to add (or subtract using negative values) the appropriate element of time to a DateTime instance. These methods and the operators listed in Table 2-4 do not modify the original DateTime; instead, they create a new instance with the modified value.

The Code

The following example demonstrates the use of operators to manipulate the DateTime and TimeSpan structures.

```
using System;

namespace Apress.VisualCSharpRecipes.Chapter02
{
    class Recipe02_08
    {
        public static void Main()
        {
            // Create a TimeSpan representing 2.5 days.
            TimeSpan timespan1 = new TimeSpan(2, 12, 0, 0);

            // Create a TimeSpan representing 4.5 days.
            TimeSpan timespan2 = new TimeSpan(4, 12, 0, 0);

            // Create a TimeSpan representing 1 week.
            TimeSpan oneWeek = timespan1 + timespan2;

            // Create a DateTime with the current date and time.
            DateTime now = DateTime.Now;

            // Create a DateTime representing 1 week ago.
            DateTime past = now - oneWeek;

            // Create a DateTime representing 1 week in the future.
            DateTime future = now + oneWeek;

            // Display the DateTime instances.
            Console.WriteLine("Now    : {0}", now);
            Console.WriteLine("Past   : {0}", past);
            Console.WriteLine("Future: {0}", future);
```

```
        // Wait to continue.
        Console.WriteLine("\nMain method complete. Press Enter");
        Console.ReadLine();
      }
   }
}
```

2-9. Sort an Array or an ArrayList

Problem

You need to sort the elements contained in an array or an ArrayList structure.

Solution

Use the ArrayList.Sort method to sort ArrayList objects and the static Array.Sort method to sort arrays.

How It Works

The simplest Sort method overload sorts the objects contained in an array or ArrayList structure as long as the objects implement the System.IComparable interface and are of the same type. All of the basic data types implement IComparable. To sort objects that do not implement IComparable, you must pass the Sort method to an object that implements the System.Collections.IComparer interface. The IComparer implementation must be capable of comparing the objects contained within the array or ArrayList. (Recipe 13-3 describes how to implement both comparable types.)

The Code

The following example demonstrates how to use the Sort methods of the ArrayList and Array classes.

```
using System;
using System.Collections;

namespace Apress.VisualCSharpRecipes.Chapter02
{
    class Recipe02_09
    {
        public static void Main()
        {
            // Create a new array and populate it.
            int[] array = { 4, 2, 9, 3 };

            // Sort the array.
            Array.Sort(array);

            // Display the contents of the sorted array.
            foreach (int i in array) { Console.WriteLine(i); }

            // Create a new ArrayList and populate it.
            ArrayList list = new ArrayList(4);
            list.Add("Michael");
            list.Add("Kate");
            list.Add("Andrea");
            list.Add("Angus");
```

```
            // Sort the ArrayList.
            list.Sort();

            // Display the contents of the sorted ArrayList.
            foreach (string s in list) { Console.WriteLine(s); }

            // Wait to continue.
            Console.WriteLine("\nMain method complete. Press Enter");
            Console.ReadLine();
        }
    }
}
```

2-10. Copy a Collection to an Array

Problem

You need to copy the contents of a collection to an array.

Solution

Use the ICollection.CopyTo method implemented by all collection classes, or use the ToArray method implemented by the ArrayList, Stack, and Queue collections.

How It Works

The ICollection.CopyTo method and the ToArray method perform roughly the same function: they perform a shallow copy of the elements contained in a collection to an array. The key difference is that CopyTo copies the collection's elements to an existing array, whereas ToArray creates a new array before copying the collection's elements into it.

The CopyTo method takes two arguments: an array and an index. The array is the target of the copy operation and must be of a type appropriate to handle the elements of the collection. If the types do not match, or no implicit conversion is possible from the collection element's type to the array element's type, a System.InvalidCastException exception is thrown. The index is the starting element of the array where the collection's elements will be copied. If the index is equal to or greater than the length of the array, or the number of collection elements exceeds the capacity of the array, a System.ArgumentException exception is thrown.

The ArrayList, Stack, and Queue classes and their generic versions also implement the ToArray method, which automatically creates an array of the correct size to accommodate a copy of all the elements of the collection. If you call ToArray with no arguments, it returns an object[] array, regardless of the type of objects contained in the collection. For convenience, the ArrayList.ToArray method has an overload to which you can pass a System.Type object that specifies the type of array that the ToArray method should create. (You must still cast the returned strongly typed array to the correct type.) The layout of the array's contents depends on which collection class you are using. For example, an array produced from a Stack object will be inverted compared to the array generated by an ArrayList object.

The Code

This example demonstrates how to copy the contents of an ArrayList structure to an array using the CopyTo method, and then shows how to use the ToArray method on the ArrayList object.

```csharp
using System;
using System.Collections;

namespace Apress.VisualCSharpRecipes.Chapter02
{
    class Recipe02_10
    {
        public static void Main()
        {
            // Create a new ArrayList and populate it.
            ArrayList list = new ArrayList(5);
            list.Add("Brenda");
            list.Add("George");
            list.Add("Justin");
            list.Add("Shaun");
            list.Add("Meaghan");

            // Create a string array and use the ICollection.CopyTo method
            // to copy the contents of the ArrayList.
            string[] array1 = new string[list.Count];
            list.CopyTo(array1, 0);

            // Use ArrayList.ToArray to create an object array from the
            // contents of the collection.
            object[] array2 = list.ToArray();

            // Use ArrayList.ToArray to create a strongly typed string
            // array from the contents of the collection.
            string[] array3 = (string[])list.ToArray(typeof(String));

            // Display the contents of the 3 arrays.
            Console.WriteLine("Array 1:");
            foreach (string s in array1)
            {
                Console.WriteLine("\t{0}",s);
            }

            Console.WriteLine("Array 2:");
            foreach (string s in array2)
            {
                Console.WriteLine("\t{0}", s);
            }

            Console.WriteLine("Array 3:");
            foreach (string s in array3)
            {
                Console.WriteLine("\t{0}", s);
            }

            // Wait to continue.
            Console.WriteLine("\nMain method complete. Press Enter");
            Console.ReadLine();
        }
    }
}
```

2-11. Use a Strongly Typed Collection

Problem

You need a collection that works with elements of a specific type so that you do not need to work with `System.Object` references in your code.

Solution

Use the appropriate collection class from the `System.Collections.Generic` namespace. When you instantiate the collection, specify the type of object the collection should contain using the generics syntax built into C# 2.0.

How It Works

The generics functionality added to .NET Framework 2.0 and supported by specific syntax in C# 2.0 make it easy to create type-safe collections and containers (see recipe 2-12). To meet the most common requirements for collection classes, the `System.Collections.Generic` namespace contains a number of predefined generic collections, including the following:

- `Dictionary`
- `LinkedList`
- `List`
- `Queue`
- `Stack`

When you instantiate one of these collections, you specify the type of object that the collection will contain by including the type name in angled brackets after the collection name; for example, `Dictionary<System.Reflection.AssemblyName>`. As a result, all members that add objects to the collection expect the objects to be of the specified type, and all members that return objects from the collection will return object references of the specified type. Using strongly typed collections and working directly with objects of the desired type simplifies development and reduces the errors that can occur when working with general `Object` references and casting them to the desired type.

The Code

The following example demonstrates the use of generic collections to create a variety of collections specifically for the management of `AssemblyName` objects. Notice that you never need to cast to or from the `Object` type.

```
using System;
using System.Reflection;
using System.Collections.Generic;

namespace Apress.VisualCSharpRecipes.Chapter02
{
    class Recipe02_11
    {
        public static void Main(string[] args)
        {
            // Create an AssemblyName object for use during the example.
            AssemblyName assembly1 = new AssemblyName("com.microsoft.crypto, " +
                "Culture=en, PublicKeyToken=a5d015c7d5a0b012, Version=1.0.0.0");
```

```
// Create and use a Dictionary of AssemblyName objects.
Dictionary<string,AssemblyName> assemblyDictionary =
    new Dictionary<string,AssemblyName>();

assemblyDictionary.Add("Crypto", assembly1);

AssemblyName ass1 = assemblyDictionary["Crypto"];

Console.WriteLine("Got AssemblyName from dictionary: {0}", ass1);

// Create and use a List of Assembly Name objects.
List<AssemblyName> assemblyList = new List<AssemblyName>();

assemblyList.Add(assembly1);

AssemblyName ass2 = assemblyList[0];

Console.WriteLine("\nFound AssemblyName in list: {0}", ass1);

// Create and use a Stack of Assembly Name objects
Stack<AssemblyName> assemblyStack = new Stack<AssemblyName>();

assemblyStack.Push(assembly1);

AssemblyName ass3 = assemblyStack.Pop();

Console.WriteLine("\nPopped AssemblyName from stack: {0}", ass1);

// Wait to continue.
Console.WriteLine("\nMain method complete. Press Enter");
Console.ReadLine();
        }
    }
}
```

2-12. Create a Generic Type

Problem

You need to create a new general-purpose type such as a collection or container that supports strong typing of the elements it contains.

Solution

Use the generics functionality added to .NET Framework 2.0. Define your class using the generics syntax provided in C# 2.0.

How It Works

You can leverage the generics capabilities of .NET Framework 2.0 in any class you define. This allows you to create general-purpose classes that can be used as type-safe instances by other programmers. When you declare your type, you identify it as a generic type by following the type name with a pair of angled brackets that contain a list of identifiers for the types used in the class. Here is an example:

```
public class MyGenericType<T1, T2, T3>
```

This declaration specifies a new class named MyGenericType, which uses three generic types in its implementation (T1, T2, and T3). When implementing the type, you substitute the generic type names into the code instead of using specific type names. For example, one method might take an argument of type T1 and return a result of type T2, as shown here:

```
public T2 MyGenericMethod(T1 arg)
```

When other people use your class and create an instance of it, they specify the actual types to use as part of the instantiation. Here is an example:

```
MyGenericType<string,Stream,string> obj = new MyGenericType<string,Stream,string>();
```

The types specified replace T1, T2, and T3 throughout the implementation, so with this instance, MyGenericMethod would actually be interpreted as follows:

```
public Stream MyGenericMethod(string arg)
```

You can also include constraints as part of your generic type definition. This allows you to make specifications such as the following:

- Only value types or only reference types can be used with the generic type.
- Only types that implement a default (empty) constructor can be used with the generic type.
- Only types that implement a specific interface can be used with the generic type.
- Only types that inherit from a specific base class can be used with the generic type.
- One generic type must be the same as another generic type (for example, T1 must be the same as T3).

For example, to specify that T1 must implement the System.IDisposable interface and provide a default constructor, that T2 must be or derive from the System.IO.Stream class, and that T3 must be the same type as T1, change the definition of MyGenericType as follows:

```
public class MyGenericType<T1, T2, T3>
    where T1 : System.IDisposable, new()
    where T2 : System.IO.Stream
    where T3 : T1
{ \* ...Implementation... *\ }
```

The Code

The following example demonstrates a simplified bag implementation that returns those objects put into it at random. A *bag* is a data structure that can contain zero or more items, including duplicates of items, but does not guarantee any ordering of the items it contains.

```
using System;
using System.Collections.Generic;

namespace Apress.VisualCSharpRecipes.Chapter02
{
    public class Bag<T>
    {
        // A list to hold the bag's contents. The list must be
        // of the same type as the bag.
        private List<T> items = new List<T>();
```

```csharp
    // A method to add an item to the bag.
    public void Add(T item)
    {
        items.Add(item);
    }

    // A method to get a random item from the bag.
    public T Remove()
    {
        T item = default(T);

        if (items.Count != 0)
        {
            // Determine which item to remove from the bag.
            Random r = new Random();
            int num = r.Next(0, items.Count);

            // Remove the item
            item = items[num];
            items.RemoveAt(num);
        }
        return item;
    }

    // A method to remove all items from the bag and return them
    // as an array.
    public T[] RemoveAll()
    {
        T[] i = items.ToArray();
        items.Clear();
        return i;
    }
}

public class Recipe02_12
{
    public static void Main(string[] args)
    {
        // Create a new bag of strings.
        Bag<string> bag = new Bag<string>();

        // Add strings to the bag.
        bag.Add("Darryl");
        bag.Add("Bodders");
        bag.Add("Gary");
        bag.Add("Mike");
        bag.Add("Nigel");
        bag.Add("Ian");

        // Take four strings from the bag and display.
        Console.WriteLine("Item 1 = {0}", bag.Remove());
        Console.WriteLine("Item 2 = {0}", bag.Remove());
        Console.WriteLine("Item 3 = {0}", bag.Remove());
        Console.WriteLine("Item 4 = {0}", bag.Remove());
```

```
            // Remove the remaining items from the bag.
            string[] s = bag.RemoveAll();

            // Wait to continue.
            Console.WriteLine("\nMain method complete. Press Enter");
            Console.ReadLine();
        }
    }
}
```

2-13. Store a Serializable Object to a File

Problem

You need to store a serializable object and its state to a file, and then deserialize it later.

Solution

Use a *formatter* to serialize the object and write it to a System.IO.FileStream object. When you need to retrieve the object, use the same type of formatter to read the serialized data from the file and deserialize the object. The .NET Framework class library includes the following formatter implementations for serializing objects to binary or SOAP format:

- System.Runtime.Serialization.Formatters.Binary.BinaryFormatter
- System.Runtime.Serialization.Formatters.Soap.SoapFormatter

How It Works

Using the BinaryFormatter and SoapFormatter classes, you can serialize an instance of any serializable type. (See recipe 13-1 for details on how to make a type serializable.) The BinaryFormatter class produces a binary data stream representing the object and its state. The SoapFormatter class produces a SOAP document.

Both the BinaryFormatter and SoapFormatter classes implement the interface System.Runtime. Serialization.IFormatter, which defines two methods: Serialize and Deserialize. The Serialize method takes a System.IO.Stream reference and a System.Object reference as arguments, serializes the Object, and writes it to the Stream. The Deserialize method takes a Stream reference as an argument, reads the serialized object data from the Stream, and returns an Object reference to a deserialized object. You must cast the returned Object reference to the correct type.

■**Caution** To call the Serialize and Deserialize methods of the BinaryFormatter class, your code must be granted the SerializationFormatter element of the permission System.Security.Permissions. SecurityPermission. To call the Serialize and Deserialize methods of the SoapFormatter class, your code must be granted full trust, because the System.Runtime.Serialization.Formatters.Soap.dll assembly in which the SoapFormatter class is declared does not allow partially trusted callers. Refer to recipe 11-1 for more information about assemblies and partially trusted callers.

The Code

The example shown here demonstrates the use of both BinaryFormatter and SoapFormatter to serialize a System.Collections.ArrayList object containing a list of people to a file. The ArrayList object is then deserialized from the files and the contents displayed to the console.

```csharp
using System;
using System.IO;
using System.Collections;
using System.Runtime.Serialization.Formatters.Soap;
using System.Runtime.Serialization.Formatters.Binary;

namespace Apress.VisualCSharpRecipes.Chapter02
{
    class Recipe02_13
    {
        // Serialize an ArrayList object to a binary file.
        private static void BinarySerialize(ArrayList list)
        {
            using (FileStream str = File.Create("people.bin"))
            {
                BinaryFormatter bf = new BinaryFormatter();
                bf.Serialize(str, list);
            }
        }

        // Deserialize an ArrayList object from a binary file.
        private static ArrayList BinaryDeserialize()
        {
            ArrayList people = null;

            using (FileStream str = File.OpenRead("people.bin"))
            {
                BinaryFormatter bf = new BinaryFormatter();
                people = (ArrayList)bf.Deserialize(str);
            }
            return people;
        }

        // Serialize an ArrayList object to a SOAP file.
        private static void SoapSerialize(ArrayList list)
        {
            using (FileStream str = File.Create("people.soap"))
            {
                SoapFormatter sf = new SoapFormatter();
                sf.Serialize(str, list);
            }
        }

        // Deserialize an ArrayList object from a SOAP file.
        private static ArrayList SoapDeserialize()
        {
            ArrayList people = null;

            using (FileStream str = File.OpenRead("people.soap"))
            {
                SoapFormatter sf = new SoapFormatter();
```

```
            people = (ArrayList)sf.Deserialize(str);
        }
        return people;
    }

    public static void Main()
    {
        // Create and configure the ArrayList to serialize
        ArrayList people = new ArrayList();
        people.Add("Graeme");
        people.Add("Lin");
        people.Add("Andy");

        // Serialize the list to a file in both binary and SOAP form.
        BinarySerialize(people);
        SoapSerialize(people);

        // Rebuild the lists of people from the binary and SOAP
        // serializations and display them to the console.
        ArrayList binaryPeople = BinaryDeserialize();
        ArrayList soapPeople = SoapDeserialize();

        Console.WriteLine("Binary people:");
        foreach (string s in binaryPeople)
        {
            Console.WriteLine("\t" + s);
        }

        Console.WriteLine("\nSOAP people:");
        foreach (string s in soapPeople)
        {
            Console.WriteLine("\t" + s);
        }

        // Wait to continue.
        Console.WriteLine("\nMain method complete. Press Enter");
        Console.ReadLine();
    }
  }
}
```

Usage

To illustrate the different results achieved using the BinaryFormatter and SoapFormatter classes, Figure 2-1 shows the contents of the people.bin file generated using the BinaryFormatter class, and Figure 2-2 shows the contents of the people.soap file generated using the SoapFormatter class.

```
00000000h: 00 01 00 00 00 FF FF FF FF 01 00 00 00 00 00 00 ; .....ÿÿÿÿ.......
00000010h: 00 04 01 00 00 00 1C 53 79 73 74 65 6D 2E 43 6F ; .......System.Co
00000020h: 6C 6C 65 63 74 69 6F 6E 73 2E 41 72 72 61 79 4C ; llections.ArrayL
00000030h: 69 73 74 03 00 00 00 06 5F 69 74 65 6D 73 05 5F ; ist....._items._
00000040h: 73 69 7A 65 08 5F 76 65 72 73 69 6F 6E 05 00 00 ; size._version...
00000050h: 08 08 09 02 00 00 03 00 00 00 03 00 00 00 10 ; ................
00000060h: 02 00 00 00 10 00 00 00 06 03 00 00 00 06 47 72 ; ..............Gr
00000070h: 61 65 6D 65 06 04 00 00 00 03 4C 69 6E 06 05 00 ; aeme......Lin...
00000080h: 00 00 04 41 6E 64 79 0D 0D 0B              ; ...Andy...
```

Figure 2-1. *Contents of the people.bin file*

```
<SOAP-ENV:Envelope xmlns:xsi="http://www.w3.org/2001/XMLSchema-instance"
xmlns:xsd="http://www.w3.org/2001/XMLSchema" xmlns:SOAP-
ENC="http://schemas.xmlsoap.org/soap/encoding/" xmlns:SOAP-
ENV="http://schemas.xmlsoap.org/soap/envelope/"
xmlns:clr="http://schemas.microsoft.com/soap/encoding/clr/1.0" SOAP-
ENV:encodingStyle="http://schemas.xmlsoap.org/soap/encoding/">
<SOAP-ENV:Body>
<a1:ArrayList id="ref-1"
xmlns:a1="http://schemas.microsoft.com/clr/ns/System.Collections">
<_items href="#ref-2"/>
<_size>3</_size>
<_version>3</_version>
</a1:ArrayList>
<SOAP-ENC:Array id="ref-2" SOAP-ENC:arrayType="xsd:anyType[16]">
<item id="ref-3" xsi:type="SOAP-ENC:string">Graeme</item>
<item id="ref-4" xsi:type="SOAP-ENC:string">Lin</item>
<item id="ref-5" xsi:type="SOAP-ENC:string">Andy</item>
</SOAP-ENC:Array>
</SOAP-ENV:Body>
</SOAP-ENV:Envelope>
```

Figure 2-2. *Contents of the people.soap file*

2-14. Read User Input from the Console

Problem

You want to read user input from the Windows console, either a line or character at a time.

Solution

Use the Read or ReadLine method of the System.Console class to read input when the user presses Enter. To read input without requiring the user to press Enter, use the Console.ReadKey method.

How It Works

The simplest way to read input from the console is to use the static Read or ReadLine methods of the Console class. These methods will both cause your application to block, waiting for the user to enter input and press Enter. In both instances, the user will see the input characters in the console. Once the user presses Enter, the Read method will return an int value representing the next character of input data, or –1 if no more data is available. The ReadLine method will return a string containing all the data entered, or an empty string if no data was entered.

.NET Framework 2.0 adds the ReadKey method to the Console class, which provides a way to read input from the console without waiting for the user to press Enter. The ReadKey method waits for the user to press a key and returns a System.ConsoleKeyInfo object to the caller. By passing true as an argument to an overload of the ReadKey method, you can also prevent the key pressed by the user from being echoed to the console.

The returned ConsoleKeyInfo object contains details about the key pressed. The details are accessible through the properties of the ConsoleKeyInfo class summarized in Table 2-5.

Table 2-5. *Properties of the* ConsoleKeyInfo *Class*

Property	Description
Key	Gets a value of the System.ConsoleKey enumeration representing the key pressed. The ConsoleKey enumeration contains values that represent all of the keys usually found on a keyboard. These include all the character and function keys; navigation and editing keys like Home, Insert, and Delete; and more modern specialized keys like the Windows key, media player control keys, browser activation keys, and browser navigation keys.
KeyChar	Gets a char value containing the Unicode character representation of the key pressed.
Modifiers	Gets a bitwise combination of values from the System.ConsoleModifiers enumeration that identifies one or more modifier keys pressed simultaneously with the console key. The members of the ConsoleModifiers enumeration are Alt, Control, and Shift.

The KeyAvailable method of the Console class returns a bool value indicating whether input is available in the input buffer without blocking your code.

The Code

The following example reads input from the console one character at a time using the ReadKey method. If the user presses F1, the program toggles in and out of "secret" mode, where input is masked by asterisks. When the user presses Escape, the console is cleared and the input the user has entered is displayed. If the user presses Alt-X or Alt-x, the example terminates.

```
using System;
using System.Collections.Generic;

namespace Apress.VisualCSharpRecipes.Chapter02
{
    class Recipe02_14
    {
        public static void Main()
        {
            // Local variable to hold the key entered by the user.
            ConsoleKeyInfo key;

            // Control whether character or asterisk is displayed.
            bool secret = false;

            // Character List for the user data entered.
            List<char> input = new List<char>();
```

```csharp
string msg = "Enter characters and press Escape to see input." +
    "\nPress F1 to enter/exit Secret mode and Alt-X to exit.";

Console.WriteLine(msg);

// Process input until the user enters "Alt-X" or "Alt-x".
do
{
    // Read a key from the console. Intercept the key so that it is not
    // displayed to the console. What is displayed is determined later
    // depending on whether the program is in secret mode.
    key = Console.ReadKey(true);

    // Switch secret mode on and off.
    if (key.Key == ConsoleKey.F1)
    {
        if (secret)
        {
            // Switch secret mode off.
            secret = false;
        }
        else
        {
            // Switch secret mode on.
            secret = true;
        }
    }

    // Handle Backspace.
    if (key.Key == ConsoleKey.Backspace)
    {
        if (input.Count > 0)
        {
            // Backspace pressed, remove the last character.
            input.RemoveAt(input.Count - 1);

            Console.Write(key.KeyChar);
            Console.Write(" ");
            Console.Write(key.KeyChar);
        }
    }
    // Handle Escape.
    else if (key.Key == ConsoleKey.Escape)
    {
        Console.Clear();
        Console.WriteLine("Input: {0}\n\n",
            new String(input.ToArray()));
        Console.WriteLine(msg);
        input.Clear();
    }
    // Handle character input.
    else if (key.Key >= ConsoleKey.A && key.Key <= ConsoleKey.Z)
    {
        input.Add(key.KeyChar);
```

```
                if (secret)
                {
                    Console.Write("*");
                }
                else
                {
                    Console.Write(key.KeyChar);
                }
            }
        } while (key.Key != ConsoleKey.X
            || key.Modifiers != ConsoleModifiers.Alt);

        // Wait to continue.
        Console.WriteLine("\n\nMain method complete. Press Enter");
        Console.ReadLine();
    }
  }
}
```

CHAPTER 3

■■■

Application Domains, Reflection, and Metadata

The power and flexibility of the Microsoft .NET Framework is enhanced by the ability to inspect and manipulate types and metadata at runtime. The recipes in this chapter describe how to use application domains, reflection, and metadata. Specifically, the recipes in this chapter describe how to do the following:

- Create application domains into which you can load assemblies that are isolated from the rest of your application (recipe 3-1)

- Create types that have the capability to cross application domain boundaries (recipe 3-2) and types that are guaranteed to be unable to cross application domain boundaries (recipe 3-4)

- Control the loading of assemblies and the instantiation of types in local and remote application domains (recipes 3-3, 3-5, 3-6, and 3-7)

- Pass simple configuration data between application domains (recipe 3-8)

- Unload application domains, which provides the only means through which you can unload assemblies at runtime (recipe 3-9)

- Inspect and test the type of an object using a variety of mechanisms built into the C# language and capabilities provided by the objects themselves (recipes 3-10 and 3-11)

- Dynamically instantiate an object and execute its methods at runtime using reflection (recipe 3-12)

- Create custom attributes (recipe 3-13), allowing you to associate metadata with your program elements and inspect the value of those custom attributes at runtime (recipe 3-14)

■**Note** An excellent reference for detailed information on all aspects of application domains and loading assemblies is *Customizing the Microsoft .NET Framework Common Language Runtime* by Steven Pratschner (Microsoft Press, 2005).

3-1. Create an Application Domain

Problem

You need to create a new application domain.

Solution

Use the `static` method `CreateDomain` of the `System.AppDomain` class.

How It Works

The simplest overload of the `CreateDomain` method takes a single `string` argument specifying a human-readable name (friendly name) for the new application domain. Other overloads allow you to specify evidence and configuration settings for the new application domain. You specify evidence using a `System.Security.Policy.Evidence` object, and you specify configuration settings using a `System.AppDomainSetup` object.

The `AppDomainSetup` class is a container of configuration information for an application domain. Table 3-1 lists some of the properties of the `AppDomainSetup` class that you will use most often when creating application domains. These properties are accessible after creation through members of the `AppDomain` object. Some have different names, and some are modifiable at runtime; refer to the .NET Framework's software development kit (SDK) documentation on the `AppDomain` class for a comprehensive discussion.

Table 3-1. *Commonly Used* `AppDomainSetup` *Properties*

Property	Description
ApplicationBase	The directory where the CLR will look during probing to resolve private assemblies. (Recipe 3-5 discusses probing.) Effectively, `ApplicationBase` is the root directory for the executing application. By default, this is the directory containing the assembly. This is readable after creation using the `AppDomain.BaseDirectory` property.
ConfigurationFile	The name of the configuration file used by code loaded into the application domain. This is readable after creation using the `AppDomain.GetData` method with the key APP_CONFIG_FILE. By default, the configuration file is stored in the same folder as the application .exe file, but if you set `ApplicationBase`, it will be in that same folder.
DisallowPublisherPolicy	Controls whether the publisher policy section of the application configuration file is taken into consideration when determining which version of a strong-named assembly to bind to. Recipe 3-5 discusses publisher policy.
PrivateBinPath	A semicolon-separated list of directories that the runtime uses when probing for private assemblies. These directories are relative to the directory specified in `ApplicationBase`. This is readable after application domain creation using the `AppDomain.RelativeSearchPath` property.

The Code

The following code demonstrates the creation and initial configuration of an application domain:

```
using System;

namespace Apress.VisualCSharpRecipes.Chapter03
{
    class Recipe03_01
    {
        public static void Main()
        {
            // Instantiate an AppDomainSetup object.
            AppDomainSetup setupInfo = new AppDomainSetup();

            // Configure the application domain setup information.
            setupInfo.ApplicationBase = @"C:\MyRootDirectory";
            setupInfo.ConfigurationFile = "MyApp.config";
            setupInfo.PrivateBinPath = "bin;plugins;external";

            // Create a new application domain passing null as the evidence
            // argument. Remember to save a reference to the new AppDomain as
            // this cannot be retrieved any other way.
            AppDomain newDomain =
                AppDomain.CreateDomain("My New AppDomain",null, setupInfo);

            // Wait to continue.
            Console.WriteLine("\nMain method complete. Press Enter.");
            Console.ReadLine();
        }
    }
}
```

■Note You must maintain a reference to the AppDomain object when you create it because no mechanism exists to enumerate existing application domains from within managed code.

3-2. Create Types That Can Be Passed Across Application Domain Boundaries

Problem

You need to pass objects across application domain boundaries as arguments or return values.

Solution

Use marshal-by-value or marshal-by-reference objects.

How It Works

The .NET Remoting system (discussed in Chapter 10) makes passing objects across application domain boundaries straightforward. However, to those unfamiliar with .NET Remoting, the results can be very different from those expected. In fact, the most confusing aspect of using multiple application domains stems from the interaction with .NET Remoting and the way objects traverse application domain boundaries.

All types fall into one of three categories: nonremotable, marshal-by-value (MBV), or marshal-by-reference (MBR). Nonremotable types cannot cross application domain boundaries and cannot be used as arguments or return values in cross-application domain calls. Recipe 3-4 discusses non-remotable types.

MBV types are serializable types. When you pass an MBV object across an application domain boundary as an argument or a return value, the .NET Remoting system serializes the object's current state, passes it to the destination application domain, and creates a new copy of the object with the same state as the original. This results in a copy of the MBV object existing in both application domains. The content of the two instances are initially identical, but they are independent; changes made to one instance are not reflected in the other instance (this applies to static members as well). This often causes confusion as you try to update the remote object but are in fact updating the local copy. If you actually want to be able to call and change an object from a remote application domain, the object needs to be an MBR type.

MBR types are those classes that derive from System.MarshalByRefObject. When you pass an MBR object across an application domain boundary as an argument or a return value, the .NET Remoting system creates a *proxy* in the destination application domain that represents the remote MBR object. To any class in the destination application domain, the proxy looks and behaves like the remote MBR object that it represents. In reality, when a call is made against the proxy, the .NET Remoting system transparently passes the call and its arguments to the remote application domain and issues the call against the original object. Any results are passed back to the caller via the proxy. Figure 3-1 illustrates the relationship between an MBR object and the objects that access it across application domains via a proxy.

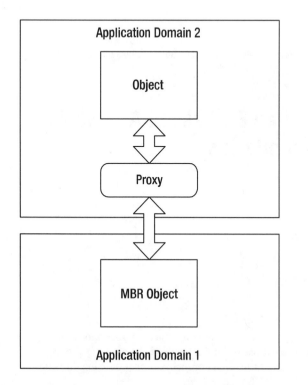

Figure 3-1. *An MBR object is accessed across application domains via a proxy.*

The Code

The following example highlights (in bold) the fundamental difference between creating classes that are passed by value (Recipe03_02MBV) and those passed by reference (Recipe03_02MBR). The code creates a new application domain and instantiates two remotable objects in it (discussed further in recipe 3-7). However, because the Recipe03_02MBV object is an MBV object, when it is created in the new application domain, it is serialized, passed across the application domain boundary, and deserialized as a new independent object in the caller's application domain. Therefore, when the code retrieves the name of the application domain hosting each object, Recipe03_02MBV returns the name of the main application domain, and Recipe03_02MBR returns the name of the new application domain in which it was created.

```
using System;

namespace Apress.VisualCSharpRecipes.Chapter03
{
    // Declare a class that is passed by value.
    [Serializable]
    public class Recipe03_02MBV
    {
        public string HomeAppDomain
        {
            get
            {
                return AppDomain.CurrentDomain.FriendlyName;
            }
        }
    }

    // Declare a class that is passed by reference.
    public class Recipe03_02MBR: MarshalByRefObject
    {
        public string HomeAppDomain
        {
            get
            {
                return AppDomain.CurrentDomain.FriendlyName;
            }
        }
    }

    public class Recipe03_02
    {
        public static void Main(string[] args)
        {
            // Create a new application domain.
            AppDomain newDomain =
                AppDomain.CreateDomain("My New AppDomain");

            // Instantiate an MBV object in the new application domain.
            Recipe03_02MBV mbvObject =
                (Recipe03_02MBV)newDomain.CreateInstanceFromAndUnwrap(
                    "Recipe03-02.exe",
                    "Apress.VisualCSharpRecipes.Chapter03.Recipe03_02MBV");

            // Instantiate an MBR object in the new application domain.
            Recipe03_02MBR mbrObject =
```

```
        (Recipe03_02MBR)newDomain.CreateInstanceFromAndUnwrap(
            "Recipe03-02.exe",
            "Apress.VisualCSharpRecipes.Chapter03.Recipe03_02MBR");

    // Display the name of the application domain in which each of
    // the objects is located.
    Console.WriteLine("Main AppDomain = {0}",
        AppDomain.CurrentDomain.FriendlyName);
    Console.WriteLine("AppDomain of MBV object = {0}",
        mbvObject.HomeAppDomain);
    Console.WriteLine("AppDomain of MBR object = {0}",
        mbrObject.HomeAppDomain);

    // Wait to continue.
    Console.WriteLine("\nMain method complete. Press Enter.");
    Console.ReadLine();
    }
  }
}
```

■**Note** Recipe 13-1 provides more details on creating serializable types, and recipe 10-16 describes how to create remotable types.

3-3. Avoid Loading Unnecessary Assemblies into Application Domains

Problem

You need to pass an object reference across multiple application domain boundaries; however, to conserve memory and avoid impacting performance, you want to ensure the common language runtime (CLR) loads only the object's type metadata into the application domains where it is required (that is, where you will actually use the object).

Solution

Wrap the object reference in a System.Runtime.Remoting.ObjectHandle, and unwrap the object reference only when you need to access the object.

How It Works

When you pass an MBV object across application domain boundaries, the runtime creates a new instance of that object in the destination application domain. This means the runtime must load the assembly containing that type metadata into the application domain. Passing MBV references across intermediate application domains can result in the runtime loading unnecessary assemblies into application domains. Once loaded, these superfluous assemblies cannot be unloaded without unloading the containing application domain. (See recipe 3-9 for more information.)

The ObjectHandle class allows you to wrap an object reference so that you can pass it between application domains without the runtime loading additional assemblies. When the object reaches the destination application domain, you can unwrap the object reference, causing the runtime to load the required assembly and allowing you to access the object as normal.

The Code

The following code contains some simple methods that demonstrate how to wrap and unwrap a System.Data.DataSet using an ObjectHandle:

```
using System;
using System.Data;
using System.Runtime.Remoting;

namespace Apress.VisualCSharpRecipes.Chapter03
{
    class Recipe03_03
    {
        // A method to wrap a Dataset.
        public ObjectHandle WrapDataSet(DataSet ds)
        {
            // Wrap the DataSet.
            ObjectHandle objHandle = new ObjectHandle(ds);

            // Return the wrapped DataSet.
            return objHandle;
        }

        // A method to unwrap a DataSet.
        public DataSet UnwrapDataSet(ObjectHandle handle)
        {
            // Unwrap the DataSet.
            DataSet ds = (System.Data.DataSet)handle.Unwrap();

            // Return the wrapped DataSet.
            return ds;
        }
    }
}
```

3-4. Create a Type That Cannot Cross Application Domain Boundaries

Problem

You need to create a type so that instances of the type are inaccessible to code in other application domains.

Solution

Ensure the type is nonremotable by making sure it is not serializable and it does not derive from the MarshalByRefObject class.

How It Works

On occasion, you will want to ensure that instances of a type cannot transcend application domain boundaries. To create a nonremotable type, ensure that it isn't serializable and that it doesn't derive (directly or indirectly) from the MarshalByRefObject class. If you take these steps, you ensure that an object's state can never be accessed from outside the application domain in which the object was instantiated—such objects cannot be used as arguments or return values in cross-application domain method calls.

Ensuring that a type isn't serializable is easy because a class doesn't inherit the ability to be serialized from its parent class. To ensure that a type isn't serializable, make sure it does not have `System.SerializableAttribute` applied to the type declaration.

Ensuring that a class cannot be passed by reference requires a little more attention. Many classes in the .NET class library derive directly or indirectly from `MarshalByRefObject`; you must be careful you don't inadvertently derive your class from one of these. Commonly used base classes that derive from `MarshalByRefObject` include `System.ComponentModel.Component`, `System.IO.Stream`, `System.IO.TextReader`, `System.IO.TextWriter`, `System.NET.WebRequest`, and `System.Net.WebResponse`. (Check the .NET Framework SDK documentation on `MarshalByRefObject`. The inheritance hierarchy listed for the class provides a complete list of classes that derive from it.)

3-5. Load an Assembly into the Current Application Domain

Problem

You need to load an assembly at runtime into the current application domain.

Solution

Use the `static Load` method or the `LoadFrom` method of the `System.Reflection.Assembly` class.

■**Note** The `Assembly.LoadWithPartialName` method has been deprecated in .NET 2.0. Instead, you should use the `Assembly.Load` method described in this recipe.

How It Works

Unlike Win32 where the referenced DLLs are loaded when the process starts, the CLR will automatically load the assemblies identified at build time as being referenced by your assembly only when the metadata for their contained types is required. However, you can also explicitly instruct the runtime to load assemblies. The `Load` and `LoadFrom` methods both result in the runtime loading an assembly into the current application domain, and both return an `Assembly` instance that represents the newly loaded assembly. The differences between each method are the arguments you must provide to identify the assembly to load and the process that the runtime undertakes to locate the specified assembly.

The `Load` method provides overloads that allow you to specify the assembly to load using one of the following:

- A `string` containing the fully or partially qualified *display name* of the assembly
- A `System.Reflection.AssemblyName` containing details of the assembly
- A `byte` array containing the raw bytes that constitute the assembly

A fully qualified display name contains the assembly's text name, version, culture, and public key token, separated by commas (for example, System.Data, Version=2.0.0.0, Culture=neutral,

PublicKeyToken=b77a5c561934e089). To specify an assembly that doesn't have a strong name, use PublicKeyToken=null. You can also specify a partial display name, but as a minimum, you must specify the assembly name (without the file extension).

In response to the Load call, the runtime undertakes an extensive process to locate and load the specified assembly. The following is a summary; consult the section "How the Runtime Locates Assemblies" in the .NET Framework SDK documentation for more details:

1. If you specify a strong-named assembly, the Load method will apply the version policy and publisher policy to enable requests for one version of an assembly to be satisfied by another version. You specify the version policy in your machine or application configuration file using <bindingRedirect> elements. You specify the publisher policy in special resource assemblies installed in the global assembly cache (GAC).

2. Once the runtime has established the correct version of an assembly to use, it attempts to load strong-named assemblies from the GAC.

3. If the assembly is not strong named or is not found in the GAC, the runtime looks for applicable <codeBase> elements in your machine and application configuration files. A <codeBase> element maps an assembly name to a file or a uniform resource locator (URL). If the assembly is strong named, <codeBase> can refer to any location including Internet-based URLs; otherwise, <codeBase> must refer to a directory relative to the application directory. If the assembly doesn't exist at the specified location, Load throws a System.IO.FileNotFoundException.

4. If no <codeBase> elements are relevant to the requested assembly, the runtime will locate the assembly using *probing*. Probing looks for the first file with the assembly's name (with either a .dll or an .exe extension) in the following locations:

   • The application root directory

   • Directories under the application root that match the assembly's name and culture

   • Directories under the application root that are specified in the private binpath

The Load method is the easiest way to locate and load assemblies but can also be expensive in terms of processing if the runtime needs to start probing many directories for a weak-named assembly. The LoadFrom method allows you to load an assembly from a specific location. If the specified file isn't found, the runtime will throw a FileNotFoundException. The runtime won't attempt to locate the assembly in the same way as the Load method—LoadFrom provides no support for the GAC, policies, <codebase> elements, or probing.

The Code

The following code demonstrates various forms of the Load and LoadFrom methods. Notice that unlike the Load method, LoadFrom requires you to specify the extension of the assembly file.

```
using System;
using System.Reflection;
using System.Globalization;

namespace Apress.VisualCSharpRecipes.Chapter03
{
    class Recipe03_05
    {
        public static void ListAssemblies()
        {
            // Get an array of the assemblies loaded into the current
            // application domain.
            Assembly[] assemblies = AppDomain.CurrentDomain.GetAssemblies();
```

```
        foreach (Assembly a in assemblies)
        {
            Console.WriteLine(a.GetName());
        }
    }

    public static void Main()
    {
        // List the assemblies in the current application domain.
        Console.WriteLine("**** BEFORE ****");
        ListAssemblies();

        // Load the System.Data assembly using a fully qualified display name.
        string name1 = "System.Data,Version=2.0.0.0," +
            "Culture=neutral,PublicKeyToken=b77a5c561934e089";
        Assembly a1 = Assembly.Load(name1);

        // Load the System.Xml assembly using an AssemblyName.
        AssemblyName name2 = new AssemblyName();
        name2.Name = "System.Xml";
        name2.Version = new Version(2, 0, 0, 0);
        name2.CultureInfo = new CultureInfo("");     //Neutral culture.
        name2.SetPublicKeyToken(
            new byte[] {0xb7, 0x7a, 0x5c, 0x56, 0x19, 0x34, 0xe0, 0x89});
        Assembly a2 = Assembly.Load(name2);

        // Load the SomeAssembly assembly using a partial display name.
        Assembly a3 = Assembly.Load("SomeAssembly");

        // Load the assembly named c:\shared\MySharedAssembly.dll.
        Assembly a4 = Assembly.LoadFrom(@"c:\shared\MySharedAssembly.dll");

        // List the assemblies in the current application domain.
        Console.WriteLine("\n\n**** AFTER ****");
        ListAssemblies();

        // Wait to continue.
        Console.WriteLine("\nMain method complete. Press Enter.");
        Console.ReadLine();
    }
  }
}
```

3-6. Execute an Assembly in a Different Application Domain

Problem

You need to execute an assembly in an application domain other than the current one.

Solution

Call the ExecuteAssembly or ExecuteAssemlyByName (in .NET 2.0) method of the AppDomain object that represents the application domain, and specify the filename of an executable assembly.

How It Works

If you have an executable assembly that you want to load and run in an application domain, the ExecuteAssembly or ExecuteAssemblyByName method provides the easiest solution. The ExecuteAssembly method provides four overloads. The simplest overload takes only a string containing the name of the executable assembly to run; you can specify a local file or a URL. Other ExecuteAssembly overloads allow you to specify evidence for the assembly (which affect code access security) and arguments to pass to the assembly's entry point (equivalent to command-line arguments).

The ExecuteAssembly method loads the specified assembly and executes the method defined in metadata as the assembly's entry point (usually the Main method). If the specified assembly isn't executable, ExecuteAssembly throws a System.MissingMethodException. The CLR doesn't start execution of the assembly in a new thread, so control won't return from the ExecuteAssembly method until the newly executed assembly exits. Because the ExecuteAssembly method loads an assembly using partial information (only the filename), the CLR won't use the GAC or probing to resolve the assembly. (See recipe 3-5 for more information.)

The ExecuteAssemblyByName method provides a similar set of overloads and takes the same argument types, but instead of taking just the filename of the executable assembly, you pass it the display name of the assembly. This overcomes the limitations inherent in ExecuteAssembly as a result of supplying only partial names. Again, see recipe 3-5 for more information on the structure of assembly display names.

The Code

The following code demonstrates how to use the ExecuteAssembly method to load and run an assembly. The Recipe03-06 class creates an AppDomain and executes itself in that AppDomain using the ExecuteAssembly method. This results in two copies of the Recipe03-06 assembly loaded into two different application domains.

```
using System;

namespace Apress.VisualCSharpRecipes.Chapter03
{
    class Recipe03_06
    {
        public static void Main(string[] args)
        {
            // For the purpose of this example, if this assembly is executing
            // in an AppDomain with the friendly name "NewAppDomain", do not
            // create a new AppDomain. This avoids an infinite loop of
            // AppDomain creation.
            if (AppDomain.CurrentDomain.FriendlyName != "NewAppDomain")
            {
                // Create a new application domain.
                AppDomain domain = AppDomain.CreateDomain("NewAppDomain");

                // Execute this assembly in the new application domain and
                // pass the array of command-line arguments.
                domain.ExecuteAssembly("Recipe03-06.exe", null, args);
            }
```

```
            // Display the command-line arguments to the screen prefixed with
            // the friendly name of the AppDomain.
            foreach (string s in args)
            {
                Console.WriteLine(AppDomain.CurrentDomain.FriendlyName + " : " + s);
            }

            // Wait to continue.
            if (AppDomain.CurrentDomain.FriendlyName != "NewAppDomain")
            {
                Console.WriteLine("\nMain method complete. Press Enter.");
                Console.ReadLine();
            }
        }
    }
}
```

Usage

If you run `Recipe03-06` using the following command:

```
Recipe03-06 Testing AppDomains
```

you will see that the command-line arguments are listed from both the existing and new application domains:

```
NewAppDomain : Testing
NewAppDomain : AppDomains
Recipe03-06.exe : Testing
Recipe03-06.exe : AppDomains
```

3-7. Instantiate a Type in a Different Application Domain

Problem

You need to instantiate a type in an application domain other than the current one.

Solution

Call the `CreateInstance` method or the `CreateInstanceFrom` method of the `AppDomain` object that represents the target application domain.

How It Works

The `ExecuteAssembly` method discussed in recipe 3-6 is straightforward to use, but when you are developing sophisticated applications that use application domains, you are likely to want more control over loading assemblies, instantiating types, and invoking object members within the application domain.

The `CreateInstance` and `CreateInstanceFrom` methods provide a variety of overloads that offer fine-grained control over the process of object instantiation. The simplest overloads assume the use of a type's default constructor, but both methods implement overloads that allow you to provide arguments to use any constructor.

The CreateInstance method loads a named assembly into the application domain using the process described for the Assembly.Load method in recipe 3-5. CreateInstance then instantiates a named type and returns a reference to the new object wrapped in an ObjectHandle (described in recipe 3-3). The CreateInstanceFrom method also instantiates a named type and returns an ObjectHandle-wrapped object reference; however, CreateInstanceFrom loads the specified assembly file into the application domain using the process described in recipe 3-5 for the Assembly.LoadFrom method.

AppDomain also provides two convenience methods named CreateInstanceAndUnwrap and CreateInstanceFromAndUnwrap that automatically extract the reference of the instantiated object from the returned ObjectHandle object; you must cast the returned object to the correct type.

■**Caution** Be aware that if you use CreateInstance or CreateInstanceFrom to instantiate MBV types in another application domain, the object will be created, but the returned object reference won't refer to that object. Because of the way MBV objects cross application domain boundaries, the reference will refer to a copy of the object created automatically in the local application domain. Only if you create an MBR type will the returned reference refer to the object in the other application domain. (See recipe 3-2 for more details about MBV and MBR types.)

A common technique to simplify the management of application domains is to use a *controller class*. A controller class is a custom MBR type. You create an application domain and then instantiate your controller class in the application domain using CreateInstance. The controller class implements the functionality required by your application to manipulate the application domain and its contents. This could include loading assemblies, creating further application domains, cleaning up prior to deleting the application domain, or enumerating program elements (something you cannot normally do from outside an application domain). It is best to create your controller class in an assembly of its own to avoid loading unnecessary classes into each application domain. You should also be careful about what types you pass as return values from your controller to your main application domain to avoid loading additional assemblies.

The Code

The following code demonstrates how to use a simplified controller class named PluginManager. When instantiated in an application domain, PluginManager allows you to instantiate classes that implement the IPlugin interface, start and stop those plug-ins, and return a list of currently loaded plug-ins.

```
using System;
using System.Reflection;
using System.Collections;
using System.Collections.Generic;
using System.Collections.Specialized;

namespace Apress.VisualCSharpRecipes.Chapter03
{
    // A common interface that all plug-ins must implement.
    public interface IPlugin
    {
        void Start();
        void Stop();
    }
```

```csharp
// A simple IPlugin implementation to demonstrate the PluginManager
// controller class.
public class SimplePlugin : IPlugin
{
    public void Start()
    {
        Console.WriteLine(AppDomain.CurrentDomain.FriendlyName +
            ": SimplePlugin starting...");
    }

    public void Stop()
    {
        Console.WriteLine(AppDomain.CurrentDomain.FriendlyName +
            ": SimplePlugin stopping...");
    }
}

// The controller class, which manages the loading and manipulation
// of plug-ins in its application domain.
public class PluginManager : MarshalByRefObject
{
    // A Dictionary to hold keyed references to IPlugin instances.
    private Dictionary<string, IPlugin> plugins =
        new Dictionary<string, IPlugin> ();

    // Default constructor.
    public PluginManager() { }

    // Constructor that loads a set of specified plug-ins on creation.
    public PluginManager(NameValueCollection pluginList)
    {
        // Load each of the specified plug-ins.
        foreach (string plugin in pluginList.Keys)
        {
            this.LoadPlugin(pluginList[plugin], plugin);
        }
    }

    // Load the specified assembly and instantiate the specified
    // IPlugin implementation from that assembly.
    public bool LoadPlugin(string assemblyName, string pluginName)
    {
        try
        {
            // Load the named private assembly.
            Assembly assembly = Assembly.Load(assemblyName);

            // Create the IPlugin instance, ignore case.
            IPlugin plugin = assembly.CreateInstance(pluginName, true)
                as IPlugin;

            if (plugin != null)
            {
                // Add new IPlugin to ListDictionary
                plugins[pluginName] = plugin;

                return true;
```

```csharp
            }
            else
            {
                return false;
            }
        }
        catch
        {
            // Return false on all exceptions for the purpose of
            // this example. Do not suppress exceptions like this
            // in production code.
            return false;
        }
    }

    public void StartPlugin(string plugin)
    {
        try
        {
            // Extract the IPlugin from the Dictionary and call Start.
            plugins[plugin].Start();
        }
        catch
        {
            // Log or handle exceptions appropriately
        }
    }

    public void StopPlugin(string plugin)
    {
        try
        {
            // Extract the IPLugin from the Dictionary and call Stop.
            plugins[plugin].Stop();
        }
        catch
        {
            // Log or handle exceptions appropriately
        }
    }

    public ArrayList GetPluginList()
    {
        // Return an enumerable list of plug-in names. Take the keys
        // and place them in an ArrayList, which supports marshal-by-value.
        return new ArrayList(plugins.Keys);
    }
}

class Recipe03_07
{
    public static void Main()
    {
        // Create a new application domain.
        AppDomain domain1 = AppDomain.CreateDomain("NewAppDomain1");
```

```
// Create a PluginManager in the new application domain using
// the default constructor.
PluginManager manager1 =
    (PluginManager)domain1.CreateInstanceAndUnwrap("Recipe03-07",
    "Apress.VisualCSharpRecipes.Chapter03.PluginManager");

// Load a new plugin into NewAppDomain1.
manager1.LoadPlugin("Recipe03-07",
    "Apress.VisualCSharpRecipes.Chapter03.SimplePlugin");

// Start and stop the plug-in in NewAppDomain1.
manager1.StartPlugin(
    "Apress.VisualCSharpRecipes.Chapter03.SimplePlugin");
manager1.StopPlugin(
    "Apress.VisualCSharpRecipes.Chapter03.SimplePlugin");

// Create a new application domain.
AppDomain domain2 = AppDomain.CreateDomain("NewAppDomain2");

// Create a ListDictionary containing a list of plug-ins to create.
NameValueCollection pluginList = new NameValueCollection();
pluginList["Apress.VisualCSharpRecipes.Chapter03.SimplePlugin"] =
    "Recipe03-07";

// Create a PluginManager in the new application domain and
// specify the default list of plug-ins to create.
PluginManager manager2 = (PluginManager)domain1.CreateInstanceAndUnwrap(
    "Recipe03-07", "Apress.VisualCSharpRecipes.Chapter03.PluginManager",
    true, 0, null, new object[] { pluginList }, null, null, null);

// Display the list of plug-ins loaded into NewAppDomain2.
Console.WriteLine("\nPlugins in NewAppDomain2:");
foreach (string s in manager2.GetPluginList())
{
    Console.WriteLine(" - " + s);
}

// Wait to continue.
Console.WriteLine("\nMain method complete. Press Enter.");
Console.ReadLine();
        }
    }
}
```

3-8. Pass Data Between Application Domains

Problem

You need a simple mechanism to pass general configuration or state data between application domains.

Solution

Use the SetData and GetData methods of the AppDomain class.

How It Works

You can pass data between application domains as arguments and return values when you invoke the methods and properties of objects that exist in other application domains. However, at times it is useful to pass data between application domains in such a way that the data is easily accessible by all code within the application domain.

Every application domain maintains a data cache that contains a set of name-value pairs. Most of the cache content reflects configuration settings of the application domain, such as the values from the AppDomainSetup object provided during application domain creation. (See recipe 3-1 for more information.) You can also use this data cache as a mechanism to exchange data between application domains or as a simple state storage mechanism for code running within the application domain.

The SetData method allows you to associate a string key with an object and store it in the application domain's data cache. The GetData method allows you to retrieve an object from the data cache using the key. If code in one application domain calls the SetData method or the GetData method to access the data cache of another application domain, the data object must support MBV or MBR semantics, or a System.Runtime.Serialization.SerializationException is thrown. (See recipe 3-3 for details on the characteristics required to allow objects to transcend application domain boundaries.)

When using the SetData or GetData methods to exchange data between application domains, you should avoid using the following keys, which are already used by the .NET Framework:

- APP_CONFIG_FILE
- APP_NAME
- APPBASE
- APP_CONFIG_BLOB
- BINPATH_PROBE_ONLY
- CACHE_BASE
- CODE_DOWNLOAD_DISABLED
- DEV_PATH
- DYNAMIC_BASE
- DISALLOW_APP
- DISALLOW_APP_REDIRECTS
- DISALLOW_APP_BASE_PROBING
- FORCE_CACHE_INSTALL
- LICENSE_FILE
- PRIVATE_BINPATH
- SHADOW_COPY_DIRS

The Code

The following example demonstrates how to use the SetData and GetData methods by passing a System.Collections.ArrayList between two application domains. After passing a list of pets to a second application domain for modification, the application displays both the original and modified lists. You will notice that the code running in the second application domain does not modify the original list because ArrayList is a pass-by-value type, meaning that the second application domain only has a *copy* of the original list. (See recipe 3-2 for more details.)

```csharp
using System;
using System.Reflection;
using System.Collections;

namespace Apress.VisualCSharpRecipes.Chapter03
{
    public class ListModifier
    {
        public ListModifier()
        {
            // Get the list from the data cache.
            ArrayList list = (ArrayList)AppDomain.CurrentDomain.GetData("Pets");

            // Modify the list.
            list.Add("turtle");
        }
    }

    class Recipe03_08
    {
        public static void Main()
        {
            // Create a new application domain.
            AppDomain domain = AppDomain.CreateDomain("Test");

            // Create an ArrayList and populate with information.
            ArrayList list = new ArrayList();
            list.Add("dog");
            list.Add("cat");
            list.Add("fish");

            // Place the list in the data cache of the new application domain.
            domain.SetData("Pets", list);

            // Instantiate a ListModifier in the new application domain.
            domain.CreateInstance("Recipe03-08",
                "Apress.VisualCSharpRecipes.Chapter03.ListModifier");

            // Get the list and display its contents.
            foreach (string s in (ArrayList)domain.GetData("Pets")) {
                Console.WriteLine(s);
            }

            // Wait to continue.
            Console.WriteLine("\nMain method complete. Press Enter.");
            Console.ReadLine();
        }
    }
}
```

3-9. Unload Assemblies and Application Domains

Problem

You need to unload assemblies or application domains at runtime.

Solution

You have no way to unload individual assemblies from a System.AppDomain. You can unload an entire application domain using the static AppDomain.Unload method, which has the effect of unloading all assemblies loaded into the application domain.

How It Works

The only way to unload an assembly is to unload the application domain in which the assembly is loaded. Unfortunately, unloading an application domain will unload all the assemblies that have been loaded into it. This might seem like a heavy-handed and inflexible approach, but with appropriate planning of your application domain, the assembly-loading structure, and the runtime dependency of your code on that application domain, it is not overly restrictive.

You unload an application domain using the static AppDomain.Unload method and passing it an AppDomain reference to the application domain you want to unload. You cannot unload the default application domain created by the CLR at start-up.

The Unload method stops any new threads from entering the specified application domain and calls the Thread.Abort method on all threads currently active in the application domain. If the thread calling the Unload method is currently running in the specified application domain (making it the target of a Thread.Abort call), a new thread starts in order to carry out the unload operation. If a problem is encountered unloading an application domain, the thread performing the unload operation throws a System.CannotUnloadAppDomainException.

While an application domain is unloading, the CLR calls the finalization method of all objects in the application domain. Depending on the number of objects and nature of their finalization methods, this can take an arbitrary amount of time. The AppDomain.IsFinalizingForUnload method returns true if the application domain is unloading and the CLR has started to finalize contained objects; otherwise, it returns false.

The Code

This code fragment demonstrates the syntax of the Unload method:

```
// Create a new application domain
AppDomain newDomain = AppDomain.CreateDomain("New Domain");

// Load assemblies into the application domain
...

// Unload the new application domains
AppDomain.Unload(newDomain);
```

3-10. Retrieve Type Information

Problem

You need to obtain a System.Type object that represents a specific type.

Solution

Use one of the following:

- The `typeof` operator
- The `static GetType` method of the `System.Type` class
- The `GetType` method of an existing instance of the type
- The `GetNestedType` or `GetNestedTypes` method of the `Type` class
- The `GetType` or `GetTypes` method of the `Assembly` class
- The `GetType`, `GetTypes`, or `FindTypes` method of the `System.Reflection.Module` class

How It Works

The `Type` class provides a starting point for working with types using reflection. A `Type` object allows you to inspect the metadata of the type, obtain details of the type's members, and create instances of the type. Because of its importance, the .NET Framework provides a variety of mechanisms for obtaining references to `Type` objects.

One method of obtaining a `Type` object for a specific type is to use the `typeof` operator shown here:

```
System.Type t1 = typeof(System.Text.StringBuilder);
```

The type name is not enclosed in quotes and must be resolvable by the compiler (meaning you must reference the assembly using a compiler switch). Because the reference is resolved at compile time, the assembly containing the type becomes a static dependency of your assembly and will be listed as such in your assembly's manifest.

An alternative to the `typeof` operator is the `static` method `Type.GetType`, which takes a string containing the type name. Because you use a string to specify the type, you can vary it at runtime, which opens the door to a world of dynamic programming opportunities using reflection (see recipe 3-12). If you specify just the type name, the runtime must be able to locate the type in an already loaded assembly. Alternatively, you can specify an assembly-qualified type name. Refer to the .NET Framework SDK documentation for the `Type.GetType` method for a complete description of how to structure assembly-qualified type names. Table 3-2 summarizes some other methods that provide access to `Type` objects.

Table 3-2. *Methods That Return* Type *Objects*

Method	Description
`Type.GetNestedType`	Gets a specified type declared as a nested type within the existing `Type` object.
`Type.GetNestedTypes`	Gets an array of `Type` objects representing the nested types declared within the existing `Type` object.
`Assembly.GetType`	Gets a `Type` object for the specified type declared within the assembly.
`Assembly.GetTypes`	Gets an array of `Type` objects representing the types declared within the assembly.
`Module.GetType`	Gets a `Type` object for the specified type declared within the module. (See recipe 1-3 for a discussion of modules.)
`Module.GetTypes`	Gets an array of `Type` objects representing the types declared within the module.
`Module.FindTypes`	Gets a filtered array of `Type` objects representing the types declared within the module. The types are filtered using a delegate that determines whether each `Type` should appear in the final array.

The Code

The following example demonstrates how to use typeof and the GetType method to return a Type object for a named type and from existing objects:

```
using System;
using System.Text;

namespace Apress.VisualCSharpRecipes.Chapter03
{
    class Recipe03_10
    {
        public static void Main()
        {
            // Obtain type information using the typeof operator.
            Type t1 = typeof(StringBuilder);

            // Obtain type information using the Type.GetType method.
            // Case sensitive, return null if not found.
            Type t2 = Type.GetType("System.String");

            // Case-sensitive, throw TypeLoadException if not found.
            Type t3 = Type.GetType("System.String", true);

            // Case-insensitive, throw TypeLoadException if not found.
            Type t4 = Type.GetType("system.string", true, true);

            // Assembly-qualifed type name.
            Type t5 = Type.GetType("System.Data.DataSet,System.Data," +
                "Version=2.0.0.0,Culture=neutral,PublicKeyToken=b77a5c561934e089");

            // Obtain type information using the Object.GetType method.
            StringBuilder sb = new StringBuilder();
            Type t6 = sb.GetType();

            // Wait to continue.
            Console.WriteLine("\nMain method complete. Press Enter.");
            Console.ReadLine();
        }
    }
}
```

3-11. Test an Object's Type

Problem

You need to test the type of an object.

Solution

Use the inherited Object.GetType method to obtain a Type for the object. You can also use the is and as operators to test an object's type.

How It Works

All types inherit the GetType method from the Object base class. As discussed in recipe 3-10, this method returns a Type reference representing the type of the object. The runtime maintains a single instance of Type for each type loaded, and all references for this type refer to this same object. This means you can compare two type references efficiently. For convenience, C# provides the is operator as a quick way to check whether an object is a specified type. In addition, is will return true if the tested object is derived from the specified class.

Both of these approaches require that the type used with the typeof and is operators be known and resolvable at compile time. A more flexible (but slower) alternative is to use the Type.GetType method to return a Type reference for a named type. The Type reference is not resolved until runtime, which causes the performance hit but allows you to change the type comparison at runtime based on the value of a string.

Finally, you can use the as operator to perform a safe cast of any object to a specified type. Unlike a standard cast that triggers a System.InvalidCastException if the object cannot be cast to the specified type, the as operator returns null. This allows you to perform safe casts that are easy to verify, but the compared type must be resolvable at runtime.

■**Note** The runtime will usually maintain more than one instance of each type depending on how assemblies are loaded into application domains. Usually, an assembly will be loaded into a specific application domain, meaning a Type instance will exist in each application domain in which the assembly is loaded. However, assemblies can also be loaded by a runtime host in a domain-neutral configuration, which means the assembly's type metadata (and Type instances) is shared across all application domains. By default, only the mscorlib assembly is loaded in a domain-neutral configuration.

The Code

The following example demonstrates the various type-testing alternatives described in this recipe:

```
using System;
using System.IO;

namespace Apress.VisualCSharpRecipes.Chapter03
{
    class Recipe03_11
    {
        // A method to test whether an object is an instance of a type
        // or a derived type.
        public static bool IsType(object obj, string type)
        {
            // Get the named type, use case-insensitive search, throw
            // an exception if the type is not found.
            Type t = Type.GetType(type, true, true);

            return t == obj.GetType() || obj.GetType().IsSubclassOf(t);
        }

        public static void Main()
        {
            // Create a new StringReader for testing.
            Object someObject = new StringReader("This is a StringReader");
```

```
        // Test if someObject is a StringReader by obtaining and
        // comparing a Type reference using the typeof operator.
        if (typeof(StringReader) == someObject.GetType())
        {
            Console.WriteLine("typeof: someObject is a StringReader");
        }

        // Test if someObject is, or is derived from, a TextReader
        // using the is operator.
        if (someObject is TextReader)
        {
            Console.WriteLine(
                "is: someObject is a TextReader or a derived class");
        }

        // Test if someObject is, or is derived from, a TextReader using
        // the Type.GetType and Type.IsSubclassOf methods.
        if (IsType(someObject, "System.IO.TextReader"))
        {
            Console.WriteLine("GetType: someObject is a TextReader");
        }

        // Use the "as" operator to perform a safe cast.
        StringReader reader = someObject as StringReader;
        if (reader != null)
        {
            Console.WriteLine("as: someObject is a StringReader");
        }

        // Wait to continue.
        Console.WriteLine("\nMain method complete. Press Enter.");
        Console.ReadLine();
    }
  }
}
```

■**Tip** The static method GetUnderlyingType of the System.Enum class allows you to retrieve the underlying type of an enumeration.

3-12. Instantiate an Object Using Reflection

Problem

You need to instantiate an object at runtime using reflection.

Solution

Obtain a Type object representing the type of object you want to instantiate, call its GetConstructor method to obtain a System.Reflection.ConstructorInfo object representing the constructor you want to use, and execute the ConstructorInfo.Invoke method.

How It Works

The first step in creating an object using reflection is to obtain a Type object that represents the type you want to instantiate. (See recipe 3-10 for details.) Once you have a Type instance, call its GetConstructor method to obtain a ConstructorInfo representing one of the type's constructors. The most commonly used overload of the GetConstructor method takes a Type array argument and returns a ConstructorInfo representing the constructor that takes the number, order, and type of arguments specified in the Type array. To obtain a ConstructorInfo representing a parameterless (default) constructor, pass an empty Type array (use the static field Type.EmptyTypes or new Type[0]); don't use null, or GetConstructor will throw a System.ArgumentNullException. If GetConstructor cannot find a constructor with a signature that matches the specified arguments, it will return null.

Once you have the desired ConstructorInfo, call its Invoke method. You must provide an object array containing the arguments you want to pass to the constructor. Invoke instantiates the new object and returns an object reference to it, which you must cast to the appropriate type.

Reflection functionality is commonly used to implement factories in which you use reflection to instantiate concrete classes that either extend a common base class or implement a common interface. Often both an interface and a common base class are used. The abstract base class implements the interface and any common functionality, and then each concrete implementation extends the base class.

No mechanism exists to formally declare that each concrete class must implement constructors with specific signatures. If you intend third parties to implement concrete classes, your documentation must specify the constructor signature called by your factory. A common approach to avoid this problem is to use a default (empty) constructor and configure the object after instantiation using properties and methods.

The Code

The following code fragment demonstrates how to instantiate a System.Text.StringBuilder object using reflection and how to specify the initial content for the StringBuilder (a string) and its capacity (an int):

```
using System;
using System.Text;
using System.Reflection;

namespace Apress.VisualCSharpRecipes.Chapter03
{
    class Recipe03_12
    {
        public static StringBuilder CreateStringBuilder()
        {
            // Obtain the Type for the StringBuilder class.
            Type type = typeof(StringBuilder);

            // Create a Type[] containing Type instances for each
            // of the constructor arguments - a string and an int.
            Type[] argTypes = new Type[] { typeof(System.String),
                typeof(System.Int32) };

            // Obtain the ConstructorInfo object.
            ConstructorInfo cInfo = type.GetConstructor(argTypes);

            // Create an object[] containing the constructor arguments.
            object[] argVals = new object[] { "Some string", 30 };
```

```
        // Create the object and cast it to StringBuilder.
        StringBuilder sb = (StringBuilder)cInfo.Invoke(argVals);

        return sb;
    }
  }
}
```

The following code demonstrates a factory to instantiate objects that implement the IPlugin interface (first used in recipe 3-7):

```
using System;
using System.Reflection;
namespace Apress.VisualCSharpRecipes.Chapter03
{
    // A common interface that all plug-ins must implement.
    public interface IPlugin
    {
        string Description { get; set; }
        void Start();
        void Stop();
    }

    // An abstract base class from which all plug-ins must derive.
    public abstract class AbstractPlugin : IPlugin
    {
        // Hold a description for the plug-in instance.
        private string description = "";

        // Sealed property to get the plug-in description.
        public string Description
        {
            get { return description; }
            set { description = value; }
        }

        // Declare the members of the IPlugin interface as abstract.
        public abstract void Start();
        public abstract void Stop();
    }

    // A simple IPlugin implementation to demonstrate the PluginFactory class.
    public class SimplePlugin : AbstractPlugin
    {
        // Implement Start method.
        public override void Start()
        {
            Console.WriteLine(Description + ": Starting...");
        }

        // Implement Stop method.
        public override void Stop()
        {
            Console.WriteLine(Description + ": Stopping...");
        }
    }
```

```csharp
// A factory to instantiate instances of IPlugin.
public sealed class PluginFactory
{
    public static IPlugin CreatePlugin(string assembly,
        string pluginName, string description)
    {
        // Obtain the Type for the specified plug-in.
        Type type = Type.GetType(pluginName + ", " + assembly);

        // Obtain the ConstructorInfo object.
        ConstructorInfo cInfo = type.GetConstructor(Type.EmptyTypes);

        // Create the object and cast it to StringBuilder.
        IPlugin plugin = cInfo.Invoke(null) as IPlugin;

        // Configure the new IPlugin.
        plugin.Description = description;

        return plugin;
    }

    public static void Main(string[] args)
    {
        // Instantiate a new IPlugin using the PluginFactory.
        IPlugin plugin = PluginFactory.CreatePlugin(
            "Recipe03-12",  // Private assembly name
            "Apress.VisualCSharpRecipes.Chapter03.SimplePlugin",
             // Plug-in class name
            "A Simple Plugin"       // Plug-in instance description
        );

        // Start and stop the new plug-in.
        plugin.Start();
        plugin.Stop();

        // Wait to continue.
        Console.WriteLine("\nMain method complete. Press Enter.");
        Console.ReadLine();
    }
}
}
```

■**Tip** The System.Activator class provides two static methods named CreateInstance and CreateInstanceFrom that instantiate objects based on Type objects or strings containing type names. The key difference between using GetConstructor and Activator is that the constructor used by Activator is implied by the constructor arguments you pass to CreateInstance or CreateInstanceFrom. Using GetConstructor, you can determine exactly which constructor you want to use to instantiate the object. See the description of the Activator class in the .NET Framework SDK documentation for more details.

3-13. Create a Custom Attribute

Problem

You need to create a custom attribute.

Solution

Create a class that derives from the `abstract` base class `System.Attribute`. Implement constructors, fields, and properties to allow users to configure the attribute. Use `System.AttributeUsageAttribute` to define the following:

- Which program elements are valid targets of the attribute

- Whether you can apply more than one instance of the attribute to a program element

- Whether the attribute is inherited by derived types

How It Works

Attributes provide a mechanism for associating declarative information (metadata) with program elements. This metadata is contained in the compiled assembly, allowing programs to retrieve it through reflection at runtime without creating an instance of the type. (See recipe 3-14 for more details.) Other programs, particularly the CLR, use this information to determine how to interact with and manage program elements.

To create a custom attribute, derive a class from the `abstract` base class `System.Attribute`. Custom attribute classes by convention should have a name ending in *Attribute* (but this is not essential). A custom attribute must have at least one `public` constructor—the automatically generated default constructor is sufficient. The constructor parameters become the attribute's mandatory (or positional) parameters. When you use the attribute, you must provide values for these parameters in the order they appear in the constructor. As with any other class, you can declare more than one constructor, giving users of the attribute the option of using different sets of positional parameters when applying the attribute. Any `public` nonconstant writable fields and properties declared by an attribute are automatically exposed as named parameters. Named parameters are optional and are specified in the format of name-value pairs where the name is the property or field name. The following example will clarify how to specify positional and named parameters.

To control how and where a user can apply your attribute, apply the attribute `AttributeUsageAttribute` to your custom attribute. `AttributeUsageAttribute` supports the one positional and two named parameters described in Table 3-3. The default values specify the value that is applied to your custom attribute if you do not apply `AttributeUsageAttribute` or do not specify a value for that particular parameter.

Table 3-3. *Members of the* `AttributeUsage` *Type*

Parameter	Type	Description	Default
ValidOn	Positional	A member of the `System.AttributeTargets` enumeration that identifies the program elements on which the attribute is valid	`AttributeTargets.All`

(Continued)

Table 3-3. *Continued*

Parameter	Type	Description	Default
AllowMultiple	Named	Whether the attribute can be specified more than once for a single element	False
Inherited	Named	Whether the attribute is inherited by derived classes or overridden members	True

The Code

The following example shows a custom attribute named AuthorAttribute, which you can use to identify the name and company of the person who created an assembly or a class. AuthorAttribute declares a single public constructor that takes a string containing the author's name. This means users of AuthorAttribute must always provide a positional string parameter containing the author's name. The Company property is public, making it an optional named parameter, but the Name property is read-only—no set accessor is declared—meaning that it isn't exposed as a named parameter.

```
using System;

namespace Apress.VisualCSharpRecipes.Chapter03
{
    [AttributeUsage(AttributeTargets.Class | AttributeTargets.Assembly,
        AllowMultiple = true, Inherited = false)]
    public class AuthorAttribute : System.Attribute
    {
        private string company; // Creator's company
        private string name;    // Creator's name

        // Declare a public constructor.
        public AuthorAttribute(string name)
        {
            this.name = name;
            company = "";
        }

        // Declare a property to get/set the company field.
        public string Company
        {
            get { return company; }
            set { company = value; }
        }

        // Declare a property to get the internal field.
        public string Name
        {
            get { return name; }
        }
    }
}
```

Usage

The following example demonstrates how to decorate types with AuthorAttribute:

```
using System;

// Declare Allen as the assembly author. Assembly attributes
// must be declared after using statements but before any other.
// Author name is a positional parameter.
// Company name is a named parameter.
[assembly: Apress.VisualCSharpRecipes.Chapter03.Author("Allen",
    Company = "Principal Objective Ltd.")]

namespace Apress.VisualCSharpRecipes.Chapter03
{
    // Declare a class authored by Allen.
    [Author("Allen", Company = "Principal Objective Ltd.")]
    public class SomeClass
    {
        // Class implementation.
    }

    // Declare a class authored by Lena.
    [Author("Lena")]
    public class SomeOtherClass
    {
        // Class implementation.
    }
}
```

3-14. Inspect the Attributes of a Program Element Using Reflection

Problem

You need to use reflection to inspect the custom attributes applied to a program element.

Solution

All program elements implement the System.Reflection.ICustomAttributeProvider interface. Call the IsDefined method of the ICustomAttributeProvider interface to determine whether an attribute is applied to a program element, or call the GetCustomAttributes method of the ICustomAttributeProvider interface to obtain objects representing the attributes applied to the program element.

How It Works

All the classes that represent program elements implement the ICustomAttributeProvider interface. This includes Assembly, Module, Type, EventInfo, FieldInfo, PropertyInfo, and MethodBase. MethodBase has two further subclasses: ConstructorInfo and MethodInfo. If you obtain instances of any of these classes, you can call the method GetCustomAttributes, which will return an object array containing the custom attributes applied to the program element. The object array contains only custom attributes, not those contained in the .NET Framework base class library.

The GetCustomAttributes method provides two overloads. The first takes a bool that controls whether GetCustomAttributes should return attributes inherited from parent classes. The second GetCustomAttributes overload takes an additional Type argument that acts as a filter, resulting in GetCustomAttributes returning only attributes of the specified type.

Alternatively, you can call the IsDefined method. IsDefined provides a single overload that takes two arguments. The first argument is a System.Type object representing the type of attribute you are interested in, and the second is a bool that indicates whether IsDefined should look for inherited attributes of the specified type. IsDefined returns a bool indicating whether the specified attribute is applied to the program element and is less expensive than calling the GetCustomAttributes method, which actually instantiates the attribute objects.

The Code

The following example uses the custom AuthorAttribute declared in recipe 3-13 and applies it to the Recipe03-14 class. The Main method calls the GetCustomAttributes method, filtering the attributes so that the method returns only AuthorAttribute instances. You can safely cast this set of attributes to AuthorAttribute references and access their members without needing to use reflection.

```
using System;

namespace Apress.VisualCSharpRecipes.Chapter03
{
    [Author("Lena")]
    [Author("Allen", Company = "Principal Objective Ltd.")]
    class Recipe03_15
    {
        public static void Main()
        {
            // Get a Type object for this class.
            Type type = typeof(Recipe03_15);

            // Get the attributes for the type. Apply a filter so that only
            // instances of AuthorAttribute are returned.
            object[] attrs =
                type.GetCustomAttributes(typeof(AuthorAttribute), true);

            // Enumerate the attributes and display their details.
            foreach (AuthorAttribute a in attrs) {
                Console.WriteLine(a.Name + ", " + a.Company);
            }

            // Wait to continue.
            Console.WriteLine("\nMain method complete. Press Enter.");
            Console.ReadLine();
        }
    }
}
```

CHAPTER 4

■■■

Threads, Processes, and Synchronization

One of the strengths of the Microsoft Windows operating system is that it allows many programs (processes) to run concurrently and allows each process to perform many tasks concurrently (using multiple threads). When you run an executable application, a new process is created. The process isolates your application from other programs running on the computer. The process provides the application with its own virtual memory and its own copies of any libraries it needs to run, allowing your application to execute as if it were the only application running on the machine.

Along with the process, an initial thread is created that runs your Main method. In single-threaded applications, this one thread steps through your code and sequentially performs each instruction. If an operation takes time to complete, such as reading a file from the Internet or doing a complex calculation, the application will be unresponsive (will *block*) until the operation is finished, at which point the thread will continue with the next operation in your program.

To avoid blocking, the main thread can create additional threads and specify which code each should start running. As a result, many threads may be running in your application's process, each running (potentially) different code and performing different operations seemingly simultaneously. In reality, unless you have multiple processors (or a single multicore processor) in your computer, the threads are not really running simultaneously. Instead, the operating system coordinates and schedules the execution of all threads across all processes; each thread is given a tiny portion (or *time slice*) of the processor's time, which gives the impression they are executing at the same time.

The difficulty of having multiple threads executing within your application arises when those threads need to access shared data and resources. If multiple threads are changing an object's state or writing to a file at the same time, your data will quickly become corrupt. To avoid problems, you must synchronize the threads to make sure they each get a chance to access the resource, but only one at a time. Synchronization is also important when waiting for a number of threads to reach a certain point of execution before proceeding with a different task and for controlling the number of threads that are at any given time actively performing a task—perhaps processing requests from client applications.

■**Note** Although it will not affect your multithreaded programming in Visual C#, it is worth noting that an operating system thread has no fixed relationship to a managed thread. The runtime host—the managed code that loads and runs the common language runtime (CLR)—controls the relationship between managed and unmanaged threads. A sophisticated runtime host, such as Microsoft SQL Server 2005, can schedule many managed threads against the same operating system thread or can perform the actions of a managed thread using different operating system threads.

This chapter describes how to control processes and threads in your own applications using the features provided by Visual C# and the Microsoft .NET Framework class library. Specifically, the recipes in this chapter describe how to do the following:

- Execute code in independent threads using features including the thread pool, asynchronous method invocation, and timers (recipes 4-1 through 4-6)

- Synchronize the execution of multiple threads using a host of synchronization techniques including monitors, events, mutexes, and semaphores (recipes 4-7 and 4-11)

- Terminate threads and know when threads have terminated (recipes 4-12 and 4-13)

- Create thread-safe instances of the .NET collection classes (recipe 4-14)

- Start and stop applications running in new processes (recipes 4-15 and 4-16)

- Ensure that only one instance of an application is able to run at any given time (recipe 4-17)

As you will see in this chapter, delegates are used extensively in multithreaded programs to wrap the method that a thread should execute or that should act as a callback when an asynchronous operation is complete. Prior to C# 2.0, it would be necessary to

1. Declare a method that matches the signature of the required delegate,

2. Create a delegate instance of the required type by passing it the name of the method, and

3. Pass the delegate instance to the new thread or asynchronous operation.

C# 2.0 adds two important new features that simplify the code you must write when using delegates:

- First, you no longer need to create a delegate instance to wrap the method you want to execute. You can pass a method name where a delegate is expected, and as long as the method signature is correct, the compiler infers the need for the delegate and creates it automatically. This is a compiler enhancement only—the intermediate language (IL) generated is as if the appropriate delegate had been instantiated. Recipes 4-1 and 4-2 (along with many others) demonstrate how to use this capability.

- Second, you no longer need to explicitly declare a method for using with the delegate. Instead, you can provide an anonymous method wherever a delegate is required. In effect, you actually write the method code at the point where you would usually pass the method name (or delegate instance). The only difference is that you use the keyword `delegate` instead of giving the method a name. This approach can reduce the need to implement methods solely for use as callbacks and event handlers, which reduces code clutter, but it can quickly become confusing if the anonymous method is longer than a couple of lines of code. Recipes 4-3 and 4-4 demonstrate how to use anonymous methods.

4-1. Execute a Method Using the Thread Pool

Problem

You need to execute a task using a thread from the runtime's thread pool.

Solution

Declare a method containing the code you want to execute. The method's signature must match that defined by the System.Threading.WaitCallback delegate; that is, it must return void and take a single object argument. Call the static method QueueUserWorkItem of the System.Threading. ThreadPool class, passing it your method name. The runtime will queue your method and execute it when a thread-pool thread becomes available.

How It Works

Applications that use many short-lived threads or maintain large numbers of concurrent threads can suffer performance degradation because of the overhead associated with the creation, operation, and destruction of threads. In addition, it is common in multithreaded systems for threads to sit idle a large portion of the time while they wait for the appropriate conditions to trigger their execution. Using a thread pool provides a common solution to improve the scalability, efficiency, and performance of multithreaded systems.

The .NET Framework provides a simple thread-pool implementation accessible through the members of the ThreadPool static class. The QueueUserWorkItem method allows you to execute a method using a thread-pool thread by placing a work item on a queue. As a thread from the thread pool becomes available, it takes the next work item from the queue and executes it. The thread performs the work assigned to it, and when it is finished, instead of terminating, the thread returns to the thread pool and takes the next work item from the work queue.

■**Tip** If you need to execute a method with a signature that does not match the WaitCallback delegate, then you must use one of the other techniques described in this chapter. See recipe 4-2 or 4-6.

The Code

The following example demonstrates how to use the ThreadPool class to execute a method named DisplayMessage. The example passes DisplayMessage to the thread pool twice, first with no arguments and then with a MessageInfo object, which allows you to control which message the new thread will display.

```
using System;
using System.Threading;

namespace Apress.VisualCSharpRecipes.Chapter04
{
    class Recipe04_01
    {

        // A private class used to pass data to the DisplayMessage method when it is
        // executed using the thread pool.
        private class MessageInfo
        {
            private int iterations;
            private string message;

            // A constructor that takes configuration settings for the thread.
            public MessageInfo(int iterations, string message)
            {
                this.iterations = iterations;
                this.message = message;
            }
```

```csharp
        // Properties to retrieve configuration settings.
        public int Iterations { get { return iterations; } }
        public string Message { get { return message; } }
    }

    // A method that conforms to the System.Threading.WaitCallback delegate
    // signature. Displays a message to the console.
    public static void DisplayMessage(object state)
    {
        // Safely cast the state argument to a MessageInfo object.
        MessageInfo config = state as MessageInfo;

        // If the config argument is null, no arguments were passed to
        // the ThreadPool.QueueUserWorkItem method; use default values.
        if (config == null)
        {
            // Display a fixed message to the console three times.
            for (int count = 0; count < 3; count++)
            {
                Console.WriteLine("A thread pool example.");

                // Sleep for the purpose of demonstration. Avoid sleeping
                // on thread-pool threads in real applications.
                Thread.Sleep(1000);
            }

        }
        else
        {
            // Display the specified message the specified number of times.
            for (int count = 0; count < config.Iterations; count++)
            {
                Console.WriteLine(config.Message);

                // Sleep for the purpose of demonstration. Avoid sleeping
                // on thread-pool threads in real applications.
                Thread.Sleep(1000);
            }
        }
    }

    public static void Main()
    {
        // Execute DisplayMessage using the thread pool and no arguments.
        ThreadPool.QueueUserWorkItem(DisplayMessage);

        // Create a MessageInfo object to pass to the DisplayMessage method.
        MessageInfo info = new MessageInfo(5,
            "A thread pool example with arguments.");

        // Execute DisplayMessage using the thread pool and providing an
        // argument.
        ThreadPool.QueueUserWorkItem(DisplayMessage, info);

        // Wait to continue.
        Console.WriteLine("Main method complete. Press Enter.");
        Console.ReadLine();
```

```
        }
    }
}
```

Notes

Using the runtime's thread pool simplifies multithreaded programming dramatically; however, be aware that the implementation is a simple, general-purpose thread pool. Before deciding to use the thread pool, consider the following points:

- Each process has one thread pool, which supports by default a maximum of 25 concurrent threads per processor. You can change the maximum number of threads using the method ThreadPool.SetMaxThreads, but some runtime hosts (Internet Information Services [IIS] and SQL Server, for example) will limit the maximum number of threads and may not allow the default value to be changed at all.

- As well as allowing you to use the thread pool to execute code directly, the runtime uses the thread pool for other purposes internally. This includes the asynchronous execution of methods (see recipe 4-2), execution of timer events (see recipes 4-3 and 4-4), and execution of wait-based methods (see recipe 4-5). All of these uses can lead to heavy contention for the thread-pool threads, meaning that the work queue can become very long. Although the work queue's maximum length is limited only by the amount of memory available to the runtime's process, an excessively long queue will result in long delays before queued work items are executed. The ThreadPool.GetAvailableThreads method returns the number of threads currently available in the thread pool. This can be useful in determining whether your application is placing too much load on the thread pool, indicating that you should increase the number of available threads using the ThreadPool.SetMaxThreads method.

- Where possible, avoid using the thread pool to execute long-running processes. The limited number of threads in the thread pool means that a handful of threads tied up with long-running processes can significantly affect the overall performance of the thread pool. Specifically, you should avoid putting thread-pool threads to sleep for any length of time.

- Thread-pool threads are background threads. You can configure threads as either foreground threads or background threads. Foreground and background threads are identical except that a background thread will not keep an application process alive. Therefore, your application will terminate automatically when the last foreground thread of your application terminates.

- You have no control over the scheduling of thread-pool threads, and you cannot prioritize work items. The thread pool handles each work item in the sequence in which you add it to the work queue.

- Once a work item is queued, it cannot be canceled or stopped.

- Do not try to use thread-pool threads to update or manipulate Windows Forms controls, because they can be updated only by the thread that created them.

4-2. Execute a Method Asynchronously

Problem

You need to start execution of a method and continue with other tasks while the method runs on a separate thread. After the method completes, you need to retrieve the method's return value.

Solution

Declare a delegate with the same signature as the method you want to execute. Create an instance of the delegate that references the method. Call the BeginInvoke method of the delegate instance to start executing your method. Use the EndInvoke method to determine the method's status as well as obtain the method's return value if complete.

How It Works

Typically, when you invoke a method, you do so synchronously, meaning that the calling code blocks until the method is complete. Most of the time, this is the expected, desired behavior because your code requires the operation to complete before it can continue. However, sometimes it is useful to execute a method asynchronously, meaning that you start the method in a separate thread and then continue with other operations.

The .NET Framework implements an asynchronous execution pattern that allows you to call any method asynchronously using a delegate. When you declare and compile a delegate, the compiler automatically generates two methods that support asynchronous execution: BeginInvoke and EndInvoke. When you call BeginInvoke on a delegate instance, the method referenced by the delegate is queued for asynchronous execution. Control returns to the caller immediately, and the referenced method executes in the context of the first available thread-pool thread.

The signature of the BeginInvoke method includes the same arguments as those specified by the delegate signature, followed by two additional arguments to support asynchronous completion. These additional arguments are as follows:

- A System.AsyncCallback delegate instance that references a method that the runtime will call when the asynchronous method completes. The method will be executed by a thread-pool thread. Passing null means no method is called and means you must use another mechanism (discussed later in this recipe) to determine when the asynchronous method is complete.

- A reference to an object that the runtime associates with the asynchronous operation for you. The asynchronous method does not use or have access to this object, but it is available to your code when the method completes, allowing you to associate useful state information with an asynchronous operation. For example, this object allows you to map results against initiated operations in situations where you initiate many asynchronous operations that use a common callback method to perform completion.

The EndInvoke method allows you to retrieve the return value of a method that was executed asynchronously, but you must first determine when it has finished. If your asynchronous method threw an exception, it will be rethrown so that you can handle it when you call EndInvoke. Here are the four techniques for determining whether an asynchronous method has finished:

- *Blocking* stops the execution of the current thread until the asynchronous method completes execution. In effect, this is much the same as synchronous execution. However, you have the flexibility to decide exactly when your code enters the blocked state, giving you the opportunity to perform some additional processing before blocking.

- *Polling* involves repeatedly testing the state of an asynchronous method to determine whether it is complete. This is a simple technique and is not particularly efficient from a processing perspective. You should avoid tight loops that consume processor time; it is best to put the polling thread to sleep for a period using Thread.Sleep between completion tests. Because polling involves maintaining a loop, the actions of the waiting thread are limited, but you can easily update some kind of progress indicator.

- *Waiting* depends on the `AsyncWaitHandle` property of the `IAsyncResult` returned by `BeginInvoke`. This object derives from the `System.Threading.WaitHandle` class signals when the asynchronous method completes. Waiting is a more efficient version of polling and in addition allows you to wait for multiple asynchronous methods to complete. You can also specify time-out values to allow your waiting thread to notify a failure if the asynchronous method takes too long or if you want to periodically update a status indicator.

- A *callback* is a method that the runtime calls when an asynchronous operation completes. The calling code does not have to take any steps to determine when the asynchronous method is complete and is free to continue with other processing. Callbacks provide the greatest flexibility but also introduce the greatest complexity, especially if you have many asynchronous operations active concurrently that all use the same callback. In such cases, you must use appropriate state objects as the last parameter of `BeginInvoke` to match the completed methods against those you initiated.

■**Caution** Even if you do not want to handle the return value of your asynchronous method, you should call `EndInvoke`; otherwise, you risk leaking memory each time you initiate an asynchronous call using `BeginInvoke`.

The Code

The following code demonstrates how to use the asynchronous execution pattern. It uses a delegate named `AsyncExampleDelegate` to execute a method named `LongRunningMethod` asynchronously. `LongRunningMethod` simulates a long-running method using a configurable delay (produced using `Thread.Sleep`). The example contains the following five methods that demonstrate the various approaches to handling asynchronous method completion:

- The `BlockingExample` method executes `LongRunningMethod` asynchronously and continues with a limited set of processing. Once this processing is complete, `BlockingExample` blocks until `LongRunningMethod` completes. To block, `BlockingExample` calls the `EndInvoke` method of the `AsyncExampleDelegate` delegate instance. If `LongRunningMethod` has already finished, `EndInvoke` returns immediately; otherwise, `BlockingExample` blocks until `LongRunningMethod` completes.

- The `PollingExample` method executes `LongRunningMethod` asynchronously and then enters a polling loop until `LongRunningMethod` completes. `PollingExample` tests the `IsCompleted` property of the `IAsyncResult` instance returned by `BeginInvoke` to determine whether `LongRunningMethod` is complete; otherwise, `PollingExample` calls `Thread.Sleep`.

- The `WaitingExample` method executes `LongRunningMethod` asynchronously and then waits until `LongRunningMethod` completes. `WaitingExample` uses the `AsyncWaitHandle` property of the `IAsyncResult` instance returned by `BeginInvoke` to obtain a `WaitHandle` and then calls its `WaitOne` method. Using a time-out allows `WaitingExample` to break out of waiting in order to perform other processing or to fail completely if the asynchronous method is taking too long.

- The `WaitAllExample` method executes `LongRunningMethod` asynchronously multiple times and then uses an array of `WaitHandle` objects to wait efficiently until all the methods are complete.

- The `CallbackExample` method executes `LongRunningMethod` asynchronously and passes an `AsyncCallback` delegate instance (that references the `CallbackHandler` method) to the `BeginInvoke` method. The referenced `CallbackHandler` method is called automatically when the asynchronous `LongRunningMethod` completes, leaving the `CallbackExample` method free to continue processing.

■**Note** For the purpose of demonstrating the various synchronization techniques, the example performs several tasks that should be avoided when using the thread pool, including putting thread-pool threads to sleep and calling long-running methods. See recipe 4-1 for more suggestions on using the thread pool appropriately.

```csharp
using System;
using System.Threading;
using System.Collections;

namespace Apress.VisualCSharpRecipes.Chapter04
{
    class Recipe04_02
    {
        // A utility method for displaying useful trace information to the
        // console along with details of the current thread.
        private static void TraceMsg(DateTime time, string msg)
        {
            Console.WriteLine("[{0,3}/{1}] - {2} : {3}",
                Thread.CurrentThread.ManagedThreadId,
                Thread.CurrentThread.IsThreadPoolThread ? "pool" : "fore",
                time.ToString("HH:mm:ss.ffff"), msg);
        }

        // A delegate that allows you to perform asynchronous execution of
        // LongRunningMethod.
        public delegate DateTime AsyncExampleDelegate(int delay, string name);

        // A simulated long-running method.
        public static DateTime LongRunningMethod(int delay, string name)
        {
            TraceMsg(DateTime.Now, name + " example - thread starting.");

            // Simulate time-consuming processing.
            Thread.Sleep(delay);

            TraceMsg(DateTime.Now, name + " example - thread stopping.");

            // Return the method's completion time.
            return DateTime.Now;
        }

        // This method executes LongRunningMethod asynchronously and continues
        // with other processing. Once the processing is complete, the method
        // blocks until LongRunningMethod completes.
        public static void BlockingExample()
        {
            Console.WriteLine(Environment.NewLine +
                "*** Running Blocking Example ***");

            // Invoke LongRunningMethod asynchronously. Pass null for both the
            // callback delegate and the asynchronous state object.
            AsyncExampleDelegate longRunningMethod = LongRunningMethod;

            IAsyncResult asyncResult = longRunningMethod.BeginInvoke(2000,
                "Blocking", null, null);
```

```
    // Perform other processing until ready to block.
    for (int count = 0; count < 3; count++)
    {
        TraceMsg(DateTime.Now,
            "Continue processing until ready to block...");

        Thread.Sleep(200);
    }

    // Block until the asynchronous method completes.
    TraceMsg(DateTime.Now,
        "Blocking until method is complete...");

    // Obtain the completion data for the asynchronous method.
    DateTime completion = DateTime.MinValue;

    try
    {
        completion = longRunningMethod.EndInvoke(asyncResult);
    }
    catch
    {
        // Catch and handle those exceptions you would if calling
        // LongRunningMethod directly.
    }

    // Display completion information
    TraceMsg(completion,"Blocking example complete.");
}

// This method executes LongRunningMethod asynchronously and then
// enters a polling loop until LongRunningMethod completes.
public static void PollingExample()
{
    Console.WriteLine(Environment.NewLine +
        "*** Running Polling Example ***");

    // Invoke LongRunningMethod asynchronously. Pass null for both the
    // callback delegate and the asynchronous state object.
    AsyncExampleDelegate longRunningMethod = LongRunningMethod;

    IAsyncResult asyncResult = longRunningMethod.BeginInvoke(2000,
        "Polling", null, null);

    // Poll the asynchronous method to test for completion. If not
    // complete, sleep for 300ms before polling again.
    TraceMsg(DateTime.Now, "Poll repeatedly until method is complete.");

    while (!asyncResult.IsCompleted)
    {
        TraceMsg(DateTime.Now, "Polling...");
        Thread.Sleep(300);
    }

    // Obtain the completion data for the asynchronous method.
    DateTime completion = DateTime.MinValue;
```

```
        try
        {
            completion = longRunningMethod.EndInvoke(asyncResult);
        }
        catch
        {
            // Catch and handle those exceptions you would if calling
            // LongRunningMethod directly.
        }

        // Display completion information.
        TraceMsg(completion, "Polling example complete.");
    }

    // This method executes LongRunningMethod asynchronously and then
    // uses a WaitHandle to wait efficiently until LongRunningMethod
    // completes. Use of a time-out allows the method to break out of
    // waiting in order to update the user interface or fail if the
    // asynchronous method is taking too long.
    public static void WaitingExample()
    {
        Console.WriteLine(Environment.NewLine +
            "*** Running Waiting Example ***");

        // Invoke LongRunningMethod asynchronously. Pass null for both the
        // callback delegate and the asynchronous state object.
        AsyncExampleDelegate longRunningMethod = LongRunningMethod;

        IAsyncResult asyncResult = longRunningMethod.BeginInvoke(2000,
            "Waiting", null, null);

        // Wait for the asynchronous method to complete. Time-out after
        // 300ms and display status to the console before continuing to
        // wait.
        TraceMsg(DateTime.Now, "Waiting until method is complete...");

        while (!asyncResult.AsyncWaitHandle.WaitOne(300, false))
        {
            TraceMsg(DateTime.Now, "Wait timeout...");
        }

        // Obtain the completion data for the asynchronous method.
        DateTime completion = DateTime.MinValue;

        try
        {
            completion = longRunningMethod.EndInvoke(asyncResult);
        }
        catch
        {
            // Catch and handle those exceptions you would if calling
            // LongRunningMethod directly.
        }

        // Display completion information.
        TraceMsg(completion, "Waiting example complete.");
    }
```

```csharp
// This method executes LongRunningMethod asynchronously multiple
// times and then uses an array of WaitHandle objects to wait
// efficiently until all of the methods are complete. Use of
// a time-out allows the method to break out of waiting in order
// to update the user interface or fail if the asynchronous
// method is taking too long.
public static void WaitAllExample()
{
    Console.WriteLine(Environment.NewLine +
        "*** Running WaitAll Example ***");

    // An ArrayList to hold the IAsyncResult instances for each of the
    // asynchronous methods started.
    ArrayList asyncResults = new ArrayList(3);

    // Invoke three LongRunningMethods asynchronously. Pass null for
    // both the callback delegate and the asynchronous state object.
    // Add the IAsyncResult instance for each method to the ArrayList.
    AsyncExampleDelegate longRunningMethod = LongRunningMethod;

    asyncResults.Add(longRunningMethod.BeginInvoke(3000,
        "WaitAll 1", null, null));

    asyncResults.Add(longRunningMethod.BeginInvoke(2500,
        "WaitAll 2", null, null));

    asyncResults.Add(longRunningMethod.BeginInvoke(1500,
        "WaitAll 3", null, null));

    // Create an array of WaitHandle objects that will be used to wait
    // for the completion of all the asynchronous methods.
    WaitHandle[] waitHandles = new WaitHandle[3];

    for (int count = 0; count < 3; count++)
    {
        waitHandles[count] =
            ((IAsyncResult)asyncResults[count]).AsyncWaitHandle;
    }

    // Wait for all three asynchronous method to complete. Time out
    // after 300ms and display status to the console before continuing
    // to wait.
    TraceMsg(DateTime.Now, "Waiting until all 3 methods are complete...");

    while (!WaitHandle.WaitAll(waitHandles, 300, false))
    {
        TraceMsg(DateTime.Now, "WaitAll timeout...");
    }

    // Inspect the completion data for each method, and determine the
    // time at which the final method completed.
    DateTime completion = DateTime.MinValue;

    foreach (IAsyncResult result in asyncResults)
    {
        try
        {
```

```
            DateTime time = longRunningMethod.EndInvoke(result);
            if (time > completion) completion = time;
        }
        catch
        {
            // Catch and handle those exceptions you would if calling
            // LongRunningMethod directly.
        }
    }

    // Display completion information
    TraceMsg(completion, "WaitAll example complete.");
}

// This method executes LongRunningMethod asynchronously and passes
// an AsyncCallback delegate instance. The referenced CallbackHandler
// method is called automatically when the asynchronous method
// completes, leaving this method free to continue processing.
public static void CallbackExample()
{
    Console.WriteLine(Environment.NewLine +
        "*** Running Callback Example ***");

    // Invoke LongRunningMethod asynchronously. Pass an AsyncCallback
    // delegate instance referencing the CallbackHandler method that
    // will be called automatically when the asynchronous method
    // completes. Pass a reference to the AsyncExampleDelegate delegate
    // instance as asynchronous state; otherwise, the callback method
    // has no access to the delegate instance in order to call
    // EndInvoke.
    AsyncExampleDelegate longRunningMethod = LongRunningMethod;

    IAsyncResult asyncResult = longRunningMethod.BeginInvoke(2000,
        "Callback", CallbackHandler, longRunningMethod);

    // Continue with other processing.
    for (int count = 0; count < 15; count++)
    {
        TraceMsg(DateTime.Now, "Continue processing...");
        Thread.Sleep(200);
    }
}

// A method to handle asynchronous completion using callbacks.
public static void CallbackHandler(IAsyncResult result)
{
    // Extract the reference to the AsyncExampleDelegate instance
    // from the IAsyncResult instance. This allows you to obtain the
    // completion data.
    AsyncExampleDelegate longRunningMethod =
        (AsyncExampleDelegate)result.AsyncState;

    // Obtain the completion data for the asynchronous method.
    DateTime completion = DateTime.MinValue;
```

```
        try
        {
            completion = longRunningMethod.EndInvoke(result);
        }
        catch
        {
            // Catch and handle those exceptions you would if calling
            // LongRunningMethod directly.
        }

        // Display completion information.
        TraceMsg(completion, "Callback example complete.");
    }

    public static void Main()
    {
        // Demonstrate the various approaches to asynchronous method completion.
        BlockingExample();
        PollingExample();
        WaitingExample();
        WaitAllExample();
        CallbackExample();

        // Wait to continue.
        Console.WriteLine(Environment.NewLine);
        Console.WriteLine("Main method complete. Press Enter.");
        Console.ReadLine();
    }
    }
}
```

4-3. Execute a Method Periodically

Problem

You need to execute a method in a separate thread periodically.

Solution

Declare a method containing the code you want to execute periodically. The method's signature must match that defined by the System.Threading.TimerCallback delegate; in other words, it must return void and take a single object argument. Create a System.Threading.Timer object and pass it the method you want to execute along with a state object that the timer will pass to your method when the timer expires. The runtime will wait until the timer expires and then call your method using a thread from the thread pool.

Tip If you are implementing a timer in a Windows Forms application, you should consider using the System.Windows.Forms.Timer, which also provides additional support in Visual Studio that allows you to drag the timer from your Toolbox onto your application. For server-based applications where you want to signal multiple listeners each time the timer fires, consider using the System.Timers.Timer class, which notifies listeners using events.

How It Works

It is often useful to execute a method at regular intervals. For example, you might need to clean a data cache every 20 minutes. The Timer class makes the periodic execution of methods straightforward, allowing you to execute a method referenced by a TimerCallback delegate at specified intervals. The referenced method executes in the context of a thread from the thread pool. (See recipe 4-1 for notes on the appropriate use of thread-pool threads.)

When you create a Timer object, you specify two time intervals. The first value specifies the millisecond delay until the Timer first executes your method. Specify 0 to execute the method immediately, and specify System.Threading.Timeout.Infinite to create the Timer in an unstarted state. The second value specifies the interval in milliseconds; then the Timer will repeatedly call your method following the initial execution. If you specify a value of 0 or Timeout.Infinite, the Timer will execute the method only once (as long as the initial delay is not Timeout.Infinite). You can specify the time intervals as int, long, uint, or System.TimeSpan values.

Once you have created a Timer object, you can modify the intervals used by the timer using the Change method, but you cannot change the method that is called. When you have finished with a Timer object, you should call its Dispose method to free system resources held by the timer. Disposing of the Timer object cancels any method that is scheduled for execution.

The Code

The TimerExample class shown next demonstrates how to use a Timer object to call a method named TimerHandler. Initially, the Timer object is configured to call TimerHandler after 2 seconds and then at 1-second intervals. The example allows you to enter a new millisecond interval in the console, which is applied using the Timer.Change method.

```csharp
using System;
using System.Threading;

namespace Apress.VisualCSharpRecipes.Chapter04
{
    class Recipe04_03
    {
        public static void Main()
        {
            // Create the state object that is passed to the TimerHandler
            // method when it is triggered. In this case, a message to display.
            string state = "Timer expired.";

            Console.WriteLine("{0} : Creating Timer.",
                DateTime.Now.ToString("HH:mm:ss.ffff"));

            // Create a Timer that fires first after 2 seconds and then every
            // second. Use an anonymous method for the timer expiry handler.
            using (Timer timer =
                new Timer(delegate(object s)
                            {Console.WriteLine("{0} : {1}",
                             DateTime.Now.ToString("HH:mm:ss.ffff"),s);
                            }
                , state, 2000, 1000))
            {
                int period;

                // Read the new timer interval from the console until the
                // user enters 0 (zero). Invalid values use a default value
                // of 0, which will stop the example.
```

```
            do
            {
                try
                {
                    period = Int32.Parse(Console.ReadLine());
                }
                catch (FormatException)
                {
                    period = 0;
                }

                // Change the timer to fire using the new interval starting
                // immediately.
                if (period > 0) timer.Change(0, period);
            } while (period > 0);
        }

        // Wait to continue.
        Console.WriteLine("Main method complete. Press Enter.");
        Console.ReadLine();
    }
  }
}
```

4-4. Execute a Method at a Specific Time

Problem

You need to execute a method in a separate thread at a specific time.

Solution

Declare a method containing the code you want to execute. The method's signature must match that defined by the System.Threading.TimerCallback delegate; that is, it must return void and take a single object argument. Create a System.Threading.Timer object, and pass it the method you want to execute along with a state object that the timer will pass to your method when the timer expires. Calculate the time difference between the current time and the desired execution time, and configure the Timer object to fire once after this period of time.

How It Works

Executing a method at a particular time is often useful. For example, you might need to back up data at 1 a.m. daily. Although primarily used for calling methods at regular intervals, the Timer object also provides the flexibility to call a method at a specific time.

When you create a Timer object, you specify two time intervals. The first value specifies the millisecond delay until the Timer first executes your method. To execute the method at a specific time, you should set this value to the difference between the current time (System.DateTime.Now) and the desired execution time. The second value specifies the interval after which the Timer will repeatedly call your method following the initial execution. If you specify a value of 0, System.Threading.Timeout.Infinite, or TimeSpan(-1), the Timer object will execute the method only once. If you need the method to execute at a specific time every day, you can easily set this figure using TimeSpan.FromDays(1), which represents the number of milliseconds in 24 hours.

The Code

The following code demonstrates how to use a Timer object to execute a method at a specified time. The RunAt method calculates the TimeSpan between the current time and a time specified on the command line (in RFC1123 format, which updates RFC822) and configures a Timer object to fire once after that period of time.

```
using System;
using System.Threading;
using System.Globalization;

namespace Apress.VisualCSharpRecipes.Chapter04
{
    class Recipe04_04
    {
        public static void RunAt(DateTime execTime)
        {
            // Calculate the difference between the specified execution
            // time and the current time.
            TimeSpan waitTime = execTime - DateTime.Now;

            if (waitTime < new TimeSpan(0)) waitTime = new TimeSpan(0);

            // Create a Timer that fires once at the specified time. Specify
            // an interval of -1 to stop the timer executing the method
            // repeatedly. Use an anonymous method for the timer expiry handler.
            new Timer(delegate(object s)
                    {
                        Console.WriteLine("{0} : {1}",
                            DateTime.Now.ToString("HH:mm:ss.ffff"), s);
                    }
                    , null, waitTime, new TimeSpan(-1));
        }

        public static void Main(string[] args)
        {
            DateTime execTime;

            // Ensure there is an execution time specified on the command line.
            if (args.Length > 0)
            {
                // Convert the string to a DateTime. Support only the RFC1123
                // DateTime pattern.
                try
                {
                    execTime = DateTime.ParseExact(args[0],"r", null);

                    Console.WriteLine("Current time    : " +
                        DateTime.Now.ToString("r"));

                    Console.WriteLine("Execution time : " +
                        execTime.ToString("r"));

                    RunAt(execTime);
                }
                catch (FormatException)
                {
```

```
            Console.WriteLine("Execution time must be of the format:\n\t"+
                CultureInfo.CurrentCulture.DateTimeFormat.RFC1123Pattern);
        }

        // Wait to continue.
        Console.WriteLine("Waiting for Timer.");
        Console.WriteLine("Main method complete. Press Enter.");
        Console.ReadLine();

    }
    else
    {
        Console.WriteLine("Specify the time you want the method to" +
            " execute using the format :\n\t " +
            CultureInfo.CurrentCulture.DateTimeFormat.RFC1123Pattern);
    }
    }
  }
}
```

4-5. Execute a Method by Signaling a WaitHandle Object

Problem

You need to execute one or more methods automatically when an object derived from System.Threading.WaitHandle is signaled.

Solution

Declare a method containing the code you want to execute. The method's signature must match that defined by the System.Threading.WaitOrTimerCallback delegate. Using the static ThreadPool.RegisterWaitForSingleObject method, register the method to execute and the WaitHandle object that will trigger execution when signaled.

How It Works

You can use classes derived from the WaitHandle class to trigger the execution of a method. Using the RegisterWaitForSingleObject method of the ThreadPool class, you can register a WaitOrTimerCallback delegate instance for execution by a thread-pool thread when a specified WaitHandle-derived object enters a signaled state. You can configure the thread pool to execute the method only once or to automatically reregister the method for execution each time the WaitHandle is signaled. If the WaitHandle is already signaled when you call RegisterWaitForSingleObject, the method will execute immediately. The Unregister method of the System.Threading.RegisteredWaitHandle object returned by the RegisterWaitForSingleObject method is used to cancel a registered wait operation.

The class most commonly used as a trigger is AutoResetEvent, which automatically returns to an unsignaled state after it is signaled. However, you can also use the ManualResetEvent, Mutex, and Semaphore classes, which require you to change the signaled state manually.

The Code

The following example demonstrates how to use an AutoResetEvent to trigger the execution of a method named EventHandler. (The AutoResetEvent class is discussed further in recipe 4-8.)

```csharp
using System;
using System.Threading;

namespace Apress.VisualCSharpRecipes.Chapter04
{
    class Recipe04_05
    {
        // A method that is executed when the AutoResetEvent is signaled
        // or the wait operation times out.
        private static void EventHandler(object state, bool timedout)
        {
            // Display appropriate message to the console based on whether
            // the wait timed out or the AutoResetEvent was signaled.
            if (timedout)
            {
                Console.WriteLine("{0} : Wait timed out.",
                    DateTime.Now.ToString("HH:mm:ss.ffff"));
            }
            else
            {
                Console.WriteLine("{0} : {1}",
                    DateTime.Now.ToString("HH:mm:ss.ffff"), state);
            }
        }

        public static void Main()
        {
            // Create the new AutoResetEvent in an unsignaled state.
            AutoResetEvent autoEvent = new AutoResetEvent(false);

            // Create the state object that is passed to the event handler
            // method when it is triggered. In this case, a message to display.
            string state = "AutoResetEvent signaled.";

            // Register the EventHandler method to wait for the AutoResetEvent to
            // be signaled. Set a time-out of 3 seconds, and configure the wait
            // operation to reset after activation (last argument).
            RegisteredWaitHandle handle = ThreadPool.RegisterWaitForSingleObject(
                autoEvent, EventHandler, state, 3000, false);

            Console.WriteLine("Press ENTER to signal the AutoResetEvent" +
                " or enter \"Cancel\" to unregister the wait operation.");

            while (Console.ReadLine().ToUpper() != "CANCEL")
            {
                // If "Cancel" has not been entered into the console, signal
                // the AutoResetEvent, which will cause the EventHandler
                // method to execute. The AutoResetEvent will automatically
                // revert to an unsignaled state.
                autoEvent.Set();
            }
```

```
            // Unregister the wait operation.
            Console.WriteLine("Unregistering wait operation.");
            handle.Unregister(null);

            // Wait to continue.
            Console.WriteLine("Main method complete. Press Enter.");
            Console.ReadLine();
        }
    }
}
```

4-6. Execute a Method Using a New Thread

Problem

You need to execute code in its own thread, and you want complete control over the thread's state and operation.

Solution

Declare a method containing the code you want to execute. The method's signature must match that defined by the System.Threading.ThreadStart or System.Threading.ParameterizedThreadStart delegate. Create a new System.Threading.Thread object, and pass the method as an argument to its constructor. Call the Thread.Start method to start the execution of your method.

How It Works

For maximum control and flexibility when creating multithreaded applications, you need to take a direct role in creating and managing threads. This is the most complex approach to multithreaded programming, but it is the only way to overcome the restrictions and limitations inherent in the approaches using thread-pool threads, as discussed in the preceding recipes. The Thread class provides the mechanism through which you create and control threads. To create and start a new thread, follow this process:

1. Define a method that matches the ThreadStart or ParameterizedThreadStart delegate. The ThreadStart delegate takes no arguments and returns void. This means you cannot easily pass data to your new thread. The ParameterizedThreadStart delegate also returns void but takes a single object as an argument, allowing you to pass data to the method you want to run. (The ParameterizedThreadStart delegate is a welcome addition to .NET 2.0.) The method you want to execute can be static or an instance method.

2. Create a new Thread object, and pass your method as an argument to the Thread constructor. The new thread has an initial state of Unstarted (a member of the System.Threading.ThreadState enumeration) and is a foreground thread by default. If you want to configure it to be a background thread, you need to set its IsBackground property to true.

3. Call Start on the Thread object, which changes its state to ThreadState.Running and begins execution of your method. If you need to pass data to your method, include it as an argument to the Start call. If you call Start more than once, it will throw a System.Threading. ThreadStateException.

The Code

The following code demonstrates how to execute a method in a new thread and shows you how to pass data to the new thread:

```
using System;
using System.Threading;

namespace Apress.VisualCSharpRecipes.Chapter04
{
    class Recipe04_06
    {

        // A utility method for displaying useful trace information to the
        // console along with details of the current thread.
        private static void TraceMsg(string msg)
        {
            Console.WriteLine("[{0,3}] - {1} : {2}",
                Thread.CurrentThread.ManagedThreadId,
                DateTime.Now.ToString("HH:mm:ss.ffff"), msg);
        }

        // A private class used to pass initialization data to a new thread.
        private class ThreadStartData
        {
            public ThreadStartData(int iterations, string message, int delay)
            {
                this.iterations = iterations;
                this.message = message;
                this.delay = delay;
            }

            // Member variables hold initialization data for a new thread.
            private readonly int iterations;
            private readonly string message;
            private readonly int delay;

            // Properties provide read-only access to initialization data.
            public int Iterations { get { return iterations; } }
            public string Message { get { return message; } }
            public int Delay { get { return delay; } }
        }

        // Declare the method that will be executed in its own thread. The
        // method displays a message to the console a specified number of
        // times, sleeping between each message for a specified duration.
        private static void DisplayMessage(object config)
        {
            ThreadStartData data = config as ThreadStartData;

            if (data != null)
            {
                for (int count = 0; count < data.Iterations; count++)
                {
                    TraceMsg(data.Message);

                    // Sleep for the specified period.
```

```
                    Thread.Sleep(data.Delay);
                }
            }
            else
            {
                TraceMsg("Invalid thread configuration.");
            }
        }

        public static void Main()
        {
            // Create a new Thread object specifying DisplayMessage
            // as the method it will execute.
            Thread thread = new Thread(DisplayMessage);

            // Create a new ThreadStartData object to configure the thread.
            ThreadStartData config =
                new ThreadStartData(5, "A thread example.", 500);

            TraceMsg("Starting new thread.");

            // Start the new thread and pass the ThreadStartData object
            // containing the initialization data.
            thread.Start(config);

            // Continue with other processing.
            for (int count = 0; count < 13; count++)
            {
                TraceMsg("Main thread continuing processing...");
                Thread.Sleep(200);
            }

            // Wait to continue.
            Console.WriteLine(Environment.NewLine);
            Console.WriteLine("Main method complete. Press Enter.");
            Console.ReadLine();
        }
    }
}
```

4-7. Synchronize the Execution of Multiple Threads Using a Monitor

Problem

You need to coordinate the activities of multiple threads to ensure the efficient use of shared resources or to ensure several threads are not updating the same shared resource at the same time.

Solution

Identify an appropriate object to use as a mechanism to control access to the shared resource/data. Use the static method Monitor.Enter to acquire a lock on the object, and use the static method Monitor.Exit to release the lock so another thread may acquire it.

How It Works

The greatest challenge in writing a multithreaded application is ensuring that the threads work in concert. This is commonly referred to as *thread synchronization* and includes the following:

- Ensuring threads access shared objects and data correctly so that they do not cause corruption
- Ensuring threads execute only when they are meant to and cause minimum overhead when they are idle

The most commonly used synchronization mechanism is the System.Threading.Monitor class. The Monitor class allows a single thread to obtain an exclusive lock on an object by calling the static method Monitor.Enter. By acquiring an exclusive lock prior to accessing a shared resource or data, you ensure that only one thread can access the resource concurrently. Once the thread has finished with the resource, release the lock to allow another thread to access it. A block of code that enforces this behavior is often referred to as a *critical section*.

■**Note** Monitors are managed-code synchronization mechanisms that do not rely on any specific operating system primitives. This ensures your code is portable should you want to run it on a non-Windows platform. This is in contrast to the synchronization mechanisms discussed in recipes 4-8, 4-9, and 4-10, which rely on Win32 operating system–based synchronization objects.

You can use any object to act as the lock; it is common to use the keyword this to obtain a lock on the current object, but it is better to use a separate object dedicated to the purpose of synchronization. The key point is that all threads attempting to access a shared resource must try to acquire the *same* lock. Other threads that attempt to acquire a lock using Monitor.Enter on the same object will block (enter a WaitSleepJoin state) and are added to the lock's *ready queue* until the thread that owns the lock releases it by calling the static method Monitor.Exit. When the owning thread calls Exit, one of the threads from the ready queue acquires the lock. If the owner of a lock does not release it by calling Exit, all other threads will block indefinitely. Therefore, it is important to place the Exit call within a finally block to ensure that it is called even if an exception occurs. To ensure threads do not wait indefinitely, you can specify a time-out value when you call Monitor.Enter.

■**Tip** Because Monitor is used so frequently in multithreaded applications, C# provides language-level support through the lock statement, which the compiler translates to the use of the Monitor class. A block of code encapsulated in a lock statement is equivalent to calling Monitor.Enter when entering the block and Monitor.Exit when exiting the block. In addition, the compiler automatically places the Monitor.Exit call in a finally block to ensure that the lock is released if an exception is thrown.

Using Monitor.Enter and Monitor.Exit is often all you will need to correctly synchronize access to a shared resource in a multithreaded application. However, when you are trying to coordinate the activation of a pool of threads to handle work items from a shared queue, Monitor.Enter and Monitor.Exit will not be sufficient. In this situation, you want a potentially large number of threads to wait efficiently until a work item becomes available without putting unnecessary load on the central processing unit (CPU). This is where you need the fine-grained synchronization control provided by the Monitor.Wait, Monitor.Pulse, and Monitor.PulseAll methods.

The thread that currently owns the lock can call Monitor.Wait, which will release the lock and place the calling thread on the lock's *wait queue*. Threads in a wait queue also have a state of WaitSleepJoin and will continue to block until a thread that owns the lock calls either the Monitor.Pulse method or the Monitor.PulseAll method. Monitor.Pulse moves one of the waiting threads from the wait queue to the ready queue, and Monitor.PulseAll moves all threads. Once a thread has moved from the wait queue to the ready queue, it can acquire the lock the next time the lock is released. It is important to understand that threads on a lock's wait queue *will not* acquire a released lock; they will wait indefinitely until you call Monitor.Pulse or Monitor.PulseAll to move them to the ready queue.

So, in practice, when your pool threads are inactive, they sit on the wait queue. As a new work item arrives, a dispatcher obtains the lock and calls Monitor.Pulse, moving one worker thread to the ready queue where it will obtain the lock as soon as the dispatcher releases it. The worker thread takes the work item, releases the lock, and processes the work item. Once the worker thread has finished with the work item, it again obtains the lock in order to take the next work item, but if there is no work item to process, the thread calls Monitor.Wait and goes back to the wait queue.

The Code

The following example demonstrates how to synchronize access to a shared resource (the console) and the activation of waiting threads using the Monitor.Wait, Monitor.Pulse, and Monitor.PulseAll methods. The example starts three worker threads that take work items from a queue and processes them. When the user presses Enter the first two times, work items (strings in the example) are added to the work queue, and Monitor.Pulse is called to release one waiting thread for each work item. The third time the user presses Enter, Monitor.PulseAll is called, releasing all waiting threads and allowing them to terminate.

```
using System;
using System.Threading;
using System.Collections.Generic;

namespace Apress.VisualCSharpRecipes.Chapter04
{
    class Recipe04_07
    {
        // Declare an object for synchronization of access to the console.
        // A static object is used because you are using it in static methods.
        private static object consoleGate = new Object();

        // Declare a Queue to represent the work queue.
        private static Queue<string> workQueue = new Queue<string>();

        // Declare a flag to indicate to activated threads that they should
        // terminate and not process more work items.
        private static bool processWorkItems = true;

        // A utility method for displaying useful trace information to the
        // console along with details of the current thread.
        private static void TraceMsg(string msg)
        {
            lock (consoleGate)
            {
                Console.WriteLine("[{0,3}/{1}] - {2} : {3}",
                    Thread.CurrentThread.ManagedThreadId,
                    Thread.CurrentThread.IsThreadPoolThread ? "pool" : "fore",
                    DateTime.Now.ToString("HH:mm:ss.ffff"), msg);
            }
        }

        // Declare the method that will be executed by each thread to process
```

```csharp
    // items from the work queue.
    private static void ProcessWorkItems()
    {
        // A local variable to hold the work item taken from the work queue.
        string workItem = null;

        TraceMsg("Thread started, processing items from queue...");

        // Process items from the work queue until termination is signaled.
        while (processWorkItems)
        {
            // Obtain the lock on the work queue.
            Monitor.Enter(workQueue);

            try
            {
                // Pop the next work item and process it, or wait if none
                // is available.
                if (workQueue.Count == 0)
                {
                    TraceMsg("No work items, waiting...");

                    // Wait until Pulse is called on the workQueue object.
                    Monitor.Wait(workQueue);
                }
                else
                {
                    // Obtain the next work item.
                    workItem = workQueue.Dequeue();
                }
            }
            finally
            {
                // Always release the lock.
                Monitor.Exit(workQueue);
            }

            // Process the work item if one was obtained.
            if (workItem != null)
            {
                // Obtain a lock on the console and display a series
                // of messages.
                lock (consoleGate)
                {
                    for (int i = 0; i < 5; i++)
                    {
                        TraceMsg("Processing " + workItem);
                        Thread.Sleep(200);
                    }
                }

                // Reset the status of the local variable.
                workItem = null;
            }
        }

        // This will be reached only if processWorkItems is false.
```

```csharp
        TraceMsg("Terminating.");
}

public static void Main()
{
    TraceMsg("Starting worker threads.");

    // Add an initial work item to the work queue.
    lock (workQueue)
    {
        workQueue.Enqueue("Work Item 1");
    }

    // Create and start three new worker threads running the
    // ProcessWorkItems method.
    for (int count = 0; count < 3; count++)
    {
        (new Thread(ProcessWorkItems)).Start();
    }

    Thread.Sleep(1500);

    // The first time the user presses Enter, add a work item and
    // activate a single thread to process it.
    TraceMsg("Press Enter to pulse one waiting thread.");
    Console.ReadLine();

    // Acquire a lock on the workQueue object.
    lock (workQueue)
    {
        // Add a work item.
        workQueue.Enqueue("Work Item 2.");

        // Pulse 1 waiting thread.
        Monitor.Pulse(workQueue);
    }

    Thread.Sleep(2000);

    // The second time the user presses Enter, add three work items and
    // activate three threads to process them.
    TraceMsg("Press Enter to pulse three waiting threads.");
    Console.ReadLine();

    // Acquire a lock on the workQueue object.
    lock (workQueue)
    {
        // Add work items to the work queue, and activate worker threads.
        workQueue.Enqueue("Work Item 3.");
        Monitor.Pulse(workQueue);
        workQueue.Enqueue("Work Item 4.");
        Monitor.Pulse(workQueue);
        workQueue.Enqueue("Work Item 5.");
        Monitor.Pulse(workQueue);
    }

    Thread.Sleep(3500);
```

```
            // The third time the user presses Enter, signal the worker threads
            // to terminate and activate them all.
            TraceMsg("Press Enter to pulse all waiting threads.");
            Console.ReadLine();

            // Acquire a lock on the workQueue object.
            lock (workQueue)
            {
                // Signal that threads should terminate.
                processWorkItems = false;

                // Pulse all waiting threads.
                Monitor.PulseAll(workQueue);
            }

            Thread.Sleep(1000);

            // Wait to continue.
            TraceMsg("Main method complete. Press Enter.");
            Console.ReadLine();
        }
    }
}
```

4-8. Synchronize the Execution of Multiple Threads Using an Event

Problem

You need a mechanism to synchronize the execution of multiple threads in order to coordinate their activities or access to shared resources.

Solution

Use the `EventWaitHandle`, `AutoResetEvent`, and `ManualResetEvent` classes from the `System.Threading` namespace.

How It Works

The `EventWaitHandle`, `AutoResetEvent`, and `ManualResetEvent` classes provide similar functionality. In fact, although the `EventWaitHandle` is new to .NET 2.0, it is the base class from which the `AutoResetEvent` and `ManualResetEvent` classes are derived. (`EventWaitHandle` inherits from `System.Threading.WaitHandle` and allows you to create named events.) All three event classes allow you to synchronize multiple threads by manipulating the state of the event between two possible values: *signaled* and *unsignaled*.

Threads requiring synchronization call static or inherited methods of the `WaitHandle` abstract base class (summarized in Table 4-1) to test the state of one or more event objects. If the events are signaled when tested, the thread continues to operate unhindered. If the events are unsignaled, the thread enters a `WaitSleepJoin` state, blocking until one or more of the events become signaled or when a given time-out expires.

Table 4-1. `WaitHandle` *Methods for Synchronizing Thread Execution*

Method	Description
WaitOne	Causes the calling thread to enter a `WaitSleepJoin` state and wait for a specific `WaitHandle` derived object to be signaled. You can also specify a time-out value. The `WaitingExample` method in recipe 4-2 demonstrates how to use the `WaitOne` method.
WaitAny	A `static` method that causes the calling thread to enter a `WaitSleepJoin` state and wait for any one of the objects in a `WaitHandle` array to be signaled. You can also specify a time-out value.
WaitAll	A `static` method that causes the calling thread to enter a `WaitSleepJoin` state and wait for all the `WaitHandle` objects in a `WaitHandle` array to be signaled. You can also specify a time-out value. The `WaitAllExample` method in recipe 4-2 demonstrates how to use the `WaitAll` method.
SignalAndWait	A `static` method that causes the calling thread to signal a specified event object and then wait on a specified event object. The signal and wait operations are carried out as an atomic operation. You can also specify a time-out value. `SignalAndWait` is new to .NET 2.0.

The key differences between the three event classes are how they transition from a signaled to an unsignaled state and their visibility. Both the `AutoResetEvent` and `ManualResetEvent` classes are local to the process in which they are declared. To signal an `AutoResetEvent` class, call its `Set` method, which will release only one thread that is waiting on the event. The `AutoResetEvent` class will then automatically return to an unsignaled state. The code in recipe 4-4 demonstrates how to use an `AutoResetEvent` class.

The `ManualResetEvent` class must be manually switched back and forth between signaled and unsignaled states using its `Set` and `Reset` methods. Calling `Set` on a `ManualResetEvent` class will set it to a signaled state, releasing all threads that are waiting on the event. Only by calling `Reset` does the `ManualResetEvent` class become unsignaled.

You can configure the `EventWaitHandle` class to operate in a manual or automatic reset mode, making it possible to act like either the `AutoResetEvent` class or the `ManualResetEvent` class. When you create the `EventWaitHandle`, you pass a value of the `System.Threading.EventResetMode` enumeration to configure the mode in which the `EventWaitHandle` will function; the two possible values are `AutoReset` and `ManualReset`. The unique benefit of the `EventWaitHandle` class is that it is not constrained to the local process. When you create an `EventWaitHandle` class, you can associate a name with it that makes it accessible to other processes, including nonmanaged Win32 code. This allows you to synchronize the activities of threads across process and application domain boundaries and synchronize access to resources that are shared by multiple processes. To obtain a reference to an existing named `EventWaitHandle`, call the static method `EventWaitHandle.OpenExisting`, and specify the name of the event.

The Code

The following example demonstrates how to use a named `EventWaitHandle` in manual mode that is initially signaled. A thread is spawned that waits on the event and then displays a message to the console—repeating the process every 2 seconds. When you press Enter, you toggle the event between a signaled and a nonsignaled state.

```csharp
using System;
using System.Threading;

namespace Apress.VisualCSharpRecipes.Chapter04
{
    class Recipe04_08
    {
        // Boolean to signal that the second thread should terminate.
        static bool terminate = false;

        // A utility method for displaying useful trace information to the
        // console along with details of the current thread.
        private static void TraceMsg(string msg)
        {
            Console.WriteLine("[{0,3}] - {1} : {2}",
                Thread.CurrentThread.ManagedThreadId,
                DateTime.Now.ToString("HH:mm:ss.ffff"), msg);
        }

        // Declare the method that will be executed on the separate thread.
        // The method waits on the EventWaitHandle before displaying a message
        // to the console and then waits two seconds and loops.
        private static void DisplayMessage()
        {
            // Obtain a handle to the EventWaitHandle with the name "EventExample".
            EventWaitHandle eventHandle =
                EventWaitHandle.OpenExisting("EventExample");

            TraceMsg("DisplayMessage Started.");

            while (!terminate)
            {
                // Wait on the EventWaitHandle, time-out after two seconds. WaitOne
                // returns true if the event is signaled; otherwise, false. The
                // first time through, the message will be displayed immediately
                // because the EventWaitHandle was created in a signaled state.
                if (eventHandle.WaitOne(2000, true))
                {
                    TraceMsg("EventWaitHandle In Signaled State.");
                }
                else
                {
                    TraceMsg("WaitOne Timed Out -- " +
                        "EventWaitHandle In Unsignaled State.");
                }
                Thread.Sleep(2000);
            }

            TraceMsg("Thread Terminating.");
        }

        public static void Main()
```

```csharp
    {
        // Create a new EventWaitHandle with an initial signaled state, in
        // manual mode, with the name "EventExample".
        using (EventWaitHandle eventWaitHandle =
            new EventWaitHandle(true, EventResetMode.ManualReset,
            "EventExample"))
        {
            // Create and start a new thread running the DisplayMesssage
            // method.
            TraceMsg("Starting DisplayMessageThread.");
            Thread trd = new Thread(DisplayMessage);
            trd.Start();

            // Allow the EventWaitHandle to be toggled between a signaled and
            // unsignaled state up to three times before ending.
            for (int count = 0; count < 3; count++)
            {
                // Wait for Enter to be pressed.
                Console.ReadLine();

                // You need to toggle the event. The only way to know the
                // current state is to wait on it with a 0 (zero) time-out
                // and test the result.
                if (eventWaitHandle.WaitOne(0, true))
                {
                    TraceMsg("Switching Event To UnSignaled State.");

                    // Event is signaled, so unsignal it.
                    eventWaitHandle.Reset();
                }
                else
                {
                    TraceMsg("Switching Event To Signaled State.");

                    // Event is unsignaled, so signal it.
                    eventWaitHandle.Set();
                }
            }

            // Terminate the DisplayMessage thread, and wait for it to
            // complete before disposing of the EventWaitHandle.
            terminate = true;
            eventWaitHandle.Set();
            trd.Join(5000);
        }

        // Wait to continue.
        Console.WriteLine(Environment.NewLine);
        Console.WriteLine("Main method complete. Press Enter.");
        Console.ReadLine();
    }
  }
}
```

4-9. Synchronize the Execution of Multiple Threads Using a Mutex

Problem

You need to coordinate the activities of multiple threads (possibly across process boundaries) to ensure the efficient use of shared resources or to ensure several threads are not updating the same shared resource at the same time.

Solution

Use the `System.Threading.Mutex` class.

How It Works

The `Mutex` has a similar purpose to the `Monitor` discussed in recipe 4-7—it provides a means to ensure only a single thread has access to a shared resource or section of code at any given time. However, unlike the `Monitor`, which is implemented fully within managed code, the `Mutex` is a wrapper around an operating system synchronization object. This, and because `Mutex`es can be given names, means you can use a `Mutex` to synchronize the activities of threads across process boundaries, even with threads running in nonmanaged Win32 code.

Like the `EventWaitHandle`, `AutoResetEvent`, and `ManualResetEvent` classes discussed in recipe 4-8, the `Mutex` is derived from `System.Threading.WaitHandle` and enables thread synchronization in a similar fashion. A `Mutex` is in either a signaled state or an unsignaled state. A thread acquires ownership of the `Mutex` at construction or by using one of the methods listed in Table 4-1. If a thread has ownership of the `Mutex`, the `Mutex` is unsignaled, meaning other threads will block if they try to acquire ownership. Ownership of the `Mutex` is released by the owning thread calling the `Mutex.ReleaseMutex` method, which signals the `Mutex` and allows another thread to acquire ownership. A thread may acquire ownership of a `Mutex` any number of times without problems, but it must release the `Mutex` an equal number of times to free it and make it available for another thread to acquire. If the thread with ownership of a `Mutex` terminates normally, the `Mutex` becomes signaled, allowing another thread to acquire ownership.

The Code

The following example demonstrates how to use a named `Mutex` to limit access to a shared resource (the console) to a single thread at any given time:

```
using System;
using System.Threading;

namespace Apress.VisualCSharpRecipes.Chapter04
{
    class Recipe04_09
    {
        // Boolean to signal that the second thread should terminate.
        static bool terminate = false;

        // A utility method for displaying useful trace information to the
        // console along with details of the current thread.
        private static void TraceMsg(string msg)
```

```
    {
        Console.WriteLine("[{0,3}] - {1} : {2}",
            Thread.CurrentThread.ManagedThreadId,
            DateTime.Now.ToString("HH:mm:ss.ffff"), msg);
    }

    // Declare the method that will be executed on the separate thread.
    // In a loop the method waits to obtain a Mutex before displaying a
    // message to the console and then waits one second before releasing the
    // Mutex.
    private static void DisplayMessage()
    {
        // Obtain a handle to the Mutex with the name "MutexExample".
        // Do not attempt to take ownership immediately.
        using (Mutex mutex = new Mutex(false, "MutexExample"))
        {
            TraceMsg("Thread started.");

            while (!terminate)
            {
                // Wait on the Mutex.
                mutex.WaitOne();

                TraceMsg("Thread owns the Mutex.");

                Thread.Sleep(1000);

                TraceMsg("Thread releasing the Mutex.");

                // Release the Mutex.
                mutex.ReleaseMutex();

                // Sleep a little to give another thread a good chance of
                // acquiring the Mutex.
                Thread.Sleep(100);
            }

            TraceMsg("Thread terminating.");
        }
    }

    public static void Main()
    {
        // Create a new Mutex with the name "MutexExample".
        using (Mutex mutex = new Mutex(false, "MutexExample"))
        {
            TraceMsg("Starting threads -- press Enter to terminate.");

            // Create and start three new threads running the
            // DisplayMesssage method.
            Thread trd1 = new Thread(DisplayMessage);
            Thread trd2 = new Thread(DisplayMessage);
            Thread trd3 = new Thread(DisplayMessage);
            trd1.Start();
            trd2.Start();
            trd3.Start();
```

```
                    // Wait for Enter to be pressed.
                    Console.ReadLine();

                    // Terminate the DisplayMessage threads, and wait for them to
                    // complete before disposing of the Mutex.
                    terminate = true;
                    trd1.Join(5000);
                    trd2.Join(5000);
                    trd3.Join(5000);
                }

                // Wait to continue.
                Console.WriteLine(Environment.NewLine);
                Console.WriteLine("Main method complete. Press Enter.");
                Console.ReadLine();
            }
        }
    }
}
```

■**Note** Recipe 4-17 demonstrates how to use a named `Mutex` as a means to ensure only a single instance of an application can be started at any given time.

4-10. Synchronize the Execution of Multiple Threads Using a Semaphore

Problem

You need to control the number of threads that can access a shared resource or section of code concurrently.

Solution

Use the System.Threading.Semaphore class.

How It Works

The Semaphore is another synchronization class derived from the System.Threading.WaitHandle class. The Semaphore is new in .NET 2.0 but will be familiar to those with Win32 programming experience. The purpose of the Semaphore is to allow a specified maximum number of threads to access a shared resource or section of code concurrently.

As with the other synchronization classes derived from WaitHandle (discussed in recipe 4-8 and recipe 4-9), a Semaphore is either in a signaled state or in an unsignaled state. Threads wait for the Semaphore to become signaled using the methods described in Table 4-1. The Semaphore maintains a count of the active threads it has allowed through and automatically switches to an unsignaled state once the maximum number of threads is reached. To release the Semaphore and allow other waiting threads the opportunity to act, a thread calls the Release method on the Semaphore object. A thread may acquire ownership of the Semaphore more than once, reducing the maximum number of threads that can be active concurrently, and must call Release the same number of times to fully release it.

The Code

The following example demonstrates how to use a named Semaphore to limit access to a shared resource (the console) to two threads at any given time. The code is similar to that used in recipe 4-9 but substitutes a Semaphore for the Mutex.

```
using System;
using System.Threading;

namespace Apress.VisualCSharpRecipes.Chapter04
{
    class Recipe04_10
    {
        // Boolean to signal that the second thread should terminate.
        static bool terminate = false;

        // A utility method for displaying useful trace information to the
        // console along with details of the current thread.
        private static void TraceMsg(string msg)
        {
            Console.WriteLine("[{0,3}] - {1} : {2}",
                Thread.CurrentThread.ManagedThreadId,
                DateTime.Now.ToString("HH:mm:ss.fffff"), msg);
        }

        // Declare the method that will be executed on the separate thread.
        // In a loop the method waits to obtain a Semaphore before displaying a
        // message to the console and then waits one second before releasing the
        // Semaphore.
        private static void DisplayMessage()
        {
            // Obtain a handle to the Semaphore with the name "SemaphoreExample".
            using (Semaphore sem = Semaphore.OpenExisting("SemaphoreExample"))
            {
                TraceMsg("Thread started.");

                while (!terminate)
                {
                    // Wait on the Semaphore.
                    sem.WaitOne();

                    TraceMsg("Thread owns the Semaphore.");

                    Thread.Sleep(1000);

                    TraceMsg("Thread releasing the Semaphore.");

                    // Release the Semaphore.
                    sem.Release();

                    // Sleep a little to give another thread a good chance of
                    // acquiring the Semaphore.
                    Thread.Sleep(100);
                }

                TraceMsg("Thread terminating.");
            }
        }
```

```
    public static void Main()
    {
        // Create a new Semaphore with the name "SemaphoreExample". The
        // Semaphore can be owned by up to two threads at the same time.
        using (Semaphore sem = new Semaphore(2,2,"SemaphoreExample"))
        {
            TraceMsg("Starting threads -- press Enter to terminate.");

            // Create and start three new threads running the
            // DisplayMesssage method.
            Thread trd1 = new Thread(DisplayMessage);
            Thread trd2 = new Thread(DisplayMessage);
            Thread trd3 = new Thread(DisplayMessage);
            trd1.Start();
            trd2.Start();
            trd3.Start();

            // Wait for Enter to be pressed.
            Console.ReadLine();

            // Terminate the DisplayMessage threads and wait for them to
            // complete before disposing of the Semaphore.
            terminate = true;
            trd1.Join(5000);
            trd2.Join(5000);
            trd3.Join(5000);
        }

        // Wait to continue.
        Console.WriteLine(Environment.NewLine);
        Console.WriteLine("Main method complete. Press Enter.");
        Console.ReadLine();
    }
  }
}
```

4-11. Synchronize Access to a Shared Data Value

Problem

You need to ensure operations on a numeric data value are executed atomically so that multiple threads accessing the value do not cause errors or corruption.

Solution

Use the static members of the System.Threading.Interlocked class.

How It Works

The Interlocked class contains several static methods that perform some simple arithmetic and comparison operations on a variety of data types and ensure the operations are carried out atomically. Table 4-2 summarizes the methods and the data types on which they can be used. Note that the methods use the ref keyword on their arguments to allow the method to update the value of the actual value type variable passed in. If the operations you want to perform are not supported by the Interlocked class, you will need to implement your own synchronization using the other approaches described in this chapter.

■**Caution** Be aware, as of the time of this writing, the reliability of the 64-bit interlocked operations on a 32-bit platform is in question.

Table 4-2. Interlocked *Methods for Synchronizing Data Access*

Method	Description
Add	Adds two int or long values and sets the value of the first argument to the sum of the two values.
CompareExchange	Compares two values; if they are the same, sets the first argument to a specified value. This method has overloads to support the comparison and exchange of int, long, float, double, object, and System.IntPtr.
Decrement	Decrements an int or long value.
Exchange	Sets the value of a variable to a specified value. This method has overloads to support the exchange of int, long, float, double, object, and System.IntPtr.
Increment	Increments an int or a long value.

The Code

The following simple example demonstrates how to use the methods of the Interlocked class. The example does not demonstrate Interlocked in the context of a multithreaded program and is provided only to clarify the syntax and effect of the various methods.

```
using System;
using System.Threading;

namespace Apress.VisualCSharpRecipes.Chapter04
{
    class Recipe04_11
    {
        public static void Main()
        {
            int firstInt = 2500;
            int secondInt = 8000;

            Console.WriteLine("firstInt initial value = {0}", firstInt);
            Console.WriteLine("secondInt initial value = {0}", secondInt);

            // Decrement firstInt in a thread-safe manner.
            // The thread-safe equivalent of firstInt = firstInt - 1.
            Interlocked.Decrement(ref firstInt);

            Console.WriteLine(Environment.NewLine);
            Console.WriteLine("firstInt after decrement = {0}", firstInt);
```

```
        // Increment secondInt in a thread-safe manner.
        // The thread-safe equivalent of secondInt = secondInt + 1.
        Interlocked.Increment(ref secondInt);

        Console.WriteLine("secondInt after increment = {0}", secondInt);

        // Add the firstInt and secondInt values, and store the result in
        // firstInt.
        // The thread-safe equivalent of firstInt = firstInt + secondInt.
        Interlocked.Add(ref firstInt, secondInt);

        Console.WriteLine(Environment.NewLine);
        Console.WriteLine("firstInt after Add = {0}", firstInt);
        Console.WriteLine("secondInt after Add = {0}", secondInt);

        // Exchange the value of firstInt with secondInt.
        // The thread-safe equivalenet of secondInt = firstInt.
        Interlocked.Exchange(ref secondInt, firstInt);

        Console.WriteLine(Environment.NewLine);
        Console.WriteLine("firstInt after Exchange = {0}", firstInt);
        Console.WriteLine("secondInt after Exchange = {0}", secondInt);

        // Compare firstInt with secondInt, and if they are equal, set
        // firstInt to 5000.
        // The thread-safe equivalenet of:
        //      if (firstInt == secondInt) firstInt = 5000
        Interlocked.CompareExchange(ref firstInt, 5000, secondInt);

        Console.WriteLine(Environment.NewLine);
        Console.WriteLine("firstInt after CompareExchange = {0}", firstInt);
        Console.WriteLine("secondInt after CompareExchange = {0}", secondInt);

        // Wait to continue.
        Console.WriteLine(Environment.NewLine);
        Console.WriteLine("Main method complete. Press Enter.");
        Console.ReadLine();
    }
  }
}
```

4-12. Know When a Thread Finishes

Problem

You need to know when a thread has finished.

Solution

Use the IsAlive property or the Join method of the Thread class.

How It Works

The easiest way to test whether a thread has finished executing is to test the Thread.IsAlive property. The IsAlive property returns true if the thread has been started but has not terminated or been aborted. The IsAlive property provides a simple test to see whether a thread has finished executing, but commonly you will need one thread to wait for another thread to complete its processing. Instead of testing IsAlive in a loop, which is inefficient, you can use the Thread.Join method.

Join causes the calling thread to block until the referenced thread terminates, at which point the calling thread will continue. You can optionally specify an int or a TimeSpan value that specifies the time, after which the Join operation will time out and execution of the calling thread will resume. If you specify a time-out value, Join returns true if the thread terminated and returns false if Join timed out.

The Code

The following example executes a second thread and then calls Join (with a time-out of 2 seconds) to wait for the second thread to terminate. Because the second thread takes about 5 seconds to execute, the Join method will always time out, and the example will display a message to the console. The example then calls Join again without a time-out and blocks until the second thread terminates.

```
using System;
using System.Threading;

namespace Apress.VisualCSharpRecipes.Chapter04
{
    class Recipe04_12
    {
        private static void DisplayMessage()
        {
            // Display a message to the console 5 times.
            for (int count = 0; count < 5; count++)
            {
                Console.WriteLine("{0} : DisplayMessage thread",
                    DateTime.Now.ToString("HH:mm:ss.ffff"));

                // Sleep for 1 second.
                Thread.Sleep(1000);
            }
        }

        public static void Main()
        {
            // Create a new Thread to run the DisplayMessage method.
            Thread thread = new Thread(DisplayMessage);

            Console.WriteLine("{0} : Starting DisplayMessage thread.",
                DateTime.Now.ToString("HH:mm:ss.ffff"));

            // Start the DisplayMessage thread.
            thread.Start();

            // Block until the DisplayMessage thread finishes, or time-out after
            // 2 seconds.
            if (!thread.Join(2000))
            {
                Console.WriteLine("{0} : Join timed out !!",
```

```
                        DateTime.Now.ToString("HH:mm:ss.fffff"));
            }

            // Block again until the DisplayMessage thread finishes with no time-out.
            thread.Join();

            // Wait to continue.
            Console.WriteLine("Main method complete. Press Enter.");
            Console.ReadLine();
        }
    }
}
```

4-13. Terminate the Execution of a Thread

Problem

You need to terminate an executing thread without waiting for it to finish on its own accord.

Solution

Call the Abort method of the Thread object you want to terminate.

How It Works

It is better to write your code so that you can signal to a thread that it should shut down and allow it to terminate naturally. Recipes 4-7, 4-8, and 4-9 demonstrate this technique (using a Boolean flag). However, sometimes you will want a more direct method of terminating an active thread.

Calling Abort on an active Thread object terminates the thread by throwing a System.Threading. ThreadAbortException in the code that the thread is running. You can pass an object as an argument to the Abort method, which is accessible to the aborted thread through the ExceptionState property of the ThreadAbortException. When called, Abort returns immediately, but the runtime determines exactly when the exception is thrown, so you cannot assume the thread has terminated by the Abort returns. You should use the techniques described in recipe 4-12 if you need to determine when the aborted thread is actually done.

The aborted thread's code can catch the ThreadAbortException to perform cleanup, but the runtime will automatically throw the exception again when exiting the catch block to ensure that the thread terminates. So, you should not write code after the catch block: it will never execute. However, calling the static Thread.ResetAbort in the catch block will cancel the abort request and allow the thread to continue executing. Once you abort a thread, you cannot restart it by calling Thread.Start.

The Code

The following example creates a new thread that continues to display messages to the console until you press Enter, at which point the thread is terminated by a call to Thread.Abort:

```
using System;
using System.Threading;

namespace Apress.VisualCSharpRecipes.Chapter04
{
    class Recipe04_13
```

```csharp
{
    private static void DisplayMessage()
    {
        try
        {
            while (true)
            {
                // Display a message to the console.
                Console.WriteLine("{0} : DisplayMessage thread active",
                    DateTime.Now.ToString("HH:mm:ss.ffff"));

                // Sleep for 1 second.
                Thread.Sleep(1000);
            }
        }
        catch (ThreadAbortException ex)
        {
            // Display a message to the console.
            Console.WriteLine("{0} : DisplayMessage thread terminating - {1}",
                DateTime.Now.ToString("HH:mm:ss.ffff"),
                (string)ex.ExceptionState);

            // Call Thread.ResetAbort here to cancel the abort request.
        }

        // This code is never executed unless Thread.ResetAbort
        // is called in the previous catch block.
        Console.WriteLine("{0} : nothing is called after the catch block",
            DateTime.Now.ToString("HH:mm:ss.ffff"));
    }

    public static void Main()
    {
        // Create a new Thread to run the DisplayMessage method.
        Thread thread = new Thread(DisplayMessage);

        Console.WriteLine("{0} : Starting DisplayMessage thread" +
            " - press Enter to terminate.",
            DateTime.Now.ToString("HH:mm:ss.ffff"));

        // Start the DisplayMessage thread.
        thread.Start();

        // Wait until Enter is pressed and terminate the thread.
        System.Console.ReadLine();

        thread.Abort("User pressed Enter");

        // Block again until the DisplayMessage thread finishes.
        thread.Join();

        // Wait to continue.
        Console.WriteLine("Main method complete. Press Enter.");
        Console.ReadLine();
    }
}
}
```

4-14. Create a Thread-Safe Collection Instance

Problem

You need multiple threads to be able to safely access the contents of a collection concurrently.

Solution

Use lock statements in your code to synchronize thread access to the collection, or to access the collection through a thread-safe wrapper.

How It Works

By default, the standard collection classes from the System.Collections, System.Collections.Specialized, and System.Collections.Generic namespaces will support multiple threads reading the collection's content concurrently. However, if more than one of these threads tries to modify the collection, you will almost certainly encounter problems. This is because the operating system can interrupt the actions of the thread while modifications to the collection have been only partially applied. This leaves the collection in an indeterminate state, which will almost certainly cause another thread accessing the collection to fail, return incorrect data, or corrupt the collection.

■**Note** Using thread synchronization introduces a performance overhead. Making collections non-thread-safe by default provides better performance for the vast majority of situations where multiple threads are not used.

The most commonly used collections from the System.Collections namespace implement a static method named Synchronized; this includes only the ArrayList, Hashtable, Queue, SortedList, and Stack classes. The Synchronized method takes a collection object of the appropriate type as an argument and returns an object that provides a synchronized wrapper around the specified collection object. The wrapper object is returned as the same type as the original collection, but all the methods and properties that read and write the collection ensure that only a single thread has access to the initial collection content concurrently. You can test whether a collection is thread-safe using the IsSynchronized property. One final note: once you get the wrapper, you should neither access the initial collection nor create a new wrapper. In both cases, you will lose thread safety.

The collection classes such as HybridDictionary, ListDictionary, and StringCollection from the System.Collections.Specialized namespace do not implement a Synchronized method. To provide thread-safe access to instances of these classes, you must implement manual synchronization using the object returned by their SyncRoot property. This property and IsSynchronized are both defined by the ICollection interface that is implemented by all collection classes from System.Collections and System.Collections.Specialized (except BitVector32); you can therefore synchronize all your collections in a fine-grained way.

However, the new 2.0 classes in the System.Collections.Generic namespace provide no built-in synchronization mechanisms, leaving it to you to implement thread synchronization manually using the techniques discussed in this chapter.

■**Caution** Often you will have multiple collections and data elements that are related and need to be updated atomically. In these instances, you should not use the synchronization mechanisms provided by the individual collection classes. This approach will introduce synchronization problems into your code such as deadlocks and race conditions. You must decide what collections and other data elements need to be managed atomically and use the techniques described in this chapter to synchronize access to these elements as a unit.

The Code

The following code snippet shows how to create a thread-safe `Hashtable` instance:

```
// Create a standard Hashtable
Hashtable hUnsync = new Hashtable();

// Create a synchronized wrapper
Hashtable hSync = Hashtable.Synchronized(hUnsync);
```

The following code snippet shows how to create a thread-safe `NameValueCollection`. Notice that the `NameValueCollection` class derives from the `NameObjectCollectionBase` class, which uses an explicit interface implementation to implement the `ICollection.SyncRoot` property. As shown, you must cast the `NameValueCollection` to an `ICollection` instance before you can access the `SyncRoot` property. Casting is not necessary with other specialized collection classes such as `HybridDictionary`, `ListDictionary`, and `StringCollection`, which do not use explicit interface implementation to implement `SyncRoot`.

```
// Create a NameValueCollection.
NameValueCollection nvCollection = new NameValueCollection();

// Obtain a lock on the NameValueCollection before modification.
lock (((ICollection)nvCollection).SyncRoot) {

    // Modify the NameValueCollection...
}
```

4-15. Start a New Process

Problem

You need to execute an application in a new process.

Solution

Call one of the `static Start` method overloads of the `System.Diagnostics.Process` class. Specify the configuration details of the process you want to start as individual arguments to the `Start` method or in a `System.Diagnostics.ProcessStartInfo` object that you pass to the `Start` method.

How It Works

The `Process` class provides a managed representation of an operating system process and provides a simple mechanism through which you can execute both managed and unmanaged applications. The `Process` class implements five `static` overloads of the `Start` method, which you use to start a new process. All these methods return a Process object that represents the newly started process. Two of these overloads are methods that allow you to specify only the name and arguments to pass to the new process. For example, the following statements both execute Notepad in a new process:

```
// Execute notepad.exe with no command-line arguments.
Process.Start("notepad.exe");
```

```
// Execute notepad.exe passing the name of the file to open as a
// command-line argument.
Process.Start("notepad.exe", "SomeFile.txt");
```

Another two overloads extend these and allow you to specify the name of a Windows user who the process should run as. You must specify the username, password, and Windows domain. The password is specified as a System.Security.SecureString for added security. (See recipe 11-18 for more information about the SecureString class.) Here is an example:

```
System.Security.SecureString mySecureString = new System.Security.SecureString();
```

```
// Obtain a password and place in SecureString (see Recipe 11-18).
```

```
// Execute notepad.exe with no command-line arguments.
Process.Start("notepad.exe", "allen", mySecureString, "MyDomain");
```

```
// Execute notepad.exe passing the name of the file to open as a
// command-line argument.
Process.Start("notepad.exe", "SomeFile.txt", "allen", mySecureString, "MyDomain");
```

The remaining static overload requires you to create a ProcessStartInfo object configured with the details of the process you want to run; using the ProcessStartInfo object provides greater control over the behavior and configuration of the new process. Table 4-3 summarizes some of the commonly used properties of the ProcessStartInfo class.

Table 4-3. *Properties of the* ProcessStartInfo *Class*

Property	Description
Arguments	The command-line arguments to pass to the new process.
Domain	A string containing the Windows domain name to which the user belongs.
ErrorDialog	If Process.Start cannot start the specified process, it will throw a System.ComponentModel.Win32Exception. If ErrorDialog is true, Start displays an error dialog box to the user before throwing the exception.
FileName	The name of the application to start. You can also specify any type of file for which you have configured an application association. For example, you could specify a file with a .doc or an .xls extension, which would cause Microsoft Word or Microsoft Excel to run.
LoadUserProfile	A bool indicating whether the user's profile should be loaded from the registry when the new process is started.
Password	A SecureString containing the password of the user.
UserName	A string containing the name of the user to use when starting the process.
WindowStyle	A member of the System.Diagnostics.ProcessWindowStyle enumeration, which controls how the window is displayed. Valid values include Hidden, Maximized, Minimized, and Normal.
WorkingDirectory	The fully qualified name of the initial directory for the new process.

When finished with a `Process` object, you should dispose of it in order to release system resources—call `Close`, call `Dispose`, or create the `Process` object within the scope of a `using` statement.

■**Note** Disposing of a `Process` object does not affect the underlying system process, which will continue to run.

The Code

The following example uses `Process` to execute Notepad in a maximized window and open a file named C:\Temp\file.txt. After creation, the example calls the `Process.WaitForExit` method, which blocks the calling thread until a process terminates or a specified time-out expires. This method returns true if the process ends before the time-out and returns false otherwise.

```
using System;
using System.Diagnostics;

namespace Apress.VisualCSharpRecipes.Chapter04
{
    class Recipe04_15
    {
        public static void Main()
        {
            // Create a ProcessStartInfo object and configure it with the
            // information required to run the new process.
            ProcessStartInfo startInfo = new ProcessStartInfo();

            startInfo.FileName = "notepad.exe";
            startInfo.Arguments = "file.txt";
            startInfo.WorkingDirectory = @"C:\Temp";
            startInfo.WindowStyle = ProcessWindowStyle.Maximized;
            startInfo.ErrorDialog = true;

            // Declare a new Process object.
            Process process;

            try
            {
                // Start the new process.
                process = Process.Start(startInfo);

                // Wait for the new process to terminate before exiting.
                Console.WriteLine("Waiting 30 seconds for process to finish.");

                if (process.WaitForExit(30000))
                {
                    Console.WriteLine("Process terminated.");
                }
                else
                {
                    Console.WriteLine("Timed out waiting for process to end.");
                }
            }
            catch (Exception ex)
            {
                Console.WriteLine("Could not start process.");
```

```
            Console.WriteLine(ex);
        }

        // Wait to continue.
        Console.WriteLine(Environment.NewLine);
        Console.WriteLine("Main method complete. Press Enter.");
        Console.ReadLine();
      }
    }
}
```

4-16. Terminate a Process

Problem

You need to terminate a process such as an application or a service.

Solution

Obtain a `Process` object representing the operating system process you want to terminate. For Windows-based applications, call `Process.CloseMainWindow` to send a close message to the application's main window. For Windows-based applications that ignore `CloseMainWindow`, or for non-Windows-based applications, call the `Process.Kill` method.

How It Works

If you start a new process from managed code using the `Process` class (discussed in recipe 4-15), you can terminate the process using the `Process` object that represents the new process. You can also obtain `Process` objects that refer to other currently running processes using the `static` methods of the `Process` class summarized in Table 4-4.

Table 4-4. *Methods for Obtaining Process References*

Method	Description
GetCurrentProcess	Returns a `Process` object representing the currently active process.
GetProcessById	Returns a `Process` object representing the process with the specified ID. This is the process ID (PID) you can get using Windows Task Manager.
GetProcesses	Returns an array of `Process` objects representing all currently active processes.
GetProcessesByName	Returns an array of `Process` objects representing all currently active processes with a specified friendly name. The friendly name is the name of the executable excluding file extension or path; for example, a friendly name could be `notepad` or `calc`.

Once you have a `Process` object representing the process you want to terminate, you need to call either the `CloseMainWindow` method or the `Kill` method. The `CloseMainWindow` method posts a `WM_CLOSE` message to a Windows-based application's main window. This method has the same effect as if the user had closed the main window using the system menu, and it gives the application the opportunity to perform its normal shutdown routine. `CloseMainWindow` will not terminate applications that do not have a main window or applications with a disabled main window—possibly because a modal dialog box is currently displayed. Under such circumstances, CloseMainWindow will return false.

CloseMainWindow returns true if the close message was successfully sent, but this does not guarantee that the process is actually terminated. For example, applications used to edit data will usually give the user the opportunity to save unsaved data if a close message is received. The user usually has the chance to cancel the close operation under such circumstances. This means CloseMainWindow will return true, but the application will still be running once the user cancels. You can use the Process.WaitForExit method to signal process termination and the Process.HasExited property to test whether a process has terminated. Alternatively, you can use the Kill method.

The Kill method simply terminates a process immediately; the user has no chance to stop the termination, and all unsaved data is lost. Kill is the only option for terminating Windows-based applications that do not respond to CloseMainWindow and for terminating non-Windows-based applications.

The Code

The following example starts a new instance of Notepad, waits 5 seconds, and then terminates the Notepad process. The example first tries to terminate the process using CloseMainWindow. If CloseMainWindow returns false, or the Notepad process is still running after CloseMainWindow is called, the example calls Kill and forces the Notepad process to terminate; you can force CloseMainWindow to return false by leaving the File Open dialog box open.

```
using System;
using System.Threading;
using System.Diagnostics;

namespace Apress.VisualCSharpRecipes.Chapter04
{
    class Recipe04_16
    {
        public static void Main()
        {
            // Create a new Process and run notepad.exe.
            using (Process process =
                Process.Start("notepad.exe",@"c:\SomeFile.txt"))
            {
                // Wait for 5 seconds and terminate the notepad process.
                Console.WriteLine(
                    "Waiting 5 seconds before terminating notepad.exe.");
                Thread.Sleep(5000);

                // Terminate notepad process.
                Console.WriteLine("Terminating Notepad with CloseMainWindow.");

                // Try to send a close message to the main window.
                if (!process.CloseMainWindow())
                {
                    // Close message did not get sent - Kill Notepad.
                    Console.WriteLine("CloseMainWindow returned false - " +
                        " terminating Notepad with Kill.");
                    process.Kill();
                }
                else
                {
                    // Close message sent successfully; wait for 2 seconds
                    // for termination confirmation before resorting to Kill.
```

```
                    if (!process.WaitForExit(2000))
                    {
                        Console.WriteLine("CloseMainWindow failed to" +
                            " terminate - terminating Notepad with Kill.");
                        process.Kill();
                    }
                }
            }

            // Wait to continue.
            Console.WriteLine("Main method complete. Press Enter.");
            Console.ReadLine();
        }
    }
}
```

4-17. Ensure That Only One Instance of an Application Can Execute Concurrently

Problem

You need to ensure that a user can have only one instance of an application running concurrently.

Solution

Create a named System.Threading.Mutex object, and have your application try to acquire ownership of it at start-up.

How It Works

The Mutex provides a mechanism for synchronizing the execution of threads across process boundaries and in addition provides a convenient mechanism through which to ensure that only a single instance of an application is running concurrently. By trying to acquire ownership of a named Mutex at start-up and exiting if the Mutex cannot be acquired, you can ensure that only one instance of your application is running.

The Code

This example uses a Mutex named MutexExample to ensure that only a single instance of the example can execute:

```
using System;
using System.Threading;

namespace Apress.VisualCSharpRecipes.Chapter04
{
    class Recipe04_17
    {
        public static void Main()
        {
```

```csharp
        // A boolean that indicates whether this application has
        // initial ownership of the Mutex.
        bool ownsMutex;

        // Attempt to create and take ownership of a Mutex named
        // MutexExample.
        using (Mutex mutex =
                    new Mutex(true, "MutexExample", out ownsMutex))
        {
            // If the application owns the Mutex it can continue to execute;
            // otherwise, the application should exit.
            if (ownsMutex)
            {
                Console.WriteLine("This application currently owns the" +
                    " mutex named MutexExample. Additional instances of" +
                    " this application will not run until you release" +
                    " the mutex by pressing Enter.");

                Console.ReadLine();

                // Release the mutex
                mutex.ReleaseMutex();
            }
            else
            {
                Console.WriteLine("Another instance of this application " +
                    " already owns the mutex named MutexExample. This" +
                    " instance of the application will terminate.");
            }
        }

        // Wait to continue.
        Console.WriteLine("Main method complete. Press Enter.");
        Console.ReadLine();
        }
    }
}
```

Note If you do not construct the Mutex in a using statement and encapsulate the body of your application in the body of the using block as shown in this example, in long-running applications the garbage collector may dispose of the Mutex if it is not referenced after initial creation. This will result in releasing the Mutex and allow additional instances of the application to execute concurrently. In these circumstances, you should include the statement System.GC.KeepAlive(mutex) to ensure the Mutex is not garbage collected. Thanks to Michael A. Covington for highlighting this possibility.

■■■

CHAPTER 5

Files, Directories, and I/O

The Microsoft .NET Framework I/O classes fall into two basic categories. First are the classes that retrieve information from the file system and allow you to perform file system operations such as copying files and moving directories. Two examples include the FileInfo and the DirectoryInfo classes. The second, and possibly more important, category includes a broad range of classes that allow you to read and write data from all types of streams. Streams can correspond to binary or text files, a file in an isolated store, a network connection, or even a memory buffer. In all cases, the way you interact with a stream is the same. This chapter describes how to use the file system classes and a wide range of stream-based classes.

The recipes in this chapter describe how to do the following:

- Retrieve or modify information about a file, directory, or a drive (recipes 5-1, 5-2, 5-4, 5-5, and 5-16)
- Copy, move, and delete files and directories (recipe 5-3)
- Show a directory tree in a Microsoft Windows-based application and use the common file dialog boxes (recipes 5-6 and 5-17)
- Read and write text and binary files (recipes 5-7 and 5-8)
- Create temporary files and files in a user-specific isolated store (recipes 5-15 and 5-18)
- Read files asynchronously (recipe 5-9)
- Search for specific files and test files for equality (recipes 5-10 and 5-11)
- Work with strings that contain path information (recipes 5-12, 5-13, and 5-14)
- Monitor the file system for changes (recipe 5-19)
- Write to a COM port (recipe 5-20)
- Generate a random filename (recipe 5-21)
- Retrieve or modify the access control lists (ACLs) of a file or directory (recipe 5-22)

5-1. Retrieve Information About a File, Directory, or Drive

Problem

You need to retrieve information about a file, directory, or drive.

Solution

Create a new System.IO.FileInfo, System.IO.DirectoryInfo, or System.IO.DriveInfo object, depending on the type of resource about which you need to retrieve information. Supply the path of the resource to the constructor, and then you will be able to retrieve information through the properties of the class.

How It Works

To create a FileInfo, DirectoryInfo, or DriveInfo object, you supply a relative or fully qualified path in the constructor. You can retrieve information through the corresponding object properties. Table 5-1 lists some of the key members that are found in these objects.

Table 5-1. *Key Members for Files, Directories, and Drives*

Member	Applies To	Description
Exists	FileInfo and DirectoryInfo	Returns true or false, depending on whether a file or a directory exists at the specified location.
Attributes	FileInfo and DirectoryInfo	Returns one or more values from the System.IO.FileAttributes enumeration, which represents the attributes of the file or the directory.
CreationTime, LastAccessTime, and LastWriteTime	FileInfo and DirectoryInfo	Return System.DateTime instances that describe when a file or a directory was created, last accessed, and last updated, respectively.
FullName, Name, and Extension	FileInfo and DirectoryInfo	Return a string that represents the fully qualified name, the directory, or the filename (with extension), and the extension on its own.
IsReadOnly	FileInfo	Returns true or false, depending on whether a file is read-only.
Length	FileInfo	Returns the file size as a number of bytes.
DirectoryName and Directory	FileInfo	DirectoryName returns the name of the parent directory as a string. Directory returns a full DirectoryInfo object that represents the parent directory and allows you to retrieve more information about it.
Parent and Root	DirectoryInfo	Return a DirectoryInfo object that represents the parent or root directory.
CreateSubdirectory	DirectoryInfo	Creates a directory with the specified name in the directory represented by the DirectoryInfo object. It also returns a new DirectoryInfo object that represents the subdirectory.
GetDirectories	DirectoryInfo	Returns an array of DirectoryInfo objects, with one element for each subdirectory contained in this directory.
GetFiles	DirectoryInfo	Returns an array of FileInfo objects, with one element for each file contained in this directory.

Member	Applies To	Description
DriveType	DriveInfo	Returns a DriveType enumeration value that represents the type of the specified drive; for example, Fixed or CD Rom.
AvailableFreeSpace	DriveInfo	Returns a long that represents the free space available in the drive.
GetDrives	DriveInfo	Returns an array of DriveInfo objects that represents the logical drives in the computer.

The following are a few points to note while working with these objects:

- FileInfo and DirectoryInfo classes derive from the abstract FileSystemInfo class, which defines common methods like CreationTime, Exists, and so on. The DriveInfo class does not inherit from this base class, so it does not provide some of the common members available in the other two classes.

- The full set of properties FileInfo and DirectoryInfo objects expose is read the first time you interrogate any property. If the file or directory changes after this point, you must call the Refresh method to update the properties. However, this is not the case for DriveInfo; each property access asks the file system for an up-to-date value.

- You will not encounter an error if you specify a path that does not correspond to an existing file, directory, or drive. Instead, you will receive an object that represents an entity that does not exist—its Exists (or IsReady property for DriveInfo) property will be false. You can use this object to manipulate the entity. However, if you attempt to read most other properties, exceptions like FileNotFoundException, DirectoryNotFoundException, and so on will be thrown.

The Code

The following console application takes a file path from a command-line argument, and then displays information about the file, the containing directory, and the drive.

```
using System;
using System.IO;

namespace Apress.VisualCSharpRecipes.Chapter05
{
    static class Recipe05_01
    {
        static void Main(string[] args)
        {
            if (args.Length == 0)
            {
                Console.WriteLine("Please supply a filename.");
                return;
            }

            // Display file information.
            FileInfo file = new FileInfo(args[0]);

            Console.WriteLine("Checking file: " + file.Name);
            Console.WriteLine("File exists: " + file.Exists.ToString());
```

```
if (file.Exists)
{
    Console.Write("File created: ");
    Console.WriteLine(file.CreationTime.ToString());
    Console.Write("File last updated: ");
    Console.WriteLine(file.LastWriteTime.ToString());
    Console.Write("File last accessed: ");
    Console.WriteLine(file.LastAccessTime.ToString());
    Console.Write("File size (bytes): ");
    Console.WriteLine(file.Length.ToString());
    Console.Write("File attribute list: ");
    Console.WriteLine(file.Attributes.ToString());
}
Console.WriteLine();

// Display directory information.
DirectoryInfo dir = file.Directory;

Console.WriteLine("Checking directory: " + dir.Name);
Console.WriteLine("In directory: " + dir.Parent.Name);
Console.Write("Directory exists: ");
Console.WriteLine(dir.Exists.ToString());

if (dir.Exists)
{
    Console.Write("Directory created: ");
    Console.WriteLine(dir.CreationTime.ToString());
    Console.Write("Directory last updated: ");
    Console.WriteLine(dir.LastWriteTime.ToString());
    Console.Write("Directory last accessed: ");
    Console.WriteLine(dir.LastAccessTime.ToString());
    Console.Write("Directory attribute list: ");
    Console.WriteLine(dir.Attributes.ToString());
    Console.WriteLine("Directory contains: " +
       dir.GetFiles().Length.ToString() + " files");
}
Console.WriteLine();

// Display drive information.
DriveInfo drv = new DriveInfo(file.FullName);

Console.Write("Drive: ");
Console.WriteLine(drv.Name);

if (drv.IsReady)
{
    Console.Write("Drive type: ");
    Console.WriteLine(drv.DriveType.ToString());
    Console.Write("Drive format: ");
    Console.WriteLine(drv.DriveFormat.ToString());
    Console.Write("Drive free space: ");
    Console.WriteLine(drv.AvailableFreeSpace.ToString());
}

// Wait to continue.
Console.WriteLine(Environment.NewLine);
Console.WriteLine("Main method complete. Press Enter.");
```

```
        Console.ReadLine();
      }
    }
}
```

Usage

If you execute the command Recipe05-01.exe c:\windows\win.ini, you might expect the following
output:

```
Checking file: win.ini
File exists: True
File created: 31.Mar.2003 5:30:00 PM
File last updated: 24.Sep.2005 11:11:13 PM
File last accessed: 10.Nov.2005 9:41:05 PM
File size (bytes): 658
File attribute list: Archive

Checking directory: windows
In directory: c:\
Directory exists: True
Directory created: 04.Jun.2005 4:47:56 PM
Directory last updated: 01.Nov.2005 10:09:45 AM
Directory last accessed: 11.Nov.2005 6:24:59 AM
Directory attribute list: Directory
Directory contains: 134 files

Drive: c:\
Drive type: Fixed
Drive format: NTFS
Drive free space: 14045097984
```

■ **Note** Instead of using the instance methods of the FileInfo and DirectoryInfo classes, you can use the
static File and Directory classes (note that a class corresponding to the DriveInfo class does not exist). The
File and Directory methods expose most of the same functionality, but they require you to submit the filename
or path with every method invocation. In cases where you need to perform multiple operations with the same file
or directory, using the FileInfo and DirectoryInfo classes will be faster, because they will perform security
checks only once. Also note that you could obtain the list of all logical drives in the computer by using the static
DriveInfo.GetDrives method.

5-2. Set File and Directory Attributes

Problem

You need to test or modify file or directory attributes.

Solution

Create a System.IO.FileInfo object for a file or a System.IO.DirectoryInfo object for a directory and use
the bitwise AND (&) and OR (|) arithmetic operators to modify the value of the Attributes property.

How It Works

The `FileInfo.Attributes` and `DirectoryInfo.Attributes` properties represent file attributes such as archive, system, hidden, read-only, compressed, and encrypted. (Refer to the MSDN reference for the full list.) Because a file can possess any combination of attributes, the `Attributes` property accepts a combination of enumerated values. To individually test for a single attribute or change a single attribute, you need to use bitwise arithmetic.

■Note The `Attributes` setting is made up (in binary) of a series of ones and zeros, such as 00010011. Each 1 represents an attribute that is present, while each 0 represents an attribute that is not. When you use a bitwise AND (&) operation, it compares each individual digit against each digit in the enumerated value. For example, if you bitwise AND a value of 00100001 (representing an individual file's archive and read-only attributes) with the enumerated value 00000001 (which represents the read-only flag), the resulting value will be 00000001—it will have a 1 only where it can be matched in both values.

The Code

The following example takes a read-only test file and checks for the read-only attribute.

```
using System;
using System.IO;

namespace Apress.VisualCSharpRecipes.Chapter05
{
    static class Recipe05_02
    {
        static void Main()
        {
            // This file has the archive and read-only attributes.
            FileInfo file = new FileInfo("data.txt");

            // This displays the string "ReadOnly, Archive "
            Console.WriteLine(file.Attributes.ToString());

            // This test fails, because other attributes are set.
            if (file.Attributes == FileAttributes.ReadOnly)
            {
                Console.WriteLine("File is read-only (faulty test).");
            }

            // This test succeeds, because it filters out just the
            // read-only attribute.
            if ((file.Attributes & FileAttributes.ReadOnly) ==
              FileAttributes.ReadOnly)
            {
                Console.WriteLine("File is read-only (correct test).");
            }

            // Wait to continue.
            Console.WriteLine(Environment.NewLine);
            Console.WriteLine("Main method complete. Press Enter.");
            Console.ReadLine();
        }
    }
}
```

When setting an attribute, you must also use bitwise arithmetic, as demonstrated in the following example. In this case, it's needed to ensure that you don't inadvertently clear the other attributes.

```
// This adds just the read-only attribute.
file.Attributes = file.Attributes | FileAttributes.ReadOnly;

// This removes just the read-only attribute.
file.Attributes = file.Attributes & ~FileAttributes.ReadOnly;
```

5-3. Copy, Move, or Delete a File or a Directory

Problem

You need to copy, move, or delete a file or directory.

Solution

Create a System.IO.FileInfo object for a file or a System.IO.DirectoryInfo object for a directory, supplying the path in the constructor. You can then use the object's methods to copy, move, and delete the file or directory.

How It Works

The FileInfo and DirectoryInfo classes include a host of valuable methods for manipulating files and directories. Table 5-2 shows methods for the FileInfo class, and Table 5-3 shows methods for the DirectoryInfo class.

Table 5-2. *Key Methods for Manipulating a* FileInfo *Object*

Method	Description
CopyTo	Copies a file to the new path and filename specified as a parameter. It also returns a new FileInfo object that represents the new (copied) file. You can supply an optional additional parameter of true to allow overwriting.
Create and CreateText	Create creates the specified file and returns a FileStream object that you can use to write to it. CreateText performs the same task, but returns a StreamWriter object that wraps the stream. For more information about writing files, see recipes 5-7 and 5-8.
Open, OpenRead, OpenText, and OpenWrite	Open a file (provided it exists). OpenRead and OpenText open a file in read-only mode, returning a FileStream or StreamReader object. OpenWrite opens a file in write-only mode, returning a FileStream object. For more information about reading files, see recipes 5-7 and 5-8.
Delete	Removes the file, if it exists.
Encrypt and Decrypt	Encrypt/decrypt a file using the current account. This applies to NTFS file systems only.
MoveTo	Moves the file to the new path and filename specified as a parameter. MoveTo can also be used to rename a file without changing its location.
Replace	Replaces contents of a file by the current FileInfo object. This method could also take a backup copy of the replaced file.

Table 5-3. *Key Methods for Manipulating a* DirectoryInfo *Object*

Method	Description
Create	Creates the specified directory. If the path specifies multiple directories that do not exist, they will all be created at once.
CreateSubdirectory	Creates a directory with the specified name in the directory represented by the DirectoryInfo object. It also returns a new DirectoryInfo object that represents the subdirectory.
Delete	Removes the directory, if it exists. If you want to delete a directory that contains other directories, you must use the overloaded Delete method that accepts a parameter named recursive and set it to true.
MoveTo	Moves the directory (contents and all) to a new path. MoveTo can also be used to rename a directory without changing its location.

The Code

One useful feature that is missing from the DirectoryInfo class is a copy method. Fortunately, you can write this logic easily enough by relying on recursive logic and the FileInfo object.

The following example contains a helper function that can copy any directory, and its contents.

```csharp
using System;
using System.IO;

namespace Apress.VisualCSharpRecipes.Chapter05
{
    static class Recipe05_03
    {
        static void Main(string[] args)
        {
            if (args.Length != 2)
            {
                Console.WriteLine("USAGE:   " +
                  " Recipe05_03 [sourcePath] [destinationPath]");
                return;
            }

            DirectoryInfo sourceDir = new DirectoryInfo(args[0]);
            DirectoryInfo destinationDir = new DirectoryInfo(args[1]);

            CopyDirectory(sourceDir, destinationDir);

            // Wait to continue.
            Console.WriteLine(Environment.NewLine);
            Console.WriteLine("Main method complete. Press Enter.");
            Console.ReadLine();
        }

        static void CopyDirectory(DirectoryInfo source,
            DirectoryInfo destination)
        {
            if (!destination.Exists)
            {
                destination.Create();
            }
```

```
        // Copy all files.
        FileInfo[] files = source.GetFiles();
        foreach (FileInfo file in files)
        {
            file.CopyTo(Path.Combine(destination.FullName,
                file.Name));
        }

        // Process subdirectories.
        DirectoryInfo[] dirs = source.GetDirectories();
        foreach (DirectoryInfo dir in dirs)
        {
            // Get destination directory.
            string destinationDir = Path.Combine(destination.FullName,
                dir.Name);

            // Call CopyDirectory() recursively.
            CopyDirectory(dir, new DirectoryInfo(destinationDir));
        }
    }
  }
}
```

5-4. Calculate the Size of a Directory

Problem

You need to calculate the size of all files contained in a directory (and optionally, its subdirectories).

Solution

Examine all the files in a directory and add together their `FileInfo.Length` properties. Use recursive logic to include the size of files in contained subdirectories.

How It Works

The `DirectoryInfo` class does not provide any property that returns size information. However, you can easily calculate the size of all files contained in a directory using the `FileInfo.Length` property.

The Code

The following example calculates the size of a directory and optionally examines contained directories recursively.

```
using System;
using System.IO;

namespace Apress.VisualCSharpRecipes.Chapter05
{
    static class Recipe05_04
    {
        static void Main(string[] args)
        {
```

```
        if (args.Length == 0)
        {
            Console.WriteLine("Please supply a directory path.");
            return;
        }

        DirectoryInfo dir = new DirectoryInfo(args[0]);
        Console.WriteLine("Total size: " +
          CalculateDirectorySize(dir, true).ToString() +
          " bytes.");

        // Wait to continue.
        Console.WriteLine(Environment.NewLine);
        Console.WriteLine("Main method complete. Press Enter.");
        Console.ReadLine();
    }

    static long CalculateDirectorySize(DirectoryInfo directory,
        bool includeSubdirectories)
    {
        long totalSize = 0;

        // Examine all contained files.
        FileInfo[] files = directory.GetFiles();
        foreach (FileInfo file in files)
        {
            totalSize += file.Length;
        }

        // Examine all contained directories.
        if (includeSubdirectories)
        {
            DirectoryInfo[] dirs = directory.GetDirectories();
            foreach (DirectoryInfo dir in dirs)
            {
                totalSize += CalculateDirectorySize(dir, true);
            }
        }

        return totalSize;
    }
  }
}
```

5-5. Retrieve Version Information for a File

Problem

You want to retrieve file version information, such as the publisher of a file, its revision number, associated comments, and so on.

Solution

Use the static GetVersionInfo method of the System.Diagnostics.FileVersionInfo class.

How It Works

The .NET Framework allows you to retrieve file information without resorting to the Windows API. Instead, you simply need to use the FileVersionInfo class and call the GetVersionInfo method with the filename as a parameter. You can then retrieve extensive information through the FileVersionInfo properties.

The Code

The FileVersionInfo properties are too numerous to list here, but the following code snippet shows an example of what you might retrieve.

```
using System;
using System.Diagnostics;

namespace Apress.VisualCSharpRecipes.Chapter05
{
    static class Recipe05_05
    {
        static void Main(string[] args)
        {
            if (args.Length == 0)
            {
                Console.WriteLine("Please supply a filename.");
                return;
            }

            FileVersionInfo info = FileVersionInfo.GetVersionInfo(args[0]);

            // Display version information.
            Console.WriteLine("Checking File: " + info.FileName);
            Console.WriteLine("Product Name: " + info.ProductName);
            Console.WriteLine("Product Version: " + info.ProductVersion);
            Console.WriteLine("Company Name: " + info.CompanyName);
            Console.WriteLine("File Version: " + info.FileVersion);
            Console.WriteLine("File Description: " + info.FileDescription);
            Console.WriteLine("Original Filename: " + info.OriginalFilename);
            Console.WriteLine("Legal Copyright: " + info.LegalCopyright);
            Console.WriteLine("InternalName: " + info.InternalName);
            Console.WriteLine("IsDebug: " + info.IsDebug);
            Console.WriteLine("IsPatched: " + info.IsPatched);
            Console.WriteLine("IsPreRelease: " + info.IsPreRelease);
            Console.WriteLine("IsPrivateBuild: " + info.IsPrivateBuild);
            Console.WriteLine("IsSpecialBuild: " + info.IsSpecialBuild);

            // Wait to continue.
            Console.WriteLine(Environment.NewLine);
            Console.WriteLine("Main method complete. Press Enter.");
            Console.ReadLine();
        }
    }
}
```

Usage

If you run the command Recipe05_05 c:\windows\explorer.exe, the example produces the following output.

```
Checking File: c:\windows\explorer.exe
Product Name: Microsoftr Windowsr Operating System
Product Version: 6.00.2900.2180
Company Name: Microsoft Corporation
File Version: 6.00.2900.2180 (xpsp_sp2_rtm.040803-2158)
File Description: Windows Explorer
Original Filename: EXPLORER.EXE
Legal Copyright: c Microsoft Corporation. All rights reserved.
InternalName: explorer
IsDebug: False
IsPatched: False
IsPreRelease: False
IsPrivateBuild: False
IsSpecialBuild: False
```

5-6. Show a Just-in-Time Directory Tree in the TreeView Control

Problem

You need to display a directory tree in a TreeView control. However, filling the directory tree structure at startup is too time-consuming.

Solution

Fill the first level of directories in the TreeView control and add a hidden dummy node to each directory branch. React to the TreeView.BeforeExpand event to fill in subdirectories in a branch just before it's displayed.

How It Works

You can use recursion to build an entire directory tree. However, scanning the file system in this way can be slow, particularly for large drives. For this reason, professional file management software programs (including Windows Explorer) use a different technique. They query the necessary directory information when the user requests it.

The TreeView control is particularly well suited to this approach because it provides a BeforeExpand event that fires before a new level of nodes is displayed. You can use a placeholder (such as an asterisk or empty TreeNode) in all the directory branches that are not filled in. This allows you to fill in parts of the directory tree as they are displayed.

To use this type of solution, you need the following three ingredients:

- A Fill method that adds a single level of directory nodes based on a single directory. You will use this method to fill directory levels as they are expanded.

- A basic Form.Load event handler that uses the Fill method to add the first level of directories for the drive.

- A TreeView.BeforeExpand event handler that reacts when the user expands a node and calls the Fill method if this directory information has not yet been added.

The Code

The following shows the full-form code for this solution.

```csharp
using System;
using System.Windows.Forms;
using System.IO;

namespace Apress.VisualCSharpRecipes.Chapter05
{
    public partial class DirectoryTree : Form
    {
        public DirectoryTree()
        {
            InitializeComponent();
        }

        private void DirectoryTree_Load(object sender, EventArgs e)
        {
            // Set the first node.
            TreeNode rootNode = new TreeNode(@"C:\");
            treeDirectory.Nodes.Add(rootNode);

            // Fill the first level and expand it.
            Fill(rootNode);
            treeDirectory.Nodes[0].Expand();
        }

        private void treeDirectory_BeforeExpand(object sender,
            TreeViewCancelEventArgs e)
        {
            // If a dummy node is found, remove it and read the
            // real directory list.
            if (e.Node.Nodes[0].Text == "*")
            {
                e.Node.Nodes.Clear();
                Fill(e.Node);
            }
        }

        private void Fill(TreeNode dirNode)
        {
            DirectoryInfo dir = new DirectoryInfo(dirNode.FullPath);

            // An exception could be thrown in this code if you don't
            // have sufficient security permissions for a file or directory.
            // You can catch and then ignore this exception.
            foreach (DirectoryInfo dirItem in dir.GetDirectories())
            {
                // Add node for the directory.
                TreeNode newNode = new TreeNode(dirItem.Name);
                dirNode.Nodes.Add(newNode);
                newNode.Nodes.Add("*");
            }
        }
    }
}
```

Figure 5-1 shows the directory tree in action.

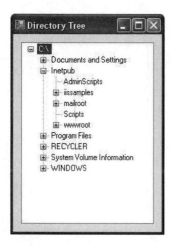

Figure 5-1. *A directory tree with the* TreeView

5-7. Read and Write a Text File

Problem

You need to write data to a sequential text file using ASCII, Unicode, or UTF-8 encoding.

Solution

Create a new System.IO.FileStream object that references the file. To write the file, wrap the FileStream in a System.IO.StreamWriter and use the overloaded Write method. To read the file, wrap the FileStream in a System.IO.StreamReader and use the Read or ReadLine method.

How It Works

The .NET Framework allows you to write or read text with any stream by using the StreamWriter and StreamReader classes. When writing data with the StreamWriter, you use the StreamWriter.Write method. This method is overloaded to support all the common C# .NET data types, including strings, chars, integers, floating-point numbers, decimals, and so on. However, the Write method always converts the supplied data to text. If you want to be able to convert the text back to its original data type, you should use the WriteLine method to make sure each value is placed on a separate line.

The way a string is represented depends on the encoding you use. The most common encodings include the following:

- ASCII, which encodes each character in a string using 7 bits. ASCII-encoded data cannot contain extended Unicode characters. When using ASCII encoding in .NET, the bits will be padded and the resulting byte array will have 1 byte for each character.

- Full Unicode (or UTF-16), which represents each character in a string using 16 bits. The resulting byte array will have 2 bytes for each character.

- UTF-7 Unicode, which uses 7 bits for ordinary ASCII characters and multiple 7-bit pairs for extended characters. This encoding is primarily for use with 7-bit protocols such as mail, and it is not regularly used.

- UTF-8 Unicode, which uses 8 bits for ordinary ASCII characters and multiple 8-bit pairs for extended characters. The resulting byte array will have 1 byte for each character (provided there are no extended characters).

The .NET Framework provides a class for each type of encoding in the System.Text namespace. When using StreamReader and StreamWriter, you can specify the encoding you want to use or simply use the default UTF-8 encoding.

When reading information, you use the Read or ReadLine method of StreamReader. The Read method reads a single character, or the number of characters you specify, and returns the data as a char or char array. The ReadLine method returns a string with the content of an entire line. The ReadToEnd method will return a string with the content starting from the current position to the end of the stream.

The Code

The following console application writes and then reads a text file.

```
using System;
using System.IO;
using System.Text;

namespace Apress.VisualCSharpRecipes.Chapter05
{
    static class Recipe05_07
    {
        static void Main()
        {
            // Create a new file.
            using (FileStream fs = new FileStream("test.txt", FileMode.Create))
            {
                // Create a writer and specify the encoding.
                // The default (UTF-8) supports special Unicode characters,
                // but encodes all standard characters in the same way as
                // ASCII encoding.
                using (StreamWriter w = new StreamWriter(fs, Encoding.UTF8))
                {
                    // Write a decimal, string, and char.
                    w.WriteLine(124.23M);
                    w.WriteLine("Test string");
                    w.WriteLine('!');
                }
            }
            Console.WriteLine("Press Enter to read the information.");
            Console.ReadLine();
```

```
        // Open the file in read-only mode.
        using (FileStream fs = new FileStream("test.txt", FileMode.Open))
        {
            using (StreamReader r = new StreamReader(fs, Encoding.UTF8))
            {
                // Read the data and convert it to the appropriate data type.
                Console.WriteLine(Decimal.Parse(r.ReadLine()));
                Console.WriteLine(r.ReadLine());
                Console.WriteLine(Char.Parse(r.ReadLine()));
            }
        }

        // Wait to continue.
        Console.WriteLine(Environment.NewLine);
        Console.WriteLine("Main method complete. Press Enter.");
        Console.ReadLine();
    }
  }
}
```

5-8. Read and Write a Binary File

Problem

You need to write data to a binary file, with strong data typing.

Solution

Create a new System.IO.FileStream object that references the file. To write the file, wrap the FileStream in a System.IO.BinaryWriter and use the overloaded Write method. To read the file, wrap the FileStream in a System.IO.BinaryReader and use the Read method that corresponds to the expected data type.

How It Works

The .NET Framework allows you to write or read binary data with any stream by using the BinaryWriter and BinaryReader classes. When writing data with the BinaryWriter, you use the BinaryWriter.Write method. This method is overloaded to support all the common C# .NET data types, including strings, chars, integers, floating-point numbers, decimals, and so on. The information will then be encoded as a series of bytes and written to the file. You can configure the encoding used for strings by using an overloaded constructor that accepts a System.Text.Encoding object, as described in recipe 5-7.

You must be particularly fastidious with data types when using binary files. This is because when you retrieve the information, you must use one of the strongly typed Read methods from the BinaryReader. For example, to retrieve decimal data, you use ReadDecimal. To read a string, you use ReadString. (The BinaryWriter always records the length of a string when it writes it to a binary file to prevent any possibility of error.)

The Code

The following console application writes and then reads a binary file.

```csharp
using System;
using System.IO;

namespace Apress.VisualCSharpRecipes.Chapter05
{
    static class Recipe05_08
    {
        static void Main()
        {
            // Create a new file and writer.
            using (FileStream fs = new FileStream("test.bin", FileMode.Create))
            {
                using (BinaryWriter w = new BinaryWriter(fs))
                {
                    // Write a decimal, two strings, and a char.
                    w.Write(124.23M);
                    w.Write("Test string");
                    w.Write("Test string 2");
                    w.Write('!');
                }
            }
            Console.WriteLine("Press Enter to read the information.");
            Console.ReadLine();

            // Open the file in read-only mode.
            using (FileStream fs = new FileStream("test.bin", FileMode.Open))
            {
                // Display the raw information in the file.
                using (StreamReader sr = new StreamReader(fs))
                {
                    Console.WriteLine(sr.ReadToEnd());
                    Console.WriteLine();

                    // Read the data and convert it to the appropriate data type.
                    fs.Position = 0;
                    using (BinaryReader br = new BinaryReader(fs))
                    {
                        Console.WriteLine(br.ReadDecimal());
                        Console.WriteLine(br.ReadString());
                        Console.WriteLine(br.ReadString());
                        Console.WriteLine(br.ReadChar());
                    }
                }
            }

            // Wait to continue.
            Console.WriteLine(Environment.NewLine);
            Console.WriteLine("Main method complete. Press Enter.");
            Console.ReadLine();
        }
    }
}
```

5-9. Read a File Asynchronously

Problem

You need to read data from a file without blocking the execution of your code. This technique is commonly used if the file is stored on a slow backing store (such as a networked drive in a wide area network).

Solution

Create a separate class that will read the file asynchronously. Start reading a block of data using the `FileStream.BeginRead` method and supply a callback method. When the callback is triggered, retrieve the data by calling `FileStream.EndRead`, process it, and read the next block asynchronously with `BeginRead`.

How It Works

The `FileStream` includes basic support for asynchronous use through the `BeginRead` and `EndRead` methods. Using these methods, you can read a block of data on one of the threads provided by the .NET Framework thread pool, without needing to directly use the threading classes in the `System.Threading` namespace.

When reading a file asynchronously, you choose the amount of data that you want to read at a time. Depending on the situation, you might want to read a very small amount of data at a time (for example, if you are copying it block by block to another file) or a relatively large amount of data (for example, if you need a certain amount of information before your processing logic can start). You specify the block size when calling `BeginRead`, and you pass a buffer where the data will be placed. Because the `BeginRead` and `EndRead` methods need to be able to access many of the same pieces of information, such as the `FileStream`, the buffer, the block size, and so on, it's usually easiest to encapsulate your asynchronous file reading code in a single class.

The Code

The following example demonstrates reading a file asynchronously. The `AsyncProcessor` class provides a public `StartProcess` method, which starts an asynchronous read. Every time the read operation finishes, the `OnCompletedRead` callback is triggered and the block of data is processed. If there is more data in the file, a new asynchronous read operation is started. `AsyncProcessor` reads 2 kilobytes (2,048 bytes) at a time.

```
using System;
using System.IO;
using System.Threading;

namespace Apress.VisualCSharpRecipes.Chapter05
{
    public class AsyncProcessor
    {
        private Stream inputStream;

        // The amount that will be read in one block (2 KB).
        private int bufferSize = 2048;
```

```csharp
    public int BufferSize
    {
        get { return bufferSize; }
        set { bufferSize = value; }
    }

    // The buffer that will hold the retrieved data.
    private byte[] buffer;

    public AsyncProcessor(string fileName)
    {
        buffer = new byte[bufferSize];

        // Open the file, specifying true for asynchronous support.
        inputStream = new FileStream(fileName, FileMode.Open,
          FileAccess.Read, FileShare.Read, bufferSize, true);
    }

    public void StartProcess()
    {

        // Start the asynchronous read, which will fill the buffer.
        inputStream.BeginRead(buffer, 0, buffer.Length,
          OnCompletedRead, null);
    }

    private void OnCompletedRead(IAsyncResult asyncResult)
    {
        // One block has been read asynchronously.
        // Retrieve the data.
        int bytesRead = inputStream.EndRead(asyncResult);

        // If no bytes are read, the stream is at the end of the file.
        if (bytesRead > 0)
        {
            // Pause to simulate processing this block of data.
            Console.WriteLine("\t[ASYNC READER]: Read one block.");
            Thread.Sleep(TimeSpan.FromMilliseconds(20));

            // Begin to read the next block asynchronously.
            inputStream.BeginRead(
            buffer, 0, buffer.Length, OnCompletedRead,
              null);
        }
        else
        {
            // End the operation.
            Console.WriteLine("\t[ASYNC READER]: Complete.");
            inputStream.Close();
        }
    }
}
}
```

Usage

The following example shows a console application that uses AsyncProcessor to read a 2-megabyte file.

```csharp
using System;
using System.IO;
using System.Threading;

namespace Apress.VisualCSharpRecipes.Chapter05
{
    static class Recipe05_09
    {
        static void Main(string[] args)
        {
            // Create a 2 MB test file.
            using (FileStream fs = new FileStream("test.txt", FileMode.Create))
            {
                fs.SetLength(1000000);
            }

            // Start the asynchronous file processor on another thread.
            AsyncProcessor asyncIO = new AsyncProcessor("test.txt");
            asyncIO.StartProcess();

            // At the same time, do some other work.
            // In this example, we simply loop for 10 seconds.
            DateTime startTime = DateTime.Now;
            while (DateTime.Now.Subtract(startTime).TotalSeconds < 10)
            {
                Console.WriteLine("[MAIN THREAD]: Doing some work.");

                // Pause to simulate a time-consuming operation.
                Thread.Sleep(TimeSpan.FromMilliseconds(100));
            }

            Console.WriteLine("[MAIN THREAD]: Complete.");
            Console.ReadLine();

            // Remove the test file.
            File.Delete("test.txt");
        }
    }
}
```

The following is an example of the output you will see when you run this test.

```
[MAIN THREAD]: Doing some work.
        [ASYNC READER]: Read one block.
        [ASYNC READER]: Read one block.
[MAIN THREAD]: Doing some work.
        [ASYNC READER]: Read one block.
        [ASYNC READER]: Read one block.
        [ASYNC READER]: Read one block.
        [ASYNC READER]: Read one block.
[MAIN THREAD]: Doing some work.
        [ASYNC READER]: Read one block.
        [ASYNC READER]: Read one block.
        [ASYNC READER]: Read one block.
        . . .
```

5-10. Find Files That Match a Wildcard Expression

Problem

You need to process multiple files based on a filter expression (such as *.dll or mysheet20??.xls).

Solution

Use the overloaded version of the System.IO.DirectoryInfo.GetFiles method that accepts a filter expression and returns an array of FileInfo objects. For searching recursively across all subdirectories, use the overloaded version that accepts the SearchOption enumeration.

How It Works

The DirectoryInfo and Directory objects both provide a way to search the directories for files that match a specific filter expression. These search expressions can use the standard ? and * wildcards. You can use a similar technique to retrieve directories that match a specified search pattern by using the overloaded DirectoryInfo.GetDirectories method. You can also use the new overload of GetFiles for searching recursively using the SearchOption.AllDirectories enumeration constant.

The Code

The following example retrieves the names of all the files in a specified directory that match a specified filter string. The directory and filter expression are submitted as command-line arguments. The code then iterates through the retrieved FileInfo collection of matching files and displays the name and size of each one.

```
using System;
using System.IO;

namespace Apress.VisualCSharpRecipes.Chapter05
{
    static class Recipe05_10
    {
        static void Main(string[] args)
        {
            if (args.Length != 2)
            {
                Console.WriteLine(
                  "USAGE:  Recipe05_10 [directory] [filterExpression]");
                return;
            }

            DirectoryInfo dir = new DirectoryInfo(args[0]);
            FileInfo[] files = dir.GetFiles(args[1]);

            // Display the name of all the files.
            foreach (FileInfo file in files)
            {
                Console.Write("Name: " + file.Name + "  ");
                Console.WriteLine("Size: " + file.Length.ToString());
            }
```

```
                // Wait to continue.
                Console.WriteLine(Environment.NewLine);
                Console.WriteLine("Main method complete. Press Enter.");
                Console.ReadLine();
            }
        }
}
```

5-11. Test Two Files for Equality

Problem

You need to quickly compare the content of two files and determine if it matches exactly.

Solution

Calculate the hash code of each file using the `System.Security.Cryptography.HashAlgorithm` class, and then compare the hash codes.

How It Works

You might compare file contents in a number of ways. For example, you could examine a portion of the file for similar data, or you could read through each file byte by byte, comparing each byte as you go. Both of these approaches are valid, but in some cases, it's more convenient to use a *hash code* algorithm.

A hash code algorithm generates a small (typically about 20 bytes) binary fingerprint for a file. While it's *possible* for different files to generate the same hash codes, that is statistically unlikely to occur. In fact, even a minor change (for example, modifying a single bit in the source file) has an approximately 50-percent chance of independently changing each bit in the hash code. For this reason, hash codes are often used in security code to detect data tampering. (Hash codes are discussed in more detail in recipes 11-14, 11-15, and 11-16.)

To create a hash code, you must first create a `HashAlgorithm` object, typically by calling the static `HashAlgorithm.Create` method. You can then call `HashAlgorithm.ComputeHash`, which returns a byte array with the hash data.

The Code

The following example demonstrates a simple console application that reads two filenames that are supplied as arguments and uses hash codes to test the files for equality. The hashes are compared by converting them into strings. Alternatively, you could compare them by iterating over the byte array and comparing each value. This approach would be slightly faster, but because the overhead of converting 20 bytes into a string is minimal, it's not required.

```
using System;
using System.IO;
using System.Security.Cryptography;

namespace Apress.VisualCSharpRecipes.Chapter05
{
    static class Recipe05_11
    {
        static void Main(string[] args)
```

```
    {
        if (args.Length != 2)
        {
            Console.WriteLine("USAGE:  Recipe05_11 [fileName] [fileName]");
            return;
        }

        Console.WriteLine("Comparing " + args[0] + " and " + args[1]);

        // Create the hashing object.
        using (HashAlgorithm hashAlg = HashAlgorithm.Create())
        {
            using (FileStream fsA = new FileStream(args[0], FileMode.Open),
                fsB = new FileStream(args[1], FileMode.Open))
            {
                // Calculate the hash for the files.
                byte[] hashBytesA = hashAlg.ComputeHash(fsA);
                byte[] hashBytesB = hashAlg.ComputeHash(fsB);

                // Compare the hashes.
                if (BitConverter.ToString(hashBytesA) ==
                    BitConverter.ToString(hashBytesB))
                {
                    Console.WriteLine("Files match.");
                }
                else
                {
                    Console.WriteLine("No match.");
                }
            }
        }

        // Wait to continue.
        Console.WriteLine(Environment.NewLine);
        Console.WriteLine("Main method complete. Press Enter.");
        Console.ReadLine();
    }
  }
}
```

5-12. Manipulate Strings Representing Filenames

Problem

You want to retrieve a portion of a path or verify that a file path is in a normal (standardized) form.

Solution

Process the path using the System.IO.Path class. You can use Path.GetFileName to retrieve a file-name from a path, Path.ChangeExtension to modify the extension portion of a path string, and Path.Combine to create a fully qualified path without worrying about whether or not your directory includes a trailing directory separation (\) character.

How It Works

File paths are often difficult to work with in code because of the many different ways to represent the same directory. For example, you might use an absolute path (C:\Temp), a UNC path (\\MyServer\\MyShare\temp), or one of many possible relative paths (C:\Temp\MyFiles\..\ or C:\Temp\MyFiles\..\..\temp).

The easiest way to handle file system paths is to use the static methods of the Path class to make sure you have the information you expect. For example, here is how you take a filename that might include a qualified path and extract just the filename:

```
string filename = @"..\System\MyFile.txt";
filename = Path.GetFileName(filename);

// Now filename = "MyFile.txt"
```

And here is how you might append the filename to a directory path using the Path.Combine method:

```
string filename = @"..\..\myfile.txt";
string fullPath = @"c:\Temp";

string filename = Path.GetFileName(filename);
string fullPath = Path.Combine(fullPath, filename);

// (fullPath is now "c:\Temp\myfile.txt")
```

The advantage of this approach is that a trailing backslash (\) is automatically added to the path name if required. The Path class also provides the following useful methods for manipulating path information:

- ChangeExtension modifies the current extension of the file in a string. If no extension is specified, the current extension will be removed.

- GetDirectoryName returns all the directory information, which is the text between the first and last directory separators (\).

- GetFileNameWithoutExtension is similar to GetFileName, but it omits the extension.

- GetFullPath has no effect on an absolute path, and it changes a relative path into an absolute path using the current directory. For example, if C:\Temp\ is the current directory, calling GetFullPath on a filename such as test.txt returns C:\Temp\test.txt.

- GetPathRoot retrieves a string with the root (for example, "C:\"), provided that information is in the string. For a relative path, it returns a null reference.

- HasExtension returns true if the path ends with an extension.

- IsPathRooted returns true if the path is an absolute path and false if it's a relative path.

■**Note** In most cases, an exception will be thrown if you try to supply an invalid path to one of these methods (for example, paths that include illegal characters). However, path names that are invalid because they contain a wildcard character (* or ?) will not cause the methods to throw an exception. You could use the Path.GetInvalidPathChars method to obtain an array of characters that are illegal in path names.

5-13. Determine If a Path Is a Directory or a File

Problem

You have a path (in the form of a string), and you want to determine whether it corresponds to a directory or a file.

Solution

Test the path with the `Directory.Exists` and the `File.Exists` methods.

How It Works

The `System.IO.Directory` and `System.IO.File` classes both provide an `Exists` method. The `Directory.Exists` method returns `true` if a supplied relative or absolute path corresponds to an existing directory, even a shared folder with an UNC name. `File.Exists` returns `true` if the path corresponds to an existing file.

The Code

The following example demonstrates how you can quickly determine if a path corresponds to a file or directory.

```
using System;
using System.IO;

namespace Apress.VisualCSharpRecipes.Chapter05
{
    static class Recipe05_13
    {
        static void Main(string[] args)
        {
            foreach (string arg in args)
            {
                Console.Write(arg);

                if (Directory.Exists(arg))
                {
                    Console.WriteLine(" is a directory");
                }
                else if (File.Exists(arg))
                {
                    Console.WriteLine(" is a file");
                }
                else
                {
                    Console.WriteLine(" does not exist");
                }
            }
```

```
                    // Wait to continue.
                    Console.WriteLine(Environment.NewLine);
                    Console.WriteLine("Main method complete. Press Enter.");
                    Console.ReadLine();
                }
            }
        }
```

5-14. Work with Relative Paths

Problem

You want to set the current working directory so that you can use relative paths in your code.

Solution

Use the static GetCurrentDirectory and SetCurrentDirectory methods of the System.IO.Directory class.

How It Works

Relative paths are automatically interpreted in relation to the current working directory. You can retrieve the current working directory by calling Directory.GetCurrentDirectory or change it using Directory.SetCurrentDirectory. In addition, you can use the static GetFullPath method of the System.IO.Path class to convert a relative path into an absolute path using the current working directory.

The Code

The following is a simple example that demonstrates working with relative paths.

```
using System;
using System.IO;

namespace Apress.VisualCSharpRecipes.Chapter05
{
    static class Recipe05_14
    {
        static void Main()
        {
            Console.WriteLine("Using: " + Directory.GetCurrentDirectory());
            Console.WriteLine("The relative path 'file.txt' " +
              "will automatically become: '" +
              Path.GetFullPath("file.txt") + "'");

            Console.WriteLine();

            Console.WriteLine("Changing current directory to c:\\");
            Directory.SetCurrentDirectory(@"c:\");

            Console.WriteLine("Now the relative path 'file.txt' " +
              "will automatically become '" +
              Path.GetFullPath("file.txt") + "'");
```

```
        // Wait to continue.
        Console.WriteLine(Environment.NewLine);
        Console.WriteLine("Main method complete. Press Enter.");
        Console.ReadLine();
    }
  }
}
```

Usage

The output for this example might be the following (if you run the application in the directory C:\temp).

```
Using: c:\temp
The relative path 'file.txt' will automatically become 'c:\temp\file.txt'

Changing current directory to c:\
The relative path 'file.txt' will automatically become 'c:\file.txt'
```

■**Caution** If you use relative paths, it's recommended that you set the working path at the start of each file interaction. Otherwise, you could introduce unnoticed security vulnerabilities that could allow a malicious user to force your application into accessing or overwriting system files by tricking it into using a different working directory.

5-15. Create a Temporary File

Problem

You need to create a file that will be placed in the user-specific temporary directory and will have a unique name, so that it will not conflict with temporary files generated by other programs.

Solution

Use the static GetTempFileName method of the System.IO.Path class, which returns a path made up of the user's temporary directory and a randomly generated filename.

How It Works

You can use a number of approaches to generate temporary files. In simple cases, you might just create a file in the application directory, possibly using a GUID or a timestamp in conjunction with a random value as the filename. However, the Path class provides a helper method that can save you some work. It creates a file with a unique filename in the current user's temporary directory which is stored in a folder like C:\Documents and Settings\[username]\Local Settings\temp by default.

The Code

The following example demonstrates creating a temporary file.

```
using System;
using System.IO;
```

```
namespace Apress.VisualCSharpRecipes.Chapter05
{
    static class Recipe05_15
    {
        static void Main()
        {
            string tempFile = Path.GetTempFileName();

            Console.WriteLine("Using " + tempFile);

            using (FileStream fs = new FileStream(tempFile, FileMode.Open))
            {
                // (Write some data.)
            }

            // Now delete the file.
            File.Delete(tempFile);

            // Wait to continue.
            Console.WriteLine(Environment.NewLine);
            Console.WriteLine("Main method complete. Press Enter.");
            Console.ReadLine();
        }
    }
}
```

5-16. Get the Total Free Space on a Drive

Problem

You need to examine a drive and determine how many bytes of free space are available.

Solution

Use the DriveInfo.AvailableFreeSpace property.

How It Works

The DriveInfo class (new to .NET Framework 2.0) provides members that let you find out the drive type, free space, and many other details of a drive. In order to create a new DriveInfo object, you need to pass the drive letter or the drive root string to the constructor, such as 'C' or "C:\" for creating a DriveInfo instance representing the C drive of the computer. You could also retrieve the list of logical drives available by using the static Directory.GetLogicalDrives method, which returns an array of strings, each containing the root of the drive, such as "C:\". For more details on each drive, you create a DriveInfo instance, passing either the root or the letter corresponding to the logical drive. If you need a detailed description of each logical drive, call the DriveInfo.GetDrives method, which returns an array of DriveInfo objects, instead of using Directory.GetLogicalDrives.

■**Note** An System.IO.IOException exception is thrown if you try to access an unavailable network drive.

The Code

The following console application shows the available free space using the DriveInfo class for the given drive or for all logical drives if no argument is passed to the application.

```csharp
using System;
using System.IO;

namespace Apress.VisualCSharpRecipes.Chapter05
{
    static class Recipe05_16
    {
        static void Main(string[] args)
        {
            if (args.Length == 1)
            {
                DriveInfo drive = new DriveInfo(args[0]);

                Console.Write("Free space in {0}-drive (in kilobytes): ", args[0]);
                Console.WriteLine(drive.AvailableFreeSpace / 1024);
                return;
            }

            foreach (DriveInfo drive in DriveInfo.GetDrives())
            {
                try
                {
                    Console.WriteLine(
                        "{0} - {1} KB",
                        drive.RootDirectory,
                        drive.AvailableFreeSpace / 1024
                        );
                }
                catch (IOException) // network drives may not be available
                {
                    Console.WriteLine(drive);
                }
            }

            // Wait to continue.
            Console.WriteLine(Environment.NewLine);
            Console.WriteLine("Main method complete. Press Enter.");
            Console.ReadLine();
        }
    }
}
```

Note In addition to the AvailableFreeSpace property, DriveInfo also defines a TotalFreeSpace property. The difference between these two properties is that AvailableFreeSpace takes into account disk quotas.

5-17. Show the Common File Dialog Boxes

Problem

You need to show the standard Windows dialog boxes for opening and saving files and for selecting a folder.

Solution

Use the OpenFileDialog, SaveFileDialog, and FolderBrowserDialog classes in the System.Windows. Forms namespace. Call the ShowDialog method to display the dialog box, examine the return value to determine whether the user clicked OK or Cancel, and retrieve the selection from the FileName or SelectedPath property.

How It Works

The .NET Framework provides objects that wrap many of the standard Windows dialog boxes, including those used for saving and selecting files and directories. These classes all inherit from System.Windows.Forms.CommonDialog and include the following:

- OpenFileDialog, which allows the user to select a file, as shown in Figure 5-2. The filename and path are provided to your code through the FileName property (or the FileNames collection, if you have enabled multiple file select by setting Multiselect to true). Additionally, you can use the Filter property to set the file format choices and set CheckFileExists to enforce validation.

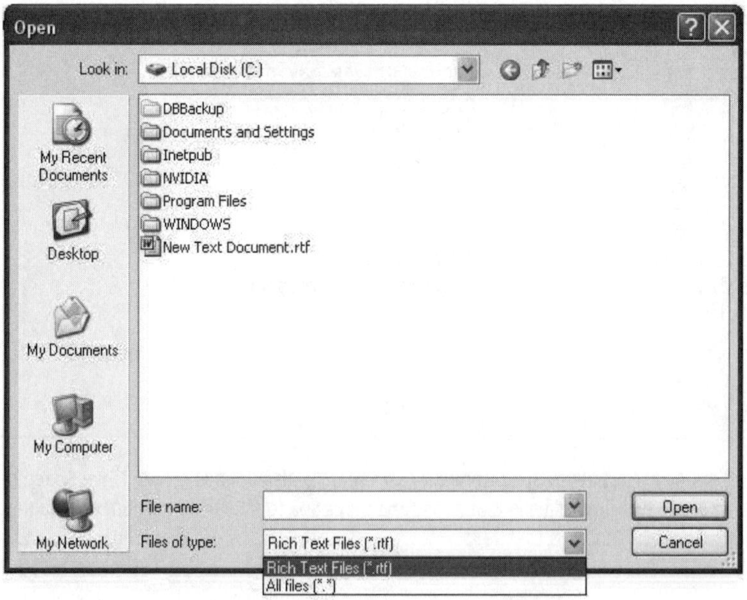

Figure 5-2. OpenFileDialog *shows the Open dialog box.*

- SaveFileDialog, which allows the user to specify a new file. The filename and path are provided to your code through the FileName property. You can also use the Filter property to set the file format choices, and set the CreatePrompt and OverwritePrompt Boolean properties to instruct .NET to display a confirmation if the user selects a new file or an existing file, respectively.

- FolderBrowserDialog, which allows the user to select (and optionally create) a directory, as shown in Figure 5-3. The selected path is provided through the SelectedPath property, and you can specify whether or not a Create New button should appear.

Figure 5-3. FolderBrowserDialog *shows the Browse for Folder dialog box.*

When using OpenFileDialog or SaveFileDialog, you need to set the filter string, which specifies the allowed file extensions. The filter string is separated with the pipe character (|) in this format:

```
[Text label] | [Extension list separated by semicolons] | [Text label]
| [Extension list separated by semicolons] |  . . .
```

You can also set the Title (form caption) and the InitialDirectory.

The Code

The following code shows a Windows-based application that allows the user to load documents into a RichTextBox, edit the content, and then save the modified document. When opening and saving a document, the OpenFileDialog and SaveFileDialog classes are used.

```csharp
using System;
using System.Windows.Forms;

namespace Apress.VisualCSharpRecipes.Chapter05
{
    public partial class MainForm : Form
    {
        public MainForm()
```

```
        {
            InitializeComponent();
        }

        private void mnuOpen_Click(object sender, EventArgs e)
        {
            OpenFileDialog dlg = new OpenFileDialog();
            dlg.Filter = "Rich Text Files (*.rtf)|*.RTF|" +
              "All files (*.*)|*.*";
            dlg.CheckFileExists = true;
            dlg.InitialDirectory = Application.StartupPath;

            if (dlg.ShowDialog() == DialogResult.OK)
            {
                rtDoc.LoadFile(dlg.FileName);
                rtDoc.Enabled = true;
            }
        }

        private void mnuSave_Click(object sender, EventArgs e)
        {
            SaveFileDialog dlg = new SaveFileDialog();
            dlg.Filter = "RichText Files (*.rtf)|*.RTF|Text Files (*.txt)|*.TXT" +
              "|All files (*.*)|*.*";
            dlg.CheckFileExists = true;
            dlg.InitialDirectory = Application.StartupPath;

            if (dlg.ShowDialog() == DialogResult.OK)
            {
                rtDoc.SaveFile(dlg.FileName);
            }
        }

        private void mnuExit_Click(object sender, EventArgs e)
        {
            this.Close();
        }
    }
}
```

5-18. Use an Isolated Store

Problem

You need to store data in a file, but your application does not have the required `FileIOPermission` for the local hard drive.

Solution

Use the `IsolatedStorageFile` and `IsolatedStorageFileStream` classes from the `System.IO.IsolatedStorage` namespace. These classes allow your application to write data to a file in a user-specific directory without needing permission to access the local hard drive directly.

How It Works

The .NET Framework includes support for isolated storage, which allows you to read and write to a user-specific virtual file system that the common language runtime (CLR) manages. When you create isolated storage files, the data is automatically serialized to a unique location in the user profile path (typically a path like C:\Documents and Settings\[username]\Local Settings\Application Data\isolated storage\[guid_identifier]).

One reason you might use isolated storage is to give a partially trusted application limited ability to store data. For example, the default CLR security policy gives local code unrestricted `FileIOPermission`, which allows it to open or write to any file. Code that you run from a remote server on the local intranet is automatically assigned fewer permissions. It lacks the `FileIOPermission`, but it has the `IsolatedStoragePermission`, giving it the ability to use isolated stores. (The security policy also limits the maximum amount of space that can be used in an isolated store.) Another reason you might use an isolated store is to better secure data. For example, data in one user's isolated store will be restricted from another nonadministrative user.

By default, each isolated store is segregated by user and assembly. That means that when the same user runs the same application, the application will access the data in the same isolated store. However, you can choose to segregate it further by application domain so that multiple `AppDomain` instances running in the same application receive different isolated stores.

The files are stored as part of a user's profile, so users can access their isolated storage files on any workstation they log on to if roaming profiles are configured on your local area network. (In this case, the store must be specifically designated as a roaming store by applying the `IsolatedStorageFile.Roaming` flag when it's created.) By letting the .NET Framework and the CLR provide these levels of isolation, you can relinquish responsibility for maintaining the separation between files, and you do not need to worry that programming oversights or misunderstandings will cause loss of critical data.

The Code

The following example shows how you can access isolated storage.

```
using System;
using System.IO;
using System.IO.IsolatedStorage;

namespace Apress.VisualCSharpRecipes.Chapter05
{
    static class Recipe05_18
    {
        static void Main(string[] args)
        {
            // Create the store for the current user.
            using (IsolatedStorageFile store =
                IsolatedStorageFile.GetUserStoreForAssembly())
            {
                // Create a folder in the root of the isolated store.
                store.CreateDirectory("MyFolder");

                // Create a file in the isolated store.
                using (Stream fs = new IsolatedStorageFileStream(
                  "MyFile.txt", FileMode.Create, store))
                {
                    StreamWriter w = new StreamWriter(fs);
```

```
                    // You can now write to the file as normal.
                    w.WriteLine("Test");
                    w.Flush();
                }

                Console.WriteLine("Current size: " +
                    store.CurrentSize.ToString());
                Console.WriteLine("Scope: " + store.Scope.ToString());

                Console.WriteLine("Contained files include:");
                string[] files = store.GetFileNames("*.*");
                foreach (string file in files)
                {
                    Console.WriteLine(file);
                }
            }

            // Wait to continue.
            Console.WriteLine(Environment.NewLine);
            Console.WriteLine("Main method complete. Press Enter.");
            Console.ReadLine();
        }
    }
}
```

The following demonstrates using multiple AppDomain instances running in the same application to receive different isolated stores.

```
// Access isolated storage for the current user and assembly
// (which is equivalent to the first example).
store = IsolatedStorageFile.GetStore(IsolatedStorageScope.User |
    IsolatedStorageScope.Assembly, null, null);

// Access isolated storage for the current user, assembly,
// and application domain. In other words, this data is
// accessible only by the current AppDomain instance.
store = IsolatedStorageFile.GetStore(IsolatedStorageScope.User |
    IsolatedStorageScope.Assembly | IsolatedStorageScope.Domain,
    null, null);
```

5-19. Monitor the File System for Changes

Problem

You need to react when a file system change is detected in a specific path (such as a file modification or creation).

Solution

Use the System.IO.FileSystemWatcher component, specify the path or file you want to monitor, and handle the Created, Deleted, Renamed, and Changed events.

How It Works

When linking together multiple applications and business processes, it's often necessary to create a program that waits idly and becomes active only when a new file is received or changed. You can create this type of program by scanning a directory periodically, but you face a key trade-off. The more often you scan, the more system resources you waste. The less often you scan, the longer it will take to detect a change. The solution is to use the `FileSystemWatcher` class to react directly to Windows file events.

To use `FileSystemWatcher`, you must create an instance and set the following properties:

- `Path` indicates the directory you want to monitor.
- `Filter` indicates the types of files you are monitoring.
- `NotifyFilter` indicates the type of changes you are monitoring.

`FileSystemWatcher` raises four key events: `Created`, `Deleted`, `Renamed`, and `Changed`. All of these events provide information through their `FileSystemEventArgs` parameter, including the name of the file (`Name`), the full path (`FullPath`), and the type of change (`ChangeType`). The `Renamed` event provides a `RenamedEventArgs` instance, which derives from `FileSystemEventArgs`, and adds information about the original filename (`OldName` and `OldFullPath`). If you need to, you can disable these events by setting the `FileSystemWatcher.EnableRaisingEvents` property to `false`. The `Created`, `Deleted`, and `Renamed` events are easy to handle. However, if you want to use the `Changed` event, you need to use the `NotifyFilter` property to indicate the types of changes you want to watch. Otherwise, your program might be swamped by an unceasing series of events as files are modified.

The `NotifyFilter` property can be set using any combination of the following values from the `System.IO.NotifyFilters` enumeration:

- `Attributes`
- `CreationTime`
- `DirectoryName`
- `FileName`
- `LastAccess`
- `LastWrite`
- `Security`
- `Size`

The Code

The following example shows a console application that handles `Created` and `Deleted` events, and tests these events by creating a test file.

```
using System;
using System.IO;
using System.Windows.Forms;

namespace Apress.VisualCSharpRecipes.Chapter05
{
    static class Recipe05_19
    {
```

```csharp
static void Main()
{
    // Configure the FileSystemWatcher.
    using (FileSystemWatcher watch = new FileSystemWatcher())
    {
        watch.Path = Application.StartupPath;
        watch.Filter = "*.*";
        watch.IncludeSubdirectories = true;

        // Attach the event handler.
        watch.Created += new FileSystemEventHandler(OnCreatedOrDeleted);
        watch.Deleted += new FileSystemEventHandler(OnCreatedOrDeleted);
        watch.EnableRaisingEvents = true;

        Console.WriteLine("Press Enter to create a file.");
        Console.ReadLine();

        if (File.Exists("test.bin"))
        {
            File.Delete("test.bin");
        }

        // Create test.bin.
        using (FileStream fs = new FileStream("test.bin", FileMode.Create))
        {
            // Do something.
        }

        Console.WriteLine("Press Enter to terminate the application.");
        Console.ReadLine();
    }

    // Wait to continue.
    Console.WriteLine(Environment.NewLine);
    Console.WriteLine("Main method complete. Press Enter.");
    Console.ReadLine();
}

// Fires when a new file is created in the directory being monitored.
private static void OnCreatedOrDeleted(object sender,
    FileSystemEventArgs e)
{
    // Display the notification information.
    Console.WriteLine("\tNOTIFICATION: " + e.FullPath +
        "' was " + e.ChangeType.ToString());
    Console.WriteLine();
}
    }
}
```

5-20. Access a COM Port

Problem

You need to send data directly to a serial port.

Solution

Use the System.IO.Ports.SerialPort class. This class represents a serial port resource and defines methods that enable communication through it.

How It Works

.NET Framework 2.0 defines a System.IO.Ports namespace that contains several classes. The central class is SerialPort. A SerialPort instance represents a serial port resource and provides methods that let you communicate through it. The SerialPort class also exposes properties that let you specify the port, baud rate, parity, and other information.

The Code

The following example demonstrates a simple console application that writes a string into the COM1 port.

```
using System;
using System.IO.Ports;

namespace Apress.VisualCSharpRecipes.Chapter05
{
    static class Recipe05_20
    {
        static void Main(string[] args)
        {
            using (SerialPort port = new SerialPort("COM1"))
            {
                // Set the properties.
                port.BaudRate = 9600;
                port.Parity = Parity.None;
                port.ReadTimeout = 10;
                port.StopBits = StopBits.One;

                // Write a message into the port.
                port.Open();
                port.Write("Hello world!");

                Console.WriteLine("Wrote to the port.");
            }

            // Wait to continue.
            Console.WriteLine(Environment.NewLine);
            Console.WriteLine("Main method complete. Press Enter.");
            Console.ReadLine();
        }
    }
}
```

5-21. Get a Random Filename

Problem

You need to get a random name for creating a folder or a file.

Solution

Use the `Path.GetRandomFileName` method, which returns a random name.

How It Works

The `System.IO.Path` class includes a new `GetRandomFileName` method, which generates a random string. You could use this string for creating a new file or folder.

The difference between `GetRandomFileName` and `GetTempFileName` (discussed in recipe 5-15) of the `Path` class is that `GetRandomFileName` just returns a random string and does not create a file, whereas `GetTempFileName` creates a new 0-byte temporary file and returns the path to the file.

5-22. Manipulate the Access Control Lists of a File or Directory

Problem

You want to modify the access control list (ACL) of a file or directory in the computer.

Solution

Use the `GetAccessControl` and `SetAccessControl` methods of the `File` or `Directory` class.

How It Works

.NET Framework 2.0 now includes support for ACLs for resources like I/O, registry, and threading classes. You can retrieve and apply the ACL for a resource by using the `GetAccessControl` and `SetAccessControl` methods defined in the corresponding resource classes. For example, the `File` and `Directory` classes define both these methods, which let you manipulate the ACLs for a file or directory.

To add or remove an ACL-associated right of a file or directory, you need to first retrieve the `FileSecurity` or `DirectorySecurity` object currently applied to the resource using the `GetAccessControl` method. Once you retrieve this object, you need to perform the required modification of the rights, and then apply the ACL back to the resource using the `SetAccessControl` method. Access rights are updated using any of the add and remove methods provided in the security class.

The Code

The following example demonstrates the effect of denying Everyone Read access to a temporary file, using a console application. An attempt to read the file after a change in the ACL triggers a security exception.

```csharp
using System;
using System.IO;
using System.Security.AccessControl;

namespace Apress.VisualCSharpRecipes.Chapter05
{
    static class Recipe05_22
    {
        static void Main(string[] args)
        {
            FileStream stream;
            string fileName;

            // Create a new file and assign full control to 'Everyone'.
            Console.WriteLine("Press any key to write a new file...");
            Console.ReadKey(true);

            fileName = Path.GetRandomFileName();
            using (stream = new FileStream(fileName, FileMode.Create))
            {
                // Do something.
            }
            Console.WriteLine("Created a new file " + fileName + ".");
            Console.WriteLine();


            // Deny 'Everyone' access to the file
            Console.WriteLine("Press any key to deny 'Everyone' " +
                "access to the file...");
            Console.ReadKey(true);
            SetRule(fileName, "Everyone",
                FileSystemRights.Read, AccessControlType.Deny);
            Console.WriteLine("Removed access rights of 'Everyone'.");
            Console.WriteLine();


            // Attempt to access file.
            Console.WriteLine("Press any key to attempt " +
                "access to the file...");
            Console.ReadKey(true);

            try
            {
                stream = new FileStream(fileName, FileMode.Create);
            }
            catch (Exception ex)
            {
                Console.WriteLine("Exception thrown: ");
                Console.WriteLine(ex.ToString());
            }
            finally
            {
                stream.Close();
                stream.Dispose();
            }
```

```csharp
        // Wait to continue.
        Console.WriteLine(Environment.NewLine);
        Console.WriteLine("Main method complete. Press Enter.");
        Console.ReadLine();
    }

    static void AddRule(string filePath, string account,
        FileSystemRights rights, AccessControlType controlType)
    {
        // Get a FileSecurity object that represents the
        // current security settings.
        FileSecurity fSecurity = File.GetAccessControl(filePath);

        // Add the FileSystemAccessRule to the security settings.
        fSecurity.AddAccessRule(new FileSystemAccessRule(account,
            rights, controlType));

        // Set the new access settings.
        File.SetAccessControl(filePath, fSecurity);
    }

    static void SetRule(string filePath, string account,
        FileSystemRights rights, AccessControlType controlType)
    {
        // Get a FileSecurity object that represents the
        // current security settings.
        FileSecurity fSecurity = File.GetAccessControl(filePath);

        // Add the FileSystemAccessRule to the security settings.
        fSecurity.ResetAccessRule(new FileSystemAccessRule(account,
            rights, controlType));

        // Set the new access settings.
        File.SetAccessControl(filePath, fSecurity);
    }

    }
}
```

■ ■ ■

CHAPTER 6

XML Processing

One of the most remarkable aspects of the Microsoft .NET Framework is its deep integration with XML. In many .NET applications, you won't even be aware you're using XML technologies—they'll just be used behind the scenes when you serialize a Microsoft ADO.NET DataSet, call a Web service, or read application settings from a Web.config configuration file. In other cases, you'll want to work directly with the System.Xml namespaces to manipulate Extensible Markup Language (XML) data. Common XML tasks don't just include parsing an XML file but also include validating it against a schema, applying an XSL transform to create a new document or Hypertext Markup Language (HTML) page, and searching intelligently with XPath. The recipes in this chapter describe how to do the following:

- Read, parse, and manipulate XML data (recipes 6-1, 6-2, 6-3, and 6-7)
- Search an XML document for specific nodes, either by name (recipe 6-4), by namespace (recipe 6-5), or by using XPath (recipe 6-6)
- Validate an XML document with an XML schema (recipe 6-8)
- Serialize an object to XML (recipe 6-9), create an XML schema for a class (recipe 6-10), and generate the source code for a class based on an XML schema (recipe 6-11)
- Transform an XML document to another document using an XSL Transformations (XSLT) stylesheet (recipe 6-12)

6-1. Show the Structure of an XML Document in a TreeView

Problem

You need to display the structure and content of an XML document in a Windows-based application.

Solution

Load the XML document using the System.Xml.XmlDocument class. Create a re-entrant method that converts a single XmlNode into a System.Windows.Forms.TreeNode, and call it recursively to walk through the entire document.

How It Works

The .NET Framework provides several different ways to process XML documents. The one you use depends in part upon your programming task. One of the most fully featured classes is XmlDocument, which provides an in-memory representation of an XML document that conforms to the W3C Document Object Model (DOM). The XmlDocument class allows you to browse through the nodes in any direction, insert and remove nodes, and change the structure on the fly. For details of the DOM specification, go to http://www.w3c.org.

■Note The XmlDocument class is not scalable for very large XML documents, because it holds the entire XML content in memory at once. If you want a more memory-efficient alternative, and you can afford to read and process the XML piece by piece, consider the XmlReader and XmlWriter classes described in recipe 6-7.

To use the XmlDocument class, simply create a new instance of the class, and call the Load method with a filename, a Stream, a TextReader, or an XmlReader object. It is also possible to read the XML from a simple string with the LoadXML method. You can even supply a string with a URL that points to an XML document on the Web using the Load method. The XmlDocument instance will be populated with the tree of elements, or *nodes*, from the source document. The entry point for accessing these nodes is the root element, which is provided through the XmlDocument.DocumentElement property. DocumentElement is an XmlElement object that can contain one or more nested XmlNode objects, which in turn can contain more XmlNode objects, and so on. An XmlNode is the basic ingredient of an XML file. Common XML nodes include elements, attributes, comments, and contained text.

When dealing with an XmlNode or a class that derives from it (such as XmlElement or XmlAttribute), you can use the following basic properties:

- ChildNodes is an XmlNodeList collection that contains the first level of nested nodes.

- Name is the name of the node.

- NodeType returns a member of the System.Xml.XmlNodeType enumeration that indicates the type of the node (element, attribute, text, and so on).

- Value is the content of the node, if it's a text or CDATA node.

- Attributes provides a collection of node objects representing the attributes applied to the element.

- InnerText retrieves a string with the concatenated value of the node and all nested nodes.

- InnerXml retrieves a string with the concatenated XML markup for all nested nodes.

- OuterXml retrieves a string with the concatenated XML markup for the current node and all nested nodes.

The Code

The following example walks through every element of an XmlDocument using the ChildNodes property and a recursive method. Each node is displayed in a TreeView control, with descriptive text that either identifies it or shows its content.

```
using System;
using System.Windows.Forms;
using System.Xml;
using System.IO;
```

```csharp
namespace Apress.VisualCSharpRecipes.Chapter06
{
    public partial class Recipe06_01 : System.Windows.Forms.Form
    {
        private void cmdLoad_Click(object sender, System.EventArgs e)
        {
            // Clear the tree.
            treeXml.Nodes.Clear();

            // Load the XML document.
            XmlDocument doc = new XmlDocument();
            try
            {
                doc.Load(txtXmlFile.Text);
            }
            catch (Exception err)
            {
                MessageBox.Show(err.Message);
                return;
            }

            // Populate the TreeView.
            ConvertXmlNodeToTreeNode(doc, treeXml.Nodes);

            // Expand all nodes.
            treeXml.Nodes[0].ExpandAll();
        }

        private void ConvertXmlNodeToTreeNode(XmlNode xmlNode,
          TreeNodeCollection treeNodes)
        {
            // Add a TreeNode node that represents this XmlNode.
            TreeNode newTreeNode = treeNodes.Add(xmlNode.Name);

            // Customize the TreeNode text based on the XmlNode
            // type and content.
            switch (xmlNode.NodeType)
            {
                case XmlNodeType.ProcessingInstruction:
                case XmlNodeType.XmlDeclaration:
                    newTreeNode.Text = "<?" + xmlNode.Name + " " +
                      xmlNode.Value + "?>";
                    break;
                case XmlNodeType.Element:
                    newTreeNode.Text = "<" + xmlNode.Name + ">";
                    break;
                case XmlNodeType.Attribute:
                    newTreeNode.Text = "ATTRIBUTE: " + xmlNode.Name;
                    break;
                case XmlNodeType.Text:
                case XmlNodeType.CDATA:
                    newTreeNode.Text = xmlNode.Value;
                    break;
                case XmlNodeType.Comment:
                    newTreeNode.Text = "<!--" + xmlNode.Value + "-->";
                    break;
            }
```

```
                    // Call this routine recursively for each attribute.
                    // (XmlAttribute is a subclass of XmlNode.)
                    if (xmlNode.Attributes != null)
                    {
                        foreach (XmlAttribute attribute in xmlNode.Attributes)
                        {
                            ConvertXmlNodeToTreeNode(attribute, newTreeNode.Nodes);
                        }
                    }

                    // Call this routine recursively for each child node.
                    // Typically, this child node represents a nested element
                    // or element content.
                    foreach (XmlNode childNode in xmlNode.ChildNodes)
                    {
                        ConvertXmlNodeToTreeNode(childNode, newTreeNode.Nodes);
                    }
                }
            }
        }
```

Usage

As an example, consider the following simple XML file (which is included with the sample code as the ProductCatalog.xml file):

```
<?xml version="1.0" ?>
<productCatalog>
    <catalogName>Jones and Jones Unique Catalog 2004</catalogName>
    <expiryDate>2005-01-01</expiryDate>

    <products>
        <product id="1001">
            <productName>Gourmet Coffee</productName>
            <description>The finest beans from rare Chilean
             plantations.</description>
            <productPrice>0.99</productPrice>
            <inStock>true</inStock>
        </product>
        <product id="1002">
            <productName>Blue China Tea Pot</productName>
            <description>A trendy update for tea drinkers.</description>
            <productPrice>102.99</productPrice>
            <inStock>true</inStock>
        </product>
    </products>
</productCatalog>
```

Figure 6-1 shows how this file will be rendered in the Recipe06_01 form.

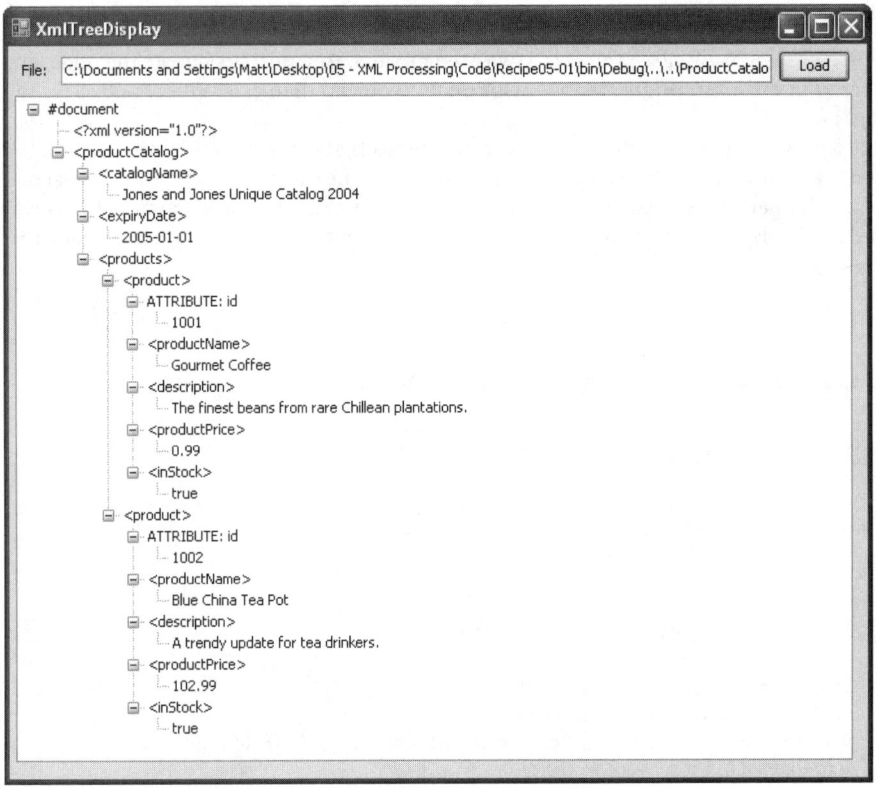

Figure 6-1. *The displayed structure of an XML document*

6-2. Insert Nodes in an XML Document

Problem

You need to modify an XML document by inserting new data, or you want to create an entirely new XML document in memory.

Solution

Create the node using the appropriate XmlDocument method (such as CreateElement, CreateAttribute, CreateNode, and so on). Then insert it using the appropriate XmlNode method (such as InsertAfter, InsertBefore, or AppendChild).

How It Works

Inserting a node into the XmlDocument class is a two-step process. You must first create the node, and then you insert it at the appropriate location. Optionally, you can then call XmlDocument.Save to persist changes.

To create a node, you use one of the XmlDocument methods starting with the word *Create*, depending on the type of node. This ensures the node will have the same namespace as the rest of the document. (Alternatively, you can supply a namespace as an additional string argument.) Next, you must find a suitable related node and use one of its insertion methods to add the new node to the tree.

The Code

The following example demonstrates this technique by programmatically creating a new XML document:

```
using System;
using System.Xml;

namespace Apress.VisualCSharpRecipes.Chapter06
{
    public class Recipe06_02
    {
        private static void Main()
        {
            // Create a new, empty document.
            XmlDocument doc = new XmlDocument();
            XmlNode docNode = doc.CreateXmlDeclaration("1.0", "UTF-8", null);
            doc.AppendChild(docNode);

            // Create and insert a new element.
            XmlNode productsNode = doc.CreateElement("products");
            doc.AppendChild(productsNode);

            // Create a nested element (with an attribute).
            XmlNode productNode = doc.CreateElement("product");
            XmlAttribute productAttribute = doc.CreateAttribute("id");
            productAttribute.Value = "1001";
            productNode.Attributes.Append(productAttribute);
            productsNode.AppendChild(productNode);

            // Create and add the subelements for this product node
            // (with contained text data).
            XmlNode nameNode = doc.CreateElement("productName");
            nameNode.AppendChild(doc.CreateTextNode("Gourmet Coffee"));
            productNode.AppendChild(nameNode);
            XmlNode priceNode = doc.CreateElement("productPrice");
            priceNode.AppendChild(doc.CreateTextNode("0.99"));
            productNode.AppendChild(priceNode);

            // Create and add another product node.
            productNode = doc.CreateElement("product");
            productAttribute = doc.CreateAttribute("id");
            productAttribute.Value = "1002";
            productNode.Attributes.Append(productAttribute);
            productsNode.AppendChild(productNode);
            nameNode = doc.CreateElement("productName");
```

```
            nameNode.AppendChild(doc.CreateTextNode("Blue China Tea Pot"));
            productNode.AppendChild(nameNode);
            priceNode = doc.CreateElement("productPrice");
            priceNode.AppendChild(doc.CreateTextNode("102.99"));
            productNode.AppendChild(priceNode);

            // Save the document (to the console window rather than a file).
            doc.Save(Console.Out);
            Console.ReadLine();
        }
    }
}
```

When you run this code, the generated XML document looks like this:

```
<?xml version="1.0"?>
<products>
  <product id="1001">
    <productName>Gourmet Coffee</productName>
    <productPrice>0.99</productPrice>
  </product>
  <product id="1002">
    <productName>Blue China Tea Pot</productName>
    <productPrice>102.99</productPrice>
  </product>
</products>
```

6-3. Quickly Append Nodes in an XML Document

Problem

You need to add nodes to an XML document without requiring lengthy, verbose code.

Solution

Create a helper function that accepts a tag name and content and can generate the entire element at once. Alternatively, use the XmlDocument.CloneNode method to copy branches of an XmlDocument.

How It Works

Inserting a single element into an XmlDocument requires several lines of code. You can shorten this code in several ways. One approach is to create a dedicated helper class with higher-level methods for adding elements and attributes. For example, you could create an AddElement method that generates a new element, inserts it, and adds any contained text—the three operations needed to insert most elements.

The Code

Here's an example of one such helper class:

```
using System;
using System.Xml;
```

```
namespace Apress.VisualCSharpRecipes.Chapter06
{
    public class XmlHelper
    {
        public static XmlNode AddElement(string tagName,
          string textContent, XmlNode parent)
        {
            XmlNode node = parent.OwnerDocument.CreateElement(tagName);
            parent.AppendChild(node);

            if (textContent != null)
            {
                XmlNode content;
                content = parent.OwnerDocument.CreateTextNode(textContent);
                node.AppendChild(content);
            }
            return node;
        }

        public static XmlNode AddAttribute(string attributeName,
          string textContent, XmlNode parent)
        {
            XmlAttribute attribute;
            attribute = parent.OwnerDocument.CreateAttribute(attributeName);
            attribute.Value = textContent;
            parent.Attributes.Append(attribute);

            return attribute;
        }
    }
}
```

You can now condense the XML-generating code from recipe 6-2 with the simpler syntax shown here:

```
public class Recipe06_03
{
    private static void Main()
    {
        // Create the basic document.
        XmlDocument doc = new XmlDocument();
        XmlNode docNode = doc.CreateXmlDeclaration("1.0", "UTF-8", null);
        doc.AppendChild(docNode);
        XmlNode products = doc.CreateElement("products");
        doc.AppendChild(products);

        // Add two products.
        XmlNode product = XmlHelper.AddElement("product", null, products);
        XmlHelper.AddAttribute("id", "1001", product);
        XmlHelper.AddElement("productName", "Gourmet Coffee", product);
        XmlHelper.AddElement("productPrice", "0.99", product);

        product = XmlHelper.AddElement("product", null, products);
        XmlHelper.AddAttribute("id", "1002", product);
        XmlHelper.AddElement("productName", "Blue China Tea Pot", product);
        XmlHelper.AddElement("productPrice", "102.99", product);
```

```
        // Save the document (to the console window rather than a file).
        doc.Save(Console.Out);
        Console.ReadLine();
    }
}
```

Alternatively, you might want to take the helper methods such as `AddAttribute` and `AddElement` and make them instance methods in a custom class you derive from `XmlDocument`.

Another approach to simplifying writing XML is to duplicate nodes using the `XmlNode.CloneNode` method. `CloneNode` accepts a Boolean `deep` parameter. If you supply `true`, `CloneNode` will duplicate the entire branch, with all nested nodes.

Here is an example that creates a new product node by copying the first node:

```
// (Add first product node.)

// Create a new element based on an existing product.
product = product.CloneNode(true);

// Modify the node data.
product.Attributes[0].Value = "1002";
product.ChildNodes[0].ChildNodes[0].Value = "Blue China Tea Pot";
product.ChildNodes[1].ChildNodes[0].Value = "102.99";

// Add the new element.
products.AppendChild(product);
```

Notice that in this case, certain assumptions are being made about the existing nodes (for example, that the first child in the item node is always the name, and the second child is always the price). If this assumption is not guaranteed to be true, you might need to examine the node name programmatically.

6-4. Find Specific Elements by Name

Problem

You need to retrieve a specific node from an `XmlDocument`, and you know its name but not its position.

Solution

Use the `XmlDocument.GetElementsByTagName` method, which searches an entire document and returns a `System.Xml.XmlNodeList` containing any matches.

How It Works

The `XmlDocument` class provides a convenient `GetElementsByTagName` method that searches an entire document for nodes that have the indicated element name. It returns the results as a collection of `XmlNode` objects.

The Code

The following code demonstrates how you could use `GetElementsByTagName` to calculate the total price of items in a catalog by retrieving all elements with the name `productPrice`:

```
using System;
using System.Xml;
```

```
namespace Apress.VisualCSharpRecipes.Chapter06
{
    public class Recipe06_04
    {
        private static void Main()
        {
            // Load the document.
            XmlDocument doc = new XmlDocument();
            doc.Load("ProductCatalog.xml");

            // Retrieve all prices.
            XmlNodeList prices = doc.GetElementsByTagName("productPrice");

            decimal totalPrice = 0;
            foreach (XmlNode price in prices)
            {
                // Get the inner text of each matching element.
                totalPrice += Decimal.Parse(price.ChildNodes[0].Value);
            }

            Console.WriteLine("Total catalog value: " + totalPrice.ToString());
            Console.ReadLine();
        }
    }
}
```

Notes

You can also search portions of an XML document by using the XmlElement.GetElementsByTagName method. It searches all the descendant nodes looking for matches. To use this method, first retrieve an XmlNode that corresponds to an element. Then cast this object to an XmlElement. The following example demonstrates how to find the price node under the first product element:

```
// Retrieve a reference to the first product.
XmlNode product = doc.GetElementsByTagName("products")[0];

// Find the price under this product.
XmlNode price = ((XmlElement)product).GetElementsByTagName("productPrice")[0];
Console.WriteLine("Price is " + price.InnerText);
```

If your elements include an attribute of type ID, you can also use a method called GetElementById to retrieve an element that has a matching ID value.

6-5. Get XML Nodes in a Specific XML Namespace

Problem

You need to retrieve nodes from a specific namespace using an XmlDocument.

Solution

Use the overload of the XmlDocument.GetElementsByTagName method that requires a namespace name as a string argument. Additionally, supply an asterisk (*) for the element name if you want to match all tags.

How It Works

Many XML documents contain nodes from more than one namespace. For example, an XML document that represents a scientific article might use a separate type of markup for denoting math equations and vector diagrams, or an XML document with information about a purchase order might aggregate client and order information with a shipping record. Similarly, an XML document that represents a business-to-business transaction might include portions from both companies, written in separate markup languages.

A common task in XML programming is to retrieve the elements found in a specific namespace. You can perform this task with the overloaded version of the `XmlDocument.GetElementsByTagName` method that requires a namespace name. You can use this method to find tags by name or to find all the tags in the specified namespace if you supply an asterisk for the tag `name` parameter.

The Code

As an example, consider the following compound XML document that includes order and client information, in two different namespaces (`http://mycompany/OrderML` and `http://mycompany/ClientML`):

```xml
<?xml version="1.0" ?>
<ord:order xmlns:ord="http://mycompany/OrderML"
 xmlns:cli="http://mycompany/ClientML">

  <cli:client>
    <cli:firstName>Sally</cli:firstName>
    <cli:lastName>Sergeyeva</cli:lastName>
  </cli:client>

  <ord:orderItem itemNumber="3211"/>
  <ord:orderItem itemNumber="1155"/>

</ord:order>
```

Here is a simple console application that selects all the tags in the `http://mycompany/OrderML` namespace:

```csharp
using System;
using System.Xml;

namespace Apress.VisualCSharpRecipes.Chapter06
{
    public class Recipe06_05
    {
        private static void Main()
        {
            // Load the document.
            XmlDocument doc = new XmlDocument();
            doc.Load("Order.xml");

            // Retrieve all order tags.
            XmlNodeList matches = doc.GetElementsByTagName("*",
              "http://mycompany/OrderML");

            // Display all the information.
            Console.WriteLine("Element \tAttributes");
            Console.WriteLine("******* \t**********");

            foreach (XmlNode node in matches)
```

```
        {
            Console.Write(node.Name + "\t");
            foreach (XmlAttribute attribute in node.Attributes)
            {
                Console.Write(attribute.Value + "  ");
            }
            Console.WriteLine();
        }
        Console.ReadLine();
    }
  }
}
```

The output of this program is as follows:

```
Element       Attributes
*******       **********
ord:order     http://mycompany/OrderML  http://mycompany/ClientML
ord:orderItem 3211
ord:orderItem 1155
```

6-6. Find Elements with an XPath Search

Problem

You need to search an XML document for nodes using advanced search criteria. For example, you might want to search a particular branch of an XML document for nodes that have certain attributes or contain a specific number of nested child nodes.

Solution

Execute an XPath expression using the SelectNodes or SelectSingleNode method of the XmlDocument class.

How It Works

The XmlNode class defines two methods that perform XPath searches: SelectNodes and SelectSingleNode. These methods operate on all contained child nodes. Because the XmlDocument inherits from XmlNode, you can call XmlDocument.SelectNodes to search an entire document.

The Code

For example, consider the following XML document, which represents an order for two items. This document includes text and numeric data, nested elements, and attributes, and so is a good way to test simple XPath expressions.

```xml
<?xml version="1.0"?>
<Order id="2004-01-30.195496">
  <Client id="ROS-930252034">
    <Name>Remarkable Office Supplies</Name>
  </Client>

  <Items>
    <Item id="1001">
      <Name>Electronic Protractor</Name>
      <Price>42.99</Price>
```

```
    </Item>
    <Item id="1002">
      <Name>Invisible Ink</Name>
      <Price>200.25</Price>
    </Item>
  </Items>
</Order>
```

Basic XPath syntax uses a pathlike notation. For example, the path /Order/Items/Item indicates an <Item> element that is nested inside an <Items> element, which, in turn, is nested in a root <Order> element. This is an absolute path. The following example uses an XPath absolute path to find the name of every item in an order:

```
using System;
using System.Xml;

namespace Apress.VisualCSharpRecipes.Chapter06
{
    public class Recipe06_06
    {
        private static void Main()
        {
            // Load the document.
            XmlDocument doc = new XmlDocument();
            doc.Load("orders.xml");

            // Retrieve the name of every item.
            // This could not be accomplished as easily with the
            // GetElementsByTagName method, because Name elements are
            // used in Item elements and Client elements, and so
            // both types would be returned.
            XmlNodeList nodes = doc.SelectNodes("/Order/Items/Item/Name");

            foreach (XmlNode node in nodes)
            {
                Console.WriteLine(node.InnerText);
            }
            Console.ReadLine();
        }
    }
}
```

The output of this program is as follows:

```
Electronic Protractor
Invisible Ink
```

Notes

XPath provides a rich and powerful search syntax, and it is impossible to explain all the variations you can use in a short recipe. However, Table 6-1 outlines some of the key ingredients in more advanced XPath expressions and includes examples that show how they would work with the order document. For a more detailed reference, refer to the W3C XPath recommendation at http://www.w3.org/TR/xpath.

Table 6-1. XPath *Expression Syntax*

Expression	Description	Example
/	Starts an absolute path that selects from the root node.	/Order/Items/Item selects all Item elements that are children of an Items element, which is itself a child of the root Order element.
//	Starts a relative path that selects nodes anywhere.	//Item/Name selects all the Name elements that are children of an Item element, regardless of where they appear in the document.
@	Selects an attribute of a node.	/Order/@id selects the attribute named id from the root Order element.
*	Selects any element in the path.	/Order/* selects both Items and Client nodes because both are contained by a root Order element.
|	Combines multiple paths.	/Order/Items/Item/Name|Order/Client/Name selects the Name nodes used to describe a Client and the Name nodes used to describe an Item.
.	Indicates the current (default) node.	If the current node is an Order, the expression ./Items refers to the related items for that order.
..	Indicates the parent node.	//Name/.. selects any element that is parent to a Name, which includes the Client and Item elements.
[ ]	Defines selection criteria that can test a contained node or an attribute value.	/Order[@id="2004-01-30.195496"] selects the Order elements with the indicated attribute value. /Order/Items/Item[Price > 50] selects products higher than $50 in price. /Order/Items/Item[Price > 50 and Name="Laser Printer"] selects products that match two criteria.
starts-with	Retrieves elements based on what text a contained element starts with.	/Order/Items/Item[starts-with (Name, "C")] finds all Item elements that have a Name element that starts with the letter *C*.
position	Retrieves elements based on position.	/Order/Items/Item[position ()=2] selects the second Item element.
count	Counts elements. You specify the name of the child element to count or an asterisk (*) for all children.	/Order/Items/Item[count(Price) = 1] retrieves Item elements that have exactly one nested Price element.

■**Note** XPath expressions and all element and attribute names you use inside them are always case-sensitive, because XML itself is case-sensitive.

6-7. Read and Write XML Without Loading an Entire Document into Memory

Problem

You need to read XML from a stream or write it to a stream. However, you want to process the information one node at a time, rather than loading it all into memory with an XmlDocument.

Solution

To write XML, create an XmlWriter that wraps a stream and use Write methods (such as WriteStartElement and WriteEndElement). To read XML, create an XmlReader that wraps a stream, and call Read to move from node to node.

How It Works

The XmlWriter and XmlReader classes read or write XML directly from a stream one node at a time. These classes do not provide the same features for navigating and manipulating your XML as XmlDocument, but they do provide higher performance and a smaller memory footprint, particularly if you need to deal with large XML documents.

Both the XmlWriter and XmlReader are abstract classes, which means you cannot create an instance of them directly. Instead, you need to create an instance of a derived class, such as XmlTextWriter. In .NET 2.0, the preferred convention is *not* to create a derived class directly. Instead, you should call the Create method of the XmlWriter or XmlReader and supply a file or stream. The Create method will return the right derived class based on the options you specify. This allows for a more flexible model. Because your code uses the base classes, it can work seamlessly with any derived class. For example, you could switch to a validating reader (as shown in the next recipe) without needing to modify your code.

To write XML to any stream, you can use the streamlined XmlWriter. It provides Write methods that write one node at a time. These include the following:

- WriteStartDocument, which writes the document prologue, and WriteEndDocument, which closes any open elements at the end of the document.

- WriteStartElement, which writes an opening tag for the element you specify. You can then add more elements nested inside this element, or you can call WriteEndElement to write the closing tag.

- WriteElementString, which writes an entire element, with an opening tag, a closing tag, and text content.

- WriteAttributeString, which writes an entire attribute for the nearest open element, with a name and value.

Using these methods usually requires less code than creating an XmlDocument by hand, as demonstrated in recipes 6-2 and 6-3.

To read the XML, you use the Read method of the XmlReader. This method advances the reader to the next node and returns true. If no more nodes can be found, it returns false. You can retrieve information about the current node through XmlReader properties, including its Name, Value, and NodeType.

To find out whether an element has attributes, you must explicitly test the HasAttributes property and then use the GetAttribute method to retrieve the attributes by name or index number. The XmlTextReader class can access only one node at a time, and it cannot move backward or jump to an arbitrary node, which gives much less flexibility than the XmlDocument class.

The Code

The following console application writes and reads a simple XML document using the XmlWriter and XmlReader classes. This is the same XML document created in recipes 6-2 and 6-3 using the XmlDocument class.

```
using System;
using System.Xml;
using System.IO;
using System.Text;

namespace Apress.VisualCSharpRecipes.Chapter06
{
    public class Recipe06_07
    {
        private static void Main()
        {
            // Create the file and writer.
            FileStream fs = new FileStream("products.xml", FileMode.Create);

            // If you want to configure additional details (like indenting,
            // encoding, and new line handling), use the overload of the Create
            // method that accepts an XmlWriterSettings object instead.
            XmlWriter w = XmlWriter.Create(fs);

            // Start the document.
            w.WriteStartDocument();
            w.WriteStartElement("products");

            // Write a product.
            w.WriteStartElement("product");
            w.WriteAttributeString("id", "1001");
            w.WriteElementString("productName", "Gourmet Coffee");
            w.WriteElementString("productPrice", "0.99");
            w.WriteEndElement();

            // Write another product.
            w.WriteStartElement("product");
            w.WriteAttributeString("id", "1002");
            w.WriteElementString("productName", "Blue China Tea Pot");
            w.WriteElementString("productPrice", "102.99");
            w.WriteEndElement();

            // End the document.
            w.WriteEndElement();
            w.WriteEndDocument();
            w.Flush();
            fs.Close();

            Console.WriteLine("Document created. " +
              "Press Enter to read the document.");
            Console.ReadLine();
```

```
        fs = new FileStream("products.xml", FileMode.Open);

        // If you want to configure additional details (like comments,
        // whitespace handling, or validation), use the overload of the Create
        // method that accepts an XmlReaderSettings object instead.
        XmlReader r = XmlReader.Create(fs);

        // Read all nodes.
        while (r.Read())
        {
            if (r.NodeType == XmlNodeType.Element)
            {
                Console.WriteLine();
                Console.WriteLine("<" + r.Name + ">");

                if (r.HasAttributes)
                {
                    for (int i = 0; i < r.AttributeCount; i++)
                    {
                        Console.WriteLine("\tATTRIBUTE: " +
                            r.GetAttribute(i));
                    }
                }
            }
            else if (r.NodeType == XmlNodeType.Text)
            {
                Console.WriteLine("\tVALUE: " + r.Value);
            }
        }
        Console.ReadLine();
    }
  }
}
```

Often, when using the XmlReader, you are searching for specific nodes, rather than processing every element as in this example. The approach used in this example does not work as well in this situation. It forces you to read element tags, text content, and CDATA sections separately, which means you need to explicitly keep track of where you are in the document. A better approach is to read the entire node and text content at once (for simple text-only nodes) by using the ReadElementString method. You can also use methods such as ReadToDescendant, ReadToFollowing, and ReadToNextSibling, all of which allow you to skip some nodes.

For example, you can use ReadToFollowing("Price"); to skip straight to the next Price element, without worrying about whitespace, comments, or other elements before it. (If a Price element cannot be found, the XmlReader moves to the end of the document, and the ReadToFollowing method returns false.)

6-8. Validate an XML Document Against a Schema

Problem

You need to validate the content of an XML document by ensuring that it conforms to an XML schema.

Solution

When you call XmlReader.Create, supply an XmlReaderSettings object that indicates you want to perform validation. Then, move through the document one node at a time by calling XmlReader.Read, catching any validation exceptions. To find all the errors in a document without catching exceptions, handle the ValidationEventHandler event on the XmlReaderSettings object given as parameter to XmlReader.

How It Works

An XML schema defines the rules that a given type of XML document must follow. The schema includes rules that define the following:

- The elements and attributes that can appear in a document
- The data types for elements and attributes
- The structure of a document, including what elements are children of other elements
- The order and number of child elements that appear in a document
- Whether elements are empty, can include text, or require fixed values

XML schema documents are beyond the scope of this chapter, but you can learn much from a simple example. This recipe uses the product catalog first presented in recipe 6-1.

At its most basic level, XML Schema Definition (XSD) defines the elements that can occur in an XML document. XSD documents are themselves written in XML, and you use a separate predefined element (named <element>) in the XSD document to indicate each element that is required in the target document. The type attribute indicates the data type. Here is an example for a product name:

```
<xsd:element name="productName" type="xsd:string" />
```

And here is an example for the product price:

```
<xsd:element name="productPrice" type="xsd:decimal" />
```

The basic schema data types are defined at http://www.w3.org/TR/xmlschema-2. They map closely to .NET data types and include string, int, long, decimal, float, dateTime, boolean, and base64Binary—to name a few of the most frequently used types.

Both the productName and productPrice are *simple types* because they contain only character data. Elements that contain nested elements are called *complex types*. You can nest them together using a <sequence> tag, if order is important, or an <all> tag if it is not. Here is how you might model the <product> element in the product catalog. Notice that attributes are always declared after elements, and they are not grouped with a <sequence> or <all> tag because order is never important:

```
<xsd:complexType name="product">
  <xsd:sequence>
    <xsd:element name="productName" type="xsd:string"/>
    <xsd:element name="productPrice" type="xsd:decimal"/>
    <xsd:element name="inStock" type="xsd:boolean"/>
  </xsd:sequence>
  <xsd:attribute name="id" type="xsd:integer"/>
</xsd:complexType>
```

By default, a listed element can occur exactly one time in a document. You can configure this behavior by specifying the maxOccurs and minOccurs attributes. Here is an example that allows an unlimited number of products in the catalog:

```
<xsd:element name="product" type="product" maxOccurs="unbounded" />
```

Here is the complete schema for the product catalog XML:

```
<?xml version="1.0"?>
<xsd:schema xmlns:xsd="http://www.w3.org/2001/XMLSchema">

    <!-- Define the complex type product. -->
    <xsd:complexType name="product">
        <xsd:sequence>
            <xsd:element name="productName" type="xsd:string"/>
            <xsd:element name="productPrice" type="xsd:decimal"/>
            <xsd:element name="inStock" type="xsd:boolean"/>
        </xsd:sequence>
        <xsd:attribute name="id" type="xsd:integer"/>
    </xsd:complexType>

    <!-- This is the structure the document must match.
        It begins with a productCatalog element that nests other elements. -->
    <xsd:element name="productCatalog">
        <xsd:complexType>
            <xsd:sequence>
                <xsd:element name="catalogName" type="xsd:string"/>
                <xsd:element name="expiryDate" type="xsd:date"/>

                <xsd:element name="products">
                    <xsd:complexType>
                        <xsd:sequence>
                            <xsd:element name="product" type="product"
                            maxOccurs="unbounded" />
                        </xsd:sequence>
                    </xsd:complexType>
                </xsd:element>
            </xsd:sequence>
        </xsd:complexType>
    </xsd:element>

</xsd:schema>
```

The XmlReader class can enforce these schema rules, providing you explicitly request a validating reader when you use the XmlReader.Create method. (Even if you do not use a validating reader, an exception will be thrown if the reader discovers XML that is not *well formed*, such as an illegal character, improperly nested tags, and so on.)

Once you have created your validating reader, the validation occurs automatically as you read through the document. As soon as an error is found, the XmlReader raises a ValidationEventHandler event with information about the error on the XmlReaderSettings object given at creation time. If you want, you can handle this event and continue processing the document to find more errors. If you do not handle this event, an XmlException will be raised when the first error is encountered and processing will be aborted.

The Code

The next example shows a utility class that displays all errors in an XML document when the ValidateXml method is called. Errors are displayed in a console window, and a final Boolean variable is returned to indicate the success or failure of the entire validation operation.

```
using System;
using System.Xml;
using System.Xml.Schema;
```

```csharp
namespace Apress.VisualCSharpRecipes.Chapter06
{
    public class ConsoleValidator
    {
        // Set to true if at least one error exists.
        private bool failed;

        public bool Failed
        {
            get {return failed;}
        }

        public bool ValidateXml(string xmlFilename, string schemaFilename)
        {
            // Set the type of validation.
            XmlReaderSettings settings = new XmlReaderSettings();
            settings.ValidationType = ValidationType.Schema;

            // Load the schema file.
            XmlSchemaSet schemas = new XmlSchemaSet();
            settings.Schemas = schemas;
            // When loading the schema, specify the namespace it validates
            // and the location of the file. Use null to use
            // the targetNamespace value from the schema.
            schemas.Add(null, schemaFilename);

            // Specify an event handler for validation errors.
            settings.ValidationEventHandler += ValidationEventHandler;

            // Create the validating reader.
            XmlReader validator = XmlReader.Create(xmlFilename, settings);

            failed = false;
            try
            {
                // Read all XML data.
                while (validator.Read()) {}
            }
            catch (XmlException err)
            {
                // This happens if the XML document includes illegal characters
                // or tags that aren't properly nested or closed.
                Console.WriteLine("A critical XML error has occurred.");
                Console.WriteLine(err.Message);
                failed = true;
            }
            finally
            {
                validator.Close();
            }

            return !failed;
        }

        private void ValidationEventHandler(object sender,
          ValidationEventArgs args)
```

```
        {
            failed = true;

            // Display the validation error.
            Console.WriteLine("Validation error: " + args.Message);
            Console.WriteLine();
        }
    }
}
```

Here is how you would use the class to validate the product catalog:

```
public class Recipe06_08
{
    private static void Main()
    {
        ConsoleValidator consoleValidator = new ConsoleValidator();
        Console.WriteLine("Validating ProductCatalog.xml.");

        bool success = consoleValidator.ValidateXml("ProductCatalog.xml",
            "ProductCatalog.xsd");
        if (!success)
            Console.WriteLine("Validation failed.");
        else
            Console.WriteLine("Validation succeeded.");

        Console.ReadLine();
    }
}
```

If the document is valid, no messages will appear, and the success variable will be set to true. But consider what happens if you use a document that breaks schema rules, such as the ProductCatalog_Invalid.xml file shown here:

```
<?xml version="1.0" ?>
<productCatalog>
    <catalogName>Acme Fall 2003 Catalog</catalogName>
    <expiryDate>Jan 1, 2004</expiryDate>

    <products>
        <product id="1001">
            <productName>Magic Ring</productName>
            <productPrice>$342.10</productPrice>
            <inStock>true</inStock>
        </product>
        <product id="1002">
            <productName>Flying Carpet</productName>
            <productPrice>982.99</productPrice>
            <inStock>Yes</inStock>
        </product>
    </products>
</productCatalog>
```

If you attempt to validate this document, the success variable will be set to false, and the output will indicate each error:

```
Validating ProductCatalog_Invalid.xml.

Validation error: The 'expiryDate' element has an invalid value according to
  its data type. [path information truncated]

Validation error: The 'productPrice' element has an invalid value according to
  its data type. [path information truncated]

Validation error: The 'inStock' element has an invalid value according to its
  data type. [path information truncated]

Validation failed.
```

Finally, if you want to validate an XML document and load it into an in-memory XmlDocument, you need to take a slightly different approach. The XmlDocument provides its own Schemas property, along with a Validate method that checks the entire document in one step. When you call Validate, you supply a delegate that points to your validation event handler.

Here is how it works:

```
XmlDocument doc = new XmlDocument();
doc.Load("Product_Catalog.xml");

// Specify the schema information.
XmlSchemaSet schemas = new XmlSchemaSet();
schemas.Add(null, schemaFilename);
doc.Schemas = schemas;

// Validate the document.
doc.Validate(new ValidationEventHandler(ValidationEventHandler));
```

6-9. Use XML Serialization with Custom Objects

Problem

You need to use XML as a serialization format. However, you don't want to process the XML directly in your code—instead, you want to interact with the data using custom objects.

Solution

Use the System.Xml.Serialization.XmlSerializer class to transfer data from your object to XML, and vice versa. You can also mark up your class code with attributes to customize its XML representation.

How It Works

The XmlSerializer class allows you to convert objects to XML data, and vice versa. This process is used natively by Web services and provides a customizable serialization mechanism that does not require a single line of custom code. The XmlSerializer class is even intelligent enough to correctly create arrays when it finds nested elements.

The only requirements for using XmlSerializer are as follows:

- The XmlSerializer serializes only properties and public variables.

- The classes you want to serialize must include a default zero-argument constructor. The XmlSerializer uses this constructor when creating the new object during deserialization.

- All class properties must be readable *and* writable. This is because XmlSerializer uses the property get accessor to retrieve information and the property set accessor to restore the data after deserialization.

■**Note** You can also store your objects in an XML-based format using .NET serialization and System.Runtime.Serialization.Formatters.Soap.SoapFormatter. In this case, you simply need to make your class serializable—you do not need to provide a default constructor or ensure all properties are writable. However, this gives you no control over the format of the serialized XML.

To use XML serialization, you must first mark up your data objects with attributes that indicate the desired XML mapping. You can find these attributes in the System.Xml.Serialization namespace and include the following:

- XmlRoot specifies the name of the root element of the XML file. By default, XmlSerializer will use the name of the class. You can apply this attribute to the class declaration.

- XmlElement indicates the element name to use for a property or public variable. By default, XmlSerializer will use the name of the property or public variable.

- XmlAttribute indicates that a property or public variable should be serialized as an attribute, not an element, and specifies the attribute name.

- XmlEnum configures the text that should be used when serializing enumerated values. If you don't use XmlEnum, the name of the enumerated constant will be used.

- XmlIgnore indicates that a property or public variable should not be serialized.

The Code

For example, consider the product catalog first shown in recipe 6-1. You can represent this XML document using ProductCatalog and Product objects. Here's the class code that you might use:

```
using System;
using System.Xml.Serialization;

namespace Apress.VisualCSharpRecipes.Chapter06
{
    [XmlRoot("productCatalog")]
    public class ProductCatalog
    {
        [XmlElement("catalogName")]
        public string CatalogName;

        // Use the date data type (and ignore the time portion in the
        // serialized XML).
        [XmlElement(ElementName="expiryDate", DataType="date")]
        public DateTime ExpiryDate;

        // Configure the name of the tag that holds all products
        // and the name of the product tag itself.
        [XmlArray("products")]
```

```
            [XmlArrayItem("product")]
            public Product[] Products;

            public ProductCatalog()
            {
                // Default constructor for deserialization.
            }

            public ProductCatalog(string catalogName, DateTime expiryDate)
            {
                this.CatalogName = catalogName;
                this.ExpiryDate = expiryDate;
            }
        }

        public class Product
        {
            [XmlElement("productName")]
            public string ProductName;

            [XmlElement("productPrice")]
            public decimal ProductPrice;

            [XmlElement("inStock")]
            public bool InStock;

            [XmlAttributeAttribute(AttributeName="id", DataType="integer")]
            public string Id;

            public Product()
            {
                // Default constructor for serialization.
            }

            public Product(string productName, decimal productPrice)
            {
                this.ProductName = productName;
                this.ProductPrice = productPrice;
            }
        }
    }
```

Notice that these classes use the XML serialization attributes to rename element names (using Pascal casing in the class member names and camel casing in the XML tag names), indicate data types that are not obvious, and specify how <product> elements will be nested in the <productCatalog>.

Using these custom classes and the XmlSerializer object, you can translate XML into objects, and vice versa. The following is the code you would need to create a new ProductCatalog object, serialize the results to an XML document, deserialize the document back to an object, and then display the XML document:

```
using System;
using System.Xml;
using System.Xml.Serialization;
using System.IO;

namespace Apress.VisualCSharpRecipes.Chapter06
{
```

```
public class Recipe06_09
{
    private static void Main()
    {
        // Create the product catalog.
        ProductCatalog catalog = new ProductCatalog("New Catalog",
          DateTime.Now.AddYears(1));
        Product[] products = new Product[2];
        products[0] = new Product("Product 1", 42.99m);
        products[1] = new Product("Product 2", 202.99m);
        catalog.Products = products;

        // Serialize the order to a file.
        XmlSerializer serializer = new XmlSerializer(typeof(ProductCatalog));
        FileStream fs = new FileStream("ProductCatalog.xml", FileMode.Create);
        serializer.Serialize(fs, catalog);
        fs.Close();

        catalog = null;

        // Deserialize the order from the file.
        fs = new FileStream("ProductCatalog.xml", FileMode.Open);
        catalog = (ProductCatalog)serializer.Deserialize(fs);

        // Serialize the order to the console window.
        serializer.Serialize(Console.Out, catalog);
        Console.ReadLine();
    }
}
}
```

6-10. Create a Schema for a .NET Class

Problem

You need to create an XML schema based on one or more C# classes. This will allow you to validate XML documents before deserializing them with the XmlSerializer.

Solution

Use the XML Schema Definition Tool (xsd.exe) command-line utility included with the .NET Framework. Specify the name of your assembly as a command-line argument, and add the /t:[TypeName] parameter to indicate the types you want to convert.

How It Works

Recipe 6-9 demonstrated how to use the XmlSerializer to serialize .NET objects to XML and deserialize XML into .NET objects. But if you want to use XML as a way to interact with other applications, business processes, or non–.NET Framework applications, you'll need an easy way to validate the XML before you attempt to deserialize it. You will also need to define an XML schema document that defines the structure and data types used in your XML format so that other applications can work with it. One quick solution is to generate an XML schema using the xsd.exe command-line utility.

The xsd.exe utility is included with the .NET Framework. If you have installed Microsoft Visual Studio .NET, you will find it in a directory like C:\Program Files\Microsoft Visual Studio .NET\ FrameworkSDK\Bin. The xsd.exe utility can generate schema documents from compiled assemblies. You simply need to supply the filename and indicate the class that represents the XML document with the / t:[TypeName] parameter.

Usage

For example, consider the `ProductCatalog` and `Product` classes shown in recipe 6-9. You could create the XML schema for a product catalog with the following command line:

```
xsd Recipe6-09.exe /t:ProductCatalog
```

You need to specify only the `ProductCatalog` class on the command line because this class represents the actual XML document. The generated schema in this example will represent a complete product catalog, with contained product items. It will be given the default filename schema0.xsd. You can now use the validation technique shown in recipe 6-8 to test whether the XML document can be successfully validated with the schema.

6-11. Generate a Class from a Schema

Problem

You need to create one or more C# classes based on an XML schema. You can then create an XML document in the appropriate format using these objects and the `XmlSerializer`.

Solution

Use the xsd.exe command-line utility included with the .NET Framework. Specify the name of your schema file as a command-line argument, and add the /c parameter to indicate you want to generate class code.

How It Works

Recipe 6-10 introduced the xsd.exe command-line utility, which you can use to generate schemas based on class definitions. The reverse operation—generating C# source code based on an XML schema document—is also possible. This is primarily useful if you want to write a certain format of XML document but you do not want to manually create the document by writing individual nodes with the `XmlDocument` class or the `XmlWriter` class. Instead, by using xsd.exe, you can generate a set of full .NET objects. You can then serialize these objects to the required XML representation using the `XmlSerializer`, as described in recipe 6-9.

To generate source code from a schema, you simply need to supply the filename of the schema document and add the /c parameter to indicate you want to generate the required classes.

Usage

For example, consider the schema shown in recipe 6-8. You can generate C# code for this schema with the following command line:

```
xsd ProductCatalog.xsd /c
```

This will generate one file (ProductCatalog.cs) with two classes: `Product` and `ProductCalalog`. These classes are similar to the ones created in recipe 6-9, except that the class member names match the XML document exactly. Optionally, you can add the `/f` parameter. If you do, the generated classes will be composed of public fields. If you do not, the generated classes will use public properties instead (which simply wrap private fields).

6-12. Perform an XSL Transform

Problem

You need to transform an XML document into another document using an XSLT stylesheet.

Solution

Use the `System.Xml.Xsl.XslCompiledTransform` class. Load the XSLT stylesheet using the `XslCompiledTransform.Load` method, and generate the output document by using the `Transform` method and supplying a source document.

How It Works

XSLT (or XSL transforms) is an XML-based language designed to transform one XML document into another document. You can use XSLT to create a new XML document with the same data but arranged in a different structure or to select a subset of the data in a document. You can also use it to create a different type of structured document. XSLT is commonly used in this manner to format an XML document into an HTML page.

The Code

XSLT is a rich language, and creating XSL transforms is beyond the scope of this book. However, you can learn how to create simple XSLT documents by looking at a basic example. This recipe transforms the orders.xml document shown in recipe 6-6 into an HTML document with a table and then displays the results. To perform this transformation, you'll need the following XSLT stylesheet:

```
<?xml version="1.0" encoding="UTF-8" ?>
<xsl:stylesheet xmlns:xsl="http://www.w3.org/1999/XSL/Transform"
    version="1.0" >

  <xsl:template match="Order">
    <html><body><p>
    Order <b><xsl:value-of select="Client/@id"/></b>
    for <xsl:value-of select="Client/Name"/></p>
    <table border="1">
    <td>ID</td><td>Name</td><td>Price</td>
    <xsl:apply-templates select="Items/Item"/>
    </table></body></html>
  </xsl:template>

  <xsl:template match="Items/Item">
    <tr>
    <td><xsl:value-of select="@id"/></td>
    <td><xsl:value-of select="Name"/></td>
```

```
      <td><xsl:value-of select="Price"/></td>
      </tr>
    </xsl:template>

</xsl:stylesheet>
```

Essentially, every XSL stylesheet consists of a set of templates. Each template matches some set of elements in the source document and then describes the contribution that the matched element will make to the resulting document. To match the template, the XSLT document uses XPath expressions, as described in recipe 6-6.

The orders.xslt stylesheet contains two template elements (as children of the root stylesheet element). The first template matches the root Order element. When the XSLT processor finds an Order element, it outputs the tags necessary to start an HTML table with appropriate column headings and inserts some data about the client using the value-of command, which outputs the text result of an XPath expression. In this case, the XPath expressions (Client/@id and Client/Name) match the id attribute and the Name element.

Next the apply-templates command branches off and performs processing of any contained Item elements. This is required because there might be multiple Item elements. Each Item element is matched using the XPath expression Items/Item. The root Order node is not specified because Order is the current node. Finally, the initial template writes the tags necessary to end the HTML document.

If you execute this transform on the sample orders.xml file shown in recipe 6-6, you will end up with the following HTML document:

```
<html>
  <body>
    <p>
    Order <b>ROS-930252034</b>
    for Remarkable Office Supplies</p>
    <table border="1">
      <td>ID</td>
      <td>Name</td>
      <td>Price</td>
      <tr>
        <td>1001</td>
        <td>Electronic Protractor</td>
        <td>42.99</td>
      </tr>
      <tr>
        <td>1002</td>
        <td>Invisible Ink</td>
        <td>200.25</td>
      </tr>
    </table>
  </body>
</html>
```

To apply an XSLT stylesheet in .NET, you use the XslCompiledTransform class. (Do not confuse this class with the similar XslTransform class—it still works but is deprecated in .NET 2.0.)

The following code shows a Windows-based application that programmatically applies the transformation and then displays the transformed file in a window using the WebBrowser control:

```
using System;
using System.Windows.Forms;
using System.Xml.Xsl;
```

```
namespace Apress.VisualCSharpRecipes.Chapter06
{
    public partial class Recipe06_12 : System.Windows.Forms.Form
    {
        private void TransformXml_Load(object sender, System.EventArgs e)
        {
            XslCompiledTransform transform = new XslCompiledTransform();

            // Load the XSL stylesheet.
            transform.Load("orders.xslt");

            // Transform orders.xml into orders.html using orders.xslt.
            transform.Transform("orders.xml", "orders.html");

            webBrowser.Navigate(Application.StartupPath + @"\orders.html");
        }
    }
}
```

Figure 6-2 shows the application.

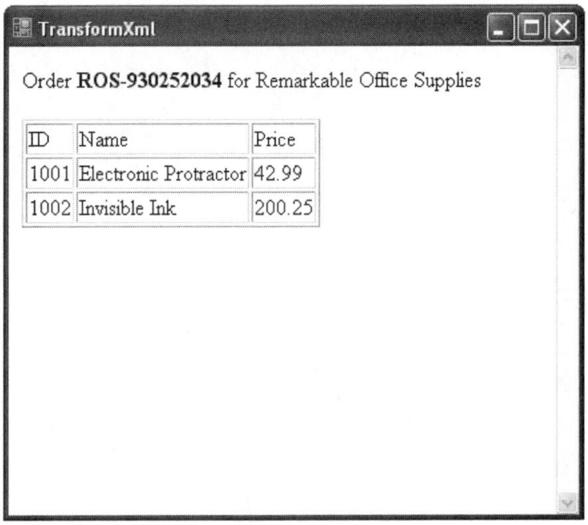

Figure 6-2. *The stylesheet output for orders.xml*

In this example, the code uses the overloaded version of the Transform method that saves the result document directly to disk, although you could receive it as a stream and process it inside your application instead. The following code shows an alternate approach that keeps the document content in memory at all times (with no external results file). The XslCompiledTransform writes the results to an XmlWriter that wraps a StringBuilder. The content is then copied from the StringBuilder into the WebBrowser through the handy WebBrowser.DocumentText property. The results are identical.

```
StringBuilder htmlContent = new StringBuilder();
XmlWriter results = XmlWriter.Create(htmlContent);
transform.Transform("orders.xml", results);
webBrowser1.DocumentText = htmlContent.ToString();
```

CHAPTER 7

Windows Forms

The Microsoft .NET Framework includes a rich set of classes for creating traditional Windows-based applications in the `System.Windows.Forms` namespace. These range from basic controls such as the `TextBox`, `Button`, and `MainMenu` classes to specialized controls such as `TreeView`, `LinkLabel`, and `NotifyIcon`. In addition, you will find all the tools you need to manage Multiple Document Interface (MDI) applications, integrate context-sensitive help, and even create multilingual user interfaces—all without needing to resort to the complexities of the Win32 API.

Most C# developers quickly find themselves at home with the Windows Forms programming model. This chapter offers a number of tips and timesaving techniques that can make your Windows programming endeavors even more productive.

■**Note** Most of the recipes in this chapter use control classes, which are defined in the `System.Windows.Forms` namespace. When introducing these classes, the full namespace name is not indicated, and `System.Windows.Forms` is assumed.

The recipes in this chapter describe how to do the following:

- Add controls to a form programmatically at runtime so that you can build forms dynamically instead of only building static forms in the Visual Studio forms designer (recipe 7-1)

- Link arbitrary data objects to controls to provide an easy way to associate data with a control without the need to maintain additional data structures (recipe 7-2)

- Process all the controls on a form in a generic way (recipe 7-3)

- Track all the forms and MDI forms in an application (recipes 7-4 and 7-5)

- Save user-based and computer-based configuration information for Windows Forms applications using the mechanisms built into the .NET Framework and Windows (recipe 7-6)

- Force a list box to always display the most recently added item, so that users do not need to scroll up and down to find it (recipe 7-7)

- Assist input validation by restricting what data a user can enter into a textbox, and implement a component-based mechanism for validating user input and reporting errors (recipes 7-8 and 7-17)

- Implement a custom autocomplete combo box so that you can make suggests for completing words as users type data (recipe 7-9)

- Allow users to sort a list view based on the values in any column (recipe 7-10)

- Avoid the need to explicitly lay out controls on a form by using the Windows Forms layout controls (recipe 7-11)

- Use part of a main menu in a context menu (recipe 7-12)

- Provide multilingual support in your Windows Forms application (recipe 7-13)

- Create forms that cannot be moved and create borderless forms that can be moved (recipes 7-14 and 7-15)

- Create an animated system tray icon for your application (recipe 7-16)

- Support drag-and-drop functionality in your Windows Forms application (recipe 7-18)

- Provide context-sensitive help to the users of your Windows Forms application (recipe 7-19)

- Display Web-based information within your Windows application and allow users to browse the Web from within your application (recipe 7-20)

■**Note** Visual Studio, with its advanced design and editing capabilities, provides the easiest and most productive way to develop Windows Forms applications. Therefore, the recipes in this chapter—unlike those in most other chapters—rely heavily on the use of Visual Studio. Instead of focusing on the library classes that provide the required functionality, or looking at the code generated by Visual Studio, these recipes focus on how to achieve the recipe's goal using the Visual Studio user interface and the code that you must write manually to complete the required functionality. The separation of generated and manual code is particularly elegant in Visual Studio 2005 due to the extensive use it makes of partial types.

7-1. Add a Control Programmatically

Problem

You need to add a control to a form at runtime, not design time.

Solution

Create an instance of the appropriate control class. Then add the control object to a form or a container control by calling `Controls.Add` on the container. (The container's `Controls` property returns a `ControlCollection` instance.)

How It Works

In a .NET form-based application, there is really no difference between creating a control at design time and creating it at runtime. When you create controls at design time (using a tool like Microsoft Visual Studio), the necessary code is added to your form class, typically in a special method named `InitializeComponent`. In .NET Framework 2.0, Visual Studio will also place this code in a separate source file using the partial type functionality. You can use the same code in your application to create controls on the fly. Just follow these steps:

1. Create an instance of the appropriate control class.

2. Configure the control properties accordingly (particularly the size and position coordinates).

3. Add the control to the form or another container. Every control implements a read-only `Controls` property that references a `ControlCollection` containing references to all of its child controls. To add a child control, invoke the `ControlCollection.Add` method.

4. If you need to handle the events for the new control, you can wire them up to existing methods.

If you need to add multiple controls to a form or container, you should call SuspendLayout on the parent control before adding the dynamic controls, and then call ResumeLayout once you have finished. This temporarily disables the layout logic used to position controls and will allow you to avoid significant performance overheads and weird flickering if many controls are being added.

The Code

The following example demonstrates the dynamic creation of a list of checkboxes. One checkbox is added for each item in a string array. All the checkboxes are added to a panel that has its AutoScroll property set to true, which gives basic scrolling support to the checkbox list.

```
using System;
using System.Windows.Forms;

namespace Apress.VisualCSharpRecipes.Chapter07
{
    public partial class Recipe07_01 : Form
    {
        public Recipe07_01()
        {
            // Initialization code is designer generated and contained
            // in a separate file using the C# 2.0 support for partial
            // classes.
            InitializeComponent();
        }

        protected override void OnLoad(EventArgs e)
        {
            // Call the OnLoad method of the base class to ensure the Load
            // event is raised correctly.
            base.OnLoad(e);

            // Create an array of strings to use as the labels for
            // the dynamic checkboxes.
            string[] foods = {"Grain", "Bread", "Beans", "Eggs",
                              "Chicken", "Milk", "Fruit", "Vegetables",
                              "Pasta", "Rice", "Fish", "Beef"};

            // Suspend the form's layout logic while multiple controls
            // are added.
            this.SuspendLayout();

            // Specify the Y coordinate of the topmost checkbox in the list.
            int topPosition = 10;

            // Create one new checkbox for each name in the list of
            // food types.
            foreach (string food in foods)
            {
                // Create a new checkbox.
                CheckBox checkBox = new CheckBox();

                // Configure the new checkbox.
                checkBox.Top = topPosition;
                checkBox.Left = 10;
                checkBox.Text = food;
```

```
                    // Set the Y coordinate of the next checkbox.
                    topPosition += 30;

                    // Add the checkbox to the panel contained by the form.
                    panel1.Controls.Add(checkBox);
                }

                // Resume the form's layout logic now that all controls
                // have been added.
                this.ResumeLayout();
            }

            [STAThread]
            public static void Main(string[] args)
            {
                Application.Run(new Recipe07_01());
            }
        }
    }
```

Usage

Figure 7-1 shows how the example will look when run.

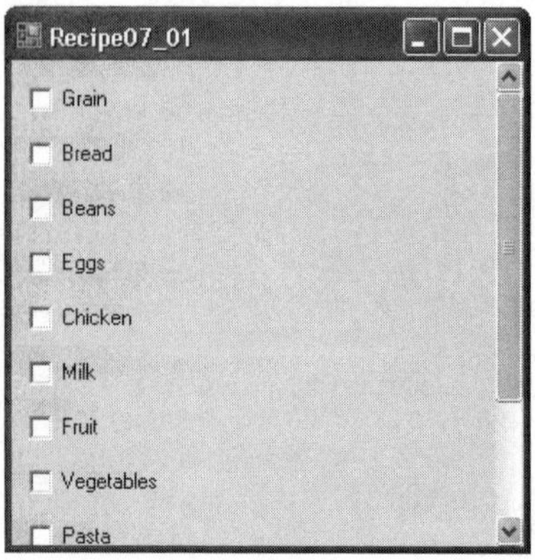

Figure 7-1. *A dynamically generated checkbox list*

7-2. Link Data to a Control

Problem

You need to link an object to a specific control (perhaps to store some arbitrary information that relates to a given display item).

Solution

Store a reference to the object in the Tag property of the control.

How It Works

Every class that derives from Control inherits a Tag property. The Tag property is not used by the control or the .NET Framework. Instead, it's reserved as a convenient storage place for application-specific information. In addition, some other classes not derived from Control also provide a Tag property. Useful examples include the ListViewItem, TreeNode, and MenuItem classes.

Because the Tag property is defined as an Object type, you can use it to store any value type or reference type, from a simple number or string to a custom object you have defined. When retrieving data from the Tag property, you must cast the Object to the correct type before use.

The Code

The following example adds a list of filenames (as ListViewItem objects) to a ListView control. The corresponding System.IO.FileInfo object for each file is stored in the Tag property of its respective ListViewItem. When a user double-clicks one of the filenames, the code retrieves the FileInfo object from the Tag property and displays the filename and size using the MessageBox static method Show.

```csharp
using System;
using System.IO;
using System.Windows.Forms;

namespace Apress.VisualCSharpRecipes.Chapter07
{
    public partial class Recipe07_02 : Form
    {
        public Recipe07_02()
        {
            // Initialization code is designer generated and contained
            // in a separate file using the C# 2.0 support for partial
            // classes.
            InitializeComponent();
        }

        protected override void OnLoad(EventArgs e)
        {
            // Call the OnLoad method of the base class to ensure the Load
            // event  is raised correctly.
            base.OnLoad(e);

            // Get all the files in the root directory.
            DirectoryInfo directory = new DirectoryInfo(@"C:\");
            FileInfo[] files = directory.GetFiles();

            // Display the name of each file in the ListView.
            foreach (FileInfo file in files)
            {
                ListViewItem item = listView1.Items.Add(file.Name);
                item.ImageIndex = 0;

                // Associate each FileInfo object with its ListViewItem.
                item.Tag = file;
            }
        }
```

```
        private void listView1_ItemActivate(object sender, EventArgs e)
        {
            // Get information from the linked FileInfo object and display
            // it using MessageBox.
            ListViewItem item = ((ListView)sender).SelectedItems[0];
            FileInfo file = (FileInfo)item.Tag;
            string info = file.FullName + " is " + file.Length + " bytes.";

            MessageBox.Show(info, "File Information");
        }

        [STAThread]
        public static void Main(string[] args)
        {
            Application.Run(new Recipe07_02());
        }
    }
}
```

Usage

Figure 7-2 shows how the example will look when run.

Figure 7-2. *Storing data in the* Tag *property*

7-3. Process All the Controls on a Form

Problem

You need to perform a generic task with all the controls on the form. For example, you may need to retrieve or clear their Text property, change their color, or resize them.

Solution

Iterate recursively through the collection of controls. Interact with each control using the properties and methods of the base Control class.

How It Works

You can iterate through the controls on a form using the Control.ControlCollection object obtained from the Form.Controls property. The ControlCollection includes all the controls that are placed directly on the form surface. However, if any of these controls are container controls (such as GroupBox, Panel, or TabPage), they might contain more controls. Thus, it's necessary to use recursive logic that searches the Controls collection of every control on the form.

The Code

The following example demonstrates the use of recursive logic to find every TextBox on a form and clears the text they contain. When a button is clicked, the code tests each control in the form's ControlCollection to determine whether it is a TextBox by using the typeof operator.

```
using System;
using System.Windows.Forms;

namespace Apress.VisualCSharpRecipes.Chapter07
{
    public partial class Recipe07_03 : Form
    {
        public Recipe07_03()
        {
            // Initialization code is designer generated and contained
            // in a separate file using the C# 2.0 support for partial
            // classes.
            InitializeComponent();
        }

        // The event handler for the button click event.
        private void cmdProcessAll_Click(object sender, System.EventArgs e)
        {
            ProcessControls(this);
        }

        private void ProcessControls(Control ctrl)
        {
            // Ignore the control unless it's a textbox.
            if (ctrl.GetType() == typeof(TextBox))
            {
                ctrl.Text = "";
            }

            // Process controls recursively.
            // This is required if controls contain other controls
            // (for example, if you use panels, group boxes, or other
            // container controls).
            foreach (Control ctrlChild in ctrl.Controls)
            {
                ProcessControls(ctrlChild);
            }
        }

        [STAThread]
        public static void Main(string[] args)
        {
            Application.Run(new Recipe07_03());
```

```
            }
        }
}
```

7-4. Track the Visible Forms in an Application

Problem

You need access to all of the open forms that are currently owned by an application.

Solution

Iterate through the FormCollection object that you get from the static property OpenForms of the Application object.

How It Works

In .NET Framework 2.0, Windows Forms applications automatically keep track of the open forms that they own. This information is accessed through the Application.OpenForms property, which returns a FormCollection object containing a Form object for each form the application owns. You can iterate through the FormCollection to access all Form objects or obtain a single Form object using its name (Form.Name) or its position in the FormCollection as an index.

The Code

The following example demonstrates the use of the Application.OpenForms property and the FormCollection it contains to manage the active forms in an application. The example allows you to create new forms with specified names. A list of active forms is displayed when you click the Refresh List button. When you click the name of a form in the list, it is made the active form.

Because of the way the FormCollection works, more than one form may have the same name. If duplicate forms have the same name, the first one found will be activated. If you try to retrieve a Form using a name that does not exist, null is returned. The following is the code for the application's main form.

```
using System;
using System.Windows.Forms;
namespace Apress.VisualCSharpRecipes.Chapter07
{
    public partial class Recipe07_04 : Form
    {
        public Recipe07_04()
        {
            // Initialization code is designer generated and contained
            // in a separate file using the C# 2.0 support for partial
            // classes.
            InitializeComponent();
        }

        // Override the OnLoad method to show the initial list of forms.
        protected override void OnLoad(EventArgs e)
        {
```

```csharp
    // Call the OnLoad method of the base class to ensure the Load
    // event is raised correctly.
    base.OnLoad(e);

    // Refresh the list to display the initial set of forms.
    this.RefreshForms();
}

// A button click event handler to create a new child form.
private void btnNewForm_Click(object sender, EventArgs e)
{
    // Create a new child form and set its name as specified.
    // If no name is specified, use a default name.
    Recipe07_04Child child = new Recipe07_04Child();

    if (this.txtFormName.Text == String.Empty)
    {
        child.Name = "Child Form";
    }
    else
    {
        child.Name = this.txtFormName.Text;
    }

    // Show the new child form.
    child.Show();
}

// List selection event handler to activate the selected form based on
// its name.
private void listForms_SelectedIndexChanged(object sender, EventArgs e)
{
    // Activate the selected form using its name as the index into the
    // collection of active forms. If there are duplicate forms with the
    // same name, the first one found will be activated.
    Form form = Application.OpenForms[this.listForms.Text];

    // If the form has been closed, using its name as an index into the
    // FormCollection will return null. In this instance, update the
    // list of forms.
    if (form != null)
    {
        // Activate the selected form.
        form.Activate();
    }
    else
    {
        // Display a message and refresh the form list.
        MessageBox.Show("Form closed; refreshing list...",
            "Form Closed");
        this.RefreshForms();
    }
}

// A button click event handler to initiate a refresh of the list of
// active forms.
private void btnRefresh_Click(object sender, EventArgs e)
```

```
        {
            RefreshForms();
        }

        // A method to perform a refresh of the list of active forms.
        private void RefreshForms()
        {
            // Clear the list and repopulate from the Application.OpenForms
            // property.
            this.listForms.Items.Clear();

            foreach (Form f in Application.OpenForms)
            {
                this.listForms.Items.Add(f.Name);
            }
        }

        [STAThread]
        public static void Main(string[] args)
        {
            Application.Run(new Recipe07_04());
        }
    }
}
```

The following is the code for the child forms you create by clicking the New Form button.

```
using System;
using System.Windows.Forms;

namespace Apress.VisualCSharpRecipes.Chapter07
{
    public partial class Recipe07_04Child : Form
    {
        public Recipe07_04Child()
        {
            InitializeComponent();
        }

        // Override the OnPaint method to correctly display the name of the
        // form.
        protected override void OnPaint(PaintEventArgs e)
        {
            // Call the OnPaint method of the base class to ensure the Paint
            // event is raised correctly.
            base.OnPaint(e);

            // Display the name of the form.
            this.lblFormName.Text = this.Name;
        }

        // A button click event handler to close the child form.
        private void btnClose_Click(object sender, EventArgs e)
        {
            this.Close();
        }
    }
}
```

Notes

Versions 1.0 and 1.1 of the .NET Framework do not provide any way of determining which forms are currently owned by an application. (The one exception is MDI applications, as described in recipe 7-5.) If you want to determine which forms exist or which forms are displayed, or you want one form to call the methods or set the properties of another form, you will need to keep track of form instances on your own.

For tracking small numbers of forms, one useful approach is to create a static class consisting of static members. Each static member holds a reference to a specific Form. If you have many forms you need to track, such as in a document-based application where the user can create multiple instances of the same form, one per document, a generic collection such as a System.Collections.Generic.Dictionary<string,Form> is very useful. This lets you map a Form object to a name.

Whichever approach you take, each Form object should register itself with the tracker class when it is first created. A logical place to put this code is in the Form.OnLoad method. Conversely, when the Form object is closed, it should deregister itself with the tracker class. Deregistration should occur in the OnClosing or OnClosed method of the Form class.

Using either of these approaches, any code that requires access to a Form object can obtain a reference to it from the members of the tracker class, and even invoke operations on the Form instance directly through the tracker class if you are sure the Form object exists.

7-5. Find All MDI Child Forms

Problem

You need to find all the forms that are currently being displayed in an MDI application.

Solution

Iterate through the forms returned by the MdiChildren collection property of the MDI parent.

How It Works

The .NET Framework includes two convenient shortcuts for managing the forms open in MDI applications: the MdiChildren and the MdiParent properties of the Form class. The MdiParent property of any MDI child returns a Form representing the containing parent window. The MdiChildren property returns an array containing all of the MDI child forms.

The Code

The following example presents an MDI parent window that allows you to create new MDI children by clicking the New item on the File menu. Each child window contains a label, which displays the date and time when the MDI child was created, and a button. When the button is clicked, the event handler walks through all the MDI child windows and displays the label text that each one contains. Notice that when the example enumerates the collection of MDI child forms, it converts the generic Form reference to the derived Recipe07-05Child form class so that it can use the LabelText property. The following is the Recipe07-05Parent class.

```
using System;
using System.Windows.Forms;

namespace Apress.VisualCSharpRecipes.Chapter07
{
```

```csharp
        // An MDI parent form.
        public partial class Recipe07_05Parent : Form
        {
            public Recipe07_05Parent()
            {
                // Initialization code is designer generated and contained
                // in a separate file using the C# 2.0 support for partial
                // classes.
                InitializeComponent();
            }

            // When the New menu item is clicked, create a new MDI child.
            private void mnuNew_Click(object sender, EventArgs e)
            {
                Recipe07_05Child frm = new Recipe07_05Child();
                frm.MdiParent = this;
                frm.Show();
            }

            [STAThread]
            public static void Main(string[] args)
            {
                Application.Run(new Recipe07_05Parent());
            }
        }
}
```

The following is the Recipe07-05Child class.

```csharp
using System;
using System.Windows.Forms;

namespace Apress.VisualCSharpRecipes.Chapter07
{
    // An MDI child form.
    public partial class Recipe07_05Child : Form
    {
        public Recipe07_05Child()
        {
            // Initialization code is designer generated and contained
            // in a separate file using the C# 2.0 support for partial
            // classes.
            InitializeComponent();
        }

        // When a button on any of the MDI child forms is clicked, display the
        // contents of a each form by enumerating the MdiChildren collection.
        private void cmdShowAllWindows_Click(object sender, EventArgs e)
        {
            foreach (Form frm in this.MdiParent.MdiChildren)
            {
                // Cast the generic Form to the Recipe07_05Child derived class
                // type.
                Recipe07_05Child child = (Recipe07_05Child)frm;
                MessageBox.Show(child.LabelText, frm.Text);
            }
        }
```

```
    // On load, set the MDI child form's label to the current date/time.
    protected override void OnLoad(EventArgs e)
    {
        // Call the OnLoad method of the base class to ensure the Load
        // event is raised correctly.
        base.OnLoad(e);

        label.Text = DateTime.Now.ToString();
    }

    // A property to provide easy access to the label data.
    public string LabelText
    {
        get { return label.Text; }
    }
    }
}
```

Usage

Figure 7-3 shows how the example will look when run.

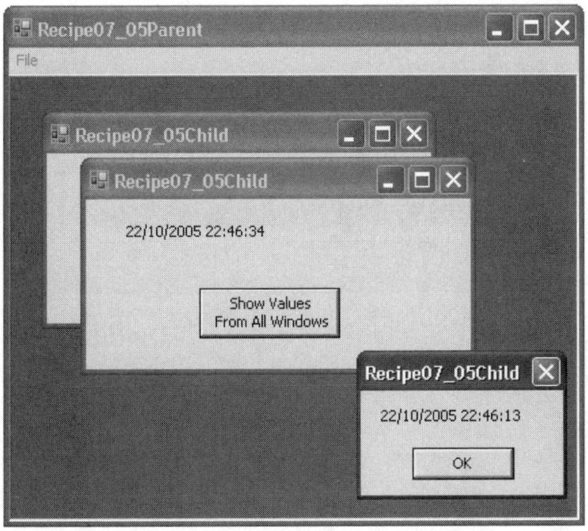

Figure 7-3. *Getting information from multiple MDI child windows*

7-6. Save Configuration Settings for a Form

Problem

You need to store configuration settings for a form so that they are remembered the next time that the form is shown.

Solution

Use the .NET Framework 2.0 Application Settings functionality, which is configurable at design time in Visual Studio.

How It Works

The Application Settings functionality in .NET Framework 2.0 provides an easy-to-use mechanism through which you can save application and user settings used to customize the appearance and operation of a Windows Forms application. You configure Application Settings through the Properties panel of each Windows control (including the main Windows Form) in your application. By expanding the ApplicationSettings property and clicking the ellipsis (three dots) to the right of (PropertyBinding), you can review and configure Application Settings for each property of the active control. See Figure 7-4 for an example.

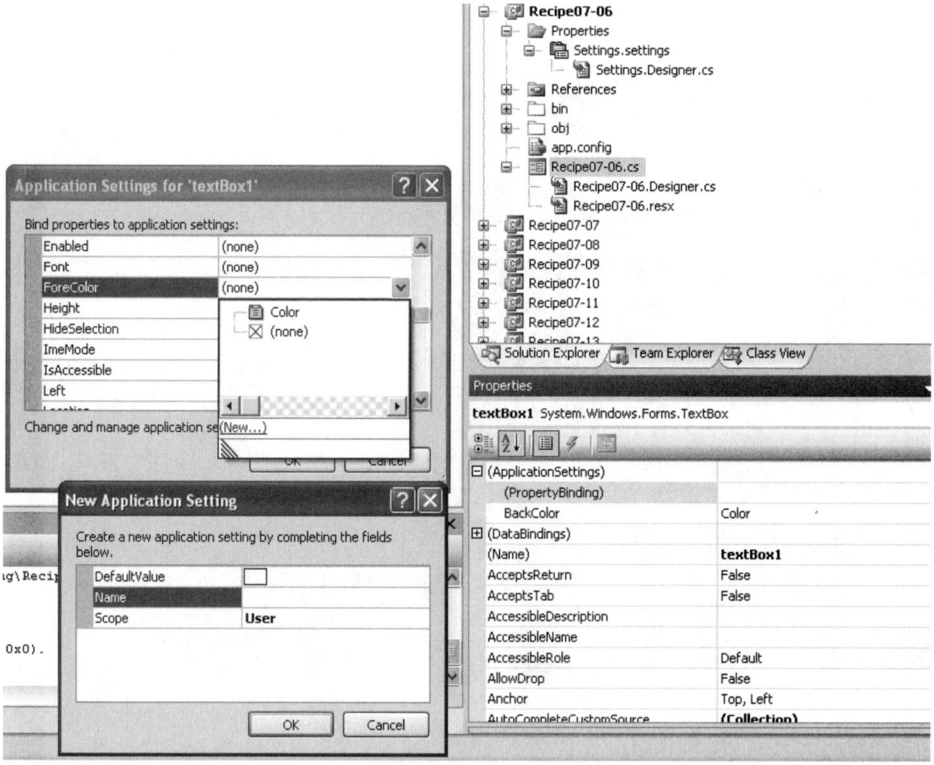

Figure 7-4. *Configuring Application Settings in Visual Studio*

When you configure a new Application Setting for a control's property, you must assign it a name, a default value, and a scope.

- The name allows you to both access the setting programmatically and reuse the Application Setting across multiple controls.

- The default value is used if the application cannot obtain a value from a configuration file at runtime.

- The scope is either User or Application.

Settings with an Application scope are stored in the application's configuration file (usually located in the same folder as the application assembly) and are read-only. The benefit of an Application scope is that you can change configuration settings by editing the configuration file without needing to recompile the application. Settings with a User scope are read-write by default and are stored as part of the user's Windows profile in a file named after the executing assembly.

When you configure your application to use Application Settings, Visual Studio actually auto-generates a wrapper class that provides access to the configuration file information, regardless of whether it is scoped as Application or User. The class is named Settings and implements the Singleton pattern (discussed in recipe 13-10); the singleton instance is accessed through Settings.Default. This class contains properties with names matching each of the Application Setting names you configured for your controls' properties. The controls will automatically read their configuration at startup, but you should store configuration changes prior to terminating your application by calling the Settings.Default.Save method.

The Code

The following example shows how to update and save Application Settings at runtime.

```
using System;
using System.ComponentModel;
using System.Windows.Forms;
using Apress.VisualCSharpRecipes.Chapter07.Properties;

namespace Apress.VisualCSharpRecipes.Chapter07
{
    public partial class Recipe07_06 : Form
    {
        public Recipe07_06()
        {
            // Initialization code is designer generated and contained
            // in a separate file using the C# 2.0 support for partial
            // classes.
            InitializeComponent();
        }

        private void Button_Click(object sender, EventArgs e)
        {
            // Change the color of the textbox depending on which button
            // was pressed.
            Button btn = sender as Button;

            if (btn != null)
            {
                // Set the background color of the textbox
                textBox1.BackColor = btn.ForeColor;

                // Update the application settings with the new value.
                Settings.Default.Color = textBox1.BackColor;
            }
        }
```

```
        protected override void OnClosing(CancelEventArgs e)
        {
            // Call the OnClosing method of the base class to ensure the
            // FormClosing event is raised correctly.
            base.OnClosing(e);

            // Update the application settings for Form.
            Settings.Default.Size = this.Size;

            // Store all application settings.
            Settings.Default.Save();
        }

        [STAThread]
        public static void Main(string[] args)
        {
            Application.Run(new Recipe07_06());
        }
    }
}
```

7-7. Force a List Box to Scroll to the Most Recently Added Item

Problem

You need to scroll a list box programmatically so that the most recently added items are visible.

Solution

Set the ListBox.TopIndex property, which sets the first visible list item.

How It Works

In some cases, you might have a list box that stores a significant amount of information or one that you add information to periodically. Often, the most recent information, which is added at the end of the list, is more important than the information at the top of the list. One solution is to scroll the list box so that recently added items are visible. The ListBox.TopIndex property enables you to do this by allowing you to specify which item is visible at the top of the list.

The Code

The following sample form includes a list box and a button. Each time the button is clicked, 20 items are added to the list box. Each time new items are added, the code sets the ListBox.TopIndex property and forces the list box to display the most recently added items. To provide better feedback, the same line is also selected.

```
using System;
using System.Windows.Forms;
```

```
namespace Apress.VisualCSharpRecipes.Chapter07
{
    public partial class Recipe07_07 : Form
    {
        // A counter to keep track of the number of items added
        // to the ListBox.
        private int counter = 0;

        public Recipe07_07()
        {
            // Initialization code is designer generated and contained
            // in a separate file using the C# 2.0 support for partial
            // classes.
            InitializeComponent();
        }

        // Button click event handler adds 20 new items to the ListBox.
        private void cmdTest_Click(object sender, EventArgs e)
        {
            // Add 20 items.
            for (int i = 0; i < 20; i++)
            {
                counter++;
                listBox1.Items.Add("Item " + counter.ToString());
            }

            // Set the TopIndex property of the ListBox to ensure the
            // most recently added items are visible.
            listBox1.TopIndex = listBox1.Items.Count - 1;
            listBox1.SelectedIndex = listBox1.Items.Count - 1;
        }

        [STAThread]
        public static void Main(string[] args)
        {
            Application.Run(new Recipe07_07());
        }
    }
}
```

7-8. Restrict a Textbox to Accepting Only Specific Input

Problem

You need to create a textbox that will reject all nonnumeric keystrokes.

Solution

Use the MaskedTextBox control and set the Mask property to configure the input that is acceptable.

How It Works

One way to ensure user input is valid is to prevent invalid data from being entered in the first place. The MaskedTextBox control facilitates this approach. The MaskedTextBox.Mask property takes a string that specifies the input mask for the control. This mask determines what type of input a user can enter at each point in the control's text area. If the user enters an incorrect character, the control will beep if the BeepOnError property is true, and the MaskInputRejected event is raised so that you can customize the handling of incorrect input.

■**Note** The MaskedTextBox control will not solve all your user-input validation problems. While it does make some types of validation easy to implement, without customization, it will not ensure some common validation requirements are met. For example, you can specify that only numeric digits can be input, but you cannot specify that they must be less than a specific value, nor can you control the overall characteristics of the input value.

The Code

The following example demonstrates the use of the MaskedTextBox control. A series of buttons allows you to change the active mask on the MaskedTextBox control and experiment with the various masks. Notice that the control tries to accommodate existing content with the new mask when the mask is changed. If the content is not allowed with the new mask, the control is cleared.

```
using System;
using System.Threading;
using System.Windows.Forms;

namespace Apress.VisualCSharpRecipes.Chapter07
{
    public partial class Recipe07_08 : Form
    {

        public Recipe07_08()
        {
            // Initialization code is designer generated and contained
            // in a separate file using the C# 2.0 support for partial
            // classes.
            InitializeComponent();
        }

        private void btnTime_Click(object sender, EventArgs e)
        {
            // Set the input mask to that of a short time.
            this.mskTextBox.UseSystemPasswordChar = false;
            this.mskTextBox.Mask = "00:00";
            this.lblActiveMask.Text = this.mskTextBox.Mask;
            this.mskTextBox.Focus();
        }

        private void btnUSZip_Click(object sender, EventArgs e)
        {
            // Set the input mask to that of a US ZIP code.
            this.mskTextBox.UseSystemPasswordChar = false;
            this.mskTextBox.Mask = "00000-9999";
            this.lblActiveMask.Text = this.mskTextBox.Mask;
            this.mskTextBox.Focus();
        }
```

```
        private void btnUKPost_Click(object sender, EventArgs e)
        {
            // Set the input mask to that of a UK postcode.
            this.mskTextBox.UseSystemPasswordChar = false;
            this.mskTextBox.Mask = ">LCCC 9LL";
            this.lblActiveMask.Text = this.mskTextBox.Mask;
            this.mskTextBox.Focus();
        }

        private void btnCurrency_Click(object sender, EventArgs e)
        {
            // Set the input mask to that of a currency.
            this.mskTextBox.UseSystemPasswordChar = false;
            this.mskTextBox.Mask = "$999,999.00";
            this.lblActiveMask.Text = this.mskTextBox.Mask;
            this.mskTextBox.Focus();
        }

        private void btnDate_Click(object sender, EventArgs e)
        {
            // Set the input mask to that of a short date.
            this.mskTextBox.UseSystemPasswordChar = false;
            this.mskTextBox.Mask = "00/00/0000";
            this.lblActiveMask.Text = this.mskTextBox.Mask;
            this.mskTextBox.Focus();
        }

        private void btnSecret_Click(object sender, EventArgs e)
        {
            // Set the input mask to that of a secret PIN.
            this.mskTextBox.UseSystemPasswordChar = true;
            this.mskTextBox.Mask = "0000";
            this.lblActiveMask.Text = this.mskTextBox.Mask;
            this.mskTextBox.Focus();
        }

        [STAThread]
        public static void Main(string[] args)
        {
            Application.Run(new Recipe07_08());
        }
    }
}
```

Notes

The MaskedTextBox used in this recipe is new to .NET Framework 2.0. In previous versions of the .NET Framework, one approach was to use a standard TextBox control and handle the KeyPress events it raises. The KeyPress event is raised after each keystroke has been received but before it is displayed. You can use the KeyPressEventArgs event parameter to effectively cancel an invalid keystroke by setting its Handled property to true.

For example, to allow only numeric input, you must allow a keystroke only if it corresponds to a number (0 through 9) or a special control key (such as Delete or the arrow keys). The keystroke character is provided to the KeyPress event through the KeyPressEventArgs.KeyChar property. You can use two static methods of the System.Char class—IsDigit and IsControl—to quickly test the character.

7-9. Use an Autocomplete Combo Box

Problem

You want to create a combo box that automatically completes what the user is typing based on the item list.

Solution

You can implement a basic autocomplete combo box by creating a custom control that overrides the OnKeyPress and OnTextChanged methods of the ComboBox object.

■**Note** The ComboBox control in .NET Framework 2.0 provides autocomplete options. You can configure the behavior using the AutoCompleteMode property of the ComboBox class.

How It Works

An autocomplete control has many different variations. For example, the control may fill in values based on a list of recent selections (as Microsoft Excel does when you are entering cell values), or the control might display a drop-down list of near matches (as Microsoft Internet Explorer does when you are typing a URL). You can create a basic autocomplete combo box by handling the KeyPress and TextChanged events, or by creating a custom class that derives from ComboBox and overrides the OnKeyPress and OnTextChanged methods.

The Code

The following example contains an AutoCompleteComboBox control that derives from ComboBox. The AutoCompleteComboBox control supports autocompletion by overriding the OnKeyPress and OnTextChanged inherited methods. In the OnKeyPress method, the combo box determines whether or not an autocomplete replacement should be made. If the user pressed a character key (such as a letter), the replacement can be made, but if the user pressed a control key (such as the backspace key, the cursor keys, and so on), no action should be taken. The OnTextChanged method performs the actual replacement after the key processing is complete. This method looks up the first match for the current text in the list of items, and then adds the rest of the matching text. After the text is added, the combo box selects the characters between the current insertion point and the end of the text. This allows the user to continue typing and replace the autocomplete text if it is not what the user wants.

```
using System;
using System.Windows.Forms;

namespace Apress.VisualCSharpRecipes.Chapter07
{
    public class AutoCompleteComboBox : ComboBox
    {
        // A private member to track if a special key is pressed, in
        // which case, any text replacement operation will be skipped.
        private bool controlKey = false;

        // Determine whether a special key was pressed.
        protected override void OnKeyPress(System.Windows.Forms.KeyPressEventArgs e)
        {
```

```
        // First call the overridden base class method.
        base.OnKeyPress(e);

        // Clear the text if the Escape key is pressed.
        if (e.KeyChar == (int)Keys.Escape)
        {
            // Clear the text.
            this.SelectedIndex = -1;
            this.Text = "";
            controlKey = true;
        }
        // Don't try to autocomplete when control key is pressed.
        else if (Char.IsControl(e.KeyChar))
        {
            controlKey = true;
        }
        // Noncontrol keys should trigger autocomplete.
        else
        {
            controlKey = false;
        }
    }

    // Perform the text substitution.
    protected override void OnTextChanged(System.EventArgs e)
    {
        // First call the overridden base class method.
        base.OnTextChanged(e);

        if (this.Text != "" && !controlKey)
        {
            // Search the current contents of the combo box for a
            // matching entry.
            string matchText = this.Text;
            int match = this.FindString(matchText);

            // If a matching entry is found, insert it now.
            if (match != -1)
            {
                this.SelectedIndex = match;

                // Select the added text so it can be replaced
                // if the user keeps typing.
                this.SelectionStart = matchText.Length;
                this.SelectionLength = this.Text.Length - this.SelectionStart;
            }
        }
    }
  }
 }
}
```

Usage

The following code demonstrates the use of the AutoCompleteComboBox by adding it to a form and filling it with a list of words. In this example, the control is added to the form manually, and the list of words is retrieved from a text file named words.txt. As an alternative, you could compile the

AutoCompleteComboBox class to a separate class library assembly, and then add it to the Visual Studio Toolbox, so you could add it to forms at design time.

```
using System;
using System.IO;
using System.Drawing;
using System.Windows.Forms;

namespace Apress.VisualCSharpRecipes.Chapter07
{
    public partial class Recipe07_09 : Form
    {
        public Recipe07_09()
        {
            // Initialization code is designer generated and contained
            // in a separate file using the C# 2.0 support for partial
            // classes.
            InitializeComponent();
        }

        protected override void OnLoad(EventArgs e)
        {
            // Call the OnLoad method of the base class to ensure the Load
            // event is raised correctly.
            base.OnLoad(e);

            // Add the AutoCompleteComboBox to the form.
            AutoCompleteComboBox combo = new AutoCompleteComboBox();
            combo.Location = new Point(10, 10);
            this.Controls.Add(combo);

            // Read the list of words from the file words.txt and add them
            // to the AutoCompleteComboBox.
            using (FileStream fs = new FileStream("words.txt", FileMode.Open))
            {
                using (StreamReader r = new StreamReader(fs))
                {
                    while (r.Peek() > -1)
                    {
                        string word = r.ReadLine();
                        combo.Items.Add(word);
                    }
                }
            }
        }

        [STAThread]
        public static void Main(string[] args)
        {
            Application.Run(new Recipe07_09());
        }
    }
}
```

Figure 7-5 shows how the AutoCompleteComboBox will look when the Recipe07-09 example is run.

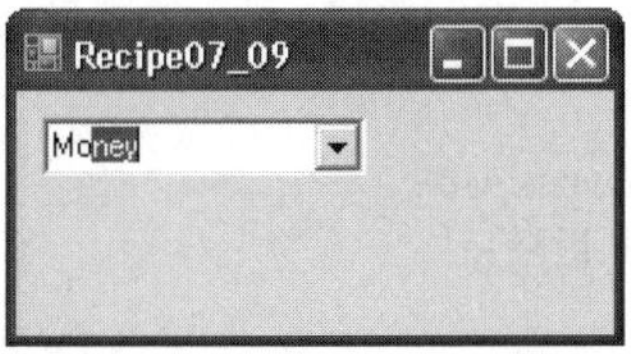

Figure 7-5. *An autocomplete combo box*

7-10. Sort a List View by Any Column

Problem

You need to sort a list view, but the built-in `ListView.Sort` method sorts based on only the first column.

Solution

Create a type that implements the `System.Collections.IComparer` interface and can sort `ListViewItem` objects. The `IComparer` type can sort based on any `ListViewItem` criteria you specify. Set the `ListView.ListViewItemSorter` property with an instance of the `IComparer` type before calling the `ListView.Sort` method.

How It Works

The `ListView` control provides a `Sort` method that orders items alphabetically based on the text in the first column. If you want to sort based on other column values or order items numerically, you need to create a custom implementation of the `IComparer` interface that can perform the work. The `IComparer` interface defines a single method named `Compare`, which takes two `object` arguments and determines which one should be ordered first. Full details of how to implement the `IComparer` interface are available in recipe 13-3.

The Code

The following example demonstrates the creation of an `IComparer` implementation named `ListViewItemComparer`. The `ListViewItemComparer` class also implements two additional properties: `Column` and `Numeric`. The `Column` property identifies the column that should be used for sorting. The `Numeric` property is a Boolean flag that can be set to `true` if you want to perform number-based comparisons instead of alphabetic comparisons.

When the user clicks a column heading, the example creates a `ListViewItemComparer` instance, configures the column to use for sorting, and assigns the `ListViewItemComparer` instance to the `ListView.ListViewItemSorter` property before calling the `ListView.Sort` method.

```
using System;
using System.Collections;
using System.Windows.Forms;

namespace Apress.VisualCSharpRecipes.Chapter07
{
    public partial class Recipe07_10 : Form
```

```csharp
{
    public Recipe07_10()
    {
        // Initialization code is designer generated and contained
        // in a separate file using the C# 2.0 support for partial
        // classes.
        InitializeComponent();
    }

    // Event handler to handle user clicks on column headings.
    private void listView1_ColumnClick(object sender, ColumnClickEventArgs e)
    {
        // Create and/or configure the ListViewItemComparer to sort based on
        // the column that was clicked.
        ListViewItemComparer sorter =
            listView1.ListViewItemSorter as ListViewItemComparer;

        if (sorter == null)
        {
            // Create a new ListViewItemComparer.
            sorter = new ListViewItemComparer(e.Column);
            listView1.ListViewItemSorter = sorter;
        }
        else
        {
            // Configure the existing ListViewItemComparer.
            sorter.Column = e.Column;
        }

        // Sort the ListView
        listView1.Sort();
    }

    [STAThread]
    public static void Main(string[] args)
    {
        Application.Run(new Recipe07_10());
    }
}

public class ListViewItemComparer : IComparer
{
    // Private members to configure comparer logic.
    private int column;
    private bool numeric = false;

    // Property to get/set the column to use for comparison.
    public int Column
    {
        get { return column; }
        set { column = value; }
    }

    // Property to get/set whether numeric comparison is required
    // as opposed to the standard alphabetic comparison.
    public bool Numeric
```

```csharp
{
    get { return numeric; }
    set { numeric = value; }
}

public ListViewItemComparer(int columnIndex)
{
    Column = columnIndex;
}

public int Compare(object x, object y)
{
    // Convert the arguments to ListViewItem objects.
    ListViewItem itemX = x as ListViewItem;
    ListViewItem itemY = y as ListViewItem;

    // Handle logic for null reference as dictated by the
    // IComparer interface. Null is considered less than
    // any other value.
    if (itemX == null && itemY == null) return 0;
    else if (itemX == null) return -1;
    else if (itemY == null) return 1;

    // Short-circuit condition where the items are references
    // to the same object.
    if (itemX == itemY) return 0;

    // Determine if numeric comparison is required.
    if (Numeric)
    {
        // Convert column text to numbers before comparing.
        // If the conversion fails, just use the value 0.
        decimal itemXVal, itemYVal;

        if (!Decimal.TryParse(itemX.SubItems[Column].Text, out itemXVal))
        {
            itemXVal = 0;
        }
        if (!Decimal.TryParse(itemY.SubItems[Column].Text, out itemYVal))
        {
            itemYVal = 0;
        }

        return Decimal.Compare(itemXVal, itemYVal);
    }
    else
    {
        // Keep the column text in its native string format
        // and perform an alphabetic comparison.
        string itemXText = itemX.SubItems[Column].Text;
        string itemYText = itemY.SubItems[Column].Text;

        return String.Compare(itemXText, itemYText);
    }
}
}
}
```

7-11. Lay Out Controls Automatically

Problem

You have a large set of controls on a form and you want them arranged automatically.

Solution

Use the FlowLayoutPanel container to dynamically arrange the controls using a horizontal or vertical flow, or use the TableLayoutPanel container to dynamically arrange the controls in a grid.

How It Works

The FlowLayoutPanel and TableLayoutPanel containers (both new to .NET Framework 2.0) simplify the design-time and runtime layout of the controls they contain. At both design time and runtime, as you add controls to one of these panels, the panel's logic determines where the control should be positioned, so you do not need to determine the exact location.

With the FlowLayoutPanel container, the FlowDirection and WrapContents properties determine where controls are positioned. FlowDirection controls the order and location of controls, and it can be set to LeftToRight, TopDown, RightToLeft, or BottomUp. The WrapContents property controls whether controls run off the edge of the panel or wrap around to form a new line of controls.

With the TableLayoutPanel container, the RowCount and ColumnCount properties control how many rows and columns are currently in the panel's grid. The GrowStyle property determines how the grid grows to accommodate more controls once it is full, and it can be set to AddRows, AddColumns, or FixedSize (which means the grid cannot grow).

Figure 7-6 shows the design-time appearance of both a TableLayoutPanel container and a FlowLayoutPanel container. The TableLayoutPanel panel is configured with three rows and three columns. The FlowLayoutPanel panel is configured to wrap contents and use left-to-right flow direction.

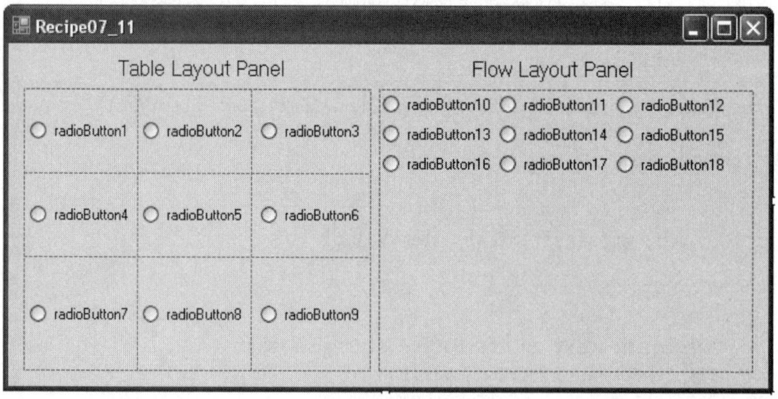

Figure 7-6. *Using a* FlowLayoutPanel *panel and a* TableLayoutPanel *panel*

7-12. Use Part of a Main Menu for a Context Menu

Problem

You need to create a context menu that shows the same menu items as those displayed as part of an application's main menu.

Solution

Use the CloneMenu method of the MenuItem class to duplicate the required portion of the main menu.

How It Works

In many applications, a control's context-sensitive menu duplicates a portion of the main menu. However, .NET does not allow you to create a MenuItem instance that is contained in more than one menu at a time.

The solution is to make a duplicate copy of a portion of the menu using the CloneMenu method. The CloneMenu method not only copies the appropriate MenuItem items (and any contained submenus), but it also registers each MenuItem object with the same event handlers. Thus, when a user clicks a cloned menu item in a context menu, the event handler will be triggered as if the user had clicked the duplicate menu item in the main menu.

The Code

The following example uses the CloneMenu method to configure the context menu for a TextBox to be a duplicate of the File menu.

```
using System;
using System.Drawing;
using System.Windows.Forms;

namespace Apress.VisualCSharpRecipes.Chapter07
{
    public partial class Recipe07_12 : Form
    {
        public Recipe07_12()
        {
            // Initialization code is designer generated and contained
            // in a separate file using the C# 2.0 support for partial
            // classes.
            InitializeComponent();
        }

        // As the main form loads, clone the required section of the main
        // menu and assign it to the ContextMenu property of the TextBox.
        protected override void OnLoad(EventArgs e)
        {
            // Call the OnLoad method of the base class to ensure the Load
            // event is raised correctly.
            base.OnLoad(e);

            ContextMenu mnuContext = new ContextMenu();
```

```
        // Copy the menu items from the File menu into a context menu.
        foreach (MenuItem mnuItem in mnuFile.MenuItems)
        {
            mnuContext.MenuItems.Add(mnuItem.CloneMenu());
        }

        // Attach the cloned menu to the TextBox.
        TextBox1.ContextMenu = mnuContext;
    }

    // Event handler to display the ContextMenu for the ListBox.
    private void TextBox1_MouseDown(object sender, MouseEventArgs e)
    {
        if (e.Button == MouseButtons.Right)
        {
            TextBox1.ContextMenu.Show(TextBox1, new Point(e.X, e.Y));
        }
    }

    // Event handler to process clicks on File/Open menu item.
    // For the purpose of the example, simply show a message box.
    private void mnuOpen_Click(object sender, EventArgs e)
    {
        MessageBox.Show("This is the event handler for Open.","Recipe07-12");
    }

    // Event handler to process clicks on File/Save menu item.
    // For the purpose of the example, simply show a message box.
    private void mnuSave_Click(object sender, EventArgs e)
    {
        MessageBox.Show("This is the event handler for Save.","Recipe07-12");
    }

    // Event handler to process clicks on File/Exit menu item.
    // For the purpose of the example, simply show a message box.
    private void mnuExit_Click(object sender, EventArgs e)
    {
        MessageBox.Show("This is the event handler for Exit.","Recipe07-12");
    }

    public static void Main(string[] args)
    {
        Application.Run(new Recipe07_12());
    }
  }
}
```

Usage

Figure 7-7 shows how the example will look when run.

Figure 7-7. *Copying part of a main menu to a context menu*

7-13. Make a Multilingual Form

Problem

You need to create a localizable form that can be deployed in more than one language.

Solution

Store all locale-specific information in resource files, which are compiled into satellite assemblies.

How It Works

The .NET Framework includes built-in support for localization through its use of resource files. The basic idea is to store information that is locale-specific (for example, button text) in a resource file. You can create resource files for each culture you need to support and compile them into satellite assemblies. When you run the application, .NET will automatically use the correct satellite assembly based on the locale settings of the current user/computer.

You can read to and write from resource files manually; they are XML files. However, Visual Studio also includes extensive design-time support for localized forms. It works like this:

1. Set the Localizable property of a Form to true using the Properties window.

2. Set the Language property of the form to the locale for which you would like to enter information. (See Figure 7-8.) Then configure the localizable properties of all the controls on the form. Instead of storing your changes in the designer-generated code for the form, Visual Studio will actually create a new resource file to hold your data.

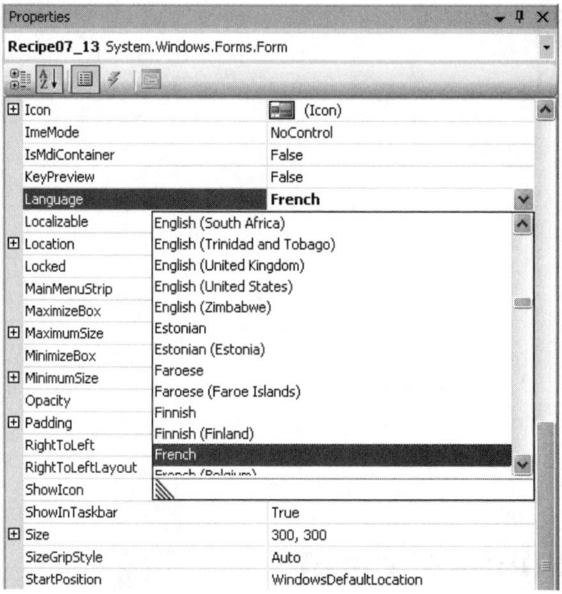

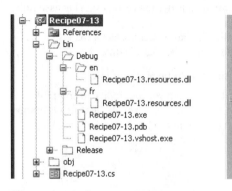

Figure 7-8. *Selecting a language for localizing a form*

3. Repeat step 2 for each language that you want to support. Each time you enter a new locale for the form's Language property, a new resource file will be generated. If you change the Language property to a locale you have already configured, your previous settings will reappear, and you will be able to modify them.

You can now compile and test your application on differently localized systems. Visual Studio will create a separate directory and satellite assembly for each resource file in the project. You can select Project ▶ Show All Files from the Visual Studio menu to see how these files are arranged, as shown in Figure 7-9.

Figure 7-9. *Satellite assembly structure*

The Code

Although you do not need to manually code any of the localization functionality, as a testing shortcut, you can force your application to adopt a specific culture by modifying the `Thread.CurrentUICulture` property of the application thread. However, you must modify this property before the form has loaded.

```
using System;
using System.Threading;
using System.Globalization;
using System.Windows.Forms;

namespace Apress.VisualCSharpRecipes.Chapter07
{
    public partial class Recipe07_13 : Form
    {
        public Recipe07_13()
        {
            // Initialization code is designer generated and contained
            // in a separate file using the C# 2.0 support for partial
            // classes.
            InitializeComponent();
        }

        [STAThread]
        public static void Main(string[] args)
        {
            Thread.CurrentThread.CurrentUICulture = new CultureInfo("fr");
            Application.Run(new Recipe07_13());
        }
    }
}
```

Usage

Figure 7-10 shows both the English and French versions of the Recipe07-13 example. As you can see, both the language and the layout of the form are different depending on the current locale.

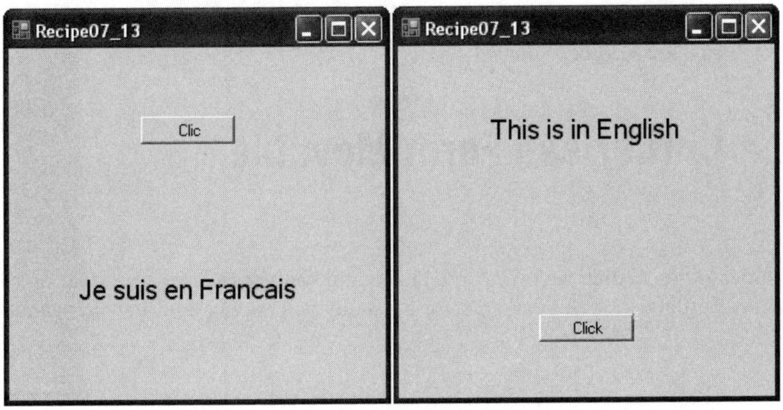

Figure 7-10. *English and French localizations of Recipe07-13*

7-14. Create a Form That Cannot Be Moved

Problem

You want to create a form that occupies a fixed location on the screen and cannot be moved.

Solution

Make a borderless form by setting the FormBorderStyle property of the Form class to the value FormBorderStyle.None.

How It Works

You can create a borderless form by setting the FormBorderStyle property of a Form to None. Borderless forms cannot be moved. However, as their name implies, they also lack any kind of border. If you want the customary blue border, you will need to add it yourself, either with manual drawing code or by using a background image.

One other approach to creating an immovable form does provide a basic control-style border. First, set the ControlBox, MinimizeBox, and MaximizeBox properties of the form to false. Then set the Text property to an empty string. The form will have a raised gray border or black line (depending on the FormBorderStyle option you use), similar to a button. Figure 7-11 shows both types of immovable forms.

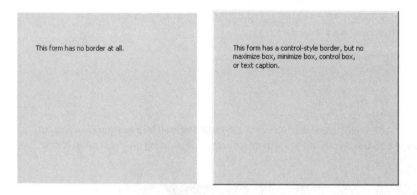

Figure 7-11. *Two types of forms that cannot be moved*

7-15. Make a Borderless Form Movable

Problem

You need to create a borderless form that can be moved. This might be the case if you are creating a custom window that has a unique look (for example, for a visually rich application such as a game or a media player).

Solution

Create another control that responds to the MouseDown, MouseUp, and MouseMove events and programmatically moves the form.

How It Works

Borderless forms omit a title bar, which makes it impossible for a user to move them. You can compensate for this shortcoming by adding a control to the form that serves the same purpose. For example, Figure 7-12 shows a form that includes a label to support dragging. The user can click on this label, and then drag the form to a new location on the screen while holding down the mouse button. As the user moves the mouse, the form moves correspondingly, as though it were "attached" to the mouse pointer.

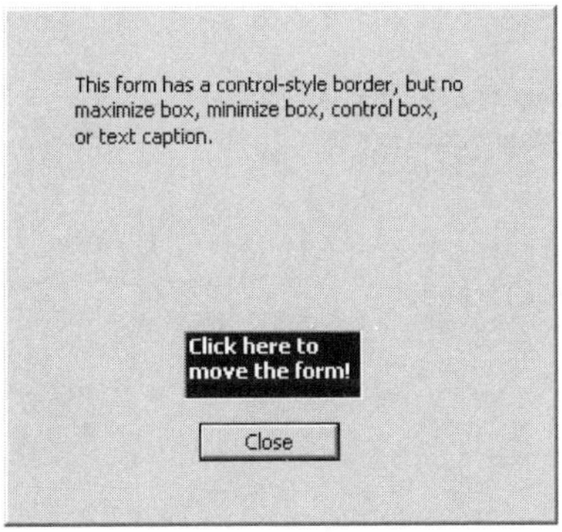

Figure 7-12. *A movable borderless form*

To implement this solution, take the following steps:

1. Create a form-level Boolean variable that tracks whether or not the form is currently being dragged.

2. When the label is clicked, the code sets the flag to indicate that the form is in drag mode. At the same time, the current mouse position is recorded. You add this logic to the event handler for the Label.MouseDown event.

3. When the user moves the mouse over the label, the form is moved correspondingly, so that the position of the mouse over the label is unchanged. You add this logic to the event handler for the Label.MouseMove event.

4. When the user releases the mouse button, the dragging mode is switched off. You add this logic to the event handler for the Label.MouseUp event.

The Code

The following example creates a borderless form that a user can move by clicking on a form control and dragging the form.

```
using System;
using System.Drawing;
using System.Windows.Forms;

namespace Apress.VisualCSharpRecipes.Chapter07
{
    public partial class Recipe07_15 : Form
    {
        // Boolean member tracks whether the form is in drag mode. If it is,
        // mouse movements over the label will be translated into form movements.
        private bool dragging;
```

```
// Stores the offset where the label is clicked.
private Point pointClicked;

public Recipe07_15()
{
    // Initialization code is designer generated and contained
    // in a separate file using the C# 2.0 support for partial
    // classes.
    InitializeComponent();
}

// MouseDown event handler for the label initiates the dragging process.
private void lblDrag_MouseDown(object sender, MouseEventArgs e)
{
    if (e.Button == MouseButtons.Left)
    {
        // Turn drag mode on and store the point clicked.
        dragging = true;
        pointClicked = new Point(e.X, e.Y);
    }
    else
    {
        dragging = false;
    }
}

// MouseMove event handler for the label processes dragging movements if
// the form is in drag mode.
private void lblDrag_MouseMove(object sender, MouseEventArgs e)
{
    if (dragging)
    {
        Point pointMoveTo;

        // Find the current mouse position in screen coordinates.
        pointMoveTo = this.PointToScreen(new Point(e.X, e.Y));

        // Compensate for the position the control was clicked.
        pointMoveTo.Offset(-pointClicked.X, -pointClicked.Y);

        // Move the form.
        this.Location = pointMoveTo;
    }
}

// MouseUp event handler for the label switches off drag mode.
private void lblDrag_MouseUp(object sender, MouseEventArgs e)
{
    dragging = false;
}

private void cmdClose_Click(object sender, EventArgs e)
{
    this.Close();
}

[STAThread]
public static void Main(string[] args)
```

```
        {
            Application.Run(new Recipe07_15());
        }
    }
}
```

7-16. Create an Animated System Tray Icon

Problem

You need to create an animated system tray icon (perhaps to indicate the status of a long-running task).

Solution

Create and show a NotifyIcon control. Use a timer that fires periodically (every second or so) and updates the NotifyIcon.Icon property.

How It Works

The .NET Framework makes it easy to show a system tray icon with the NotifyIcon component. You simply need to add this component to a form and supply an icon by setting the Icon property. Optionally, you can add a linked context menu through the ContextMenu property. The NotifyIcon component automatically displays its context menu when it's right-clicked. You can animate a system tray icon by swapping the icon periodically.

The Code

The following example uses eight icons, each of which shows a moon graphic in a different stage of fullness. By moving from one image to another, the illusion of animation is created.

```
using System;
using System.Drawing;
using System.Windows.Forms;

namespace Apress.VisualCSharpRecipes.Chapter07
{
    public partial class Recipe07_16 : Form
    {
        // An array to hold the set of Icons used to create the
        // animation effect.
        private Icon[] images = new Icon[8];

        // An integer to identify the current icon to display.
        int offset = 0;

        public Recipe07_16()
        {
            // Initialization code is designer generated and contained
            // in a separate file using the C# 2.0 support for partial
            // classes.
            InitializeComponent();
        }
```

```
        protected override void OnLoad(EventArgs e)
        {
            // Call the OnLoad method of the base class to ensure the Load
            // event is raised correctly.
            base.OnLoad(e);

            // Load the basic set of eight icons.
            images[0] = new Icon("moon01.ico");
            images[1] = new Icon("moon02.ico");
            images[2] = new Icon("moon03.ico");
            images[3] = new Icon("moon04.ico");
            images[4] = new Icon("moon05.ico");
            images[5] = new Icon("moon06.ico");
            images[6] = new Icon("moon07.ico");
            images[7] = new Icon("moon08.ico");
        }

        private void timer_Elapsed(object sender, System.Timers.ElapsedEventArgs e)
        {
            // Change the icon. This event handler fires once every second
            // (1000 ms).
            notifyIcon.Icon = images[offset];
            offset++;
            if (offset > 7) offset = 0;
        }

        [STAThread]
        public static void Main(string[] args)
        {
            Application.Run(new Recipe07_16());
        }
    }
}
```

7-17. Validate an Input Control

Problem

You need to alert the user of invalid input in a control, such as a TextBox.

Solution

Use the ErrorProvider component to display an error icon next to the offending control. Check for errors before allowing the user to continue.

How It Works

You can perform validation in a Windows-based application in a number of ways. One approach is to refuse any invalid character as the user presses a key, by using a MaskedTextBox control, as shown in recipe 7-8. Another approach is to respond to control validation events and prevent users from changing focus from one control to another if an error exists. A less invasive approach is to simply flag the offending control in some way, so that the user can review all the errors at once. You can use this approach by adding the ErrorProvider component to your form.

The ErrorProvider is a special property extender component that displays error icons next to invalid controls. You show the error icon next to a control by using the ErrorProvider.SetError method and specifying the appropriate control and a string error message. The ErrorProvider will then show a warning icon to the right of the control. When the user hovers the mouse above the warning icon, the detailed message appears.

You need to add only one ErrorProvider component to your form, and you can use it to display an error icon next to any control. To add the ErrorProvider, drag it on the form or into the component tray, or create it manually in code.

The Code

The following example checks the value that a user has entered into a textbox whenever the textbox loses focus. The code validates this textbox using a regular expression that checks to see if the value corresponds to the format of a valid e-mail address (see recipe 2-5 for more details on regular expressions). If validation fails, the ErrorProvider is used to display an error message. If the text is valid, any existing error message is cleared from the ErrorProvider. Finally, the Click event handler for the OK button steps through all the controls on the form and verifies that none of them have errors before allowing the example to continue. In this example, an empty textbox is allowed, although it would be a simple matter to perform additional checks when the OK button is pressed for situations where empty textboxes are not acceptable.

```
using System;
using System.Windows.Forms;
using System.Text.RegularExpressions;

namespace Apress.VisualCSharpRecipes.Chapter07
{
    public partial class Recipe07_17 : Form
    {
        public Recipe07_17()
        {
            // Initialization code is designer generated and contained
            // in a separate file using the C# 2.0 support for partial
            // classes.
            InitializeComponent();
        }

        // Button click event handler ensures the ErrorProvider is not
        // reporting any error for each control before proceeding.
        private void Button1_Click(object sender, EventArgs e)
        {
            string errorText = "";
            bool invalidInput = false;

            foreach (Control ctrl in this.Controls)
            {
                if (errProvider.GetError(ctrl) != "")
                {
                    errorText += "   * " + errProvider.GetError(ctrl) + "\n";
                    invalidInput = true;
                }
            }

            if (invalidInput)
            {
                MessageBox.Show(
```

```
                        "The form contains the following unresolved errors:\n\n" +
                        errorText, "Invalid Input", MessageBoxButtons.OK,
                        MessageBoxIcon.Warning);
                }
                else
                {
                    this.Close();
                }
            }

            // When the TextBox loses focus, check that the contents are a valid
            // e-mail address.
            private void txtEmail_Leave(object sender, EventArgs e)
            {
                // Create a regular expression to check for valid e-mail addresses.
                Regex regex;
                regex = new Regex(@"^[\w-]+@([\w-]+\.)+[\w-]+$");

                // Validate the text from the control that raised the event.
                Control ctrl = (Control)sender;
                if (regex.IsMatch(ctrl.Text) || ctrl.Text == "")
                {
                    errProvider.SetError(ctrl, "");
                }
                else
                {
                    errProvider.SetError(ctrl, "This is not a valid email address.");
                }
            }

            [STAThread]
            public static void Main(string[] args)
            {
                Application.Run(new Recipe07_17());
            }
        }
    }
```

Usage

Figure 7-13 shows how the ErrorProvider control indicates an input error for the TextBox control when Recipe07-17 is run.

Figure 7-13. *A validated form with the* ErrorProvider

7-18. Use a Drag-and-Drop Operation

Problem

You need to use the drag-and-drop feature to exchange information between two controls (possibly in separate windows or in separate applications).

Solution

Start a drag-and-drop operation using the DoDragDrop method of the Control class, and then respond to the DragEnter and DragDrop events.

How It Works

A drag-and-drop operation allows the user to transfer information from one place to another by clicking an item and dragging it to another location. A drag-and-drop operation consists of the following three basic steps:

1. The user clicks a control, holds down the mouse button, and begins dragging. If the control supports the drag-and-drop feature, it sets aside some information.

2. The user drags the mouse over another control. If this control accepts the dragged type of content, the mouse cursor changes to the special drag-and-drop icon (arrow and page). Otherwise, the mouse cursor becomes a circle with a line drawn through it.

3. When the user releases the mouse button, the data is sent to the control, which can then process it appropriately.

To support drag-and-drop functionality, you must handle the DragEnter, DragDrop, and (typically) MouseDown events. To start a drag-and-drop operation, you call the source control's DoDragDrop method. At this point, you submit the data and specify the type of operations that will be supported (copying, moving, and so on). Controls that can receive dragged data must have the AllowDrop property set to true. These controls will receive a DragEnter event when the mouse drags the data over them. At this point, you can examine the data that is being dragged, decide whether the control can accept the drop, and set the DragEventArgs.Effect property accordingly. The final step is to respond to the DragDrop event, which occurs when the user releases the mouse button.

■**Note** It is very important that the Main method of your Windows application be annotated with the STAThread attribute if your application will provide drag-and-drop functionality.

The Code

The following example allows you to drag content between two textboxes, as well as to and from other applications that support drag-and-drop operations.

```
using System;
using System.Windows.Forms;

namespace Apress.VisualCSharpRecipes.Chapter07
{
    public partial class Recipe07_18 : Form
    {
```

```csharp
public Recipe07_18()
{
    // Initialization code is designer generated and contained
    // in a separate file using the C# 2.0 support for partial
    // classes.
    InitializeComponent();
}

private void TextBox_MouseDown(object sender, MouseEventArgs e)
{
    TextBox txt = (TextBox)sender;
    txt.SelectAll();
    txt.DoDragDrop(txt.Text, DragDropEffects.Copy);
}

private void TextBox_DragEnter(object sender, DragEventArgs e)
{
    if (e.Data.GetDataPresent(DataFormats.Text))
    {
        e.Effect = DragDropEffects.Copy;
    }
    else
    {
        e.Effect = DragDropEffects.None;
    }
}

private void TextBox_DragDrop(object sender, DragEventArgs e)
{
    TextBox txt = (TextBox)sender;
    txt.Text = (string)e.Data.GetData(DataFormats.Text);
}

[STAThread]
public static void Main(string[] args)
{
    Application.Run(new Recipe07_18());
}
    }
}
```

7-19. Use Context-Sensitive Help

Problem

You want to display a specific help file topic depending on the currently selected control.

Solution

Use the System.Windows.Forms.HelpProvider component, and set the HelpKeyword and HelpNavigator extended properties for each control.

How It Works

The .NET Framework provides support for context-sensitive help through the HelpProvider class. The HelpProvider class is a special extender control. You add it to the component tray of a form, and it extends all the controls on the form with a few additional properties, including HelpNavigator and HelpKeyword. For example, Figure 7-14 shows a form that has two controls and a HelpProvider named helpProvider1. The ListBox control, which is currently selected, has several help-specific properties that are provided through HelpProvider.

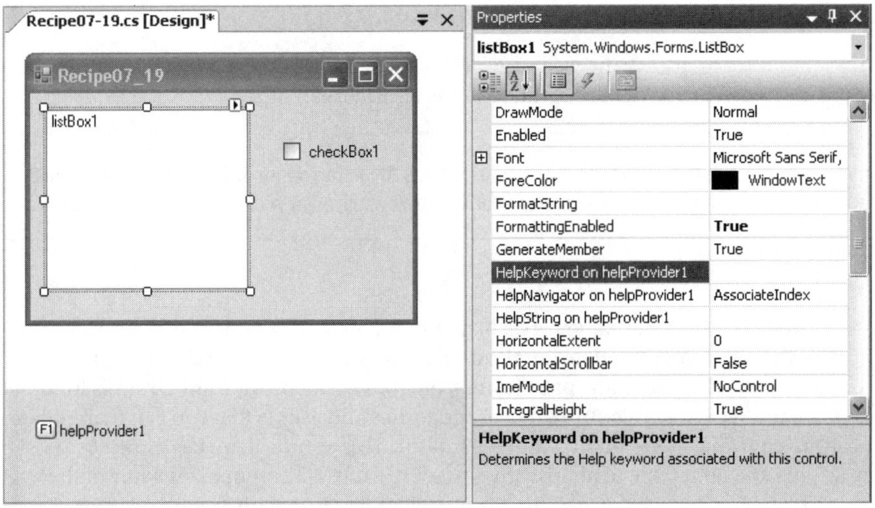

Figure 7-14. *The* HelpProvider *extender properties*

To use context-sensitive help with HelpProvider, you simply need to follow these three steps:

1. Set the HelpProvider.HelpNamespace property with the name of the help file. (For example, an HTML help file might be named myhelp.chm.)

2. For every control that requires context-sensitive help, set the HelpNavigator extender property to HelpNavigator.Topic.

3. For every control that requires context-sensitive help, set the HelpKeyword extender property with the name of the topic that should be linked to this control. (The topic names are specific to the help file and can be configured in your help authoring tools.)

If the user presses the F1 key while a control has focus, the help file will be launched automatically, and the linked topic will be displayed in the help window. If the user presses F1 while positioned on a control that does not have a linked help topic, the help settings for the containing control will be used (for example, a group box or a panel). If there are no containing controls or the containing control does not have any help settings, the form's help settings will be used. You can also use the HelpProvider methods to set or modify context-sensitive help mapping at runtime.

7-20. Display a Web Page in a Windows-Based Application

Problem

You want to display a web page and provide web-navigation capabilities within your Windows Forms application.

Solution

Use the WebBrowser control to display the web page and other standard controls like buttons and textboxes to allow the user to control the operation of the WebBrowser.

■**Caution** The WebBrowser control is a managed wrapper around the WebBrowser ActiveX control. This means that you must ensure you annotate the Main method of your Windows application with the STAThread attribute.

How It Works

The WebBrowser control (new to .NET Framework 2.0) makes it a trivial task to embed highly functional web browser capabilities into your Windows applications. The WebBrowser control is responsible for the display of web pages and maintaining page history, but it does not provide any controls for user interaction. Instead, the WebBrowser control exposes properties and events that you can manipulate programmatically to control the operation of the WebBrowser. This approach makes the WebBrowser control highly flexible and adaptable to almost any situation. Table 7-1 summarizes some of the WebBrowser members related to web navigation that you will find particularly useful.

Table 7-1. *Commonly Used Members of the* WebBrowser *Control*

Member	Description
Property	
AllowNavigation	Controls whether the WebBrowser can navigate to another page after its initial page has been loaded
CanGoBack	Indicates whether the WebBrowser currently holds back page history, which would allow the GoBack method to succeed
CanGoForward	Indicates whether the WebBrowser currently holds forward page history, which would allow the GoForward method to succeed
IsBusy	Indicates whether the WebBrowser is currently busy downloading a page
Url	Holds the URL of the currently displayed/downloading page
Method	
GoBack	Displays the previous page in the page history
GoForward	Displays the next page in the page history
GoHome	Displays the home page of the current user as configured in Windows
Navigate	Displays the web page at the specified URL
Stop	Stops the current WebBrowser activity
Event	
DocumentCompleted	Signals that the active download has completed and the document is displayed in the WebBrowser

You can also use the `WebBrowser.DocumentText` property to set (or get) the currently displayed HTML contents of the `WebBrowser`. To manipulate the contents using the Document Object Model (DOM), get an `HtmlDocument` instance via the `Document` property.

The Code

The following example uses the `WebBrowser` control to allow users to navigate to a web page whose address is entered into a `TextBox`. Buttons also allow users to move forward and backward through page history and navigate directly to their personal home page.

```csharp
using System;
using System.Windows.Forms;

namespace Apress.VisualCSharpRecipes.Chapter07
{
    public partial class Recipe07_20 : Form
    {
        public Recipe07_20()
        {
            // Initialization code is designer generated and contained
            // in a separate file using the C# 2.0 support for partial
            // classes.
            InitializeComponent();
        }

        private void goButton_Click(object sender, EventArgs e)
        {
            // Navigate to the URL specified in the textbox.
            webBrowser1.Navigate(textURL.Text);
        }

        private void homeButton_Click(object sender, EventArgs e)
        {
            // Navigate to the current user's home page.
            webBrowser1.GoHome();
        }

        protected override void OnLoad(EventArgs e)
        {
            // Call the OnLoad method of the base class to ensure the Load
            // event is raised correctly.
            base.OnLoad(e);

            // Navigate to the Apress home page when the application first
            // loads.
            webBrowser1.Navigate("http://www.apress.com");
        }

        private void backButton_Click(object sender, EventArgs e)
        {
            // Go to the previous page in the WebBrowser history.
            webBrowser1.GoBack();
        }
```

```csharp
        private void forwarButton_Click(object sender, EventArgs e)
        {
            // Go to the next page in the WebBrowser history.
            webBrowser1.GoForward();
        }

        // Event handler to perform general interface maintenance once a document
        // has been loaded into the WebBrowser.
        private void webBrowser1_DocumentCompleted(object sender,
            WebBrowserDocumentCompletedEventArgs e)
        {
            // Update the content of the TextBox to reflect the current URL.
            textURL.Text = webBrowser1.Url.ToString();

            // Enable or disable the Back button depending on whether the
            // WebBrowser has back history.
            if (webBrowser1.CanGoBack)
            {
                backButton.Enabled = true;
            }
            else
            {
                backButton.Enabled = false;
            }

            // Enable or disable the Forward button depending on whether the
            // WebBrowser has forward history.
            if (webBrowser1.CanGoForward)
            {
                forwarButton.Enabled = true;
            }
            else
            {
                forwarButton.Enabled = false;
            }
        }

        [STAThread]
        public static void Main(string[] args)
        {
            Application.Run(new Recipe07_20());
        }
    }
}
```

■ ■ ■

CHAPTER 8

Graphics, Multimedia, and Printing

Graphics, video, sound, and printing are the hallmarks of a traditional rich client on the Microsoft Windows operating system. When it comes to multimedia, the Microsoft .NET Framework delivers a compromise, providing support for some of these features while ignoring others. For example, you will find a sophisticated set of tools for two-dimensional drawing and event-based printing with GDI+ and the types in the System.Drawing namespaces. These classes wrap GDI32.dll and USER32.dll, which provide the native Graphics Device Interface (GDI) functions in the Windows application programming interface (API), and they make it much easier to draw complex shapes, work with coordinates and transforms, and process images. On the other hand, if you want to show a video file or get information about the current print jobs, you will need to look beyond the .NET Framework.

This chapter presents recipes that show you how to use built-in .NET features and, where necessary, native Win32 libraries via P/Invoke or COM Interop. The recipes in this chapter describe how to do the following:

- Find the fonts installed in your system (recipe 8-1)

- Perform hit testing with shapes (recipe 8-2)

- Create an irregularly shaped form or control (recipe 8-3)

- Create a sprite that could be moved around (recipe 8-4)

- Display an image that could be made to scroll (recipe 8-5), learn how to capture the image of the desktop (recipe 8-6), and create a thumbnail for an existing image (recipe 8-8)

- Enable double buffering to increase performance while redrawing (recipe 8-7)

- Play a beep or a system-defined sound (recipe 8-9), play a WAV file (recipe 8-10), play a non-WAV file such as an MP3 file (recipe 8-11), and play an animation with DirectShow (recipe 8-12)

- Retrieve information about the printers installed in the machine (recipe 8-13), print a simple document (recipe 8-14), print a document having multiple pages (recipe 8-15), print wrapped text (recipe 8-16), show a print preview (recipe 8-17), and manage print jobs (recipe 8-18)

8-1. Find All Installed Fonts

Problem

You need to retrieve a list of all the fonts installed on the current computer.

Solution

Create a new instance of the System.Drawing.Text.InstalledFontCollection class, which contains a collection of FontFamily objects representing all the installed fonts.

How It Works

The InstalledFontCollection class allows you to retrieve information about currently installed fonts. It derives from the FontCollection class, which allows you to get a list of font families as a collection in the Families property.

The Code

The following code shows a form that iterates through the font collection when it is first created. Every time it finds a font, it creates a new Label control that will display the font name in the given font face (at a size of 14 points). The Label is added to a Panel control named pnlFonts with AutoScroll set to true, allowing the user to scroll through the list of available fonts.

```
using System;
using System.Drawing;
using System.Windows.Forms;
using System.Drawing.Text;

namespace Apress.VisualCSharpRecipes.Chapter08
{
    public partial class Recipe08_01: Form
    {
        public Recipe08_01()
        {
            InitializeComponent();
        }

        private void Recipe08_01_Load(object sender, EventArgs e)
        {
            // Create the font collection.
            using (InstalledFontCollection fontFamilies =
                new InstalledFontCollection())
            {
                // Iterate through all font families.
                int offset = 10;
                foreach (FontFamily family in fontFamilies.Families)
                {
                    try
                    {
                        // Create a label that will display text in this font.
                        Label fontLabel = new Label();
                        fontLabel.Text = family.Name;
                        fontLabel.Font = new Font(family, 14);
                        fontLabel.Left = 10;
                        fontLabel.Width = pnlFonts.Width;
                        fontLabel.Top = offset;

                        // Add the label to a scrollable Panel.
                        pnlFonts.Controls.Add(fontLabel);
                        offset += 30;
                    }
```

```
catch
{
    // An error will occur if the selected font does
    // not support normal style (the default used when
    // creating a Font object). This problem can be
    // harmlessly ignored.
}
                }
            }
        }
    }
}
```

Figure 8-1 shows this simple test application.

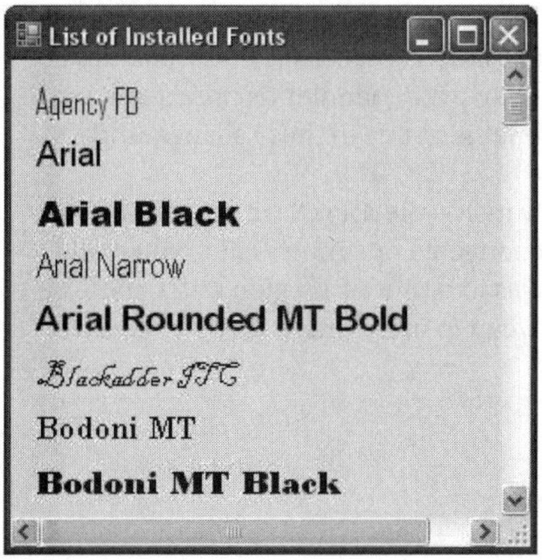

Figure 8-1. *A list of installed fonts*

8-2. Perform Hit Testing with Shapes

Problem

You need to detect whether a user clicks inside a shape.

Solution

Test the point where the user clicked with methods such as Rectangle.Contains and Region.IsVisible (in the System.Drawing namespace) or GraphicsPath.IsVisible (in the System.Drawing.Drawing2D namespace), depending on the type of shape.

How It Works

Often, if you use GDI+ to draw shapes on a form, you need to be able to determine when a user clicks inside a given shape. The .NET Framework provides three methods to help with this task:

- The Rectangle.Contains method, which takes a point and returns true if the point is inside a given rectangle. In many cases, you can retrieve a rectangle for another type of shape. For example, you can use Image.GetBounds to retrieve the invisible rectangle that represents the image boundaries. The Rectangle struct is a member of the System.Drawing namespace.

- The GraphicsPath.IsVisible method, which takes a point and returns true if the point is inside the area defined by a closed GraphicsPath. Because a GraphicsPath can contain multiple lines, shapes, and figures, this approach is useful if you want to test whether a point is contained inside a nonrectangular region. The GraphicsPath class is a member of the System.Drawing. Drawing2D namespace.

- The Region.IsVisible method, which takes a point and returns true if the point is inside the area defined by a Region. A Region, like the GraphicsPath, can represent a complex nonrectangular shape. Region is a member of the System.Drawing namespace.

The Code

The following example shows a form that creates a Rectangle and a GraphicsPath. By default, these two shapes are given light-blue backgrounds. However, an event handler responds to the Form.MouseMove event, checks to see whether the mouse pointer is in one of these shapes, and updates the background to bright pink if the pointer is there.

Note that the highlighting operation takes place directly inside the MouseMove event handler. The painting is performed only if the current selection has changed. For simpler code, you could invalidate the entire form every time the mouse pointer moves in or out of a region and handle all the drawing in the Form.Paint event handler, but this would lead to more drawing and generate additional flicker as the entire form is repainted.

```
using System;
using System.Drawing;
using System.Windows.Forms;
using System.Drawing.Drawing2D;

namespace Apress.VisualCSharpRecipes.Chapter08
{
    public partial class Recipe08_02 : Form
    {
        // Define the shapes used on this form.
        private GraphicsPath path;
        private Rectangle rectangle;

        // Define the flags that track where the mouse pointer is.
        private bool inPath = false;
        private bool inRectangle = false;

        // Define the brushes used for painting the shapes.
        Brush highlightBrush = Brushes.HotPink;
        Brush defaultBrush = Brushes.LightBlue;

        public Recipe08_02()
        {
            InitializeComponent();
        }
```

```csharp
private void Recipe08_02_Load(object sender, EventArgs e)
{
    // Create the shapes that will be displayed.
    path = new GraphicsPath();
    path.AddEllipse(10, 10, 100, 60);
    path.AddCurve(new Point[] {new Point(50, 50),
            new Point(10,33), new Point(80,43)});
    path.AddLine(50, 120, 250, 80);
    path.AddLine(120, 40, 110, 50);
    path.CloseFigure();

    rectangle = new Rectangle(100, 170, 220, 120);
}

private void Recipe08_02_Paint(object sender, PaintEventArgs e)
{
    Graphics g = e.Graphics;

    // Paint the shapes according to the current selection.
    if (inPath)
    {
        g.FillPath(highlightBrush, path);
        g.FillRectangle(defaultBrush, rectangle);
    }
    else if (inRectangle)
    {
        g.FillRectangle(highlightBrush, rectangle);
        g.FillPath(defaultBrush, path);
    }
    else
    {
        g.FillPath(defaultBrush, path);
        g.FillRectangle(defaultBrush, rectangle);
    }
    g.DrawPath(Pens.Black, path);
    g.DrawRectangle(Pens.Black, rectangle);
}

private void Recipe08_02_MouseMove(object sender, MouseEventArgs e)
{
    using (Graphics g = this.CreateGraphics())
    {
        // Perform hit testing with rectangle.
        if (rectangle.Contains(e.X, e.Y))
        {
            if (!inRectangle)
            {
                inRectangle = true;

                // Highlight the rectangle.
                g.FillRectangle(highlightBrush, rectangle);
                g.DrawRectangle(Pens.Black, rectangle);
            }
        }
        else if (inRectangle)
        {
            inRectangle = false;
```

```
                    // Restore the unhighlighted rectangle.
                    g.FillRectangle(defaultBrush, rectangle);
                    g.DrawRectangle(Pens.Black, rectangle);
                }

                // Perform hit testing with path.
                if (path.IsVisible(e.X, e.Y))
                {
                    if (!inPath)
                    {
                        inPath = true;

                        // Highlight the path.
                        g.FillPath(highlightBrush, path);
                        g.DrawPath(Pens.Black, path);
                    }
                }
                else if (inPath)
                {
                    inPath = false;

                    // Restore the unhighlighted path.
                    g.FillPath(defaultBrush, path);
                    g.DrawPath(Pens.Black, path);
                }
            }
        }
    }
}
```

Figure 8-2 shows the application in action.

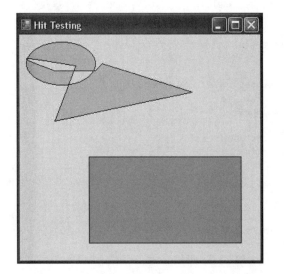

Figure 8-2. *Hit testing with a* Rectangle *and a* GraphicsPath *object*

8-3. Create an Irregularly Shaped Control

Problem

You need to create a nonrectangular form or control.

Solution

Create a new `System.Drawing.Region` object that has the shape you want for the form, and assign it to the `Form.Region` or `Control.Region` property.

How It Works

To create a nonrectangular form or control, you first need to define the shape you want. The easiest approach is to use the `System.Drawing.Drawing2D.GraphicsPath` object, which can accommodate any combination of ellipses, rectangles, closed curves, and even strings. You can add shapes to a `GraphicsPath` instance using methods such as `AddEllipse`, `AddRectangle`, `AddClosedCurve`, and `AddString`. Once you are finished defining the shape you want, you can create a `Region` object from this `GraphicsPath`—just submit the `GraphicsPath` in the `Region` class constructor. Finally, you can assign the `Region` to the `Form.Region` property or the `Control.Region` property.

The Code

The following example creates an irregularly shaped form (shown in Figure 8-3) using two curves made of multiple points, which are converted into a closed figure using the `GraphicsPath.CloseAllFigures` method.

```
using System;
using System.Drawing;
using System.Windows.Forms;
using System.Drawing.Drawing2D;

namespace Apress.VisualCSharpRecipes.Chapter08
{
    public partial class Recipe08_03 : Form
    {
        public Recipe08_03()
        {
            InitializeComponent();
        }

        private void Recipe08_03_Load(object sender, EventArgs e)
        {
            GraphicsPath path = new GraphicsPath();

            Point[] pointsA = new Point[]
                {
                    new Point(0, 0),
                    new Point(40, 60),
                    new Point(this.Width - 100, 10)
                };
            path.AddCurve(pointsA);
```

```
            Point[] pointsB = new Point[]
                {
                    new Point(this.Width - 40, this.Height - 60),
                    new Point(this.Width, this.Height),
                    new Point(10, this.Height)
                };
            path.AddCurve(pointsB);

            path.CloseAllFigures();

            this.Region = new Region(path);
        }

        private void cmdClose_Click(object sender, EventArgs e)
        {
            this.Close();
        }
    }
}
```

■ Note Another method for creating nonrectangular forms (not controls) is using the `BackgroundImage` and `TransparentKey` properties available in the `Form` class. However, this method could cause display problems when monitors are set to a color depth greater than 24-bit. For more information about this topic, refer to the Microsoft Developer Network (MSDN) documentation.

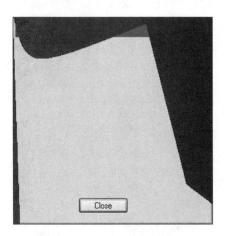

Figure 8-3. *A nonrectangular form*

For an example that demonstrates a nonrectangular control, refer to recipe 8-4.

8-4. Create a Movable Sprite

Problem

You need to create a shape the user can manipulate on a form, perhaps by dragging it, resizing it, or otherwise interacting with it.

Solution

Create a custom control, and override the painting logic to draw a shape. Assign your shape to the Control.Region property. You can then use this Region to perform hit testing.

How It Works

If you need to create a complex user interface that incorporates many custom-drawn elements, you need a way to track these elements and allow the user to interact with them. The easiest approach in .NET is to create a dedicated control by deriving a class from System.Windows.Forms.Control. You can then customize the way this control is painted in the way its basic set of events is raised.

The Code

The following example shows a control that represents a simple ellipse shape on a form. All controls are associated with a rectangular region on a form, so the EllipseShape control generates an ellipse that fills these boundaries (provided through the Control.ClientRectangle property). Once the shape has been generated, the Control.Region property is set according to the bounds on the ellipse. This ensures events such as MouseMove, MouseDown, Click, and so on, will occur only if the mouse is over the ellipse, not the entire client rectangle.

The following code shows the full EllipseShape code:

```
using System;
using System.Drawing;
using System.Windows.Forms;
using System.Drawing.Drawing2D;

namespace Apress.VisualCSharpRecipes.Chapter08
{
    public partial class EllipseShape : Control
    {
        public EllipseShape()
        {
            InitializeComponent();
        }

        private GraphicsPath path = null;

        private void RefreshPath()
        {
            // Create the GraphicsPath for the shape (in this case
            // an ellipse that fits inside the full control area)
            // and apply it to the control by setting
            // the Region property.
            path = new GraphicsPath();
            path.AddEllipse(this.ClientRectangle);
            this.Region = new Region(path);
        }
```

```
        protected override void OnPaint(PaintEventArgs e)
        {
            base.OnPaint(e);
            if (path != null)
            {
                e.Graphics.SmoothingMode = SmoothingMode.AntiAlias;
                e.Graphics.FillPath(new SolidBrush(this.BackColor), path);
                e.Graphics.DrawPath(new Pen(this.ForeColor, 4), path);
            }
        }

        protected override void OnResize(System.EventArgs e)
        {
            base.OnResize(e);
            RefreshPath();
            this.Invalidate();
        }
    }
}
```

You could define the EllipseShape control in a separate class library assembly so you could add it to the Microsoft Visual Studio .NET Toolbox and use it at design time. However, even without taking this step, it is easy to create a simple test application. The following Windows Forms application creates two ellipses and allows the user to drag both of them around the form, simply by holding the mouse down and moving the pointer.

```
using System;
using System.Drawing;
using System.Windows.Forms;

namespace Apress.VisualCSharpRecipes.Chapter08
{
    public partial class Recipe08_04 : Form
    {
        public Recipe08_04()
        {
            InitializeComponent();
        }

        // Tracks when drag mode is on.
        private bool isDraggingA = false;
        private bool isDraggingB = false;

        // The ellipse shape controls.
        private EllipseShape ellipseA, ellipseB;

        private void Recipe08_04_Load(object sender, EventArgs e)
        {
            // Create and configure both ellipses.
            ellipseA = new EllipseShape();
            ellipseA.Width = ellipseA.Height = 100;
            ellipseA.Top = ellipseA.Left = 30;
            ellipseA.BackColor = Color.Red;
            this.Controls.Add(ellipseA);

            ellipseB = new EllipseShape();
            ellipseB.Width = ellipseB.Height = 100;
            ellipseB.Top = ellipseB.Left = 130;
```

```csharp
        ellipseB.BackColor = Color.Azure;
        this.Controls.Add(ellipseB);

        // Attach both ellipses to the same set of event handlers.
        ellipseA.MouseDown += Ellipse_MouseDown;
        ellipseA.MouseUp += Ellipse_MouseUp;
        ellipseA.MouseMove += Ellipse_MouseMove;

        ellipseB.MouseDown += Ellipse_MouseDown;
        ellipseB.MouseUp += Ellipse_MouseUp;
        ellipseB.MouseMove += Ellipse_MouseMove;
    }

    private void Ellipse_MouseDown(object sender, MouseEventArgs e)
    {
        // Get the ellipse that triggered this event.
        Control control = (Control)sender;

        if (e.Button == MouseButtons.Left)
        {
            control.Tag = new Point(e.X, e.Y);
            if (control == ellipseA)
            {
                isDraggingA = true;
            }
            else
            {
                isDraggingB = true;
            }
        }
    }

    private void Ellipse_MouseUp(object sender, MouseEventArgs e)
    {
        isDraggingA = false;
        isDraggingB = false;
    }

    private void Ellipse_MouseMove(object sender, MouseEventArgs e)
    {
        // Get the ellipse that triggered this event.
        Control control = (Control)sender;

        if ((isDraggingA && control == ellipseA) ||
         (isDraggingB && control == ellipseB))
        {
            // Get the offset.
            Point point = (Point)control.Tag;

            // Move the control.
            control.Left = e.X + control.Left - point.X;
            control.Top = e.Y + control.Top - point.Y;
        }
    }
}
}
```

Figure 8-4 shows the user about to drag an ellipse.

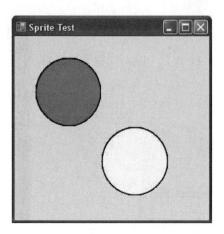

Figure 8-4. *Dragging custom shape controls on a form*

8-5. Create a Scrollable Image

Problem

You need to create a scrollable picture with dynamic content.

Solution

Leverage the automatic scroll capabilities of the `System.Windows.Forms.Panel` control by setting `Panel.AutoScroll` to true and placing a `System.Windows.Forms.PictureBox` control with the image content inside the `Panel`.

How It Works

The `Panel` control has built-in scrolling support, as shown in recipe 8-1. If you place any controls in it that extend beyond its bounds and you set `Panel.AutoScroll` to true, the panel will show scroll bars that allow the user to move through the content. This works particularly well with large images. You can load or create the image in memory, assign it to a picture box (which has no intrinsic support for scrolling), and then show the picture box inside the panel. The only consideration you need to remember is to make sure you set the picture box dimensions equal to the full size of the image you want to show.

The Code

The following example creates an image that represents a document. The image is generated as an in-memory bitmap, and several lines of text are added using the `Graphics.DrawString` method. The image is then bound to a picture box, which is shown in a scrollable panel, as shown in Figure 8-5.

```
using System;
using System.Drawing;
using System.Windows.Forms;
```

```
namespace Apress.VisualCSharpRecipes.Chapter08
{
    public partial class Recipe08_05 : Form
    {
        public Recipe08_05()
        {
            InitializeComponent();
        }

        private void Recipe08_05_Load(object sender, EventArgs e)
        {
            string text = "The quick brown fox jumps over the lazy dog.";
            using (Font font = new Font("Tahoma", 20))
            {
                // Create an in-memory bitmap.
                Bitmap b = new Bitmap(600, 600);
                using (Graphics g = Graphics.FromImage(b))
                {
                    g.FillRectangle(Brushes.White, new Rectangle(0, 0,
                        b.Width, b.Height));

                    // Draw several lines of text on the bitmap.
                    for (int i = 0; i < 10; i++)
                    {
                        g.DrawString(text, font, Brushes.Black,
                            50, 50 + i * 60);
                    }
                }

                // Display the bitmap in the picture box.
                pictureBox1.BackgroundImage = b;
                pictureBox1.Size = b.Size;
            }
        }
    }
}
```

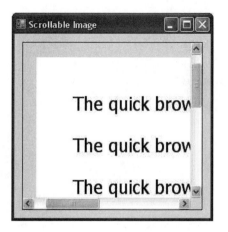

Figure 8-5. *Adding scrolling support to custom content*

8-6. Perform a Screen Capture

Problem

You need to take a snapshot of the current desktop.

Solution

Use the CopyFromScreen method of the Graphics class to copy screen contents.

How It Works

The Graphics class now includes CopyFromScreen methods that copy color data from the screen onto the drawing surface represented by a Graphics object. This method requires you to pass the source and destination points and the size of the image to be copied.

The Code

The following example captures the screen and displays it in a picture box. It first creates a new Bitmap object and then invokes CopyFromScreen to draw onto the Bitmap. After drawing, the image is assigned to the picture box, as shown in Figure 8-6.

```
using System;
using System.Drawing;
using System.Windows.Forms;

namespace Apress.VisualCSharpRecipes.Chapter08
{
    public partial class Recipe08_06 : Form
    {
        public Recipe08_06()
        {
            InitializeComponent();
        }

        private void cmdCapture_Click(object sender, EventArgs e)
        {
            Bitmap screen = new Bitmap(Screen.PrimaryScreen.Bounds.Width,
                Screen.PrimaryScreen.Bounds.Height);

            using (Graphics g = Graphics.FromImage(screen))
            {
                g.CopyFromScreen(0, 0, 0, 0, screen.Size);
            }

            pictureBox1.Image = screen;
        }
    }
}
```

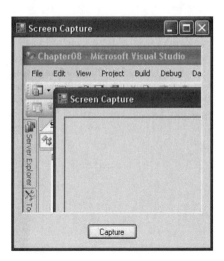

Figure 8-6. *Capturing the screen contents*

8-7. Use Double Buffering to Increase Redraw Speed

Problem

You need to optimize drawing for a form or an authored control that is frequently refreshed, and you want to reduce flicker.

Solution

Set the DoubleBuffered property of the form to true.

How It Works

In some applications you need to repaint a form or control frequently. This is commonly the case when creating animations. For example, you might use a timer to invalidate your form every second. Your painting code could then redraw an image at a new location, creating the illusion of motion. The problem with this approach is that every time you invalidate the form, Windows repaints the window background (clearing the form) and then runs your painting code, which draws the graphic element by element. This can cause substantial on-screen flicker.

   Double buffering is a technique you can implement to reduce this flicker. With double buffering, your drawing logic writes to an in-memory bitmap, which is copied to the form at the end of the drawing operation in a single, seamless repaint operation. Flickering is reduced dramatically.

   The .NET Framework 2.0 provides a default double buffering mechanism for forms and controls. You can enable this by setting the DoubleBuffered property of your form or control to true or by using the SetStyle method.

The Code

The following example sets the DoubleBuffered property of the form to true and shows an animation of an image alternately growing and shrinking on the page. The drawing logic takes place in the
Form.Paint event handler, and a timer invalidates the form in a preset interval so that the image can
be redrawn. The user can choose whether to enable double buffering through a checkbox on the
form. Without double buffering, the form flickers noticeably. When double buffering is enabled,
however, the image grows and shrinks with smooth, flicker-free animation.

```csharp
using System;
using System.Drawing;
using System.Windows.Forms;
using System.Drawing.Drawing2D;

namespace Apress.VisualCSharpRecipes.Chapter08
{
    public partial class Recipe08_07 : Form
    {
        public Recipe08_07()
        {
            InitializeComponent();
        }

        // Track the image size and the type of animation
        // (expanding or shrinking).
        private bool isShrinking = false;
        private int imageSize = 0;

        // Store the logo that will be painted on the form.
        private Image image;

        private void Recipe08_07_Load(object sender, EventArgs e)
        {
            // Load the logo image from the file.
            image = Image.FromFile("test.jpg");

            // Start the timer that invalidates the form.
            tmrRefresh.Start();
        }

        private void tmrRefresh_Tick(object sender, EventArgs e)
        {
            // Change the desired image size according to the animation mode.
            if (isShrinking)
            {
                imageSize--;
            }
            else
            {
                imageSize++;
            }

            // Change the sizing direction if it nears the form border.
            if (imageSize > (this.Width - 150))
            {
                isShrinking = true;
            }
            else if (imageSize < 1)
```

```
        {
            isShrinking = false;
        }

        // Repaint the form.
        this.Invalidate();
    }

    private void Recipe08_07_Paint(object sender, PaintEventArgs e)
    {
        Graphics g;

        g = e.Graphics;

        g.SmoothingMode = SmoothingMode.HighQuality;

        // Draw the background.
        g.FillRectangle(Brushes.Yellow, new Rectangle(new Point(0, 0),
        this.ClientSize));

        // Draw the logo image.
        g.DrawImage(image, 50, 50, 50 + imageSize, 50 + imageSize);
    }

    private void chkUseDoubleBuffering_CheckedChanged(object sender, EventArgs e)
    {
        this.DoubleBuffered = chkUseDoubleBuffering.Checked;
    }
    }
}
```

■**Note** You could also choose to manually handle double buffering. For more information, refer to the WinFX documentation at MSDN.

8-8. Show a Thumbnail for an Image

Problem

You need to show thumbnails (small representations of pictures) for the images in a directory.

Solution

Read the image from the file using the static FromFile method of the System.Drawing.Image class. You can then retrieve a thumbnail using the Image.GetThumbnailImage method.

How It Works

The Image class provides the functionality for generating thumbnails through the GetThumbnailImage method. You simply need to pass the width and height of the thumbnail you want (in pixels), and the Image class will create a new Image object that fits these criteria. Antialiasing is used when reducing the image to ensure the best possible image quality, although some blurriness and loss of detail is inevitable. (*Antialiasing* is the process of removing jagged edges, often in resized graphics, by adding shading with an intermediate color.) In addition, you can supply a notification callback, allowing you to create thumbnails asynchronously.

When generating a thumbnail, it is important to ensure that the aspect ratio remains constant. For example, if you reduce a 200×100 picture to a 50×50 thumbnail, the width will be compressed to one quarter and the height will be compressed to one half, distorting the image. To ensure that the aspect ratio remains constant, you can change either the width or the height to a fixed size and then adjust the other dimension proportionately.

The Code

The following example reads a bitmap file and generates a thumbnail that is not greater than 200×200 pixels while preserving the original aspect ratio:

```
using System;
using System.Drawing;
using System.Windows.Forms;

namespace Apress.VisualCSharpRecipes.Chapter08
{
    public partial class Recipe08_08 : Form
    {
        public Recipe08_08()
        {
            InitializeComponent();
        }

        Image thumbnail;

        private void Recipe08_08_Load(object sender, EventArgs e)
        {
            using (Image img = Image.FromFile("test.jpg"))
            {
                int thumbnailWidth = 0, thumbnailHeight = 0;

                // Adjust the largest dimension to 200 pixels.
                // This ensures that a thumbnail will not be larger than
                // 200x200 pixels.
                // If you are showing multiple thumbnails, you would reserve a
                // 200x200 pixel square for each one.
                if (img.Width > img.Height)
                {
                    thumbnailWidth = 200;
                    thumbnailHeight = Convert.ToInt32(((200F / img.Width) *
                        img.Height));
                }
                else
                {
                    thumbnailHeight = 200;
                    thumbnailWidth = Convert.ToInt32(((200F / img.Height) *
                        img.Width));
                }

                thumbnail = img.GetThumbnailImage(thumbnailWidth, thumbnailHeight,
                    null, IntPtr.Zero);
            }
        }
    }
```

```
        private void Recipe08_08_Paint(object sender, PaintEventArgs e)
        {
            e.Graphics.DrawImage(thumbnail, 10, 10);
        }
    }
}
```

8-9. Play a Simple Beep or System Sound

Problem

You need to play a simple system-defined beep or sound.

Solution

Use the new managed Beep method of the Console class or the Play method of the SystemSound class.

How It Works

The .NET Framework 2.0 now has new additions such as the Beep method in the Console class and a new namespace System.Media, which provides classes for playing sound files.

Overloads of the Console.Beep method let you play a beep with the default frequency and duration or with a frequency and duration you specify. Frequency is represented in hertz (and must range from 37 to 32,767), and the duration is represented in milliseconds. Internally, these methods invoke the Beep Win32 function and use the computer's internal speaker. Thus, if the computer does not have an internal speaker, no sound will be produced.

The System.Media namespace contains the SystemSound, SystemSounds, and SoundPlayer classes. The SystemSound class represents a Windows sound event, such as an asterisk, beep, question, and so on. It also defines a Play method, which lets you play the sound associated with it.

The SystemSounds class defines properties that let you obtain the SystemSound instance of a specific Windows sound event. For example, it defines an Asterisk property that returns a SystemSound instance associated with the asterisk Windows sound event.

The SoundPlayer class lets you play WAV files. For more information on how to play a WAV file using this class, refer to recipe 8-10.

The Code

The following example plays two different beeps and the asterisk sound in succession, using the Console and SystemSound classes:

```
using System;
using System.Windows.Forms;
using System.Media;

namespace Apress.VisualCSharpRecipes.Chapter08
{
    public partial class Recipe08_09 : Form
    {
        public Recipe08_09()
        {
            InitializeComponent();
        }
```

```
        private void Recipe08_09_Load(object sender, EventArgs e)
        {
            // Play a beep with default frequency
            // and duration (800 and 200, respectively)
            Console.Beep();

            // Play a beep with frequency as 200 and duration as 300
            Console.Beep(200, 300);

            // Play the sound associated with the Asterisk event
            SystemSounds.Asterisk.Play();
        }
    }
}
```

8-10. Play a WAV File

Problem

You need to play a WAV file.

Solution

Create a new instance of the System.Media.SoundPlayer class, pass the location or stream of the WAV file, and invoke the Play method.

How It Works

The .NET Framework 2.0 defines a new System.Media namespace that contains a SoundPlayer class. SoundPlayer contains constructors that let you specify the location of a WAV file or its stream. Once you have created an instance, you just need to invoke the Play method to play the file. The Play method creates a new thread to play the sound and is thus asynchronous (unless a stream is used). For playing the sound synchronously, use the PlaySync method. Note that SoundPlayer supports only the WAV format.

Before a file is played, it is loaded into memory. You can load a file in advance by invoking the Load or LoadSync method depending upon whether you want the operation to be asynchronous or synchronous.

The Code

The following example shows a simple form that allows users to open any WAV file and play it:

```
using System;
using System.Windows.Forms;
using System.Media;

namespace Apress.VisualCSharpRecipes.Chapter08
{
    public partial class Recipe08_10 : Form
    {
        public Recipe08_10()
        {
            InitializeComponent();
        }
```

```
private void cmdOpen_Click(object sender, EventArgs e)
{
    // Allow the user to choose a file.
    OpenFileDialog openDialog = new OpenFileDialog();
    openDialog.Filter = "WAV Files|*.wav|All Files|*.*";

    if (DialogResult.OK == openDialog.ShowDialog())
    {
        SoundPlayer player = new SoundPlayer(openDialog.FileName);

        try
        {
            player.Play();
        }
        catch (Exception)
        {
            MessageBox.Show("An error occurred while playing media.");
        }
        finally
        {
            player.Dispose();
        }
    }
}
```

8-11. Play a Sound File

Problem

You need to play a non-WAV format audio file such as an MP3 file.

Solution

Use the ActiveMovie COM component included with Windows Media Player, which supports WAV and MP3 audio.

How It Works

The ActiveMovie Quartz library provides a COM component that can play various types of audio files, including the WAV and MP3 formats. The Quartz type library is provided through quartz.dll and is included as a part of Microsoft DirectX with Media Player and the Windows operating system.

The first step for using the library is to generate an interop class that can manage the interaction between your .NET application and the unmanaged Quartz library. You can generate a C# class with this interop code using the Type Library Importer utility (Tlbimp.exe) and the following command line, where [WindowsDir] is the path for your installation of Windows:

```
tlbimp [WindowsDir]\system32\quartz.dll /out:QuartzTypeLib.dll
```

Alternatively, you can generate the interop class using Visual Studio .NET by adding a reference. Simply right-click your project in the Solution Explorer, and choose Add Reference from the context menu. Then select the COM tab, and scroll down to select ActiveMovie Control Type Library, as shown in Figure 8-7.

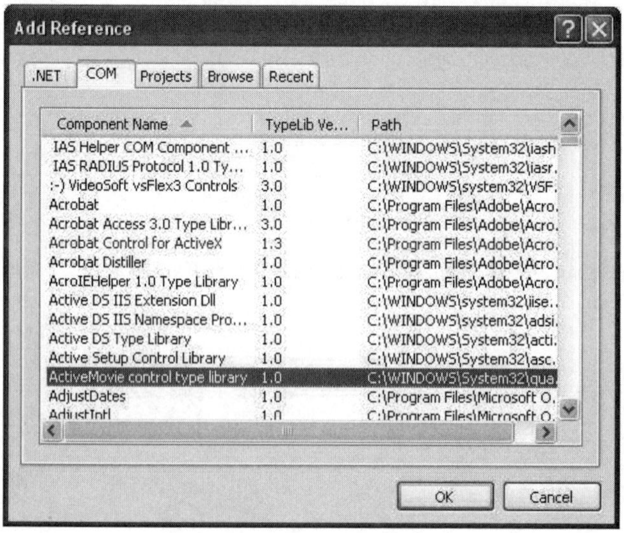

Figure 8-7. *Adding the Quartz interop class*

Once the interop class is generated, you can work with the IMediaControl interface. You can specify the file you want to play using RenderFile, and you can control playback using methods such as Run, Stop, and Pause. The actual playback takes place on a separate thread, so it will not block your code.

The Code

The following example shows a simple form that allows you to open any audio file and play it.

You can also use the Quartz library to show movie files, as demonstrated in recipe 8-12.

```csharp
using System;
using System.Windows.Forms;
using QuartzTypeLib;

namespace Apress.VisualCSharpRecipes.Chapter08
{
    public partial class Recipe08_11 : Form
    {
        public Recipe08_11()
        {
            InitializeComponent();
        }

        private void cmdOpen_Click(object sender, EventArgs e)
        {
```

```
        // Allow the user to choose a file.
        OpenFileDialog openFileDialog = new OpenFileDialog();
        openFileDialog.Filter =
            "Media Files|*.wav;*.mp3;*.mp2;*.wma|All Files|*.*";

        if (DialogResult.OK == openFileDialog.ShowDialog())
        {
            // Access the IMediaControl interface.
            QuartzTypeLib.FilgraphManager graphManager =
              new QuartzTypeLib.FilgraphManager();
            QuartzTypeLib.IMediaControl mc =
              (QuartzTypeLib.IMediaControl)graphManager;

            // Specify the file.
            mc.RenderFile(openFileDialog.FileName);

            // Start playing the audio asynchronously.
            mc.Run();
        }
    }
  }
}
```

8-12. Show an Animation with DirectShow

Problem

You need to play a video file (such as an MPEG, an AVI, or a WMV file) in a Windows Forms application.

Solution

Use the ActiveMovie COM component included with Windows Media Player. Bind the video output to a picture box on your form by setting the IVideoWindow.Owner property to the PictureBox.Handle property.

How It Works

Although the .NET Framework does not include any managed classes for interacting with video files, you can leverage the functionality of DirectShow using the COM-based Quartz library included with Windows Media Player and the Windows operating system. For information about creating an interop assembly for the Quartz type library, refer to the instructions in recipe 8-11.

Once you have created the interop assembly, you can use the IMediaControl interface to load and play a movie. This is essentially the same technique demonstrated in recipe 8-11 with audio files. However, if you want to show the video window inside your application interface (rather than in a separate stand-alone window), you must also use the IVideoWindow interface. The core FilgraphManager object can be cast to both the IMediaControl interface and the IVideoWindow interface—and several other interfaces are also supported, such as IBasicAudio (which allows you to configure balance and volume settings). With the IVideoWindow interface, you can bind the video output to a control on your form, such as a Panel or a PictureBox. To do so, set the IVideoWindow.Owner property to the handle for the control, which you can retrieve using the Control.Handle property. Then, call IVideoWindow. SetWindowPosition to set the window size and location. You can call this method to change the video size during playback (for example, if the form is resized).

The Code

The following example shows a simple form that allows users to open any video file and play it back in the provided picture box. The picture box is anchored to all sides of the form, so it changes size as the form resizes. The code responds to the PictureBox.SizeChanged event to change the size of the corresponding video window.

```
using System;
using System.Windows.Forms;
using QuartzTypeLib;

namespace Apress.VisualCSharpRecipes.Chapter08
{
    public partial class Recipe08_12 : Form
    {
        public Recipe08_12()
        {
            InitializeComponent();
        }

        // Define constants used for specifying the window style.
        private const int WS_CHILD = 0x40000000;
        private const int WS_CLIPCHILDREN = 0x2000000;

        // Hold a form-level reference to the media control interface,
        // so the code can control playback of the currently loaded
        // movie.
        private IMediaControl mc = null;

        // Hold a form-level reference to the video window in case it
        // needs to be resized.
        private IVideoWindow videoWindow = null;

        private void cmdOpen_Click(object sender, EventArgs e)
        {
            // Allow the user to choose a file.
            OpenFileDialog openFileDialog = new OpenFileDialog();
            openFileDialog.Filter =
            "Media Files|*.mpg;*.avi;*.wma;*.mov;*.wav;*.mp2;*.mp3|" +
            "All Files|*.*";

            if (DialogResult.OK == openFileDialog.ShowDialog())
            {
                // Stop the playback for the current movie, if it exists.
                if (mc != null) mc.Stop();

                // Load the movie file.
                FilgraphManager graphManager = new FilgraphManager();
                graphManager.RenderFile(openFileDialog.FileName);
```

```csharp
            // Attach the view to a picture box on the form.
            try
            {
                videoWindow = (IVideoWindow)graphManager;
                videoWindow.Owner = (int)pictureBox1.Handle;
                videoWindow.WindowStyle = WS_CHILD | WS_CLIPCHILDREN;
                videoWindow.SetWindowPosition(
                  pictureBox1.ClientRectangle.Left,
                  pictureBox1.ClientRectangle.Top,
                  pictureBox1.ClientRectangle.Width,
                  pictureBox1.ClientRectangle.Height);
            }
            catch
            {
                // An error can occur if the file does not have a video
                // source (for example, an MP3 file.)
                // You can ignore this error and still allow playback to
                // continue (without any visualization).
            }

            // Start the playback (asynchronously).
            mc = (IMediaControl)graphManager;
            mc.Run();
        }
    }

    private void pictureBox1_SizeChanged(object sender, EventArgs e)
    {
        if (videoWindow != null)
        {
            try
            {
                videoWindow.SetWindowPosition(
                    pictureBox1.ClientRectangle.Left,
                    pictureBox1.ClientRectangle.Top,
                    pictureBox1.ClientRectangle.Width,
                    pictureBox1.ClientRectangle.Height);
            }
            catch
            {
                // Ignore the exception thrown when resizing the form
                // when the file does not have a video source.
            }
        }
    }
}
```

Figure 8-8 shows an example of the output you will see.

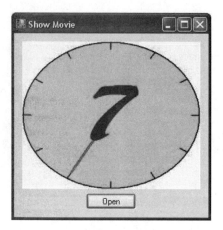

Figure 8-8. *Playing a video file*

8-13. Retrieve Information About the Installed Printers

Problem

You need to retrieve a list of available printers.

Solution

Read the names in the `InstalledPrinters` collection of the `System.Drawing.Printing.PrinterSettings` class.

How It Works

The `PrinterSettings` class encapsulates the settings for a printer and information about the printer. For example, you can use the `PrinterSettings` class to determine supported paper sizes, paper sources, and resolutions and check for the ability to print color or double-sided (*duplexed*) pages. In addition, you can retrieve default page settings for margins, page orientation, and so on.

The `PrinterSettings` class provides a static `InstalledPrinters` string collection, which includes the name of every printer installed on the computer. If you want to find out more information about the settings for a specific printer, you simply need to create a `PrinterSettings` instance and set the `PrinterName` property accordingly.

The Code

The following code shows a console application that finds all the printers installed on a computer and displays information about the paper sizes and the resolutions supported by each one.

You do not need to take this approach when creating an application that provides printing features. As you will see in recipe 8-14, you can use the `PrintDialog` class to prompt the user to choose a printer and its settings. The `PrintDialog` class can automatically apply its settings to the appropriate `PrintDocument` without any additional code.

```csharp
using System;
using System.Drawing.Printing;

namespace Apress.VisualCSharpRecipes.Chapter08
{
    class Recipe08_13
    {
        static void Main(string[] args)
        {
            foreach (string printerName in PrinterSettings.InstalledPrinters)
            {
                // Display the printer name.
                Console.WriteLine("Printer: {0}", printerName);

                // Retrieve the printer settings.
                PrinterSettings printer = new PrinterSettings();
                printer.PrinterName = printerName;

                // Check that this is a valid printer.
                // (This step might be required if you read the printer name
                // from a user-supplied value or a registry or configuration file
                // setting.)
                if (printer.IsValid)
                {
                    // Display the list of valid resolutions.
                    Console.WriteLine("Supported Resolutions:");

                    foreach (PrinterResolution resolution in
                      printer.PrinterResolutions)
                    {
                        Console.WriteLine("  {0}", resolution);
                    }
                    Console.WriteLine();

                    // Display the list of valid paper sizes.
                    Console.WriteLine("Supported Paper Sizes:");

                    foreach (PaperSize size in printer.PaperSizes)
                    {
                        if (Enum.IsDefined(size.Kind.GetType(), size.Kind))
                        {
                            Console.WriteLine("  {0}", size);
                        }
                    }
                    Console.WriteLine();
                }
            }
            Console.ReadLine();
        }
    }
}
```

Usage

Here is the type of output this utility displays:

```
Printer: HP LaserJet 5L
Supported Resolutions:
  [PrinterResolution High]
  [PrinterResolution Medium]
  [PrinterResolution Low]
  [PrinterResolution Draft]
  [PrinterResolution X=600 Y=600]
  [PrinterResolution X=300 Y=300]

Supported Paper Sizes:
  [PaperSize Letter Kind=Letter Height=1100 Width=850]
  [PaperSize Legal Kind=Legal Height=1400 Width=850]
  [PaperSize Executive Kind=Executive Height=1050 Width=725]
  [PaperSize A4 Kind=A4 Height=1169 Width=827]
  [PaperSize Envelope #10 Kind=Number10Envelope Height=950 Width=412]
  [PaperSize Envelope DL Kind=DLEnvelope Height=866 Width=433]
  [PaperSize Envelope C5 Kind=C5Envelope Height=902 Width=638]
  [PaperSize Envelope B5 Kind=B5Envelope Height=984 Width=693]
  [PaperSize Envelope Monarch Kind=MonarchEnvelope Height=750 Width=387]

Printer: Generic PostScript Printer
. . .
```

■Note You can print a document in almost any type of application. However, your application must include a reference to the System.Drawing.dll assembly. If you are using a project type in Visual Studio .NET that would not normally have this reference (such as a console application), you must add it.

8-14. Print a Simple Document

Problem

You need to print text or images.

Solution

Create a PrintDocument and write a handler for the PrintDocument.PrintPage event that uses the DrawString and DrawImage methods of the Graphics class to print data to the page.

How It Works

.NET uses an asynchronous event-based printing model. To print a document, you create a System. Drawing.Printing.PrintDocument instance, configure its properties, and then call its Print method, which schedules the print job. The common language runtime (CLR) will then fire the BeginPrint, PrintPage, and EndPrint events of the PrintDocument class on a new thread. You handle these events and use the provided System.Drawing.Graphics object to output data to the page. Graphics and text are written to a page in the same way as you draw to a window using GDI+. However, you might need to track your position on a page, because every Graphics class method requires explicit coordinates that indicate where to draw.

You configure printer settings through the `PrintDocument.PrinterSettings` and `PrintDocument.`
`DefaultPageSettings` properties. The `PrinterSettings` property returns a full `PrinterSettings` object
(as described in recipe 8-11), which identifies the printer that will be used. The `DefaultPageSettings`
property provides a full `PageSettings` object that specifies printer resolution, margins, orientation,
and so on. You can configure these properties in code, or you can use the `System.Windows.Forms.`
`PrintDialog` class to let the user make the changes using the standard Windows Print dialog box
(shown in Figure 8-9). In the Print dialog box, the user can select a printer and choose the number
of copies. The user can also click the Properties button to configure advanced settings such as page
layout and printer resolution. Finally, the user can either accept or cancel the print operation by
clicking OK or Cancel.

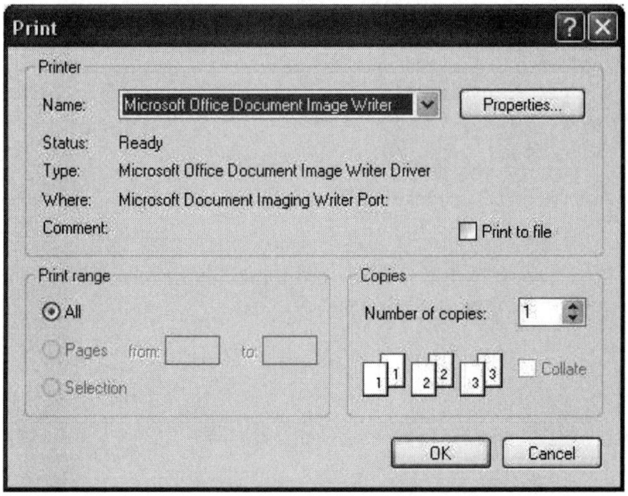

Figure 8-9. *Using the* `PrintDialog` *class*

Before using the `PrintDialog` class, you must explicitly attach it to a `PrintDocument` object by
setting the `PrintDialog.Document` property. Then, any changes the user makes in the Print dialog
box will be automatically applied to the `PrintDocument` object.

The Code

The following example provides a form with a single button. When the user clicks the button, the
application creates a new `PrintDocument`, allows the user to configure print settings, and then starts
an asynchronous print operation (provided the user clicks OK). An event handler responds to the
`PrintPage` event and writes several lines of text and an image.

This example has one limitation: it can print only a single page. To print more complex documents and span multiple pages, you will probably want to create a specialized class that encapsulates
the document information, the current page, and so on. Recipe 8-15 demonstrates this technique.

```
using System;
using System.Drawing;
using System.Windows.Forms;
using System.Drawing.Printing;
using System.IO;
```

```csharp
namespace Apress.VisualCSharpRecipes.Chapter08
{
    public partial class Recipe08_14 : Form
    {
        public Recipe08_14()
        {
            InitializeComponent();
        }

        private void cmdPrint_Click(object sender, EventArgs e)
        {
            // Create the document and attach an event handler.
            PrintDocument doc = new PrintDocument();
            doc.PrintPage += this.Doc_PrintPage;

            // Allow the user to choose a printer and specify other settings.
            PrintDialog dlgSettings = new PrintDialog();
            dlgSettings.Document = doc;

            // If the user clicked OK, print the document.
            if (dlgSettings.ShowDialog() == DialogResult.OK)
            {

                // This method returns immediately, before the print job starts.
                // The PrintPage event will fire asynchronously.
                doc.Print();
            }
        }

        private void Doc_PrintPage(object sender, PrintPageEventArgs e)
        {
            // Define the font.
            using (Font font = new Font("Arial", 30))
            {
                // Determine the position on the page.
                // In this case, we read the margin settings
                // (although there is nothing that prevents your code
                // from going outside the margin bounds.)
                float x = e.MarginBounds.Left;
                float y = e.MarginBounds.Top;

                // Determine the height of a line (based on the font used).
                float lineHeight = font.GetHeight(e.Graphics);

                // Print five lines of text.
                for (int i = 0; i < 5; i++)
                {

                    // Draw the text with a black brush,
                    // using the font and coordinates we have determined.
                    e.Graphics.DrawString("This is line " + i.ToString(),
                        font, Brushes.Black, x, y);

                    // Move down the equivalent spacing of one line.
                    y += lineHeight;
                }
                y += lineHeight;
```

```
                // Draw an image.
                e.Graphics.DrawImage(
                    Image.FromFile(
                        Path.Combine(Application.StartupPath,"test.jpg")
                        ),
                    x, y);
            }
        }
    }
}
```

8-15. Print a Multipage Document

Problem

You need to print complex documents with multiple pages and possibly print several different documents at once.

Solution

Place the information you want to print into a custom class that derives from PrintDocument, and in the PrintPage event handler, set the PrintPageEventArgs.HasMorePages property to true as long as pages are remaining.

How It Works

The PrintDocument.PrintPage event is triggered to let you to print only a single page. If you need to print more pages, you need to set the PrintPageEventArgs.HasMorePages property to true in the PrintPage event handler. As long as HasMorePages is set to true, the PrintDocument class will continue firing PrintPage events. However, it is up to you to track which page you are on, what data should be placed on each page, and what is the last page for which HasMorePage is not set to true. To facilitate this tracking, it is a good idea to create a custom class.

The Code

The following example shows a class called TextDocument. This class inherits from PrintDocument and adds three properties. Text stores an array of text lines, PageNumber reflects the last printed page, and Offset indicates the last line that was printed from the Text array.

```
public class TextDocument : PrintDocument {

    private string[] text;
    private int pageNumber;
    private int offset;

    public string[] Text {
        get {return text;}
        set {text = value;}
    }

    public int PageNumber {
        get {return pageNumber;}
        set {pageNumber = value;}
    }
```

```
    public int Offset {
        get {return offset;}
        set {offset = value;}
    }

    public TextDocument(string[] text) {
        this.Text = text;
    }
}
```

Depending on the type of material you are printing, you might want to modify this class. For example, you could store an array of image data, some content that should be used as a header or footer on each page, font information, or even the name of a file from which you want to read the information. Encapsulating the information in a single class makes it easier to print more than one document at the same time. This is especially important because the printing process runs in a new dedicated thread. As a consequence, the user is able to keep working in the application and therefore update your data while the pages are printing. So, this dedicated class should contain a copy of the data to print to avoid any concurrency problems.

The code that initiates printing is the same as in recipe 8-14, only now it creates a TextDocument instance instead of a PrintDocument instance. The PrintPage event handler keeps track of the current line and checks whether the page has space before attempting to print the next line. If a new page is needed, the HasMorePages property is set to true and the PrintPage event fires again for the next page. If not, the print operation is deemed complete. This simple code sample also takes into account whether a line fits into the width of the page; refer to recipe 8-16 for a solution to this problem.

The full form code is as follows:

```
using System;
using System.Drawing;
using System.Windows.Forms;
using System.Drawing.Printing;

namespace Apress.VisualCSharpRecipes.Chapter08
{
    public partial class Recipe08_15 : Form
    {
        public Recipe08_15()
        {
            InitializeComponent();
        }

        private void cmdPrint_Click(object sender, EventArgs e)
        {
            // Create a document with 100 lines.
            string[] printText = new string[101];
            for (int i = 0; i < 101; i++)
            {
                printText[i] = i.ToString();
                printText[i] +=
                    ": The quick brown fox jumps over the lazy dog.";
            }

            PrintDocument doc = new TextDocument(printText);
            doc.PrintPage += this.Doc_PrintPage;

            PrintDialog dlgSettings = new PrintDialog();
            dlgSettings.Document = doc;
```

```
        // If the user clicked OK, print the document.
        if (dlgSettings.ShowDialog() == DialogResult.OK)
        {
            doc.Print();
        }
    }

    private void Doc_PrintPage(object sender, PrintPageEventArgs e)
    {
        // Retrieve the document that sent this event.
        TextDocument doc = (TextDocument)sender;

        // Define the font and determine the line height.
        using (Font font = new Font("Arial", 10))
        {
            float lineHeight = font.GetHeight(e.Graphics);

            // Create variables to hold position on page.
            float x = e.MarginBounds.Left;
            float y = e.MarginBounds.Top;

            // Increment the page counter (to reflect the page that
            // is about to be printed).
            doc.PageNumber += 1;

            // Print all the information that can fit on the page.
            // This loop ends when the next line would go over the
            // margin bounds, or there are no more lines to print.

            while ((y + lineHeight) < e.MarginBounds.Bottom &&
              doc.Offset <= doc.Text.GetUpperBound(0))
            {
                e.Graphics.DrawString(doc.Text[doc.Offset], font,
                  Brushes.Black, x, y);

                // Move to the next line of data.
                doc.Offset += 1;

                // Move the equivalent of one line down the page.
                y += lineHeight;
            }

            if (doc.Offset < doc.Text.GetUpperBound(0))
            {
                // There is still at least one more page.
                // Signal this event to fire again.
                e.HasMorePages = true;
            }
            else
            {
                // Printing is complete.
                doc.Offset = 0;
            }
        }
    }
  }
}
```

8-16. Print Wrapped Text

Problem

You need to parse a large block of text into distinct lines that fit on one page.

Solution

Use the `Graphics.DrawString` method overload that accepts a bounding rectangle.

How It Works

Often, you will need to break a large block of text into separate lines that can be printed individually on a page. The .NET Framework can perform this task automatically, provided you use a version of the `Graphics.DrawString` method that accepts a bounding rectangle. You specify a rectangle that represents where you want the text to be displayed. The text is then wrapped automatically to fit within those confines.

The Code

The following code demonstrates this approach, using the bounding rectangle that represents the printable portion of the page. It prints a large block of text from a textbox on the form.

```
using System;
using System.Drawing;
using System.Windows.Forms;
using System.Drawing.Printing;

namespace Apress.VisualCSharpRecipes.Chapter08
{
    public partial class Recipe08_16 : Form
    {
        public Recipe08_16()
        {
            InitializeComponent();
        }

        private void cmdPrint_Click(object sender, EventArgs e)
        {
            // Create the document and attach an event handler.
            string text = "Windows Server 2003 builds on the core strengths " +
                "of the Windows family of operating systems--security, " +
                "manageability, reliability, availability, and scalability. " +
                "Windows Server 2003 provides an application environment to " +
                "build, deploy, manage, and run XML Web services. " +
                "Additionally, advances in Windows Server 2003 provide many " +
                "benefits for developing applications.";
            PrintDocument doc = new ParagraphDocument(text);
            doc.PrintPage += this.Doc_PrintPage;
```

```
            // Allow the user to choose a printer and specify other settings.
            PrintDialog dlgSettings = new PrintDialog();
            dlgSettings.Document = doc;

            // If the user clicked OK, print the document.
            if (dlgSettings.ShowDialog() == DialogResult.OK)
            {
                doc.Print();
            }
        }

        private void Doc_PrintPage(object sender, PrintPageEventArgs e)
        {
            // Retrieve the document that sent this event.
            ParagraphDocument doc = (ParagraphDocument)sender;

            // Define the font and text.
            using (Font font = new Font("Arial", 15))
            {
                e.Graphics.DrawString(doc.Text, font, Brushes.Black,
                    e.MarginBounds, StringFormat.GenericDefault);
            }
        }
    }

    public class ParagraphDocument : PrintDocument
    {
        private string text;
        public string Text
        {
            get { return text; }
            set { text = value; }
        }

        public ParagraphDocument(string text)
        {
            this.Text = text;
        }
    }
}
```

Figure 8-10 shows the wrapped text.

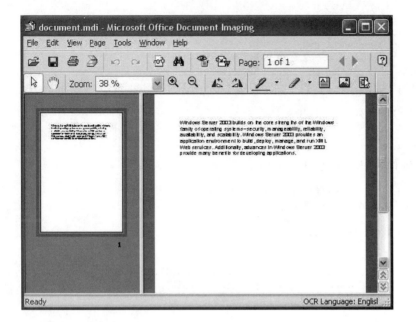

Figure 8-10. *The printed document with wrapping*

8-17. Show a Dynamic Print Preview

Problem

You need to use an on-screen preview that shows how a printed document will look.

Solution

Use `PrintPreviewDialog` or `PrintPreviewControl` (both of which are found in the `System.Windows.Forms` namespace).

How It Works

.NET provides two elements of user interface that can take a `PrintDocument` instance, run your printing code, and use it to generate a graphical on-screen preview:

- The `PrintPreviewDialog`, which shows a preview in a stand-alone form
- The `PrintPreviewControl`, which shows a preview in a control that can be embedded in one of your own custom forms

To use a stand-alone print preview form, you simply create a `PrintPreviewDialog` object, assign its `Document` property, and call the `Show` method:

```
PrintPreviewDialog dlgPreview = new PrintPreviewDialog();
dlgPreview.Document = doc;
dlgPreview.Show();
```

The Print Preview window (shown in Figure 8-11) provides all the controls the user needs to move from page to page, zoom in, and so on. The window even provides a print button that allows the user to send the document directly to the printer. You can tailor the window to some extent by modifying the `PrintPreviewDialog` properties.

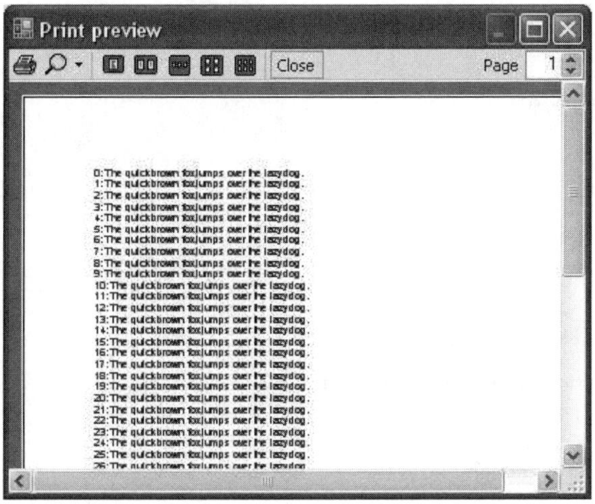

Figure 8-11. *Using the* `PrintPreviewDialog` *control*

You can also add a `PrintPreviewControl` control to any of your forms to show a preview alongside other information. In this case, you do not need to call the `Show` method. As soon as you set the `PrintPreviewControl.Document` property, the preview is generated. To clear the preview, set the `Document` property to `null`, and to refresh the preview, simply reassign the `Document` property. `PrintPreviewControl` shows only the preview pages, not any additional controls. However, you can add your own controls for zooming, tiling multiple pages, and so on. You simply need to adjust the `PrintPreviewControl` properties accordingly.

The Code

For example, consider the form shown in Figure 8-12. It incorporates a `PrintPreviewControl` and allows the user to select a zoom setting.

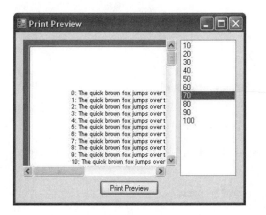

Figure 8-12. *Using the* `PrintPreviewControl` *in a custom window*

Here is the complete form code:

```csharp
using System;
using System.Drawing;
using System.Windows.Forms;
using System.Drawing.Printing;

namespace Apress.VisualCSharpRecipes.Chapter08
{
    public partial class Recipe08_17 : Form
    {
        public Recipe08_17()
        {
            InitializeComponent();
        }

        private PrintDocument doc;
        // (PrintDocument.PrintPage event handler code omitted.
        // See code in recipe 8-15.)

        private void Recipe08_17_Load(object sender, EventArgs e)
        {
            // Set the allowed zoom settings.
            for (int i = 1; i <= 10; i++)
            {
                lstZoom.Items.Add((i * 10).ToString());
            }

            // Create a document with 100 lines.
            string[] printText = new string[100];
            for (int i = 0; i < 100; i++)
            {
                printText[i] = i.ToString();
                printText[i] += ": The quick brown fox jumps over the lazy dog.";
            }

            doc = new TextDocument(printText);
            doc.PrintPage += this.Doc_PrintPage;

            lstZoom.Text = "100";
            printPreviewControl.Zoom = 1;
            printPreviewControl.Document = doc;
            printPreviewControl.Rows = 2;
        }

        private void cmdPrint_Click(object sender, EventArgs e)
        {
            // Set the zoom.
            printPreviewControl.Zoom = Single.Parse(lstZoom.Text) / 100;

            // Show the full two pages, one above the other.
            printPreviewControl.Rows = 2;

            // Rebind the PrintDocument to refresh the preview.
            printPreviewControl.Document = doc;
        }
    }
}
```

```
    // (TextDocument class code omitted. See recipe 8-15.)
}
```

8-18. Manage Print Jobs

Problem

You need to pause or resume a print job or a print queue.

Solution

Use WMI. You can retrieve information from the print queue using a query with the Win32_PrintJob class, and you can use the Pause and Resume methods of the WMI Win32_PrintJob and Win32_Printer classes to manage the queue.

How It Works

WMI allows you to retrieve a vast amount of system information using a querylike syntax. One of the tasks you can perform with WMI is to retrieve a list of outstanding print jobs, along with information about each one. You can also perform operations such as printing and resuming a job or all the jobs for a printer. To use WMI, you need to add a reference to the System.Management.dll assembly.

The Code

The following code shows a Windows application that interacts with the print queue. It performs a WMI query to get a list of all the outstanding jobs on the computer and displays the job ID for each one in a list box. When the user selects the item, a more complete WMI query is performed, and additional details about the print job are displayed in a textbox. Finally, the user can click the Pause and Resume button after selecting a job to change its status.

    Remember that Windows permissions might prevent you from pausing or removing a print job created by another user. In fact, permissions might even prevent you from retrieving status information and could cause a security exception to be thrown.

```
using System;
using System.Drawing;
using System.Windows.Forms;
using System.Management;
using System.Collections;
using System.Text;

namespace Apress.VisualCSharpRecipes.Chapter08
{
    public partial class Recipe08_18 : Form
    {
        public PrintQueueTest()
        {
            InitializeComponent();
        }

        private void cmdRefresh_Click(object sender, EventArgs e)
        {
            // Select all the outstanding print jobs.
```

```
        string query = "SELECT * FROM Win32_PrintJob";
        using (ManagementObjectSearcher jobQuery =
          new ManagementObjectSearcher(query))
        {
            using (ManagementObjectCollection jobs = jobQuery.Get())
            {
                // Add the jobs in the queue to the list box.
                lstJobs.Items.Clear();
                txtJobInfo.Text = "";
                foreach (ManagementObject job in jobs)
                {
                    lstJobs.Items.Add(job["JobID"]);
                }
            }
        }
    }

    private void Recipe08_18_Load(object sender, EventArgs e)
    {
        cmdRefresh_Click(null, null);
    }

    // This helper method performs a WMI query and returns the
    // WMI job for the currently selected list box item.
    private ManagementObject GetSelectedJob()
    {
        try
        {
            // Select the matching print job.
            string query = "SELECT * FROM Win32_PrintJob " +
              "WHERE JobID='" + lstJobs.Text + "'";
            ManagementObject job = null;
            using (ManagementObjectSearcher jobQuery =
              new ManagementObjectSearcher(query))
            {
                ManagementObjectCollection jobs = jobQuery.Get();
                IEnumerator enumerator = jobs.GetEnumerator();
                enumerator.MoveNext();
                job = (ManagementObject)enumerator.Current;
            }
            return job;
        }
        catch (InvalidOperationException)
        {
            // The Current property of the enumerator is invalid
            return null;
        }
    }

    private void lstJobs_SelectedIndexChanged(object sender, EventArgs e)
    {
      ManagementObject job = GetSelectedJob();
      if (job == null)
      {
          txtJobInfo.Text = "";
          return;
      }
```

```
        // Display job information.
        StringBuilder jobInfo = new StringBuilder();
        jobInfo.AppendFormat("Document: {0}", job["Document"].ToString());
        jobInfo.Append(Environment.NewLine);
        jobInfo.AppendFormat("DriverName: {0}", job["DriverName"].ToString());
        jobInfo.Append(Environment.NewLine);
        jobInfo.AppendFormat("Status: {0}", job["Status"].ToString());
        jobInfo.Append(Environment.NewLine);
        jobInfo.AppendFormat("Owner: {0}", job["Owner"].ToString());
        jobInfo.Append(Environment.NewLine);

        jobInfo.AppendFormat("PagesPrinted: {0}", job["PagesPrinted"].ToString());
        jobInfo.Append(Environment.NewLine);
        jobInfo.AppendFormat("TotalPages: {0}", job["TotalPages"].ToString());

        if (job["JobStatus"] != null)
        {
            txtJobInfo.Text += Environment.NewLine;
            txtJobInfo.Text += "JobStatus: " + job["JobStatus"].ToString();
        }
        if (job["StartTime"] != null)
        {
            jobInfo.Append(Environment.NewLine);
            jobInfo.AppendFormat("StartTime: {0}", job["StartTime"].ToString());
        }

        txtJobInfo.Text = jobInfo.ToString();
    }

    private void cmdPause_Click(object sender, EventArgs e)
    {
        if (lstJobs.SelectedIndex == -1) return;
        ManagementObject job = GetSelectedJob();
        if (job == null) return;

        // Attempt to pause the job.
        int returnValue = Int32.Parse(
          job.InvokeMethod("Pause", null).ToString());

        // Display information about the return value.
        if (returnValue == 0)
        {
            MessageBox.Show("Successfully paused job.");
        }
        else
        {
            MessageBox.Show("Unrecognized return value when pausing job.");
        }
    }

    private void cmdResume_Click(object sender, EventArgs e)
    {
        if (lstJobs.SelectedIndex == -1) return;
        ManagementObject job = GetSelectedJob();
        if (job == null) return;
```

```csharp
            if ((Int32.Parse(job["StatusMask"].ToString()) & 1) == 1)
            {
                // Attempt to resume the job.
                int returnValue = Int32.Parse(
                  job.InvokeMethod("Resume", null).ToString());

                // Display information about the return value.
                if (returnValue == 0)
                {
                    MessageBox.Show("Successfully resumed job.");
                }
                else if (returnValue == 5)
                {
                    MessageBox.Show("Access denied.");
                }
                else
                {
                    MessageBox.Show(
                        "Unrecognized return value when resuming job.");
                }
            }
        }
    }
}
```

Figure 8-13 shows the window for this application.

Figure 8-13. *Retrieving information from the print queue*

■Note Other WMI methods you might use in a printing scenario include AddPrinterConnection, SetDefaultPrinter, CancelAllJobs, and PrintTestPage, all of which work with the Win32_Printer class. For more information about using WMI to retrieve information about Windows hardware, refer to the MSDN documentation.

CHAPTER 9

■■■

Database Access

In the Microsoft .NET Framework, access to a wide variety of data sources is enabled through a group of classes collectively named Microsoft ADO.NET. Each type of data source is supported through the provision of a data provider. Each data provider contains a set of classes that not only implement a standard set of interfaces (defined in the System.Data namespace), but also provide functionality unique to the data source they support. These classes include representations of connections, commands, properties, data adapters, and data readers through which you interact with a data source.

■**Note** ADO.NET is an extensive subsection of the .NET Framework class library and includes a great deal of advanced functionality. For comprehensive coverage of ADO.NET, read David Sceppa's excellent book *Microsoft ADO.NET Core Reference* (Microsoft Press, 2002). An updated edition of this book to cover .NET Framework 2.0 is due out in early 2006.

Table 9-1 lists the data providers included as standard with the .NET Framework.

Table 9-1. *.NET Framework Data Provider Implementations*

Data Provider	Description
.NET Framework Data Provider for ODBC	Provides connectivity (via COM Interop) to any data source that implements an ODBC interface. This includes Microsoft SQL Server, Oracle, and Microsoft Access databases. Data provider classes are contained in the System.Data.Odbc namespace and have the prefix Odbc.
.NET Framework Data Provider for OLE DB	Provides connectivity (via COM Interop) to any data source that implements an OLE DB interface. This includes Microsoft SQL Server, MSDE, Oracle, and Jet databases. Data provider classes are contained in the System.Data.OleDb namespace and have the prefix OleDb.
.NET Framework Data Provider for Oracle	Provides optimized connectivity to Oracle databases via Oracle client software version 8.1.7 or later. Data provider classes are contained in the System.Data.OracleClient namespace and have the prefix Oracle.

(Continued)

Table 9-1. *Continued*

Data Provider	Description
.NET Framework Data Provider for SQL Server	Provides optimized connectivity to Microsoft SQL Server version 7 and later (including MSDE) by communicating directly with the SQL Server data source, without the need to use ODBC or OLE DB. Data provider classes are contained in the System.Data.SqlClient namespace and have the prefix Sql.
.NET Compact Framework Data Provider for SQL Server CE	Provides connectivity to Microsoft SQL Server CE. Data provider classes are contained in the System.Data.SqlServerCe namespace and have the prefix SqlCe.

■**Tip** Where possible, the recipes in this chapter are programmed against the interfaces defined in the System.Data namespace. This approach makes it easier to apply the solutions to any database. Adopting this approach in your own code will make it more portable. However, the data provider classes that implement these interfaces often implement additional functionality specific to their own database. Generally, you must trade off portability against access to proprietary functionality when it comes to database code. Recipe 9-10 describes how you can use the System.Data.Common.DbProviderFactory and associated classes (new to .NET Framework 2.0) to write generic code that is not tied to a specific database implementation.

This chapter describes some of the most commonly used aspects of ADO.NET. The recipes in this chapter describe how to do the following:

- Create, configure, open, and close database connections (recipe 9-1)

- Employ connection pooling to improve the performance and scalability of applications that use database connections (recipe 9-2)

- Create and securely store database connection strings (recipes 9-3 and 9-4)

- Execute SQL commands and stored procedures, and use parameters to improve their flexibility (recipes 9-5 and 9-6)

- Process the results returned by database queries as either a set of rows or as XML (recipes 9-7 and 9-8)

- Execute database operations asynchronously, allowing your main code to continue with other tasks while the database operation executes in the background (recipe 9-9)

- Write generic ADO.NET code that can be configured to work against any relational database for which a data provider is available (recipe 9-10)

- Discover all instances of SQL Server 2000 and SQL Server 2005 available on a network (recipe 9-11)

9-1. Connect to a Database

Problem

You need to open a connection to a database.

Solution

Create a connection object appropriate to the type of database to which you need to connect. All connection objects implement the `System.Data.IDbConnection` interface. Configure the connection object by setting its `ConnectionString` property. Open the connection by calling the connection object's `Open` method.

How It Works

The first step in database access is to open a connection to the database. The `IDbConnection` interface represents a database connection, and each data provider includes a unique implementation. Here is the list of `IDbConnection` implementations for the five standard data providers:

- `System.Data.Odbc.OdbcConnection`
- `System.Data.OleDb.OleDbConnection`
- `System.Data.OracleClient.OracleConnection`
- `System.Data.SqlServerCe.SqlCeConnection`
- `System.Data.SqlClient.SqlConnection`

You configure a connection object using a connection string. A connection string is a set of semicolon-separated name-value pairs. You can supply a connection string either as a constructor argument or by setting a connection object's `ConnectionString` property before opening the connection. Each connection class implementation requires that you provide different information in the connection string. Refer to the `ConnectionString` property documentation for each implementation to see the values you can specify. Possible settings include the following:

- The name of the target database server
- The name of the database to open initially
- Connection time-out values
- Connection-pooling behavior (see recipe 9-2)
- Authentication mechanisms to use when connecting to secured databases, including provision of a username and password if needed

Once configured, call the connection object's Open method to open the connection to the database. You can then use the connection object to execute commands against the data source (discussed in recipe 9-3). The properties of a connection object also allow you to retrieve information about the state of a connection and the settings used to open the connection. When you're finished with a connection, you should always call its Close method to free the underlying database connection and system resources. IDbConnection extends System.IDisposable, meaning that each connection class implements the Dispose method. Dispose automatically calls Close, making the using statement a very clean and efficient way of using connection objects in your code.

You achieve optimum scalability by opening your database connection as late as possible and closing it as soon as you have finished. This ensures that you do not tie up database connections for long periods, so you give all code the maximum opportunity to obtain a connection. This is especially important if you are using connection pooling.

The Code

The following example demonstrates how to use both the SqlConnection and OleDbConnection classes to open a connection to a Microsoft SQL Server database running on the local machine that uses integrated Windows security.

```
using System;
using System.Data;
using System.Data.SqlClient;
using System.Data.OleDb;

namespace Apress.VisualCSharpRecipes.Chapter09
{
    class Recipe09_01
    {
        public static void SqlConnectionExample()
        {
            // Create an empty SqlConnection object.
            using (SqlConnection con = new SqlConnection())
            {
                // Configure the SqlConnection object's connection string.
                con.ConnectionString =
                    @"Data Source=.\sqlexpress;" + // local SQL Server instance
                    "Database=Northwind;" +        // the sample Northwind DB
                    "Integrated Security=SSPI";    // integrated Windows security

                // Open the database connection.
                con.Open();

                // Display information about the connection.
                if (con.State == ConnectionState.Open)
                {
                    Console.WriteLine("SqlConnection Information:");
                    Console.WriteLine("  Connection State = " + con.State);
                    Console.WriteLine("  Connection String = " +
                        con.ConnectionString);
                    Console.WriteLine("  Database Source = " + con.DataSource);
                    Console.WriteLine("  Database = " + con.Database);
                    Console.WriteLine("  Server Version = " + con.ServerVersion);
                    Console.WriteLine("  Workstation Id = " + con.WorkstationId);
                    Console.WriteLine("  Timeout = " + con.ConnectionTimeout);
                    Console.WriteLine("  Packet Size = " + con.PacketSize);
                }
```

```csharp
            else
            {
                Console.WriteLine("SqlConnection failed to open.");
                Console.WriteLine("  Connection State = " + con.State);
            }
            // At the end of the using block Dispose() calls Close().
        }
    }

    public static void OleDbConnectionExample()
    {

        // Create an empty OleDbConnection object.
        using (OleDbConnection con = new OleDbConnection())
        {
            // Configure the OleDbConnection object's connection string.
            con.ConnectionString =
                "Provider=SQLOLEDB;" +         // OLE DB Provider for SQL Server
                @"Data Source=.\sqlexpress;" + // local SQL Server instance
                "Initial Catalog=Northwind;" + // the sample Northwind DB
                "Integrated Security=SSPI";      // integrated Windows security

            // Open the database connection.
            con.Open();

            // Display information about the connection.
            if (con.State == ConnectionState.Open)
            {
                Console.WriteLine("OleDbConnection Information:");
                Console.WriteLine("  Connection State = " + con.State);
                Console.WriteLine("  Connection String = " +
                    con.ConnectionString);
                Console.WriteLine("  Database Source = " + con.DataSource);
                Console.WriteLine("  Database = " + con.Database);
                Console.WriteLine("  Server Version = " + con.ServerVersion);
                Console.WriteLine("  Timeout = " + con.ConnectionTimeout);
            }
            else
            {
                Console.WriteLine("OleDbConnection failed to open.");
                Console.WriteLine("  Connection State = " + con.State);
            }
            // At the end of the using block Dispose() calls Close().
        }
    }

    public static void Main()
    {
        // Open connection using SqlConnection.
        SqlConnectionExample();
        Console.WriteLine(Environment.NewLine);

        // Open connection using OleDbConnection.
        OleDbConnectionExample();

        // Wait to continue.
        Console.WriteLine(Environment.NewLine);
```

```
                Console.WriteLine("Main method complete. Press Enter.");
                Console.ReadLine();
            }
        }
}
```

9-2. Use Connection Pooling

Problem

You need to use a pool of database connections to improve application performance and scalability.

Solution

Configure the connection pool using settings in the connection string of a connection object.

How It Works

Connection pooling significantly reduces the overhead associated with creating and destroying database connections. Connection pooling also improves the scalability of solutions by reducing the number of concurrent connections a database must maintain. Many of these connections sit idle for a significant portion of their lifetimes. With connection pooling, instead of creating and opening a new connection object whenever you need one, you take an already open connection from the connection pool. When you have finished using the connection, instead of closing it, you return it to the pool and allow other code to use it.

The SQL Server and Oracle data providers encapsulate connection-pooling functionality that they enable by default. One connection pool exists for each unique connection string you specify when you open a new connection. Each time you open a new connection with a connection string that you used previously, the connection is taken from the existing pool. Only if you specify a different connection string will the data provider create a new connection pool. You can control some characteristics of your pool using the connection string settings described in Table 9-2.

■ Note Once created, a pool exists until your process terminates.

Table 9-2. *Connection String Settings That Control Connection Pooling*

Setting	Description
Connection Lifetime	Specifies the maximum time in seconds that a connection is allowed to live in the pool before it's closed. The age of a connection is tested only when the connection is returned to the pool. This setting is useful for minimizing pool size if the pool is not heavily used and also ensures optimal load balancing is achieved in clustered database environments. The default value is 0, which means connections exist for the life of the current process.
Connection Reset	Supported only by the SQL Server data provider. Specifies whether connections are reset as they are taken from the pool. A value of True (the default) ensures a connection's state is reset but requires an additional communication with the database.

Setting	Description
Max Pool Size	Specifies the maximum number of connections that should be in the pool. Connections are created and added to the pool as required until this value is reached. If a request for a connection is made but there are no free connections, the caller will block until a connection becomes available. The default value is 100.
Min Pool Size	Specifies the minimum number of connections that should be in the pool. On pool creation, this number of connections is created and added to the pool. During periodic maintenance, or when a connection is requested, connections are added to the pool to ensure the minimum number of connections is available. The default value is 0.
Pooling	Set to False to obtain a nonpooled connection. The default value is True.

The Code

The following example demonstrates the configuration of a connection pool that contains a minimum of 5 and a maximum of 15 connections. Connections expire after 10 minutes (600 seconds) and are reset each time a connection is obtained from the pool. The example also demonstrates how to use the Pooling setting to obtain a connection object that is not from a pool. This is useful if your application uses a single long-lived connection to a database.

```csharp
using System;
using System.Data.SqlClient;

namespace Apress.VisualCSharpRecipes.Chapter09
{
    class Recipe09_02
    {
        public static void Main()
        {
            // Obtain a pooled connection.
            using (SqlConnection con = new SqlConnection())
            {
                // Configure the SqlConnection object's connection string.
                con.ConnectionString =
                    @"Data Source = .\sqlexpress;" +// local SQL Server instance
                    "Database = Northwind;" +        // the sample Northwind DB
                    "Integrated Security = SSPI;" + // integrated Windows security
                    "Min Pool Size = 5;" +           // configure minimum pool size
                    "Max Pool Size = 15;" +          // configure maximum pool size
                    "Connection Reset = True;" +     // reset connections each use
                    "Connection Lifetime = 600";     // set max connection lifetime

                // Open the database connection.
                con.Open();

                // Access the database. . .

                // At the end of the using block, the Dispose calls Close, which
                // returns the connection to the pool for reuse.
            }

            // Obtain a nonpooled connection.
            using (SqlConnection con = new SqlConnection())
```

```
        {
            // Configure the SqlConnection object's connection string.
            con.ConnectionString =
                @"Data Source = .\sqlexpress;" +//local SQL Server instance
                "Database = Northwind;" +        //the sample Northwind DB
                "Integrated Security = SSPI;" + //integrated Windows security
                "Pooling = False";               //specify nonpooled connection

            // Open the database connection.
            con.Open();

            // Access the database. . .

            // At the end of the using block, the Dispose calls Close, which
            // closes the nonpooled connection.
        }

        // Wait to continue.
        Console.WriteLine(Environment.NewLine);
        Console.WriteLine("Main method complete. Press Enter.");
        Console.ReadLine();
    }
  }
}
```

Notes

The ODBC and OLE DB data providers also support connection pooling, but they do not implement connection pooling within managed .NET classes, and you do not configure the pool in the same way as you do for the SQL Server or Oracle data providers. ODBC connection pooling is managed by the ODBC Driver Manager and configured using the ODBC Data Source Administrator tool in the Control Panel. OLE DB connection pooling is managed by the native OLE DB implementation. The most you can do is disable pooling by including the setting OLE DB Services=-4; in your connection string.

The SQL Server CE data provider does not support connection pooling, because SQL Server CE supports only a single concurrent connection.

9-3. Create a Database Connection String Programmatically

Problem

You need to programmatically create or modify a syntactically correct connection string by working with its component parts or by parsing a given connection string.

Solution

Use the System.Data.Common.DbConnectionStringBuilder class or one of its strongly typed subclasses that form part of an ADO.NET data provider.

How It Works

Connection strings are String objects that contain a set of configuration parameters in the form of name-value pairs separated by semicolons. These configuration parameters instruct the ADO.NET infrastructure how to open a connection to the data source you want to access and how to handle the life cycle of connections to that data source. As a developer, you will often simply define your connection string by hand and store it in a configuration file (see recipe 9-4). However, at times, you may want to build a connection string from component elements entered by a user, or you may want to parse an existing connection string into its component parts to allow you to manipulate it programmatically. The DbConnectionStringBuilder class (new to .NET Framework 2.0) and the classes derived from it provide both these capabilities.

DbConnectionStringBuilder is a class used to create connection strings from name-value pairs or to parse connection strings, but it does not enforce any logic on which configuration parameters are valid. Instead, each data provider (except the SQL Server CE data provider) includes a unique implementation derived from DbConnectionStringBuilder that accurately enforces the configuration rules for a connection string of that type. Here is the list of available DbConnectionStringBuilder implementations for standard data providers:

- System.Data.Odbc.OdbcConnectionStringBuilder

- System.Data.OleDb.OleDbConnectionStringBuilder

- System.Data.OracleClient.OracleConnectionStringBuilder

- System.Data.SqlClient.SqlConnectionStringBuilder

Each of these classes exposes properties for getting and setting the possible parameters for a connection string of that type. To parse an existing connection string, pass it as an argument when creating the DbConnectionStringBuilder derived class or set the ConnectionString property. If this string contains a keyword not supported by the type of connection, an ArgumentException exception is thrown.

The Code

The following example demonstrates the use of the SqlConnectionStringBuilder class to parse and construct SQL Server connection strings.

```
using System;
using System.Data.SqlClient;

namespace Apress.VisualCSharpRecipes.Chapter09
{
    class Recipe09_03
    {
        public static void Main(string[] args)
        {
            string conString = @"Data Source=.\sqlexpress;" +
                "Database=Northwind;Integrated Security=SSPI;" +
                "Min Pool Size=5;Max Pool Size=15;Connection Reset=True;" +
                "Connection Lifetime=600;";

            // Parse the SQL Server connection string and display the component
            // configuration parameters.
            SqlConnectionStringBuilder sb1 =
                new SqlConnectionStringBuilder(conString);
```

```
                    Console.WriteLine("Parsed SQL Connection String Parameters:");
                    Console.WriteLine("  Database Source = " + sb1.DataSource);
                    Console.WriteLine("  Database = " + sb1.InitialCatalog);
                    Console.WriteLine("  Use Integrated Security = "
                        + sb1.IntegratedSecurity);
                    Console.WriteLine("  Min Pool Size = " + sb1.MinPoolSize);
                    Console.WriteLine("  Max Pool Size = " + sb1.MinPoolSize);
                    Console.WriteLine("  Lifetime = " + sb1.LoadBalanceTimeout);
                    Console.WriteLine("  Connection Reset = " + sb1.ConnectionReset);

                    // Build a connection string from component parameters and display it.
                    SqlConnectionStringBuilder sb2 =
                        new SqlConnectionStringBuilder(conString);

                    sb2.DataSource = @".\sqlexpress";
                    sb2.InitialCatalog = "Northwind";
                    sb2.IntegratedSecurity = true;
                    sb2.MinPoolSize = 5;
                    sb2.MinPoolSize = 15;
                    sb2.LoadBalanceTimeout = 600;
                    sb2.ConnectionReset = true;

                    Console.WriteLine(Environment.NewLine);
                    Console.WriteLine("Constructed connection string:");
                    Console.WriteLine("   " + sb2.ConnectionString);

                    // Wait to continue.
                    Console.WriteLine(Environment.NewLine);
                    Console.WriteLine("Main method complete. Press Enter.");
                    Console.ReadLine();
                }
            }
        }
```

9-4. Store a Database Connection String Securely

Problem

You need to store a database connection string securely.

Solution

Store the connection string in an encrypted section of the application's configuration file.

■Note Protected configuration—the .NET Framework feature that lets you encrypt configuration information—relies on the key storage facilities of the Data Protection API (DPAPI) to store the secret key used to encrypt the configuration file. This solves the very difficult problem of code-based secret key management.

How It Works

Database connection strings often contain secret information, or at the very least information that would be valuable to someone trying to attack your system. As such, you should not store connection strings in plaintext, nor is it sufficient to hard-code them into the application code. Strings embedded in an assembly can easily be retrieved using a disassembler. Version 2.0 of the .NET Framework adds a number of classes and capabilities that make storing and retrieving encrypted connection strings in your application's configuration trivial.

Unencrypted connection strings are stored in the machine or application configuration file in the <connectionStrings> section in the format shown here:

```
<configuration>
    <connectionStrings>
        <add name="ConnectionString1" connectionString="Data Source=.\sqlexpress
;Database=Northwind;Integrated Security=SSPI;Min Pool Size=5;Max Pool Size=15;Co
nnection Reset=True;Connection Lifetime=600;"
            providerName="System.Data.SqlClient" />
    </connectionStrings>
</configuration>
```

The easiest way to read this connection string is to use the indexed ConnectionStrings property of the System.Configuration.ConfigurationManager class. Specifying the name of the connection string you want as the property index will return a System.Configuration.ConnectionStringSettings object. The ConnectionStringSettings.ConnectionString property gets the connection string, and the ConnectionStringSettings.ProviderName property gets the provider name that you can use to create a data provider factory (see recipe 9-10). This process will work regardless of whether the connection string has been encrypted or written in plaintext.

To write a connection string to the application's configuration file, you must first obtain a System.Configuration.Configuration object, which represents the application's configuration file. The easiest way to do this is by calling the System.Configuration.ConfigurationManager. OpenExeConfiguration method. You should then create and configure a new System.Configuration. ConnectionStringSettings object to represent the stored connection string. You should provide a name, connection string, and data provider name for storage. Add the ConnectionStringSettings object to the Configuration's ConnectionStringsSection collection available through the Configuration. ConnectionStrings property. Finally, save the updated file by calling the Configuration.Save method.

To encrypt the connection strings section of the configuration file, before saving the file, you must configure the ConnectionStringsSection collection. To do this, call the ConnectionStringsSection. SectionInformation.ProtectSection method and pass it a string containing the name of the protected configuration provider to use: either RsaProtectedConfigurationProvider or DPAPIProtectedConfigurationProvider. To disable encryption, call the SectionInformation. Unprotect method.

■**Note** To use the classes from the System.Configuration namespace discussed in this recipe, you must add a reference to the System.Configuration.dll assembly when you build your application.

The Code

The following example demonstrates the writing of an encrypted connection string to the application's configuration file and the subsequent reading and use of that connection string.

```
using System;
using System.Configuration;
using System.Data.SqlClient;
```

```csharp
namespace Apress.VisualCSharpRecipes.Chapter09
{
    class Recipe09_04
    {
        private static void WriteEncryptedConnectionStringSection(
            string name, string constring, string provider)
        {
            // Get the configuration file for the current application. Specify
            // the ConfigurationUserLevel.None argument so that we get the
            // configuration settings that apply to all users.
            Configuration config = ConfigurationManager.OpenExeConfiguration(
                ConfigurationUserLevel.None);

            // Get the connectionStrings section from the configuration file.
            ConnectionStringsSection section = config.ConnectionStrings;

            // If the connectionString section does not exist, create it.
            if (section == null)
            {
                section = new ConnectionStringsSection();
                config.Sections.Add("connectionSettings", section);
            }

            // If it is not already encrypted, configure the connectionStrings
            // section to be encrypted using the standard RSA Proected
            // Configuration Provider.
            if (!section.SectionInformation.IsProtected)
            {
                // Remove this statement to write the connection string in clear
                // text for the purpose of testing.
                section.SectionInformation.ProtectSection(
                    "RsaProtectedConfigurationProvider");
            }

            // Create a new connection string element and add it to the
            // connection string configuration section.
            ConnectionStringSettings cs =
                new ConnectionStringSettings(name, constring, provider);
            section.ConnectionStrings.Add(cs);

            // Force the connection string section to be saved.
            section.SectionInformation.ForceSave = true;

            // Save the updated configuration file.
            config.Save(ConfigurationSaveMode.Full);
        }

        public static void Main(string[] args)
        {
            // The connection string information to be written to the
            // configuration file.
            string conName = "ConnectionString1";
            string conString = @"Data Source=.\sqlexpress;" +
                "Database=Northwind;Integrated Security=SSPI;" +
                "Min Pool Size=5;Max Pool Size=15;Connection Reset=True;" +
                "Connection Lifetime=600;";
            string providerName = "System.Data.SqlClient";
```

```
        // Write the new connection string to the application's
        // configuration file.
        WriteEncryptedConnectionStringSection(conName, conString, providerName);

        // Read the encrypted connection string settings from the
        // application's configuration file.
        ConnectionStringSettings cs2 =
            ConfigurationManager.ConnectionStrings["ConnectionString1"];

        // Use the connection string to create a new SQL Server connection.
        using (SqlConnection con = new SqlConnection(cs2.ConnectionString))
        {
            // Issue database commands/queries. . .

        }

        // Wait to continue.
        Console.WriteLine(Environment.NewLine);
        Console.WriteLine("Main method complete. Press Enter.");
        Console.ReadLine();
    }
  }
}
```

9-5. Execute a SQL Command or Stored Procedure

Problem

You need to execute a SQL command or stored procedure on a database.

Solution

Create a command object appropriate to the type of database you intend to use. All command objects implement the System.Data.IDbCommand interface. Configure the command object by setting its CommandType and CommandText properties. Execute the command using the ExecuteNonQuery, ExecuteReader, or ExecuteScalar method, depending on the type of command and its expected results.

How It Works

The IDbCommand interface represents a database command, and each data provider includes a unique implementation. Here is the list of IDbCommand implementations for the five standard data providers:

- System.Data.Odbc.OdbcCommand
- System.Data.OleDb.OleDbCommand
- System.Data.OracleClient.OracleCommand
- System.Data.SqlServerCe.SqlCeCommand
- System.Data.SqlClient.SqlCommand

To execute a command against a database, you must have an open connection (discussed in recipe 9-1) and a properly configured command object appropriate to the type of database you are

```
public static void UpdatePriceLevelUnitsProc()
{
  try
  {
    string queryStringUnits = "dbo.pUpdatePriceLevelUnits";
    using (SqlConnection connection = new SqlConnection (
@"Trusted_Connection=true;server=WDC\SQLEXPRESS;database=DrilTracR" ))
    {
    SqlCommand commandUnits = new SqlCommand ( queryStringUnits, connection );
    connection.Open ();
SqlDataReader reader = commandUnits.ExecuteReader ();
reader.Read ();
reader.Close ();
connection.Close ();    }
  } // end try
catch (System.Exception ex)
{
        System.Windows.Forms.MessageBox.Show ( "Error in Customer.cs form: Module =
UpdatePriceLevelProc.\n", ex.Message );
}
}       // End procedure
```

	return before timing out and raising an exception. Defaults to 30 seconds.
CommandType	A value of the System.Data.CommandType enumeration that specifies the type of command represented by the command object. For most data providers, valid values are StoredProcedure, when you want to execute a stored procedure, and Text, when you want to execute a SQL text command. If you are using the OLE DB data provider, you can specify TableDirect when you want to return the entire contents of one or more tables; refer to the .NET Framework SDK documentation for more details. Defaults to Text.
Connection	An IDbConnection instance that provides the connection to the database on which you will execute the command. If you create the command using the IDbConnection.CreateCommand method, this property will be automatically set to the IDbConnection instance from which you created the command.
Parameters	A System.Data.IDataParameterCollection instance containing the set of parameters to substitute into the command. (See recipe 9-6 for details on how to use parameters.)
Transaction	A System.Data.IDbTransaction instance representing the transaction into which to enlist the command. (See the .NET Framework SDK documentation for details about transactions.)

Once you have configured your command object, you can execute it in a number of ways, depending on the nature of the command, the type of data returned by the command, and the format in which you want to process the data.

- To execute a command that does not return database data (such as INSERT, DELETE, or CREATE TABLE), call ExecuteNonQuery. For the UPDATE, INSERT, and DELETE commands, the ExecuteNonQuery method returns an int that specifies the number of rows affected by the command. For other commands, such as CREATE TABLE, ExecuteNonQuery returns the value –1.

- To execute a command that returns a result set, such as a SELECT statement or stored procedure, use the ExecuteReader method. ExecuteReader returns an IDataReader instance (discussed in recipe 9-7) through which you have access to the result data. Most data providers also allow you to execute multiple SQL commands in a single call to the ExecuteReader method, as demonstrated in the example in this recipe, which also shows how to access each result set.

- If you want to execute a query but only need the value from the first column of the first row of result data, use the ExecuteScalar method. The value is returned as an object reference that you must cast to the correct type.

■**Note** The `IDbCommand` implementations included in the Oracle and SQL data providers implement additional command execution methods. Recipe 9-8 describes how to use the `ExecuteXmlReader` method provided by the `SqlCommand` class. Refer to the .NET Framework's SDK documentation for details on the additional `ExecuteOracleNonQuery` and `ExecuteOracleScalar` methods provided by the `OracleCommand` class.

The Code

The following example demonstrates the use of command objects to update a database record, run a stored procedure, and obtain a scalar value.

```
using System;
using System.Data;
using System.Data.SqlClient;

namespace Apress.VisualCSharpRecipes.Chapter09
{
    class Recipe09_05
    {
        public static void ExecuteNonQueryExample(IDbConnection con)
        {
            // Create and configure a new command.
            IDbCommand com = con.CreateCommand();
            com.CommandType = CommandType.Text;
            com.CommandText = "UPDATE Employees SET Title = 'Sales Director'" +
                " WHERE EmployeeId = '5'";

            // Execute the command and process the result.
            int result = com.ExecuteNonQuery();

            if (result == 1)
            {
                Console.WriteLine("Employee title updated.");
            }
            else
            {
                Console.WriteLine("Employee title not updated.");
            }
        }

        public static void ExecuteReaderExample(IDbConnection con)
        {
            // Create and configure a new command.
            IDbCommand com = con.CreateCommand();
            com.CommandType = CommandType.StoredProcedure;
            com.CommandText = "Ten Most Expensive Products";

            // Execute the command and process the results
            using (IDataReader reader = com.ExecuteReader())
            {
                Console.WriteLine("Price of the Ten Most Expensive Products.");

                while (reader.Read())
                {
                    // Display the product details.
                    Console.WriteLine("  {0} = {1}",
```

```
                        reader["TenMostExpensiveProducts"],
                        reader["UnitPrice"]);
            }
        }
    }

    public static void ExecuteScalarExample(IDbConnection con)
    {
        // Create and configure a new command.
        IDbCommand com = con.CreateCommand();
        com.CommandType = CommandType.Text;
        com.CommandText = "SELECT COUNT(*) FROM Employees";

        // Execute the command and cast the result.
        int result = (int)com.ExecuteScalar();

        Console.WriteLine("Employee count = " + result);
    }

    public static void Main()
    {
        // Create a new SqlConnection object.
        using (SqlConnection con = new SqlConnection())
        {
            // Configure the SqlConnection object's connection string.
            con.ConnectionString = @"Data Source = .\sqlexpress;" +
                "Database = Northwind; Integrated Security=SSPI";

            // Open the database connection and execute the example
            // commands through the connection.
            con.Open();

            ExecuteNonQueryExample(con);
            Console.WriteLine(Environment.NewLine);

            ExecuteReaderExample(con);
            Console.WriteLine(Environment.NewLine);

            ExecuteScalarExample(con);
        }

        // Wait to continue.
        Console.WriteLine(Environment.NewLine);
        Console.WriteLine("Main method complete. Press Enter.");
        Console.ReadLine();
    }
}
}
```

9-6. Use Parameters in a SQL Command or Stored Procedure

Problem

You need to set the arguments of a stored procedure or use parameters in a SQL command to improve flexibility.

Solution

Create parameter objects appropriate to the type of command object you intend to execute. All parameter objects implement the `System.Data.IDataParameter` interface. Configure the parameter objects' data types, values, and directions and add them to the command object's parameter collection using the `IDbCommand.Parameters.Add` method.

How It Works

All command objects support the use of parameters, so you can do the following:

- Set the arguments of stored procedures.
- Receive stored procedure return values.
- Substitute values into text commands at runtime.

The `IDataParameter` interface represents a parameter, and each data provider includes a unique implementation. Here is the list of `IDataParameter` implementations for the five standard data providers:

- `System.Data.Odbc.OdbcParameter`
- `System.Data.OleDb.OleDbParameter`
- `System.Data.OracleClient.OracleParameter`
- `System.Data.SqlServerCe.SqlCeParameter`
- `System.Data.SqlClient.SqlParameter`

To use parameters with a text command, you must identify where to substitute the parameter's value within the command. The ODBC, OLE DB, and SQL Server CE data providers support positional parameters; the location of each argument is identified by a question mark (?). For example, the following command identifies two locations to be substituted with parameter values.

```
UPDATE Employees SET Title = ? WHERE EmployeeId = ?
```

The SQL Server and Oracle data providers support named parameters, which allow you to identify each parameter location using a name preceded by the at symbol (@). Here is the equivalent command using named parameters:

```
UPDATE Employees SET Title = @title WHERE EmployeeId = @id
```

To specify the parameter values to substitute into a command, you must create parameter objects of the correct type and add them to the command object's parameter collection accessible through the `Parameters` property. You can add named parameters in any order, but you must add positional parameters in the same order they appear in the text command. When you execute your command, the value of each parameter is substituted into the command string before the command is executed against the data source. You can create parameter objects in the following ways:

- Use the IDbCommand.CreateParameter method.

- Use the IDbCommand.Parameters.Add method.

- Use System.Data.Common.DbProviderFactory.

- Directly create parameter objects using constructors and configure them using constructor arguments or through setting their properties. (This approach ties you to a specific database provider.)

A parameter object's properties describe everything about a parameter that the command object needs to use the parameter object when executing a command against a data source. Table 9-4 describes the properties that you will use most frequently when configuring parameters.

Table 9-4. *Commonly Used Parameter Properties*

Property	Description
DbType	A value of the System.Data.DbType enumeration that specifies the type of data contained in the parameter. Commonly used values include String, Int32, DateTime, and Currency.
Direction	A value from the System.Data.ParameterDirection enumeration that indicates the direction in which the parameter is used to pass data. Valid values are Input, InputOutput, Output, and ReturnValue.
IsNullable	A bool that indicates whether the parameter accepts null values.
ParameterName	A string containing the name of the parameter.
Value	An object containing the value of the parameter.

When using parameters to execute stored procedures, you must provide parameter objects to satisfy each argument required by the stored procedure, including both input and output arguments. You must set the Direction property of each parameter as described in Table 9-4; parameters are Input by default. If a stored procedure has a return value, the parameter to hold the return value (with a Direction property equal to ReturnValue) must be the first parameter added to the parameter collection.

The Code

The following example demonstrates the use of parameters in SQL commands. The ParameterizedCommandExample method demonstrates the use of parameters in a SQL Server UPDATE statement. The ParameterizedCommandExample method's arguments include an open SqlConnection and two strings. The values of the two strings are substituted into the UPDATE command using parameters. The StoredProcedureExample method demonstrates the use of parameters to call a stored procedure.

```
using System;
using System.Data;
using System.Data.SqlClient;

namespace Apress.VisualCSharpRecipes.Chapter09
{
    class Recipe09_06
    {
```

```csharp
public static void ParameterizedCommandExample(SqlConnection con,
    string employeeID, string title)
{
    // Create and configure a new command containing 2 named parameters.
    using (SqlCommand com = con.CreateCommand())
    {
        com.CommandType = CommandType.Text;
        com.CommandText = "UPDATE Employees SET Title = @title" +
            " WHERE EmployeeId = @id";

        // Create a SqlParameter object for the title parameter.
        SqlParameter p1 = com.CreateParameter();
        p1.ParameterName = "@title";
        p1.SqlDbType = SqlDbType.VarChar;
        p1.Value = title;
        com.Parameters.Add(p1);

        // Use a shorthand syntax to add the id parameter.
        com.Parameters.Add("@id", SqlDbType.Int).Value = employeeID;

        // Execute the command and process the result.
        int result = com.ExecuteNonQuery();

        if (result == 1)
        {
            Console.WriteLine("Employee {0} title updated to {1}.",
                employeeID, title);
        }
        else
        {
            Console.WriteLine("Employee {0} title not updated.",
                employeeID);
        }
    }
}

public static void StoredProcedureExample(SqlConnection con,
    string category, string year)
{
    // Create and configure a new command.
    using (SqlCommand com = con.CreateCommand())
    {
        com.CommandType = CommandType.StoredProcedure;
        com.CommandText = "SalesByCategory";

        // Create a SqlParameter object for the category parameter.
        com.Parameters.Add("@CategoryName", SqlDbType.NVarChar).Value =
            category;

        // Create a SqlParameter object for the year parameter.
        com.Parameters.Add("@OrdYear", SqlDbType.NVarChar).Value = year;

        // Execute the command and process the results.
        using (IDataReader reader = com.ExecuteReader())
        {
            Console.WriteLine("Sales By Category ({0}).", year);
```

```
                        while (reader.Read())
                        {
                            // Display the product details.
                            Console.WriteLine("  {0} = {1}",
                                reader["ProductName"],
                                reader["TotalPurchase"]);
                        }
                    }
                }
            }

            public static void Main()
            {
                // Create a new SqlConnection object.
                using (SqlConnection con = new SqlConnection())
                {
                    // Configure the SqlConnection object's connection string.
                    con.ConnectionString = @"Data Source = .\sqlexpress;" +
                        "Database = Northwind; Integrated Security=SSPI";

                    // Open the database connection and execute the example
                    // commands through the connection.
                    con.Open();

                    ParameterizedCommandExample(con, "5", "Cleaner");
                    Console.WriteLine(Environment.NewLine);

                    StoredProcedureExample(con, "Seafood", "1999");
                    Console.WriteLine(Environment.NewLine);
                }

                // Wait to continue.
                Console.WriteLine(Environment.NewLine);
                Console.WriteLine("Main method complete. Press Enter.");
                Console.ReadLine();
            }
        }
    }
```

9-7. Process the Results of a SQL Query Using a Data Reader

Problem

You need to process the data contained in a System.Data.IDataReader instance returned when you execute the IDbCommand.ExecuteReader method (discussed in recipe 9-5).

Solution

Use the members of the IDataReader instance to move through the rows in the result set sequentially and access the individual data items contained in each row.

How It Works

The IDataReader interface represents a data reader, which is a forward-only, read-only mechanism for accessing the results of a SQL query. Each data provider includes a unique IDataReader implementation. Here is the list of IDataReader implementations for the five standard data providers:

- System.Data.Odbc.OdbcDataReader
- System.Data.OleDb.OleDbDataReader
- System.Data.OracleClient.OracleDataReader
- System.Data.SqlServerCe.SqlCeDataReader
- System.Data.SqlClient.SqlDataReader

The IDataReader interface extends the System.Data.IDataRecord interface. Together, these interfaces declare the functionality that provides access to both the data and the structure of the data contained in the result set. Table 9-5 describes some of the commonly used members of the IDataReader and IDataRecord interfaces.

Table 9-5. *Commonly Used Members of Data Reader Classes*

Member	Description
Property	
FieldCount	Gets the number of columns in the current row.
IsClosed	Returns true if the IDataReader is closed; false if it's currently open.
Item	Returns an object representing the value of the specified column in the current row. Columns can be specified using a zero-based integer index or a string containing the column name. You must cast the returned value to the appropriate type. This is the indexer for data record and reader classes.
Method	
GetDataTypeName	Gets the name of the data source data type for a specified column.
GetFieldType	Gets a System.Type instance representing the data type of the value contained in the column specified using a zero-based integer index.
GetName	Gets the name of the column specified by using a zero-based integer index.
GetOrdinal	Gets the zero-based column ordinal for the column with the specified name.
GetSchemaTable	Returns a System.Data.DataTable instance that contains metadata describing the columns contained in the IDataReader.
IsDBNull	Returns true if the value in the specified column contains a data source null value; otherwise, it returns false.
NextResult	If the IDataReader includes multiple result sets because multiple statements were executed, NextResult moves to the next set of results. By default, the IDataReader is positioned on the first result set.
Read	Advances the reader to the next record. The reader always starts prior to the first record.

In addition to those members listed in Table 9-5, the data reader provides a set of methods for retrieving typed data from the current row. Each of the following methods takes an integer argument that identifies the zero-based index of the column from which the data should be returned: GetBoolean, GetByte, GetBytes, GetChar, GetChars, GetDateTime, GetDecimal, GetDouble, GetFloat, GetGuid, GetInt16, GetInt32, GetInt64, GetString, GetValue, and GetValues.

The SQL Server and Oracle data readers also include methods for retrieving data as data source–specific data types. For example, the SqlDataReader includes methods such as GetSqlByte, GetSqlDecimal, and GetSqlMoney, and the OracleDataReader includes methods such as GetOracleLob, GetOracleNumber, and GetOracleMonthSpan. Refer to the .NET Framework SDK documentation for more details.

When you have finished with a data reader, you should always call its Close method so that you can use the database connection again. IDataReader extends System.IDisposable, meaning that each data reader class implements the Dispose method. Dispose automatically calls Close, making the using statement a very clean and efficient way of using data readers.

The Code

The following example demonstrates the use of a data reader to process the contents of two result sets returned by executing a batch query containing two SELECT queries. The first result set is enumerated and displayed to the console. The second result set is inspected for metadata information, which is then displayed.

```csharp
using System;
using System.Data;
using System.Data.SqlClient;

namespace Apress.VisualCSharpRecipes.Chapter09
{
    class Recipe09_07
    {
        public static void Main()
        {
            // Create a new SqlConnection object.
            using (SqlConnection con = new SqlConnection())
            {
                // Configure the SqlConnection object's connection string.
                con.ConnectionString = @"Data Source = .\sqlexpress;" +
                    "Database = Northwind; Integrated Security=SSPI";

                // Create and configure a new command.
                using (SqlCommand com = con.CreateCommand())
                {
                    com.CommandType = CommandType.Text;
                    com.CommandText = "SELECT BirthDate,FirstName,LastName FROM "+
                        "Employees ORDER BY BirthDate;SELECT * FROM Employees";

                    // Open the database connection and execute the example
                    // commands through the connection.
                    con.Open();

                    // Execute the command and obtain a SqlReader.
                    using (SqlDataReader reader = com.ExecuteReader())
                    {
                        // Process the first set of results and display the
                        // content of the result set.
                        Console.WriteLine("Employee Birthdays (By Age).");

                        while (reader.Read())
                        {
                            Console.WriteLine("  {0,18:D} - {1} {2}",
                                reader.GetDateTime(0),  // Retrieve typed data
                                reader["FirstName"],    // Use string index
```

```
                    reader[2]);                    // Use ordinal index
            }
            Console.WriteLine(Environment.NewLine);

            // Process the second set of results and display details
            // about the columns and data types in the result set.
            reader.NextResult();
            Console.WriteLine("Employee Table Metadata.");
            for (int field = 0; field < reader.FieldCount; field++)
            {
                Console.WriteLine("  Column Name:{0}  Type:{1}",
                    reader.GetName(field),
                    reader.GetDataTypeName(field));
            }
        }
      }
    }
  }

      // Wait to continue.
      Console.WriteLine(Environment.NewLine);
      Console.WriteLine("Main method complete. Press Enter.");
      Console.ReadLine();
    }
  }
}
```

9-8. Obtain an XML Document from a SQL Server Query

Problem

You need to execute a query against a SQL Server 2000 (or later) database and retrieve the results as XML.

Solution

Specify the FOR XML clause in your SQL query to return the results as XML. Execute the command using the ExecuteXmlReader method of the System.Data.SqlClient.SqlCommand class, which returns a System.Xml.XmlReader object through which you can access the returned XML data.

How It Works

SQL Server 2000 (and later versions) provides direct support for XML. You simply need to add the clause FOR XML AUTO to the end of a SQL query to indicate that the results should be returned as XML. By default, the XML representation is not a full XML document. Instead, it simply returns the result of each record in a separate element, with all the fields as attributes. For example, this query:

```
SELECT CustomerID, CompanyName FROM Customers FOR XML AUTO
```

returns XML with the following structure:

```
<Customers CustomerID="ALFKI" CompanyName="Alfreds Futterkiste"/>
<Customers CustomerID="ANTON" CompanyName="Antonio Moreno Taquería"/>
<Customers CustomerID="GOURL" CompanyName="Gourmet Lanchonetes"/>
```

Alternatively, you can add the ELEMENTS keyword to the end of a query to structure the results using nested elements rather than attributes. For example, this query:

```
SELECT CustomerID, CompanyName FROM Customers FOR XML AUTO, ELEMENTS
```

returns XML with the following structure:

```
<Customers>
  <CustomerID>ALFKI</CustomerID>
  <CompanyName>Alfreds Futterkiste</CompanyName>
</Customers>
<Customers>
  <CustomerID>ANTON</CustomerID>
  <CompanyName>Antonio Moreno Taquería</CompanyName>
</Customers>
<Customers>
  <CustomerID>GOURL</CustomerID>
  <CompanyName>Gourmet Lanchonetes</CompanyName>
</Customers>
```

■**Tip** You can also fine-tune the format in more detail using the FOR XML EXPLICIT syntax. For example, this allows you to convert some fields to attributes and others to elements. Refer to SQL Server Books Online for more information.

When the ExecuteXmlReader command returns, the connection cannot be used for any other commands while the XmlReader is open. You should process the results as quickly as possible, and you must always close the XmlReader. Instead of working with the XmlReader and accessing the data sequentially, you can read the XML data into a System.Xml.XmlDocument. This way, all the data is retrieved into memory, and the database connection can be closed. You can then continue to interact with the XML document. (Chapter 6 contains numerous examples of how to use the XmlReader and XmlDocument classes.)

The Code

The following example demonstrates how to retrieve results as XML using the FOR XML clause and the ExecuteXmlReader method.

```csharp
using System;
using System.Xml;
using System.Data;
using System.Data.SqlClient;

namespace Apress.VisualCSharpRecipes.Chapter09
{
    class Recipe09_08
    {
        public static void ConnectedExample()
        {
            // Create a new SqlConnection object.
            using (SqlConnection con = new SqlConnection())
            {
                // Configure the SqlConnection object's connection string.
                con.ConnectionString = @"Data Source = .\sqlexpress;" +
                    "Database = Northwind; Integrated Security=SSPI";
```

```csharp
        // Create and configure a new command that includes the
        // FOR XML AUTO clause.
        using (SqlCommand com = con.CreateCommand())
        {
            com.CommandType = CommandType.Text;
            com.CommandText = "SELECT CustomerID, CompanyName" +
                " FROM Customers FOR XML AUTO";

            // Open the database connection.
            con.Open();

            // Execute the command and retrieve an XmlReader to access
            // the results.
            using (XmlReader reader = com.ExecuteXmlReader())
            {
                while (reader.Read())
                {
                    Console.Write("Element: " + reader.Name);
                    if (reader.HasAttributes)
                    {
                        for (int i = 0; i < reader.AttributeCount; i++)
                        {
                            reader.MoveToAttribute(i);
                            Console.Write("  {0}: {1}",
                                reader.Name, reader.Value);
                        }

                        // Move the XmlReader back to the element node.
                        reader.MoveToElement();
                        Console.WriteLine(Environment.NewLine);
                    }
                }
            }
        }
    }
}

public static void DisconnectedExample()
{
    XmlDocument doc = new XmlDocument();

    // Create a new SqlConnection object.
    using (SqlConnection con = new SqlConnection())
    {
        // Configure the SqlConnection object's connection string.
        con.ConnectionString = @"Data Source = .\sqlexpress;" +
            "Database = Northwind; Integrated Security=SSPI";

        // Create and configure a new command that includes the
        // FOR XML AUTO clause.
        SqlCommand com = con.CreateCommand();
        com.CommandType = CommandType.Text;
        com.CommandText =
            "SELECT CustomerID, CompanyName FROM Customers FOR XML AUTO";

        // Open the database connection.
        con.Open();
```

```
                    // Load the XML data into the XmlDocument. Must first create a
                    // root element into which to place each result row element.
                    XmlReader reader = com.ExecuteXmlReader();
                    doc.LoadXml("<results></results>");

                    // Create an XmlNode from the next XML element read from the
                    // reader.
                    XmlNode newNode = doc.ReadNode(reader);

                    while (newNode != null)
                    {
                        doc.DocumentElement.AppendChild(newNode);
                        newNode = doc.ReadNode(reader);
                    }
                }

                // Process the disconnected XmlDocument.
                Console.WriteLine(doc.OuterXml);
            }

            public static void Main(string[] args)
            {
                ConnectedExample();
                Console.WriteLine(Environment.NewLine);

                DisconnectedExample();
                Console.WriteLine(Environment.NewLine);

                // Wait to continue.
                Console.WriteLine(Environment.NewLine);
                Console.WriteLine("Main method complete. Press Enter.");
                Console.ReadLine();
            }
        }
    }
```

9-9. Perform Asynchronous Database Operations Against SQL Server

Problem

You need to execute a query or command against a SQL Server database as a background task while your application continues with other processing.

Solution

Use the `BeginExecuteNonQuery`, `BeginExecuteReader`, or `BeginExecuteXmlReader` method of the `System.Data.SqlClient.SqlCommand` class to start the database operation as a background task. These methods all return a `System.IAsyncResult` object that you can use to determine the operation's status or use thread synchronization to wait for completion. Use the `IAsyncResult` object and the corresponding `EndExecuteNonQuery`, `EndExecuteReader`, or `EndExecuteXmlReader` method to obtain the result of the operation.

Note Only the `SqlCommand` class supports the asynchronous operations described in this recipe. The equivalent command classes for the Oracle, SQL Server CE, ODBC, and OLE DB data providers do not provide this functionality.

How It Works

You will usually execute operations against databases synchronously, meaning that the calling code blocks until the operation is complete. Synchronous calls are most common because your code will usually require the result of the operation before it can continue. However, sometimes it's useful to execute a database operation asynchronously, meaning that you start the method in a separate thread and then continue with other operations.

Note To execute asynchronous operations over a `System.Data.SqlClient.SqlConnection` connection, you must specify the value `Asynchronous Processing=true` in its connection string.

As of .NET Framework 2.0, the `SqlCommand` class implements the asynchronous execution pattern similar to that discussed in recipe 4-2. As with the general asynchronous execution pattern described in recipe 4-2, the arguments of the asynchronous execution methods (`BeginExecuteNonQuery`, `BeginExecuteReader`, and `BeginExecuteXmlReader`) are the same as those of the synchronous variants (`ExecuteNonQuery`, `ExecuteReader`, and `ExecuteXmlReader`), but they take the following two additional arguments to support asynchronous completion:

- A `System.AsyncCallback` delegate instance that references a method that the runtime will call when the asynchronous operation completes. The method is executed in the context of a thread-pool thread. Passing `null` means that no method is called and you must use another completion mechanism (discussed later in this recipe) to determine when the asynchronous operation is complete.

- An `object` reference that the runtime associates with the asynchronous operation. The asynchronous operation does not use nor have access to this object, but it's available to your code when the operation completes, allowing you to associate useful state information with an asynchronous operation. For example, this object allows you to map results against initiated operations in situations where you initiate many asynchronous operations that use a common callback method to perform completion.

The `EndExecuteNonQuery`, `EndExecuteReader`, and `EndExecuteXmlReader` methods allow you to retrieve the return value of an operation that was executed asynchronously, but you must first determine when it has finished. Here are the four techniques for determining if an asynchronous method has finished:

- *Blocking*: This method stops the execution of the current thread until the asynchronous operation completes execution. In effect, this is much the same as synchronous execution. However, you do have the flexibility to decide exactly when your code enters the blocked state, giving you the opportunity to carry out some additional processing before blocking.

- *Polling*: This method involves repeatedly testing the state of an asynchronous operation to determine if it's complete. This is a very simple technique and is not particularly efficient from a processing perspective. You should avoid tight loops that consume processor time. It's best to put the polling thread to sleep for a period using `Thread.Sleep` between completion tests. Because polling involves maintaining a loop, the actions of the waiting thread are limited, but you can easily update some kind of progress indicator.

- *Waiting*: This method uses an object derived from the System.Threading.WaitHandle class to signal when the asynchronous method completes. Waiting is a more efficient version of polling and in addition allows you to wait for multiple asynchronous operations to complete. You can also specify time-out values to allow your waiting thread to fail if the asynchronous operation takes too long, or if you want to periodically update a status indicator.

- *Callback*: This a method that the runtime calls when an asynchronous operation completes. The calling code does not need to take any steps to determine when the asynchronous operation is complete and is free to continue with other processing. Callbacks provide the greatest flexibility, but also introduce the greatest complexity, especially if you have many concurrently active asynchronous operations that all use the same callback. In such cases, you must use appropriate state objects to match completed methods against those you initiated.

■**Caution** When using the asynchronous capabilities of the SQL Server data provider, you must ensure that your code does not inadvertently dispose of objects that are still being used by other threads. Pay particular attention to SqlConnection and SqlCommand objects.

The Code

Recipe 4-2 provides examples of all of the completion techniques summarized in the preceding list. The following example demonstrates the use of an asynchronous call to execute a stored procedure on a SQL Server database. The code uses a callback to process the returned result set.

```
using System;
using System.Data;
using System.Threading;
using System.Data.SqlClient;

namespace Apress.VisualCSharpRecipes.Chapter09
{
    class Recipe09_09
    {
        // A method to handle asynchronous completion using callbacks.
        public static void CallbackHandler(IAsyncResult result)
        {
            // Obtain a reference to the SqlCommand used to initiate the
            // asynchronous operation.
            using (SqlCommand cmd = result.AsyncState as SqlCommand)
            {
                // Obtain the result of the stored procedure.
                using (SqlDataReader reader = cmd.EndExecuteReader(result))
                {
                    // Display the results of the stored procedure to the console.
                    lock (Console.Out)
                    {
                        Console.WriteLine(
                            "Price of the Ten Most Expensive Products:");

                        while (reader.Read())
                        {
                            // Display the product details.
                            Console.WriteLine("  {0} = {1}",
                                reader["TenMostExpensiveProducts"],
                                reader["UnitPrice"]);
                        }
                    }
                }
            }
        }
    }
}
```

```
                }
            }
        }

        public static void Main()
        {
            // Create a new SqlConnection object.
            using (SqlConnection con = new SqlConnection())
            {
                // Configure the SqlConnection object's connection string.
                // You must specify Asynchronous Processing=true to support
                // asynchronous operations over the connection.
                con.ConnectionString = @"Data Source = .\sqlexpress;" +
                    "Database = Northwind; Integrated Security=SSPI;" +
                    "Asynchronous Processing=true";

                // Create and configure a new command to run a stored procedure.
                // Do not wrap it in a using statement because the asynchronous
                // completion handler will dispose of the SqlCommand object.
                SqlCommand cmd = con.CreateCommand();
                cmd.CommandType = CommandType.StoredProcedure;
                cmd.CommandText = "Ten Most Expensive Products";

                // Open the database connection and execute the command
                // asynchronously. Pass the reference to the SqlCommand
                // used to initiate the asynchronous operation.
                con.Open();
                cmd.BeginExecuteReader(CallbackHandler, cmd);

                // Continue with other processing.
                for (int count = 0; count < 10; count++)
                {
                    lock (Console.Out)
                    {
                        Console.WriteLine("{0} : Continue processing...",
                            DateTime.Now.ToString("HH:mm:ss.ffff"));
                    }
                    Thread.Sleep(500);
                }
            }

            // Wait to continue.
            Console.WriteLine(Environment.NewLine);
            Console.WriteLine("Main method complete. Press Enter.");
            Console.ReadLine();
        }
    }
}
```

9-10. Write Database-Independent Code

Problem

You need to write code that can be configured to work against any relational database supported by
an ADO.NET data provider.

Solution

Program to the ADO.NET data provider interfaces in the System.Data namespace, as opposed to the concrete implementations, and do not rely on features and data types that are unique to specific database implementations. Use factory classes and methods to instantiate the data provider objects you need to use.

How It Works

Using a specific data provider implementation (the SQL Server data provider, for example) simplifies your code and may be appropriate if you need to support only a single type of database or require access to specific features provided by that data provider, such as the asynchronous execution for SQL Server detailed in recipe 9-9. However, if you program your application against a specific data provider implementation, you will need to rewrite and test those sections of your code if you want to use a different data provider at some point in the future.

Table 9-6 contains a summary of the main interfaces you must program against when writing generic ADO.NET code that will work with any relational database's data provider. The table also explains how to create objects of the appropriate type that implement the interface. Many of the recipes in this chapter demonstrate the use of ADO.NET data provider interfaces over specific implementation, as highlighted in the table.

Table 9-6. *Data Provider Interfaces*

Interface	Description	Demonstrated In
IDbConnection	Represents a connection to a relational database. You must program the logic to create a connection object of the appropriate type based on your applications configuration information, or use the DbProviderFactory.CreateConnection factory method (discussed in this recipe).	Recipe 9-1
IDbCommand	Represents a SQL command that is issued to a relational database. You can create IDbCommand objects of the appropriate type using the IDbConnection.CreateCommand or DbProviderFactory.CreateCommand factory method.	Recipe 9-5
IDataParameter	Represents a parameter to an IDbCommand object. You can create IDataParameter objects of the correct type using the IDbCommand.CreateParameter, IDbCommand.Parameters.Add, or DbProviderFactory.CreateParameter factory method.	Recipe 9-6
IDataReader	Represents the result set of a database query and provides access to the contained rows and columns. An object of the correct type will be returned when you call the IDbCommand.ExecuteReader method.	Recipes 9-5 and 9-6
IDbDataAdapter	Represents the set of commands used to fill a System.Data.DataSet from a relational database and to update the database based on changes to the DataSet. You must program the logic to create a data adapter object of the appropriate type based on your applications configuration information, or use the DbProviderFactory.CreateAdapter factory method (discussed in this recipe).	

The `System.Data.Common.DbProviderFactory` class is new to .NET Framework 2.0 and provides a set of factory methods for creating all types of data provider objects, making it very useful for implementing generic database code. Most important, `DbProviderFactory` provides a mechanism for obtaining an initial `IDbConnection` instance, which is the critical starting point to writing generic ADO.NET code. Each of the standard data provider implementations (except the SQL Server CE data provider) includes a unique factory class derived from `DbProviderFactory`. Here is the list of `DbProviderFactory` subclasses:

- `System.Data.Odbc.OdbcFactory`
- `System.Data.OleDb.OleDbFactory`
- `System.Data.OracleClient.OracleClientFactory`
- `System.Data.SqlClient.SqlClientFactory`

You can obtain an instance of the appropriate `DbProviderFactory` subclass using the `DbProviderFactories` class, which is effectively a factory of factories. Each data provider factory is described by configuration information in the machine.config file similar to that shown here for the SQL Server data adapter. This can be changed or overridden by application-specific configuration information if required.

```
<configuration>
 <system.data>
    <DbProviderFactories>
      <add name="SqlClient Data Provider" invariant="System.Data.SqlClient" ➥
description=".Net Framework Data Provider for SqlServer" type= ➥
"System.Data.SqlClient.SqlClientFactory, System.Data, Version=2.0.0.0, ➥
Culture=neutral, PublicKeyToken=b77a5c561934e089" />
      <add name="Odbc Data Provider" ... />
      <add name="OleDb Data Provider" ... />
      <add name="OracleClient Data Provider" ... />
      <add name="SQL Server CE Data ... />
    </DbProviderFactories>
  </system.data>
</configuration>
```

You can enumerate the available data provider factories by calling `DbProviderFactories.GetFactoryClasses`, which returns a `System.Data.DataTable` containing the following columns:

- `Name`, which contains a human-readable name for the provider factory. Taken from the name attribute in the configuration information.
- `Description`, which contains a human-readable description for the provider factory. Taken from the description attribute of the configuration information.
- `InvariantName`, which contains the unique name used to refer to the data provider factory programmatically. Taken from the invariant attribute of the configuration information.
- `AssemblyQualifiedName`, which contains the fully qualified name of the `DbProviderFactory` class for the data provider. Taken from the type attribute of the configuration information.

Normally, you would allow the provider to be selected at install time or the first time the application was run, and then store the settings as user or application configuration data. The most important piece of information is the `InvariantName`, which you pass to the `DbProviderFactories.GetFactory` method to obtain the `DbProviderFactory` implementation you will use to create your `IDbConnection` instances.

■**Note** Prior to .NET Framework 2.0, it was difficult to write generic ADO.NET code because each data provider implemented its own exception class that did not extend a common base class. In .NET Framework 2.0, the `System.Data.Common.DbException` class has been added as the base class of all data provider-specific exceptions, making generic handling of database exceptions a reality.

The Code

The following example demonstrates the enumeration of all data providers configured for the local machine and application. It then uses the `DbProviderFactories` class to instantiate a `DbProviderFactory` object (actually a `SqlClientFactory`) from which it creates the appropriate `IDbConnection`. It then uses the factory methods of the data provider interfaces to create other required objects, resulting in code that is completely generic.

```
using System;
using System.Data;
using System.Data.Common;

namespace Apress.VisualCSharpRecipes.Chapter09
{
    class Recipe09_10
    {
        public static void Main(string[] args)
        {
            // Obtain the list of ADO.NET data providers registered in the
            // machine and application configuration file.
            using (DataTable providers = DbProviderFactories.GetFactoryClasses())
            {
                // Enumerate the set of data providers and display details.
                Console.WriteLine("Available ADO.NET Data Providers:");
                foreach (DataRow prov in providers.Rows)
                {
                    Console.WriteLine(" Name:{0}", prov["Name"]);
                    Console.WriteLine("   Description:{0}",
                        prov["Description"]);
                    Console.WriteLine("   Invariant Name:{0}",
                        prov["InvariantName"]);
                }
            }

            // Obtain the DbProviderFactory for SQL Server. The provider to use
            // could be selected by the user or read from a configuration file.
            // In this case, we simply pass the invariant name.
            DbProviderFactory factory =
                DbProviderFactories.GetFactory("System.Data.SqlClient");

            // Use the DbProviderFactory to create the initial IDbConnection, and
            // then the data provider interface factory methods for other objects.
            using (IDbConnection con = factory.CreateConnection())
            {
                // Normally, read the connection string from secure storage.
                // See recipe 9-3. In this case, use a default value.
                con.ConnectionString = @"Data Source = .\sqlexpress;" +
                    "Database = Northwind; Integrated Security=SSPI";
```

```
            // Create and configure a new command.
            using (IDbCommand com = con.CreateCommand())
            {
                com.CommandType = CommandType.StoredProcedure;
                com.CommandText = "Ten Most Expensive Products";

                // Open the connection.
                con.Open();

                // Execute the command and process the results.
                using (IDataReader reader = com.ExecuteReader())
                {
                    Console.WriteLine(Environment.NewLine);
                    Console.WriteLine("Price of the Ten Most
                        Expensive Products.");

                    while (reader.Read())
                    {
                        // Display the product details.
                        Console.WriteLine("  {0} = {1}",
                            reader["TenMostExpensiveProducts"],
                            reader["UnitPrice"]);
                    }
                }
            }

        // Wait to continue.
        Console.WriteLine(Environment.NewLine);
        Console.WriteLine("Main method complete. Press Enter.");
        Console.ReadLine();
        }
    }
}
```

9-11. Discover All Instances of SQL Server on Your Network

Problem

You need to obtain a list of all instances of SQL Server 2000 or SQL Server 2005 that are accessible on the network.

Solution

Use the GetDataSources method of the System.Data.Sql.SqlDataSourceEnumerator class.

■**Note** Your code needs to be granted FullTrust to be able to execute the GetDataSources method.

How It Works

The addition of the new SqlDataSourceEnumerator class in .NET Framework 2.0 makes it easy to enumerate the SQL Server instances accessible on the network. In previous versions of the .NET Framework, you needed to create a COM Interop library to access the SQLDMO library to achieve this.

In .NET Framework 2.0, you simply obtain the singleton SqlDataSourceEnumerator instance via the static property SqlDataSourceEnumerator.Instance and call its GetDataSources method. The GetDataSources method returns a System.Data.DataTable that contains a set of System.Data.DataRow objects. Each DataRow represents a single SQL Server instance and contains the following columns:

- ServerName, which contains the name of the server where the SQL Server instance is hosted.

- InstanceName, which contains the name of the SQL Server instance or the empty string if the SQL Server is the default instance.

- IsClustered, which indicates whether the SQL Server instance is part of a cluster.

- Version, which contains the version of the SQL Server instance (8.00.x for SQL Server 2000 or 9.00.x for SQL Server 2005).

■**Caution** It is possible to configure SQL Server 2005 to be invisible to the GetDataSources method by disabling the SQL Server Browser. Therefore, you cannot assume that a SQL Server instance does not exist because you could not discover it.

The Code

The following example demonstrates the use of the SqlDataSourceEnumerator class to discover and display details of all SQL Server instances accessible (and visible) on the network.

```
using System;
using System.Data;
using System.Data.Sql;

namespace Apress.VisualCSharpRecipes.Chapter09
{
    class Recipe09_11
    {
        public static void Main(string[] args)
        {
            // Obtain the DataTable of SQL Server instances.
            using (DataTable SqlSources =
                SqlDataSourceEnumerator.Instance.GetDataSources())
            {
                // Enumerate the set of SQL Servers and display details.
                Console.WriteLine("Discover SQL Server Instances:");
                foreach (DataRow source in SqlSources.Rows)
                {
                    Console.WriteLine(" Server Name:{0}", source["ServerName"]);
                    Console.WriteLine("   Instance Name:{0}",
                        source["InstanceName"]);
                    Console.WriteLine("   Is Clustered:{0}",
                        source["IsClustered"]);
                    Console.WriteLine("   Version:{0}", source["Version"]);
                }
            }
        }
```

```
        // Wait to continue.
        Console.WriteLine(Environment.NewLine);
        Console.WriteLine("Main method complete. Press Enter.");
        Console.ReadLine();
    }
  }
}
```

CHAPTER 10

■■■

Networking and Remoting

The Microsoft .NET Framework includes a full set of classes for network programming. These classes support everything from socket-based programming with Transmission Control Protocol/Internet Protocol (TCP/IP) to downloading files and HTML pages from the Web over Hypertext Transfer Protocol (HTTP). Not only do these networking classes provide you with a rich set of tried-and-tested tools to use in your own distributed applications, they are also the foundation on which two high-level distributed programming models integral to the .NET Framework are built: Remoting and XML Web services.

Although Remoting and XML Web services share many similarities (for example, they both abstract cross-process and cross-machine calls as method invocations on remote objects), they also have fundamental differences. XML Web services are built using cross-platform standards and are based on the concept of XML messaging. XML Web services are executed by the ASP.NET runtime, which means they gain ASP.NET features such as output caching. This also means that XML Web services are fundamentally stateless. Overall, XML Web services are best suited when you need to cross platform boundaries (for example, with a Java client calling an ASP.NET Web service) or trust boundaries (for example, in business-to-business transactions).

Remoting is a .NET-specific technology for distributed objects and is the successor to Distributed Component Object Model (DCOM). It's ideal for in-house systems in which all applications are built on the .NET platform, such as the backbone of an internal order-processing system. Remoting allows for different types of communication, including leaner binary messages and more efficient TCP/IP connections, which aren't supported by XML Web services. In addition, Remoting is the only technology that supports stateful objects and bidirectional communication through callbacks. It's also the only technology that allows you to send custom .NET objects over the wire.

The recipes in this chapter describe how to do the following:

- Obtain configuration and network statistic information about the network interfaces on a computer as well as detect when network configuration changes occur (recipes 10-1 and 10-2)

- Download files from File Transfer Protocol (FTP) and HTTP servers (recipes 10-3, 10-4, and 10-6)

- Respond to HTTP requests from within your application (recipe 10-5)

- Send e-mail messages with attachments using Simple Mail Transfer Protocol (SMTP) (recipe 10-7)

- Use the Domain Name System (DNS) to resolve a host name into an Internet Protocol (IP) address (recipe 10-8)

- Ping an IP address to determine whether it is accessible and calculate round-trip communication speeds by sending it an Internet Control Message Protocol (ICMP) Echo request (recipe 10-9)

- Communicate between programs through the direct use of TCP in both synchronous and asynchronous communication models (recipes 10-10 and 10-11)

- Communicate using User Datagram Protocol (UDP) datagrams where the connection-oriented and reliable TCP represents unnecessary overhead (recipe 10-12)

- Write Web service proxy classes that read the Web service uniform resource locator (URL) from a configuration file, thus avoiding the need to rebuild code if the URL changes (recipe 10-13)

- Provide credentials to allow a proxy class to authenticate against a secured Web service (recipe 10-14)

- Call a Web service method asynchronously to avoid the calling code blocking and waiting for the Web service to respond (recipe 10-15)

- Create remotable objects and register them with the .NET Framework's Remoting infrastructure (recipes 10-16 and 10-17)

- Host a remote object in Internet Information Services (IIS) (recipe 10-18)

- Control the lifetime and versioning of remotable objects (recipes 10-19 and 10-20)

10-1. Obtain Information About the Local Network Interface

Problem

You need to obtain information about the network adapters and network configuration of the local machine.

Solution

Call the static method GetAllNetworkInterfaces of the System.Net.NetworkInformation. NetworkInterface class to get an array of objects derived from the abstract class NetworkInterface. Each object represents a network interface available on the local machine. Use the members of each NetworkInterface object to retrieve configuration information and network statistics for that interface.

How It Works

The addition of the System.Net.NetworkInformation namespace in the .NET Framework 2.0 provides easy access to information about network configuration and statistics that was not readily available to .NET applications previously.

The primary means of retrieving network information are the properties and methods of the NetworkInterface class. You do not instantiate NetworkInterface objects directly. Instead, you call the static method NetworkInterface.GetAllNetworkInterfaces, which returns an array of NetworkInterface objects. Each object represents a single network interface on the local machine. You can then obtain network information and statistics about the interface using the NetworkInterface members described in Table 10-1.

Tip The `System.Net.NetworkInformation.IPGlobalProperties` class (new to .NET 2.0) also provides access to useful information about the network configuration of the local computer.

Table 10-1. *Members of the* `NetworkInterface` *Class*

Member	Description
Properties	
`Description`	Gets a `string` that provides a general description of the interface.
`Id`	Gets a `string` that contains the identifier of the interface.
`IsReceiveOnly`	Gets a `bool` indicating whether the interface can only receive or can both send and receive data.
`Name`	Gets a `string` containing the name of the interface.
`NetworkInterfaceType`	Gets a value from the `System.Net.NetworkInformation.NetworkInterfaceType` enumeration that identifies the type of interface. Common values include `Ethernet`, `FastEthernetT`, and `Loopback`.
`OperationalStatus`	Gets a value from the `System.Net.NetworkInformation.OperationalStatus` enumeration that identifies the status of the interface. Common values include `Down` and `Up`.
`Speed`	Gets a `long` that identifies the speed (in bits per second) of the interface as reported by the adapter, not based on dynamic calculation.
`SupportsMulticast`	Gets a `bool` indicating whether the interface is enabled to receive multicast packets.
Methods	
`GetIPProperties`	Returns a `System.Net.NetworkInformation.IPInterfaceProperties` object that provides access to the TCP/IP configuration information for the interface. Properties of the `IPInterfaceProperties` object provide access to WINS, DNS, gateway, and IP address configuration.
`GetIPv4Statistics`	Returns a `System.Net.NetworkInformation.IPv4InterfaceStatistics` object that provides access to the TCP/IP v4 statistics for the interface. The properties of the `IPv4InterfaceStatistics` object provide access to information about bytes sent and received, packets sent and received, discarded packets, and packets with errors.
`GetPhysicalAddress`	Returns a `System.Net.NetworkInformation.PhysicalAddress` object that provides access to the physical address of the interface. You can obtain the physical address as a byte array using the method `PhysicalAddress.GetAddressBytes` or as a `string` using `PhysicalAddress.ToString`.
`Supports`	Returns a `bool` indicating whether the interface supports a specified protocol. You specify the protocol using a value from the `System.Net.NetworkInformation.NetworkInterfaceComponent` enumeration. Possible values include `IPv4` and `IPv6`.

The `NetworkInterface` class also provides two other `static` members that you will find useful:

- The `static` property `LoopbackInterfaceIndex` returns an `int` identifying the index of the loopback interface within the `NetworkInterface` array returned by `GetAllNetworkInterfaces`.

- The `static` method `GetIsNetworkAvailable` returns a `bool` indicating whether any network connection is available, that is, has an `OperationalStatus` value of `Up`.

The Code

The following example uses the members of the NetworkInterface class to display information about all the network interfaces on the local machine:

```
using System;
using System.Net.NetworkInformation;

namespace Apress.VisualCSharpRecipes.Chapter10
{
    class Recipe10_01
    {
        static void Main()
        {
            // Only proceed if there is a network available.
            if (NetworkInterface.GetIsNetworkAvailable())
            {
                // Get the set of all NetworkInterface objects for the local
                // machine.
                NetworkInterface[] interfaces =
                    NetworkInterface.GetAllNetworkInterfaces();

                // Iterate through the interfaces and display information.
                foreach (NetworkInterface ni in interfaces)
                {
                    // Report basic interface information.
                    Console.WriteLine("Interface Name: {0}", ni.Name);
                    Console.WriteLine("    Description: {0}", ni.Description);
                    Console.WriteLine("    ID: {0}", ni.Id);
                    Console.WriteLine("    Type: {0}", ni.NetworkInterfaceType);
                    Console.WriteLine("    Speed: {0}", ni.Speed);
                    Console.WriteLine("    Status: {0}", ni.OperationalStatus);

                    // Report physical address.
                    Console.WriteLine("    Physical Address: {0}",
                        ni.GetPhysicalAddress().ToString());

                    // Report network statistics for the interface.
                    Console.WriteLine("    Bytes Sent: {0}",
                        ni.GetIPv4Statistics().BytesSent);
                    Console.WriteLine("    Bytes Received: {0}",
                        ni.GetIPv4Statistics().BytesReceived);

                    // Report IP configuration.
                    Console.WriteLine("    IP Addresses:");
                    foreach (UnicastIPAddressInformation addr
                        in ni.GetIPProperties().UnicastAddresses)
                    {
                        Console.WriteLine("        - {0} (lease expires {1})",
                            addr.Address,
                            DateTime.Now +
                            new TimeSpan(0, 0, (int)addr.DhcpLeaseLifetime));
                    }

                    Console.WriteLine(Environment.NewLine);
                }
            }
        }
```

```
            else
            {
                Console.WriteLine("No network available.");
            }

            // Wait to continue.
            Console.WriteLine(Environment.NewLine);
            Console.WriteLine("Main method complete. Press Enter");
            Console.ReadLine();
        }
    }
}
```

10-2. Detect Changes in Network Connectivity

Problem

You need a mechanism to check whether changes to the network occur during the life of your application.

Solution

Add handlers to the static NetworkAddressChanged and NetworkAvailabilityChanged events implemented by the System.Net.NetworkInformation.NetworkChange class.

How It Works

The NetworkChange class (new to the .NET Framework 2.0) provides an easy-to-use mechanism that allows applications to be aware of changes to network addresses and general network availability. This allows your applications to adapt dynamically to the availability and configuration of the network.

The NetworkAvailabilityChanged event fires when a change occurs to general network availability. An instance of the NetworkAvailabilityChangedEventHandler delegate is needed to handle this event and is passed a NetworkAvailabilityEventArgs object when the event fires. The NetworkAvailabilityEventArgs.IsAvailable property returns a bool indicating whether the network is available or unavailable following the change.

The NetworkAddressChanged event fires when the IP address of a network interface changes. An instance of the NetworkAddressChangedEventHandler delegate is required to handle these events. No event-specific arguments are passed to the event handler, which must call NetworkInterface. GetAllNetworkInterfaces (discussed in recipe 10-1) to determine what has changed and to take appropriate action.

The Code

The following example demonstrates how to use handlers that catch NetworkAddressChanged and NetworkAvailabilityChanged events and then displays status information to the console:

```
using System;
using System.Net.NetworkInformation;
```

```csharp
namespace Apress.VisualCSharpRecipes.Chapter10
{
    class Recipe10_02
    {
        // Declare a method to handle NetworkAvailabilityChanged events.
        private static void NetworkAvailabilityChanged(
            object sender, NetworkAvailabilityEventArgs e)
        {
            // Report whether the network is now available or unavailable.
            if (e.IsAvailable)
            {
                Console.WriteLine("Network Available");
            }
            else
            {
                Console.WriteLine("Network Unavailable");
            }
        }

        // Declare a method to handle NetworkAdressChanged events.
        private static void NetworkAddressChanged(object sender, EventArgs e)
        {
            Console.WriteLine("Current IP Addresses:");

            // Iterate through the interfaces and display information.
            foreach (NetworkInterface ni in
                NetworkInterface.GetAllNetworkInterfaces())
            {
                foreach (UnicastIPAddressInformation addr
                    in ni.GetIPProperties().UnicastAddresses)
                {
                    Console.WriteLine("    - {0} (lease expires {1})",
                        addr.Address, DateTime.Now +
                        new TimeSpan(0, 0, (int)addr.DhcpLeaseLifetime));
                }
            }
        }

        static void Main(string[] args)
        {
            // Add the handlers to the NetworkChange events.
            NetworkChange.NetworkAvailabilityChanged +=
                NetworkAvailabilityChanged;
            NetworkChange.NetworkAddressChanged +=
                NetworkAddressChanged;

            // Wait to continue.
            Console.WriteLine(Environment.NewLine);
            Console.WriteLine("Press Enter to stop waiting for network events");
            Console.ReadLine();
        }
    }
}
```

10-3. Download Data over HTTP or FTP

Problem

You need a quick, simple way to download data from the Internet using HTTP or FTP.

Solution

Use the methods of the `System.Net.WebClient` class.

How It Works

The .NET Framework provides several mechanisms for transferring data over the Internet. One of the easiest approaches is to use the `System.Net.WebClient` class. `WebClient` provides many high-level methods that simplify the transfer of data by specifying the source as a uniform resource identifier (URI); Table 10-2 summarizes them. The URI can specify that a file (file://), FTP (ftp://), or HTTP (http:// or https://) scheme be used to download the resource.

Table 10-2. *Data Download Methods of the* `WebClient` *Class*

Method	Description
OpenRead	Returns a `System.IO.Stream` that provides access to the data from a specified URI.
OpenReadAsync	Same as `OpenRead` but performs the data transfer using a thread-pool thread so that the calling thread does not block. Add an event handler to the `OpenReadCompleted` event to receive notification that the operation has completed. (This is new to the .NET Framework 2.0.)
DownloadData	Returns a `byte` array that contains the data from a specified URI.
DownloadDataAsync	Same as `DownloadData` but performs the data transfer using a thread-pool thread so that the calling thread does not block. Add an event handler to the `DownloadDataCompleted` event to receive notification that the operation has completed. (This is new to the .NET Framework 2.0.)
DownloadFile	Downloads data from a specified URI and saves it to a specified local file.
DownloadFileAsync	Same as `DownloadFile` but performs the data transfer using a thread-pool thread so that the calling thread does not block. Add an event handler to the `DownLoadFileCompleted` event to receive notification that the operation has completed. (This is new to the .NET Framework 2.0.)
DownloadString	Returns a `string` that contains the data from a specified URI. (This is new to the .NET Framework 2.0.)
DownloadStringAsync	Same as `DownloadString` but performs the data transfer using a thread-pool thread so that the calling thread does not block. Add an event handler to the `DownloadStringCompleted` event to receive notification that the operation has completed. (This is new to the .NET Framework 2.0.)

The asynchronous download methods added in version 2.0 of the .NET Framework allow you to download data as a background task using a thread from the thread pool (discussed in recipe 4-1). When the download is finished or fails, the thread calls the appropriate `OnXXX` virtual methods that raise the corresponding event on the `WebClient` object, which you can handle using a method that matches the signature of the `System.ComponentModel.AsyncCompletedEventHandler` delegate if you don't want to derive a type from `WebClient` and override the virtual method. However, the `WebClient` object can handle only a single concurrent asynchronous download, making a `WebClient` object suitable for the background download of large single sets of data but not for the download of many files concurrently. (You could, of course, create multiple `WebClient` objects to handle multiple downloads.) You can cancel the outstanding asynchronous download using the method `CancelAsync`.

Tip The `WebClient` class derives from `System.ComponentModel.Component`, so you can add it to the Visual Studio 2005 Form Designer Toolbox in order to allow you to easily set the properties or define the event handlers in a Windows Forms–based application.

The Code

The following example downloads a specified resource from a URI as a string and, since it is an HTML page, parses it for any fully qualified URLs that refer to GIF files. It then downloads each of these files to the local hard drive.

```
using System;
using System.IO;
using System.Net;
using System.Text.RegularExpressions;

namespace Apress.VisualCSharpRecipes.Chapter10
{
    class Recipe10_03
    {
        private static void Main()
        {
            // Specify the URI of the resource to parse.
            string remoteUri = "http://www.apress.com";

            // Create a WebClient to perform the download.
            WebClient client = new WebClient();

            Console.WriteLine("Downloading {0}", remoteUri);

            // Perform the download getting the resource as a string.
            string str = client.DownloadString(remoteUri);

            // Use a regular expression to extract all fully qualified
            // URIs that refer to GIF files.
            MatchCollection matches =
                Regex.Matches(str,@"http\S+[^-,;:?]\.gif");

            // Try to download each referenced .gif file.
            foreach(Match match in matches)
            {
                foreach(Group grp in match.Groups)
                {
                    // Determine the local filename.
                    string file =
                        grp.Value.Substring(grp.Value.LastIndexOf('/')+1);

                    try
                    {
                        // Download and store the file.
```

```
                    Console.WriteLine("Downloading {0} to file {1}",
                        grp.Value, file);

                    client.DownloadFile(new Uri(grp.Value), file);
                }
                catch
                {
                    Console.WriteLine("Failed to download {0}", grp.Value);
                }
            }
        }

        // Wait to continue.
        Console.WriteLine(Environment.NewLine);
        Console.WriteLine("Main method complete. Press Enter");
        Console.ReadLine();
    }
}
```

■**Note** The regular expression used in the example is simple and is not designed to cater to all possible URL structures. Recipes 2-5 and 2-6 discuss regular expressions.

Notes

You may also want to upload data to resources specified as a URI, although this technique is not as commonly used. The WebClient class also provides methods for performing uploads that are equivalent to the download methods discussed previously.

- OpenWrite
- OpenWriteAsync
- UploadData
- UploadDataAsync
- UploadFile
- UploadFileAsync
- UploadString
- UploadStringAsync

10-4. Download a File and Process It Using a Stream

Problem

You need to retrieve a file from a web site, but you do not want or do not have permission to save it directly to the hard drive. Instead, you want to process the data in your application directly in memory.

Solution

Use the System.Net.WebRequest class to create your request, the System.Net.WebResponse class to retrieve the response from the web server, and some form of reader (typically a System.IO.StreamReader for HTML or text data or a System.IO.BinaryReader for a binary file) to parse the response data.

■**Tip** You could also use the OpenRead method of the System.Net.WebClient class to open a stream. However, the additional capabilities of the WebRequest and WebResponse classes give you more control over the operation of the network request.

How It Works

Opening and downloading a stream of data from the Web using the WebRequest and WebResponse classes takes the following four basic steps:

1. Use the static method Create of the WebRequest class to specify the page you want. This method returns a WebRequest-derived object, depending on the type of URI you specify. For example, if you use an HTTP URI (with the scheme http:// or https://), you will create an HttpWebRequest instance. If you use a file system URI (with the scheme file://), you will create a FileWebRequest instance. In the .NET Framework 2.0, you can also use an FTP URL (with the scheme ftp://), which will create an FtpWebRequest.

2. Use the GetResponse method of the WebRequest object to return a WebResponse object for the page. If the request times out, a System.Net.WebException will be thrown. You can configure the time-out for the network request through the WebRequest.Timeout property in milliseconds (the default value is 100000).

3. Create a StreamReader or a BinaryReader that wraps the stream returned by the WebResponse.GetResponseStream method.

4. Perform any steps you need to with the stream contents.

The Code

The following example retrieves and displays a graphic and the HTML content of a web page. Figure 10-1 shows the output.

```
using System;
using System.Net;
using System.IO;
using System.Drawing;
using System.Windows.Forms;

namespace Apress.VisualCSharpRecipes.Chapter10
{
    public partial class Recipe10_04 : Form
    {
        public Recipe10_04()
        {
            InitializeComponent();
        }

        protected override void OnLoad(EventArgs e)
        {
            base.OnLoad(e);
```

```
        string picUri = "http://www.apress.com/img/img05/Hex_RGB4.jpg";
        string htmlUri = "http://www.apress.com";

        // Create the requests.
        WebRequest requestPic = WebRequest.Create(picUri);
        WebRequest requestHtml = WebRequest.Create(htmlUri);

        // Get the responses.
        // This takes the most significant amount of time, particularly
        // if the file is large, because the whole response is retrieved.
        WebResponse responsePic = requestPic.GetResponse();
        WebResponse responseHtml = requestHtml.GetResponse();

        // Read the image from the response stream.
        pictureBox1.Image = Image.FromStream(responsePic.GetResponseStream());

        // Read the text from the response stream.
        using (StreamReader r =
            new StreamReader(responseHtml.GetResponseStream()))
        {
            textBox1.Text = r.ReadToEnd();
        }
    }

    [STAThread]
    public static void Main(string[] args)
    {
        Application.Run(new Recipe10_04());
    }
  }
}
```

Figure 10-1. *Downloading content from the Web using a Stream*

10-5. Respond to HTTP Requests from Your Application

Problem

You want your application to be able to respond to HTTP requests programmatically.

Solution

Use the new `System.Net.HttpListener` class provided by the .NET Framework 2.0.

■**Note** Your application must be running on Windows XP Service Pack 2 (or later) or Windows 2003 to use the `HttpListener` class; otherwise, a `System.PlatformNotSupportedException` will be thrown when you try to instantiate it. You should check the `bool` returned by the `static` property `HttpListener.IsSupported` to check whether support is available.

How It Works

The `HttpListener` class provides an easy-to-use mechanism through which your programs can accept and respond to HTTP requests. To use the `HttpListener` class, follow these steps:

1. Instantiate an `HttpListener` object.

2. Configure the URI prefixes that the `HttpListener` object will handle using the `Prefixes` property. The `Prefixes` property returns a `System.Net.HttpListenerPrefixCollection` collection to which you can add URI prefixes (as `strings`) using the `Add` method. Each prefix must end with a forward slash (/), or an `System.ArgumentException` is thrown. If you specify a URL prefix that is already being handled, a `System.Net.HttpListenerException` is thrown. When a client makes a request, the request will be handled by the listener configured with the prefix that most closely matches the client's requested URL.

3. Start the `HttpListener` object by calling its `Start` method. You must call `Start` before the `HttpListener` object can accept and process HTTP requests.

4. Accept client requests using the `GetContext` method of the `HttpListener` object. The `GetContext` method will block the calling thread until a request is received and then returns a `System.Net.HttpListenerContext` object. Alternatively, you can use the `BeginGetContext` and `EndGetContext` methods to listen for requests on a thread-pool thread. When a request is received, the `System.AsynchCallback` delegate specified as the argument to the `BeginGetContext` method will be called and passed the `HttpListenerContext` object. Regardless of how it is obtained, the `HttpListenerContext` objects implements three read-only properties critical to the handling of a client request:

   - The `Request` property returns a `System.Net.HttpListenerRequest` through which you can access details of the client's request.

   - The `Response` property returns a `System.Net.HttpListenerResponse` through which you can configure the response to send to the client.

   - The `User` property returns an instance of a type implementing `System.Security.Principal.IPrincipal`, which you can use to obtain identity, authentication, and authorization information about the user associated with the request.

5. Configure the HTTP response through the members of the HttpListenerResponse object accessible through the HttpListenerContext.Response property.

6. Send the response by calling the Close method of the HttpListenerResponse object.

7. Once you have finished processing HTTP requests, call Stop on the HttpListener object to stop accepting more requests. Call Close to shut down the HttpListener object, which will wait until all outstanding requests have been processed, or call Abort to terminate the HttpListener object without waiting for requests to be complete.

The Code

The following example demonstrates how to use the HttpListener class to process HTTP requests. The example starts listening for five requests concurrently using the asynchronous BeginGetContext method and handles the response to each request by calling the RequestHandler method. Each time a request is handled, a new call is made to BeginGetContext so that you always have the capacity to handle up to five requests.

To open a connection to the example from your browser, enter the URL http://localhost:19080/VisualCSharpRecipes/ or http://localhost:20000/Recipe10-05/, and you will see the response from the appropriate request handler.

```
using System;
using System.IO;
using System.Net;
using System.Text;
using System.Threading;

namespace Apress.VisualCSharpRecipes.Chapter10
{
    class Recipe10_05
    {
        // Configure the maximum number of request that can be
        // handled concurrently.
        private static int maxRequestHandlers = 5;

        // An integer used to assign each HTTP request handler a unique
        // identifier.
        private static int requestHandlerID = 0;

        // The HttpListener is the class that provides all the capabilities
        // to receive and process HTTP requests.
        private static HttpListener listener;

        // A method to asynchronously process individual requests and send
        // responses.
        private static void RequestHandler(IAsyncResult result)
        {
            Console.WriteLine("{0}: Activated.", result.AsyncState);

            try
            {
                // Obtain the HttpListenerContext for the new request.
                HttpListenerContext context = listener.EndGetContext(result);

                Console.WriteLine("{0}: Processing HTTP Request from {1} ({2}).",
                    result.AsyncState,
                    context.Request.UserHostName,
                    context.Request.RemoteEndPoint);
```

```csharp
                // Build the response using a StreamWriter feeding the
                // Response.OutputStream.
                StreamWriter sw =
                    new StreamWriter(context.Response.OutputStream, Encoding.UTF8);

                sw.WriteLine("<html>");
                sw.WriteLine("<head>");
                sw.WriteLine("<title>Visual C# Recipes</title>");
                sw.WriteLine("</head>");
                sw.WriteLine("<body>");
                sw.WriteLine("Recipe 10-5: " + result.AsyncState);
                sw.WriteLine("</body>");
                sw.WriteLine("</html>");
                sw.Flush();

                // Configure the Response.
                context.Response.ContentType = "text/html";
                context.Response.ContentEncoding = Encoding.UTF8;

                // Close the Response to send it to the client.
                context.Response.Close();

                Console.WriteLine("{0}: Sent HTTP response.", result.AsyncState);
            }
            catch (ObjectDisposedException)
            {
                Console.WriteLine("{0}: HttpListener disposed--shutting down.",
                    result.AsyncState);
            }
            finally
            {
                // Start another handler if unless the HttpListener is closing.
                if (listener.IsListening)
                {
                    Console.WriteLine("{0}: Creating new request handler.",
                        result.AsyncState);

                    listener.BeginGetContext(RequestHandler, "RequestHandler_" +
                        Interlocked.Increment(ref requestHandlerID));
                }
            }
        }
    }

    public static void Main(string[] args)
    {
        // Quit gracefully if this feature is not supported.
        if (!HttpListener.IsSupported)
        {
            Console.WriteLine(
                "You must be running this example on Windows XP SP2, ",
                "Windows Server 2003, or higher to create ",
                "an HttpListener.");
            return;
        }

        // Create the HttpListener.
        using (listener = new HttpListener())
```

```
    {
        // Configure the URI prefixes that will map to the HttpListener.
        listener.Prefixes.Add(
            "http://localhost:19080/VisualCSharpRecipes/");
        listener.Prefixes.Add(
            "http://localhost:20000/Recipe10-05/");

        // Start the HttpListener before listening for incoming requests.
        Console.WriteLine("Starting HTTP Server");
        listener.Start();
        Console.WriteLine("HTTP Server started");
        Console.WriteLine(Environment.NewLine);

        // Create a number of asynchronous request handlers up to
        // the configurable maximum. Give each a unique identifier.
        for (int count = 0; count < maxRequestHandlers; count++)
        {
            listener.BeginGetContext(RequestHandler, "RequestHandler_" +
                Interlocked.Increment(ref requestHandlerID));
        }

        // Wait for the user to stop the HttpListener.
        Console.WriteLine("Press Enter to stop the HTTP Server");
        Console.ReadLine();

        // Stop accepting new requests.
        listener.Stop();

        // Terminate the HttpListener without processing current requests.
        listener.Abort();
    }

    // Wait to continue.
    Console.WriteLine(Environment.NewLine);
    Console.WriteLine("Main method complete. Press Enter");
    Console.ReadLine();
    }
  }
}
```

10-6. Get an HTML Page from a Site That Requires Authentication

Problem

You need to retrieve a file from a web site, but the web site requires that you provide credentials for the purpose of authentication.

Solution

Use the System.Net.WebRequest and System.Net.WebResponse classes as described in recipe 10-4. Before making the request, configure the WebRequest.Credentials and WebRequest.Certificates properties with the necessary authentication information.

■**Tip** You could also use the `System.Net.WebClient` class (discussed in recipe 10-3), which also has `Credentials` and `Certificates` properties that allow you to associate user credentials with a web request.

How It Works

Some web sites require user authentication information. When connecting through a browser, this information might be submitted transparently (for example, on a local intranet site that uses Windows integrated authentication), or the browser might request this information with a login dialog box. When accessing a web page programmatically, your code needs to submit this information. The approach you use depends on the type of authentication implemented by the web site:

- If the web site is using basic or digest authentication, you can transmit a username and password combination by manually creating a new `System.Net.NetworkCredential` object and assigning it to the `WebRequest.Credentials` property. With digest authentication, you may also supply a domain name.

- If the web site is using Windows integrated authentication, you can take the same approach and manually create a new `System.Net.NetworkCredential` object. Alternatively, you can retrieve the current user login information from the `System.Net.CredentialCache` object using the `DefaultCredentials` property.

- If the web site requires a client certificate, you can load the certificate from a file using the `System.Security.Cryptography.X509Certificates.X509Certificate2` class and add that to the `HttpWebRequest.ClientCertificates` collection.

- In the .NET Framework 2.0, you can load an X.509 certificate from a certificate store using the class `System.Security.Cryptography.X509Certificates.X509Store` defined in the `System.Security.dll` assembly. You can either find a certificate in the store programmatically using the `X509Store.Certificates.Find` method or present the user with a Windows dialog box and allow them to select the certificate. To present a dialog box, pass a collection of X.509 certificates contained in an `X509Certificate2Collection` object to the `SelectFromCollection` method of the `System.Security.Cryptography.X509Certificates.X509Certificate2UI` class.

The Code

The following example demonstrates all four of the basic approaches described previously. Note that you need to add a reference to the `System.Security.dll` assembly.

```
using System;
using System.Net;
using System.Security.Cryptography.X509Certificates;

namespace Apress.VisualCSharpRecipes.Chapter10
{
    class Recipe10_06
    {
        public static void Main()
        {
            // Create a WebRequest that authenticates the user with a
            // username and password combination over basic authentication.
            WebRequest requestA = WebRequest.Create("http://www.somesite.com");
            requestA.Credentials = new NetworkCredential("userName", "password");
            requestA.PreAuthenticate = true;
```

```
// Create a WebRequest that authenticates the current user
// with Windows integrated authentication.
WebRequest requestB = WebRequest.Create("http://www.somesite.com");
requestB.Credentials = CredentialCache.DefaultCredentials;
requestB.PreAuthenticate = true;

// Create a WebRequest that authenticates the user with a client
// certificate loaded from a file.
HttpWebRequest requestC =
    (HttpWebRequest)WebRequest.Create("http://www.somesite.com");
X509Certificate cert1 =
    X509Certificate.CreateFromCertFile(@"..\..\TestCertificate.cer");
requestC.ClientCertificates.Add(cert1);

// Create a WebRequest that authenticates the user with a client
// certificate loaded from a certificate store. Try to find a
// certificate with a specific subject, but if it is not found
// present the user with a dialog so they can select the certificate
// to use from their personal store.
HttpWebRequest requestD =
    (HttpWebRequest)WebRequest.Create("http://www.somesite.com");
X509Store store = new X509Store();
X509Certificate2Collection certs =
    store.Certificates.Find(X509FindType.FindBySubjectName,
    "Allen Jones", false);

if (certs.Count == 1)
{
    requestD.ClientCertificates.Add(certs[0]);
}
else
{
    certs = X509Certificate2UI.SelectFromCollection(
        store.Certificates,
        "Select Certificate",
        "Select the certificate to use for authentication.",
        X509SelectionFlag.SingleSelection);

    if (certs.Count != 0)
    {
        requestD.ClientCertificates.Add(certs[0]);
    }
}

// Now issue the request and process the responses...
        }
    }
}
```

10-7. Send E-mail Using SMTP

Problem

You need to send e-mail using an SMTP server.

Solution

Use the SmtpClient and MailMessage classes in the System.Net.Mail namespace.

Note In version 1.0 and 1.1 of the .NET Framework, you would send SMTP mail using the SmtpMail and MailMessage classes in the System.Web.Mail namespace from the System.Web.dll assembly. The SmtpClient and MailMessage classes discussed in this recipe are new to the System.dll assembly in the .NET Framework 2.0, and both simplify and extend the functionality provided by earlier versions.

How It Works

An instance of the SmtpClient class provides the mechanism through which you communicate with the SMTP server. You configure the SmtpClient using the properties described in Table 10-3.

Table 10-3. *Properties of the* SmtpClient *Class*

Property	Description
ClientCertificates	Gets a System.Security.Cryptography.X509Certificates. X509CertificatesCollection to which you add the certificates to use for communicating with the SMTP server (if required).
Credentials	Gets or sets an implementation of the System.Net.ICredentialsByHost interface that represents the credentials to use to gain access to the SMTP server. The CredentialCache and NetworkCredential classes implement the ICredentialsByHost interface. Use NetworkCredential if you want to specify a single set of credentials and CredentialCache if you want to specify more than one.
EnableSsl	Gets or sets a bool value that indicates whether the SmtpClient should use Secure Sockets Layer (SSL) to communicate with the SMTP server.
Host	Gets or sets a string containing the host name or IP address of the SMTP server to use to send e-mail.
Port	Gets or sets an int value containing the port number to connect to on the SMTP server. The default value is 25.
Timeout	Gets or sets an int value containing the time-out in milliseconds when attempting to send e-mail. The default is 100 seconds.
UseDefaultCredentials	Gets or sets a bool value indicating whether the default user credentials are used when communicating with the SMTP server. If true, the credentials passed to the SMTP server are automatically obtained from the static property CredentialCache.DefaultCredentials.

Tip You can specify default settings for the SmtpClient in the <mailSettings> section of your machine or application configuration files. Configurable default values include the host, port, username, and password.

Mail messages are represented by MailMessage objects, which you instantiate and then configure using the members summarized in Table 10-4.

Tip For simple mail messages, the MailMessage class provides a constructor that allows you to specify the from, to, subject, and body information for the mail message as string arguments—allowing you to create a complete mail message in a single call.

Table 10-4. *Properties of the* MailMessage *Class*

Property	Description
Attachments	Gets or sets a System.Net.Mail.AttachmentCollection containing the set of attachments for the e-mail message. A System.Net.Mail.Attachment object represents each attachment. You can create Attachment objects from files or streams, and you can configure the encoding and content type for each attachment.
Bcc	Gets or sets a System.Net.Mail.MailAddressCollection containing the blind carbon copy addresses for the e-mail message. The MailAddressCollection contains one or more MailAddress objects.
Body	Gets or sets a string value that contains the body text of the e-mail message.
BodyEncoding	Gets or sets a System.Text.Encoding object that specifies the encoding for the body of the e-mail message. The default value is null resulting in a default encoding of us-ascii, which is equivalent to the Encoding object returned by the static property Encoding.ASCII.
CC	Gets or sets a System.Net.Mail.MailAddressCollection containing the carbon copy addresses for the e-mail message. The MailAddressCollection contains one or more MailAddress objects.
From	Gets or sets a System.Net.Mail.MailAddress containing the from address for the e-mail message.
IsBodyHtml	Gets or sets a bool value identifying whether the body of the e-mail message contains HTML.
ReplyTo	Gets or sets a System.Net.Mail.MailAddress containing the reply address for the e-mail message.
Subject	Gets or sets a string containing the subject for the e-mail message.
SubjectEncoding	Gets or sets a System.Text.Encoding object that specifies the encoding used to encode the body of the e-mail subject. The default value is null resulting in a default encoding of us-ascii, which is equivalent to the Encoding object returned by the static property Encoding.ASCII.
To	Gets or sets a System.Net.Mail.MailAddressCollection containing the destination addresses for the e-mail message. The MailAddressCollection contains one or more MailAddress objects.

Once you have configured the SmtpClient, you can send your MailMessage objects using the SmtpClient.Send method, which will cause your code to block until the send operation is completed or fails. Alternatively, you can send mail using a thread from the thread pool by calling the SendAsync method. When you call SendAsync, your code will be free to continue other processing while the e-mail is sent. Add an event handler to the SendCompleted event to receive notification that the asynchronous send has completed.

■**Note** Remember that you can't use SMTP to retrieve e-mail. For this task, you need the Post Office Protocol 3 (POP3) or the Internet Message Access Protocol (IMAP), neither of which is exposed natively in the .NET Framework.

The Code

The following example demonstrates how to use the SmtpClient class to send an e-mail message with multiple attachments to a set of recipients whose e-mail addresses are specified as command-line arguments:

```csharp
using System;
using System.Net;
using System.Net.Mail;

namespace Apress.VisualCSharpRecipes.Chapter10
{
    class Recipe10_07
    {
        public static void Main(string[] args)
        {
            // Create and configure the SmtpClient that will send the mail.
            // Specify the host name of the SMTP server and the port used
            // to send mail.
            SmtpClient client = new SmtpClient("mail.somecompany.com", 25);

            // Configure the SmtpClient with the credentials used to connect
            // to the SMTP server.
            client.Credentials =
                new NetworkCredential("user@somecompany.com", "password");

            // Create the MailMessage to represent the e-mail being sent.
            using (MailMessage msg = new MailMessage())
            {
                // Configure the e-mail sender and subject.
                msg.From = new MailAddress("author@visual-csharp-recipes.com");
                msg.Subject = "Greetings from Visual C# Recipes";

                // Configure the e-mail body.
                msg.Body = "This is a message from Recipe 10-07 of" +
                    " Visual C# Recipes. Attached is the source file " +
                    " and the binary for the recipe.";

                // Attach the files to the e-mail message and set their MIME type.
                msg.Attachments.Add(
                    new Attachment(@"..\..\Recipe10-07.cs","text/plain"));
                msg.Attachments.Add(
                    new Attachment(@".\Recipe10-07.exe",
                    "application/octet-stream"));

                // Iterate through the set of recipients specified on the
                // command line. Add all addresses with the correct structure as
                //   recipients.
                foreach (string str in args)
                {
                    // Create a MailAddress from each value on the command line
                    // and add it to the set of recipients.
                    try
                    {
                        msg.To.Add(new MailAddress(str));
                    }
                    catch (FormatException ex)
                    {
                        // Proceed to the next specified recipient.
                        Console.WriteLine("{0}: Error -- {1}", str, ex.Message);
                        continue;
                    }
                }
```

```
            // Send the message.
            client.Send(msg);
        }

        // Wait to continue.
        Console.WriteLine(Environment.NewLine);
        Console.WriteLine("Main method complete. Press Enter");
        Console.ReadLine();
    }
  }
}
```

10-8. Resolve a Host Name to an IP Address

Problem

You want to determine the IP address for a computer based on its fully qualified domain name by performing a DNS query.

Solution

In version 2.0 of the .NET Framework, use the method GetHostEntry of the System.Net.Dns class, and pass the computer's fully qualified domain name as a string parameter.

■**Note** In version 1.0 and 1.1 of the .NET Framework, you should use the method GetHostByName of the Dns class, but it is marked as obsolete in version 2.0.

How It Works

On the Internet, the human-readable names that refer to computers are mapped to IP addresses, which is what TCP/IP requires in order to communicate between computers. For example, the name www.apress.com might be mapped to the IP address 65.19.150.100. To determine the IP address for a given name, the computer contacts a DNS server. The name or IP address of the DNS server contacted is configured as part of a computer's network configuration.

The entire process of name resolution is transparent if you use the System.Net.Dns class, which allows you to retrieve the IP address for a host name by calling GetHostEntry.

■**Tip** The Dns class also provides the BeginGetHostEntry and EndGetHostEntry methods that allow you to resolve IP addresses asynchronously. Also, the static method GetHostName returns the computer name of the local machine.

The Code

The following example retrieves the IP addresses of all computers whose fully qualified domain names are specified as command-line arguments:

```
using System;
using System.Net;
```

```csharp
namespace Apress.VisualCSharpRecipes.Chapter10
{
    class Recipe10_08
    {
        public static void Main(string[] args)
        {
            foreach (string comp in args)
            {
                try
                {
                    // Retrieve the DNS entry for the specified computer.
                    IPAddress[] addresses = Dns.GetHostEntry(comp).AddressList;

                    // The DNS entry may contain more than one IP address. Iterate
                    // through them and display each one along with the type of
                    // address (AddressFamily).
                    foreach (IPAddress address in addresses)
                    {
                        Console.WriteLine("{0} = {1} ({2})",
                            comp, address, address.AddressFamily);
                    }
                }
                catch (Exception ex)
                {
                    Console.WriteLine("{0} = Error ({1})", comp, ex.Message);
                }
            }

            // Wait to continue.
            Console.WriteLine(Environment.NewLine);
            Console.WriteLine("Main method complete. Press Enter");
            Console.ReadLine();
        }
    }
}
```

Usage

Running the example with the following command line:

```
recipe10-08 www.apress.com www.microsoft.com localhost somejunk
```

will produce the following output. Notice that multiple IP addresses are returned for some host names.

```
www.apress.com = 65.19.150.100 (InterNetwork)
www.microsoft.com = 207.46.198.30 (InterNetwork)
www.microsoft.com = 207.46.20.30 (InterNetwork)
www.microsoft.com = 207.46.20.60 (InterNetwork)
www.microsoft.com = 207.46.18.30 (InterNetwork)
www.microsoft.com = 207.46.19.30 (InterNetwork)
www.microsoft.com = 207.46.19.60 (InterNetwork)
www.microsoft.com = 207.46.199.30 (InterNetwork)
www.microsoft.com = 207.46.198.60 (InterNetwork)
localhost = 127.0.0.1 (InterNetwork)
somejunk = Error (No such host is known)
```

10-9. Ping an IP Address

Problem

You want to check to see whether a computer is online and accessible and gauge its response time.

Solution

Send a ping message. This message is sent using the ICMP, accessible through the Send method of the System.Net.NetworkInformation.Ping class.

■**Note** The Ping class is new to the .NET Framework 2.0. To send a ping message in earlier versions of the .NET Framework, you had to undertake significant effort to manually create an ICMP request message using raw sockets and lengthy code.

How It Works

A ping message contacts a device at a specific IP address, passing it a test packet, and requests that the remote device respond by echoing back the packet. To gauge the connection latency between two computers, you can measure the time taken for a ping response to be received.

■**Caution** Many commercial Web sites do not respond to ping requests because they represent an unnecessary processing overhead and are often used in denial of service attacks. The firewall that protects the site will usually filter them out before they reach the specified destination. This will cause your ping request to time out.

The Ping class allows you to send ping messages using the Send method. The Send method provides a number of overloads, which allow you to specify some or all of the following:

- The IP address or host name of the target computer. You can specify this as a string or a System.Net.IPAddress object.

- The number of milliseconds to wait for a response before the request times out (specified as an int) with the default set to 5000.

- A byte array of up to 65,500 data bytes that is sent with the ping request and that should be returned in the response.

- A System.Net.NetworkInformation.PingOptions object that specifies time-to-live and fragmentation options for the transmission of the ping message.

The Send method will return a System.Net.NetworkInformation.PingReply object. The Status property of the PingReply will contain a value from the System.Net.NetworkInformation.IPStatus enumeration from which you can determine the result of the ping request. The most common values will be Success and TimedOut. If the host name you pass to the Send method cannot be resolved, Send will throw an exception, but you must look at the InnerException to determine the cause of the problem.

The Ping class also provides a SendAsync method that performs the ping request using a thread-pool thread so that the calling thread does not block. When the ping is finished or fails because of a time-out, the thread raises the PingCompleted event on the Ping object, which you can handle using a method that matches the signature of the System.Net.NetworkInformation.PingCompletedEventHandler delegate. However, the Ping object can handle only a single concurrent request; otherwise, it will throw a System.InvalidOperationException.

■**Tip** The `Ping` class derives from `System.ComponentModel.Component`, so you can add it to the Visual Studio 2005 Form Designer Toolbox in order to allow you to easily set the properties or define the event handlers in a Windows Forms–based application.

The Code

The following example pings the computers whose domain names or IP addresses are specified as command-line arguments:

```
using System;
using System.Net.NetworkInformation;

namespace Apress.VisualCSharpRecipes.Chapter10
{
    class Recipe10_09
    {
        public static void Main(string[] args)
        {
            // Create an instance of the Ping class.
            using (Ping ping = new Ping())
            {
                Console.WriteLine("Pinging:");

                foreach (string comp in args)
                {
                    try
                    {
                        Console.Write("    {0}...", comp);

                        // Ping the specified computer with a time-out of 100ms.
                        PingReply reply = ping.Send(comp, 100);

                        if (reply.Status == IPStatus.Success)
                        {
                            Console.WriteLine("Success - IP Address:{0} Time:{1}ms",
                                reply.Address, reply.RoundtripTime);
                        }
                        else
                        {
                            Console.WriteLine(reply.Status);
                        }
                    }
                    catch (Exception ex)
                    {
                        Console.WriteLine("Error ({0})",
                            ex.InnerException.Message);
                    }
                }
            }
        }
    }
```

```
            // Wait to continue.
            Console.WriteLine(Environment.NewLine);
            Console.WriteLine("Main method complete. Press Enter");
            Console.ReadLine();
        }
    }
}
```

Usage

Running the example with the following command line:

```
recipe10-09 www.apress.com www.google.com localhost somejunk
```

will produce the following output:

```
Pinging:
    www.apress.com...TimedOut
    www.google.com...Success - IP Address:216.239.59.104 Time:42ms
    localhost...Success - IP Address:127.0.0.1 Time:0ms
    somejunk...Error (No such host is known)
```

10-10. Communicate Using TCP

Problem

You need to send data between two computers on a network using a TCP/IP connection.

Solution

One computer (the server) must begin listening using the `System.Net.Sockets.TcpListener` class. Another computer (the client) connects to it using the `System.Net.Sockets.TcpClient` class. Once a connection is established, both computers can communicate using the `System.Net.Sockets.NetworkStream` class.

How It Works

TCP is a reliable, connection-oriented protocol that allows two computers to communicate over a network. It provides built-in flow control, sequencing, and error handling, which makes it reliable and easy to program.

To create a TCP connection, one computer must act as the server and start listening on a specific endpoint. (An *endpoint* is a combination of an IP address and a port number.) The other computer must act as a client and send a connection request to the endpoint on which the first computer is listening. Once the connection is established, the two computers can take turns exchanging messages. .NET makes this process easy through its stream abstraction. Both computers simply write to and read from a `System.Net.Sockets.NetworkStream` to transmit data.

■Note Even though a TCP connection always requires a server and a client, an individual application could be both. For example, in a peer-to-peer application, one thread is dedicated to listening for incoming requests (acting as a server), and another thread is dedicated to initiating outgoing connections (acting as a client). In the examples provided with this chapter, the client and server are provided as separate applications and are placed in separate subdirectories.

Once a TCP connection is established, the two computers can send any type of data by writing it to the NetworkStream. However, it's a good idea to begin designing a networked application by defining the application-level protocol that clients and servers will use to communicate. This protocol includes constants that represent the allowable commands, ensuring that your application code doesn't include hard-coded communication strings.

The Code

In this example, the defined protocol is basic. You would add more constants depending on the type of application. For example, in a file transfer application, you might include a client message for requesting a file. The server might then respond with an acknowledgment and return file details such as the file size. These constants should be compiled into a separate class library assembly, which must be referenced by both the client and server. Here is the code for the shared protocol:

```
namespace Apress.VisualCSharpRecipes.Chapter10
{
    public class Recipe10_10Shared
    {
        public const string AcknowledgeOK = "OK";
        public const string AcknowledgeCancel = "Cancel";
        public const string Disconnect = "Bye";
        public const string RequestConnect = "Hello";
    }
}
```

The following code is a template for a basic TCP server. It listens on a fixed port, accepts the first incoming connection, and then waits for the client to request a disconnect. At this point, the server could call the TcpListener.AcceptTcpClient method again to wait for the next client, but instead it simply shuts down.

```
using System;
using System.IO;
using System.Net;
using System.Net.Sockets;

namespace Apress.VisualCSharpRecipes.Chapter10
{
    public class Recipe10_10Server
    {
        public static void Main()
        {
            // Create a new listener on port 8000.
            TcpListener listener =
                new TcpListener(IPAddress.Parse("127.0.0.1"), 8000);

            Console.WriteLine("About to initialize port.");
            listener.Start();
            Console.WriteLine("Listening for a connection...");
```

```
try
{
    // Wait for a connection request, and return a TcpClient
    // initialized for communication.
    using (TcpClient client = listener.AcceptTcpClient())
    {
        Console.WriteLine("Connection accepted.");

        // Retrieve the network stream.
        NetworkStream stream = client.GetStream();

        // Create a BinaryWriter for writing to the stream.
        using (BinaryWriter w = new BinaryWriter(stream))
        {
            // Create a BinaryReader for reading from the stream.
            using (BinaryReader r = new BinaryReader(stream))
            {
                if (r.ReadString() ==
                    Recipe10_10Shared.RequestConnect)
                {
                    w.Write(Recipe10_10Shared.AcknowledgeOK);
                    Console.WriteLine("Connection completed.");

                    while (r.ReadString() !=
                        Recipe10_10Shared.Disconnect) { }

                    Console.WriteLine(Environment.NewLine);
                    Console.WriteLine("Disconnect request received.");
                }
                else
                {
                    Console.WriteLine("Can't complete connection.");
                }
            }
        }
    }

    Console.WriteLine("Connection closed.");
}
catch (Exception ex)
{
    Console.WriteLine(ex.ToString());
}
finally
{
    // Close the underlying socket (stop listening for new requests).
    listener.Stop();
    Console.WriteLine("Listener stopped.");
}

// Wait to continue.
Console.WriteLine(Environment.NewLine);
Console.WriteLine("Main method complete. Press Enter");
Console.ReadLine();
        }
    }
}
```

The following code is a template for a basic TCP client. It contacts the server at the specified IP address and port. In this example, the loopback address (127.0.0.1) is used, which always points to the local computer. Keep in mind that a TCP connection requires two ports: one at the server end and one at the client end. However, only the server port to connect to needs to be specified. The outgoing client port can be chosen dynamically at runtime from the available ports, which is what the TcpClient class will do by default.

```
using System;
using System.IO;
using System.Net;
using System.Net.Sockets;

namespace Apress.VisualCSharpRecipes.Chapter10
{
    public class Recipe10_10Client
    {
        public static void Main()
        {
            TcpClient client = new TcpClient();

            try
            {
                Console.WriteLine("Attempting to connect to the server ",
                    "on port 8000.");
                client.Connect(IPAddress.Parse("127.0.0.1"), 8000);
                Console.WriteLine("Connection established.");

                // Retrieve the network stream.
                NetworkStream stream = client.GetStream();

                // Create a BinaryWriter for writing to the stream.
                using (BinaryWriter w = new BinaryWriter(stream))
                {
                    // Create a BinaryReader for reading from the stream.
                    using (BinaryReader r = new BinaryReader(stream))
                    {
                        // Start a dialogue.
                        w.Write(Recipe10_10Shared.RequestConnect);

                        if (r.ReadString() == Recipe10_10Shared.AcknowledgeOK)
                        {
                            Console.WriteLine("Connected.");
                            Console.WriteLine("Press Enter to disconnect.");
                            Console.ReadLine();
                            Console.WriteLine("Disconnecting...");
                            w.Write(Recipe10_10Shared.Disconnect);
                        }
                        else
                        {
                            Console.WriteLine("Connection not completed.");
                        }
                    }
                }
            }
            catch (Exception err)
            {
                Console.WriteLine(err.ToString());
```

```
        }
        finally
        {
            // Close the connection socket.
            client.Close();
            Console.WriteLine("Port closed.");
        }

        // Wait to continue.
        Console.WriteLine(Environment.NewLine);
        Console.WriteLine("Main method complete. Press Enter");
        Console.ReadLine();
    }
  }
}
```

Usage

Here's a sample connection transcript on the server side:

```
About to initialize port.
Listening for a connection...
Connection accepted.
Connection completed.

Disconnect request received.
Connection closed.
Listener stopped.
```

And here's a sample connection transcript on the client side:

```
Attempting to connect to the server on port 8000.
Connection established.
Connected.
Press Enter to disconnect.

Disconnecting...
Port closed.
```

10-11. Create a Multithreaded TCP Server That Supports Asynchronous Communications

Problem

You need to handle multiple network requests concurrently or perform a network data transfer as a background task while your program continues with other processing.

Solution

Use the method `AcceptTcpClient` of the `System.Net.Sockets.TcpListener` class to accept connections. Every time a new client connects, start a new thread to handle the connection. Alternatively, use the `TcpListener.BeginAcceptTcpClient` to accept a new client connection on a thread-pool thread using the asynchronous execution pattern (discussed in recipe 4-2).

To start a background task to handle the asynchronous sending of data, you can use the BeginWrite method of the System.Net.Sockets.NetworkStream class and supply a callback method—each time the callback is triggered, send more data.

How It Works

A single TCP endpoint (IP address and port) can serve multiple connections. In fact, the operating system takes care of most of the work for you. All you need to do is create a worker object on the server that will handle each connection on a separate thread. The TcpListener.AcceptTcpClient method returns a TcpClient when a connection is established. This should be passed off to a threaded worker object so that the worker can communicate with the remote client.

Alternatively, call the TcpListener.BeginAcceptTcpClient method to start an asynchronous operation using a thread-pool thread that waits in the background for a client to connect. BeginAcceptTcpClient follows the asynchronous execution pattern, allowing you to wait for the operation to complete or specify a callback that the .NET runtime will call when a client connects. (See recipe 4-2 for details on the options available.) Whichever mechanism you use, once BeginAcceptTcpClient has completed, call EndAcceptTcpClient to obtain the newly created TcpClient object.

To exchange network data asynchronously, you can use the NetworkStream class, which includes basic support for asynchronous communication through the BeginRead and BeginWrite methods. Using these methods, you can send or receive a block of data on one of the threads provided by the thread pool, without blocking your code. When sending data asynchronously, you must send raw binary data (an array of bytes). It's up to you to choose the amount you want to send or receive at a time.

One advantage of this approach when sending files is that the entire content of the file does not have to be held in memory at once. Instead, it is retrieved just before a new block is sent. Another advantage is that the server can abort the transfer operation easily at any time.

The Code

The following example demonstrates various techniques for handling network connections and communications asynchronously. The server (Recipe10-11Server) starts a thread-pool thread listening for new connections using the TcpListener.BeginAcceptTcpClient method and specifying a callback method to handle the new connections. Every time a client connects to the server, the callback method obtains the new TcpClient object and passes it to a new threaded ClientHandler object to handle client communications.

The ClientHandler object waits for the client to request data and then sends a large amount of data (read from a file) to the client. This data is sent asynchronously, which means ClientHandler could continue to perform other tasks. In this example, it simply monitors the network stream for messages sent from the client. The client reads only a third of the data before sending a disconnect message to the server, which terminates the remainder of the file transfer and drops the client connection.

Here is the code for the shared protocol:

```
namespace Apress.VisualCSharpRecipes.Chapter10
{
    public class Recipe10_11Shared
    {
        public const string AcknowledgeOK = "OK";
        public const string AcknowledgeCancel = "Cancel";
        public const string Disconnect = "Bye";
        public const string RequestConnect = "Hello";
        public const string RequestData = "Data";
```

```
        }
}
```

Here is the server code:

```csharp
using System;
using System.IO;
using System.Net;
using System.Threading;
using System.Net.Sockets;

namespace Apress.VisualCSharpRecipes.Chapter10
{
    public class Recipe10_11Server
    {
        // A flag used to indicate whether the server is shutting down.
        private static bool terminate;
        public static bool Terminate { get { return terminate; } }

        // A variable to track the identity of each client connection.
        private static int ClientNumber = 0;

        // A single TcpListener will accept all incoming client connections.
        private static TcpListener listener;

        public static void Main()
        {
            // Create a 100Kb test file for use in the example. This file will be
            // sent to clients that connect.
            using (FileStream fs = new FileStream("test.bin", FileMode.Create))
            {
                fs.SetLength(100000);
            }

            try
            {
                // Create a TcpListener that will accept incoming client
                // connections on port 8000 of the local machine.
                listener = new TcpListener(IPAddress.Parse("127.0.0.1"), 8000);

                Console.WriteLine("Starting TcpListener...");

                // Start the TcpListener accepting connections.
                terminate = false;
                listener.Start();

                // Begin asynchronously listening for client connections. When a
                // new connection is established, call the ConnectionHandler
                // method to process the new connection.
                listener.BeginAcceptTcpClient(ConnectionHandler, null);

                // Keep the server active until the user presses Enter.
                Console.WriteLine("Server awaiting connections. " +
                    "Press Enter to stop server.");
                Console.ReadLine();
            }
            finally
```

```
    {
        // Shut down the TcpListener. This will cause any outstanding
        // asynchronous requests to stop and throw an exception in
        // the ConnectionHandler when EndAcceptTcpClient is called.
        // More robust termination synchronization may be desired here,
        // but for the purpose of this example ClientHandler threads are
        // all background threads and will terminate automatically when
        // the main thread terminates. This is suitable for our needs.
        Console.WriteLine("Server stopping...");
        terminate = true;
        if (listener != null) listener.Stop();
    }

    // Wait to continue.
    Console.WriteLine(Environment.NewLine);
    Console.WriteLine("Server stopped. Press Enter");
    Console.ReadLine();
}

// A method to handle the callback when a connection is established
// from a client. This is a simple way to implement a dispatcher
// but lacks the control and scalability required when implementing
// full-blown asynchronous server applications.
private static void ConnectionHandler(IAsyncResult result)
{
    TcpClient client = null;

    // Always end the asynchronous operation to avoid leaks.
    try
    {
        // Get the TcpClient that represents the new client connection.
        client = listener.EndAcceptTcpClient(result);
    }
    catch (ObjectDisposedException)
    {
        // Server is shutting down and the outstanding asynchronous
        // request calls the completion method with this exception.
        // The exception is thrown when EndAcceptTcpClient is called.
        // Do nothing and return.
        return;
    }

    Console.WriteLine("Dispatcher: New connection accepted.");

    // Begin asynchronously listening for the next client
    // connection.
    listener.BeginAcceptTcpClient(ConnectionHandler, null);

    if (client != null)
    {
        // Determine the identifier for the new client connection.
        Interlocked.Increment(ref ClientNumber);
        string clientName = "Client " + ClientNumber.ToString();

        Console.WriteLine("Dispatcher: Creating client handler ({0})."
            , clientName);
```

```csharp
                // Create a new ClientHandler to handle this connection.
                new ClientHandler(client, clientName);
            }
        }
    }
}

// A class that encapsulates the logic to handle a client connection.
public class ClientHandler
{
    // The TcpClient that represents the connection to the client.
    private TcpClient client;

    // An ID that uniquely identifies this ClientHandler.
    private string ID;

    // The amount of data that will be written in one block (2 KB).
    private int bufferSize = 2048;

    // The buffer that holds the data to write.
    private byte[] buffer;

    // Used to read data from the local file.
    private FileStream fileStream;

    // A signal to stop sending data to the client.
    private bool stopDataTransfer;

    internal ClientHandler(TcpClient client, string ID)
    {
        this.buffer = new byte[bufferSize];
        this.client = client;
        this.ID = ID;

        // Create a new background thread to handle the client connection
        // so that we do not consume a thread-pool thread for a long time
        // and also so that it will be terminated when the main thread ends.
        Thread thread = new Thread(ProcessConnection);
        thread.IsBackground = true;
        thread.Start();
    }

    private void ProcessConnection()
    {
        using (client)
        {
            // Create a BinaryReader to receive messages from the client. At
            // the end of the using block, it will close both the BinaryReader
            // and the underlying NetworkStream.
            using (BinaryReader reader = new BinaryReader(client.GetStream()))
            {
                if (reader.ReadString() == Recipe10_11Shared.RequestConnect)
                {
                    // Create a BinaryWriter to send messages to the client.
                    // At the end of the using block, it will close both the
                    // BinaryWriter and the underlying NetworkStream.
                    using (BinaryWriter writer =
                        new BinaryWriter(client.GetStream()))
```

```csharp
        {
            writer.Write(Recipe10_11Shared.AcknowledgeOK);
            Console.WriteLine(ID + ": Connection established.");

            string message = "";

            while (message != Recipe10_11Shared.Disconnect)
            {
                try
                {
                    // Read the message from the client.
                    message = reader.ReadString();
                }
                catch
                {
                    // For the purpose of the example, any
                    // exception should be taken as a
                    // client disconnect.
                    message = Recipe10_11Shared.Disconnect;
                }

                if (message == Recipe10_11Shared.RequestData)
                {
                    Console.WriteLine(ID + ": Requested data. ",
                        "Sending...");

                    // The filename could be supplied by the
                    // client, but in this example a test file
                    // is hard-coded.
                    fileStream = new FileStream("test.bin",
                        FileMode.Open, FileAccess.Read);

                    // Send the file size--this is how the client
                    // knows how much to read.
                    writer.Write(fileStream.Length.ToString());

                    // Start an asynchronous send operation.
                    stopDataTransfer = false;
                    StreamData(null);
                }
                else if (message == Recipe10_11Shared.Disconnect)
                {
                    Console.WriteLine(ID +
                        ": Client disconnecting...");
                    stopDataTransfer = true;
                }
                else
                {
                    Console.WriteLine(ID + ": Unknown command.");
                }
            }
        }
    }
    else
    {
        Console.WriteLine(ID +
            ": Could not establish connection.");
```

```
                }
            }
        }

        Console.WriteLine(ID + ": Client connection closed.");
    }

    private void StreamData(IAsyncResult asyncResult)
    {
        // Always complete outstanding asynchronous operations to avoid leaks.
        if (asyncResult != null)
        {
            try
            {
                client.GetStream().EndWrite(asyncResult);
            }
            catch
            {
                // For the purpose of the example, any exception obtaining
                // or writing to the network should just terminate the
                // download.
                fileStream.Close();
                return;
            }
        }

        if (!stopDataTransfer && !Recipe10_11Server.Terminate)
        {
            // Read the next block from the file.
            int bytesRead = fileStream.Read(buffer, 0, buffer.Length);

            // If no bytes are read, the stream is at the end of the file.
            if (bytesRead > 0)
            {
                Console.WriteLine(ID + ": Streaming next block.");

                // Write the next block to the network stream.
                client.GetStream().BeginWrite(buffer, 0, buffer.Length,
                    StreamData, null);
            }
            else
            {
                // End the operation.
                Console.WriteLine(ID + ": File streaming complete.");
                fileStream.Close();
            }
        }
        else
        {
            // Client disconnected.
            Console.WriteLine(ID + ": Client disconnected.");
            fileStream.Close();
        }
    }
}
}
```

And here is the client code:

```
using System;
using System.Net;
using System.Net.Sockets;
using System.IO;

namespace Apress.VisualCSharpRecipes.Chapter10
{
    public class Recipe10_11Client
    {
        private static void Main()
        {
            using (TcpClient client = new TcpClient())
            {
                Console.WriteLine("Attempting to connect to the server ",
                    "on port 8000.");

                // Connect to the server.
                client.Connect(IPAddress.Parse("127.0.0.1"), 8000);

                // Retrieve the network stream from the TcpClient.
                using (NetworkStream networkStream = client.GetStream())
                {
                    // Create a BinaryWriter for writing to the stream.
                    using (BinaryWriter writer = new BinaryWriter(networkStream))
                    {
                        // Start a dialogue.
                        writer.Write(Recipe10_11Shared.RequestConnect);

                        // Create a BinaryReader for reading from the stream.
                        using (BinaryReader reader =
                            new BinaryReader(networkStream))
                        {
                            if (reader.ReadString() ==
                                Recipe10_11Shared.AcknowledgeOK)
                            {
                                Console.WriteLine("Connection established." +
                                    "Press Enter to download data.");

                                Console.ReadLine();

                                // Send message requesting data to server.
                                writer.Write(Recipe10_11Shared.RequestData);

                                // The server should respond with the size of
                                // the data it will send. Assume it does.
                                int fileSize = int.Parse(reader.ReadString());

                                // Only get part of the data then carry out a
                                // premature disconnect.
                                for (int i = 0; i < fileSize / 3; i++)
                                {
                                    Console.Write(networkStream.ReadByte());
                                }

                                Console.WriteLine(Environment.NewLine);
```

```
                    Console.WriteLine("Press Enter to disconnect.");
                    Console.ReadLine();
                    Console.WriteLine("Disconnecting...");
                    writer.Write(Recipe10_11Shared.Disconnect);
                }
                else
                {
                    Console.WriteLine("Connection not established.");
                }
            }
        }
    }
}

    // Wait to continue.
    Console.WriteLine(Environment.NewLine);
    Console.WriteLine("Connection closed. Press Enter");
    Console.ReadLine();
        }
    }
}
```

10-12. Communicate Using UDP

Problem

You need to send data between two computers on a network using a UDP stream.

Solution

Use the `System.Net.Sockets.UdpClient` class, and use two threads: one to send data and the other to receive it.

How It Works

UDP is a connectionless protocol that doesn't include any flow control or error checking. Unlike TCP, UDP shouldn't be used where reliable communication is required. However, because of its lower overhead, UDP is often used for "chatty" applications where it is acceptable to lose some messages. For example, imagine you want to create a network in which individual clients send information about the current temperature at their locations to a server every few minutes. You might use UDP in this case because the communication frequency is high and the damage caused by losing a packet is trivial (because the server can just continue to use the last received temperature reading).

The Code

The application shown in the following code uses two threads: one to receive messages and one to send them. The application stops when the user presses the Enter key without any text to send. Notice that UDP applications cannot use the `NetworkStream` abstraction that TCP applications can. Instead, they must convert all data to a stream of bytes using an encoding class, as described in recipe 2-2.

```csharp
using System;
using System.Text;
using System.Net;
using System.Net.Sockets;
using System.Threading;

namespace Apress.VisualCSharpRecipes.Chapter10
{
    class Recipe10_12
    {
        private static int localPort;

        private static void Main()
        {
            // Define endpoint where messages are sent.
            Console.Write("Connect to IP: ");
            string IP = Console.ReadLine();
            Console.Write("Connect to port: ");
            int port = Int32.Parse(Console.ReadLine());

            IPEndPoint remoteEndPoint =
                new IPEndPoint(IPAddress.Parse(IP), port);

            // Define local endpoint (where messages are received).
            Console.Write("Local port for listening: ");
            localPort = Int32.Parse(Console.ReadLine());

            // Create a new thread for receiving incoming messages.
            Thread receiveThread = new Thread(ReceiveData);
            receiveThread.IsBackground = true;
            receiveThread.Start();

            UdpClient client = new UdpClient();

            Console.WriteLine("Type message and press Enter to send:");

            try
            {
                string text;

                do
                {
                    text = Console.ReadLine();

                    // Send the text to the remote client.
                    if (text.Length != 0)
                    {
                        // Encode the data to binary using UTF8 encoding.
                        byte[] data = Encoding.UTF8.GetBytes(text);

                        // Send the text to the remote client.
                        client.Send(data, data.Length, remoteEndPoint);
                    }
                } while (text.Length != 0);
            }
            catch (Exception err)
            {
```

```
            Console.WriteLine(err.ToString());
        }
        finally
        {
            client.Close();
        }

        // Wait to continue.
        Console.WriteLine(Environment.NewLine);
        Console.WriteLine("Main method complete. Press Enter");
        Console.ReadLine();
    }

    private static void ReceiveData()
    {
        UdpClient client = new UdpClient(localPort);

        while (true)
        {
            try
            {
                // Receive bytes.
                IPEndPoint anyIP = new IPEndPoint(IPAddress.Any, 0);
                byte[] data = client.Receive(ref anyIP);

                // Convert bytes to text using UTF8 encoding.
                string text = Encoding.UTF8.GetString(data);

                // Display the retrieved text.
                Console.WriteLine(">> " + text);
            }
            catch (Exception err)
            {
                Console.WriteLine(err.ToString());
            }
        }
    }
}
```

Usage

To test this application, load two instances at the same time. On computer A, specify the IP address for computer B. On computer B, specify the address for computer A. You can then send text messages back and forth at will. You can test this application with clients on the local computer using the loopback alias 127.0.0.1, provided you use different listening ports. For example, imagine a situation with two UDP clients, client A and client B. Here's a sample transcript for client A:

```
Connect to IP: 127.0.0.1
Connect to port: 8001
Local port for listening: 8080

Hi there!
```

And here's the corresponding transcript for client B (with the received message):

```
Connect to IP: 127.0.0.1
Connect to port: 8080
Local port for listening: 8001

>> Hi there!
```

10-13. Avoid Hard-Coding the XML Web Service URL

Problem

You need to use an XML Web service located at a URL that might change after you deploy the client application.

Solution

Use a dynamic URL, which will be retrieved automatically from the client application's configuration file. You can configure a dynamic URL in the URL Behavior section of a web reference's properties in Microsoft Visual Studio or by using the /urlkey parameter with the Web Services Description Language tool (wsdl.exe).

How It Works

When you create a Web reference in Visual Studio 2005, the automatically generated proxy class is configured to use a dynamic URL as the address of the referenced Web service. The actual URL used to contact the Web service at runtime is read from your application's configuration file. This allows you to easily change the location of the Web service without recompiling your code. The automatically generated configuration section looks something like the following, where the value attribute contains the URL of the Web service:

```
<applicationSettings>
    <Recipe10_13.Properties.Settings>
        <setting name="Recipe10_13_MyWebService_MyWebService" serializeAs="String">
            <value>http://localhost/TestWebService/MyWebService.asmx</value>
        </setting>
    </Recipe10_13.Properties.Settings>
</applicationSettings>
```

In previous releases of Visual Studio, dynamic URLs were not the default behavior. In these cases you can configure the setting by looking at the URL Behavior option in the Properties window for the web reference, as shown in Figure 10-2.

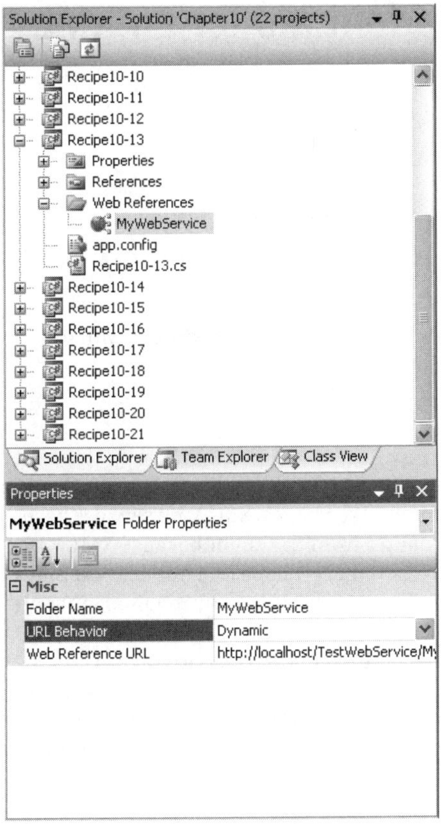

Figure 10-2. *Configuring a dynamic URL for a Web service in Visual Studio*

If you use wsdl.exe from the command line to generate your Web service proxy class, it uses a static URL by default. To configure wsdl.exe to use a dynamic URL, you must use the /urlkey parameter and specify the configuration setting name that the proxy class should read from the configuration file. For example:

```
wsdl http://localhost/TestWebService/MyWebService.asmx?WSDL /urlkey:MyWebService
```

Whether you're using Visual Studio or wsdl.exe, the automatically generated proxy class is coded in such a way that if the class doesn't find the configuration parameter containing a dynamic URL, it defaults to the static URL that was used during development.

■**Tip** You can always manually override the URL setting in your code by modifying the Url property of the proxy class after you instantiate it.

10-14. Set Authentication Credentials for an XML Web Service

Problem

You want an XML Web service client to submit logon credentials for IIS authentication.

Solution

Configure the `Credentials` and `Certificates` properties of the Web service's proxy class with the appropriate credentials prior to calling a Web service method.

How It Works

You can configure XML Web services, like Web pages, to require users to authenticate using credentials such as usernames and passwords or X.509 certificates. Unlike Web pages, XML Web services have no built-in method for retrieving authentication information from the client because XML Web services are executed by other applications, not directly by the user. Thus, the application that's interacting with the XML Web service bears the responsibility for submitting any required authentication information.

Similar to the `System.Net.WebRequest` discussed in recipe 10-6, the Web service proxy classes automatically generated by Visual Studio and the Web Services Description Language tool (wsdl.exe) implement `Credentials` and `ClientCertificates` properties. Using these properties allows you to associate user credentials with Web method calls. The approach you use depends on the type of authentication implemented by the Web service:

- If the Web service is using basic or digest authentication, you can transmit a username and password combination by manually creating a new `System.Net.NetworkCredential` object and assigning it to the proxy's `Credentials` property. With digest authentication, you may also supply a domain name.

- If the Web service is using Windows integrated authentication, you can take the same approach and manually create a new `NetworkCredential` object. Alternatively, you can configure the proxy to use the current user login information by setting the proxy's `UseDefaultCredentials` property to true.

- If the Web service requires a client certificate, you can load the certificate from a file using the `System.Security.Cryptography.X509Certificates.X509Certificate2` class and add that to the proxy's `ClientCertificates` collection.

- In the .NET Framework 2.0, you can load an X.509 certificate from a certificate store using the class `System.Security.Cryptography.X509Certificates.X509Store`. You can either find a certificate in the store programmatically using the `X509Store.Certificates.Find` method or present the user with a Windows dialog box using `X509Store.Certificates.Select` and allow them to select the certificate.

■**Tip** To add more than one set of credentials to a proxy, create a `CredentialCache` object and add multiple `NetworkCredential` objects to the credential collection using the `Add` method. `Add` also allows you to specify the URI, port, and authentication mechanism for which each `NetworkCredential` object should be used. Then assign the `CredentialCache` object to the proxy's `Credentials` property.

The Code

The following XML Web service provides a simple user authentication test. GetIISUser returns the user that was authenticated by IIS. If anonymous access is allowed, the result will be an empty string because no authentication will be performed. If anonymous access is denied, the result will be a string in the form [DomainName]\[UserName] or [ComputerName]\[UserName].

```
public class AuthenticationTest : System.Web.Services.WebService {

    // Retrieves the authenticated IIS user.
    [WebMethod()]
    public string GetIISUser() {
        return User.Identity.Name;
    }
}
```

The following example shows how a client can access an XML Web service that uses basic authentication, Windows integrated authentication, and X.509 certificate–based authentication:

```
using System;
using System.Net;
using Recipe10_14.MyWebService;
using System.Security.Cryptography.X509Certificates;

namespace Apress.VisualCSharpRecipes.Chapter10
{
    class Recipe10_14
    {
        public static void Main()
        {
            // Create a Web service proxy. For the purpose of the example, set
            // the ConnectionGroupName to a unique value to stop the
            // ServicePointManager reusing the connection in future requests.
            MyWebService proxy1 = new MyWebService();
            proxy1.ConnectionGroupName = "Test1";

            // Configure the proxy with a set of credentials for use over basic
            // authentication.
            CredentialCache cache = new CredentialCache();
            cache.Add(new Uri(proxy1.Url), "Basic",
                new NetworkCredential("user", "password"));
            proxy1.Credentials = cache;

            // Try to call the GetIISUser Web method.
            try
            {
                Console.WriteLine("Authenticated user = {0}", proxy1.GetIISUser());
            }
            catch (WebException)
            {
                Console.WriteLine("Basic authentication failed");
            }

            // Create a proxy that authenticates the current user
            // with Windows integrated authentication.
            MyWebService proxy2 = new MyWebService();
            proxy2.ConnectionGroupName = "Test2";
            proxy2.Credentials = CredentialCache.DefaultCredentials;
```

```
            try
            {
                Console.WriteLine("Authenticated user = {0}", proxy2.GetIISUser());
            }
            catch (WebException)
            {
                Console.WriteLine("Integrated Windows authentication failed");
            }

            // Create a proxy that authenticates the user with a client
            // certificate loaded from a file.
            MyWebService proxy3 = new MyWebService();
            proxy3.ConnectionGroupName = "Test3";
            X509Certificate cert1 =
                X509Certificate.CreateFromCertFile(@"..\..\TestCertificate.cer");
            proxy3.ClientCertificates.Add(cert1);
            try
            {
                Console.WriteLine("Authenticated user = {0}", proxy3.GetIISUser());
            }
            catch (WebException)
            {
                Console.WriteLine("Certificate authentication failed");
            }

            // Wait to continue.
            Console.WriteLine(Environment.NewLine);
            Console.WriteLine("Main method complete. Press Enter");
            Console.ReadLine();
        }
    }
}
```

10-15. Call a Web Method Asynchronously

Problem

You need to invoke a Web method on another thread so that your program can continue with other tasks (such as updating the user interface) while waiting for the response.

Solution

Use the proxy class's built-in asynchronous method and asynchronous completion event, which are automatically generated for every Web method supported by the XML Web service. The method is named XXXAsync, and the completion event is named XXXCompleted, where XXX is the name of the original, synchronous method.

How It Works

The automatically generated proxy class has the features you need to call any Web method asynchronously. For example, consider the Wait Web method shown in the following code, which pauses for a random number of seconds between a lower and an upper value:

```
// Returns the specified string after a random delay
// between a lower and upper bound.
[WebMethod()]
public string Echo(string str, int lower, int upper)
{
    // Sleep for a random period of time between the specified
    // lower and upper boundaries.
    Random rand = new Random();
    Thread.Sleep(rand.Next(lower,upper));

    // Echo back the specified string.
    return str;
}
```

The proxy class generated for the Web service that exposes the Echo method will also implement a method named EchoAsync, an event named EchoCompleted, an event argument data class named EchoCompletedEventArgs, and a delegate named EchoCompletedEventHandler. Together, these program elements allow you to call the Echo web method asynchronously and handle the result—regardless of whether the call fails or succeeds. All Web methods follow the same model; only the names are changed. Each of these elements is described here:

- The EchoAsync method takes the same arguments as the Echo method, with the option of providing an additional object argument that can be used for general state information. This extra state is passed to the EchoCompletedEventHandler (described next) when the asynchronous call completes and is often used to match completed events to original calls. When you call EchoAsync, the .NET Framework returns control immediately to the calling code so that it can continue processing but executes the method on a thread from the thread pool.

- When the EchoAsync method completes, the proxy raises the EchoCompleted event using a thread from the thread pool. To handle these events, you must add an EchoCompletedEventHandler delegate to the event. The EchoCompletedEventHandler delegate declares two arguments. The first argument is an object that is a reference to the sender (or source) of the event, which is the proxy object. The second argument is an EchoCompletedEventArgs object, which is discussed next.

- The EchoCompletedEventArgs class provides access to the result of the asynchronous operation. The Cancelled property indicates whether the operation was canceled by a call to the CancelAsynch method, Error contains any exception that was raised that caused the asynchronous operation to fail, UserState contains the user state object (if any) that was passed to the EchoAsync method, and Result is of the same type returned by Echo and contains the result of the asynchronous call if it succeeded.

■**Note** The asynchronous model described in this recipe is new to the Web service proxy code generated by Visual Studio 2005. In earlier versions of Visual Studio and in the code generated by the Web Services Description Language tool (wsdl.exe), a different asynchronous model is implemented. Instead of an XXXAsync method and the use of events, the proxy would have BeginXXX and EndXXX methods. This old approach had the benefit of providing you with System.Threading.WaitHandle objects for the asynchronous operations, which you could use for multithreaded synchronization.

The Code

The following example demonstrates how to call a Web method named Echo asynchronously using the automatically generated EchoAsync method of the proxy. The EchoAsync method is called three times, and the second instance is canceled before it has a chance to complete. The EchoCompletedHandler method processes the results of the three asynchronous method calls.

```csharp
using System;
using System.Threading;
using Recipe10_15.MyWebService;

namespace Apress.VisualCSharpRecipes.Chapter10
{
    class Recipe10_15
    {
        private static void Main()
        {
            // Create a proxy through which to execute the methods of
            // the Web service.
            MyWebService proxy = new MyWebService();

            // Add an event handler to the EchoCompleted event.
            proxy.EchoCompleted += EchoCompletedHandler;

            // Call Echo three times asynchronously.
            proxy.EchoAsync("Echo String 1", 7000, 10000, "Test1");
            proxy.EchoAsync("Echo String 2", 5000, 10000, "Test2");
            proxy.EchoAsync("Echo String 3", 1000, 10000, "Test3");

            // Quickly cancel the second asynchronous operation.
            proxy.CancelAsync("Test2");

            // Wait to continue.
            Console.WriteLine(Environment.NewLine);
            Console.WriteLine("Main method complete. Press Enter");
            Console.ReadLine();
        }

        // A method to handle asynchronous Echo completion events.
        private static void EchoCompletedHandler(object sender,
            EchoCompletedEventArgs args)
        {
            if (args.Error != null)
            {
                Console.WriteLine("{0}: {1}", args.UserState,args.Error.Message);
            }
            else if (args.Cancelled)
            {
                Console.WriteLine("{0}: operation cancelled before completion.",
                    args.UserState);
            }
            else
            {
                Console.WriteLine("{0}: Succeeded, echoed string = {1}.",
                    args.UserState, args.Result);
            }
        }
    }
}
```

10-16. Make an Object Remotable

Problem

You need to create a class that can be accessed from another application or another computer on the network. However, you don't need cross-platform compatibility, and you want optimum performance.

Solution

Make the class remotable by deriving from `System.MarshalByRefObject`, and create a component host that registers the class with the .NET Remoting infrastructure.

How It Works

Remoting allows you to make an object accessible across process and machine boundaries. While XML Web services are ideal when you need to share functionality across platforms or trust boundaries, Remoting is the best-performing choice for a closed system in which all components are built on .NET and the Windows operating system. To use .NET Remoting, you need the following ingredients, each of which must reside in a separate assembly:

- *A remotable object*: This object can be accessed from other applications and computers and must derive from the `System.MarshalByRefObject`.

- *A component host*: This application registers the remotable type with the .NET Remoting infrastructure using the `RemotingConfiguration` class from the `System.Runtime.Remoting` namespace. You can use any type of long-running .NET Framework application for a component host (including Windows Forms–based applications, Windows services, console applications, and even IIS). As long as the component host is running, remote clients can create or connect to existing instances of the remotable object. The component host never interacts with the remotable objects directly. All it does is register the appropriate types with the .NET Remoting infrastructure. After this point, clients can create object instances, and the server application can continue with other tasks. However, when the component host is closed, any remotable objects will be destroyed, and no more hosted objects can be created.

- *A client application*: This application can create or connect to instances of the remotable class in the component host process and interact with them. The client uses the `RemotingConfiguration` class to register the types it wants to access remotely. The client application uses the `RemotingConfiguration.Configure` method to register the remote objects it wants to call. Once this step is taken, the client can create the object exactly as it would create a local object. However, the object will actually be created in the component host.

Figure 10-3 shows how these three parts interact. This example has only one client. However, it's also possible for multiple clients to create instances of the remotable class at the same time. In this case, you can configure the Remoting host whether each client has its own remotable object instance or whether all clients share a single instance.

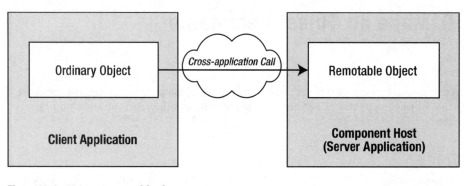

Figure 10-3. *Using a remotable class*

■Note Ideally, the remote object won't retain any state. This characteristic allows you to use *single-call activation*, in which object instances are created at the beginning of each method call and released at the end, much like an XML Web service. This ensures your objects consume the fewest possible server resources and saves you from the added complexity of implementing a lease policy to configure object lifetime.

The Code

The following example demonstrates the declaration of a remotable class that reads data from the Authors table of the pubs database and returns a System.Data.DataTable. Notice that the only Remoting-specific code is the derivation of the class from the System.MarshalByRef class.

```csharp
using System;
using System.Data;
using System.Data.SqlClient;

namespace Apress.VisualCSharpRecipes.Chapter10
{
    // Define a class that extends MarshalByRefObject, making it remotable.
    public class Recipe10_16 : MarshalByRefObject
    {
        private static string connectionString = @"Data Source=.\SQLEXPRESS;" +
            "Initial Catalog=PUBS;Integrated Security=SSPI";

        // The DataTable returned by this method is serializable, meaning that the
        // data will be physically passed back to the caller across the network.
        public DataTable GetAuthors()
        {
            string SQL = "SELECT * FROM Authors";

            // Create ADO.NET objects to execute the DB query.
            SqlConnection con = new SqlConnection(connectionString);
            SqlCommand com = new SqlCommand(SQL, con);
            SqlDataAdapter adapter = new SqlDataAdapter(com);
            DataSet ds = new DataSet();

            // Execute the command.
            try
            {
                con.Open();
```

```
            adapter.Fill(ds, "Authors");
        }
        catch (Exception err)
        {
            Console.WriteLine(err.ToString());
        }
        finally
        {
            con.Close();
        }

        // Return the first DataTable in the DataSet to the caller.
        return ds.Tables[0];
    }

    // This method allows you to verify that the object is running remotely.
    public string GetHostLocation()
    {
        return AppDomain.CurrentDomain.FriendlyName;
    }
    }
}
```

Usage

To use the Recipe10_16 class remotely, you must host it and then create a client that uses the remote object. Here is the code for a simple console component host:

```
using System;
using System.Runtime.Remoting;

namespace Apress.VisualCSharpRecipes.Chapter10
{
    class Recipe10_16Host
    {
        private static void Main()
        {
            // Register the remotable classes defined in the specified
            // configuration file.
            RemotingConfiguration.Configure("Recipe10-16Host.exe.config");

            // As long as this application is running, the registered remote
            // objects will be accessible.
            Console.Clear();
            Console.WriteLine("Press Enter to shut down the host.");
            Console.ReadLine();
        }
    }
}
```

The component host uses the following configuration file (Recipe10-16Host.exe.config) to configure the classes it will support, the ports it will support for network communication, and the URI that the client will use to access the object. This Recipe10-16 assembly containing the implementation of the remote object class must be in the global assembly cache (GAC) or in the same directory as the server application. The configuration file also configures the remote object to use single-call activation, meaning that a new object is created for each client call.

```xml
<?xml version="1.0" encoding="utf-8" ?>
<configuration>
    <system.runtime.remoting>
        <application>

            <!-- Define the remotable types. -->
            <service>
                <wellknown
                    mode = "SingleCall"
                    type = "Apress.VisualCSharpRecipes.Chapter10.Recipe10_16, ➥
Recipe10-16"
                    objectUri = "Recipe10-16" />
            </service>

            <!-- Define the protocol used for network access.
            You can use tcp or http channels. -->
            <channels>
                <channel ref="tcp" port="19080" />
            </channels>

        </application>
    </system.runtime.remoting>
</configuration>
```

The following code shows a simple client that uses the remote object created earlier. Notice that in this example, the configuration of the Remoting infrastructure is performed programmatically instead of using the configuration file. You should avoid such an approach when using static configuration values because using configuration files provides more flexibility. However, if you want to dynamically configure the Remoting infrastructure, you will need to be familiar with the approach demonstrated here. Unfortunately, a complete discussion is beyond the scope of this book; for detailed information, see *Advanced .NET Remoting, Second Edition* by Ingo Rammer and Mario Szpuszta (Apress, 2004). Note that as with the host, the assembly containing the declaration of the class that will be accessed remotely must still be accessible to the client application, either in the local folder or in the local GAC.

```csharp
using System;
using System.Runtime.Remoting;
using System.Runtime.Remoting.Channels;
using System.Runtime.Remoting.Channels.Tcp;
using System.Data;

namespace Apress.VisualCSharpRecipes.Chapter10
{
    class Recipe10_16Client
    {
        public static void Main()
        {
            // Register a new TCP Remoting channel to communicate with the
            // remote object.
            ChannelServices.RegisterChannel(new TcpChannel());

            // Register the classes that will be accessed remotely.
            RemotingConfiguration.RegisterWellKnownClientType(
                typeof(Recipe10_16), @"tcp://localhost:19080/Recipe10-16");
```

```
        // Now any attempts to instantiate the Recipe10_16
        // class will actually create a proxy to a remote instance.

        // Interact with the remote object through a proxy.
        Recipe10_16 proxy = new Recipe10_16();

        // Display the name of the component host application domain
        // where the object executes.
        Console.WriteLine("Object executing in: " + proxy.GetHostLocation());

        // Get the DataTable from the remote object and display its contents.
        DataTable dt = proxy.GetAuthors();

        foreach (DataRow row in dt.Rows)
        {
            Console.WriteLine(row[1]);
        }

        // Wait to continue.
        Console.WriteLine(Environment.NewLine);
        Console.WriteLine("Main method complete. Press Enter");
        Console.ReadLine();
    }
  }
}
```

10-17. Register All the Remotable Classes in an Assembly

Problem

You want to register all the remotable classes that are defined in an assembly without having to specify them in a configuration file.

Solution

Load the assembly with the remotable classes using reflection. Loop through all its public types, and use the RemotingConfiguration.RegisterWellKnownServiceType method to register every remotable class.

How It Works

.NET makes it equally easy to register remotable classes through a configuration file or program-matically with code. The type being registered must extend MarshalByRefObject, and then you call RemotingConfiguration.RegisterWellKnownServiceType, passing on the type, the URI on which remote clients can connect to the type, and a value of the System.Runtime.Remoting.WellKnownObjectMode enumeration, which describes how the Remoting infrastructure should map client calls to object instances. The possible values are SingleCall, in which every incoming call is serviced by a new object, and Singleton, in which every incoming call is serviced by the same object. When using singleton objects, accurate state management and thread synchronization become critical.

The Code

The following server code searches for remotable classes in an assembly that is specified as a command-line argument. Each class derived from MarshalByRefObject is registered, and then the example displays the channel where the remotable object is available.

```
using System;
using System.Reflection;
using System.Runtime.Remoting;
using System.Runtime.Remoting.Channels;
using System.Runtime.Remoting.Channels.Tcp;

namespace Apress.VisualCSharpRecipes.Chapter10
{
    class Recipe10_17
    {
        public static void Main(string[] args)
        {
            // Ensure there is an argument, we is assumed to be a valid
            // filename.
            if (args.Length != 1) return;

            // Register a new TCP Remoting channel to communicate with the
            // remote object.
            ChannelServices.RegisterChannel(new TcpChannel(19080));

            // Get the registered Remoting channel.
            TcpChannel channel =
                (TcpChannel)ChannelServices.RegisteredChannels[0];

            // Create an Assembly object representing the assembly
            // where remotable classes are defined.
            Assembly assembly = Assembly.LoadFrom(args[0]);

            // Process all the public types in the specified assembly.
            foreach (Type type in assembly.GetExportedTypes())
            {
                // Check if the type is remotable.
                if (type.IsSubclassOf(typeof(MarshalByRefObject)))
                {
                    // Register each type using the type name as the URI
                    // (like ProductsDB).
                    Console.WriteLine("Registering {0}", type.Name);
                    RemotingConfiguration.RegisterWellKnownServiceType(
                        type,
                        type.Name,
                        WellKnownObjectMode.SingleCall);

                    // Determine the URL where this type is published.
                    string[] urls = channel.GetUrlsForUri(type.Name);
                    Console.WriteLine(urls[0]);
                }
            }

            // As long as this application is running, the registered remote
            // objects will be accessible.
            Console.WriteLine(Environment.NewLine);
            Console.WriteLine("Press Enter to shut down the host.");
```

```
            Console.ReadLine();
        }
    }
}
```

■**Note** The preceding code determines whether a class is remotable by examining whether it derives from MarshalByRefObject. This approach always works, but it could lead you to expose some types that you don't want to make remotable. For example, the System.Windows.Forms.Form object derives indirectly from MarshalByRefObject. This means if your remote object library contains any forms, they will be exposed remotely. To avoid this problem, don't include remotable types in your assembly unless you want to make them publicly available. Or, identify the types you want to register with a custom attribute. You could then check for this attribute before registering a type.

10-18. Host a Remote Object in IIS

Problem

You want to create a remotable object in IIS (perhaps so that you can use SSL or IIS authentication) instead of a dedicated component host.

Solution

Place the configuration file and assembly in a virtual directory, and modify the object URI so that it ends in .rem or .soap.

How It Works

Instead of creating a dedicated component host, you can host a remotable class in IIS. This allows you to ensure that the remotable classes will always be available, and it allows you to use IIS features such as SSL encryption and integrated Windows authentication.

To host a remotable class in IIS, you must first create a virtual directory. The virtual directory will contain two things: a configuration file named Web.config that registers the remotable classes and a Bin directory where you must place the corresponding class library assembly (or install the assembly in the GAC).

The configuration file for hosting in IIS is quite similar to the configuration file you use with a custom component host. However, you must follow several additional rules:

- You must use the HTTP channel (although you can use the binary formatter for smaller message sizes).

- You cannot specify a specific port number for listening. IIS listens on all the ports you have configured in IIS Manager. Typically, this will be ports 80 and 443 (for secure SSL communication).

- The object URI must end with .rem or .soap.

- The configuration file must be named Web.config, or it will be ignored.

The Code

Here's an example Web.config file that registers the remote class shown in recipe 10-16:

```
<?xml version="1.0" encoding="utf-8" ?>
<configuration>
    <system.runtime.remoting>
        <application>

            <!-- Define the remotable types. -->
            <service>
                <wellknown
                    mode = "SingleCall"
                    type = "Apress.VisualCSharpRecipes.Chapter10.Recipe10_16, ➥
Recipe10-16"
                    objectUri = "Recipe10-16.rem" />
            </service>

            <!-- Define the protocol used for network access.
            You can use only the http channel. -->
            <channels>
                <channel ref="http"/>
            </channels>

            <!-- Uncomment the following tags to use the binary formatter
                 (instead of the default SOAP formatter). -->
            <!--
            <serverProviders>
                <formatter ref="binary"/>
            </serverProviders>
            -->


        </application>
    </system.runtime.remoting>
</configuration>
```

Usage

A client can use an object hosted in IIS in the same way as an object hosted in a custom component host. However, the virtual directory name will become part of the object URI. For example, if the Web.config file shown in the preceding code is hosted in the virtual directory `http://localhost/ RemoteObjects`, the full URL will be `http://localhost/RemoteObjects/Recipe10-16.rem`.

Note When hosting an object with IIS, the account used to execute the object is the ASP.NET account defined in the Machine.config file. If this account doesn't have the rights to access the database (which is the default situation), you will receive an error when you try this example. Look at the .NET Framework for documentation on the `<processModel>` tag.

10-19. Control the Lifetime of a Remote Object

Problem

You want to configure how long a singleton or client-activated object lives while not in use.

Solution

Configure a lease policy by using configuration file settings, override the `MarshalByRefObject.InitializeLifetimeService` method, or implement a custom lease provider.

How It Works

If a remotable object uses single-call activation, it will be automatically destroyed at the end of each method call. This behavior changes with client-activated and singleton objects, which are given a longer lifetime dictated by a *lifetime lease*. With the default settings, a remote object will be automatically destroyed if it's inactive for 2 minutes, provided it has been in existence for at least 5 minutes.

The component host, remote object, and client each have the opportunity to change lifetime settings, as described here:

- The component host can specify different lease lifetime defaults in the configuration file using the `<lifetime>` tag. The `leaseTime` attribute of the tag specifies the default lifetime for all hosted object. The `renewOnCallTime` attribute specifies the amount of time by which the lease is extended when a call is made against a hosted object. You can specify the values for both attributes as positive integers with a time unit suffix for days (D), hours (H), minutes (M), or seconds (S). For example, 10 hours is 10H, and 30 seconds is 30S.

- The remote class can override its `InitializeLifetimeService` method (inherited from `MarshalByRefObject`) to modify its initial lease settings by configuring and returning an object that implements the `System.Runtime.Remoting.Lifetime.ILease` interface. You obtain an `ILease` instance by calling the base class method `InitializeLifetimeService`. Then configure the returned `ILease` by setting the `InitialLeaseTime` and `RenewOnCallTime` properties to the desired values using `System.TimeSpan` objects. If you want the object to have an unlimited lifetime, simply return a `null` reference instead of an `ILease` object. This is most commonly the case if you are creating a singleton object that needs to run independently (and permanently), even if clients aren't currently using it.

- The client can call the `MarshalByRefObject.GetLifetimeService` method on a specific remote object to retrieve an `ILease` instance. The client can then call the `ILease.Renew` method to specify a minimum amount of time the object should be kept alive.

The Code

The following example demonstrates how to use a component host's configuration file to control lifetime leases. The configuration gives each hosted object an initial lifetime of 10 minutes, and each time a member of the object is invoked, the lifetime is set to be at least 3 minutes.

```
<configuration>
  <system.runtime.remoting>
    <application>

      <service>
        <wellknown
            mode = "Singleton"
            type="Apress.VisualCSharpRecipes.Chapter10.Recipe10_19,Recipe10-19"
            objectUri = "Recipe10-19" />
      </service>

      <channels>
        <channel ref="tcp" port="19080" />
      </channels>
```

```
        <lifetime leaseTime = "10M"
                  renewOnCallTime = "3M" />

    </application>
  </system.runtime.remoting>
</configuration>
```

The following example demonstrates how to use the second approach outlined where the remotable object overrides the InitializeLifetimeService method and takes control of its own lifetime. The example shows a remotable object that gives itself a default 10-minute lifetime and 5-minute renewal time.

```
using System;
using System.Data;
using System.Data.SqlClient;
using System.Runtime.Remoting.Lifetime;

namespace Apress.VisualCSharpRecipes.Chapter10
{
    // Define a class that extends MarshalByRefObject, making it remotable.
    public class Recipe10_19 : MarshalByRefObject
    {
        public override object InitializeLifetimeService()
        {
            ILease lease = (ILease)base.InitializeLifetimeService();

            // Lease can only be configured if it is in an initial state.
            if (lease.CurrentState == LeaseState.Initial)
            {
                lease.InitialLeaseTime = TimeSpan.FromMinutes(10);
                lease.RenewOnCallTime = TimeSpan.FromMinutes(5);
            }
            return lease;
        }

        ...

    }
}
```

10-20. Control Versioning for Remote Objects

Problem

You want to create a component host that can host more than one version of the same object.

Solution

Install all versions of the remotable object into the GAC, and explicitly register each version at a different URI endpoint. See recipe 1-14 for details on how to manage the assemblies in the GAC.

How It Works

.NET Remoting doesn't include any intrinsic support for versioning. When a client creates a remote object, the component host automatically uses the version in the local directory or, in the case of a shared assembly, the latest version from the GAC. To support multiple versions, you have three choices:

- *Create separate component host applications*: Each component host will host a different version of the remote object assembly and will register its version with a different URI. This approach forces you to run multiple component host applications at once and is most practical if you are using IIS hosting (as described in recipe 10-18).

- *Create an entirely new remote object assembly (instead of simply changing the version)*: You can then register the classes from both assemblies at different URIs by using the same component host.

- *Install all versions of the remote object assembly in the GAC*: You can now create a component host that maps different URIs to specific versions of the remote object assembly.

The Code

The last option is the most flexible in cases where you need to support multiple versions. The following configuration file registers two versions of the RemoteObjects assembly at two different endpoints. Notice that you need to include the exact version number and public key token when using assemblies from the GAC. You can find this information by viewing the assembly in the Windows Explorer GAC plug-in (browse to C:\[WindowsDir]\Assembly). The client configuration file won't change at all (aside from updating the URI, if required). The client "chooses" the version it wants to use by using the corresponding URI.

```
<configuration>
  <system.runtime.remoting>
    <application>
      <service>
        <!-- The type information is split over two lines to accommodate the
             bounds of the page. In the configuration file, this information
             must all be placed on a single line. -->

        <wellknown mode="SingleCall"
          type="RemoteObjects.RemoteObject, RemoteObjects, Version 1.0.0.1,
              Culture=neutral, PublicKeyToken=8b5ed84fd25209e1"
          objectUri="RemoteObj" />

        <wellknown mode="SingleCall"
          type="RemoteObjects.RemoteObject, RemoteObjects, Version 2.0.0.1,
              Culture=neutral, PublicKeyToken=8b5ed84fd25209e1"
          objectUri="RemoteObj_2.0" />
      </service>
      <channels>
        <channel ref="tcp" port="19080" />
      </channels>
    </application>
  </system.runtime.remoting>
</configuration>
```

CHAPTER 11

■■■

Security and Cryptography

A principal goal of the Microsoft .NET Framework is to make computing more secure, especially with respect to the use of mobile code and distributed systems. Most modern operating systems (including Microsoft Windows) support user-based security, allowing you to control the actions and resources to which a user has access. However, in the highly connected world resulting from the proliferation of computer networks, particularly the Internet, it's insufficient to base security solely on the identity of a system's user. In the interest of security, code should not automatically receive the same level of trust that you assign to the person running the code.

The .NET Framework incorporates two complementary security models that address many of the issues associated with user and code security: code access security (CAS) and role-based security (RBS). CAS and RBS do not replace or duplicate the security facilities provided by the underlying operating system. They are platform-independent mechanisms that provide additional security capabilities to augment and enhance the overall security of your managed solutions. CAS uses information about the source and origin of an assembly (*evidence*) gathered at runtime to determine which actions and resources code from the assembly can access (*permissions*). The .NET Framework *security policy*—a hierarchical set of configurable rules—defines the mapping between evidence and permissions. The building blocks of security policy are *code groups*, which allow you to configure the mapping between evidence and permissions. The set of permissions granted to an assembly as a result of the security policy is known as the assembly's *grant set*.

The .NET Framework class library uses permission *demands* to protect its most important functionality from unauthorized access. A demand forces the common language runtime (CLR) to ensure that the whole stack of code calling a protected method has a specific permission. CAS ensures that the runtime capabilities of code depend on the level of trust you place in the creator and source of the code, not the level of trust you place in the user running the code.

Following a more traditional security model, RBS allows you to make runtime decisions based on the identity and roles of the user on whose behalf an application is running. On the Windows operating system, this equates to making decisions based on the Windows username and the Windows groups to which that user belongs. However, RBS provides a generic security mechanism that is independent of the underlying operating system, allowing you (with some development) to integrate with any user account system.

Another important aspect of the security features provided by the .NET Framework is *cryptography*. Cryptography is one of the most complex aspects of software development that any developer will use. The theory of modern cryptographic techniques is extremely difficult to understand and requires a level of mathematical knowledge that relatively few people have or need. Fortunately, the Microsoft .NET Framework class library provides easy-to-use implementations of the most commonly used cryptographic techniques and support for the most popular and well-understood algorithms.

This chapter provides a wide variety of recipes that cover some of the more commonly used security capabilities provided by the .NET Framework. As you read the recipes in this chapter and think about how to apply the techniques to your own code, keep in mind that individual security features are rarely effective when implemented in isolation. In particular, cryptography does not equal security; the use of cryptography is merely one small element of creating a secure solution.

The recipes in this chapter describe how to do the following:

- Develop strong-named assemblies that can still be called by partially trusted code (recipe 11-1)

- Configure the .NET Framework security policy to turn off CAS completely or turn off only execution permission checks (recipes 11-2 and 11-3)

- Request specific code access permissions for your assemblies, determine at runtime what permissions the current assembly has, and inspect third-party assemblies to determine what permissions they need in order to run correctly (recipes 11-4, 11-5, 11-6, and 11-7)

- Control inheritance and member overrides using CAS (recipe 11-8)

- Inspect the evidence presented by an assembly to the runtime when the assembly is loaded (recipe 11-9)

- Integrate with Windows security to determine if a user is a member of a specific Windows group, restrict which users can execute your code, and impersonate other Windows users (recipes 11-10, 11-11, and 11-12)

- Generate random numbers that are nondeterministic and are suitable for use in security-sensitive applications (recipe 11-13)

- Use hash codes and keyed hash codes to store user passwords and determine if files have changed (recipes 11-14, 11-15, 11-16, and 11-17)

- Use encryption to protect sensitive data both in memory and when it is stored to disk (recipes 11-18 and 11-19)

■Note For a broader explanation of secure programming and where cryptography fits in the overall security landscape, read *Writing Secure Code, Second Edition*, by Michael Howard and David LeBlanc (Microsoft Press, 2003), a modern classic of computer literature that contains a wealth of practical field-tested information. For more comprehensive coverage of the .NET security classes, see *Programming .NET Security* by Adam Freeman and Allen Jones (O'Reilly and Associates, 2003). Although not yet updated for .NET Framework 2.0, *Programming .NET Security* provides easily understood descriptions of security fundamentals, covers all the .NET security classes in detail, and demonstrates how to extend most aspects of the security framework.

11-1. Allow Partially Trusted Code to Use Your Strong-Named Assembly

Problem

You need to write a shared assembly that is accessible to partially trusted code. (By default, the runtime does not allow partially trusted code to access the types and members contained in a strong-named assembly.)

Solution

Apply the assembly-level attribute `System.Security.AllowPartiallyTrustedCallersAttribute` to your shared assembly.

How It Works

To minimize the security risks posed by malicious code, the runtime does not allow assemblies granted only partial trust to access strong-named assemblies. This restriction dramatically reduces the opportunity for malicious code to attack your system, but the reasoning behind such a heavy-handed approach requires some explanation.

Assemblies that contain important functionality that is shared between multiple applications are usually strong-named and often installed in the global assembly cache (GAC). This is particularly true of the assemblies that constitute the .NET Framework class library. Other strong-named assemblies from well-known and widely distributed products will also be in the GAC and accessible to managed applications. The high chance that certain assemblies will be present in the GAC, their easy accessibility, and their importance to many different applications makes strong-named assemblies the most likely target for any type of subversive activity by malicious managed code.

Generally, the code most likely to be malicious is that which is loaded from remote locations, such as the Internet, over which you have little or no control. Under the default security policy in version 1.*x* and 2.0 of the .NET Framework, all code run from the local machine has full trust, whereas code loaded from remote locations has only partial trust. Stopping partially trusted code from accessing strong-named assemblies means that partially trusted code has no opportunity to use the features of the assembly for malicious purposes, and cannot probe and explore the assembly to find exploitable holes. Of course, this theory hinges on the assumption that you correctly administer your security policy. If you simply assign all code full trust, not only will any assembly be able to access your strong-named assembly, but the code will also be able to access all of the functionality of the .NET Framework and even Win32 or any COM object through P/Invoke and COM Interop. That would be a security disaster!

■Note If you design, implement, and test your shared assembly correctly using CAS to restrict access to important members, you do not need to impose a blanket restriction to prevent partially trusted code from using your assembly. However, for an assembly of any significance, it's impossible to prove there are no security holes that malicious code can exploit. Therefore, you should carefully consider the need to allow partially trusted code to access your strong-named assembly before applying AllowPartiallyTrustedCallersAttribute. However, you might have no choice. If you are exposing public classes that provide events, you must apply this attribute. If you do not, an assembly that is not strong-named will be allowed to register a handler for one of your events, but when it is called, a security exception will be thrown. Code in an assembly that is not strong-named is not allowed to call code in a strong-named assembly.

The runtime stops partially trusted code from accessing strong-named assemblies by placing an implicit `LinkDemand` for the `FullTrust` permission set on every `public` and `protected` member of every publicly accessible type defined in the assembly. This means that only assemblies granted the permissions equivalent to the `FullTrust` permission set are able to access the types and members from the strong-named assembly. Applying `AllowPartiallyTrustedCallersAttribute` to your strong-named assembly signals the runtime not to enforce the `LinkDemand` on the contained types and members.

■**Note** The runtime is responsible for enforcing the implicit LinkDemand security actions required to protect strong-named assemblies. The C# assembler does not generate declarative LinkDemand statements at compile time.

The Code

The following code fragment shows the application of the attribute AllowPartiallyTrustedCallersAttribute. Notice that you must prefix the attribute with assembly: to signal to the compiler that the target of the attribute is the assembly (also called a *global attribute*). In addition, you do not need to include the Attribute part of the attribute name, although you can if you want to add it. Because you target the assembly, the attribute must be positioned after any top-level using statements, but before any namespace or type declarations.

```
using System.Security;

[assembly:AllowPartiallyTrustedCallers]

namespace Apress.VisualCSharpRecipes.Chapter11
{
    public class Recipe11-01 {

        // Implementation code. . .
    }
}
```

■**Tip** It's common practice to contain all global attributes in a file separate from the rest of your application code. Microsoft Visual Studio uses this approach, creating a file named AssemblyInfo.cs to contain all global attributes.

Notes

If, after applying AllowPartiallyTrustedCallersAttribute to your assembly, you want to restrict partially trusted code from calling only specific members, you should implement a LinkDemand for the FullTrust permission set on the necessary members, as shown in the following code fragment.

```
[System.Security.Permissions.PermissionSetAttribute
    (System.Security.Permissions.SecurityAction.LinkDemand, Name="FullTrust")]

public void SomeMethod() {
    // Method code. . .
}
```

11-2. Disable Code Access Security

Problem

You need to turn off all code access security (CAS) checks.

Solution

Use the Code Access Security Policy tool (Caspol.exe) and execute the command caspol -s off from the command line to temporarily disable code access security checks.

■**Note** You could permanently turn off CAS in .NET Framework versions 1.0 and 1.1 both programmatically and using Caspol.exe. In .NET Framework 2.0, you can turn off CAS only temporarily and only by using Caspol.exe.

How It Works

In some cases, code-level security might not be of interest to you. For example, when you are debugging code, you might want to exclude the possible interference caused by CAS. On rare occasions, the need for performance might outweigh the need for security. CAS is a key element of the .NET runtime's security model and one that sets it apart from many other computing platforms. Although CAS was implemented with performance in mind and has been used prudently throughout the .NET class library, some overhead is associated with each security demand and resulting stack walk that the runtime must execute to check every caller in the chain of execution.

■**Note** You should disable CAS only for performance reasons after you have exhausted all other possible measures to achieve the performance characteristics your application requires. Profiling your code will usually identify areas where you can improve performance significantly without the need to disable CAS. In addition, you should ensure that your system resources have appropriate protection using operating system security mechanisms, such as Windows access control lists (ACLs), before disabling CAS.

In these situations, you can temporarily disable CAS and remove the overhead and possible interference caused by code-level security checks. Turning off CAS has the effect of giving all code the ability to perform any action supported by the .NET Framework (equivalent to the `FullTrust` permission set). This includes the ability to load other code, call native libraries, and use pointers to access memory directly.

Caspol.exe is a utility provided with the .NET Framework that allows you to configure all aspects of your code access security policy from the command line. When you enter the command `caspol -s off` from the command line, you will see the following message indicating that CAS has been temporarily disabled:

```
Microsoft (r) .NET Framework CasPol 2.0.50727.42
Copyright (c) Microsoft Corporation. Al rights reserved.

CAS enforcement is being turned off temporarily. Press <enter> when you want to
restore the setting back on.
```

As the message states, CAS enforcement is off until you press Enter, or until the console in which Caspol.exe is running terminates.

Notes

In versions 1.0 and 1.1 of the .NET Framework, running the command `caspol -s off` turned off CAS enforcement permanently until you turned it on again using the command `caspol -s on`. In addition, it was possible to turn CAS on and off programmatically using the `System.Security.SecurityManager` class. The `SecurityManager` class contains a set of `static` methods that provide access to critical security functionality and data. This includes the `SecurityEnabled` property, which turns CAS checks on and off.

To disable CAS, your code must run as a Windows Administrator and must have the `ControlPolicy` element of the permission `System.Security.Permissions.SecurityPermission`. Naturally, you do not need any specific permissions to enable CAS.

Changing SecurityEnabled will not affect the enforcement of CAS in existing processes, nor will it affect new processes until you call the SavePolicy method, which saves the state of SecurityEnabled to the Windows registry. Unfortunately, the .NET Framework does not guarantee that changes to SecurityEnabled will correctly affect the operation of CAS in the current process, so you must change SecurityEnabled, and then launch a new process to achieve reliable and expected operation. The current on/off state of CAS is stored in the Windows registry in the key HKEY_LOCAL_MACHINE\SOFTWARE \Microsoft\.NETFramework\Security\Policy as part of a set of flags contained in the Global Settings value. If the key does not exist, CAS defaults to on. Because CAS can no longer be permanently turned off in .NET Framework 2.0, this registry key is no longer used to control CAS.

The following example will work only on .NET Framework versions 1.0 and 1.1. It contains two methods (CasOn and CasOff) that demonstrate the code required to turn CAS on and off programmatically and persist the configuration change.

```
using System.Security;

namespace Apress.VisualCSharpRecipes.Chapter11
{
    class Recipe11_02
    {
        // A method to turn on CAS and persist the change.
        public void CasOn()
        {
            // Turn on CAS checks.
            SecurityManager.SecurityEnabled = true;

            // Persist the configuration change.
            SecurityManager.SavePolicy();
        }

        // A method to turn off CAS and persist the change.
        public void CasOff()
        {
            // Turn off CAS checks.
            SecurityManager.SecurityEnabled = false;

            // Persist the configuration change.
            SecurityManager.SavePolicy();
        }
    }
}
```

11-3. Disable Execution Permission Checks

Problem

You need to load assemblies at runtime without the runtime checking them for execution permission.

Solution

In code, set the property CheckExecutionRights of the class System.Security.SecurityManager to false and persist the change by calling SecurityManager.SavePolicy. Alternatively, use the Code Access Security Policy tool (Caspol.exe), and execute the command caspol -e off from the command line.

How It Works

As the runtime loads each assembly, it ensures that the assembly's grant set (the permissions assigned to the assembly based on the security policy) includes the Execution element of SecurityPermission. The runtime implements a lazy policy resolution process, meaning that the grant set of an assembly is not calculated until the first time a security demand is made against the assembly. Not only does execution permission checking force the runtime to check that every assembly has the execution permission, but it also indirectly causes policy resolution for every assembly loaded, effectively negating the benefits of lazy policy resolution. These factors can introduce a noticeable delay as assemblies are loaded, especially when the runtime loads a number of assemblies together, as it does at application startup.

In many situations, simply allowing code to load and run is not a significant risk, as long as all other important operations and resources are correctly secured using CAS and operating system security. The SecurityManager class contains a set of static methods that provide access to critical security functionality and data. This includes the CheckExecutionRights property, which turns on and off execution permission checks.

To modify the value of CheckExecutionRights, your code must have the ControlPolicy element of SecurityPermission. The change will affect the current process immediately, allowing you to load assemblies at runtime without the runtime checking them for execution permission. However, the change will not affect other existing processes. You must call the SavePolicy method to persist the change to the Windows registry for it to affect new processes.

The Code

The following example contains two methods (ExecutionCheckOn and ExecutionCheckOff) that demonstrate the code required to turn execution permission checks on and off and persist the configuration change.

```csharp
using System.Security;

namespace Apress.VisualCSharpRecipes.Chapter11
{
    class Recipe11_03
    {
        // A method to turn on execution permission checking
        // and persist the change.
        public void ExecutionCheckOn()
        {
            // Turn on execution permission checks.
            SecurityManager.CheckExecutionRights = true;

            // Persist the configuration change.
            SecurityManager.SavePolicy();
        }

        // A method to turn off execution permission checking
        // and persist the change.
        public void ExecutionCheckOff()
        {
            // Turn off execution permission checks.
            SecurityManager.CheckExecutionRights = false;

            // Persist the configuration change.
            SecurityManager.SavePolicy();
        }
    }
}
```

Notes

The .NET runtime allows you to turn off the automatic checks for execution permissions from within code or by using Caspol.exe. When you enter the command `caspol -e off` or its counterpart `caspol -e on` from the command line, the Caspol.exe utility actually sets the `CheckExecutionRights` property of the `SecurityManager` class before calling `SecurityManager.SavePolicy`.

11-4. Ensure the Runtime Grants Specific Permissions to Your Assembly

Problem

You need to ensure that the runtime grants your assembly those code access permissions that are critical to the successful operation of your application.

Solution

In your assembly, use permission requests to specify the code access permissions that your assembly must have. You declare permission requests using assembly-level code access permission attributes.

How It Works

The name *permission request* is a little misleading given that the runtime will never grant permissions to an assembly unless security policy dictates that the assembly should have those permissions. However, naming aside, permission requests serve an essential purpose, and although the way the runtime handles permission requests might initially seem strange, the nature of CAS does not allow for any obvious alternative.

Permission requests identify permissions that your code *must* have to function. For example, if you wrote a movie player that your customers could use to download and view movies from your web server, it would be disastrous if the user's security policy did not allow your player to open a network connection to your media server. Your player would load and run, but as soon as the user tried to connect to your server to play a movie, the application would crash with the exception `System.Security.SecurityException`. The solution is to include in your assembly a permission request for the code access permission required to open a network connection to your server (`System.Net.WebPermission` or `System.Net.SocketPermission`, depending on the type of connection you need to open).

The runtime honors permission requests using the premise that it's better that your code never load than to load and fail sometime later when it tries to perform an action that it does not have permission to perform. Therefore, if after security policy resolution the runtime determines that the grant set of your assembly does not satisfy the assembly's permission requests, the runtime will fail to load the assembly and will instead throw the exception `System.Security.Policy.PolicyException`. Since your own code failed to load, the runtime will handle this security exception during the assembly loading and transform it into a `System.IO.FileLoadException` exception that will terminate your program.

When you try to load an assembly from within code (either automatically or manually), and the loaded assembly contains permission requests that the security policy does not satisfy, the method you use to load the assembly will throw a `PolicyException` exception, which you must handle appropriately.

To declare a permission request, you must use the attribute counterpart of the code access permission that you need to request. All code access permissions have an attribute counterpart that you use to construct declarative security statements, including permission requests. For example, the attribute counterpart of SocketPermission is SocketPermissionAttribute, and the attribute counterpart of WebPermission is WebPermissionAttribute. All permissions and their attribute counterparts follow the same naming convention and are members of the same namespace.

When making a permission request, it's important to remember the following:

- You must declare the permission request after any top-level using statements but before any namespace or type declarations.

- The attribute must target the assembly, so you must prefix the attribute name with assembly.

- You do not need to include the Attribute portion of an attribute's name, although you can.

- You must specify SecurityAction.RequestMinimum as the first positional argument of the attribute. This value identifies the statement as a permission request.

- You must configure the attribute to represent the code access permission you want to request using the attribute's properties. Refer to the .NET Framework SDK documentation for details of the properties implemented by each code access security attribute.

- The permission request statements do not end with a semicolon (;).

- To make more than one permission request, simply include multiple permission request statements.

The Code

The following example is a console application that includes two permission requests: one for SocketPermission and the other for SecurityPermission. If you try to execute the PermissionRequestExample application and your security policy does not grant the assembly the requested permissions, you will get a PolicyException exception, and the application will not execute. Using the default security policy, this will happen if you run the assembly from a network share, because assemblies loaded from the intranet zone are not granted SocketPermission.

```csharp
using System;
using System.Net;
using System.Security.Permissions;

// Permission request for a SocketPermission that allows the code to open
// a TCP connection to the specified host and port.
[assembly:SocketPermission(SecurityAction.RequestMinimum,
    Access = "Connect", Host = "www.fabrikam.com",
    Port = "3538", Transport = "Tcp")]

// Permission request for the UnmanagedCode element of SecurityPermission,
// which controls the code's ability to execute unmanaged code.
[assembly:SecurityPermission(SecurityAction.RequestMinimum,
    UnmanagedCode = true)]

namespace Apress.VisualCSharpRecipes.Chapter11
{
    class Recipe11_04
    {
        public static void Main()
        {
            // Do something. . .
```

```
        // Wait to continue.
        Console.WriteLine("Main method complete. Press Enter.");
        Console.ReadLine();
      }
    }
}
```

11-5. Limit the Permissions Granted to Your Assembly

Problem

You need to restrict the code access permissions granted to your assembly, ensuring that people and other software can never use your code as a mechanism through which to perform undesirable or malicious actions.

Solution

Use declarative security statements to specify optional permission requests and permission refusal requests in your assembly. Optional permission requests define the maximum set of permissions that the runtime will grant to your assembly. Permission refusal requests specify particular permissions that the runtime should not grant to your assembly.

How It Works

In the interest of security, it's ideal if your code has only those code access permissions required to perform its function. This minimizes the opportunities for people and other code to use your code to carry out malicious or undesirable actions. The problem is that the runtime resolves an assembly's permissions using security policy, which a user or an administrator configures. Security policy could be different in every location where your application is run, and you have no control over what permissions the security policy assigns to your code.

Although you cannot control security policy in all locations where your code runs, the .NET Framework provides two mechanisms through which you can reject permissions granted to your assembly:

- *Refuse request*: This allows you to identify specific permissions that you do not want the runtime to grant to your assembly. After policy resolution, if the final grant set of an assembly contains any permission specified in a refuse request, the runtime removes that permission.

- *Optional permission request*: This defines the maximum set of permissions that the runtime can grant to your assembly. If the final grant set of an assembly contains any permissions other than those specified in the optional permission request, the runtime removes those permissions. Unlike as with a minimum permission request (discussed in recipe 11-4), the runtime will not refuse to load your assembly if it cannot grant all of the permissions specified in the optional request.

You can think of a refuse request and an optional request as alternative ways to achieve the same result. The approach you use depends on how many permissions you want to reject. If you want to reject only a handful of permissions, a refuse request is easier to code. However, if you want to reject a large number of permissions, it's easier to code an optional request for the few permissions you want, which will automatically reject the rest.

You include optional and refuse requests in your code using declarative security statements with the same syntax as the minimum permission requests discussed in recipe 11-4. The only difference is the value of the System.Security.Permissions.SecurityAction that you pass to the permission attribute's constructor. Use SecurityAction.RequestOptional to declare an optional permission request and SecurityAction.RequestRefuse to declare a refuse request. As with minimal permission requests, you must declare optional and refuse requests as global attributes by beginning the permission attribute name with the prefix assembly. In addition, all requests must appear after any top-level using statements but before any namespace or type declarations.

The Code

The code shown here demonstrates an optional permission request for the Internet permission set. The Internet permission set is a named permission set defined by the default security policy. When the runtime loads the example, it will not grant the assembly any permission that is not included within the Internet permission set. (Consult the .NET Framework SDK documentation for details of the permissions contained in the Internet permission set.)

```
using System.Security.Permissions;

[assembly:PermissionSet(SecurityAction.RequestOptional, Name = "Internet")]

namespace Apress.VisualCSharpRecipes.Chapter11
{
    class Recipe11_05_OptionalRequest
    {
        // Class implementation. . .
    }
}
```

In contrast to the preceding example, the following example uses a refuse request to single out the permission System.Security.Permissions.FileIOPermission—representing write access to the C: drive—for refusal.

```
using System.Security.Permissions;

[assembly:FileIOPermission(SecurityAction.RequestRefuse, Write = @"C:\")]

namespace Apress.VisualCSharpRecipes.Chapter11
{
    class Recipe11_05_RefuseRequest
    {
        // Class implementation. . .
    }
}
```

11-6. View the Permissions Required by an Assembly

Problem

You need to view the permissions that an assembly must be granted in order to run correctly.

Solution

Use the Permissions Calculator (Permcalc.exe) supplied with the .NET Framework SDK version 2.0 or the Permissions View tool (Permview.exe) supplied with the .NET Framework SDK versions 1.0 and 1.1.

How It Works

To configure security policy correctly, you need to know the code access permission requirements of the assemblies you intend to run. This is true of both executable assemblies and libraries that you access from your own applications. With libraries, it's also important to know which permissions the assembly refuses so that you do not try to use the library to perform a restricted action, which would result in a System.Security.SecurityException exception.

The Permissions View tool (Permview.exe) supplied with the .NET Framework SDK versions 1.0 and 1.1 allows you to view the minimal, optional, and refuse permission requests made by an assembly. By specifying the /decl switch, you can view all of the declarative security statements contained in an assembly, including declarative demands and asserts. This can give you a good insight into what the assembly is trying to do and allow you to configure security policy appropriately. However, Permview.exe does not show the imperative security operations contained within the assembly.

The Permissions Calculator (Permcalc.exe) supplied with the .NET Framework SDK version 2.0 overcomes this limitation. Permcalc.exe walks through an assembly and provides an estimate of the permissions the assembly requires to run, regardless of whether they are declarative or imperative.

■**Note** The Permissions View tool (Permview.exe) is not supplied with the .NET Framework SDK version 2.0. Permview.exe from previous versions of the .NET Framework do not work correctly with .NET 2.0 assemblies. This is unfortunate, as Permcalc.exe does not provide a direct replacement for some of the useful functionality provided by Permview.exe. Although Permcalc.exe can determine both the imperative and declarative demands an assembly makes, it does not report the minimal, optional, and refusal requests made within an assembly.

The Code

The following example shows a class that declares a minimum, optional, and refusal request, as well as a number of imperative security demands.

```
using System;
using System.Net;
using System.Security.Permissions;

// Minimum permission request for SocketPermission.
[assembly: SocketPermission(SecurityAction.RequestMinimum,
    Unrestricted = true)]

// Optional permission request for IsolatedStorageFilePermission.
[assembly: IsolatedStorageFilePermission(SecurityAction.RequestOptional,
    Unrestricted = true)]

// Refuse request for ReflectionPermission.
[assembly: ReflectionPermission(SecurityAction.RequestRefuse,
    Unrestricted = true)]

namespace Apress.VisualCSharpRecipes.Chapter11
{
    class Recipe11_06
```

```
{
    public static void Main()
    {
        // Create and configure a FileIOPermission object that represents
        // write access to the C:\Data folder.
        FileIOPermission fileIOPerm =
            new FileIOPermission(FileIOPermissionAccess.Write, @"C:\Data");

        // Make the demand.
        fileIOPerm.Demand();

        // Do something. . .

        // Wait to continue.
        Console.WriteLine("Main method complete. Press Enter.");
        Console.ReadLine();
    }
}
}
```

Usage

Executing the command `permview Recipe11-06.exe` will generate the following output. Although this output is not particularly user-friendly, you can decipher it to determine the declarative permission requests made by an assembly. Each of the three types of permission requests—minimum, optional, and refused—is listed under a separate heading and is structured as the XML representation of a `System.Security.PermissionSet` object.

```
Microsoft (R) .NET Framework Permission Request Viewer.
Version 1.1.4322.573
Copyright (C) Microsoft Corporation 1998-2002. All rights reserved.

minimal permission set:
<PermissionSet class=System.Security.PermissionSet" version="1">
  <IPermission class="System.Net.SocketPermission, System, Version=1.
0.5000.0, Culture=neutral, PublicKeyToken=b77a5c561934e089" version="
1" Unrestricted="true"/>
</PermissionSet>

optional permission set:
<PermissionSet class="System.Security.PermissionSet" version="1">
  <IPermission class="System.Security.Permissions.IsolatedStorageFilePermission,
mscorlib, Version=1.0.5000.0, Culture=neutral, PublicKeyToken=b77a5c5
61934e089" version="1" Unrestricted="true"/>
</PermissionSet>

refused permission set:
<PermissionSet class="System.Security.PermissionSet" version="1">
  <IPermission class="System.Security.Permissions.ReflectionPermission,
mscorlib, Version=1.0.5000.0, Culture=neutral, PublicKeyToken=b77a5c5
61934e089" version="1" Unrestricted="true"/>
</PermissionSet>
```

Executing the command `permcalc -sandbox Recipe11-06.exe` will generate a file named sandbox.PermCalc.xml that contains XML representations of the permissions required by the assembly. Where the exact requirements of a permission cannot be determined (because it is based on runtime data), Permcalc.exe reports that unrestricted permissions of that type are required. You can instead default to the Internet zone permissions using the `-Internet` flag. Here are the contents of sandbox.PermCalc.xml when run against the sample code.

```xml
<?xml version="1.0"?>
<Sandbox>
  <PermissionSet version="1" class="System.Security.PermissionSet">
    <IPermission Write="C:\Data" version="1"
        class="System.Security.Permissions.FileIOPermission, mscorlib,
        Version=2.0.0.0, Culture=neutral,
        PublicKeyToken=b77a5c561934e089" />
    <IPermission version="1" class="System.Security.Permissions.SecurityPermission,
        mscorlib, Version=2.0.0.0, Culture=neutral,
        PublicKeyToken=b77a5c561934e089" Flags="Execution" />
    <IPermission version="1" class="System.Security.Permissions.UIPermission,
        mscorlib, Version=2.0.0.0, Culture=neutral,
        PublicKeyToken=b77a5c561934e089" Unrestricted="true" />
    <IPermission version="1" class="System.Net.SocketPermission, System,
        Version=2.0.0.0, Culture=neutral, PublicKeyToken=b77a5c561934e089"
        Unrestricted="true" />
  </PermissionSet>
</Sandbox>
```

11-7. Determine at Runtime If Your Code Has a Specific Permission

Problem

You need to determine at runtime if your assembly has a specific permission.

Solution

Instantiate and configure the permission you want to test for, and then pass it as an argument to the static method `IsGranted` of the class `System.Security.SecurityManager`.

How It Works

Using minimum permission requests, you can ensure that the runtime grants your assembly a specified set of permissions. As a result, when your code is running, you can safely assume that it has the requested minimum permissions. However, you might want to implement opportunistic functionality that your application offers only if the runtime grants your assembly appropriate permissions. This approach is partially formalized using optional permission requests, which allow you to define a set of permissions that your code could use if the security policy granted them, but are not essential for the successful operation of your code. (Recipe 11-5 provides more details on using optional permission requests.)

The problem with optional permission requests is that the runtime has no ability to communicate to your assembly which of the requested optional permissions it has granted. You can try to use a protected operation and fail gracefully if the call results in the exception

System.Security.SecurityException. However, it's more efficient to determine in advance if you have the necessary permissions. You can then build logic into your code to avoid invoking secured members that will cause stack walks and raise security exceptions.

■**Note** IsGranted checks the grant set only of the calling assembly. It does not do a full stack walk to evaluate the grant set of other assemblies on the call stack.

The Code

The following example demonstrates how to use the IsGranted method to determine if the assembly has write permission to the directory C:\Data. You could make such a call each time you needed to test for the permission, but it's more efficient to use the returned Boolean value to set a configuration flag indicating whether to allow users to save files.

```
using System.Security;
using System.Security.Permissions;

namespace Apress.VisualCSharpRecipes.Chapter11
{
    class Recipe11_07
    {
        // Define a variable to indicate whether the assembly has write
        // access to the C:\Data folder.
        private bool canWrite = false;

        public Recipe11_07()
        {
            // Create and configure a FileIOPermission object that represents
            // write access to the C:\Data folder.
            FileIOPermission fileIOPerm =
                new FileIOPermission(FileIOPermissionAccess.Write, @"C:\Data");

            // Test if the current assembly has the specified permission.
            canWrite = SecurityManager.IsGranted(fileIOPerm);
        }
    }
}
```

11-8. Restrict Who Can Extend Your Classes and Override Class Members

Problem

You need to control what code can extend your classes through inheritance and which class members a derived class can override.

Solution

Use declarative security statements to apply the SecurityAction.InheritanceDemand to the declarations of the classes and members that you need to protect.

■Note In .NET Framework 2.0, assemblies granted `FullTrust` can extend a class regardless of the security demands implemented on the class. This means that the `InheritanceDemand` is useful in environments where assembly permissions are closely managed, because you can still ensure that malicious or unauthorized code cannot extend your critical business classes. However, the `InheritanceDemand` does not allow you to protect classes that you develop and distribute to other environments, as part of a packaged product, for example. Although this may seem like a useful feature has been lost, there were always ways for a determined programmer to write and run fully trusted assemblies to overcome the `InheritanceDemand`. The approach taken in .NET 2.0 is simply to avoid people placing too much confidence in a security feature that was at best an inconvenience to the determined hacker.

How It Works

Language modifiers such as `sealed`, `public`, `private`, and `virtual` give you a level of control over the ability of classes to inherit from your class and override its members. However, these modifiers are inflexible, providing no selectivity in restricting which code can extend a class or override its members. For example, you might want to allow only code written by your company or department to extend business-critical classes. By applying an `InheritanceDemand` to your class or member declaration, you can specify runtime permissions that a class must have to extend your class or override particular members. Remember that the permissions of a class are the permissions of the assembly in which the class is declared.

Although you can demand any permission or permission set in your `InheritanceDemand`, it's more common to demand identity permissions. Identity permissions represent evidence presented to the runtime by an assembly. If an assembly presents certain types of evidence at load time, the runtime will automatically assign the assembly the appropriate identity permission. Identity permissions allow you to use regular imperative and declarative security statements to base security decisions directly on code identity, without the need to evaluate evidence objects directly. Table 11-1 lists the type of identity permission generated for each type of evidence. (Evidence types are members of the `System.Security.Policy` namespace, and identity permission types are members of the `System.Security.Permissions` namespace.)

Table 11-1. *Evidence Classes That Generate Identity Permissions*

Evidence Class	Identity Permission
ApplicationDirectory	None
Hash	None
Publisher	PublisherIdentityPermission
Site	SiteIdentityPermission
StrongName	StrongNameIdentityPermission
Url	UrlIdentityPermission
Zone	ZoneIdentityPermission

■Note The runtime assigns identity permissions to an assembly based on the evidence presented by the assembly. You cannot assign additional identity permissions to an assembly through the configuration of security policy.

You must use declarative security syntax to implement an `InheritanceDemand`, and so you must use the attribute counterpart of the permission class that you want to demand. All permission classes, including `InheritanceDemand`, have an attribute counterpart that you use to construct declarative security statements. For example, the attribute counterpart of PublisherIdentityPermission is PublisherIdentityPermissionAttribute, and the attribute counterpart of StrongNameIdentityPermission is StrongNameIdentityPermissionAttribute. All permissions and their attribute counterparts follow the same naming convention and are members of the same namespace.

To control which code can extend your class, apply the InheritanceDemand to the class declaration using one of the permissions listed in Table 11-1. To control which code can override specific members of a class, apply the InheritanceDemand to the member declaration.

The Code

The following example demonstrates the use of an InheritanceDemand on both a class and a method. Applying a PublisherIdentityPermissionAttribute to the Recipe11_08 class means only classes in assemblies signed by the publisher certificate contained in the pubcert.cer file (or assemblies granted FullTrust) can extend the class. The contents of the pubcert.cer file are read at compile time, and the necessary certificate information is built into the assembly metadata. To demonstrate that other permissions can also be used with an InheritanceDemand, the PermissionSetAttribute is used to allow only classes granted the FullTrust permission set to override the method SomeProtectedMethod.

```
using System.Security.Permissions;

namespace Apress.VisualCSharpRecipes.Chapter11
{
    [PublisherIdentityPermission(SecurityAction.InheritanceDemand,
        CertFile = "pubcert.cer")]
    public class Recipe11_08
    {
        [PermissionSet(SecurityAction.InheritanceDemand, Name="FullTrust")]
        public void SomeProtectedMethod ()
        {
            // Method implementation. . .
        }
    }
}
```

11-9. Inspect an Assembly's Evidence

Problem

You need to inspect the evidence that the runtime assigned to an assembly.

Solution

Obtain a System.Reflection.Assembly object that represents the assembly in which you are interested. Get the System.Security.Policy.Evidence collection from the Evidence property of the Assembly object, and access the contained evidence objects using the GetEnumerator, GetHostEnumerator, or GetAssemblyEnumerator method of the Evidence class.

How It Works

The Evidence class represents a collection of evidence objects. The read-only Evidence property of the Assembly class returns an Evidence collection object that contains all of the evidence objects that the runtime assigned to the assembly as the assembly was loaded.

The Evidence class actually contains two collections, representing different types of evidence:

- *Host evidence* includes those evidence objects assigned to the assembly by the runtime or the trusted code that loaded the assembly.

- *Assembly evidence* represents custom evidence objects embedded into the assembly at build time.

The Evidence class implements three methods for enumerating the evidence objects it contains: GetEnumerator, GetHostEnumerator, and GetAssemblyEnumerator. The GetHostEnumerator and GetAssemblyEnumerator methods return a System.Collections.IEnumerator instance that enumerates only those evidence objects from the appropriate collection. The GetEnumerator method returns an IEnumerator instance that enumerates *all* of the evidence objects contained in the Evidence collection.

■**Note** Evidence classes do not extend a standard base class or implement a standard interface. Therefore, when working with evidence programmatically, you need to test the type of each object and know what particular types you are seeking. (See recipe 3-11 for details on how to test the type of an object at runtime.)

The Code

The following example demonstrates how to display the host and assembly evidence of an assembly to the console. The example relies on the fact that all standard evidence classes override the Object. ToString method to display a useful representation of the evidence object's state. Although interesting, this example does not always show the evidence that an assembly would have when loaded from within your program. The runtime host (such as the Microsoft ASP.NET or Internet Explorer runtime host) is free to assign additional host evidence as it loads an assembly.

```
using System;
using System.Reflection;
using System.Collections;
using System.Security.Policy;

namespace Apress.VisualCSharpRecipes.Chapter11
{
    public class Recipe11_09
    {
        public static void Main(string[] args)
        {
            // Load the specified assembly.
            Assembly a = Assembly.LoadFrom(args[0]);

            // Get the Evidence collection from the
            // loaded assembly.
            Evidence e = a.Evidence;

            // Display the Host Evidence.
            IEnumerator x = e.GetHostEnumerator();
            Console.WriteLine("HOST EVIDENCE COLLECTION:");
            while(x.MoveNext())
            {
                Console.WriteLine(x.Current.ToString());
                Console.WriteLine("Press Enter to see next evidence.");
                Console.ReadLine();
            }
```

```
            // Display the Assembly Evidence.
            x = e.GetAssemblyEnumerator();
            Console.WriteLine("ASSEMBLY EVIDENCE COLLECTION:");
            while(x.MoveNext())
            {
                Console.WriteLine(x.Current.ToString());
                Console.WriteLine("Press Enter to see next evidence.");
                Console.ReadLine();
            }

            // Wait to continue.
            Console.WriteLine("Main method complete. Press Enter.");
            Console.ReadLine();
        }
    }
}
```

■**Note** All of the standard evidence classes provided by the .NET Framework are immutable, ensuring that you cannot change their values after the runtime has created them and assigned them to the assembly. In addition, you cannot add or remove items while you are enumerating across the contents of a collection using an IEnumerator; otherwise, the MoveNext method throws a System.InvalidOperationException exception.

11-10. Determine If the Current User Is a Member of a Specific Windows Group

Problem

You need to determine if the current user of your application is a member of a specific Windows user group.

Solution

Obtain a System.Security.Principal.WindowsIdentity object representing the current Windows user by calling the static method WindowsIdentity.GetCurrent. Create a System.Security.Principal. WindowsPrincipal class using the WindowsIdentity class, and then call the method IsInRole of the WindowsPrincipal object.

How It Works

The role-based security (RBS) mechanism of the .NET Framework abstracts the user-based security features of the underlying operating system through the following two key interfaces:

- The System.Security.Principal.IIdentity interface, which represents the entity on whose behalf code is running; for example, a user or service account.

- The System.Security.Principal.IPrincipal interface, which represents the entity's IIdentity and the set of roles to which the entity belongs. A *role* is simply a categorization used to group entities with similar security capabilities, such as a Windows user group.

To integrate RBS with Windows user security, the .NET Framework provides the following two Windows-specific classes that implement the IIdentity and IPrincipal interfaces:

- `System.Security.Principal.WindowsIdentity`, which implements the `IIdentity` interface and represents a Windows user.

- `System.Security.Principal.WindowsPrincipal`, which implements `IPrincipal` and represents the set of Windows groups to which the user belongs.

Because .NET RBS is a generic solution designed to be platform-independent, you have no access to the features and capabilities of the Windows user account through the `IIdentity` and `IPrincipal` interfaces, and you must frequently use the `WindowsIdentity` and `WindowsPrincipal` objects directly.

To determine if the current user is a member of a specific Windows group, you must first call the `static` method `WindowsIdentity.GetCurrent`. The `GetCurrent` method returns a `WindowsIdentity` object that represents the Windows user on whose behalf the current thread is running. An overload of the `GetCurrent` method new to .NET Framework 2.0 takes a `bool` argument and allows you to control what is returned by `GetCurrent` if the current thread is impersonating a user different from the one associated with the process. If the argument is `true`, `GetCurrent` returns a `WindowsIdentity` representing the impersonated user, or it returns `null` if the thread is not impersonating a user. If the argument is `false`, `GetCurrent` returns the `WindowsIdentity` of the thread if it is not impersonating a user, or it returns the `WindowsIdentity` of the process if the thread is currently impersonating a user.

Note The `WindowsIdentity` class provides overloaded constructors that, when running on Microsoft Windows Server 2003 or later platforms, allow you to obtain a `WindowsIdentity` object representing a named user. You can use this `WindowsIdentity` object and the process described in this recipe to determine if that user is a member of a specific Windows group. If you try to use one of these constructors when running on an earlier version of Windows, the `WindowsIdentity` constructor will throw an exception. On Windows platforms preceding Windows Server 2003, you must use native code to obtain a Windows access token representing the desired user. You can then use this access token to instantiate a `WindowsIdentity` object. Recipe 11-12 explains how to obtain Windows access tokens for specific users.

Once you have a `WindowsIdentity`, instantiate a new `WindowsPrincipal` object, passing the `WindowsIdentity` object as an argument to the constructor. Finally, call the `IsInRole` method of the `WindowsPrincipal` object to test if the user is in a specific group (role). `IsInRole` returns `true` if the user is a member of the specified group; otherwise, it returns `false`. The `IsInRole` method provides four overloads:

- The first overload takes a `string` containing the name of the group for which you want to test. The group name must be of the form `[DomainName]\[GroupName]` for domain-based groups and `[MachineName]\[GroupName]` for locally defined groups. If you want to test for membership of a standard Windows group, use the form `BUILTIN\[GroupName]` or the other overload that takes a value from the `System.Security.Principal.WindowsBuiltInRole` enumeration. `IsInRole` performs a case-insensitive test for the specified group name.

- The second `IsInRole` overload accepts an `int`, which specifies a Windows role identifier (RID). RIDs provide a mechanism to identify groups that is independent of language and localization.

- The third `IsInRole` overload accepts a member of the `System.Security.Principal.WindowsBuiltInRole` enumeration. The `WindowsBuiltInRole` enumeration defines a set of members that represent each of the built-in Windows groups.

- The fourth `IsInRole` overload (new to .NET Framework 2.0) accepts a `System.Security.Principal.SecurityIdentifier` object that represents the security identifier (SID) of the group for which you want to test.

Table 11-2 lists the name, RID, and `WindowsBuiltInRole` value for each of the standard Windows groups.

Table 11-2. *Windows Built-In Account Names and Identifiers*

Account Name	RID (Hex)	WindowsBuiltInRole Value
BUILTIN\Account Operators	0x224	AccountOperator
BUILTIN\Administrators	0x220	Administrator
BUILTIN\Backup Operators	0x227	BackupOperator
BUILTIN\Guests	0x222	Guest
BUILTIN\Power Users	0x223	PowerUser
BUILTIN\Print Operators	0x226	PrintOperator
BUILTIN\Replicators	0x228	Replicator
BUILTIN\Server Operators	0x225	SystemOperator
BUILTIN\Users	0x221	User

The Code

The following example demonstrates how to test whether the current user is a member of a set of named Windows groups. You specify the groups that you want to test for as command-line arguments. Remember to prefix the group name with the machine or domain name, or `BUILTIN` for standard Windows groups.

```csharp
using System;
using System.Security.Principal;

namespace Apress.VisualCSharpRecipes.Chapter11
{
    class Recipe11_10
    {
        public static void Main (string[] args)
        {
            // Obtain a WindowsIdentity object representing the currently
            // logged on Windows user.
            WindowsIdentity identity = WindowsIdentity.GetCurrent();

            // Create a WindowsPrincipal object that represents the security
            // capabilities of the specified WindowsIdentity; in this case,
            // the Windows groups to which the current user belongs.
            WindowsPrincipal principal = new WindowsPrincipal(identity);

            // Iterate through the group names specified as command-line
            // arguments and test to see if the current user is a member of
            // each one.
            foreach (string role in args)
            {
                Console.WriteLine("Is {0} a member of {1}? = {2}",
                    identity.Name, role, principal.IsInRole(role));
            }

            // Wait to continue.
            Console.WriteLine("\nMain method complete. Press Enter.");
            Console.ReadLine();
```

```
        }
      }
   }
}
```

Usage

If you run this example as a user named Darryl on a computer named MACHINE using this command:

```
Recipe11-10 BUILTIN\Administrators BUILTIN\Users MACHINE\Accountants
```

you will see console output similar to the following:

```
Is MACHINE\Darryl a member of BUILTIN\Administrators? = False
Is MACHINE\Darryl a member of BUILTIN\Users? = True
Is MACHINE\Darryl a member of MACHINE\Accountants? = True
```

11-11. Restrict Which Users Can Execute Your Code

Problem

You need to restrict which users can execute elements of your code based on the user's name or the roles of which the user is a member.

Solution

Use the permission class `System.Security.Permissions.PrincipalPermission` and its attribute counterpart `System.Security.Permissions.PrincipalPermissionAttribute` to protect your program elements with RBS demands.

How It Works

The .NET Framework supports both imperative and declarative RBS demands. The class `PrincipalPermission` provides support for imperative security statements, and its attribute counterpart `PrincipalPermissionAttribute` provides support for declarative security statements. RBS demands use the same syntax as CAS demands, but RBS demands specify the name the current user must have, or more commonly, the roles of which the user must be a member. An RBS demand instructs the runtime to look at the name and roles of the current user, and if that user does not meet the requirements of the demand, the runtime throws a `System.Security.SecurityException` exception.

To make an imperative security demand, you must first create a `PrincipalPermission` object specifying the username and role name you want to demand, and then you must call its Demand method. You can specify only a single username and role name per demand. If either the username or the role name is `null`, any value will satisfy the demand. Unlike with code access permissions, an RBS demand does not result in a stack walk; the runtime evaluates only the username and roles of the current user.

To make a declarative security demand, you must annotate the class or member you want to protect with a correctly configured `PrincipalPermissionAttribute` attribute. Class-level demands apply to all members of the class, unless a member-specific demand overrides the class demand.

Generally, you are free to choose whether to implement imperative or declarative demands. However, imperative security demands allow you to integrate RBS demands with code logic to achieve more sophisticated demand behavior. In addition, if you do not know the role or usernames to demand at compile time, you must use imperative demands. Declarative demands have the advantage that they are separate from code logic and easier to identify. In addition, you can view declarative demands using the Permview.exe tool (discussed in recipe 11-6). Whether you implement imperative or declarative demands, you must ensure that the runtime has access to the name and roles for the current user to evaluate the demand correctly.

The `System.Threading.Thread` class represents an operating system thread running managed code. The `static` property `CurrentPrincipal` of the `Thread` class contains an `IPrincipal` instance representing the user on whose behalf the managed thread is running. At the operating system level, each thread also has an associated Windows access token, which represents the Windows account on whose behalf the thread is running. The `IPrincipal` instance and the Windows access token are two separate entities. Windows uses its access token to enforce operating system security, whereas the .NET runtime uses its `IPrincipal` instance to evaluate application-level RBS demands. Although they may, and often do, represent the same user, this is by no means always the case.

The benefit of this approach is that you can implement a user and an RBS model within your application using a proprietary user accounts database, without the need for all users to have Windows user accounts. This is a particularly useful approach in large-scale, publicly accessible Internet applications.

By default, the `Thread.CurrentPrincipal` property is undefined. Because obtaining user-related information can be time-consuming, and only a minority of applications use this information, the .NET designers opted for lazy initialization of the `CurrentPrincipal` property. The first time code gets the `Thread.CurrentPrincipal` property, the runtime assigns an `IPrincipal` instance to the property using the following logic:

- If the application domain in which the current thread is executing has a default principal, the runtime assigns this principal to the `Thread.CurrentPrincipal` property. By default, application domains do not have default principals. You can set the default principal of an application domain by calling the method `SetThreadPrincipal` on a `System.AppDomain` object that represents the application domain you want to configure. Code must have the `ControlPrincipal` element of `SecurityPermission` to call `SetThreadPrincipal`. You can set the default principal only once for each application domain; a second call to `SetThreadPrincipal` results in the exception `System.Security.Policy.PolicyException`.

- If the application domain does not have a default principal, the application domain's principal policy determines which `IPrincipal` implementation to create and assign to `Thread.CurrentPrincipal`. To configure principal policy for an application domain, obtain an `AppDomain` object that represents the application domain and call the object's `SetPrincipalPolicy` method. The `SetPrincipalPolicy` method accepts a member of the enumeration `System.Security.Principal.PrincipalPolicy`, which specifies the type of `IPrincipal` object to assign to `Thread.CurrentPrincipal`. Code must have the `ControlPrincipal` element of `SecurityPermission` to call `SetPrincipalPolicy`. Table 11-3 lists the available `PrincipalPolicy` values; the default value is `UnauthenticatedPrincipal`.

- If your code has the `ControlPrincipal` element of `SecurityPermission`, you can instantiate your own `IPrincipal` object and assign it to the `Thread.CurrentPrincipal` property directly. This will prevent the runtime from assigning default `IPrincipal` objects or creating new ones based on principal policy.

Table 11-3. *Members of the* PrincipalPolicy *Enumeration*

Member Name	Description
NoPrincipal	No IPrincipal object is created. Thread.CurrentPrincipal returns a null reference.
UnauthenticatedPrincipal	An empty System.Security.Principal.GenericPrincipal object is created and assigned to Thread.CurrentPrincipal.
WindowsPrincipal	A WindowsPrincipal object representing the currently logged-on Windows user is created and assigned to Thread.CurrentPrincipal.

Whatever method you use to establish the IPrincipal for the current thread, you must do so before you use RBS demands, or the correct user (IPrincipal) information will not be available for the runtime to process the demand. Normally, when running on the Windows platform, you would set the principal policy of an application domain to PrincipalPolicy.WindowsPrincipal (as shown here) to obtain Windows user information.

```
// Obtain a reference to the current application domain.
AppDomain appDomain = System.AppDomain.CurrentDomain;

// Configure the current application domain to use Windows-based principals.
appDomain.SetPrincipalPolicy(
    System.Security.Principal.PrincipalPolicy.WindowsPrincipal);
```

The Code

The following example demonstrates the use of imperative and declarative RBS demands. The example shows three methods protected using imperative RBS demands (Method1, Method2, and Method3), and then three other methods protected using the equivalent declarative RBS demands (Method4, Method5, and Method6).

```
using System;
using System.Security.Permissions;

namespace Apress.VisualCSharpRecipes.Chapter11
{
    class Recipe11_11
    {
        public static void Method1()
        {
            // An imperative role-based security demand for the current principal
            // to represent an identity with the name Anya. The roles of the
            // principal are irrelevant.
            PrincipalPermission perm =
                new PrincipalPermission(@"MACHINE\Anya", null);

            // Make the demand.
            perm.Demand();
        }

        public static void Method2()
        {
            // An imperative role-based security demand for the current principal
            // to be a member of the roles Managers OR Developers. If the
            // principal is a member of either role, access is granted. Using the
            // PrincipalPermission, you can express only an OR type relationship.
            // This is because the PrincipalPolicy.Intersect method always
```

```
        // returns an empty permission unless the two inputs are the same.
        // However, you can use code logic to implement more complex
        // conditions. In this case, the name of the identity is irrelevant.
        PrincipalPermission perm1 =
            new PrincipalPermission(null, @"MACHINE\Managers");

        PrincipalPermission perm2 =
            new PrincipalPermission(null, @"MACHINE\Developers");

        // Make the demand.
        perm1.Union(perm2).Demand();
    }

    public static void Method3()
    {
        // An imperative role-based security demand for the current principal
        // to represent an identity with the name Anya AND be a member of the
        // Managers role.
        PrincipalPermission perm =
            new PrincipalPermission(@"MACHINE\Anya", @"MACHINE\Managers");

        // Make the demand
        perm.Demand();
    }

    // A declarative role-based security demand for the current principal
    // to represent an identity with the name Anya. The roles of the
    // principal are irrelevant.
    [PrincipalPermission(SecurityAction.Demand, Name = @"MACHINE\Anya")]
    public static void Method4()
    {
        // Method implementation. . .
    }

    // A declarative role-based security demand for the current principal
    // to be a member of the roles Managers OR Developers. If the
    // principal is a member of either role, access is granted. You
    // can express only an OR type relationship, not an AND relationship.
    // The name of the identity is irrelevant.
    [PrincipalPermission(SecurityAction.Demand, Role = @"MACHINE\Managers")]
    [PrincipalPermission(SecurityAction.Demand, Role = @"MACHINE\Developers")]
    public static void Method5()
    {
        // Method implementation. . .
    }

    // A declarative role-based security demand for the current principal
    // to represent an identity with the name Anya AND be a member of the
    // Managers role.
    [PrincipalPermission(SecurityAction.Demand, Name = @"MACHINE\Anya",
        Role = @"MACHINE\Managers")]
    public static void Method6()
    {
        // Method implementation. . .
    }
    }
}
```

11-12. Impersonate a Windows User

Problem

You need your code to run in the context of a Windows user other than the currently active user account.

Solution

Obtain a `System.Security.Principal.WindowsIdentity` object representing the Windows user you need to impersonate, and then call the `Impersonate` method of the `WindowsIdentity` object.

How It Works

Every Windows thread has an associated *access token*, which represents the Windows account on whose behalf the thread is running. The Windows operating system uses the access token to determine whether a thread has the appropriate permissions to perform protected operations on behalf of the account, such as read and write files, reboot the system, and change the system time.

By default, a managed application runs in the context of the Windows account that executed the application. This is normally desirable behavior, but sometimes you will want to run an application in the context of a different Windows account. This is particularly true in the case of server-side applications that process transactions on behalf of the users remotely connected to the server.

It's common for a server application to run in the context of a Windows account created specifically for the application—a service account. This service account will have minimal permissions to access system resources. Enabling the application to operate as though it were the connected user permits the application to access the operations and resources appropriate to that user's security clearance. When an application assumes the identity of another user, it's known as *impersonation*. Correctly implemented, impersonation simplifies security administration and application design, while maintaining user accountability.

■**Note** As discussed in recipe 11-11, a thread's Windows access token and its .NET principal are separate entities and can represent different users. The impersonation technique described in this recipe changes only the Windows access token of the current thread; it does not change the thread's principal. To change the thread's principal, code must have the `ControlPrincipal` element of `SecurityPermission` and assign a new `System.Security.Principal.IPrincipal` object to the `CurrentPrincipal` property of the current `System.Threading.Thread`.

The `System.Security.Principal.WindowsIdentity` class provides the functionality through which you invoke impersonation. However, the exact process depends on which version of Windows your application is running. If it's running on Windows Server 2003 or later, the `WindowsIdentity` class supports constructor overloads that create `WindowsIdentity` objects based on the account name of the user you want to impersonate. On all previous versions of Windows, you must first obtain a `System.IntPtr` containing a reference to a Windows access token that represents the user to impersonate. To obtain the access token reference, you must use a native method such as the `LogonUser` function from the Win32 API.

■**Caution** A major issue with performing impersonation on Microsoft Windows 2000 and Windows NT is that an account must have the Windows privilege SE_TCB_NAME to execute LogonUser. This requires you to configure Windows security policy and grant the account the right to "act as part of operating system." This grants the account a very high level of trust. You should never grant the privilege SE_TCB_NAME directly to user accounts. The requirement for an account to have the SE_TCB_NAME privilege no longer exists for Windows 2003 and Windows XP.

Once you have a WindowsIdentity object representing the user you want to impersonate, call its Impersonate method. From that point on, all actions your code performs occur in the context of the impersonated Windows account. The Impersonate method returns a System.Security.Principal. WindowsSecurityContext object, which represents the active account prior to impersonation. To revert to the original account, call the Undo method of this WindowsSecurityContext object.

The Code

The following example demonstrates impersonation of a Windows user. The example uses the LogonUser function of the Win32 API to obtain a Windows access token for the specified user, impersonates the user, and then reverts to the original user context.

```
using System;
using System.IO;
using System.Security.Principal;
using System.Security.Permissions;
using System.Runtime.InteropServices;

// Ensure the assembly has permission to execute unmanaged code
// and control the thread principal.
[assembly:SecurityPermission(SecurityAction.RequestMinimum,
    UnmanagedCode=true, ControlPrincipal=true)]

namespace Apress.VisualCSharpRecipes.Chapter11
{
    class Recipe11_12
    {
        // Define some constants for use with the LogonUser function.
        const int LOGON32_PROVIDER_DEFAULT = 0;
        const int LOGON32_LOGON_INTERACTIVE = 2;

        // Import the Win32 LogonUser function from advapi32.dll. Specify
        // "SetLastError = true" to correctly support access to Win32 error
        // codes.
        [DllImport("advapi32.dll", SetLastError=true, CharSet=CharSet.Unicode)]
        static extern bool LogonUser(string userName, string domain,
            string password, int logonType, int logonProvider,
            ref IntPtr accessToken);

        public static void Main(string[] args)
        {
            // Create a new IntPtr to hold the access token returned by the
            // LogonUser function.
            IntPtr accessToken = IntPtr.Zero;

            // Call LogonUser to obtain an access token for the specified user.
            // The accessToken variable is passed to LogonUser by reference and
```

```csharp
            // will contain a reference to the Windows access token if
            // LogonUser is successful.
            bool success = LogonUser(
                args[0],                    // username to log on.
                ".",                        // use the local account database.
                args[1],                    // user's password.
                LOGON32_LOGON_INTERACTIVE,  // create an interactive login.
                LOGON32_PROVIDER_DEFAULT,   // use the default logon provider.
                ref accessToken             // receives access token handle.
            );

            // If the LogonUser return code is zero, an error has occurred.
            // Display the error and exit.
            if (!success)
            {
                Console.WriteLine("LogonUser returned error {0}",
                    Marshal.GetLastWin32Error());
            }
            else
            {
                // Create a new WindowsIdentity from the Windows access token.
                WindowsIdentity identity = new WindowsIdentity(accessToken);

                // Display the active identity.
                Console.WriteLine("Identity before impersonation = {0}",
                    WindowsIdentity.GetCurrent().Name);

                // Impersonate the specified user, saving a reference to the
                // returned WindowsImpersonationContext, which contains the
                // information necessary to revert to the original user
                // context.
                WindowsImpersonationContext impContext =
                    identity.Impersonate();

                // Display the active identity.
                Console.WriteLine("Identity during impersonation = {0}",
                    WindowsIdentity.GetCurrent().Name);

                // ****************************************
                // Perform actions as the impersonated user.
                // ****************************************

                // Revert to the original Windows user using the
                // WindowsImpersonationContext object.
                impContext.Undo();

                // Display the active identity.
                Console.WriteLine("Identity after impersonation  = {0}",
                    WindowsIdentity.GetCurrent().Name);

                // Wait to continue.
                Console.WriteLine("\nMain method complete. Press Enter.");
                Console.ReadLine();
            }
        }
    }
}
```

Usage

The example expects two command-line arguments: the account name of the user on the local machine to impersonate and the account's password. For example, the command `Recipe11-12 Bob password` impersonates the user Bob, as long as that user exists in the local accounts database and his password is "password."

11-13. Create a Cryptographically Random Number

Problem

You need to create a random number that is suitable for use in cryptographic and security applications.

Solution

Use a cryptographic random number generator such as the `System.Security.Cryptography.RNGCryptoServiceProvider` class.

How It Works

The `System.Random` class is a pseudo-random number generator that uses a mathematical algorithm to simulate the generation of random numbers. In fact, the algorithm it uses is deterministic, meaning that you can always calculate what the next number will be based on the previously generated number. This means that numbers generated by the `Random` class are unsuitable for use in situations in which security is a priority, such as generating encryption keys and passwords.

When you need a nondeterministic random number for use in cryptographic or security-related applications, you must use a random number generator derived from the class `System.Security.Cryptography.RandomNumberGenerator`. The `RandomNumberGenerator` class is an abstract class from which all concrete .NET random number generator classes should inherit. Currently, the `RNGCryptoServiceProvider` class is the only concrete implementation provided. The `RNGCryptoServiceProvider` class provides a managed wrapper around the `CryptGenRandom` function of the Win32 CryptoAPI, and you can use it to fill `byte` arrays with cryptographically random `byte` values.

■**Note** The numbers produced by the `RNGCryptoServiceProvider` class are not truly random. However, they are sufficiently random to meet the requirements of cryptography and security applications in most commercial and government environments.

As is the case with many of the .NET cryptography classes, the `RandomNumberGenerator` base class is a factory for the concrete implementation classes that derive from it. Calling `RandomNumberGenerator.Create("System.Security.Cryptography.RNGCryptoServiceProvider")` will return an instance of `RNGCryptoServiceProvider` that you can use to generate random numbers. In addition, because `RNGCryptoServiceProvider` is the only concrete implementation provided, it's the default class created if you call the `Create` method without arguments, as in `RandomNumberGenerator.Create()`.

Once you have a `RandomNumberGenerator` instance, the method `GetBytes` fills a `byte` array with random `byte` values. As an alternative, you can use the `GetNonZeroBytes` method if you need random data that contains no zero values.

The Code

The following example instantiates an RNGCryptoServiceProvider object and uses it to generate random values.

```
using System;
using System.Security.Cryptography;

namespace Apress.VisualCSharpRecipes.Chapter11
{
    class Recipe11_13
    {
        public static void Main() {

            // Create a byte array to hold the random data.
            byte[] number = new byte[32];

            // Instantiate the default random number generator.
            RandomNumberGenerator rng = RandomNumberGenerator.Create();

            // Generate 32 bytes of random data.
            rng.GetBytes(number);

            // Display the random number.
            Console.WriteLine(BitConverter.ToString(number));

            // Wait to continue.
            Console.WriteLine("\nMain method complete. Press Enter.");
            Console.ReadLine();
        }
    }
}
```

■**Note** The computational effort required to generate a random number with RNGCryptoServiceProvider is significantly greater than that required by Random. For everyday purposes, the use of RNGCryptoServiceProvider is overkill. You should consider the quantity of random numbers you need to generate and the purpose of the numbers before deciding to use RNGCryptoServiceProvider. Excessive and unnecessary use of the RNGCryptoServiceProvider class could have a noticeable effect on application performance if many random numbers are generated.

11-14. Calculate the Hash Code of a Password

Problem

You need to store a user's password securely so that you can use it to authenticate the user in the future.

Solution

Create and store a cryptographic hash code of the password using a hashing algorithm class derived from the System.Security.Cryptography.HashAlgorithm class. On future authentication attempts, generate the hash of the password entered by the user and compare it to the stored hash code.

> ■**Caution** You should never store a user's plaintext password, because it is a major security risk and one that most users would not appreciate, given that many of them will use the same password to access multiple systems.

How It Works

Hashing algorithms are one-way cryptographic functions that take plaintext of variable length and generate a fixed-size numeric value. They are *one-way* because it's nearly impossible to derive the original plaintext from the hash code. Hashing algorithms are deterministic; applying the same hashing algorithm to a specific piece of plaintext always generates the same hash code. This makes hash codes useful for determining if two blocks of plaintext (passwords in this case) are the same. The design of hashing algorithms ensures that the chance of two different pieces of plaintext generating the same hash code is extremely small (although not impossible). In addition, there is no correlation between the similarity of two pieces of plaintext and their hash codes; minor differences in the plaintext cause significant differences in the resulting hash codes.

When using passwords to authenticate a user, you are not concerned with the content of the password that the user enters. You need to know only that the entered password matches the password that you have recorded for that user in your accounts database.

The nature of hashing algorithms makes them ideal for storing passwords securely. When the user provides a new password, you must create the hash code of the password and store it, and then discard the plaintext password. Each time the user tries to authenticate with your application, calculate the hash code of the password that user provides and compare it with the hash code you have stored.

> ■**Note** People regularly ask how to obtain a password from a hash code. The simple answer is that you cannot. The whole purpose of a hash code is to act as a token that you can freely store without creating security holes. If a user forgets a password, you cannot derive it from the stored hash code. Rather, you must either reset the account to some default value or generate a new password for the user.

Generating hash codes is simple in the .NET Framework. The abstract class `HashAlgorithm` provides a base from which all concrete hashing algorithm implementations derive. The .NET Framework class library includes the seven hashing algorithm implementations listed in Table 11-4; each implementation class is a member of the `System.Security.Cryptography` namespace. The classes with names ending in `CryptoServiceProvider` wrap functionality provided by the native Win32 CryptoAPI, whereas those with names ending in `Managed` are fully implemented in managed code.

Table 11-4. *Hashing Algorithm Implementations*

Algorithm Name	Class Name	Hash Code Size (in Bits)
MD5	MD5CryptoServiceProvider	128
RIPEMD160 or RIPEMD-160 (new in .NET 2.0)	RIPEMD160Managed	160
SHA or SHA1	SHA1CryptoServiceProvider	160
SHA1Managed	SHA1Managed	160
SHA256 or SHA-256	SHA256Managed	256
SHA384 or SHA-384	SHA384Managed	384
SHA512 or SHA-512	SHA512Managed	512

Although you can create instances of the hashing algorithm classes directly, the HashAlgorithm base class is a factory for the concrete implementation classes that derive from it. Calling the static method HashAlgorithm.Create will return an object of the specified type. Using the factory approach allows you to write generic code that can work with any hashing algorithm implementation. Note that unlike in recipe 11-13, you do not pass the class name as parameter to the factory; instead, you pass the algorithm name.

Once you have a HashAlgorithm object, its ComputeHash method accepts a byte array argument containing plaintext and returns a new byte array containing the generated hash code. Table 11-4 shows the size of hash code (in bits) generated by each hashing algorithm class.

■**Note** The SHA1Managed algorithm cannot be implemented using the factory approach. It must be instantiated directly.

The Code

The example shown here demonstrates the creation of a hash code from a string, such as a password. The application expects two command-line arguments: the name of the hashing algorithm to use and the string from which to generate the hash. Because the HashAlgorithm.ComputeHash method requires a byte array, you must first byte-encode the input string using the class System.Text.Encoding, which provides mechanisms for converting strings to and from various character-encoding formats.

```
using System;
using System.Text;
using System.Security.Cryptography;

namespace Apress.VisualCSharpRecipes.Chapter11
{
    class Recipe11_14
    {
        public static void Main(string[] args)
        {
            // Create a HashAlgorithm of the type specified by the first
            // command-line argument.
            HashAlgorithm hashAlg = null;
            if (args[0].CompareTo("SHA1Managed") == 0)
            {
                hashAlg = new SHA1Managed();
            }
            else
            {
                hashAlg = HashAlgorithm.Create(args[0]);
            }

            using (hashAlg)
            {
                // Convert the password string, provided as the second
                // command-line argument, to an array of bytes.
                byte[] pwordData = Encoding.Default.GetBytes(args[1]);

                // Generate the hash code of the password.
                byte[] hash = hashAlg.ComputeHash(pwordData);

                // Display the hash code of the password to the console.
                Console.WriteLine(BitConverter.ToString(hash));
```

```
                // Wait to continue.
                Console.WriteLine("\nMain method complete. Press Enter.");
                Console.ReadLine();
            }
        }
    }
}
```

Usage

Running the following command:

```
Recipe11-14 SHA1 ThisIsMyPassword
```

will display the following hash code to the console:

```
30-B8-BD-58-29-88-89-00-D1-5D-2B-BE-62-70-D9-BC-65-B0-70-2F
```

In contrast, executing this command:

```
Recipe11-14 RIPEMD-160 ThisIsMyPassword
```

will display the following hash code:

```
0C-39-3B-2E-8A-4E-D3-DD-FB-E3-C8-05-E4-62-6F-6B-76-7C-7A-49
```

11-15. Calculate the Hash Code of a File

Problem

You need to determine if the contents of a file have changed over time.

Solution

Create a cryptographic hash code of the file's contents using the ComputeHash method of the System.
Security.Cryptography.HashAlgorithm class. Store the hash code for future comparison against
newly generated hash codes.

How It Works

As well as allowing you to store passwords securely (discussed in recipe 11-14), hash codes provide
an excellent means of determining if a file has changed. By calculating and storing the cryptographic
hash of a file, you can later recalculate the hash of the file to determine if the file has changed in the
interim. A hashing algorithm will produce a very different hash code even if the file has been changed
only slightly, and the chances of two different files resulting in the same hash code are extremely small.

■**Caution** Standard hash codes are not suitable for sending with a file to ensure the integrity of the file's contents.
If someone intercepts the file in transit, that person can easily change the file and recalculate the hash code, leaving
the recipient none the wiser. Recipe 11-17 discusses a variant of the hash code—a keyed hash code—that is
suitable for ensuring the integrity of a file in transit.

The HashAlgorithm class makes it easy to generate the hash code of a file. First, instantiate one of the concrete hashing algorithm implementations derived from the HashAlgorithm class. To instantiate the desired hashing algorithm class, pass the name of the hashing algorithm to the HashAlgorithm.Create method, as described in recipe 11-14. See Table 11-4 for a list of valid hashing algorithm names. Then, instead of passing a byte array to the ComputeHash method, you pass a System.IO.Stream object representing the file from which you want to generate the hash code. The HashAlgorithm object handles the process of reading data from the Stream and returns a byte array containing the hash code for the file.

The Code

The example shown here demonstrates the generation of a hash code from a file. The application expects two command-line arguments: the name of the hashing algorithm to use and the name of the file from which the hash is calculated.

```
using System;
using System.IO;
using System.Security.Cryptography;

namespace Apress.VisualCSharpRecipes.Chapter11
{
    class Recipe11_15
    {
        public static void Main(string[] args)
        {
            // Create a HashAlgorithm of the type specified by the first
            // command-line argument.
            using (HashAlgorithm hashAlg = HashAlgorithm.Create(args[0]))
            {
                // Open a FileStream to the file specified by the second
                // command-line argument.
                using (Stream file =
                    new FileStream(args[1], FileMode.Open, FileAccess.Read))
                {
                    // Generate the hash code of the file's contents.
                    byte[] hash = hashAlg.ComputeHash(file);

                    // Display the hash code of the file to the console.
                    Console.WriteLine(BitConverter.ToString(hash));
                }

                // Wait to continue.
                Console.WriteLine("\nMain method complete. Press Enter.");
                Console.ReadLine();
            }
        }
    }
}
```

Usage

Running this command:

```
Recipe11-15 SHA1 Recipe11-15.exe
```

will display the following hash code to the console:

```
CA-67-A5-2D-EC-E9-FC-45-AE-97-E9-E1-38-CB-17-86-BB-17-EE-30
```

In contrast, executing this command:

```
Recipe11-15 RIPEMD-160 Recipe11-15.exe
```

will display the following hash code:

```
E1-6E-FA-BB-89-BA-DA-83-20-D5-CA-EC-FC-3D-52-13-86-B9-41-7C
```

11-16. Verify a Hash Code

Problem

You need to verify a password or confirm that a file remains unchanged by comparing two hash codes.

Solution

Convert both the old and the new hash codes to hexadecimal code strings, Base64 strings, or `byte` arrays and compare them.

How It Works

You can use hash codes to determine if two pieces of data (such as passwords or files) are the same, without the need to store, or even maintain access to, the original data. To determine if data changes over time, you must generate and store the original data's hash code. Later, you can generate another hash code for the data and compare the old and new hash codes, which will show if any change has occurred. The format in which you store the original hash code will determine the most appropriate way to verify a newly generated hash code against the stored one.

■**Note** The recipes in this chapter use the `ToString` method of the class `System.BitConverter` to convert `byte` arrays to hexadecimal string values for display. Although easy to use and appropriate for display purposes, you might find this approach inappropriate for use when storing hash codes, because it places a hyphen (-) between each byte value (for example, 4D-79-3A-C9-. . .). In addition, the `BitConverter` class does not provide a method to parse such a string representation back into a `byte` array.

Hash codes are often stored in text files, either as hexadecimal strings (for example, 89D22213170A9CFF09A392F00E2C6C4EDC1B0EF9), or as Base64-encoded strings (for example, idIiExcKnP8Jo5LwDixsTtwbDvk=). Alternatively, hash codes may be stored in databases as raw byte values. Regardless of how you store your hash code, the first step in comparing old and new hash codes is to get them both into a common form.

The Code

This following example contains three methods that use different approaches to compare hash codes:

- VerifyHexHash: This method converts a new hash code (a byte array) to a hexadecimal string for comparison to an old hash code. Other than the BitConverter.ToString method, the .NET Framework class library does not provide an easy method to convert a byte array to a hexadecimal string. You must program a loop to step through the elements of the byte array, convert each individual byte to a string, and append the string to the hexadecimal string representation of the hash code. The use of a System.Text.StringBuilder avoids the unnecessary creation of new strings each time the loop appends the next byte value to the result string. (See recipe 2-1 for more details.)

- VerifyB64Hash: This method takes a new hash code as a byte array and the old hash code as a Base64-encoded string. The method encodes the new hash code as a Base64 string and performs a straightforward string comparison of the two values.

- VerifyByteHash: This method compares two hash codes represented as byte arrays. The .NET Framework class library does not include a method that performs this type of comparison, and so you must program a loop to compare the elements of the two arrays. This code uses a few timesaving techniques, namely ensuring that the byte arrays are the same length before starting to compare them and returning false on the first difference found.

```csharp
using System;
using System.Text;

namespace Apress.VisualCSharpRecipes.Chapter11
{
    class Recipe11_16
    {
        // A method to compare a newly generated hash code with an
        // existing hash code that's represented by a hex code string
        public static bool VerifyHexHash(byte[] hash, string oldHashString)
        {
            // Create a string representation of the hash code bytes.
            StringBuilder newHashString = new StringBuilder(hash.Length);

            // Append each byte as a two-character uppercase hex string.
            foreach (byte b in hash)
            {
                newHashString.AppendFormat("{0:X2}", b);
            }

            // Compare the string representations of the old and new hash
            // codes and return the result.
            return (oldHashString == newHashString.ToString());
        }

        // A method to compare a newly generated hash code with an
        // existing hash code that's represented by a Base64-encoded string.
        private static bool VerifyB64Hash(byte[] hash, string oldHashString)
        {
            // Create a Base64 representation of the hash code bytes.
            string newHashString = Convert.ToBase64String(hash);

            // Compare the string representations of the old and new hash
            // codes and return the result.
            return (oldHashString == newHashString);
        }
```

```
        // A method to compare a newly generated hash code with an
        // existing hash code represented by a byte array.
        private static bool VerifyByteHash(byte[] hash, byte[] oldHash)
        {
            // If either array is null or the arrays are different lengths,
            // then they are not equal.
            if (hash == null || oldHash == null || hash.Length != oldHash.Length)
                return false;

            // Step through the byte arrays and compare each byte value.
            for (int count = 0; count < hash.Length; count++)
            {
                if (hash[count] != oldHash[count]) return false;
            }

            // Hash codes are equal.
            return true;
        }
    }
}
```

11-17. Ensure Data Integrity Using a Keyed Hash Code

Problem

You need to transmit a file to someone and provide the recipient with a means to verify the integrity of the file and its source.

Solution

Share a secret key with the intended recipient. This key would ideally be a randomly generated number, but it could also be a phrase that you and the recipient agree to use. Use the key with one of the keyed hashing algorithm classes derived from the `System.Security.Cryptography.KeyedHashAlgorithm` class to create a keyed hash code. Send the hash code with the file. On receipt of the file, the recipient will generate the keyed hash code of the file using the shared secret key. If the hash codes are equal, the recipient knows that the file is from you and that it has not changed in transit.

How It Works

Hash codes are useful for comparing two pieces of data to determine if they are the same, even if you no longer have access to the original data. However, you cannot use a hash code to reassure the recipient of data as to the data's integrity. If someone could intercept the data, that person could replace the data and generate a new hash code. When the recipient verifies the hash code, it will seem correct, even though the data is actually nothing like what you sent originally.

A simple and efficient solution to the problem of data integrity is a *keyed hash code*. A keyed hash code is similar to a normal hash code (discussed in recipes 11-14 and 11-15); however, the keyed hash code incorporates an element of secret data—a *key*—known only to the sender and the receiver. Without the key, a person cannot generate the correct hash code from a given set of data. When you successfully verify a keyed hash code, you can be certain that only someone who knows the secret key could generate the hash code.

■**Caution** The secret key must remain secret. Anyone who knows the secret key can generate valid keyed hash codes, meaning that you would be unable to determine if someone else who knew the key had changed the content of a document. For this reason, you should not transmit or store the secret key with the document whose integrity you are trying to protect.

Generating keyed hash codes is similar to generating normal hash codes. The abstract class System.Security.Cryptography.KeyedHashAlgorithm extends the class System.Security.Cryptography. HashAlgorithm and provides a base class from which all concrete keyed hashing algorithm implementations must derive. The .NET Framework class library includes the seven keyed hashing algorithm implementations listed in Table 11-5. Each implementation is a member of the namespace System.Security.Cryptography.

Table 11-5. *Keyed Hashing Algorithm Implementations*

Algorithm/Class Name	Key Size (in Bits)	Hash Code Size (in Bits)
HMACMD5 (new in .NET 2.0)	Any	128
HMACRIPEMD160 (new in .NET 2.0)	Any	160
HMACSHA1	Any	160
HMACSHA256 (new in .NET 2.0)	Any	256
HMACSHA384 (new in .NET 2.0)	Any	384
HMACSHA512 (new in .NET 2.0)	Any	512
MACTripleDES	128, 192	64

As with the standard hashing algorithms, you can either create keyed hashing algorithm objects directly or use the static factory method KeyedHashAlgorithm.Create and pass the algorithm name as an argument. Using the factory approach allows you to write generic code that can work with any keyed hashing algorithm implementation, but as shown in Table 11-5, MACTripleDES supports fixed key lengths that you must accommodate in generic code.

If you use constructors to instantiate a keyed hashing object, you can pass the secret key to the constructor. Using the factory approach, you must set the key using the Key property inherited from the KeyedHashAlgorithm class. Then call the ComputeHash method and pass either a byte array or a System.IO.Stream object. The keyed hashing algorithm will process the input data and return a byte array containing the keyed hash code. Table 11-5 shows the size of hash code generated by each keyed hashing algorithm.

The Code

The following example demonstrates the generation of a keyed hash code from a file. The example uses the given class to generate the keyed hash code, and then displays it to the console. The example requires three command-line arguments: the name of the file from which the hash is calculated, the name of the class to instantiate, and the key to use when calculating the hash.

```
using System;
using System.IO;
using System.Text;
using System.Security.Cryptography;
```

```
namespace Apress.VisualCSharpRecipes.Chapter11
{
    class Recipe11_17
    {
        public static void Main(string[] args)
        {
            // Create a byte array from the key string, which is the
            // second command-line argument.
            byte[] key = Encoding.Unicode.GetBytes(args[2]);

            // Create a KeyedHashAlgorithm derived object to generate the keyed
            // hash code for the input file. Pass the byte array representing the
            // key to the constructor.
            using (KeyedHashAlgorithm hashAlg = KeyedHashAlgorithm.Create(args[1]))
            {
                // Assign the key.
                hashAlg.Key = key;

                // Open a FileStream to read the input file. The filename is
                // specified by the first command-line argument.
                using (Stream file =
                    new FileStream(args[0], FileMode.Open, FileAccess.Read))
                {
                    // Generate the keyed hash code of the file's contents.
                    byte[] hash = hashAlg.ComputeHash(file);

                    // Display the keyed hash code to the console.
                    Console.WriteLine(BitConverter.ToString(hash));
                }
            }

            // Wait to continue.
            Console.WriteLine("\nMain method complete. Press Enter.");
            Console.ReadLine();
        }
    }
}
```

Usage

Executing the following command:

`Recipe11-17 Recipe11-17.exe HMACSHA1 secretKey`

will display the following hash code to the console:

`2E-5B-9B-2C-91-42-BA-4E-98-DF-39-F6-AE-89-B6-44-61-FB-32-E7`

In contrast, executing this command:

`Recipe11-17 Recipe11-17.exe HMACSHA1 anotherKey`

will display the following hash code to the console:

`EF-64-79-3A-3C-A4-44-01-AD-9E-94-2A-B4-58-CF-42-84-3E-27-91`

11-18. Work with Security-Sensitive Strings in Memory

Problem

You need to work with sensitive string data, such as passwords or credit card numbers, in memory and need to minimize the risk of other people or processes accessing that data.

Solution

Use the class System.Security.SecureString to hold the sensitive data values in memory.

How It Works

Storing sensitive data such as passwords, personal details, and banking information in memory as String objects is insecure for many reasons, including the following:

- String objects are not encrypted.

- The immutability of String objects means that whenever you change the String, the old String value is left in memory until it is garbage-collected and later overwritten.

- Because the garbage collector is free to reorganize the contents of the managed heap, multiple copies of your sensitive data may be present on the heap.

- If part of your process address space is swapped to disk or a memory dump is written to disk, a copy of your data may be stored on the disk.

Each of these factors increases the opportunities for others to access your sensitive data. In .NET Framework versions 1.0 and 1.1, one solution to these problems is to use byte arrays to hold an encrypted version of the sensitive data. You have much better control over a byte array than you do with a string; principally, you can wipe the array any time you like. The .NET Framework 2.0 introduces the SecureString class to simplify the task of working with sensitive string data in memory.

You create a SecureString as either initially empty or from a pointer to a character (char) array. Then you manipulate the contents of the SecureString one character at a time using the methods AppendChar, InsertAt, RemoveAt, and SetAt. As you add characters to the SecureString, they are encrypted using the capabilities of the Data Protection API.

■**Note** The SecureString class uses features of Data Protection API (DPAPI) and is available only on Windows 2000 SP3 and later operating system versions.

The SecureString class also provides a method named MakeReadOnly. As the name suggests, calling MakeReadOnly configures the SecureString to no longer allow its value to be changed. Attempting to modify a SecureString marked as read-only results in the exception System.InvalidOperationException being thrown. Once you have set the SecureString to read-only, it cannot be undone.

The SecureString class has a ToString method, but this does not retrieve a string representation of the contained data. Instead, the class System.Runtime.InteropServices.Marshal implements a number of static methods that take a SecureString object; decrypts it; converts it to a binary string, a block of ANSI, or a block of Unicode data; and returns a System.IntPtr object that points to the converted data.

At any time, you can call the SecureString.Clear method to clear the sensitive data, and when you have finished with the SecureString object, call its Dispose method to clear the data and free the memory. SecureString implements System.IDisposable.

■**Note** Although it might seem that the benefits of the SecureString class are limited, because there is no way in Windows Forms applications to get such a secured string from the GUI without first retrieving a nonsecured String through a TextBox or another control, it is likely that third parties and future additions to the .NET Framework will use the SecureString class to handle sensitive data. This is already the case in System.Diagnostics. ProcessStartInfo, where using a SecureString, you can set the Password property to the password of the user context in which the new process should be run.

The Code

The following example reads a username and password from the console and starts Notepad.exe as the specified user. The password is masked on input and stored in a SecureString in memory, maximizing the chances of the password remaining secret.

```csharp
using System;
using System.Security;
using System.Diagnostics;

namespace Apress.VisualCSharpRecipes.Chapter11
{
    class Recipe11_18
    {
        public static SecureString ReadString()
        {
            // Create a new emtpty SecureString.
            SecureString str = new SecureString();

            // Read the string from the console one
            // character at a time without displaying it.
            ConsoleKeyInfo nextChar = Console.ReadKey(true);

            // Read characters until Enter is pressed.
            while (nextChar.Key != ConsoleKey.Enter)
            {
                if (nextChar.Key == ConsoleKey.Backspace)
                {
                    if (str.Length > 0)
                    {
                        // Backspace pressed, remove the last character.
                        str.RemoveAt(str.Length - 1);

                        Console.Write(nextChar.KeyChar);
                        Console.Write(" ");
                        Console.Write(nextChar.KeyChar);
                    }
                    else
                    {
                        Console.Beep();
                    }
```

```csharp
            }
            else
            {
                // Append the character to the SecureString and
                // display a masked character.
                str.AppendChar(nextChar.KeyChar);
                Console.Write("*");
            }

            // Read the next character.
            nextChar = Console.ReadKey(true);
        }

        // String entry finished. Make it read-only.
        str.MakeReadOnly();
        return str;
    }

    public static void Main()
    {
        string user = "";

        // Get the username under which Notepad.exe will be run.
        Console.Write("Enter the user name: ");
        user = Console.ReadLine();

        // Get the user's password as a SecureString.
        Console.Write("Enter the user's password: ");
        using (SecureString pword = ReadString())
        {
            // Start Notepad as the specified user.
            ProcessStartInfo startInfo = new ProcessStartInfo();

            startInfo.FileName = "notepad.exe";
            startInfo.UserName = user;
            startInfo.Password = pword;
            startInfo.UseShellExecute = false;

            // Create a new Process object.
            using (Process process = new Process())
            {
                // Assign the ProcessStartInfo to the Process object.
                process.StartInfo = startInfo;

                try
                {
                    // Start the new process.
                    process.Start();
                }
                catch (Exception ex)
                {
                    Console.WriteLine("\n\nCould not start Notepad process.");
                    Console.WriteLine(ex);
                }
            }
        }
    }
```

```
        // Wait to continue.
        Console.WriteLine("\n\nMain method complete. Press Enter.");
        Console.ReadLine();
    }
  }
}
```

11-19. Encrypt and Decrypt Data Using the Data Protection API

Problem

You need a convenient way to securely encrypt data without the headache associated with key management.

Solution

Use the ProtectedData and ProtectedMemory classes of the System.Security.Cryptography name-space in .NET Framework 2.0 to access the encryption and key management capabilities provided by the Data Protection API (DPAPI).

How It Works

Given that the .NET Framework provides you with well-tested implementations of the most widely used and trusted encryption algorithms, the biggest challenge you face when using cryptography is key management, namely the effective generation, storage, and sharing of keys to facilitate the use of cryptography. In fact, key management is the biggest problem facing most people when they want to securely store or transmit data using cryptographic techniques. If implemented incorrectly, key management can easily render useless all of your efforts to encrypt your data.

DPAPI provides encryption and decryption services without the need for you to worry about key management. DPAPI automatically generates keys based on Windows user credentials, stores keys securely as part of your profile, and even provides automated key expiry without losing access to previously encrypted data.

Note DPAPI is suitable for many common uses of cryptography in Windows applications, but will not help you in situations that require you to distribute or share secret or public keys with other users.

In versions 1.0 and 1.1 of the .NET Framework, you needed to use P/Invoke to work with DPAPI. .NET Framework 2.0 introduces in System.Security.dll two managed classes that provide easy access to the encryption and decryption capabilities of DPAPI: ProtectedData and ProtectedMemory. Both classes allow you to encrypt a byte array by passing it to the static method Protect, and decrypt a byte array of encrypted data by passing it the static method Unprotect. The difference in the classes is in the scope that they allow you to specify when you encrypt and decrypt data.

Caution You must use ProtectedData if you intend to store encrypted data and reboot your machine before decrypting it. ProtectedMemory will be unable to decrypt data that was encrypted before a reboot.

When you call `ProtectedData.Protect`, you specify a value from the enumeration `System.Security.Cryptography.DataProtectionScope`. The following are the possible values:

- `CurrentUser`, which means that only code running in the context of the current user can decrypt the data

- `LocalMachine`, which means that any code running on the same computer can decrypt the data

When you call `ProtectedMemory.Protect`, you specify a value from the enumeration `System.Security.Cryptography.MemoryProtectionScope`. The possible values are as follows:

- `CrossProcess`, which means that any code in any process can decrypt the encrypted data

- `SameLogon`, which means that only code running in the same user context can decrypt the data

- `SameProcess`, which means that only code running in the same process can decrypt the data

Both classes allow you to specify additional data (*entropy*) when you encrypt your data. Entropy makes certain types of cryptographic attacks less likely to succeed. If you choose to use entropy when you protect data, you must use the same entropy value when you unprotect the data. It is not essential that you keep the entropy data secret, so it can be stored freely without encryption.

The Code

The following example demonstrates the use of the `ProtectedData` class to encrypt a string entered at the console by the user. Note that you need to reference the `System.Security.dll` assembly.

```
using System;
using System.Text;
using System.Security.Cryptography;

namespace Apress.VisualCSharpRecipes.Chapter11
{
    class Recipe11_19
    {
        public static void Main()
        {
            // Read the string from the console.
            Console.Write("Enter the string to encrypt: ");
            string str = Console.ReadLine();

            // Create a byte array of entropy to use in the encryption process.
            byte[] entropy = { 0, 1, 2, 3, 4, 5, 6, 7, 8 };

            // Encrypt the entered string after converting it to
            // a byte array. Use CurrentUser scope so that only
            // the current user can decrypt the data.
            byte[] enc = ProtectedData.Protect(Encoding.Unicode.GetBytes(str),
                entropy, DataProtectionScope.LocalMachine);

            // Display the encrypted data to the console.
            Console.WriteLine("\nEncrypted string = {0}",
                BitConverter.ToString(enc));

            // Attempt to decrypt the data using CurrentUser scope.
            byte[] dec = ProtectedData.Unprotect(enc,
                entropy, DataProtectionScope.CurrentUser);
```

```
        // Display the data decrypted using CurrentUser scope.
        Console.WriteLine("\nDecrypted data using CurrentUser scope = {0}",
            Encoding.Unicode.GetString(dec));

        // Wait to continue.
        Console.WriteLine("\nMain method complete. Press Enter.");
        Console.ReadLine();
    }
  }
}
```

CHAPTER 12

Unmanaged Code Interoperability

The Microsoft .NET Framework is an extremely ambitious platform, combining a managed runtime (the common language runtime, or CLR), a platform for hosting web applications (Microsoft ASP.NET), and an extensive class library for building all types of applications. However, as expansive as the .NET Framework is, it does not duplicate all the features that are available in unmanaged code. Currently, the .NET Framework does not include every function that is available in the Win32 API, and many businesses are using complex proprietary solutions that they have built with COM-based languages such as Microsoft Visual Basic 6 and Visual C++ 6.

Fortunately, Microsoft does not intend for businesses to abandon the code base they have built up when they move to the .NET platform. Instead, the .NET Framework is equipped with interoperability features that allow you to use legacy code from .NET Framework applications and even access .NET assemblies as though they were COM components. The recipes in this chapter describe how to do the following:

- Call functions defined in a DLL, get the handles for a control or window, invoke an unmanaged function that uses a structure, invoke unmanaged callback functions, and retrieve unmanaged error information (recipes 12-1 through 12-5)

- Use COM components from .NET Framework applications, release COM components, and use optional parameters (recipes 12-6 through 12-8)

- Use ActiveX controls from .NET Framework applications (recipe 12-9)

- Expose the functionality of a .NET assembly as a COM component (recipe 12-10)

12-1. Call a Function in an Unmanaged DLL

Problem

You need to call a C function in a DLL. This function might be a part of the Win32 API or your own legacy code.

Solution

Declare a method in your C# code that you will use to access the unmanaged function. Declare this method as both `extern` and `static`, and apply the attribute `System.Runtime.InteropServices.DllImportAttribute` to specify the DLL file and the name of the unmanaged function.

How It Works

To use a C function from an external library, all you need to do is declare it appropriately. The common language runtime (CLR) automatically handles the rest, including loading the DLL into memory when the function is called and marshaling the parameters from .NET data types to C data types. The .NET service that supports this cross-platform execution is named PInvoke (Platform Invoke), and the process is usually seamless. Occasionally, you will need to do a little more work, such as when you need to support in-memory structures, callbacks, or mutable strings.

PInvoke is often used to access functionality in the Win32 API, particularly Win32 features that are not present in the set of managed classes that make up the .NET Framework. Three core libraries make up the Win32 API:

- Kernel32.dll includes operating system-specific functionality such as process loading, context switching, and file and memory I/O.

- User32.dll includes functionality for manipulating windows, menus, dialog boxes, icons, and so on.

- GDI32.dll includes graphical capabilities for drawing directly on windows, menus, and control surfaces, as well as for printing.

As an example, consider the Win32 API functions used for writing and reading INI files, such as GetPrivateProfileString and WritePrivateProfileString, in Kernel32.dll. The .NET Framework does not include any classes that wrap this functionality. However, you can import these functions using the attribute DllImportAttribute, like this:

```
[DllImport("kernel32.DLL", EntryPoint="WritePrivateProfileString")]
private static extern bool WritePrivateProfileString(string lpAppName,
    string lpKeyName, string lpString, string lpFileName);
```

The arguments specified in the signature of the WritePrivateProfileString method must match the DLL method, or a runtime error will occur when you attempt to invoke it. Remember that you do not define any method body, because the declaration refers to a method in the DLL. The EntryPoint portion of the attribute DllImportAttribute is optional in this example. You do not need to specify the EntryPoint when the declared function name matches the function name in the external library.

The Code

The following is an example of using some Win32 API functions to get INI file information. It declares the unmanaged functions used and exposes public methods to call them. (Other Win32 API functions for getting INI file information not shown in this example include those that retrieve all the sections in an INI file.) The code first displays the current value of a key in the INI file, modifies it, retrieves the new value, and then writes the default value.

```
using System;
using System.Runtime.InteropServices;
using System.Text;

namespace Apress.VisualCSharpRecipes.Chapter12
{
    class Recipe12_01
    {
        // Declare the unmanaged functions.
        [DllImport("kernel32.dll", EntryPoint = "GetPrivateProfileString")]
        private static extern int GetPrivateProfileString(string lpAppName,
            string lpKeyName, string lpDefault, StringBuilder lpReturnedString,
            int nSize, string lpFileName);
```

```csharp
[DllImport("kernel32.dll", EntryPoint = "WritePrivateProfileString")]
private static extern bool WritePrivateProfileString(string lpAppName,
  string lpKeyName, string lpString, string lpFileName);

static void Main(string[] args)
{
    string val;

    // Obtain current value.
    val = GetIniValue("SampleSection", "Key1", "\\initest.ini");
    Console.WriteLine("Value of Key1 in [SampleSection] is: "
        + val);

    // Write a new value.
    WriteIniValue("SampleSection", "Key1", "New Value",
        "\\initest.ini");

    // Obtain the new value.
    val = GetIniValue("SampleSection", "Key1", "\\initest.ini");
    Console.WriteLine("Value of Key1 in [SampleSection] is now: "
        + val);

    // Write original value.
    WriteIniValue("SampleSection", "Key1", "Value1",
        "\\initest.ini");

    // Wait to continue.
    Console.WriteLine(Environment.NewLine);
    Console.WriteLine("Main method complete. Press Enter.");
    Console.ReadLine();
}

public static string GetIniValue(string section, string key,
    string filename)
{
    int chars = 256;
    StringBuilder buffer = new StringBuilder(chars);
    string sDefault = "";
    if (GetPrivateProfileString(section, key, sDefault,
      buffer, chars, filename) != 0)
    {
        return buffer.ToString();
    }
    else
    {
        return null;
    }
}

public static bool WriteIniValue(string section, string key,
    string value, string filename)
{
    return WritePrivateProfileString(section, key, value, filename);
}
    }
}
```

> **Note** The GetPrivateProfileString method is declared with one StringBuilder parameter (lpReturnedString). This is because this string must be mutable; when the call completes, it will contain the returned INI file information. Whenever you need a mutable string, you must substitute StringBuilder in place of the String class. Often, you will need to create the StringBuilder object with a character buffer of a set size, and then pass the size of the buffer to the function as another parameter. You can specify the number of characters in the StringBuilder constructor. See recipe 2-1 for more information about using the StringBuilder class.

Usage

You can test this program quite easily. First, in the application folder, create the inittest.ini file shown here:

```
[SampleSection]
Key1=Value1
```

Now, execute Recipe12-01.exe. You will get an output such as this:

```
Value of Key1 in [SampleSection] is: Value1
Value of Key1 in [SampleSection] is now: New Value


Main method complete. Press Enter.
```

12-2. Get the Handle for a Control, Window, or File

Problem

You need to call an unmanaged function that requires the handle for a control, a window, or a file.

Solution

Many classes, including all Control-derived classes and the FileStream class, return the handle of the unmanaged Windows object they are wrapping as an IntPtr through a property named Handle. Other classes also provide similar information; for example, the System.Diagnostics.Process class provides a Process.MainWindowHandle property in addition to the Handle property.

How It Works

The .NET Framework does not hide underlying details such as the operating system handles used for controls and windows. Although you usually will not use this information, you can retrieve it if you need to call an unmanaged function that requires it. Many Microsoft Windows API functions, for example, require control or window handles.

The Code

As an example, consider the Windows-based application shown in Figure 12-1. It consists of a single window that always stays on top of all other windows regardless of focus. (This behavior is enforced by setting the Form.TopMost property to true.) The form also includes a timer that periodically calls the unmanaged GetForegroundWindow and GetWindowText WinAPI functions to determine which window is currently active.

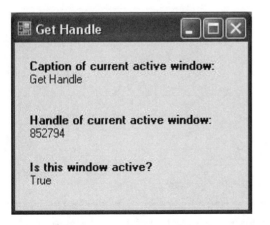

Figure 12-1. *Retrieving information about the active window*

One additional detail in this example is that the code also uses the Form.Handle property to get the handle of the main application form. It then compares with the handle of the active form to test if the current application has focus. The following is the complete code for this form.

```csharp
using System;
using System.Windows.Forms;
using System.Runtime.InteropServices;
using System.Text;

namespace Apress.VisualCSharpRecipes.Chapter12
{
    public partial class ActiveWindowInfo : Form
    {
        public ActiveWindowInfo()
        {
            InitializeComponent();
        }

        // Declare external functions.
        [DllImport("user32.dll")]
        private static extern IntPtr GetForegroundWindow();

        [DllImport("user32.dll")]
        private static extern int GetWindowText(IntPtr hWnd,
            StringBuilder text, int count);

        private void tmrRefresh_Tick(object sender, EventArgs e)
        {
            int chars = 256;
            StringBuilder buff = new StringBuilder(chars);

            // Obtain the handle of the active window.
            IntPtr handle = GetForegroundWindow();

            // Update the controls.
            if (GetWindowText(handle, buff, chars) > 0)
            {
                lblCaption.Text = buff.ToString();
```

```
        lblHandle.Text = handle.ToString();
        if (handle == this.Handle)
        {
            lblCurrent.Text = "True";
        }
        else
        {
            lblCurrent.Text = "False";
        }
    }
  }
 }
}
```

■**Caution** The Windows Forms infrastructure manages window handles for forms and controls transparently. Changing some of their properties can force the CLR to create a new native window behind the scenes, and a new handle gets wrapped with a different handle. For that reason, you should always retrieve the handle before you use it (rather than storing it in a member variable for a long period of time).

12-3. Call an Unmanaged Function That Uses a Structure

Problem

You need to call an unmanaged function that accepts a structure as a parameter.

Solution

Define the structure in your C# code. Use the attribute `System.Runtime.InteropServices.StructLayoutAttribute` to configure how the structure fields are laid out in memory. Use the `static` `SizeOf` method of the `System.Runtime.Interop.Marshal` class if you need to determine the size of the unmanaged structure in bytes.

How It Works

In pure C# code, you are not able to directly control how type fields are laid out once the memory is allocated. Instead, the CLR is free to arrange fields to optimize performance, especially in the context of moving memory around during garbage collection. This can cause problems when interacting with legacy C functions that expect structures to be laid out sequentially in memory to follow their definition in include files. Fortunately, the .NET Framework allows you to solve this problem by using the attribute `StructLayoutAttribute`, which lets you specify how the members of a given class or structure should be arranged in memory.

The Code

As an example, consider the unmanaged `GetVersionEx` function provided in the Kernel32.dll file. This function accepts a pointer to an `OSVERSIONINFO` structure and uses it to return information about the current operating system version. To use the `OSVERSIONINFO` structure in C# code, you must define it with the attribute `StructLayoutAttribute`, as shown here:

```
[StructLayout(LayoutKind.Sequential)]
public class OSVersionInfo {

    public int dwOSVersionInfoSize;
    public int dwMajorVersion;
    public int dwMinorVersion;
    public int dwBuildNumber;
    public int dwPlatformId;
    [MarshalAs(UnmanagedType.ByValTStr, SizeConst=128)]
    public String szCSDVersion;
}
```

Notice that this structure also uses the attribute System.Runtime.InteropServices.
MarshalAsAttribute, which is required for fixed-length strings. In this example, MarshalAsAttribute
specifies the string will be passed by value and will contain a buffer of exactly 128 characters, as specified
in the OSVERSIONINFO structure. This example uses sequential layout, which means the data types in
the structure are laid out in the order they are listed in the class or structure. When using sequential
layout, you can also configure the packing for the structure by specifying a named Pack field in the
StructLayoutAttribute constructor. The default is 8, which means the structure will be packed on
8-byte boundaries.

Instead of using sequential layout, you could use LayoutKind.Explicit; in which case, you
must define the byte offset of each field using FieldOffsetAttribute. This layout is useful when
dealing with an irregularly packed structure or one where you want to omit some of the fields that
you do not want to use. Here is an example that defines the OSVersionInfo class with explicit layout:

```
[StructLayout(LayoutKind.Explicit)]
public class OSVersionInfo {

    [FieldOffset(0)]public int dwOSVersionInfoSize;
    [FieldOffset(4)]public int dwMajorVersion;
    [FieldOffset(8)]public int dwMinorVersion;
    [FieldOffset(12)]public int dwBuildNumber;
    [FieldOffset(16)]public int dwPlatformId;
    [MarshalAs(UnmanagedType.ByValTStr, SizeConst=128)]
    [FieldOffset(20)]public String szCSDVersion;
}
```

Now that you've defined the structure used by the GetVersionEx function, you can declare the
function and then use it. The following console application shows all the code you will need. Notice
that InAttribute and OutAttribute are applied to the OSVersionInfo parameter to indicate that
marshaling should be performed on this structure when it is passed to the function and when it is
returned from the function. In addition, the code uses the Marshal.SizeOf method to calculate the
size the marshaled structure will occupy in memory.

```
using System;
using System.Runtime.InteropServices;

namespace Apress.VisualCSharpRecipes.Chapter12
{
    class Recipe12_03
    {
        // Declare the external function.
        [DllImport("kernel32.dll")]
        public static extern bool GetVersionEx([In, Out] OSVersionInfo osvi);

        static void Main(string[] args)
        {
```

```
            OSVersionInfo osvi = new OSVersionInfo();
            osvi.dwOSVersionInfoSize = Marshal.SizeOf(osvi);

            // Obtain the OS version information.
            GetVersionEx(osvi);

            // Display the version information.
            Console.WriteLine("Class size: " + osvi.dwOSVersionInfoSize);
            Console.WriteLine("Major Version: " + osvi.dwMajorVersion);
            Console.WriteLine("Minor Version: " + osvi.dwMinorVersion);
            Console.WriteLine("Build Number: " + osvi.dwBuildNumber);
            Console.WriteLine("Platform Id: " + osvi.dwPlatformId);
            Console.WriteLine("CSD Version: " + osvi.szCSDVersion);
            Console.WriteLine("Platform: " + Environment.OSVersion.Platform);
            Console.WriteLine("Version: " + Environment.OSVersion.Version);

            // Wait to continue.
            Console.WriteLine(Environment.NewLine);
            Console.WriteLine("Main method complete. Press Enter.");
            Console.ReadLine();
        }
    }

    // Define the structure and specify the layout type as sequential.
    [StructLayout(LayoutKind.Sequential)]
    public class OSVersionInfo
    {
        public int dwOSVersionInfoSize;
        public int dwMajorVersion;
        public int dwMinorVersion;
        public int dwBuildNumber;
        public int dwPlatformId;
        [MarshalAs(UnmanagedType.ByValTStr, SizeConst = 128)]
        public String szCSDVersion;
    }
}
```

Usage

If you run this application on a Windows XP system, you will see information such as this:

```
Class size: 148
Major Version: 5
Minor Version: 1
Build Number: 2600
Platform Id: 2
CSD Version: Service Pack 2
Platform: Win32NT
Version: 5.1.2600.131072
```

12-4. Call an Unmanaged Function That Uses a Callback

Problem

You need to call an unmanaged function and allow it to call a method in your code.

Solution

Create a delegate that has the required signature for the callback. Use this delegate when defining and using the unmanaged function.

How It Works

Many of the Win32 API functions use callbacks. For example, if you want to retrieve the name of all the top-level windows that are currently open, you can call the unmanaged EnumWindows function in the User32.dll file. When calling EnumWindows, you need to supply a pointer to a function in your code. The Windows operating system will then call this function repeatedly, once for each top-level window that it finds, and pass the window handle to your code.

The .NET Framework allows you to handle callback scenarios like this without resorting to pointers and unsafe code blocks. Instead, you can define and use a delegate that points to your call-back function. When you pass the delegate to the EnumWindows function, for example, the CLR will automatically marshal the delegate to the expected unmanaged function pointer.

The Code

Following is a console application that uses EnumWindows with a callback to display the name of every open window.

```
using System;
using System.Text;
using System.Runtime.InteropServices;

namespace Apress.VisualCSharpRecipes.Chapter12
{
    class Recipe12_04
    {
        // The signature for the callback method.
        public delegate bool CallBack(IntPtr hwnd, int lParam);

        // The unmanaged function that will trigger the callback
        // as it enumerates the open windows.
        [DllImport("user32.dll")]
        public static extern int EnumWindows(CallBack callback, int param);

        [DllImport("user32.dll")]
        public static extern int GetWindowText(IntPtr hWnd,
            StringBuilder lpString, int nMaxCount);
```

```
static void Main(string[] args)
{
    // Request that the operating system enumerate all windows,
    // and trigger your callback with the handle of each one.
    EnumWindows(DisplayWindowInfo, 0);

    // Wait to continue.
    Console.WriteLine(Environment.NewLine);
    Console.WriteLine("Main method complete. Press Enter.");
    Console.ReadLine();
}

// The method that will receive the callback. The second
// parameter is not used, but is needed to match the
// callback's signature.
public static bool DisplayWindowInfo(IntPtr hWnd, int lParam)
{
    int chars = 100;
    StringBuilder buf = new StringBuilder(chars);
    if (GetWindowText(hWnd, buf, chars) != 0)
    {
        Console.WriteLine(buf);
    }
    return true;
}
}
}
```

12-5. Retrieve Unmanaged Error Information

Problem

You need to retrieve error information (either an error code or a text message) explaining why a Win32 API call failed.

Solution

On the declaration of the unmanaged method, set the SetLastError field of the DllImportAttribute to true. If an error occurs when you execute the method, call the static Marshal.GetLastWin32Error method to retrieve the error code. To get a text description for a specific error code, use the unmanaged FormatMessage function.

How It Works

You cannot retrieve error information directly using the unmanaged GetLastError function. The problem is that the error code returned by GetLastError might not reflect the error caused by the unmanaged function you are using. Instead, it might be set by other .NET Framework classes or the CLR. You can retrieve the error information safely using the static Marshal.GetLastWin32Error method. This method should be called immediately after the unmanaged call, and it will return the error information only once. (Subsequent calls to GetLastWin32Error will simply return the error code 127.) In addition, you must specifically set the SetLastError field of the DllImportAttribute to true to indicate that errors from this function should be cached.

```
[DllImport("user32.dll", SetLastError=true)]
```

You can extract additional information from the Win32 error code using the unmanaged
FormatMessage function from the Kernel32.dll file.

The Code

The following console application attempts to show a message box, but submits an invalid window
handle. The error information is retrieved with Marshal.GetLastWin32Error, and the corresponding
text information is retrieved using FormatMessage.

```csharp
using System;
using System.Runtime.InteropServices;

namespace Apress.VisualCSharpRecipes.Chapter12
{
    class Recipe12_05
    {
        // Declare the unmanaged functions.
        [DllImport("kernel32.dll")]
        private static extern int FormatMessage(int dwFlags, int lpSource,
          int dwMessageId, int dwLanguageId, ref String lpBuffer, int nSize,
          int Arguments);

        [DllImport("user32.dll", SetLastError = true)]
        public static extern int MessageBox(IntPtr hWnd, string pText,
          string pCaption, int uType);

        static void Main(string[] args)
        {
            // Invoke the MessageBox function passing an invalid
            // window handle and thus force an error.
            IntPtr badWindowHandle = (IntPtr)453;
            MessageBox(badWindowHandle, "Message", "Caption", 0);

            // Obtain the error information.
            int errorCode = Marshal.GetLastWin32Error();
            Console.WriteLine(errorCode);
            Console.WriteLine(GetErrorMessage(errorCode));

            // Wait to continue.
            Console.WriteLine(Environment.NewLine);
            Console.WriteLine("Main method complete. Press Enter.");
            Console.ReadLine();
        }

        // GetErrorMessage formats and returns an error message
        // corresponding to the input errorCode.
        public static string GetErrorMessage(int errorCode)
        {
            int FORMAT_MESSAGE_ALLOCATE_BUFFER = 0x00000100;
            int FORMAT_MESSAGE_IGNORE_INSERTS = 0x00000200;
            int FORMAT_MESSAGE_FROM_SYSTEM = 0x00001000;

            int messageSize = 255;
            string lpMsgBuf = "";
            int dwFlags = FORMAT_MESSAGE_ALLOCATE_BUFFER |
              FORMAT_MESSAGE_FROM_SYSTEM | FORMAT_MESSAGE_IGNORE_INSERTS;
```

```
            int retVal = FormatMessage(dwFlags, 0, errorCode, 0,
              ref lpMsgBuf, messageSize, 0);

            if (0 == retVal)
            {
                return null;
            }
            else
            {
                return lpMsgBuf;
            }
        }
    }
}
```

Usage

Here is the output generated by the preceding program:

```
1400
Invalid window handle.
```

12-6. Use a COM Component in a .NET Client

Problem

You need to use a COM component in a .NET client.

Solution

Use a primary interop assembly (PIA), if one is available. Otherwise, generate a runtime callable wrapper (RCW) using the Type Library Importer (Tlbimp.exe) or the Add Reference feature in Visual Studio .NET.

How It Works

The .NET Framework includes extensive support for COM interoperability. To allow .NET clients to interact with a COM component, .NET uses an RCW—a special .NET proxy class that sits between your .NET code and the COM component. The RCW handles all the details, including marshaling data types, using the traditional COM interfaces, and handling COM events.

You have the following three options for using an RCW:

- Obtain an RCW from the author of the original COM component. In this case, the RCW is created from a PIA provided by the publisher, as Microsoft does for Microsoft Office.

- Generate an RCW using the Tlbimp.exe command-line utility or Visual Studio .NET.

- Create your own RCW using the types in the System.Runtime.InteropServices namespace. (This can be an extremely tedious and complicated process.)

If you want to use Visual Studio .NET to generate an RCW, you simply need to select Project ➤ Add Reference from the menu, and then select the appropriate component from the COM tab.

When you click OK, the PIA will be generated and added to your project references. After that, you can use the Object Browser to inspect the namespaces and classes that are available.

If you are not using Visual Studio .NET, you can create a wrapper assembly using the Tlbimp.exe command-line utility that is included with the .NET Framework. The only mandatory piece of information is the filename that contains the COM component. For example, the following statement creates an RCW with the default filename and namespace, assuming that the MyCOMComponent.dll file is in the current directory.

```
tlbimp MyCOMComponent.dll
```

Assuming that `MyCOMComponent` has a type library named `MyClasses`, the generated RCW file will have the name MyClasses.dll and will expose its classes through a namespace named `MyClasses`. You can also configure these options with command-line parameters, as described in the MSDN reference. For example, you can use `/out:[Filename]` to specify a different assembly filename and `/namespace:[Namespace]` to set a different namespace for the generated classes. You can also specify a key file using `/keyfile[keyfilename]` so that the component will be signed and given a strong name, allowing it to be placed in the global assembly cache (GAC). Use the `/primary` parameter to create a PIA.

If possible, you should always use a PIA instead of generating your own RCW. PIAs are more likely to work as expected, because they are created by the original component publisher. They might also include additional .NET refinements or enhancements. If a PIA is registered on your system for a COM component, Visual Studio .NET will automatically use that PIA when you add a reference to the COM component. For example, the .NET Framework includes an adodb.dll assembly that allows you to use the ADO classic COM objects. If you add a reference to the Microsoft ActiveX Data Objects component, this PIA will be used automatically; no new RCW will be generated. Similarly, Microsoft Office 2003 provides a PIA that improves .NET support for Office Automation. However, you must download this assembly from the MSDN web site (at `http://msdn.microsoft.com/downloads/list/office.asp`).

The Code

The following example shows how you can use COM Interop to access the classic ADO objects from a .NET Framework application.

```
using System;

namespace Apress.VisualCSharpRecipes.Chapter12
{
    class Recipe12_06
    {
        static void Main(string[] args)
        {
            // Create a new ADODB connection.
            ADODB.Connection con = new ADODB.Connection();
            string connectionString = "Provider=SQLOLEDB.1;" +
              "Data Source=localhost;" +
              "Initial Catalog=Northwind;Integrated Security=SSPI";
            con.Open(connectionString, null, null, 0);

            // Execute a SELECT query.
            object recordsAffected;
            ADODB.Recordset rs = con.Execute("SELECT * From Customers",
              out recordsAffected, 0);
```

```
            // Print out the results.
            while (rs.EOF != true)
            {
                Console.WriteLine(rs.Fields["CustomerID"].Value);
                rs.MoveNext();
            }

            // Wait to continue.
            Console.WriteLine(Environment.NewLine);
            Console.WriteLine("Main method complete. Press Enter.");
            Console.ReadLine();
        }
    }
}
```

12-7. Release a COM Component Quickly

Problem

You need to ensure that a COM component is removed from memory immediately, without waiting for garbage collection to take place, or you need to make sure that COM objects are released in a specific order.

Solution

Release the reference to the underlying COM object using the static `Marshal.FinalReleaseComObject` method and passing the appropriate RCW.

How It Works

COM uses reference counting to determine when objects should be released. When you use an RCW, the reference will be held to the underlying COM object even when the object variable goes out of scope. The reference will be released only when the garbage collector disposes of the RCW object. As a result, you cannot control when or in what order COM objects will be released from memory.

To get around this limitation, you usually use the `Marshal.ReleaseComObject` method. However, if the COM object's pointer is marshaled several times, you need to repeatedly call this method to decrease the count to zero. However, the `FinalReleaseComObject` method allows you to release all references in one go, by setting the reference count of the supplied RCW to zero. This means that you do not need to loop and invoke `ReleaseComObject` to completely release an RCW.

For example, in the ADO example in recipe 12-6, you could release the underlying ADO `Recordset` and `Connection` objects by adding these two lines to the end of your code:

```
System.Runtime.InteropServices.Marshal.FinalReleaseComObject(rs);
System.Runtime.InteropServices.Marshal.FinalReleaseComObject(con);
```

■**Note** The `ReleaseComObject` method does not actually release the COM object; it just decrements the reference count. If the reference count reaches zero, the COM object will be released. `FinalReleaseComObject` works by setting the reference count of an RCW to zero. It thus bypasses the internal count logic and releases all references.

12-8. Use Optional Parameters

Problem

You need to call a method in a COM component without supplying all the required parameters.

Solution

Use the `Type.Missing` field.

How It Works

The .NET Framework is designed with a heavy use of method overloading. Most methods are overloaded several times so that you can call the version that requires only the parameters you choose to supply. COM, on the other hand, does not support method overloading. Instead, COM components usually use methods with a long list of optional parameters. Unfortunately, C# does not support optional parameters, which means C# developers are often forced to supply numerous additional or irrelevant values when accessing a COM component. And because COM parameters are often passed by reference, your code cannot simply pass a `null` reference. Instead, it must declare an object variable and then pass that variable.

You can mitigate the problem to some extent by supplying the `Type.Missing` field whenever you wish to omit an optional parameter. If you need to pass a parameter by reference, you can simply declare a single object variable, set it equal to `Type.Missing`, and use it in all cases, like this:

```
private static object n = Type.Missing;
```

The Code

The following example uses the Microsoft Word COM objects to programmatically create and show a document. Many of the methods the example uses require optional parameters passed by reference. You will notice that the use of the `Type.Missing` field simplifies this code greatly. Each use is emphasized in the code listing.

```
using System;

namespace Apress.VisualCSharpRecipes.Chapter12
{
    class Recipe12_08
    {
        private static object n = Type.Missing;

        static void Main(string[] args)
        {
            // Start Word in the background.
            Word.ApplicationClass app = new Word.ApplicationClass();
            app.DisplayAlerts = Word.WdAlertLevel.wdAlertsNone;

            // Create a new document (this is not visible to the user).
            Word.Document doc = app.Documents.Add(ref n, ref n, ref n,
              ref n);
```

```
            Console.WriteLine();
            Console.WriteLine("Creating new document.");
            Console.WriteLine();

            // Add a heading and two lines of text.
            Word.Range range = doc.Paragraphs.Add(ref n).Range;
            range.InsertBefore("Test Document");
            string style = "Heading 1";
            object objStyle = style;
            range.set_Style(ref objStyle);

            range = doc.Paragraphs.Add(ref n).Range;
            range.InsertBefore("Line one.\nLine two.");
            range.Font.Bold = 1;

            // Show a print preview, and make Word visible.
            doc.PrintPreview();
            app.Visible = true;

            // Wait to continue.
            Console.WriteLine(Environment.NewLine);
            Console.WriteLine("Main method complete. Press Enter.");
            Console.ReadLine();
        }
    }
}
```

12-9. Use an ActiveX Control in a .NET Client

Problem

You need to place an ActiveX control on a form or a user control in a .NET Framework application.

Solution

Use an RCW exactly as you would with an ordinary COM component (see recipe 12-6). To work with the ActiveX control at design time, add it to the Visual Studio .NET Toolbox.

How It Works

The .NET Framework includes the same support for all COM components, including ActiveX controls. The key difference is that the RCW class for an ActiveX control derives from the special .NET Framework type System.Windows.Forms.AxHost. You add the AxHost control to your form, and it communicates with the ActiveX control "behind the scenes." Because AxHost derives from System.Windows.Forms. Control, it provides the standard .NET control properties, methods, and events, such as Location, Size, Anchor, and so on. In the case of an autogenerated RCW, the AxHost classes will always begin with the letters Ax.

You can create an RCW for an ActiveX control as you would for any other COM component, as described in recipe 12-6: use the Type Library Exporter (Tlbimp.exe) command-line utility or use the Add Reference feature in Visual Studio .NET and create the control programmatically. However, an easier approach in Visual Studio .NET is to add the ActiveX control to the Toolbox.

Nothing happens to your project when you add an ActiveX control to the Toolbox. However, you can use the Toolbox icon to add an instance of the control to your form. The first time you do this, Visual Studio .NET will create the interop assembly and add it to your project. For example, if you add the Microsoft Masked Edit control, Visual Studio .NET creates an RCW assembly with a name such as AxInterop.MSMask.dll. Here is the code you might expect to see in the hidden designer region that creates the control instance and adds it to the form:

```
this.axMaskEdBox1 = new AxMSMask.AxMaskEdBox();
((System.ComponentModel.ISupportInitialize)(this.axMaskEdBox1)).BeginInit();

//
// axMaskEdBox1
//
this.axMaskEdBox1.Location = new System.Drawing.Point(16, 12);
this.axMaskEdBox1.Name = "axMaskEdBox1";
this.axMaskEdBox1.OcxState = ((System.Windows.Forms.AxHost.State)
  (resources.GetObject("axMaskEdBox1.OcxState")));

this.axMaskEdBox1.Size = new System.Drawing.Size(112, 20);
this.axMaskEdBox1.TabIndex = 0;

this.Controls.Add(this.axMaskEdBox1);
```

Notice that the custom properties for the ActiveX control are not applied directly through property set statements. Instead, they are restored as a group when the control sets its persisted OcxState property. However, your code can use the control's properties directly.

12-10. Expose a .NET Component Through COM

Problem

You need to create a .NET component that can be called by a COM client.

Solution

Create an assembly that follows certain restrictions identified in this recipe. Export a type library for this assembly using the Type Library Exporter (Tlbexp.exe) command-line utility.

How It Works

The .NET Framework includes support for COM clients to use .NET components. When a COM client needs to create a .NET object, the CLR creates the managed object and a COM callable wrapper (CCW) that wraps the object. The COM client interacts with the managed object through the CCW. The runtime creates only one CCW for a managed object, regardless of how many COM clients are using it.

Types that need to be accessed by COM clients must meet certain requirements:

- The managed type (class, interface, struct, or enum) must be `public`.

- If the COM client needs to create the object, it must have a `public` default constructor. COM does not support parameterized constructors.

- The members of the type that are being accessed must be `public` instance members. `Private`, `protected`, `internal`, and `static` members are not accessible to COM clients.

In addition, you should consider the following recommendations:

- You should not create inheritance relationships between classes, because these relationships will not be visible to COM clients (although .NET will attempt to simulate this by declaring a shared base class interface).

- The classes you are exposing should implement an interface. For added versioning control, you can use the attribute `System.Runtime.InteropServices.GuidAttribute` to specify the GUID that should be assigned to an interface.

- Ideally, you should give the managed assembly a strong name so that it can be installed into the GAC and shared among multiple clients.

In order for a COM client to create the .NET object, it requires a type library (a .tlb file). The type library can be generated from an assembly using the Tlbexp.exe command-line utility. Here is an example of the syntax you use:

```
tlbexp ManagedLibrary.dll
```

Once you generate the type library, you can reference it from the unmanaged development tool. With Visual Basic 6, you reference the .tlb file from the Project ➤ References dialog box. In Visual C++ 6, you can use the `#import` statement to import the type definitions from the type library.

CHAPTER 13

■■■

Commonly Used Interfaces and Patterns

The recipes in this chapter show you how to implement patterns you will use frequently during the development of Microsoft .NET Framework applications. Some of these patterns are formalized using interfaces defined in the .NET Framework class library. Others are less rigid, but still require you to take specific approaches to their design and implementation of your types. The recipes in this chapter describe how to do the following:

- Create serializable types that you can easily store to disk, send across the network, or pass by value across application domain boundaries (recipe 13-1)

- Provide a mechanism that creates accurate and complete copies (clones) of objects (recipe 13-2)

- Implement types that are easy to compare and sort (recipe 13-3)

- Support the enumeration of the elements contained in custom collections using the built-in iterator capability of C# 2.0 or by creating a custom iterator (recipes 13-4 and 13-5)

- Ensure that a type that uses unmanaged resources correctly releases those resources when they are no longer needed (recipe 13-6)

- Display string representations of objects that vary based on format specifiers (recipe 13-7)

- Correctly implement custom exception and event argument types, which you will use frequently in the development of your applications (recipes 13-8 and 13-9)

- Implement the commonly used Singleton and Observer design patterns using the built-in features of C# and the .NET Framework class library (recipes 13-10 and 13-11)

13-1. Implement a Serializable Type

Problem

You need to implement a custom type that is serializable, allowing you to do the following:

- Store instances of the type to persistent storage (for example, a file or a database).

- Transmit instances of the type across a network.

- Pass instances of the type "by value" across application domain boundaries.

Solution

For serialization of simple types, apply the attribute `System.SerializableAttribute` to the type declaration. For types that are more complex, or to control the content and structure of the serialized data, implement the interface `System.Runtime.Serialization.ISerializable`.

How It Works

Recipe 2-13 showed how to serialize and deserialize an object using the formatter classes provided with the .NET Framework class library. However, types are not serializable by default. To implement a custom type that is serializable, you must apply the attribute `SerializableAttribute` to your type declaration. As long as all of the data fields in your type are serializable types, applying `SerializableAttribute` is all you need to do to make your custom type serializable. If you are implementing a custom class that derives from a base class, the base class must also be serializable.

■**Caution** Classes that derive from a serializable type don't inherit the attribute `SerializableAttribute`. To make derived types serializable, you must explicitly declare them as serializable by applying the `SerializableAttribute` attribute.

Each formatter class contains the logic necessary to serialize types decorated with `SerializableAttribute` and will correctly serialize all `public`, `protected`, and `private` fields. You can exclude specific fields from serialization by applying the attribute `System.NonSerializedAttribute` to those fields. As a rule, you should exclude the following fields from serialization:

- Fields that contain nonserializable data types

- Fields that contain values that might be invalid when the object is deserialized, such as database connections, memory addresses, thread IDs, and unmanaged resource handles

- Fields that contain sensitive or secret information, such as passwords, encryption keys, and the personal details of people and organizations

- Fields that contain data that is easily re-creatable or retrievable from other sources, especially if the data is large

If you exclude fields from serialization, you must implement your type to compensate for the fact that some data will not be present when an object is deserialized. Unfortunately, you cannot create or retrieve the missing data fields in an instance constructor, because formatters do not call constructors during the process of deserializing objects. The best approach for achieving fine-grained control of the serialization of your custom types is to use the attributes from the `System.Runtime.Serialization` namespace described in Table 13-1. These attributes allow you to identify methods of the serializable type that the serialization process should execute before and after serialization and deserialization. Any method annotated with one of these attributes must take a single `System.Runtime.Serialization.StreamingContext` argument, which contains details about the source or intended destination of the serialized object so that you can determine what to serialize. For example, you might be happy to serialize secret data if it's destined for another application domain in the same process, but not if the data will be written to a file.

Table 13-1. *Attributes to Customize the Serialization and Deserialization Processs*

Attribute	Description
OnSerializingAttribute	Apply this attribute to a method to have it executed before the object is serialized. This is useful if you need to modify object state before it is serialized. For example, you may need to convert a DateTime field to UTC time for storage.
OnSerializedAttribute	Apply this attribute to a method to have it executed after the object is serialized. This is useful in case you need to revert the object state to what it was before the method annotated with OnSerializingAttribute was run.
OnDeserializingAttribute	Apply this attribute to a method to have it executed before the object is deserialized. This is useful if you need to modify the object state prior to deserialization.
OnDeserializedAttribute	Apply this attribute to a method to have it executed after the object is deserialized. This is useful if you need to re-create additional object state that depends on the data that was deserialized with the object or modify the deserialized state before the object is used.

As types evolve, you often add new member variables to support new features. This new state causes a problem when deserializing old objects because the new member variables are not part of the serialized object. .NET Framework 2.0 introduces the attribute System.Runtime.Serialization.OptionalFieldAttribute. When you create a new version of a type and add data members, annotate them with OptionalFieldAttribute, and the deserialization process will not fail if they are not present. You can then use a method annotated with OnDeserializedAttribute (see Table 13-1) to configure the new member variables appropriately.

For the majority of custom types, the mechanisms described will be sufficient to meet your serialization needs. If you require more control over the serialization process, you can implement the interface ISerializable. The formatter classes use different logic when serializing and deserializing instances of types that implement ISerializable. To implement ISerializable correctly you must do the following:

- Declare that your type implements ISerializable.

- Apply the attribute SerializableAttribute to your type declaration as just described. Do not use NonSerializedAttribute because it will have no effect.

- Implement the ISerializable.GetObjectData method (used during serialization), which takes the argument types System.Runtime.Serialization.SerializationInfo and System.Runtime.Serialization.StreamingContext.

- Implement a nonpublic constructor (used during deserialization) that accepts the same arguments as the GetObjectData method. Remember that if you plan to derive classes from your serializable class, you should make the constructor protected.

- If you are creating a serializable class from a base class that also implements ISerializable, your type's GetObjectData method and deserialization constructor must call the equivalent method and constructor in the parent class.

During serialization, the formatter calls the GetObjectData method and passes it SerializationInfo and StreamingContext references as arguments. Your type must populate the SerializationInfo object with the data you want to serialize. The SerializationInfo class acts as a list of field/value pairs and provides the AddValue method to let you store a field with its value. In each call to AddValue, you must specify a name for the field/value pair; you use this name during deserialization to retrieve the value of each field. The AddValue method has 16 overloads that allow you to add values of different data types to the SerializationInfo object.

The StreamingContext object, as described earlier, provides information about the purpose and destination of the serialized data, allowing you to choose which data to serialize.

When a formatter deserializes an instance of your type, it calls the deserialization constructor, again passing a SerializationInfo and a StreamingContext reference as arguments. Your type must extract the serialized data from the SerializationInfo object using one of the SerializationInfo. Get* methods; for example, using GetString, GetInt32, or GetBoolean. During deserialization, the StreamingContext object provides information about the source of the serialized data, allowing you to mirror the logic you implemented for serialization.

■**Note** During standard serialization operations, the formatters do not use the capabilities of the StreamingContext object to provide specifics about the source, destination, and purpose of serialized data. However, if you wish to perform customized serialization, your code can configure the formatter's StreamingContext object prior to initiating serialization and deserialization. Consult the .NET Framework SDK documentation for details of the StreamingContext class.

The Code

This following example demonstrates a serializable Employee class that implements the ISerializable interface. In this example, the Employee class does not serialize the address field if the provided StreamingContext object specifies that the destination of the serialized data is a file. The Main method demonstrates the serialization and deserialization of an Employee object.

```
using System;
using System.IO;
using System.Text;
using System.Runtime.Serialization;
using System.Runtime.Serialization.Formatters.Binary;

namespace Apress.VisualCSharpRecipes.Chapter13
{
    [Serializable]
    public class Employee : ISerializable
    {
        private string name;
        private int age;
        private string address;

        // Simple Employee constructor.
        public Employee(string name, int age, string address)
        {
            this.name = name;
            this.age = age;
            this.address = address;
        }

        // Constructor required to enable a formatter to deserialize an
        // Employee object. You should declare the constructor private or at
        // least protected to ensure it is not called unnecessarily.
        private Employee(SerializationInfo info, StreamingContext context)
        {
            // Extract the name and age of the Employee, which will always be
            // present in the serialized data regardless of the value of the
            // StreamingContext.
```

```csharp
        name = info.GetString("Name");
        age = info.GetInt32("Age");

        // Attempt to extract the Employee's address and fail gracefully
        // if it is not available.
        try
        {
            address = info.GetString("Address");
        }
        catch (SerializationException)
        {
            address = null;
        }
    }

    // Public property to provide access to employee's name.
    public string Name
    {
        get { return name; }
        set { name = value; }
    }

    // Public property to provide access to employee's age.
    public int Age
    {
        get { return age; }
        set { age = value; }
    }

    // Public property to provide access to employee's address.
    // Uses lazy initialization to establish address because
    // a deserialized object will not have an address value.
    public string Address
    {
        get
        {
            if (address == null)
            {
                // Load the address from persistent storage.
                // In this case, set it to an empty string.
                address = String.Empty;
            }
            return address;
        }

        set
        {
            address = value;
        }
    }

    // Declared by the ISerializable interface, the GetObjectData method
    // provides the mechanism with which a formatter obtains the object
    // data that it should serialize.
    public void GetObjectData(SerializationInfo inf, StreamingContext con)
    {
        // Always serialize the Employee's name and age.
```

```csharp
        inf.AddValue("Name", name);
        inf.AddValue("Age", age);

        // Don't serialize the Employee's address if the StreamingContext
        // indicates that the serialized data is to be written to a file.
        if ((con.State & StreamingContextStates.File) == 0)
        {
            inf.AddValue("Address", address);
        }
    }

    // Override Object.ToString to return a string representation of the
    // Employee state.
    public override string ToString()
    {
        StringBuilder str = new StringBuilder();

        str.AppendFormat("Name: {0}\r\n", Name);
        str.AppendFormat("Age: {0}\r\n", Age);
        str.AppendFormat("Address: {0}\r\n", Address);

        return str.ToString();
    }
}

// A class to demonstrate the use of Employee.
Public class Recipe13_01
{
    public static void Main(string[] args)
    {
        // Create an Employee object representing Roger.
        Employee roger = new Employee("Roger", 56, "London");

        // Display Roger.
        Console.WriteLine(roger);

        // Serialize Roger specifying another application domain as the
        // destination of the serialized data. All data including Roger's
        // address is serialized.
        Stream str = File.Create("roger.bin");
        BinaryFormatter bf = new BinaryFormatter();
        bf.Context =
            new StreamingContext(StreamingContextStates.CrossAppDomain);
        bf.Serialize(str, roger);
        str.Close();

        // Deserialize and display Roger.
        str = File.OpenRead("roger.bin");
        bf = new BinaryFormatter();
        roger = (Employee)bf.Deserialize(str);
        str.Close();
        Console.WriteLine(roger);

        // Serialize Roger specifying a file as the destination of the
        // serialized data. In this case, Roger's address is not included
        // in the serialized data.
        str = File.Create("roger.bin");
```

```
        bf = new BinaryFormatter();
        bf.Context = new StreamingContext(StreamingContextStates.File);
        bf.Serialize(str, roger);
        str.Close();

        // Deserialize and display Roger.
        str = File.OpenRead("roger.bin");
        bf = new BinaryFormatter();
        roger = (Employee)bf.Deserialize(str);
        str.Close();
        Console.WriteLine(roger);

        // Wait to continue.
        Console.WriteLine(Environment.NewLine);
        Console.WriteLine("Main method complete. Press Enter");
        Console.ReadLine();
    }
  }
}
```

13-2. Implement a Cloneable Type

Problem

You need to create a custom type that provides a simple mechanism for programmers to create copies of type instances.

Solution

Implement the System.ICloneable interface.

How It Works

When you assign one value type to another, you create a copy of the value. No link exists between the two values—a change to one will not affect the other. However, when you assign one reference type to another (excluding strings, which receive special treatment by the runtime), you do not create a new copy of the reference type. Instead, both reference types refer to the same object, and changes to the value of the object are reflected in both references. To create a true copy of a reference type, you must *clone* the object to which it refers.

The ICloneable interface identifies a type as cloneable and declares the Clone method as the mechanism through which you obtain a clone of an object. The Clone method takes no arguments and returns a System.Object, regardless of the implementing type. This means that once you clone an object, you must explicitly cast the clone to the correct type.

The approach you take to implementing the Clone method for a custom type depends on the data members declared within the type. If the custom type contains only value-type (int, byte, and so on) and System.String data members, you can implement the Clone method by instantiating a new object and setting its data members to the same values as the current object. The Object class (from which all types derive) includes the protected method MemberwiseClone, which automates this process.

If your custom type contains reference-type data members, you must decide whether your Clone method will perform a *shallow copy* or a *deep copy*. A shallow copy means that any reference-type data members in the clone will refer to the same objects as the equivalent reference-type data members in the original object. A deep copy means that you must create clones of the entire object graph so that the reference-type data members of the clone refer to physically independent copies (clones) of the objects referenced by the original object.

A shallow copy is easy to implement using the MemberwiseClone method just described. However, a deep copy is often what programmers expect when they first clone an object, but it's rarely what they get. This is especially true of the collection classes in the System.Collections namespace, which all implement shallow copies in their Clone methods. Although it would often be useful if these collections implemented a deep copy, there are two key reasons why types (especially generic collection classes) do not implement deep copies:

- Creating a clone of a large object graph is processor-intensive and memory-intensive.

- General-purpose collections can contain wide and deep object graphs consisting of any type of object. Creating a deep-copy implementation to cater to such variety is not feasible because some objects in the collection might not be cloneable, and others might contain circular references, which would send the cloning process into an infinite loop.

For strongly typed collections in which the nature of the contained elements are understood and controlled, a deep copy can be a very useful feature; for example, the System.Xml.XmlNode implements a deep copy in its Clone method. This allows you to create true copies of entire XML object hierarchies with a single statement.

■**Tip** If you need to clone an object that does not implement ICloneable but is serializable, you can often serialize and then deserialize the object to achieve the same result as cloning. However, be aware that the serialization process might not serialize all data members (as discussed in recipe 13-1). Likewise, if you create a custom serializable type, you can potentially use the serialization process just described to perform a deep copy within your ICloneable.Clone method implementation. To clone a serializable object, use the class System.Runtime. Serialization.Formatters.Binary.BinaryFormatter to serialize the object to, and then deserialize the object from a System.IO.MemoryStream object.

The Code

The following example demonstrates various approaches to cloning. The simple class named Employee contains only string and int members, and so relies on the inherited MemberwiseClone method to create a clone. The Team class contains an implementation of the Clone method that performs a deep copy. The Team class contains a collection of Employee objects, representing a team of people. When you call the Clone method of a Team object, the method creates a clone of every contained Employee object and adds it to the cloned Team object. The Team class provides a private constructor to simplify the code in the Clone method. The use of constructors is a common approach to simplify the cloning process.

```
using System;
using System.Text;
using System.Collections.Generic;

namespace Apress.VisualCSharpRecipes.Chapter13
{
    public class Employee : ICloneable
    {
        public string Name;
        public string Title;
        public int Age;
```

```csharp
    // Simple Employee constructor.
    public Employee(string name, string title, int age)
    {
        Name = name;
        Title = title;
        Age = age;
    }

    // Create a clone using the Object.MemberwiseClone method because the
    // Employee class contains only string and value types.
    public object Clone()
    {
        return MemberwiseClone();
    }

    // Returns a string representation of the Employee object.
    public override string ToString()
    {
        return string.Format("{0} ({1}) - Age {2}", Name, Title, Age);
    }
}

public class Team : ICloneable
{
    // A List to hold the Employee team members.
    public List<Employee> TeamMembers =
        new List<Employee>();

    public Team()
    {
    }

    // Private constructor called by the Clone method to create a new Team
    // object and populate its List with clones of Employee objects from
    // a provided List.
    private Team(List<Employee> members)
    {
        foreach (Employee e in members)
        {
            // Clone the individual employee objects and
            // add them to the List.
            TeamMembers.Add((Employee)e.Clone());
        }
    }

    // Adds an Employee object to the Team.
    public void AddMember(Employee member)
    {
        TeamMembers.Add(member);
    }

    // Override Object.ToString to return a string representation of the
    // entire Team.
    public override string ToString()
    {
        StringBuilder str = new StringBuilder();
```

```csharp
        foreach (Employee e in TeamMembers)
        {
            str.AppendFormat("  {0}\r\n", e);
        }

        return str.ToString();
    }

    // Implementation of ICloneable.Clone.
    public object Clone()
    {
        // Create a deep copy of the team by calling the private Team
        // constructor and passing the ArrayList containing team members.
        return new Team(this.TeamMembers);

        // The following command would create a shallow copy of the Team.
        // return MemberwiseClone();
    }
}

// A class to demonstrate the use of Employee.
Public class Recipe13_02
{
    public static void Main()
    {
        // Create the original team.
        Team team = new Team();
        team.AddMember(new Employee("Frank", "Developer", 34));
        team.AddMember(new Employee("Kathy", "Tester", 78));
        team.AddMember(new Employee("Chris", "Support", 18));

        // Clone the original team.
        Team clone = (Team)team.Clone();

        // Display the original team.
        Console.WriteLine("Original Team:");
        Console.WriteLine(team);

        // Display the cloned team.
        Console.WriteLine("Clone Team:");
        Console.WriteLine(clone);

        // Make change.
        Console.WriteLine("*** Make a change to original team ***");
        Console.WriteLine(Environment.NewLine);
        team.TeamMembers[0].Name = "Luke";
        team.TeamMembers[0].Title = "Manager";
        team.TeamMembers[0].Age = 44;

        // Display the original team.
        Console.WriteLine("Original Team:");
        Console.WriteLine(team);

        // Display the cloned team.
        Console.WriteLine("Clone Team:");
        Console.WriteLine(clone);
```

```
        // Wait to continue.
        Console.WriteLine(Environment.NewLine);
        Console.WriteLine("Main method complete. Press Enter");
        Console.ReadLine();
    }
  }
}
```

13-3. Implement a Comparable Type

Problem

You need to provide a mechanism that allows you to compare custom types, enabling you to easily sort collections containing instances of those types.

Solution

To provide a standard comparison mechanism for a type, implement the generic `System.IComparable<T>` interface. To support the comparison of a type based on more than one characteristic, create separate types that implement the generic `System.Collections.Generic.IComparer<T>` interface.

■**Caution** The `System.IComparable` and `System.Collections.IComparer` interfaces available prior to .NET Framework 2.0 do not use generics to ensure type safety. When working with .NET Framework 1.0 or 1.1, you must take extra precautions to ensure the objects passed to the methods of these interfaces are of the appropriate type.

How It Works

If you need to sort your type into only a single order, such as ascending ID number, or alphabetically based on surname, you should implement the `IComparable<T>` interface. `IComparable<T>` defines a single method named `CompareTo`, shown here.

```
int CompareTo(T other);
```

According to the specification of the `CompareTo` method, the object (`other`) passed to the method must be an object of the same type as that being called, or `CompareTo` must throw a `System.ArgumentException` exception. This is less important in .NET Framework 2.0, given that the implementation of `IComparable` uses generics and is type-safe, ensuring that the argument is of the correct type. The value returned by `CompareTo` should be calculated as follows:

- If the current object is less than `other`, return less than zero (for example, –1).

- If the current object has the same value as `other`, return zero.

- If the current object is greater than `other`, return greater than zero (for example, 1).

What these comparisons mean depends on the type implementing the `IComparable` interface. For example, if you were sorting people based on their surname, you would do a `String` comparison on this field. However, if you wanted to sort by birthday, you would need to perform a comparison of the corresponding `System.DateTime` fields.

To support a variety of sort orders for a particular type, you must implement separate helper types that implement the IComparer<T> interface, which defines the Compare method shown here.

```
int Compare(T x, T y);
```

These helper types must encapsulate the necessary logic to compare two objects and return a value based on the following logic:

- If x is less than y, return less than zero (for example, –1).

- If x has the same value as y, return zero.

- If x is greater than y, return greater than zero (for example, 1).

The Code

The Newspaper class listed here demonstrates the implementation of both the IComparable and IComparer interfaces. The Newspaper.CompareTo method performs a case-insensitive comparison of two Newspaper objects based on their name fields. A private nested class named AscendingCirculationComparer implements IComparer and compares two Newspaper objects based on their circulation fields. An AscendingCirculationComparer object is obtained using the static Newspaper.CirculationSorter property.

The Main method shown here demonstrates the comparison and sorting capabilities provided by implementing the IComparable and IComparer interfaces. The method creates a System.Collections. ArrayList collection containing five Newspaper objects. Main then sorts the ArrayList twice using the ArrayList.Sort method. The first Sort operation uses the default Newspaper comparison mechanism provided by the IComparable.CompareTo method. The second Sort operation uses an AscendingCirculationComparer object to perform comparisons through its implementation of the IComparer.Compare method.

```
using System;
using System.Collections.Generic;

namespace Apress.VisualCSharpRecipes.Chapter13
{
    public class Newspaper : IComparable<Newspaper>
    {
        private string name;
        private int circulation;

        private class AscendingCirculationComparer : IComparer<Newspaper>
        {
            // Implementation of IComparer.Compare. The generic definition of
            // IComparer allows us to ensure both arguments are Newspaper
            // objects.
            public int Compare(Newspaper x, Newspaper y)
            {
                // Handle logic for null reference as dictated by the
                // IComparer interface. Null is considered less than
                // any other value.
                if (x == null && y == null) return 0;
                else if (x == null) return -1;
                else if (y == null) return 1;

                // Short-circuit condition where x and y are references
                // to the same object.
                if (x == y) return 0;
```

```
            // Compare the circulation figures. IComparer dictates that:
            //      return less than zero if x < y
            //      return zero if x = y
            //      return greater than zero if x > y
            // This logic is easily implemented using integer arithmetic.
            return x.circulation - y.circulation;
        }
    }

    // Simple Newspaper constructor.
    public Newspaper(string name, int circulation)
    {
        this.name = name;
        this.circulation = circulation;
    }

    // Declare a read-only property that returns an instance of the
    // AscendingCirculationComparer.
    public static IComparer<Newspaper> CirculationSorter
    {
        get { return new AscendingCirculationComparer(); }
    }

    // Override Object.ToString.
    public override string ToString()
    {
        return string.Format("{0}: Circulation = {1}", name, circulation);
    }

    // Implementation of IComparable.CompareTo. The generic definition
    // of IComparable allows us to ensure that the argument provided
    // must be a Newspaper object. Comparison is based on a
    // case-insensitive comparison of the Newspaper names.
    public int CompareTo(Newspaper other)
    {
        // IComparable dictates that an object is always considered greater
        // than null.
        if (other == null) return 1;

        // Short-circuit the case where the other Newspaper object is a
        // reference to this one.
        if (other == this) return 0;

        // Calculate return value by performing a case-insensitive
        // comparison of the Newspaper names.

        // Because the Newspaper name is a string, the easiest approach
        // is to rely on the comparison capabilities of the String
        // class, which perform culture-sensitive string comparisons.
        return string.Compare(this.name, other.name, true);
    }
}

// A class to demonstrate the use of Newspaper.
Public class Recipe13_03
{
    public static void Main()
```

```
        {
            List<Newspaper> newspapers = new List<Newspaper>();

            newspapers.Add(new Newspaper("The Echo", 125780));
            newspapers.Add(new Newspaper("The Times", 55230));
            newspapers.Add(new Newspaper("The Gazette", 235950));
            newspapers.Add(new Newspaper("The Sun", 88760));
            newspapers.Add(new Newspaper("The Herald", 5670));

            Console.Clear();
            Console.WriteLine("Unsorted newspaper list:");
            foreach (Newspaper n in newspapers)
            {
                Console.WriteLine("  " + n);
            }

            Console.WriteLine(Environment.NewLine);
            Console.WriteLine("Newspaper list sorted by name (default order):");
            newspapers.Sort();
            foreach (Newspaper n in newspapers)
            {
                Console.WriteLine("  " + n);
            }

            Console.WriteLine(Environment.NewLine);
            Console.WriteLine("Newspaper list sorted by circulation:");
            newspapers.Sort(Newspaper.CirculationSorter);
            foreach (Newspaper n in newspapers)
            {
                Console.WriteLine("  " + n);
            }

            // Wait to continue.
            Console.WriteLine(Environment.NewLine);
            Console.WriteLine("Main method complete. Press Enter");
            Console.ReadLine();
        }
    }
}
```

Usage

Running the example will produce the results shown here. The first list of newspapers is unsorted, the second is sorted using the IComparable interface, and the third is sorted using a comparer class that implements IComparer.

```
Unsorted newspaper list:
  The Echo: Circulation = 125780
  The Times: Circulation = 55230
  The Gazette: Circulation = 235950
  The Sun: Circulation = 88760
  The Herald: Circulation = 5670

Newspaper list sorted by name (default order):
  The Echo: Circulation = 125780
  The Gazette: Circulation = 235950
```

```
The Herald: Circulation = 5670
The Sun: Circulation = 88760
The Times: Circulation = 55230

Newspaper list sorted by circulation:
The Herald: Circulation = 5670
The Times: Circulation = 55230
The Sun: Circulation = 88760
The Echo: Circulation = 125780
The Gazette: Circulation = 235950
```

13-4. Implement an Enumerable Collection

Problem

You need to create a collection type whose contents you can enumerate using a foreach statement.

Solution

Implement the generic interface System.Collections.Generic.IEnumerable<T> on your collection type. The GetEnumerator method of the IEnumerable interface returns an *enumerator*, which is an object that implements the interface System.Collections.Generic.IEnumerator<T>. Within the GetEnumerator method, traverse the items in the collection using whatever logic is appropriate to your data structure and return the next value using the yield return statement. The C# compiler will automatically generate the necessary code to enable enumeration across the contents of your type.

■**Caution** The IEnumerable and IEnumerator interfaces from the System.Collections.Generic namespace discussed in this recipe are new to .NET Framework 2.0. The interfaces from which these two interfaces inherit are also named IEnumerable and IEnumerator but are located in the System.Collections namespace. To implement an enumerable collection in .Net Framework 1.0 or 1.1, see recipe 13-5.

How It Works

A numeric indexer allows you to iterate through the elements of most standard collections using a for loop. However, this technique does not always provide an appropriate abstraction for nonlinear data structures, such as trees and multidimensional collections. The foreach statement provides an easy-to-use and syntactically elegant mechanism for iterating through a collection of objects, regardless of their internal structures.

In order to support foreach semantics, the type containing the collection of objects should implement the IEnumerable<T> interface. The IEnumerable<T> interface declares a single method named GetEnumerator, which takes no arguments and returns an object that implements IEnumerator<T>. Prior to .NET Framework 2.0, you would need to implement a separate class that could correctly traverse the elements of the collection and maintain appropriate state to support the executing foreach loop. You would create an instance of this class and return it when the GetEnumerator method was called. In .NET Framework 2.0, you do not need to do this, as the C# compiler elegantly automates this relatively complex coding task through the use of the new yield return statement.

All you need to do in your GetEnumerator method is write the code necessary to iterate through the items in your collection using logic appropriate to the data structure. Each time you want to return an item, call the yield return statement and specify the value to return. The compiler generates code that returns the specified value and maintains appropriate state for the next time a value is requested. If you need to stop partway through the enumeration, call the yield break statement instead, and the enumeration will terminate as if it had reached the end of the collection.

■**Tip** You do not actually need to explicitly implement IEnumerable on your type to make it enumerable. As long as it has a GetEnumerator method that returns an IEnumerator instance, the compiler will allow you to use the type in a foreach statement. However, it is always good practice to explicitly declare the capabilities of a type by declaring the interfaces it implements, as it allows users of your class to more easily understand its capabilities and purpose.

The GetEnumerator method is used automatically whenever you use an instance of your collection type in a foreach statement. However, if you want to provide multiple ways to enumerate the items in your collection, you can implement multiple methods or properties that are declared to return IEnumerable<T> instances. Within the body of the member, use the yield return statement just mentioned, and the C# compiler will generate the appropriate code automatically. To use one of the alternative enumerations from a foreach statement, you must directly reference the appropriate member, as in this example:

```
foreach (node n in Tree.BreadthFirst)
```

The Code

The following example demonstrates the creation of an enumerable collection using the IEnumerable<T> and IEnumerator<T> interfaces in conjunction with the yield return and yield break statements. The Team class, which represents a team of people, is a collection of enumerable TeamMember objects.

```
using System;
using System.Collections.Generic;

namespace Apress.VisualCSharpRecipes.Chapter13
{
    // The TeamMember class represents an individual team member.
    public class TeamMember
    {
        public string Name;
        public string Title;

        // Simple TeamMember constructor.
        public TeamMember(string name, string title)
        {
            Name = name;
            Title = title;
        }

        // Returns a string representation of the TeamMember.
        public override string ToString()
        {
            return string.Format("{0} ({1})", Name, Title);
        }
    }
```

```
// Team class represents a collection of TeamMember objects.
public class Team
{
    // A List to contain the TeamMember objects.
    private List<TeamMember> teamMembers = new List<TeamMember>();

    // Implement the GetEnumerator method, which will support
    // iteration across the entire team member List.
    public IEnumerator<TeamMember> GetEnumerator()
    {
        foreach (TeamMember tm in teamMembers)
        {
            yield return tm;
        }
    }

    // Implement the Reverse method, which will iterate through
    // the team members in alphabetical order.
    public IEnumerable<TeamMember> Reverse
    {
        get
        {
            for (int c = teamMembers.Count - 1; c >= 0; c--)
            {
                yield return teamMembers[c];
            }
        }
    }

    // Implement the FirstTwo method, which will stop the iteration
    // after only the first two team members.
    public IEnumerable<TeamMember> FirstTwo
    {
        get
        {
            int count = 0;

            foreach (TeamMember tm in teamMembers)
            {
                if (count >= 2)
                {
                    // Terminate the iterator.
                    yield break;
                }
                else
                {
                    // Return the TeamMember and maintain the iterator.
                    count++;
                    yield return tm;
                }
            }
        }
    }
}
```

```csharp
        // Adds a TeamMember object to the Team.
        public void AddMember(TeamMember member)
        {
            teamMembers.Add(member);
        }
    }

    // A class to demonstrate the use of Team.
    Public class Recipe13_04
    {
        public static void Main()
        {
            // Create and populate a new Team.
            Team team = new Team();
            team.AddMember(new TeamMember("Curly", "Clown"));
            team.AddMember(new TeamMember("Nick", "Knife Thrower"));
            team.AddMember(new TeamMember("Nancy", "Strong Man"));

            // Enumerate the entire Team using the default iterator.
            Console.Clear();
            Console.WriteLine("Enumerate using default iterator:");
            foreach (TeamMember member in team)
            {
                Console.WriteLine("  " + member.ToString());
            }

            // Enumerate the first 2 Team members only.
            Console.WriteLine(Environment.NewLine);
            Console.WriteLine("Enumerate using the FirstTwo iterator:");
            foreach (TeamMember member in team.FirstTwo)
            {
                Console.WriteLine("   " + member.ToString());
            }

            // Enumerate the entire Team in reverse order.
            Console.WriteLine(Environment.NewLine);
            Console.WriteLine("Enumerate using the Reverse iterator:");
            foreach (TeamMember member in team.Reverse)
            {
                Console.WriteLine("  " + member.ToString());
            }

            // Wait to continue.
            Console.WriteLine(Environment.NewLine);
            Console.WriteLine("Main method complete. Press Enter");
            Console.ReadLine();
        }
    }
}
```

13-5. Implement an Enumerable Type Using a Custom Iterator

Problem

You need to create an enumerable type but do not want to rely on the built-in iterator support provided by .NET Framework 2.0 (described in recipe 13-4).

Solution

Implement the interface System.Collections.IEnumerable on your collection type. The GetEnumerator method of the IEnumerable interface returns an *enumerator*, which is an object that implements the interface System.Collections.IEnumerator. The IEnumerator interface defines the methods used by the foreach statement to enumerate the collection.

Implement a private inner class within the enumerable type that implements the interface IEnumerator and can iterate over the enumerable type while maintaining appropriate state information. In the GetEnumerator method of the enumerable type, create and return an instance of the iterator class.

How It Works

The automatic iterator support built into C# 2.0 is very powerful and will be sufficient in the majority of cases. However, in some cases, you may want to take direct control of the implementation of your collection's iterators. For example, you may want an iterator that supports changes to the underlying collection during enumeration.

Whatever your reason, the basic model of an enumerable collection is the same as that described in recipe 13-4. Your enumerable type should implement the IEnumerable interface, which requires you to implement a method named GetEnumerator. However, instead of using the yield return statement in GetEnumerator, you must instantiate and return an object that implements the IEnumerator interface. The IEnumerator interface provides a read-only, forward-only cursor for accessing the members of the underlying collection. Table 13-2 describes the members of the IEnumerator interface. The IEnumerator instance returned by GetEnumerator is your custom iterator—the object that actually supports enumeration of the collection's data elements.

Table 13-2. *Members of the* IEnumerator *Interface*

Member	Description
Current	Property that returns the current data element. When the enumerator is created, Current refers to a position preceding the first data element. This means you must call MoveNext before using Current. If Current is called and the enumerator is positioned before the first element or after the last element in the data collection, Current must throw a System.InvalidOperationException.
MoveNext	Method that moves the enumerator to the next data element in the collection. Returns true if there are more elements; otherwise, it returns false. If the underlying source of data changes during the life of the enumerator, MoveNext must throw an InvalidOperationException.
Reset	Method that moves the enumerator to a position preceding the first element in the data collection. If the underlying source of data changes during the life of the enumerator, Reset must throw an InvalidOperationException.

If your collection class contains different types of data that you want to enumerate separately, implementing the IEnumerable interface on the collection class is insufficient. In this case, you would implement a number of properties that returned different IEnumerator instances.

The Code

The TeamMember, Team, and TeamMemberEnumerator classes in the following example demonstrate the implementation of a custom iterator using the IEnumerable and IEnumerator interfaces. The TeamMember class represents a member of a team. The Team class, which represents a team of people, is a collection of TeamMember objects. Team implements the IEnumerable interface and declares a separate class, named TeamMemberEnumerator, to provide enumeration functionality. Team implements the *Observer pattern* using delegate and event members to notify all TeamMemberEnumerator objects if their underlying Team changes. (See recipe 13-11 for a detailed description of the Observer pattern.) The TeamMemberEnumerator class is a private nested class, so you cannot create instances of it other than through the Team.GetEnumerator method.

```
using System;
using System.Collections;

namespace Apress.VisualCSharpRecipes.Chapter13
{
    // TeamMember class represents an individual team member.
    public class TeamMember
    {
        public string Name;
        public string Title;

        // Simple TeamMember constructor.
        public TeamMember(string name, string title)
        {
            Name = name;
            Title = title;
        }

        // Returns a string representation of the TeamMember.
        public override string ToString()
        {
            return string.Format("{0} ({1})", Name, Title);
        }
    }

    // Team class represents a collection of TeamMember objects. Implements
    // the IEnumerable interface to support enumerating TeamMember objects.
    public class Team : IEnumerable
    {
        // TeamMemberEnumerator is a private nested class that provides
        // the functionality to enumerate the TeamMembers contained in
        // a Team collection. As a nested class, TeamMemberEnumerator
        // has access to the private members of the Team class.
        private class TeamMemberEnumerator : IEnumerator
        {
            // The Team that this object is enumerating.
            private Team sourceTeam;

            // Boolean to indicate whether underlying Team has changed
            // and so is invalid for further enumeration.
            private bool teamInvalid = false;
```

```csharp
// Integer to identify the current TeamMember. Provides
// the index of the TeamMember in the underlying ArrayList
// used by the Team collection. Initialize to -1, which is
// the index prior to the first element.
private int currentMember = -1;

// Constructor takes a reference to the Team that is the source
// of enumerated data.
internal TeamMemberEnumerator(Team team)
{
    this.sourceTeam = team;

    // Register with sourceTeam for change notifications.
    sourceTeam.TeamChange +=
        new TeamChangedEventHandler(this.TeamChange);
}

// Implement the IEnumerator.Current property.
public object Current
{
    get
    {
        // If the TeamMemberEnumerator is positioned before
        // the first element or after the last element, then
        // throw an exception.
        if (currentMember == -1 ||
            currentMember > (sourceTeam.teamMembers.Count - 1))
        {
            throw new InvalidOperationException();
        }

        //Otherwise, return the current TeamMember.
        return sourceTeam.teamMembers[currentMember];
    }
}

// Implement the IEnumerator.MoveNext method.
public bool MoveNext()
{
    // If underlying Team is invalid, throw exception.
    if (teamInvalid)
    {
        throw new InvalidOperationException("Team modified");
    }

    // Otherwise, progress to the next TeamMember.
    currentMember++;

    // Return false if we have moved past the last TeamMember.
    if (currentMember > (sourceTeam.teamMembers.Count - 1))
    {
        return false;
    }
```

```
        else
        {
            return true;
        }
    }

    // Implement the IEnumerator.Reset method.
    // This method resets the position of the TeamMemberEnumerator
    // to the beginning of the TeamMembers collection.
    public void Reset()
    {
        // If underlying Team is invalid, throw exception.
        if (teamInvalid)
        {
            throw new InvalidOperationException("Team modified");
        }

        // Move the currentMember pointer back to the index
        // preceding the first element.
        currentMember = -1;
    }

    // An event handler to handle notifications that the underlying
    // Team collection has changed.
    internal void TeamChange(Team t, EventArgs e)
    {
        // Signal that the underlying Team is now invalid.
        teamInvalid = true;
    }
}

// A delegate that specifies the signature that all team change event
// handler methods must implement.
public delegate void TeamChangedEventHandler(Team t, EventArgs e);

// An ArrayList to contain the TeamMember objects.
private ArrayList teamMembers;

// The event used to notify TeamMemberEnumerators that the Team
// has changed.
public event TeamChangedEventHandler TeamChange;

// Team constructor.
public Team()
{
    teamMembers = new ArrayList();
}

// Implement the IEnumerable.GetEnumerator method.
public IEnumerator GetEnumerator()
{
    return new TeamMemberEnumerator(this);
}

// Adds a TeamMember object to the Team.
public void AddMember(TeamMember member)
```

```csharp
        {
            teamMembers.Add(member);

            // Notify listeners that the list has changed.
            if (TeamChange != null)
            {
                TeamChange(this, null);
            }
        }
    }
}

// A class to demonstrate the use of Team.
Public class Recipe13_05
{
    public static void Main()
    {
        // Create a new Team.
        Team team = new Team();
        team.AddMember(new TeamMember("Curly", "Clown"));
        team.AddMember(new TeamMember("Nick", "Knife Thrower"));
        team.AddMember(new TeamMember("Nancy", "Strong Man"));

        // Enumerate the Team.
        Console.Clear();
        Console.WriteLine("Enumerate with foreach loop:");
        foreach (TeamMember member in team)
        {
            Console.WriteLine(member.ToString());
        }

        // Enumerate using a While loop.
        Console.WriteLine(Environment.NewLine);
        Console.WriteLine("Enumerate with while loop:");
        IEnumerator e = team.GetEnumerator();
        while (e.MoveNext())
        {
            Console.WriteLine(e.Current);
        }

        // Enumerate the Team and try to add a Team Member.
        // (This will cause an exception to be thrown.)
        Console.WriteLine(Environment.NewLine);
        Console.WriteLine("Modify while enumerating:");
        foreach (TeamMember member in team)
        {
            Console.WriteLine(member.ToString());
            team.AddMember(new TeamMember("Stumpy", "Lion Tamer"));
        }

        // Wait to continue.
        Console.WriteLine(Environment.NewLine);
        Console.WriteLine("Main method complete. Press Enter");
        Console.ReadLine();
    }
}
}
```

13-6. Implement a Disposable Class

Problem

You need to create a class that references unmanaged resources and provide a mechanism for users of the class to free those unmanaged resources deterministically.

Solution

Implement the System.IDisposable interface, and release the unmanaged resources when client code calls the IDisposable.Dispose method.

How It Works

An unreferenced object continues to exist on the managed heap and consume resources until the garbage collector releases the object and reclaims the resources. The garbage collector will automatically free managed resources (such as memory), but it will not free unmanaged resources (such as file handles and database connections) referenced by managed objects. If an object contains data members that reference unmanaged resources, the object must free those resources explicitly.

One solution is to declare a destructor—or finalizer—for the class (*destructor* is a C++ term equivalent to the more general .NET term *finalizer*). Prior to reclaiming the memory consumed by an instance of the class, the garbage collector calls the object's finalizer. The finalizer can take the necessary steps to release any unmanaged resources. Unfortunately, because the garbage collector uses a single thread to execute all finalizers, use of finalizers can have a detrimental effect on the efficiency of the garbage collection process, which will affect the performance of your application. In addition, you cannot control when the runtime frees unmanaged resources because you cannot call an object's finalizer directly, and you have only limited control over the activities of the garbage collector using the System.GC class.

As a complementary mechanism to using finalizers, the .NET Framework defines the *Dispose pattern* as a means to provide deterministic control over when to free unmanaged resources. To implement the Dispose pattern, a class must implement the IDisposable interface, which declares a single method named Dispose. In the Dispose method, you must implement the code necessary to release any unmanaged resources and remove the object from the list of objects eligible for finalization if a finalizer has been defined.

Instances of classes that implement the Dispose pattern are called *disposable objects*. When code has finished with a disposable object, it calls the object's Dispose method to free all resources and make it unusable, but still relies on the garbage collector to eventually release the object memory. It's important to understand that the runtime does not enforce disposal of objects; it's the responsibility of the client to call the Dispose method. However, because the .NET Framework class library uses the Dispose pattern extensively, C# provides the using statement to simplify the correct use of disposable objects. The following code shows the structure of a using statement:

```
using (FileStream fileStream = new FileStream("SomeFile.txt", FileMode.Open)) {
    // Do something with the fileStream object.
}
```

When the code reaches the end of the block in which the disposable object was declared, the object's Dispose method is automatically called, even if an exception is raised. Here are some points to consider when implementing the Dispose pattern:

- Client code should be able to call the Dispose method repeatedly with no adverse effects.

- In multithreaded applications, it's important that only one thread execute the Dispose method concurrently. It's normally the responsibility of the client code to ensure thread synchronization, although you could decide to implement synchronization within the Dispose method.

- The Dispose method should not throw exceptions.

- Because the Dispose method does all necessary cleaning up, you do not need to call the object's finalizer. Your Dispose method should call the GC.SuppressFinalize method to ensure the finalizer is not called during garbage collection.

- Implement a finalizer that calls the unmanaged cleanup part of your Dispose method as a safety mechanism in case client code does not call Dispose correctly. However, avoid referencing managed objects in finalizers, because you cannot be certain of the object's state.

- If a disposable class extends another disposable class, the Dispose method of the child must call the Dispose method of its base class. Wrap the child's code in a try block and call the parent's Dispose method in a finally clause to ensure execution.

- Other instance methods and properties of the class should throw a System.ObjectDisposedException exception if client code attempts to execute a method on an already disposed object.

The Code

The following example demonstrates a common implementation of the Dispose pattern.

```
using System;

namespace Apress.VisualCSharpRecipes.Chapter13
{
    // Implement the IDisposable interface.
    public class DisposeExample : IDisposable
    {
        // Private data member to signal if the object has already been
        // disposed.
        bool isDisposed = false;

        // Private data member that holds the handle to an unmanaged resource.
        private IntPtr resourceHandle;

        // Constructor.
        public DisposeExample()
        {
            // Constructor code obtains reference to unmanaged resource.
            resourceHandle = default(IntPtr);
        }

        // Destructor / Finalizer. Because Dispose calls GC.SuppressFinalize,
        // this method is called by the garbage collection process only if
        // the consumer of the object does not call Dispose as it should.
        ~DisposeExample()
        {
            // Call the Dispose method as opposed to duplicating the code to
            // clean up any unmanaged resources. Use the protected Dispose
            // overload and pass a value of "false" to indicate that Dispose is
            // being called during the garbage collection process, not by
```

```
        // consumer code.
        Dispose(false);
    }


    // Public implementation of the IDisposable.Dispose method, called
    // by the consumer of the object in order to free unmanaged resources
    // deterministically.
    public void Dispose()
    {
        // Call the protected Dispose overload and pass a value of "true"
        // to indicate that Dispose is being called by consumer code, not
        // by the garbage collector.
        Dispose(true);

        // Because the Dispose method performs all necessary cleanup,
        // ensure the garbage collector does not call the class destructor.
        GC.SuppressFinalize(this);
    }


    // Protected overload of the Dispose method. The disposing argument
    // signals whether the method is called by consumer code (true), or by
    // the garbage collector (false). Note that this method is not part of
    // the IDisposable interface because it has a different signature to the
    // parameterless Dispose method.
    protected virtual void Dispose(bool disposing)
    {
        // Don't try to Dispose of the object twice.
        if (!isDisposed)
        {
            // Determine if consumer code or the garbage collector is
            // calling. Avoid referencing other managed objects during
            // finalization.
            if (disposing)
            {
                // Method called by consumer code. Call the Dispose method
                // of any managed data members that implement the
                // IDisposable interface.
                // ...
            }

            // Whether called by consumer code or the garbage collector,
            // free all unmanaged resources and set the value of managed
            // data members to null.
            // Close(resourceHandle);

            // In the case of an inherited type, call base.Dispose(disposing).
        }

        // Signal that this object has been disposed.
        isDisposed = true;
    }


    // Before executing any functionality, ensure that Dispose has not
    // already been executed on the object.
    public void SomeMethod()
    {
        // Throw an exception if the object has already been disposed.
```

```
            if (isDisposed)
            {
                throw new ObjectDisposedException("DisposeExample");
            }

            // Execute method functionality.
            // . . .
        }
    }

    // A class to demonstrate the use of DisposeExample.
    Public class Recipe13_06
    {
        public static void Main()
        {
            // The using statement ensures the Dispose method is called
            // even if an exception occurs.
            using (DisposeExample d = new DisposeExample())
            {
                // Do something with d.
            }

            // Wait to continue.
            Console.WriteLine(Environment.NewLine);
            Console.WriteLine("Main method complete. Press Enter");
            Console.ReadLine();
        }
    }
}
```

13-7. Implement a Formattable Type

Problem

You need to implement a type that can create different string representations of its content based on the use of format specifiers, for use in formatted strings.

Solution

Implement the System.IFormattable interface.

How It Works

The following code fragment demonstrates the use of format specifiers in the WriteLine method of the System.Console class. The codes in the braces (emphasized in the example) are the format specifiers.

```
double a = 345678.5678;
uint b = 12000;
byte c = 254;
Console.WriteLine("a = {0}, b = {1}, and c = {2}", a, b, c);
Console.WriteLine("a = {0:c0}, b = {1:n4}, and c = {2,10:x5}", a, b, c);
```

When run on a machine configured with English (U.K.) regional settings, this code will result in the output shown here.

```
a = 345678.5678, b = 12000, and c = 254
a = £345,679, b = 12,000.0000, and c =       000fe
```

As you can see, changing the contents of the format specifiers changes the format of the output significantly, even though the data has not changed. To enable support for format specifiers in your own types, you must implement the IFormattable interface. IFormattable declares a single method named ToString with the following signature:

```
string ToString(string format, IFormatProvider formatProvider);
```

The format argument is a System.String containing a *format string*. The format string is the portion of the format specifier that follows the colon. For example, in the format specifier {2,10:x5} used in the previous example, x5 is the format string. The format string contains the instructions the IFormattable instance should use when it's generating the string representation of its content. The .NET Framework documentation for IFormattable states that types that implement IFormattable must support the G (general) format string, but that the other supported format strings depend on the implementation. The format argument will be null if the format specifier does not include a format string component; for example, {0} or {1,20}.

The formatProvider argument is a reference to an instance of a type that implements System. IFormatProvider, and which provides access to information about the cultural and regional preferences to use when generating the string representation of the IFormattable object. This information includes data such as the appropriate currency symbol or number of decimal places to use. By default, formatProvider is null, which means you should use the current thread's regional and cultural settings, available through the static method CurrentCulture of the System.Globalization. CultureInfo class. Some methods that generate formatted strings, such as String.Format, allow you to specify an alternative IFormatProvider to use such as CultureInfo, DateTimeFormatInfo, or NumberFormatInfo.

The .NET Framework uses IFormattable primarily to support the formatting of value types, but it can be used to good effect with any type.

The Code

The following example contains a class named Person that implements the IFormattable interface. The Person class contains the title and names of a person and will render the person's name in different formats depending on the format strings provided. The Person class does not make use of regional and cultural settings provided by the formatProvider argument. The Main method demonstrates how to use the formatting capabilities of the Person class.

```csharp
using System;

namespace Apress.VisualCSharpRecipes.Chapter13
{
    public class Person : IFormattable
    {
        // Private members to hold the person's title and name details.
        private string title;
        private string[] names;

        // Constructor used to set the person's title and names.
        public Person(string title, params string[] names)
        {
```

```csharp
        this.title = title;
        this.names = names;
    }

    // Override the Object.ToString method to return the person's
    // name using the general format.
    public override string ToString()
    {
        return ToString("G", null);
    }

    // Implementation of the IFormattable.ToString method to return the
    // person's name in different forms based on the format string
    // provided.
    public string ToString(string format, IFormatProvider formatProvider)
    {
        string result = null;

        // Use the general format if none is specified.
        if (format == null) format = "G";

        // The contents of the format string determine the format of the
        // name returned.
        switch (format.ToUpper()[0])
        {
            case 'S':
                // Use short form - first initial and surname.
                result = names[0][0] + ". " + names[names.Length - 1];
                break;

            case 'P':
                // Use polite form - title, initials, and surname
                // Add the person's title to the result.
                if (title != null && title.Length != 0)
                {
                    result = title + ". ";
                }
                // Add the person's initials and surname.
                for (int count = 0; count < names.Length; count++)
                {
                    if (count != (names.Length - 1))
                    {
                        result += names[count][0] + ". ";
                    }
                    else
                    {
                        result += names[count];
                    }
                }
                break;

            case 'I':
                // Use informal form - first name only.
                result = names[0];
                break;
```

```
                    case 'G':
                    default:
                        // Use general/default form - first name and surname.
                        result = names[0] + " " + names[names.Length - 1];
                        break;
                }
                return result;
            }
        }

        // A class to demonstrate the use of Person.
        Public class Recipe13_07
        {
            public static void Main()
            {
                // Create a Person object representing a man with the name
                // Mr. Richard Glen David Peters.
                Person person =
                    new Person("Mr", "Richard", "Glen", "David", "Peters");

                // Display the person's name using a variety of format strings.
                System.Console.WriteLine("Dear {0:G},", person);
                System.Console.WriteLine("Dear {0:P},", person);
                System.Console.WriteLine("Dear {0:I},", person);
                System.Console.WriteLine("Dear {0},", person);
                System.Console.WriteLine("Dear {0:S},", person);

                // Wait to continue.
                Console.WriteLine(Environment.NewLine);
                Console.WriteLine("Main method complete. Press Enter");
                Console.ReadLine();
            }
        }
    }
```

Usage

When executed, the preceding example produces the following output:

```
Dear Richard Peters,
Dear Mr. R. G. D. Peters,
Dear Richard,
Dear Richard Peters,
Dear R. Peters,
```

13-8. Implement a Custom Exception Class

Problem

You need to create a custom exception class so that you can use the runtime's exception-handling mechanism to handle application-specific exceptions.

Solution

Create a serializable class that extends the System.Exception class. Add support for any custom data members required by the exception, including constructors and properties required to manipulate the data members.

Tip If you need to define a number of custom exceptions for use in a single application or library, you should define a single custom exception that extends System.Exception and use this as a common base class for all of your other custom exceptions. There is very little point in extending System.Application, as is often recommended. Doing so simply introduces another level in your exception hierarchy and provides little if any benefit when handling your exception classes—after all, catching a nonspecific exception like ApplicationException is just as bad a practice as catching Exception.

How It Works

Exception classes are unique in the fact that you do not declare new classes solely to implement new or extended functionality. The runtime's exception-handling mechanism—exposed by the C# statements try, catch, and finally—works based on the *type* of exception thrown, not the functional or data members implemented by the thrown exception.

If you need to throw an exception, you should use an existing exception class from the .NET Framework class library, if a suitable one exists. For example, some useful exceptions include the following:

- System.ArgumentNullException, when code passes a null argument value to your method that does not support null arguments

- System.ArgumentOutOfRangeException, when code passes an inappropriately large or small argument value to your method

- System.FormatException, when code attempts to pass your method a String argument containing incorrectly formatted data

If none of the existing exception classes meets your needs, or you feel your application would benefit from using application-specific exceptions, it's a simple matter to create your own exception class. In order to integrate your custom exception with the runtime's exception-handling mechanism and remain consistent with the pattern implemented by .NET Framework–defined exception classes, you should do the following:

- Give your exception class a meaningful name ending in the word *Exception*, such as TypeMismatchException or RecordNotFoundException.

- Mark your exception class as sealed if you do not intend other exception classes to extend it.

- Implement additional data members and properties to support custom information that the exception class should provide.

- Implement three public constructors with the signatures shown here and ensure they call the base class constructor.

```
public CustomException() : base() {}
public CustomException(string msg): base(msg) {}
public CustomException(string msg, Exception inner) : base(msg, inner) {}
```

- Make your exception class serializable so that the runtime can marshal instances of your exception across application domain and machine boundaries. Applying the attribute System. SerializableAttribute is sufficient for exception classes that do not implement custom data members. However, because Exception implements the interface System.Runtime. Serialization.ISerializable, if your exception declares custom data members, you must override the ISerializable.GetObjectData method of the Exception class as well as implement a deserialization constructor with this signature. If your exception class is sealed, mark the deserialization constructor as private; otherwise, mark it as protected. The GetObjectData method and deserialization constructor must call the equivalent base class method to allow the base class to serialize and deserialize its data correctly. (See recipe 13-1 for details on making classes serializable.)

■**Tip** In large applications, you will usually implement quite a few custom exception classes. It pays to put signifi- cant thought into how you organize your custom exceptions and how code will use them. Generally, avoid creating new exception classes unless code will make specific efforts to catch that exception; use data members to achieve informational granularity, not additional exception classes. In addition, avoid deep class hierarchies when possible in favor of broad, shallow hierarchies.

The Code

The following example is a custom exception named CustomException that extends Exception and declares two custom data members: a string named stringInfo and a bool named booleanInfo.

```
using System;
using System.Runtime.Serialization;

namespace Apress.VisualCSharpRecipes.Chapter13
{
    // Mark CustomException as Serializable.
    [Serializable]
    public sealed class CustomException : Exception
    {
        // Custom data members for CustomException.
        private string stringInfo;
        private bool booleanInfo;

        // Three standard constructors and simply call the base class
        // constructor (System.Exception).
        public CustomException() : base() { }

        public CustomException(string message) : base(message) { }

        public CustomException(string message, Exception inner)
            : base(message, inner) { }

        // The deserialization constructor required by the ISerialization
        // interface. Because CustomException is sealed, this constructor
        // is private. If CustomException were not sealed, this constructor
        // should be declared as protected so that derived classes can call
        // it during deserialization.
        private CustomException(SerializationInfo info,
            StreamingContext context) : base(info, context)
        {
```

```csharp
        // Deserialize each custom data member.
        stringInfo = info.GetString("StringInfo");
        booleanInfo = info.GetBoolean("BooleanInfo");
    }

    // Additional constructors to allow code to set the custom data
    // members.
    public CustomException(string message, string stringInfo,
        bool booleanInfo) : this(message)
    {
        this.stringInfo = stringInfo;
        this.booleanInfo = booleanInfo;
    }

    public CustomException(string message, Exception inner,
        string stringInfo, bool booleanInfo): this(message, inner)
    {
        this.stringInfo = stringInfo;
        this.booleanInfo = booleanInfo;
    }

    // Read-only properties that provide access to the custom data members.
    public string StringInfo
    {
        get { return stringInfo; }
    }

    public bool BooleanInfo
    {
        get { return booleanInfo; }
    }

    // The GetObjectData method (declared in the ISerializable interface)
    // is used during serialization of CustomException. Because
    // CustomException declares custom data members, it must override the
    // base class implementation of GetObjectData.
    public override void GetObjectData(SerializationInfo info,
        StreamingContext context)
    {
        // Serialize the custom data members.
        info.AddValue("StringInfo", stringInfo);
        info.AddValue("BooleanInfo", booleanInfo);

        // Call the base class to serialize its members.
        base.GetObjectData(info, context);
    }

    // Override the base class Message property to include the custom data
    // members.
    public override string Message
    {
        get
        {
            string message = base.Message;
            if (stringInfo != null)
            {
                message += Environment.NewLine +
```

```
                        stringInfo + " = " + booleanInfo;
                }
                return message;
            }
        }
    }

    // A class to demonstrate the use of CustomException.
    Public class Recipe13_08
    {
        public static void Main()
        {
            try
            {
                // Create and throw a CustomException object.
                throw new CustomException("Some error",
                    "SomeCustomMessage", true);
            }
            catch (CustomException ex)
            {
                Console.WriteLine(ex.Message);
            }

            // Wait to continue.
            Console.WriteLine(Environment.NewLine);
            Console.WriteLine("Main method complete. Press Enter");
            Console.ReadLine();
        }
    }
}
```

13-9. Implement a Custom Event Argument

Problem

When you raise an event, you need to pass an event-specific state to the event handlers.

Solution

Create a custom event argument class derived from the System.EventArg class. When you raise the event, create an instance of your event argument class and pass it to the event handlers.

How It Works

When you declare your own event types, you will often want to pass event-specific state to any listening event handlers. To create a custom event argument class that complies with the *Event pattern* defined by the .NET Framework, you should do the following:

- Derive your custom event argument class from the EventArgs class. The EventArgs class contains no data and is used with events that do not need to pass event state.

- Give your event argument class a meaningful name ending in *EventArgs*, such as DiskFullEventArgs or MailReceivedEventArgs.

- Mark your argument class as sealed if you do not intend other event argument classes to extend it.

- Implement additional data members and properties to support event state that you need to pass to event handlers. It's best to make event state immutable, so you should use private readonly data members and use public properties to provide read-only access to the data members.

- Implement a public constructor that allows you to set the initial configuration of the event state.

- Make your event argument class serializable so that the runtime can marshal instances of it across application domain and machine boundaries. Applying the attribute System. SerializableAttribute is usually sufficient for event argument classes. However, if your class has special serialization requirements, you must also implement the interface System.Runtime. Serialization.ISerializable. (See recipe 13-1 for details on making classes serializable.)

The Code

The following example demonstrates the implementation of an event argument class named MailReceivedEventArgs. Theoretically, an e-mail server passes instances of the MailReceivedEventArgs class to event handlers in response to the receipt of an e-mail message. The MailReceivedEventArgs class contains information about the sender and subject of the received e-mail message.

```
using System;

namespace Apress.VisualCSharpRecipes.Chapter13
{
    [Serializable]
    public sealed class MailReceivedEventArgs : EventArgs
    {
        // Private read-only members that hold the event state that is to be
        // distributed to all event handlers. The MailReceivedEventArgs class
        // will specify who sent the received mail and what the subject is.
        private readonly string from;
        private readonly string subject;

        // Constructor, initializes event state.
        public MailReceivedEventArgs(string from, string subject)
        {
            this.from = from;
            this.subject = subject;
        }

        // Read-only properties to provide access to event state.
        public string From { get { return from; } }
        public string Subject { get { return subject; } }
    }

    // A class to demonstrate the use of MailReceivedEventArgs.
    Public class Recipe13_09
    {
        public static void Main()
        {
            MailReceivedEventArgs args =
                new MailReceivedEventArgs("Danielle", "Your book");
```

```
            Console.WriteLine("From: {0}, Subject: {1}", args.From, args.Subject);

            // Wait to continue.
            Console.WriteLine(Environment.NewLine);
            Console.WriteLine("Main method complete. Press Enter");
            Console.ReadLine();
        }
    }
}
```

13-10. Implement the Singleton Pattern

Problem

You need to ensure that only a single instance of a type exists at any given time and that the single instance is accessible to all elements of your application.

Solution

Implement the type using the *Singleton pattern*.

How It Works

Of all the identified patterns, the Singleton pattern is perhaps the most widely known and commonly used. The purpose of the Singleton pattern is to ensure that only one instance of a type exists at a given time and to provide global access to the functionality of that single instance. You can implement the type using the Singleton pattern by doing the following:

- Implement a private static member within the type to hold a reference to the single instance of the type.

- Implement a publicly accessible static property in the type to provide read-only access to the singleton instance.

- Implement only a private constructor so that code cannot create additional instances of the type.

The Code

The following example demonstrates an implementation of the Singleton pattern for a class named SingletonExample.

```
using System;

namespace Apress.VisualCSharpRecipes.Chapter13
{
    public class SingletonExample
    {
        // A static member to hold a reference to the singleton instance.
        private static SingletonExample instance;

        // A static constructor to create the singleton instance. Another
        // alternative is to use lazy initialization in the Instance property.
        static SingletonExample()
```

```
    {
        instance = new SingletonExample();
    }

    // A private constructor to stop code from creating additional
    // instances of the singleton type.
    private SingletonExample() { }

    // A public property to provide access to the singleton instance.
    public static SingletonExample Instance
    {
        get { return instance; }
    }

    // Public methods that provide singleton functionality.
    public void SomeMethod1() { /*..*/ }
    public void SomeMethod2() { /*..*/ }
    }
}
```

Usage

To invoke the functionality of the SingletonExample class, you can obtain a reference to the singleton using the Instance property and then call its methods. Alternatively, you can execute members of the singleton directly through the Instance property. The following code shows both approaches.

```
// Obtain reference to singleton and invoke methods
SingletonExample s = SingletonExample.Instance;
s.SomeMethod1();

// Execute singleton functionality without a reference
SingletonExample.Instance.SomeMethod2();
```

13-11. Implement the Observer Pattern

Problem

You need to implement an efficient mechanism for an object (the subject) to notify other objects (the observers) about changes to its state.

Solution

Implement the *Observer pattern* using delegate types as type-safe function pointers and event types to manage and notify the set of observers.

How It Works

The traditional approach to implementing the Observer pattern is to implement two interfaces: one to represent an observer (IObserver) and the other to represent the subject (ISubject). Objects that implement IObserver register with the subject, indicating that they want to be notified of important events (such as state changes) affecting the subject. The subject is responsible for managing the list of registered observers and notifying them in response to events affecting the subject. The subject usually notifies observers by calling a `Notify` method declared in the `IObserver` interface. The subject might pass data to the observer as part of the `Notify` method, or the observer might need to call a method declared in the `ISubject` interface to obtain additional details about the event.

Although you are free to implement the Observer pattern in C# using the approach just described, the Observer pattern is so pervasive in modern software solutions that C# and the .NET Framework include event and delegate types to simplify its implementation. The use of events and delegates means that you do not need to declare `IObserver` and `ISubject` interfaces. In addition, you do not need to implement the logic necessary to manage and notify the set of registered observers—the area where most coding errors occur.

The .NET Framework uses one particular implementation of the event-based and delegate-based Observer pattern so frequently that it has been given its own name: the *Event pattern*. (Pattern purists might prefer the name *Event idiom*, but Event pattern is the name most commonly used in Microsoft documentation.)

The Code

The example for this recipe contains a complete implementation of the Event pattern, which includes the following types:

- `Thermostat` class (the subject of the example), which keeps track of the current temperature and notifies observers when a temperature change occurs

- `TemperatureChangeEventArgs` class, which is a custom implementation of the `System.EventArgs` class used to encapsulate temperature change data for distribution during the notification of observers

- `TemperatureEventHandler` delegate, which defines the signature of the method that all observers of a `Thermostat` object must implement, and which a `Thermostat` object will call in the event of temperature changes

- `TemperatureChangeObserver` and `TemperatureAverageObserver` classes, which are observers of the `Thermostat` class

The `TemperatureChangeEventArgs` class (in the following listing) derives from the class `System.EventArgs`. The custom event argument class should contain all of the data that the subject needs to pass to its observers when it notifies them of an event. If you do not need to pass data with your event notifications, you do not need to define a new argument class; simply pass `EventArgs.Empty` or `null` as the argument when you raise the event. (See recipe 13-9 for details on implementing custom event argument classes.)

```
namespace Apress.VisualCSharpRecipes.Chapter13
{
    // An event argument class that contains information about a temperature
    // change event. An instance of this class is passed with every event.
    public class TemperatureChangedEventArgs : EventArgs
    {
        // Private data members contain the old and new temperature readings.
        private readonly int oldTemperature, newTemperature;

        // Constructor that takes the old and new temperature values.
        public TemperatureChangedEventArgs(int oldTemp, int newTemp)
        {
            oldTemperature = oldTemp;
            newTemperature = newTemp;
        }
```

```
        // Read-only properties provide access to the temperature values.
        public int OldTemperature { get { return oldTemperature; } }
        public int NewTemperature { get { return newTemperature; } }
    }
}
```

The following code shows the declaration of the TemperatureEventHandler delegate. Based on this declaration, all observers must implement a method (the name is unimportant), which returns void and takes two arguments: an Object instance as the first argument and a TemperatureChangeEventArgs object as the second. During notification, the Object argument is a reference to the Thermostat object that raises the event, and the TemperatureChangeEventArgs argument contains data about the old and new temperature values.

```
namespace Apress.VisualCSharpRecipes.Chapter13
{
    // A delegate that specifies the signature that all temperature event
    // handler methods must implement.
    public delegate void TemperatureChangedEventHandler(Object sender,
        TemperatureChangeEventArgs args);
}
```

For the purpose of demonstrating the Observer pattern, the example contains two different observer types: TemperatureAverageObserver and TemperatureChangeObserver. Both classes have the same basic implementation. TemperatureAverageObserver keeps a count of the number of temperature change events and the sum of the temperature values, and displays an average temperature when each event occurs. TemperatureChangeObserver displays information about the change in temperature each time a temperature change event occurs.

The following listing shows the TemperatureChangeObserver and TemperatureAverageObserver classes. Notice that the constructors take references to the Thermostat object that the TemperatureChangeObserver or TemperatureAverageObserver object should observe. When you instantiate an observer, pass it a reference to the subject. The observer must create a delegate instance containing a reference to the observer's event-handler method. To register as an observer, the observer object must then add its delegate instance to the subject using the subject's public event member. This is made even easier with the simplified delegate syntax provided by C# 2.0, where it is no longer required to explicitly instantiate a delegate to wrap the listening method.

Once the TemperatureChangeObserver or TemperatureAverageObserver object has registered its delegate instance with the Thermostat object, you need to maintain a reference to this Thermostat object only if you want to stop observing it later on. In addition, you do not need to maintain a reference to the subject, because a reference to the event source is included as the first argument each time the Thermostat object raises an event through the TemperatureChange method.

```
namespace Apress.VisualCSharpRecipes.Chapter13
{
    // A Thermostat observer that displays information about the change in
    // temperature when a temperature change event occurs.
    public class TemperatureChangeObserver
    {
        // A constructor that takes a reference to the Thermostat object that
        // the TemperatureChangeObserver object should observe.
        public TemperatureChangeObserver(Thermostat t)
        {
            // Create a new TemperatureChangedEventHandler delegate instance and
            // register it with the specified Thermostat.
            t.TemperatureChanged += this.TemperatureChange;
        }
```

```
            // The method to handle temperature change events.
            public void TemperatureChange(Object sender,
                TemperatureChangedEventArgs temp)
            {
                Console.WriteLine ("ChangeObserver: Old={0}, New={1}, Change={2}",
                    temp.OldTemperature, temp.NewTemperature,
                    temp.NewTemperature - temp.OldTemperature);
            }
        }

        // A Thermostat observer that displays information about the average
        // temperature when a temperature change event occurs.
        public class TemperatureAverageObserver
        {
            // Sum contains the running total of temperature readings.
            // Count contains the number of temperature events received.
            private int sum = 0, count = 0;

            // A constructor that takes a reference to the Thermostat object that
            // the TemperatureAverageObserver object should observe.
            public TemperatureAverageObserver(Thermostat t)
            {
                // Create a new TemperatureChangedEventHandler delegate instance and
                // register it with the specified Thermostat.
                t.TemperatureChanged += this.TemperatureChange;
            }

            // The method to handle temperature change events.
            public void TemperatureChange(Object sender,
                TemperatureChangedEventArgs temp)
            {
                count++;
                sum += temp.NewTemperature;

                Console.WriteLine
                    ("AverageObserver: Average={0:F}", (double)sum / (double)count);
            }
        }
    }
}
```

Finally, the Thermostat class is the observed object in this Observer (Event) pattern. In theory, a monitoring device sets the current temperature by calling the Temperature property on a Thermostat object. This causes the Thermostat object to raise its TemperatureChange event and send a TemperatureChangeEventArgs object to each observer.

The example contains a Recipe13_11 class that defines a Main method to drive the example. After creating a Thermostat object and two different observer objects, the Main method repeatedly prompts you to enter a temperature. Each time you enter a new temperature, the Thermostat object notifies the listeners, which display information to the console. The following is the code for the Thermostat class.

```
namespace Apress.VisualCSharpRecipes.Chapter13
{
    // A class that represents a Thermostat, which is the source of temperature
    // change events. In the Observer pattern, a Thermostat object is the
    // Subject that Observers listen to for change notifications.
    public class Thermostat
    {
```

```csharp
        // Private field to hold current temperature.
        private int temperature = 0;

        // The event used to maintain a list of observer delegates and raise
        // a temperature change event when a temperature change occurs.
        public event TemperatureChangedEventHandler TemperatureChanged;

        // A protected method used to raise the TemperatureChanged event.
        // Because events can be triggered only from within the containing
        // type, using a protected method to raise the event allows derived
        // classes to provide customized behavior and still be able to raise
        // the base class event.
        virtual protected void OnTemperatureChanged
            (TemperatureChangedEventArgs args)
        {
            // Notify all observers. A test for null indicates whether any
            // observers are registered.
            if (TemperatureChanged != null)
            {
                TemperatureChanged(this, args);
            }
        }

        // Public property to get and set the current temperature. The "set"
        // side of the property is responsible for raising the temperature
        // change event to notify all observers of a change in temperature.
        public int Temperature
        {
            get { return temperature; }

            set
            {
                // Create a new event argument object containing the old and
                // new temperatures.
                TemperatureChangedEventArgs args =
                    new TemperatureChangedEventArgs(temperature, value);

                // Update the current temperature.
                temperature = value;

                // Raise the temperature change event.
                OnTemperatureChanged(args);
            }
        }
    }

// A class to demonstrate the use of the Observer pattern.
public class Recipe13_11
{
    public static void Main()
    {
        // Create a Thermostat instance.
        Thermostat t = new Thermostat();

        // Create the Thermostat observers.
        new TemperatureChangeObserver(t);
        new TemperatureAverageObserver(t);
```

```
            // Loop, getting temperature readings from the user.
            // Any noninteger value will terminate the loop.
            do
            {
                Console.WriteLine(Environment.NewLine);
                Console.Write("Enter current temperature: ");

                try
                {
                    // Convert the user's input to an integer and use it to set
                    // the current temperature of the Thermostat.
                    t.Temperature = Int32.Parse(Console.ReadLine());
                }
                catch (Exception)
                {
                    // Use the exception condition to trigger termination.
                    Console.WriteLine("Terminating Observer Pattern Example.");

                    // Wait to continue.
                    Console.WriteLine(Environment.NewLine);
                    Console.WriteLine("Main method complete. Press Enter");
                    Console.ReadLine();
                    return;
                }
            } while (true);
        }
    }
}
```

Usage

The following listing shows the kind of output you should expect if you build and run the previous example. The bold values show your input.

```
Enter current temperature: 50
ChangeObserver: Old=0, New=50, Change=50
AverageObserver: Average=50.00

Enter current temperature: 20
ChangeObserver: Old=50, New=20, Change=-30
AverageObserver: Average=35.00

Enter current temperature: 40
ChangeObserver: Old=20, New=40, Change=20
AverageObserver: Average=36.67
```

CHAPTER 14

■ ■ ■

Windows Integration

The intention of the Microsoft .NET Framework is to run on a wide variety of operating systems to improve code mobility and simplify cross-platform integration. At the time this book was written, versions of the .NET Framework were available for various operating systems, including Microsoft Windows, FreeBSD, Linux, and Mac OS X. However, many of these implementations are yet to be widely adopted. Microsoft Windows is currently the operating system on which the .NET Framework is most commonly installed. Therefore, the recipes in this chapter describe how to perform the following tasks that are specific to the Windows operating system:

- Retrieve runtime environment information (recipes 14-1 and 14-2)
- Write to the Windows event log (recipe 14-3)
- Read, write, and search the Windows registry (recipe 14-4 and 14-5)
- Create and install Windows services (recipes 14-6 and 14-7)
- Create a shortcut on the Windows Start menu or desktop (recipe 14-8)

■**Note** The majority of functionality discussed in this chapter is protected by code access security permissions enforced by the common language runtime (CLR). See the .NET Framework software development kit (SDK) documentation for the specific permissions required to execute each member.

14-1. Access Runtime Environment Information

Problem

You need to access information about the runtime environment in which your application is running.

Solution

Use the members of the System.Environment class.

How It Works

The static Environment class provides a set of static members that you can use to obtain (and in some cases modify) information about the environment in which an application is running. Table 14-1 describes some of the most commonly used Environment members.

Table 14-1. *Commonly Used Members of the* Environment *Class*

Member	Description
Properties	
CommandLine	Gets a string containing the command line used to execute the current application, including the application name; see recipe 1-5 for details.
CurrentDirectory	Gets and sets a string containing the current application directory. Initially, this property will contain the name of the directory in which the application was started.
HasShutdownStarted	Gets a bool that indicates whether the CLR has started to shut down or the current application domain has started unloading.
MachineName	Gets a string containing the name of the machine.
OSVersion	Gets a System.OperatingSystem object that contains information about the platform and version of the underlying operating system. See the paragraph following this table for more details.
ProcessorCount	Gets the number of processors on the machine.
SystemDirectory	Gets a string containing the fully qualified path of the system directory, that is, the system32 subdirectory of the Windows installation folder.
TickCount	Gets an int representing the number of milliseconds that have elapsed since the system was started.
UserDomainName	Gets a string containing the Windows domain name to which the current user belongs. This will be the same as MachineName if the user has logged in on a machine account instead of a domain account.
UserInteractive	Gets a bool indicating whether the application is running in user interactive mode; in other words, its forms and message boxes will be visible to the logged-on user. UserInteractive will return false when the application is running as a service or is a Web application.
UserName	Gets a string containing the name of the user that started the current thread, which can be different from the logged-on user in case of impersonation.
Version	Gets a System.Version object that contains information about the version of the CLR.
Methods	
ExpandEnvironmentVariables	Replaces the names of environment variables in a string with the value of the variable; see recipe 14-2 for details.
GetCommandLineArgs	Returns a string array containing all elements of the command line used to execute the current application, including the application name; see recipe 1-5 for details.
GetEnvironmentVariable	Returns a string containing the value of a specified environment variable; see recipe 14-2 for details.
GetEnvironmentVariables	Returns an object implementing System.Collections.IDictionary, which contains all environment variables and their values; see recipe 14-2 for details.

Member	Description
GetFolderPath	Returns a string containing the path to a special system folder specified using the System.Environment.SpecialFolder enumeration. This includes folders for the Internet cache, cookies, history, desktop, and favorites; see the .NET Framework SDK documentation for a complete list of values.
GetLogicalDrives	Returns a string array containing the names of all logical drives, including network mapped drives. Note that each drive has the following syntax: <drive letter>:\.

The System.OperatingSystem object returned by OSVersion contains four properties:.

- The Platform property returns a value of the System.PlatformID enumeration identifying the current operating system; valid values are Unix, Win32NT, Win32S, Win32Windows, and WinCE.

- The ServicePack property returns a string identifying the service pack level installed on the computer. If no service packs are installed, or service packs are not supported, an empty string is returned.

- The Version property returns a System.Version object that identifies the specific operating system version.

- The VersionString property returns concatenated string summary of the Platform, ServicePack, and Version properties.

To determine the operating system on which you are running, you must use both the platform and the version information as detailed in Table 14-2.

Table 14-2. *Determining the Current Operating System*

PlatformID	Major Version	Minor Version	Operating System
Win32Windows	4	10	Windows 98
Win32Windows	4	90	Windows ME
Win32NT	4	0	Windows NT 4
Win32NT	5	0	Windows 2000
Win32NT	5	1	Windows XP
Win32NT	5	2	Windows Server 2003

The Code

The following example uses the Environment class to display information about the current environment to the console:

```
using System;

namespace Apress.VisualCSharpRecipes.Chapter14
{
    class Recipe14_01
    {
        public static void Main()
        {
            // Command line.
            Console.WriteLine("Command line : " + Environment.CommandLine);
```

```csharp
        // OS and CLR version information.
        Console.WriteLine(Environment.NewLine);
        Console.WriteLine("OS PlatformID : " +
            Environment.OSVersion.Platform);
        Console.WriteLine("OS Major Version : " +
            Environment.OSVersion.Version.Major);
        Console.WriteLine("OS Minor Version : " +
            Environment.OSVersion.Version.Minor);
        Console.WriteLine("CLR Version : " + Environment.Version);

        // User, machine, and domain name information.
        Console.WriteLine(Environment.NewLine);
        Console.WriteLine("User Name : " + Environment.UserName);
        Console.WriteLine("Domain Name : " + Environment.UserDomainName);
        Console.WriteLine("Machine name : " + Environment.MachineName);

        // Other environment information.
        Console.WriteLine(Environment.NewLine);
        Console.WriteLine("Is interactive? : "
            + Environment.UserInteractive);
        Console.WriteLine("Shutting down? : "
            + Environment.HasShutdownStarted);
        Console.WriteLine("Ticks since startup : "
            + Environment.TickCount);

        // Display the names of all logical drives.
        Console.WriteLine(Environment.NewLine);
        foreach (string s in Environment.GetLogicalDrives())
        {
            Console.WriteLine("Logical drive : " + s);
        }

        // Standard folder information.
        Console.WriteLine(Environment.NewLine);
        Console.WriteLine("Current folder : "
            + Environment.CurrentDirectory);
        Console.WriteLine("System folder : "
            + Environment.SystemDirectory);

        // Enumerate all special folders and display them.
        Console.WriteLine(Environment.NewLine);
        foreach (Environment.SpecialFolder s in
            Enum.GetValues(typeof(Environment.SpecialFolder)))
        {
            Console.WriteLine("{0} folder : {1}",
                s, Environment.GetFolderPath(s));
        }

        // Wait to continue.
        Console.WriteLine(Environment.NewLine);
        Console.WriteLine("Main method complete. Press Enter.");
        Console.ReadLine();
    }
  }
}
```

14-2. Retrieve the Value of an Environment Variable

Problem

You need to retrieve the value of an environment variable for use in your application.

Solution

Use the GetEnvironmentVariable, GetEnvironmentVariables, and ExpandEnvironmentVariables methods of the Environment class.

How It Works

The GetEnvironmentVariable method allows you to retrieve a string containing the value of a single named environment variable, whereas the GetEnvironmentVariables method returns an object implementing IDictionary that contains the names and values of all environment variables as strings. The .NET Framework 2.0 introduces an additional overload of the GetEnvironmentVariables method that takes a System.EnvironmentVariableTarget argument, allowing you to specify a subset of environment variables to return based on the target of the variable: Machine, Process, or User.

The ExpandEnvironmentVariables method provides a simple mechanism for substituting the value of an environment variable into a string by including the variable name enclosed in percent signs (%) within the string.

The Code

Here is an example that demonstrates how to use all three methods:

```
using System;
using System.Collections;

namespace Apress.VisualCSharpRecipes.Chapter14
{
    class Recipe14_02
    {
        public static void Main()
        {
            // Retrieve a named environment variable.
            Console.WriteLine("Path = " +
                Environment.GetEnvironmentVariable("Path"));
            Console.WriteLine(Environment.NewLine);

            // Substitute the value of named environment variables.
            Console.WriteLine(Environment.ExpandEnvironmentVariables(
                    "The Path on %computername% is %Path%"));
            Console.WriteLine(Environment.NewLine);

            // Retrieve all environment variables targeted at the process and
            // display the values of all that begin with the letter U.
            IDictionary vars = Environment.GetEnvironmentVariables(
                EnvironmentVariableTarget.Process);
```

```
            foreach (string s in vars.Keys)
            {
                if (s.ToUpper().StartsWith("U"))
                {
                    Console.WriteLine(s + " = " + vars[s]);
                }
            }

            // Wait to continue.
            Console.WriteLine(Environment.NewLine);
            Console.WriteLine("Main method complete. Press Enter.");
            Console.ReadLine();
        }
    }
}
```

14-3. Write an Event to the Windows Event Log

Problem

You need to write an event to the Windows event log.

Solution

Use the members of the System.Diagnostics.EventLog class to create a log (if required), register an event source, and write events.

How It Works

You can write to the Windows event log using the static methods of the EventLog class, or you can create an EventLog object and use its members. Whichever approach you choose, before writing to the event log you must decide which log you will use and register an event source against that log. The event source is simply a string that uniquely identifies your application. An event source may be registered against only one log at a time.

By default, the event log contains three separate logs: Application, System, and Security. Usually, you will write to the Application log, but you might decide your application warrants a custom log in which to write events. You do not need to explicitly create a custom log; when you register an event source against a log, if the specified log doesn't exist, it's created automatically.

Once you have decided on the destination log and registered an event source, you can start to write event log entries using the WriteEntry method. WriteEntry provides a variety of overloads that allow you to specify some or all of the following values:

- A string containing the event source for the log entry (static versions of WriteEntry only).

- A string containing the message for the log entry.

- A value from the System.Diagnostics.EventLogEntryType enumeration, which identifies the type of log entry. Valid values are Error, FailureAudit, Information, SuccessAudit, and Warning.

- An int that specifies an application-specific event ID for the log entry.

- A short that specifies an application-specific subcategory for the log entry.

- A byte array containing any raw data to associate with the log entry.

■Note The methods of the `EventLog` class also provide overloads that support the writing of events to the event log of remote machines; see the .NET Framework SDK documentation for more information.

The Code

The following example demonstrates how to use the `static` members of `EventLog` class to write an entry to the event log of the local machine:

```
using System;
using System.Diagnostics;

namespace Apress.VisualCSharpRecipes.Chapter14
{
    class Recipe14_03
    {
        public static void Main ()
        {
            // If it does not exist, register an event source for this
            // application against the Application log of the local machine.
            // Trying to register an event source that already exists on the
            // specified machine will throw a System.ArgumentException.
            if (!EventLog.SourceExists("Visual C# 2005 Recipes"))
            {
                EventLog.CreateEventSource("Visual C# 2005 Recipes",
                    "Application");
            }

            // Write an event to the event log.
            EventLog.WriteEntry(
                "Visual C# 2005 Recipes",        // Registered event source
                "A simple test event.",          // Event entry message
                EventLogEntryType.Information,    // Event type
                1,                               // Application-specific ID
                0,                               // Application-specific category
                new byte[] {10, 55, 200}         // Event data
            );

            // Wait to continue.
            Console.WriteLine(Environment.NewLine);
            Console.WriteLine("Main method complete. Press Enter.");
            Console.ReadLine();
        }
    }
}
```

14-4. Read and Write to the Windows Registry

Problem

You need to read information from, or write information to, the Windows registry.

Solution

Use the methods GetValue and SetValue of the Microsoft.Win32.Registry class.

■**Tip** The GetValue and SetValue methods open a registry key, get or set its value, and close the key each time they are called. This means they are inefficient when used to perform many read or write operations. The GetValue and SetValue methods of the Microsoft.Win32.RegistryKey class discussed in recipe 14-5 will provide better performance if you need to perform many read or write operations on the registry.

How It Works

The GetValue and SetValue methods (new to .NET 2.0) allow you to read and write named values in named registry keys. GetValue takes three arguments:

- A string containing the fully qualified name of the key you want to read. The key name must start with one of the following root key names:

  - HKEY_CLASSES_ROOT

  - HKEY_CURRENT_CONFIG

  - HKEY_CURRENT_USER

  - HKEY_DYN_DATA

  - HKEY_LOCAL_MACHINE

  - HKEY_PERFORMANCE_DATA

  - HKEY_USERS

- A string containing the name of the value in the key you want to read.

- An object containing the default value to return if the named value is not present in the key.

GetValue returns an object containing either the data read from the registry or the default value specified as the third argument if the named value is not found. If the specified key does not exist, GetValue returns null.

SetValue offers two overloads. The most functional expects the following arguments:

- A string containing the fully qualified name of the key you want to write. The key must start with one of the root key names specified previously.

- A string containing the name of the value in the key you want to write.

- An object containing the value to write.

- An element of the Microsoft.Win32.RegistyValueKind enumeration that specifies the registry data type that should be used to hold the data.

If the registry key specified in the SetValue call does not exist, it is automatically created.

The Code

The following example demonstrates how to use GetValue and SetValue to read from and write to the registry. Every time the example is run, it reads usage information from the registry and displays it to the screen. The example also updates the stored usage information, which you can see the next time you run the example.

```csharp
using System;
using Microsoft.Win32;

namespace Apress.VisualCSharpRecipes.Chapter14
{
    class Recipe14_04
    {
        public static void Main(String[] args)
        {
            // Variables to hold usage information read from registry.
            string lastUser;
            string lastRun;
            int runCount;

            // Read the name of the last user to run the application from the
            // registry. This is stored as the default value of the key and is
            // accessed by not specifying a value name. Cast the returned Object
            // to a string.
            lastUser = (string)Registry.GetValue(
                @"HKEY_CURRENT_USER\Software\Apress\Visual C# 2005 Recipes",
                "", "Nobody");

            // If lastUser is null, it means that the specified registry key
            // does not exist.
            if (lastUser == null)
            {
                // Set initial values for the usage information.
                lastUser = "Nobody";
                lastRun = "Never";
                runCount = 0;
            }
            else
            {
                // Read the last run date and specify a default value of
                // "Never". Cast the returned Object to string.
                lastRun = (string)Registry.GetValue(
                    @"HKEY_CURRENT_USER\Software\Apress\Visual C# 2005 Recipes",
                    "LastRun", "Never");

                // Read the run count value and specify a default value of
                // 0 (zero). Cast the Object to Int32, and assign to an int.
                runCount = (Int32)Registry.GetValue(
                    @"HKEY_CURRENT_USER\Software\Apress\Visual C# 2005 Recipes",
                    "RunCount", 0);
            }

            // Display the usage information.
            Console.WriteLine("Last user name: " + lastUser);
            Console.WriteLine("Last run date/time: " + lastRun);
            Console.WriteLine("Previous executions: " + runCount);

            // Update the usage information. It doesn't matter if the registry
            // key exists or not, SetValue will automatically create it.
```

```
            // Update the "last user" information with the current username.
            // Specify that this should be stored as the default value
            // for the key by using an empty string as the value name.
            Registry.SetValue(
                @"HKEY_CURRENT_USER\Software\Apress\Visual C# 2005 Recipes",
                "", Environment.UserName, RegistryValueKind.String);

            // Update the "last run" information with the current date and time.
            // Specify that this should be stored as a string value in the
            // registry.
            Registry.SetValue(
                @"HKEY_CURRENT_USER\Software\Apress\Visual C# 2005 Recipes",
                "LastRun", DateTime.Now.ToString(), RegistryValueKind.String);

            // Update the usage count information. Specify that this should
            // be stored as an integer value in the registry.
            Registry.SetValue(
                @"HKEY_CURRENT_USER\Software\Apress\Visual C# 2005 Recipes",
                "RunCount", ++runCount, RegistryValueKind.DWord);

            // Wait to continue.
            Console.WriteLine(Environment.NewLine);
            Console.WriteLine("Main method complete. Press Enter.");
            Console.ReadLine();
        }
    }
}
```

14-5. Search the Windows Registry

Problem

You need to search the Windows registry for a key that contains a specific value or content.

Solution

Use the Microsoft.Win32.Registry class to obtain a Microsoft.Win32.RegistryKey object that represents the root key of a registry hive you want to search. Use the members of this RegistryKey object to navigate through and enumerate the registry key hierarchy as well as to read the names and content of values held in the keys.

How It Works

You must first obtain a RegistryKey object that represents a base-level key and navigate through the hierarchy of RegistryKey objects as required. The Registry class implements a set of seven static fields that return RegistryKey objects representing base-level registry keys; Table 14-3 describes the registry location to where each of these fields maps.

Table 14-3. *Static Fields of the* Registry *Class*

Field	Registry Mapping
ClassesRoot	HKEY_CLASSES_ROOT
CurrentConfig	HKEY_CURRENT_CONFIG
CurrentUser	HKEY_CURRENT_USER
DynData	HKEY_DYN_DATA
LocalMachine	HKEY_LOCAL_MACHINE
PerformanceData	HKEY_PERFORMANCE_DATA
Users	HKEY_USERS

■**Tip** The static method RegistryKey.OpenRemoteBaseKey allows you to open a registry base key on a remote machine. See the .NET Framework SDK documentation for details of its use.

Once you have the base-level RegistryKey object, you must navigate through its child subkeys recursively. To support navigation, the RegistryKey class allows you to do the following:

- Get the number of immediate subkeys using the SubKeyCount property.

- Get a string array containing the names of all subkeys using the GetSubKeyNames method.

- Get a RegistryKey reference to a subkey using the OpenSubKey method. The OpenSubKey method provides two overloads: the first opens the named key as read-only; the second accepts a bool argument that, if true, will open a writable RegistryKey object.

Once you obtain a RegistryKey, you can create, read, update, and delete subkeys and values using the methods listed in Table 14-4. Methods that modify the contents of the key require you to have a writable RegistryKey object.

Table 14-4. RegistryKey *Methods to Create, Read, Update, and Delete Registry Keys and Values*

Method	Description
CreateSubKey	Creates a new subkey with the specified name and returns a writable RegistryKey object. If the specified subkey already exists, CreateSubKey returns a writable reference to the existing subkey.
DeleteSubKey	Deletes the subkey with the specified name, which must be empty of subkeys (but not values); otherwise, a System.InvalidOperationException is thrown.
DeleteSubKeyTree	Deletes the subkey with the specified name along with all of its subkeys.
DeleteValue	Deletes the value with the specified name from the current key.
GetValue	Returns the value with the specified name from the current key. The value is returned as an object, which you must cast to the appropriate type. The simplest form of GetValue returns null if the specified value doesn't exist. An overload allows you to specify a default value to return (instead of null) if the named value doesn't exist.
GetValueKind	Returns the registry data type of the value with the specified name in the current key. The value is returned as a member of the Microsoft.Win32.RegistryValueKind enumeration.

(Continued)

Table 14-4. *Continued*

Method	Description
GetValueNames	Returns a string array containing the names of all values in the current registry key.
SetValue	Creates (or updates) the value with the specified name. In 2.0, you can specify the data type used to store the value with the overload that takes a RegistryValueKind as last parameter. If you don't provide such a value kind, one will be calculated automatically, based on the managed type of the object you pass as value to set.

The RegistryKey class implements IDisposable; you should call the IDisposable.Dispose method to free operating system resources when you have finished with the RegistryKey object.

The Code

The following example takes a single command-line argument and recursively searches the CurrentUser hive of the registry looking for keys with names matching the supplied argument. When the example finds a match, it displays all string type values contained in the key to the console.

```csharp
using System;
using Microsoft.Win32;

namespace Apress.VisualCSharpRecipes.Chapter14
{
    class Recipe14_05
    {
        public static void SearchSubKeys(RegistryKey root, String searchKey)
        {
            // Loop through all subkeys contained in the current key.
            foreach (string keyname in root.GetSubKeyNames())
            {
                try
                {
                    using (RegistryKey key = root.OpenSubKey(keyname))
                    {
                        if (keyname == searchKey) PrintKeyValues(key);
                        SearchSubKeys(key, searchKey);
                    }
                }
                catch (System.Security.SecurityException)
                {
                    // Ignore SecurityException for the purpose of the example.
                    // Some subkeys of HKEY_CURRENT_USER are secured and will
                    // throw a SecurityException when opened.
                }
            }
        }

        public static void PrintKeyValues(RegistryKey key)
        {
            // Display the name of the matching subkey and the number of
            // values it contains.
            Console.WriteLine("Registry key found : {0} contains {1} values",
                key.Name, key.ValueCount);
```

```
            // Loop through the values and display.
            foreach (string valuename in key.GetValueNames())
            {
                if (key.GetValue(valuename) is String)
                {
                    Console.WriteLine("  Value : {0} = {1}",
                        valuename, key.GetValue(valuename));
                }
            }
        }
    }

    public static void Main(String[] args)
    {
        if (args.Length > 0)
        {
            // Open the CurrentUser base key.
            using (RegistryKey root = Registry.CurrentUser)
            {
                // Search recursively through the registry for any keys
                // with the specified name.
                SearchSubKeys(root, args[0]);
            }
        }

        // Wait to continue.
        Console.WriteLine(Environment.NewLine);
        Console.WriteLine("Main method complete. Press Enter.");
        Console.ReadLine();
    }
}
}
```

Usage

Running the example using the command Recipe14-05 Environment will display output similar to the following when executed using the command on a machine running Windows XP:

```
Registry key found : HKEY_CURRENT_USER\Environment contains 2 values
  Value : TEMP = C:\Documents and Settings\Allen\Local Settings\Temp
  Value : TMP = C:\Documents and Settings\Allen\Local Settings\Temp
```

14-6. Create a Windows Service

Problem

You need to create an application that will run as a Windows service.

Solution

Create a class that extends System.ServiceProcess.ServiceBase. Use the inherited properties to control the behavior of your service, and override inherited methods to implement the functionality required. Implement a Main method that creates an instance of your service class and passes it to the static ServiceBase.Run method.

■**Note** The ServiceBase class is defined in the System.Serviceprocess.dll assembly, so you must include a reference to this assembly when you build your service class.

How It Works

To create a Windows service manually, you must implement a class derived from the ServiceBase class. The ServiceBase class provides the base functionality that allows the Windows Service Control Manager (SCM) to configure the service, operate the service as a background task, and control the life cycle of the service. The SCM also controls how other applications can control the service programmatically.

■**Tip** If you are using Microsoft Visual Studio, you can use the Windows Service project template to create a Windows service. The template provides the basic code infrastructure required by a Windows service class, which you can extend with your custom functionality.

To control your service, the SCM uses the eight protected methods inherited from ServiceBase class described in Table 14-5. You should override these virtual methods to implement the functionality and behavior required by your service. Not all services must support all control messages. The CanXXX properties inherited from the ServiceBase class declare to the SCM which control messages your service supports; Table 14-5 specifies the property that controls each operation.

Table 14-5. *Methods That Control the Operation of a Service*

Method	Description
OnStart	All services must support the OnStart method, which the SCM calls to start the service. The SCM passes a string array containing arguments specified for the service. These arguments can be specified when the ServiceController. Start method is called and are usually configured in the service's property window in Windows Control Panel. However, they are rarely used because it is better for the service to retrieve its configuration information directly from the Windows registry. The OnStart method must normally return within 30 seconds, or the SCM will abort the service. Your service must call the RequestAdditionalTime method of the ServiceBase class if it requires more time; specify the additional milliseconds required as an int.
OnStop	Called by the SCM to stop a service—the SCM will call OnStop only if the CanStop property is set to true.
OnPause	Called by the SCM to pause a service—the SCM will call OnPause only if the CanPauseAndContinue property is set to true.
OnContinue	Called by the SCM to continue a paused service—the SCM will call OnContinue only if the CanPauseAndContinue property is set to true.
OnShutdown	Called by the SCM when the system is shutting down—the SCM will call OnShutdown only if the CanShutdown property is set to true.
OnPowerEvent	Called by the SCM when a system-level power status change occurs, such as a laptop going into suspend mode. The SCM will call OnPowerEvent only if the CanHandlePowerEvent property is set to true.

Method	Description
OnCustomCommand	Allows you to extend the service control mechanism with custom control messages; see the .NET Framework SDK documentation for more details.
OnSessionChange	Called by the SCM when a change event is received from the Terminal Services session or when users log on and off on the local machine. A System.ServiceProcess.SessionChangeDescription object passed as an argument by the SCM contains details of what type of session change occurred. The SCM will call OnSessionChange only if the CanHandleSessionChangeEvent property is set to true. This method is new in the .NET Framework 2.0.

As mentioned in Table 14-5, the OnStart method is expected to return within 30 seconds, so you should not use OnStart to perform lengthy initialization tasks where you can avoid it. A service class should implement a constructor that performs initialization, including configuring the inherited properties of the ServiceBase class. In addition to the properties that declare the control messages supported by a service, the ServiceBase class implements three other important properties:

- ServiceName is the name used internally by the SCM to identify the service and must be set before the service is run.

- AutoLog controls whether the service automatically writes entries to the event log when it receives any of the OnStart, OnStop, OnPause, and OnContinue control messages from Table 14-5.

- EventLog provides access to an EventLog object that's preconfigured with an event source name that's the same as the ServiceName property registered against the Application log. (See recipe 14-3 for more information about the EventLog class.)

The final step in creating a service is to implement a static Main method. The Main method must create an instance of your service class and pass it as an argument to the static method ServiceBase.Run.

The Code

The following Windows service example uses a configurable System.Timers.Timer to write an entry to the Windows event log periodically. You can start, pause, and stop the service using the Services application in the Control Panel.

```
using System;
using System.Timers;
using System.ServiceProcess;

namespace Apress.VisualCSharpRecipes.Chapter14
{
    class Recipe14_06 : ServiceBase
    {
        // A Timer that controls how frequently the example writes to the
        // event log.
        private System.Timers.Timer timer;

        public Recipe14_06()
        {
            // Set the ServiceBase.ServiceName property.
            ServiceName = "Recipe 14_06 Service";
```

```
        // Configure the level of control available on the service.
        CanStop = true;
        CanPauseAndContinue = true;
        CanHandleSessionChangeEvent = true;

        // Configure the service to log important events to the
        // Application event log automatically.
        AutoLog = true;
    }

    // The method executed when the timer expires and writes an
    // entry to the Application event log.
    private void WriteLogEntry(object sender, ElapsedEventArgs e)
    {
        // Use the EventLog object automatically configured by the
        // ServiceBase class to write to the event log.
        EventLog.WriteEntry("Recipe14_06 Service active : " + e.SignalTime);
    }

    protected override void OnStart(string[] args)
    {
        // Obtain the interval between log entry writes from the first
        // argument. Use 5000 milliseconds by default and enforce a 1000
        // millisecond minimum.
        double interval;

        try
        {
            interval = Double.Parse(args[0]);
            interval = Math.Max(1000, interval);
        }
        catch
        {
            interval = 5000;
        }

        EventLog.WriteEntry(String.Format("Recipe14_06 Service starting. " +
            "Writing log entries every {0} milliseconds...", interval));

        // Create, configure, and start a System.Timers.Timer to
        // periodically call the WriteLogEntry method. The Start
        // and Stop methods of the System.Timers.Timer class
        // make starting, pausing, resuming, and stopping the
        // service straightforward.
        timer = new Timer();
        timer.Interval = interval;
        timer.AutoReset = true;
        timer.Elapsed += new ElapsedEventHandler(WriteLogEntry);
        timer.Start();
    }

    protected override void OnStop()
    {
        EventLog.WriteEntry("Recipe14_06 Service stopping...");
        timer.Stop();
```

```
        // Free system resources used by the Timer object.
        timer.Dispose();
        timer = null;
    }

    protected override void OnPause()
    {
        if (timer != null)
        {
            EventLog.WriteEntry("Recipe14_06 Service pausing...");
            timer.Stop();
        }
    }

    protected override void OnContinue()
    {
        if (timer != null)
        {
            EventLog.WriteEntry("Recipe14_06 Service resuming...");
            timer.Start();
        }
    }

    protected override void OnSessionChange(SessionChangeDescription change)
    {
        EventLog.WriteEntry("Recipe14_06 Session change..." +
            change.Reason);
    }

    public static void Main()
    {
        // Create an instance of the Recipe14_06 class that will write
        // an entry to the Application event log. Pass the object to the
        // static ServiceBase.Run method.
        ServiceBase.Run(new Recipe14_06());
    }
  }
}
```

Usage

If you want to run multiple services in a single process, you must create an array of ServiceBase objects and pass it to the ServiceBase.Run method. Although service classes have a Main method, you can't execute service code directly; attempting to run a service class directly results in Windows displaying the Windows Service Start Failure message box, as shown in Figure 14-1. Recipe 14-7 describes what you must do to install your service before it will execute.

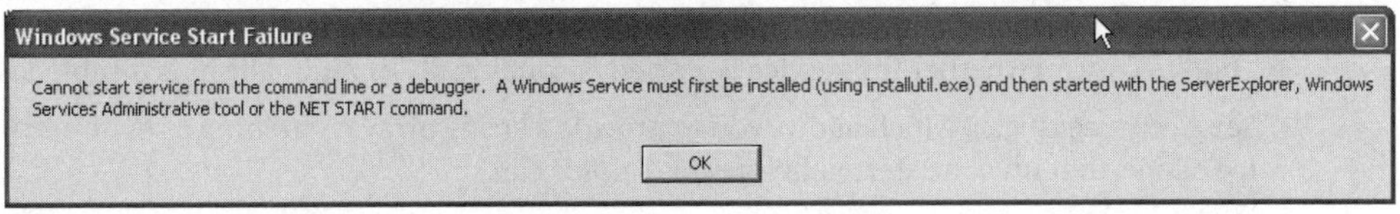

Windows Service Start Failure

Cannot start service from the command line or a debugger. A Windows Service must first be installed (using installutil.exe) and then started with the ServerExplorer, Windows Services Administrative tool or the NET START command.

[OK]

Figure 14-1. *The Windows Service Start Failure message box*

14-7. Create a Windows Service Installer

Problem

You have created a Windows service application and need to install it.

Solution

Add a new class to your Windows service project that extends the `System.Configuration.Install.Installer` class to create an installer class containing the information necessary to install and configure your service class. Use the Installer tool (Installutil.exe) to perform the installation, which is installed as part of the .NET Framework.

■**Note** You must create the installer class in the same assembly as the service class for the service to install and function correctly.

How It Works

As recipe 14-6 points out, you cannot run service classes directly. The high level of integration with the Windows operating system and the information stored about the service in the Windows registry means services require explicit installation.

If you have Microsoft Visual Studio .NET, you can create an installation component for your service automatically by right-clicking in the design view of your service class and selecting Add Installer from the context menu. You can call this installation component by using deployment projects or by using the Installer tool to install your service. You can also create installer components for Windows services manually by following these steps:

1. In your project, create a class derived from the `Installer` class.

2. Apply the attribute `System.ComponentModel.RunInstallerAttribute(true)` to the installer class.

3. In the constructor of the installer class, create a single instance of the `System.ServiceProcess.ServiceProcessInstaller` class. Set the `Account`, `User`, and `Password` properties of `ServiceProcessInstaller` to configure the account under which your service will run. This account must already exist.

4. In the constructor of the installer class, create one instance of the `System.ServiceProcess.ServiceInstaller` class for each individual service you want to install. Use the properties of the `ServiceInstaller` objects to configure information about each service, including the following:

    - `ServiceName`, which specifies the name Windows uses internally to identify the service. This must be the same as the value assigned to the `ServiceBase.ServiceName` property.

    - `DisplayName`, which provides a user-friendly name for the service.

    - `StartType`, which uses values of the `System.ServiceProcess.ServiceStartMode` enumeration to control whether the service is started automatically or manually or is disabled.

    - `ServiceDependsUpon`, which allows you to provide a string array containing a set of service names that must be started before this service can start.

5. Add the `ServiceProcessInstaller` object and all `ServiceInstaller` objects to the `System.Configuration.Install.InstallerCollection` object accessed through the `Installers` property, which is inherited by your installer class from the `Installer` base class.

The Code

The following example is an installer for the Recipe14_06 Windows service created in recipe 14-6. The sample project contains the code from recipe 14-6 and for the installer class. This is necessary for the service installation to function correctly. To compile the example, you must reference two additional assemblies: System.Configuration.Install.dll and System.ServiceProcess.dll.

```
using System.Configuration.Install;
using System.ServiceProcess;
using System.ComponentModel;

namespace Apress.VisualCSharpRecipes.Chapter14
{
    [RunInstaller(true)]
    public class Recipe14_07 : Installer
    {
        public Recipe14_07()
        {
            // Instantiate and configure a ServiceProcessInstaller.
            ServiceProcessInstaller ServiceExampleProcess =
                new ServiceProcessInstaller();
            ServiceExampleProcess.Account = ServiceAccount.LocalSystem;

            // Instantiate and configure a ServiceInstaller.
            ServiceInstaller ServiceExampleInstaller =
                new ServiceInstaller();
            ServiceExampleInstaller.DisplayName =
                "Visual C# 2005 Recipes Service Example";
            ServiceExampleInstaller.ServiceName = "Recipe 14_06 Service";
            ServiceExampleInstaller.StartType = ServiceStartMode.Automatic;

            // Add both the ServiceProcessInstaller and ServiceInstaller to
            // the Installers collection, which is inherited from the
            // Installer base class.
            Installers.Add(ServiceExampleInstaller);
            Installers.Add(ServiceExampleProcess);
        }
    }
}
```

Usage

To install the Recipe14_06 service, build the project, navigate to the directory where Recipe14-07.exe is located (bin\debug by default), and execute the command Installutil Recipe14-07.exe. You can then see and control the Recipe14_06 service using the Windows Computer Management console. However, despite specifying a StartType of Automatic, the service is initially installed unstarted; you must start the service manually (or restart your computer) before the service will write entries to the event log. Once the service is running, you can view the entries it writes to the Application event log using the Event Viewer application. To uninstall the Recipe14_06 service, add the /u switch to the Installutil command as follows: Installutil /u Recipe14-07.exe.

■Tip If you have the Service application from the Control Panel open when you uninstall the service, the service will not uninstall completely until you close the Service application. Once you close the Service application, you can reinstall the service; otherwise, you will get an error telling you that the installation failed because the service is scheduled for deletion.

14-8. Create a Shortcut on the Desktop or Start Menu

Problem

You need to create a shortcut on the user's Windows desktop or Start menu.

Solution

Use COM Interop to access the functionality of the Windows Script Host. Create and configure an IWshShortcut instance that represents the shortcut. The folder in which you save the shortcut determines whether it appears on the desktop or in the Start menu.

How It Works

The .NET Framework class library does not include the functionality to create desktop or Start menu shortcuts; however, this is relatively easy to do using the Windows Script Host component accessed through COM Interop. Chapter 15 describes how to create an interop assembly that provides access to a COM component. If you are using Visual Studio, add a reference to the Windows Script Host Object Model listed in the COM tab of the Add Reference dialog box. If you don't have Visual Studio .NET, use the Type Library Importer (Tlbimp.exe) to create an interop assembly for the wshom.ocx file, which is usually located in the Windows\System32 folder. (You can obtain the latest version of the Windows Script Host from http://msdn.microsoft.com/scripting. At the time of this writing, the latest version is 5.6.)

Once you have generated and imported the interop assembly into your project, follow these steps to create a desktop or Start menu shortcut.

1. Instantiate a WshShell object, which provides access to the Windows shell.

2. Use the SpecialFolders property of the WshShell object to determine the correct path of the folder where you want to put the shortcut. You must specify the name of the folder you want as an index to the SpecialFolders property. For example, to create a desktop shortcut, specify the value Desktop, and to create a start menu shortcut, specify StartMenu. Using the SpecialFolders property, you can obtain the path to any of the special system folders. If the specified folder does not exist on the platform you are running on, SpecialFolders returns an empty string. Other commonly used values include AllUsersDesktop and AllUsersStartMenu; you can find the full list of special folder names in the section on the SpecialFolders property in the Windows Script Host documentation.

3. Call the CreateShortcut method of the WshShell object, and provide the fully qualified filename of the shortcut file you want to create. The file should have the extension .lnk. CreateShortcut will return an IWshShortcut instance.

4. Use the properties of the IWshShortcut instance to configure the shortcut. You can configure properties such as the executable that the shortcut references, a description for the shortcut, a hotkey sequence, and the icon displayed for the shortcut.

5. Call the Save method of the IWshShortcut instance to write the shortcut to disk. The shortcut will appear either on the desktop or in the Start menu (or elsewhere) depending on the path specified when the IWshShortcut instance was created.

The Code

The following example class creates a shortcut to Notepad.exe on both the desktop and Start menu of the current user. The example creates both shortcuts by calling the CreateShortcut method and specifying a different destination folder for each shortcut file. This approach makes it possible to create the shortcut file in any of the special folders returned by the WshShell.SpecialFolders property.

```csharp
using System;
using System.IO;
using IWshRuntimeLibrary;

namespace Apress.VisualCSharpRecipes.Chapter14
{
    class Recipe14_08
    {
        public static void CreateShortcut(string destination)
        {
            // Create a WshShell instance through which to access the
            // functionality of the Windows shell.
            WshShell wshShell = new WshShell();

            // Assemble a fully qualified name that places the Notepad.lnk
            // file in the specified destination folder. You could use the
            // System.Environment.GetFolderPath method to obtain a path, but
            // the WshShell.SpecialFolders method provides access to a wider
            // range of folders. You need to create a temporary object reference
            // to the destination string to satisfy the requirements of the
            // Item method signature.
            object destFolder = (object)destination;
            string fileName = Path.Combine(
                (string)wshShell.SpecialFolders.Item(ref destFolder),
                "Notepad.lnk"
            );

            // Create the shortcut object. Nothing is created in the
            // destination folder until the shortcut is saved.
            IWshShortcut shortcut =
                (IWshShortcut)wshShell.CreateShortcut(fileName);

            // Configure the fully qualified name to the executable.
            // Use the Environment class for simplicity.
            shortcut.TargetPath = Path.Combine(
                Environment.GetFolderPath(Environment.SpecialFolder.System),
                "notepad.exe"
            );

            // Set the working directory to the Personal (My Documents) folder.
            shortcut.WorkingDirectory =
                Environment.GetFolderPath(Environment.SpecialFolder.Personal);

            // Provide a description for the shortcut.
            shortcut.Description = "Notepad Text Editor";

            // Assign a hotkey to the shortcut.
            shortcut.Hotkey = "CTRL+ALT+N";
```

```
            // Configure Notepad to always start maximized.
            shortcut.WindowStyle = 3;

            // Configure the shortcut to display the first icon in Notepad.exe.
            shortcut.IconLocation = "notepad.exe, 0";

            // Save the configured shortcut file.
            shortcut.Save();
        }

        public static void Main()
        {
            // Create the Notepad shortcut on the desktop.
            CreateShortcut("Desktop");

            // Create the Notepad shortcut on the Windows Start menu of
            // the current user.
            CreateShortcut("StartMenu");

            // Wait to continue.
            Console.WriteLine(Environment.NewLine);
            Console.WriteLine("Main method complete. Press Enter.");
            Console.ReadLine();
        }
    }
}
```

Acronyms

ACL
access control list

API
Application Programming Interface

ASCII
American Standard Code for Information Interchange

CA
certificate authority

CAS
code access security

CCW
COM callable wrapper

CLR
common language runtime

COM
Component Object Model

CPU
central processing unit

CSP
cryptographic service provider

CSS
Cascading Style Sheets

DB
database

DCOM
Distributed Component Object Model

DLL
dynamic link library

DNS
Domain Name System

DOM
Document Object Model

DPAPI
Data Protection Application Programming Interface

FTP
File Transfer Protocol

GAC
global assembly cache

GC
garbage collector

GDI
Graphical Device Interface

GUI
graphical user interface

HTML
Hypertext Markup Language

HTTP
Hypertext Transfer Protocol

HTTPS
Hypertext Transfer Protocol over Secure Sockets Layer (HTTP over SSL)

I/O
input/output

ICMP

Internet Control Message Protocol

IIS

Internet Information Services

IL

intermediate language

IMAP

Internet Message Access Protocol

IP

Internet Protocol

JIT

just in time

MAPI

Messaging Application Programming Interface

MBR

marshal by reference

MBV

marshal by value

MDI

Multiple Document Interface

MIME

Multipurpose Internet Mail Extensions

MSDE

Microsoft SQL Server Desktop Engine

MSDN

Microsoft Developer Network

MSIL

Microsoft Intermediate Language

OS

operating system

PIA

primary interop assembly

PID

process identifier

POP3

Post Office Protocol 3

RBS

role-based security

RCW

runtime callable wrapper

RFC

Request For Comment

RID

role identifier

RPC

remote procedure call

SCM

Service Control Manager

SDK

software development kit

SID

security identifier

SMTP

Simple Mail Transfer Protocol

SOAP

Simple Object Access Protocol

SPC

software publisher certificate

SQL

Structured Query Language

SSL
Secure Sockets Layer

TCP
Transmission Control Protocol

UDP
User Datagram Protocol

URI
uniform resource identifier

URL
uniform resource locator

URN
uniform resource name

UTF
Unicode Transformation Format

W3C
World Wide Web Consortium

WMI
Windows Management Instrumentation

WSDL
Web Service Description Language

XML
Extensible Markup Language

XSD
XML Schema Definition

XSL
Extensible Style Language

XSLT
Extensible Style Language Transformation

Index

forums.apress.com

JOIN THE APRESS FORUMS AND BE PART OF OUR COMMUNITY. You'll find discussions that cover topics of interest to IT professionals, programmers, and enthusiasts just like you. If you post a query to one of our forums, you can expect that some of the best minds in the business—especially Apress authors, who all write with *The Expert's Voice™*—will chime in to help you. Why not aim to become one of our most valuable participants (MVPs) and win cool stuff? Here's a sampling of what you'll find:

DATABASES

Data drives everything.

Share information, exchange ideas, and discuss any database programming or administration issues.

INTERNET TECHNOLOGIES AND NETWORKING

Try living without plumbing (and eventually IPv6).

Talk about networking topics including protocols, design, administration, wireless, wired, storage, backup, certifications, trends, and new technologies.

JAVA

We've come a long way from the old Oak tree.

Hang out and discuss Java in whatever flavor you choose: J2SE, J2EE, J2ME, Jakarta, and so on.

MAC OS X

All about the Zen of OS X.

OS X is both the present and the future for Mac apps. Make suggestions, offer up ideas, or boast about your new hardware.

OPEN SOURCE

Source code is good; understanding (open) source is better.

Discuss open source technologies and related topics such as PHP, MySQL, Linux, Perl, Apache, Python, and more.

PROGRAMMING/BUSINESS

Unfortunately, it is.

Talk about the Apress line of books that cover software methodology, best practices, and how programmers interact with the "suits."

WEB DEVELOPMENT/DESIGN

Ugly doesn't cut it anymore, and CGI is absurd.

Help is in sight for your site. Find design solutions for your projects and get ideas for building an interactive Web site.

SECURITY

Lots of bad guys out there—the good guys need help.

Discuss computer and network security issues here. Just don't let anyone else know the answers!

TECHNOLOGY IN ACTION

Cool things. Fun things.

It's after hours. It's time to play. Whether you're into LEGO® MINDSTORMS™ or turning an old PC into a DVR, this is where technology turns into fun.

WINDOWS

No defenestration here.

Ask questions about all aspects of Windows programming, get help on Microsoft technologies covered in Apress books, or provide feedback on any Apress Windows book.

HOW TO PARTICIPATE:

Go to the Apress Forums site at **http://forums.apress.com/**.

Click the New User link.